P9-BJC-630

Ecuador
& the Galápagos Islands

Rob Rachowiecki
Danny Palmerlee

LONELY PLANET PUBLICATIONS
Melbourne • Oakland • London • Paris

ECUADOR

83°W **82°W** **81°W** **80°W** **79°W**

1°N

0 — 40 — 80km
0 — 25 — 50mi

Equator

1°S

2°S

3°S

4°S

5°S

PACIFIC OCEAN

Quito
A springlike climate graces this Andean capital of colonial churches, interesting museums and fine restaurants

Saquisilí
Every Thursday, this small village hosts one of the country's largest local markets

Isla de la Plata
Nicknamed the 'poor person's Galápagos,' this island is home to colonies of breeding seabirds and, from June through October, mating humpback whales

Montañita
This podunk coastal village has Ecuador's best surf, great pancakes, cheap sleeps and plenty of sun-soakin' international travelers

El Nariz del Diablo
Ride the thrice-weekly train down 'The Devil's Nose' – an amazing feat of railroad engineering

Ingapirca
Ecuador's pre-Columbian population left its mark at Ecuador's best-known Inca site

Cuenca
This is the country's third-largest city and is a charming step back in time

Vilcabamba
Locally dubbed the 'valley of longevity,' the pleasant climate here attracts visitors simply wanting to relax

San Lorenzo
ESMERALDAS
Atacames
Punta Galera
Rio Esmeraldas
Rio Cayapas
Rio Touchi

Pedernales
Punta Ballena
Cabo Pasado
Santo Domingo de los Colorados
Bahía de Caráquez
Embalse Daule-Peripa
Manta
PORTOVIEJO
Quevedo
Cabo San Lorenzo
Isla de la Plata
Jipijapa
Volcán Chimborazo 6310m
Puerto Lopez
GUARANDA
Montañita
Rio Daule
Rio Quevedo
Rio Babahoyo
BABAHOYO
Manglaralto
GUAYAQUIL
Milagro
Santa Elena Peninsula
La Libertad
Salinas
Alausí
Ingapirca
Playas
AZOGUES
Gualaceo
CUENCA
Parque Nacional Cajas
Golfo de Guayaquil
Isla Puná
Panamericana
Cordillera de los Andes
MACHALA
Huaquillas
TUMBES
Olmedo
Catamayo
LOJA
ZAMORA
Rio Catamayo
Vilcabamba
Macará
Sullana
PERU
Zumba

Elevation
5000m
4000m
3000m
2000m
1000m
Sea Level

78°W 77°W 76°W 75°W

Pasto

COLOMBIA

1°N

Ipiales

TULCÁN

Río Caqueta

Puerto Asís

Otavalo

Ecuador's most famous crafts market boasts bargains galore!

Río Santiago

IBARRA

Otavalo

Río San Miguel

LAGO AGRIO

Jungle Lodges

Rustic but comfortable jungle hotels on Río Napo and other rivers offer guided wildlife-watching opportunities

Equator

QUITO

San Juan

Cordillera de los Andes

Panamericana

Parque Nacional Cotopaxi

Río Quijos

Río Coca

Río Aguarico

Cuyabeno

Limoncocha

COCA

Río Napo

1°S

Volcán Cotopaxi 5897m

Saquisilí

LATACUNGA

Río Napo

Río Payamino

TENA   Misahuallí

Río Shiripuno

Parque Nacional Cotopaxi

The Andean scenery here is dominated by the cone-shaped Volcán Cotopaxi

AMBATO

Baños

Volcán Tungurahua 5016m

RIOBAMBA

PUYO

Río Tiguiño

Río Conanaco

Río Curaray

Río Cunambo

Río Pintoyacu

Tena

Not only a good base for jungle trips, Tena has become the nation's premier kayaking and river-rafting destination

MACAS

Río Pastaza

Río Cushuimi

Río Yuápa

PERU

2°S

Galápagos Islands

A nature-lover's paradise, these islands are famous for unique and fearless wildlife

92°W 91°W 90°W

Río Zamora

PACIFIC OCEAN

Isla Pinta (Abingdon)

Isla Marchena (Bindloe)

Isla Genovesa (Tower)

Equator   Equator

Río Cenepa

Volcán Wolf 1707m

Isla San Salvador (Santiago or James)

Isla Baltra

Isla Fernandina (Narborough)

Isla Pinzón (Duncan)

Isla Santa Cruz (Indefatigable)

Isla San Cristóbal (Chatham)

Isla Santa Fe (Barrington)

Isla Isabela (Albemarle)

Puerto Villamil

Puerto Ayora

PUERTO BAQUERIZO MORENO

1°S   1°S

Isla Tortuga

Isla Santa María (Floreana or Charles)

Isla Española (Hood)

92°W 91°W 90°W   *same scale as main map*

Contents – Text

GUAYAQUIL & THE SOUTH COAST   324

THE GALÁPAGOS ISLANDS   360

LANGUAGE   391

GLOSSARY   398

THANKS   399

INDEX   407

MAP LEGEND   back page

METRIC CONVERSION   inside back cover

Contents – Maps

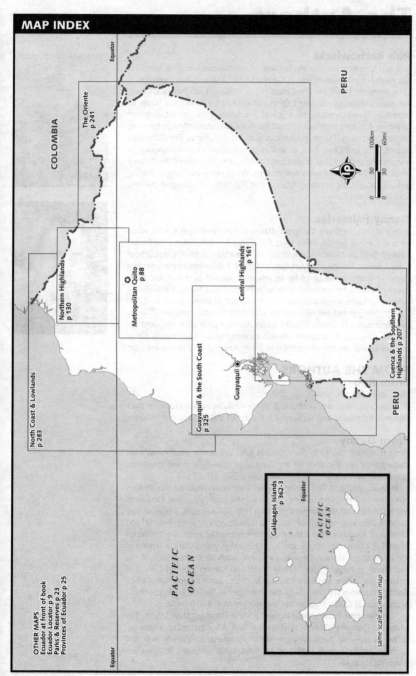

MAP INDEX

The Authors

Rob Rachowiecki

Rob was born near London and became an avid traveler during his teens. He has visited countries as diverse as Greenland and Thailand, but specializes in Latin American travel. He spent most of the 1980s in Latin America, traveling, mountaineering, teaching English and working for Wilderness Travel, an adventure-travel company. His first visit to Ecuador led to his authorship of *Climbing & Hiking in Ecuador* (Bradt Publications), soon followed by many editions of Lonely Planet guidebooks such as *Ecuador & the Galápagos Islands*, *Peru* and *Costa Rica*, as well as contributions to *South America on a shoestring* and *Trekking in the Central Andes*. This has enabled him to keep revisiting Latin America every few months. When not researching or leading treks, he makes his home in Arizona and has three school-aged children, Julia, Alison and Davy.

Danny Palmerlee

Born and raised in Gilroy, California, Danny began traveling at age 12, when he and a friend floated down Uvas Creek in a bathtub. Since then he has trekked through Montana and Wyoming, traveled extensively throughout Latin America, Europe and Morocco, and spent a debauched year running a hostel in Scotland. Much of his travels were funded by a lucrative body jewelry business he coowned with an entrepreneurial friend. His enduring passion for Latin America (especially the concept of *mañana*) has kept him busy traveling in and writing about the region for the past three years. Danny has contributed to Lonely Planet's *South America on a shoestring* and *Argentina, Uruguay & Paraguay*. He also coordinated *Mexico's Pacific Coast* and will coordinate the new edition of *South America on a shoestring*.

FROM THE AUTHORS
From Rob

Dedication: For Juls, always.

Thanks to Alejandro Lecaro and Victor Chiluiza in Guayaquil for their fabulous hospitality and for teaching me about the panama-hat industry.

From Danny

First off, a huge thanks to the countless folks in Ecuador who, rather than throwing me out the door for my barrage of seemingly stupid questions, helped me immensely.

In Quito, thanks to Tara Lambert, Xavier Bermeo and Rubén Alava for their friendship and tips, and to Cindy Smith (at the South American Explorers), Mark Thurber and Jean Brown for all their help. In Guayaquil, a huge *abrazo* to Anita Manrique and special thanks to Isabelle Dorion, Simon Peñafiel and Director of Tourism Joseph Garzozi. For their wonderful generosity and heaps of advice, I owe many thanks to Tom Quesenberry and Mariela Tenorio in Mindo, Rodrigo Mora in Otavalo, Andy and Michelle in Chugchilán, Kevin and Diane in Puerto López, Randy Smith and Ramiro Viteri in Coca and Johanna Buenaño in San Cristóbal. Thanks also to Jaime Burgos in Atacames, Karina Astudillo in Loja, Maribel at the Municipio de Turismo in Manta, Marta Mondragón in Quito, Rosa Jordan and Aussies Matt and Ronelle.

On the home front, special thanks to Steve Donziger, Dave Walsh, Tim Metz and Carolyn Hubbard – next one's on me. A big glasses-up, of course, to my *Ecuador & the Galápagos Islands compañeros*, Wendy, Rob and Graham. Finally, a huge thanks to my folks, Leslie and Dan, for their unwavering support.

This Book

The previous editions of *Ecuador & the Galápagos Islands* were written and updated by Rob Rachowiecki. This edition was updated by Rob Rachowiecki, who worked on the front chapters, and Danny Palmerlee, who did the regional chapters.

FROM THE PUBLISHER

This edition of *Ecuador & the Galápagos Islands* was produced in Lonely Planet's Melbourne office. Nancy Ianni coordinated the editing, with assistance from Emily Coles, Melanie Dankel, Quentin Frayne, Anne Mulvaney, Alan Murphy, Tegan Murray, Julia Taylor and Katrina Webb. The mapping was coordinated by Barbara Benson, with assistance from Karen Fry, Jack Gavran and Laurie Mikkelsen.

The book was designed by David Kemp. Ruth Askevold designed the cover, with artwork by Gerilyn Attebery.

This title was commissioned and developed in the US office by Wendy Smith; Graham Neale commissioned and developed the maps. Andrew Weatherill managed the book through production.

THANKS
Many thanks to the travelers who used the last edition and wrote to us with helpful hints, advice and interesting anecdotes. Your names appear in the back of this book.

Foreword

ABOUT LONELY PLANET GUIDEBOOKS

The story begins with a classic travel adventure: Tony and Maureen Wheeler's 1972 journey across Europe and Asia to Australia. There was no useful information about the overland trail then, so Tony and Maureen published the first Lonely Planet guidebook to meet a growing need.

From a kitchen table, Lonely Planet has grown to become the largest independent travel publisher in the world, with offices in Melbourne (Australia), Oakland (USA), London (UK) and Paris (France).

Today Lonely Planet guidebooks cover the globe. There is an ever-growing list of books and information in a variety of media. Some things haven't changed. The main aim is still to make it possible for adventurous travelers to get out there – to explore and better understand the world.

At Lonely Planet we believe travelers can make a positive contribution to the countries they visit – if they respect their host communities and spend their money wisely. Since 1986 a percentage of the income from each book has been donated to aid projects and human rights campaigns, and, more recently, to wildlife conservation.

Although inclusion in a guidebook usually implies a recommendation we cannot list every good place. Exclusion does not necessarily imply criticism. In fact there are a number of reasons why we might exclude a place – sometimes it is simply inappropriate to encourage an influx of travelers.

UPDATES & READER FEEDBACK

Things change – prices go up, schedules change, good places go bad and bad places go bankrupt. Nothing stays the same. So, if you find things better or worse, recently opened or long-since closed, please tell us and help make the next edition even more accurate and useful.

Lonely Planet thoroughly updates each guidebook as often as possible – usually every two years, although for some destinations the gap can be longer. Between editions, up-to-date information is available in our free, monthly email bulletin *Comet* (**w** www.lonelyplanet.com/newsletters). You can also check out the *Thorn Tree* bulletin board and *Postcards* section of our website, which carry unverified, but fascinating, reports from travellers.

Tell us about it! We genuinely value your feedback. A well-travelled team at Lonely Planet reads and acknowledges every email and letter we receive and ensures that every morsel of information finds its way to the relevant authors, editors and cartographers.

Everyone who writes to us will find their name listed in the next edition of the appropriate guidebook. The very best contributions will be rewarded with a free guidebook.

We may edit, reproduce and incorporate your comments in Lonely Planet products such as guidebooks, websites and digital products, so let us know if you don't want your comments reproduced or your name acknowledged.

How to contact Lonely Planet:
Online: **e** talk2us@lonelyplanet.com.au, **w** www.lonelyplanet.com
Australia: Locked Bag 1, Footscray, Victoria 3011
UK: 72-82 Rosebery Ave, London, EC1R 4RW
USA: 150 Linden St, Oakland, CA 94607

Introduction

Fabulous things come in small packages. Ecuador is the most diminutive of the Andean countries, yet it offers more physical and cultural diversity than almost any country on the planet. Add to that an extensive user-friendly bus system and you end up with a country that is both exciting and easy to travel in.

The beautifully preserved colonial capital of Quito is a World Heritage site brimming with amazing architecture. Perched in the highlands at 2850m above sea level, it enjoys a refreshing climate year-round and attracts many visitors seeking the Spanish-language courses that are offered in scores of schools.

From the capital you can travel by frequent buses to Andean Indian markets, remote jungle towns and warm Pacific beaches. In fact, starting from Quito, you can get to most points in this tropical country in less than a day by public transportation.

Any journey in the highlands is dominated by magnificent glacier-clad volcanoes, including Cotopaxi, which at 5897m is one of the highest active volcanoes in the world. Climbers from all over the world get all worked up at the opportunity to set personal altitude records on this and many other peaks. Further south, hiking around the country's highest peak, Chimborazo (6310m), gives

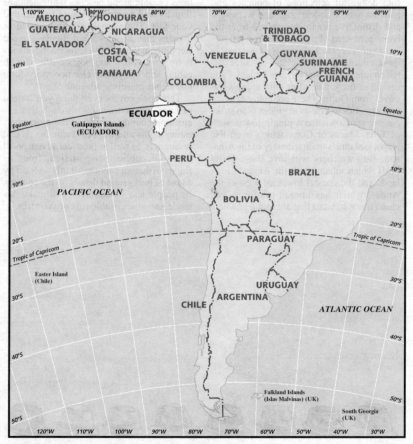

you the chance to chat with the incredibly tough children who spend their days herding a handful of sheep in the *páramo* (Andean grasslands). Wildlife enthusiasts can spend time trekking in Cajas National Park, with its unique high-altitude forests full of strange fungi, abundant flowers and rare endemic birds. There is even a section of Inca Trail to be hiked here, attesting to the huge extent of the Inca empire, descendants of which still live in lonely Andean hamlets where even the ubiquitous Coca Cola isn't available.

The highlands have many colorful Indian markets – some are world famous and deservedly so, others are rarely visited by foreigners but are no less interesting. Shoppers and seekers of handicrafts and curios will find delightful selections of ponchos and panama hats, woodcarvings and weavings, and distinctive ornaments carved from the ivory-hard seed of the native tagua palm.

Jungle travel in Ecuador is easier than in most countries because the distance between jungle sites and cities is far less – you can be in the jungle after only a day's bus travel from Quito. There are many exciting opportunities to hire local guides or to strike out on your own from jungle towns such as Tena, Macas or Coca, which is on Río Napo, Ecuador's main tributary of the Amazon. Bird-watchers will love the colorful birds which inhabit both the Amazon lowlands and the coastal lowlands west of the Andes, which has unique rainforest and cloud forest habitats that are found nowhere else on earth. With over 1500 species of birds, tiny Ecuador is home to about one-sixth of all the bird species on the planet.

The coast, too, has much to offer. You can visit a picturesque fishing village and watch the fishers expertly return their traditional balsa-wood rafts through the ocean breakers to the sandy shore, or help them pull in their nets in return for some of the catch. You can surf some of the most exciting waves in the world or, if this just seems too strenuous, you can laze on the beach in the equatorial sun, swim in the warm seas and, in the evening, listen to salsa music in a local bar.

The Galápagos Islands, 1000km off the coast of Ecuador, are high on the list of destinations for travelers interested in wildlife. Here you can swim with penguins and sea lions or walk along beaches while pelicans flap by and huge iguanas scurry around your feet. The animals are so unafraid of humans that at times it's difficult to avoid stepping on them. Travel around the islands is by small ships and boats outfitted with cabins and everything else necessary for a marvelous maritime adventure.

This book covers everything you'll need to know about traveling through this enchanting country, including the most interesting sights and the best-value hotels and restaurants, as well as practical advice on all forms of public transportation, from air flights to dugout canoes. All this – set off by a host of background details on the country, its people and its culture – will make this guide an indispensable part of your trip.

Facts about Ecuador

HISTORY

Most histories of Ecuador begin with the Inca expansion from Peru in the 15th century. Archaeological evidence, however, indicates the presence of people in Ecuador for many thousands of years before then.

It is generally accepted that Asian nomads crossing the Bering Strait some 25,000 years ago began reaching South America by about 12,000 BC. It is believed that several thousand years later, trans-Pacific colonization by the island dwellers of Polynesia added to the population.

Although Stone Age tools found in the Quito area have been dated to 9000 BC, the oldest signs of a more developed culture are burial sites found in Santa Elena that date to 6000 BC. The most ancient, widespread artefacts date to 3200 BC (the Valdivia period) and consist mainly of ceramics (especially small figurines) found in the central coastal area of Ecuador. Examples of these can be seen in the major museums of Quito and Guayaquil.

Early Tribes

The history of pre-Inca Ecuador is lost in a tangle of time and legend. Generally speaking, the main populations lived on the coast and in the highlands. The earliest historical details we have date to the 11th century AD, when there were two dominant tribes: the expansionist Caras, who resided in the coastal areas, and the peaceful Quitus, who lived in the highlands.

The Caras, led by Shyri, conquered the Quitus, which seems to have been accomplished by peaceful expansion rather than by bloody warfare. The Cara-Quitu peoples became collectively known as the Shyri nation and were the dominant force in the Ecuadorian highlands until about 1300, by which time the Puruhá, of the southern highlands, had also risen to power under the Duchicela lineage.

Conflict was avoided by the marriage of a Shyri princess, the only child of a king Caran of the Shyris, to Duchicela, the eldest son of the king of the Puruhás. This Duchicela-Shyri alliance proved successful, and the Duchicela line ruled more or less peacefully for about 150 years.

The Inca Empire

When the Inca expansion began, Duchicela's descendants still dominated the north, and the south was in the hands of the Cañari people. The Cañari defended themselves bitterly against the Inca invaders, and it was some years before the Inca Tupac-Yupanqui was able to subdue them and turn his attention to the north. During this time he fathered a son, Huayna Capac, by a Cañari princess.

The subjugation of the north took many years, and Huayna Capac grew up in Ecuador. He succeeded his father to the Inca throne and spent years traveling throughout his empire, from Bolivia to Ecuador, constantly putting down uprisings from all sides. Wherever possible, he strengthened his position by marriage; his union with Paccha, the daughter of the defeated Cacha Duchicela, produced a son, Atahualpa.

The year 1526 is major in Ecuadorian history. Huayna Capac died and left his empire not to one son, as was traditional, but to two: Huáscar of Cuzco and Atahualpa of Quito. Thus the Inca Empire was divided for the first time. In the same year, on September 21, the first Spaniards landed in northern Ecuador near what is now Esmeraldas. They were led south by the pilot Bartolomé Ruiz de Andrade on an exploratory mission for Francisco Pizarro, who remained further north.

Meanwhile, the rivalry between Huayna Capac's two sons worsened. The Inca of Cuzco, Huáscar, went to war against the Inca of Quito, Atahualpa. After several years of fighting, Atahualpa finally defeated Huáscar near Ambato and was thus the sole ruler of the weakened and still-divided Inca Empire when Pizarro arrived in 1532 with plans to conquer the Incas.

The Spanish Conquest

Pizarro's advance was rapid and dramatic. His horse-riding, armour-wearing, cannon-firing conquistadors were believed to be godlike, and although they were few in number, they spread terror among the Indians. In late 1532, a summit meeting was arranged between Pizarro and Atahualpa. Although Atahualpa was prepared to negotiate with the Spaniards, Pizarro had other ideas. When the Inca arrived at the pre-arranged meeting place (Cajamarca, in Peru) on November 16, the conquistadors captured him and massacred most of his poorly armed guards.

Atahualpa was held for ransom, and incalculable quantities of gold, silver and other valuables poured into Cajamarca. Instead of being released when the ransom was paid, the Inca was put through a sham trial and sentenced to death. Atahualpa was charged with incest (marrying one's sister was traditional in the Inca culture), polygamy, worship of false gods and crimes against the king, and he was executed on August 29, 1533. His death effectively brought the Inca Empire to an end.

Despite the death of Atahualpa, his general Rumiñahui continued to fight against the Spaniards for two more years. Pizarro's lieutenant Sebastián de Benalcázar finally battled his way to Quito in late 1534, only to find the city razed to the ground by Rumiñahui, who preferred to destroy the city rather than leave it in the hands of the conquistadors.

Quito was refounded on December 6, 1534, and Rumiñahui was captured, tortured and executed in January 1535. The most important Inca site in Ecuador, which remains partially intact today and can be visited, is at Ingapirca, to the north of Cuenca.

The Colonial Era

From 1535 onward, the colonial era proceeded with the usual intrigues among the Spanish conquistadors, but with no major uprisings by the Ecuadorian Indians. Francisco Pizarro made his brother Gonzalo the governor of Quito in 1540. Hoping to conquer the Amazon and find more gold, Gonzalo sent his lieutenant Francisco de Orellana away from Quito to prospect in 1541. The lieutenant and his force ended up floating all the way to the Atlantic, becoming the first party known to descend the Amazon and thus cross the continent. This feat took almost a year and is still commemorated in Ecuador today.

Lima, in Peru, was the seat of the political administration of Ecuador during the first centuries of colonial rule. Ecuador was originally known as a *gobernación* (province), but in 1563, it became known as the Audiencia de Quito, a more important political division. In 1739, the Audiencia de Quito was transferred from the viceroyalty of Peru, of which it was a part, to the viceroyalty of Colombia (then known as Nueva Grenada).

Ecuador remained a peaceful colony during these centuries, and agriculture and the arts flourished. Various new agricultural products were introduced from Europe, including cattle and bananas, which still remain important in Ecuador today. There was the prolific construction of churches and monasteries, which were decorated with unique carvings and paintings, the result of a blend of Spanish and Indian art influences. This so-called 'Quito School of Art,' still admired by visitors today, has left an indelible stamp on the colonial buildings of the time.

Life was comfortable for the ruling colonialists, but the Indians (and later, the *mestizos,* or people of mixed Spanish and Indian descent) were treated abysmally under their rule. A system of forced labor was not only tolerated but encouraged, and it is no surprise that by the 18th century there were several uprisings of the Indians against the Spanish ruling classes. Both poor and rich died in violent fighting.

One of the best-remembered heroes of the early revolutionary period is Eugenio Espejo, born in Quito in 1747 to an Indian father and a mulatto mother. Espejo was a brilliant man who obtained his doctorate by the age of 20 and became a major literary voice for independence. He wrote political satire, founded a liberal newspaper and spoke out strongly against colonialism. He was imprisoned several times and died in jail in 1795.

Independence

The first serious attempt to liberate Ecuador from Spanish rule was by a partisan group led by Juan Pío Montúfar on August 10, 1809. The group managed to take Quito and install a government, which lasted only 24 days before royalist troops (loyal to Spain) were able to regain control.

Independence was finally achieved by Simón Bolívar, the Venezuelan liberator who marched southward from Caracas, freed Colombia in 1819 and supported the people of Guayaquil when they claimed independence on October 9, 1820. It took almost two years before Ecuador was entirely liberated from Spanish rule. The decisive battle was fought on May 24, 1822, when one of Bolívar's finest officers, Field Marshal Sucre, defeated the royalists at the Battle of Pichincha and took Quito.

Bolívar's idealistic dream was to form a united South America, and he began by amalgamating Venezuela, Colombia and Ecuador into the independent nation of Gran Colombia. This lasted only eight years, with Ecuador becoming fully independent in 1830. In the same year, a treaty was signed with Peru, drawing up a boundary between the two nations. This boundary was shown on all Ecuadorian maps prior to 1999. (In 1942, after a war between Ecuador and Peru, the border was redrawn but was not officially acknowledged by Ecuadorian authorities until a peace treaty was signed with Peru in late 1998.)

Political Development

Independent Ecuador's internal history has been a typically Latin American turmoil of open political warfare between liberals and conservatives. Quito has emerged as the main center for the church-backed conservatives, while Guayaquil has traditionally been associated with liberal and socialist beliefs. This rivalry continues on a social level today; quiteños (people from Quito) have nicknamed guayaquileños (people from Guayaquil) 'monos' (literally 'monkeys'), and the lively coastal people think of the highland inhabitants as very staid and dull.

The rivalry between the political groups has frequently escalated to extreme violence; conservative President García Moreno was shot and killed in 1875, and liberal President Eloy Alfaro was killed and burned by a mob in Quito in 1912. The military began to take control, and the 20th century saw almost as many military as civilian periods of rule for the country.

Ecuador's most recent period of democracy began in 1979, when President Jaime Roldos Aguilera was elected. He died in an airplane crash in 1981, and his term of office was completed by his vice president, Osvaldo Hurtado Larrea.

In 1984, the conservative León Febres Cordero was elected, followed in 1988 by Rodrigo Borja, a social democrat, whose government then leaned to the left. The 1992 elections resulted in the victory of another conservative – Sixto Durán Ballén, a quiteño of the Republican Unity Party. President Durán's right-wing government attempted to tackle the deficit and reduce inflation, but ran into opposition from trade unions, who opposed privatization proposals, and from indigenous and environmental groups, who opposed the destruction of their homelands and the Amazon rainforest by oil exploration. Widespread protests created major problems for the administration, which was also plagued with corruption scandals, one of which involved Vice President Alberto Dahik, who resigned and left Ecuador after being accused of depositing state funds into private bank accounts.

Political Turmoil

The contenders in the 1996 election were two firebrand politicians from Guayaquil, both known for their brash, macho attitudes. The right-wing Jaime Nebot was defeated by the populist Abdala Bucaram, who received about 54% of the vote and was nicknamed 'El Loco' (The Madman) for his fiery, curse-laden style of oration and his penchant for performing at rock concerts as part of his campaign. Bucaram promised cheap public housing, lower prices for food staples and free medicine; but instead he promptly devalued Ecuador's currency, the sucre, and increased living costs while carousing in nightclubs. Within a few months, massive strikes led by trade unions and Conaie (Confederation of Indigenous Nationalities of Ecuador) paralyzed the country. Congress declared Bucaram 'mentally unfit,' terminated his presidency, and Bucaram fled to Panama.

After Bucaram was ousted, his vice president, Rosalía Arteaga, became Ecuador's first female president, albeit for less than two days. Congress voted overwhelmingly to replace her with Fabián Alarcón, the head of congress. He led the government until elections were held again in 1998, when quiteño Jamil Mahuad of the Popular Democracy party defeated businessman Alvaro Noboa by less than 5% of the popular vote.

Mahuad, educated at Harvard, was widely seen as an honest politician who could pull Ecuador out of its worst economic crisis since the early 20th century. His reputation was badly tarnished by a banking scandal, however, and by late 1999, his popularity ratings had dropped to single

The Border Dispute with Peru

A glance at any Ecuadorian map published before 1998 will show Ecuador's claim to a large section of jungle extending beyond Iquitos. The basis of this claim has a long history. After independence in 1822, the new republic of Ecuador claimed lands as far south as Río Marañon (in northern Peru) and as far east as the present border with Brazil. This remote and difficult-to-control area was slowly settled by increasing numbers of Peruvians (as well as by a few Colombians and Brazilians). Ecuador gradually lost lands to these countries. In 1941, matters came to a head and war with Peru broke out. Each country accused the other of beginning the aggression. The following year, a treaty signed at Río de Janeiro ended the war and Peru was allotted a huge section of what had been Ecuador.

The Ecuadorians never officially accepted the full terms of this treaty, claiming that the treaty was bulldozed through when most of the world was occupied with WWII; that Peru invaded the country; that the limits of the treaty were geographically invalid; and that the land was theirs anyway. However, the border as drawn up by the 1942 treaty was internationally accepted.

This dispute resulted in armed skirmishes every few years. The last major battles were in early 1981, when several soldiers were killed and aircraft shot down; and in early 1995, when several dozen soldiers were killed on both sides. Some political observers suggest that the wars served politicians by increasing their national popularity during periods of internal crisis or during election years.

Finally, leaders of both countries agreed to a compromise, whereby Ecuador gained a square kilometer of land that was previously Peru's. President Mahuad of Ecuador and President Fujimori of Peru signed a binding peace treaty in 1998, and the countries have not only improved their diplomatic relationship, they have also improved their economic relationship with more trade.

For travelers, the peace treaty means that there are more functioning border crossings between the two countries in remote regions, which were previously strictly controlled.

digits. The year 1999 also saw a disastrous devaluation of the sucre, and Mahuad announced that the only way to stop this downward economic spiral was to dollarize the economy (see the boxed text 'Ecuador's Dollarization' in the Facts for the Visitor chapter).

This announcement led to a national strike and a march of thousands of poor protesters on government buildings in Quito, led by the leaders of Conaie and a contingent of mainly junior military officers. After the marchers took over the Congress building on January 20, 2000, Antonio Vargas, the leader of Conaie, along with army colonel Lucio Gutiérrez and former supreme court president Carlos Solorzano, briefly formed a governing triumvirate. A few hours later, Mahuad resigned, and his vice president, Gustavo Noboa, backed by most of the military, assumed power, making him Ecuador's fifth president in fewer than three years. Mahuad's most lasting legacy was his peace treaty with Peru (see the boxed text 'The Border Dispute with Peru'.)

Noboa was generally seen as one of the few honest politicians in a country where political corruption is the norm. He soon announced that plans for dollarization would continue and began austerity measures to stabilize the economy in order to obtain US$2 billion in aid from the International Monetary Fund (IMF) and other international lenders. In December 2000, the cost of gasoline went up 25%, bus fares by as much as 75%, and some cooking fuels doubled in price.

In early January 2001, teachers and students protested the price hikes with demonstrations in Quito and other major cities. They were immediately supported by labor unions and Indian groups. Later in January, 5000 Indian protesters set up camp in Quito's Salesian University. Others erected roadblocks on major highways; some schools closed down; and the country was effectively paralyzed. Antonio Vargas, leader of Conaie, together with other Indian leaders, was arrested and held for several days. They were eventually released, but on February 2, 2001, the president announced a national state of emergency. The tense situation was defused after the government and Indian leaders agreed to reduce the costs of cooking fuel and bus fares for students and senior citizens, and place a year-long moratorium on further fuel price increases.

Strikes are frequent in Ecuador. In mid-2001, doctors went on strike for higher pay, and medical services were reduced to basic essentials in public hospitals, although patients who could afford the higher cost of private clinics were able to obtain services. Banana workers struck in August 2001, resulting in a $28 million loss of crops.

The main news in 2002 was the election, which was won by Lucio Gutiérrez, the army colonel who helped to oust President Mahuad in January 2000. A citizen of the Oriente town of Tena, Gutiérrez attracted the popular vote with his nontraditional socio-political background. He took office in January 2003, with the realization that his supporters and detractors alike agreed upon one thing – Gutiérrez was going to have a difficult job in front of him.

GEOGRAPHY

Despite its small size, Ecuador is one of the world's most varied countries. At 283,560 sq km, it is about the size of New Zealand or the US state of Nevada, and it's somewhat larger than the UK. Ecuador straddles the equator on the Pacific coast of South America and is bordered by Colombia to the north and Peru to the south and east. The country is divided into three regions. The Andean range, with Chimborazo (6310m) as Ecuador's highest peak, runs north to south, splitting the country into the western coastal lowlands and the eastern jungles of the upper Amazon Basin, locally called the Oriente.

The central highlands contain two somewhat parallel volcanic mountain ranges, each about 400km long, with a valley nestled between them, appropriately dubbed 'The Avenue of the Volcanoes' by the German explorer Alexander von Humboldt, who visited in 1802. Within the valley is the capital, Quito (at 2850m, the world's second-highest national capital after La Paz, Bolivia), as well as other towns and tiny villages that are often of great interest for their Indian markets and fiestas. This region has the highest population density in the country.

The western coastal lowlands used to be heavily forested, but most of the natural vegetation has been destroyed for agriculture, and the mangroves have been hacked out in order to create shrimp ponds. The western provinces of Los Ríos, Manabí and El Oro are the most intensively farmed in Ecuador. The beaches are blessed with warm water year-round and provide good surfing, but are not as pretty as the beaches of the Caribbean.

The eastern lowlands of the Oriente still retain much of their virgin rainforest, but oil

El Niño

At irregular intervals, usually between two to seven years, the warm eastbound central Pacific currents of January through April are more pronounced and may flow for a longer period, causing the El Niño phenomenon. This is characterized by abnormally high oceanic temperatures during the coastal rainy season. The warmer seas bring flooding rain and storms to the coast. Other effects attributed to El Niño may be experienced worldwide.

A particularly extreme El Niño occurred from late 1982 through early 1983, causing severe problems for the wildlife of the Galápagos Islands and for the coastal fishing industry, as well as flooding much of Peru's north coast. This was repeated in 1997–98, with grave consequences for the Ecuadorian and northern Peruvian coasts – landslides wiped out major roads and cut off villages for weeks on end. The bus journey from the Ecuadorian border to Lima, normally under 24 hours, grew to four days during the worst months.

The climatological phenomenon is named El Niño (The Baby Boy) because it usually gets under way at year's end, or about the time the Christ child was born. For all its disruptiveness, El Niño is still far from being fully understood by climatologists. However, the US National Oceanographic and Atmospheric Administration (NOAA) now has a website explaining what is known about the El Niño phenomenon and is making some attempt at forecasting future events. You can find the site at **W** www.pmel.noaa.gov/tao/elnino/nino-home.html.

exploitation and colonization are seriously threatening this habitat. The population of the Oriente has more than tripled since the late 1970s.

In addition, Ecuador owns the Galápagos Islands, which are on the equator about 1000km west of the mainland.

CLIMATE

Ecuador's climate consists of wet and dry seasons, with significant variation among the different geographical regions.

The Galápagos and the coast are influenced by ocean currents. The warm central

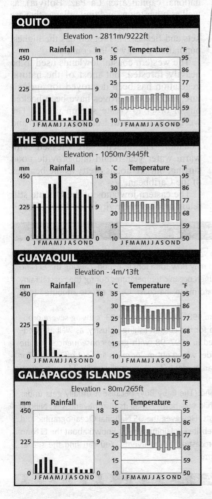

Pacific current causes a hot, rainy, humid season from January through April, when torrential downpours often disrupt communications. Daytime high temperatures average 30°C (86°F), and this is when locals visit the beach to cool off. From May to December, cool currents from the south keep temperatures a few degrees lower, and it rarely rains, although it is often gray, damp and overcast, especially in July and August.

The highland dry season is from June through September, with another short, dry season around Christmas. It doesn't rain daily in the wet season, however. April, the wettest month, averages one rainy day in two. Daytime temperatures in Quito average a high of 21°C (70°F) and a low of 8°C (48°F) year-round.

In the Oriente, it rains during most months, especially during the afternoon and evening. August and December through March are usually the driest months, and April through June are the wettest – with regional variations. It's almost as hot as the coast.

Remember the Ecuadorian adage that all four seasons can be experienced in one day, and the most predictable aspect of Ecuador's weather is its unpredictability.

ECOLOGY & ENVIRONMENT

Deforestation is Ecuador's severest environmental problem. In the highlands, almost all of the natural forest cover has disappeared – only a few pockets of forest remain, mainly in private nature reserves. Along the coast, once-plentiful mangrove forests have all but vanished, too. These forests harbor a great diversity of marine and shore life, but they have been removed to make artificial ponds in which shrimp are reared for export.

About 95% of the forests of the western slopes and lowlands have become agricultural land, mostly banana plantations. These forests are host to more species than almost anywhere on the planet, and many of them are endemic. Countless species have surely become extinct even before they have been identified. An effort is now being made to conserve what little there is left in both private and national reserves.

Although much of the rainforest in the Ecuadorian Amazon remains standing, it is being seriously threatened by fragmentation.

Since the discovery of oil, roads have been built, colonists have followed and the destruction of the forest has increased exponentially. The main drive behind the destruction is logging for short-term timber sales, followed by cattle ranching.

Clearly, these problems are linked tightly with Ecuador's economy. Oil, bananas and shrimp are the nation's top three exports. However, the serious environmental damage caused by the production of these and other products requires that their value be carefully examined.

Apart from the direct loss of tropical forest, and the plants and animals that depend upon it, deforestation also leads to other severe environmental degradation (see the boxed text 'Why Conserve the Rainforest?' later in this chapter for more information). The loss of forest cover allows for soil erosion, which is then washed into rivers. The increased amount of silt in the rivers make them less able to support microorganisms, and this affects the rest of the food chain.

Attempts to combat erosion and desertification using artificial fertilizers also contributes to the pollution of rivers, as do oil spills in the rainforest. Many indigenous inhabitants use the rivers as a source of drinking water and food, and their livelihoods are directly threatened by these and other pollutants. Other water-related problems are caused by improper and poorly regulated mining in the coastal areas and inadequate sewage-disposal facilities in the major cities. Unfortunately, government policies allow oil exploration and encourage the colonization and clearing of land with little regard for forests, rivers, wildlife or residents.

FLORA & FAUNA

Part of the reason that Ecuador is one of the most species-rich nations on the globe is that it is a tropical country. Scientists realize that the tropics harbor a much greater diversity of organisms than do more temperate countries, but the reasons for this variation are still a matter of debate and research. The most commonly held belief is that the tropics acted as a refuge for plants and animals during the many ice ages that affected more temperate regions – in other words, the much longer and relatively stable climatic history of the tropics has enabled speciation

to occur. This may well be part of the answer, but ecologists also offer various other, more technical, theories.

A better-understood reason for Ecuador's biodiversity is simply that there are a great number of different habitats within the borders of the small country. Obviously, the cold, high Andes support species very different from the low tropical rainforests, and when all the intermediate areas are included and the coastal region added, the result is a wealth of habitats, ecosystems and wildlife. Ecologists have labeled Ecuador one of the world's 'megadiversity hotspots.' This has attracted increasing numbers of nature lovers from all over the world.

Habitats

Ecologists use a system called Holdridge Life Zones to classify the type of vegetation found in a given area. Climatic data, such as temperature, rainfall and the variation of the two throughout the year, are analyzed and combined with information on latitudinal regions and altitudinal belts to give 116 life zones on earth. Some two-dozen tropical life zones are found in Ecuador. These are often named according to forest type and altitude, and so there are dry, moist, wet and rain forests in tropical, premontane, lower montane, montane and subalpine areas. Within each life zone, several types of habitat may occur. Thus, Ecuador has many habitats, each with particular associations of plants and animals. Some of the most important or interesting are described here.

Mangrove Swamps Mangroves are trees that have evolved the remarkable ability to grow in salt water. The red mangrove is the most common in Ecuador, and like other mangroves, it has a broadly spreading system of intertwining stilt roots to support the tree in the unstable sandy or silty soils of the shoreline.

Mangroves form forests and are good colonizing species – their stilt roots trap sediments and build up rich organic soil, which in turn supports other plants. In between the roots, a protected habitat is provided for many types of fish, as well as mollusks, crustaceans and other invertebrates. The branches provide nesting areas for seabirds, such as pelicans and frigatebirds. Mangroves are found primarily in the far northern and southern coastal regions of the country – the shrimp industry has extensively destroyed the mangroves on most of Ecuador's coastline, endangering the breeding grounds of many species. For more information, see the boxed text 'Maltreated Mangroves' in the North Coast & Lowlands chapter.

Tropical Dry Forests This habitat is fast disappearing and is found in hot coastal areas with well-defined wet and dry seasons. Tropical dry-forest trees lose their leaves during the dry season and tend to grow in a less-concentrated pattern than those in rainforests, creating a more open habitat. It is estimated that only 1% of tropical dry forest remains undisturbed. The only extensive example in Ecuador is in Parque Nacional Machalilla; see that section in the North Coast & Lowlands chapter for a more in-depth description of this type of forest.

Tropical Cloud Forests These types of forest are found in remote valleys at higher elevations, and comparatively little is known about them. They are called cloud forests because they trap (and help create) clouds, which drench the forest in a fine mist, allowing some particularly delicate forms of plant life to survive. Cloud-forest trees are adapted to steep rocky soils and a harsh climate. They have a characteristically low, gnarled growth of dense, small-leaved canopies and moss-covered branches, and support a host of plants, such as orchids, ferns and bromeliads. These aerial plants, which gather their moisture and some nutrients without ground roots, are collectively termed epiphytes.

The dense vegetation at all levels of this forest gives it a mysterious and delicate fairy-tale appearance. Cloud forests are the home of such rare species as the woolly tapir, the Andean spectacled bear and the puma. This habitat is particularly important as a source of freshwater and as an impediment to erosion.

Páramo The high-altitude grasslands and scrublands, known as the *páramo*, lie above the cloud forests. The páramo is the natural 'sponge' of the Andes – it catches and gradually releases much of the water that is eventually used by city dwellers in the highlands. The páramo covers over 10% of Ecuador's land area and is characterized by a harsh climate, high levels of ultraviolet light and wet, peaty soils. It is an extremely specialized highland habitat unique to the neotropics (tropical America) and is found only in the area starting from the highlands of Costa Rica at 10°N to northern Peru at 10°S. Similarly elevated grasslands in other parts of the world differ in their climates and evolutionary history, and have different assemblages of plants and animals.

The páramo has a limited flora that is dominated by cushion plants, hard grasses and small herbaceous plants. These plants have adapted well to the harsh environment, and consequently, the vegetation looks strange and interesting. Major adaptations include small, thick leaves, which are less susceptible to frost; curved leaves with heavy, waxy skins to reflect extreme solar radiation; an insulating fine, hairy down on the plant's surface; a rosette leaf formation, which prevents the leaves from shading one another during photosynthesis and which protects the delicate center of the plant; and compactness, so the plant grows close to the ground, where the temperature is more constant and the wind is less strong.

Not all páramo plants are so compact, however. The giant *Espeletia* are a weird sight as their loosely arranged stands float into view in a typical páramo mist. They are as high as a person, hence the local nickname *frailejones,* meaning 'gray friars.' They are an unmistakable feature of the northern Ecuadorian páramo, particularly in the El Ángel region, near Tulcán.

The páramo is also characterized by dense thickets of small trees. These are often of the *Polylepis* species, which, with Himalayan pines, share the world altitudinal record for trees. They were once extensive, but fire and grazing have pushed them back into small pockets. Instead, spiky, resistant tussock grass, locally called *ichu,* is commonly encountered. It grows in large clumps and makes walking uncomfortable.

Rainforests Of all the tropical habitats found in Ecuador, the rainforest seems to attract the most attention from visitors. It is very different from temperate forests, which have relatively few species. If you stand in one spot and look around, you'll see scores of different species of trees, and you'll often have to walk only several hundred meters to find another example of any particular species.

Visitors to the rainforest are often bewildered by the huge variety of plants and animals. Useful field guides are few, with the exception of those for mammals and birds. For this reason, it is worth investing in a guided natural-history tour if you are particularly interested in learning about the fantastic flora and fauna – although no guide will be able to answer all your questions!

The Galápagos Islands

Between 700 and 800 species of vascular plants have been recorded in the Galápagos, of which over 250 species are endemic. In addition, about 500 nonvascular plants (mosses, lichens and liverworts) have been described. There are six different vegetation zones, beginning with the shore and ending with the highlands. These are the littoral, arid, transition, Scalesia, Miconia and fern-sedge zones. Each zone supports different and distinctive plant species.

The littoral zone contains species such as mangroves, saltbush and sesuvium, which are able to tolerate relatively high quantities of salt in their environment. Immediately beyond the littoral zone is the arid zone, where many of the islands' cactus species are found, including forests of the giant prickly pear cactus. Trees such as the ghostly looking *palo santo*, the *palo verde* and the spiny acacias are also found here, as is the yellow cordia shrub.

The transition zone has decreasing numbers of the arid zone trees and increasing numbers of perennial herbs, smaller shrubs and lichens. The vegetation is varied and thick. This zone gives way to a cloud-forest type of vegetation, and the dominant tree is the endemic *Scalesia*. The trees are covered with smaller plants such as bromeliads, ferns, mosses, liverworts and orchids.

Next is the treeless high-altitude Miconia zone, characterized by dense endemic shrubs, liverworts and ferns. This zone is found only on the southern slopes of Santa Cruz and San Cristóbal. Finally, the fern-sedge zone is at the highest altitude and contains mainly ferns and grasses, including the Galápagos tree fern, which grows up to 3m high.

Flora

There are about 25,000 species of vascular plants in Ecuador, and new species are being discovered every year. This number is exceptionally high when compared to the 17,000 species found in the entire North American continent. A few of the most important plants are mentioned under Habitats, previous.

Fauna

For more detailed information about the wildlife of the Galápagos Islands, see the Galápagos Wildlife Guide special section.

Birds People from all over the world come to Ecuador because of the great number of species recorded here – over 1500, or approximately twice the number found in any one of the continents of North America, Europe or Australia. It's impossible to give a precise number, as new species of bird are often reported. Most birds added to the Ecuadorian list are already known from other South American countries. Occasionally, however, a species new to science is discovered – a very rare event in the world of birds. It is likely that bird species exist in Ecuador that have never been described by scientists.

Many visitors are interested in seeing the birds typical of Ecuador, such as the Andean condor, which is considered to be the largest flying bird in the world. With a wingspan of 3m and a weight of 10kg, it is certainly a magnificent bird. In 1880, the British mountaineer Edward Whymper noted that he commonly saw a dozen on the wing at the same time. Today, there are only a few hundred pairs left in the Ecuadorian highlands, so you shouldn't expect to see them frequently.

Other birds of the highlands include the carunculated caracara, a large member of the falcon family. It has bright orange-red facial skin, a yellowish bill and legs, and white thighs and underparts; it is otherwise black. This bird is often seen in the páramo of Parque Nacional Cotopaxi (see the Central Highlands chapter). Also frequently sighted here is the Andean lapwing – unmistakable with its harsh and noisy call; its reddish eyes, legs and bill; and its brown, white and black-striped wing pattern, which is particularly noticeable in flight.

The rufous-collared sparrow, readily identified by the chestnut collar on the back of its neck, replaces the similar house sparrow known in other continents.

For many visitors, the diminutive hummingbirds are the most delightful birds to observe. About 120 species have been recorded in Ecuador, and their exquisite beauty is matched by extravagant names, such as green-tailed goldenthroat, spangled coquette, fawn-breasted brilliant and amethyst-throated sunangel.

Hummingbirds beat their wings up to 80 times per second in a figure-eight pattern, thus producing the hum for which they are named. This exceptionally rapid wingbeat enables them to hover in place while feeding on nectar, or even to fly backward. These tiny birds must feed frequently in order to gain the energy they need to keep them flying. Species such as the Andean hillstar, living in the páramo, have evolved an amazing strategy to survive a cold night: they lower their body temperature by about 25°C, thus lowering their metabolism drastically.

For bird-watchers, a trip to the Galápagos Islands is very rewarding. About half of the 58 resident species are endemic to the islands, and most of the Galápagos birds have either lost, or not evolved, a fear of humans. Therefore, travelers can walk among colonies of blue-footed boobies or magnificent frigatebirds without causing them to be alarmed and fly off.

Serious bird-watchers enjoy the Ecuadorian coast. A local ornithologist claims that there are twice as many endemic species within 50km of Guayaquil than there are in the Galápagos Islands, but many of these are small and not as visually exciting.

Mammals There are some 300 species of mammals recorded in the country. These vary from monkeys in the Amazonian lowlands to the rare Andean spectacled bear in the highlands. The most diverse mammals are the bats, of which there are well over 100 species in Ecuador alone.

Visitors to protected areas of the Amazonian lowlands may see one or more of the several species of monkeys found in Ecuador, including the howler, spider, woolly, titi, capuchin and squirrel monkeys, as well as tamarins and marmosets. New World monkeys have been studied comparatively little, and their names are still under constant study and revision.

The male howler monkeys are heard as often as they are seen; their eerie vocalizations carry long distances and have been likened to a baby crying or to the wind moaning through the trees. Many visitors are unable to believe that they are hearing a monkey when they first listen to the mournful sound.

Other tropical specialities include two species of sloths. The diurnal three-toed sloth is more commonly seen than the nocturnal two-toed sloth. They are usually found hanging motionless from tree limbs or progressing at a painfully slow speed along a branch toward a particularly succulent bunch of leaves, which are their primary food source. Leaf digestion takes several days, and sloths defecate about once a week. Sloths are most fastidious with their toilet habits, always climbing down from their tree to deposit their weekly bowel movement on the ground. Why they go to all this trouble is one of the mysteries of mammalian life in the tropics.

Mammals commonly seen in the highlands include deer, rabbits and squirrels. Foxes are also occasionally sighted. There are far fewer species of mammals in the highlands than in the lowlands. The mammals most commonly associated with the Andes are llamas, but there are far fewer in Ecuador than in Peru or Bolivia. They can be seen occasionally on the outskirts of Quito, and there is a huge flock near the entrance of Parque Nacional Cotopaxi. Others are seen in and around remote Andean villages. Llamas are exclusively domesticated and are used primarily as pack animals, although their skin and meat is occasionally used in remote areas. Their wild relative, the lovely *vicuña*, has been reintroduced to the Chimborazo area and can occasionally be spotted there, although not elsewhere.

Other possible mammal sightings include anteaters, armadillos, agoutis (large rodents), capybaras (even larger rodents, some weighing up to 65kg), peccaries (wild pigs) and otters. River dolphins are occasionally sighted in Amazonian tributaries. Other exotic mammals, such as ocelots, jaguars, tapirs, pumas and spectacled bears, are very rarely seen.

Insects Many thousands of insect species have been recorded in Ecuador; undoubtedly, tens of thousands more remain undiscovered.

Butterflies, of which there are some 4500 species in Ecuador, are among the first insects that the visitor to the tropics notices. Perhaps the most dazzling are the morphos. With their 15cm wingspan and electric-blue upper wings, they lazily flap and glide along tropical rivers in a shimmering display. When they land, however, their wings close and only the brown underwings are visible. In an instant their colors change from outrageously flaunting to modestly camouflaging.

Camouflage plays an important part in many insects' lives. Some resting butterflies look exactly like green or brown leaves; others look like the scaly bark of the tree on which they are resting. Caterpillars are often masters of disguise. Some species mimic twigs; another is capable of constricting certain muscles to make itself look like the head of a viper, and yet another species looks so much like bird droppings that it rarely gets attacked by predators.

Any walk through a tropical forest will almost invariably allow the observer to study many different types of ants. Particularly interesting are the leaf-cutter ants, which can be seen marching in columns along the forest floor carrying pieces of leaves like little parasols above their heads. The leaf segments are taken into the ants' underground colony, and there, the leaves are allowed to rot into a mulch. The ants tend their mulch gardens carefully and allow a certain species of fungus to grow there. The fruiting bodies of the fungus are then used to feed the ant colony, which can exceed a million ants.

Amphibians & Reptiles These creatures form a fascinating part of the Ecuadorian fauna. The approximately 360 species of amphibians include tree frogs that spend their entire life cycle in trees. Some of them have solved the problem of where to lay their eggs by doing so in the water trapped in bromeliads, which are cuplike plants that live high up in the forest canopy.

Dendrobatids, better known by their colloquial name of poison-arrow frogs, are among the most brightly colored species of frog. Some are bright red with black dots, others are red with blue legs and still others are bright green with black markings. Some species have skin glands exuding toxins that can cause paralysis and death in many animals, including humans. *Dendrobatids* have long been used by Latin American forest Indians to provide a poison with which to dip the tips of their hunting arrows; the toxins are effective when introduced into the bloodstream (as with arrows), but they have little effect when a frog is casually touched.

Nearly 350 reptile species are recorded in Ecuador, about 100 more than are found in the whole of North America. Snakes, much talked about but seldom seen, make up roughly half of these. They usually slither away into the undergrowth when people are coming, so only a few fortunate visitors are able to catch a glimpse of one. Perhaps Ecuador's most feared snake is the fer-de-lance, which is very poisonous and can be fatal to humans. It often lives in overgrown, brushy fields, so workers clearing these fields are the most frequent victims. Tourists are rarely bitten.

Fish Recent inventories of Amazonian fish have shown surprisingly high biodiversity, with about 2500 species in the whole Amazon Basin and roughly 1000 species in Ecuador. Some of them are fearsome. The electric eel can produce shocks of 600 volts; a school of piranha can devour a large animal in minutes; stingrays can deliver a crippling sting; and the tiny candirú catfish can swim up the human urethra and become lodged there by erecting its sharp spines. Despite these horror stories, most Amazonian rivers are safe to swim in. Follow the example of the locals: Shuffle your feet as you enter the water to scare off the bottom-dwelling stingrays; wear a bathing suit to avoid having a candirú swim up your urethra; and don't swim with open, bleeding cuts or in areas where fish are being cleaned, because piranhas are attracted to blood and guts.

Conservation

The environment has never had a reliable watchdog within the Ecuadorian government, with various offices being created, shunted around, renamed and closed down during past administrations. Although there is currently a Department of Environmental Management within the Ministry of Agriculture,

Ecuador lacks the financial resources to commit itself to strong government-funded conservation programmes. Therefore, various international conservation agencies have provided much-needed expertise and economic support. The focus of conservation work is financial support to train and equip local park rangers, educate the population,

Why Conserve the Rainforest?

The loss of the world's tropical forests is an acute problem; it is happening so rapidly that most will probably disappear within decades. Two important questions arise: Why are habitats such as the tropical rainforests so important, and what can be done to prevent their loss?

Roughly half of the 1.7 million known species on earth live in tropical rainforests, such as those of Parque Nacional Yasuní (see The Oriente chapter). Scientists predict that millions more species remain to be discovered, principally in the world's remaining rainforests, which have the greatest biodiversity of all habitats. This incredible array of living things cannot exist unless the rainforest is protected; deforestation will result in countless extinctions.

Medicines ranging from anaesthetics to antibiotics, from contraceptives to cures for heart disease, have been extracted from rainforest flora. Knowledge of countless other medicinal uses of plants is being lost as remaining rainforest tribal groups are assimilated into the Western way of life, or destroyed by disease or genocide. Other pharmaceutical treasures remain locked up in tropical forests, unknown to anyone, and may never be discovered.

Many tropical crops suffer from a lack of genetic diversity because agriculturalists have bred monocultural strains that are high yielding, easy to harvest and that taste good. If these monocultures are attacked by a new disease or pest epidemic, they could be destroyed because resistant strains have been bred out of the population. Crops such as bananas are also found in the wild in tropical forests. In the event of an epidemic, scientists could seek out disease-resistant wild strains to breed into the commercially raised crops. Deforestation leads to loss of the genetic diversity that may help species adapt to a changing world.

The survival of tropical rainforests is also vital to the indigenous cultures who live within them. In Ecuador, the Huaorani, Shuar, Cofan, Secoya and Cayapa, as well as other Indian groups, still live in a more or less traditional manner, relying on the rainforest to maintain a way of life that has persisted in similar forms for centuries.

Worldwide climatic patterns are moderated by rainforests and their destruction is a major contributing factor to global warming, which, if left unchecked, could lead to disastrous changes to our world. These include the melting of ice caps, causing a rise in ocean levels and the flooding of coastal cities; and the desertification of the world's breadbasket regions.

These are good reasons for rainforest preservation, but the economic importance of forest use by the developing nations that own these forests must also be considered. Rainforests provide resources in the way of lumber, pastureland and possible mineral wealth, but this is a short-sighted view.

The long-term importance of rainforests as a resource of biodiversity, genetic variation and pharmaceutical wealth is recognized both by the countries that own the forests and by the rest of the world. Efforts are under way to find further economic value in standing rainforest. One way is by protecting it in national preserves and making it accessible to tourists. Ecotourism is becoming increasingly important for the economy of nations such as Ecuador.

People are more likely to visit Ecuador to see monkeys in the forest than cows in a pasture. Apart from spending money on tourism, people passing time in the tropics become more understanding of the natural beauty within forests and of the importance of preserving them. As a result, visitors return home and become goodwill ambassadors for tropical forests.

Other innovative projects for the sustainable development of tropical forests are being organized. The *tagua* nut is now harvested sustainably. This South American rainforest product is as hard as ivory and is used to carve ornaments and make buttons, which are bought by clothing manufacturers. Brazil nuts are also harvested. Debt-for-nature swaps have been initiated by conservation organizations. Iguana farms, orchid plantations, the export of tropical butterfly pupae, wickerwork from aerial roots and the seed harvesting of ornamental plants are some of the other projects being explored.

PARKS & RESERVES

Reserva Ecológica de Manglares Cayapas Mataje

COLOMBIA

Reserva Ecológica El Ángel

Reserva Ecológica Cotacachi-Cayapas

Reserva Ecológica Mache Chindul

Reserva Biológica Guandera

Reserva Biológica Bilsa

Reserva Biológica Maquipucuna

Reserva Biológica Los Cedros

Reserva Ecológica Cayambe-Coca

Equator

Reserva Geobotánica Pululahua

Reserva Bellavista

QUITO

Reserva Biológica Limoncocha

Reserva Produccín Faunística Cuyabeno

PACIFIC OCEAN

Refugio de Vida Silvestre Pasochoa

Reserva Ecológica Antisana

Parque Nacional Sumaco-Galeras

Río Napa

Area Nacional de Recreación El Boliche

Reserva Ecológica Los Ilinizas

Parque Nacional Cotopaxi

Parque Nacional Machalilla

La Reserva de Producción Faunística Chimborazo

Parque Nacional Llanganates

Parque Nacional Yasuní

Reserva Ecológica de Manglares Churute

Río Pastaza

GUAYAQUIL

Parque Nacional Sangay

PERU

Refugio de Vida Silvestre Isla Santa Clara

CUENCA

Parque Nacional Cajas

Río Santiago

Galápagos Islands   *same scale as main map*

PACIFIC OCEAN   Equator

Parque Nacional Galápagos

Parque Nacional Podocarpus

Panamericana

0   50   100km
0   30   60mi

---

fund research and develop low-impact and sustainable practices, such as responsible tourism.

By far the biggest environmental non-governmental organization (NGO) within Ecuador is the Fundación Natura, which was one of the first to become involved in improving the system of protected areas in the country and has developed its own cloud-forest reserve – Pasochoa, near Quito. The Fundación Natura also has an environmental education programme and arranges campaigns on specific conservation issues. Because it is Ecuador's biggest and best-known NGO, it tends to receive a large share of international funding and has been criticized by smaller, grassroots NGOs as having a top-heavy bureaucracy.

Local conservation groups have blossomed since the late 1980s. Groups on the coast are particularly concerned with defending the mangrove forests and have been forging cooperative links with shell and crab collectors, who are being affected by mangrove destruction. Some groups have been quite successful in providing legal protection for these forests. Other groups have concentrated on improving environmental data collection and training members in the disciplines needed to create a strong information base for national conservation research.

The Amazon region has been an important focus for small NGOs in recent years. They focus not only on the environment, but also on the protection of the rights of indigenous inhabitants. In the past decade, organizations protecting the fast-diminishing and unique forests on the western slopes of the Ecuadorian Andes have also become important.

Several small groups have been established to protect specific natural areas. These groups go on to involve communities around the reserves through environmental education, agroforestry and community development projects. Such community involvement at the grassroots level is essential for viable conservation in Ecuador.

The role of indigenous organizations should also be recognized as an effective voice in environmental protection. The struggle they have been engaged in to secure land rights, particularly in the Amazon regions, has gone a long way toward securing the future of the tropical forests in that area.

In the Galápagos Islands, the Charles Darwin Foundation is a long-established and tireless protector of the archipelago. Conservation, scientific research and the education of both locals and international visitors are among its main goals.

National Parks

Ecuador's first *parque nacional* (national park) was the Galápagos, formed in 1959, but it was not until the mid- to late 1970s that a comprehensive national park system began to be established on the mainland. The first mainland park was Cotopaxi, established in 1975, followed by Machalilla, Yasuní and Sangay in 1979, and Podocarpus in 1982. The most important recent addition was Cajas in 1996, among several others, as well as reserves of various kinds and a few national monuments and recreation areas. New reserves and parks are added regularly. In addition, local conservation organizations have set aside private nature reserves. All of Ecuador's major ecosystems are partly protected in one (or more) of these areas.

The national parks do not have much of a tourist infrastructure. There are almost no hostels, drive-in camping grounds, restaurants, ranger stations, museums, scenic overlooks or information centers. Many are inhabited by native peoples who were living in the area for generations before it achieved park or reserve status. Some of the parks and reserves are remote, difficult to reach and lack almost all facilities.

Nevertheless, adventurous travelers can visit most of them, and details are given in the appropriate sections of this book. Entrance fees vary, and Ecuadorians pay only a small fraction of the fee charged to foreign visitors. On the mainland, most highland parks charge $10, and most lowland parks charge $20 per visitor, but these fees are valid for a week and allow in-and-out privileges. Some parks charge less, and others give discounts in low seasons. In the Galápagos Islands, the park fee is $100. Only cash is accepted; no credit cards or traveler's checks.

Some of the funds are supposedly used to better protect the parks by paying for and equipping park rangers and so forth, although most of the money unfortunately ends up in a bureaucratic wasteland. All of these areas are susceptible to interests that are incompatible with full protection: oil drilling, logging, mining, ranching and colonization. Despite this, the national parks do preserve large tracts of pristine habitat, and many travelers visit at least one park or reserve during their stay in Ecuador.

GOVERNMENT & POLITICS

Ecuador is a republic with a democratic government headed by a president. All literate citizens over 18 have the right to vote, and the president must receive over 50% of the vote to be elected. With about 15 different political parties, 50% of the vote is rarely achieved, in which case there is a second round between the top two contenders. A president governs for four years and cannot be re-elected. The president is also the head of the armed forces and appoints his own cabinet ministers.

The legislative branch of government consists of a single Chamber of Representatives (or congress), which appoints the justices of the Supreme Court. There are 123 representatives, 79 of which are popularly elected by all national citizens to serve four-year terms, and 44 of which are popularly elected according to province (two per province) for four-year terms.

There are 22 provinces, each with democratically elected prefects and a governor appointed by the president. The provinces are subdivided into smaller political units, called *cantones;* each canton has a democratically elected *alcalde,* or mayor.

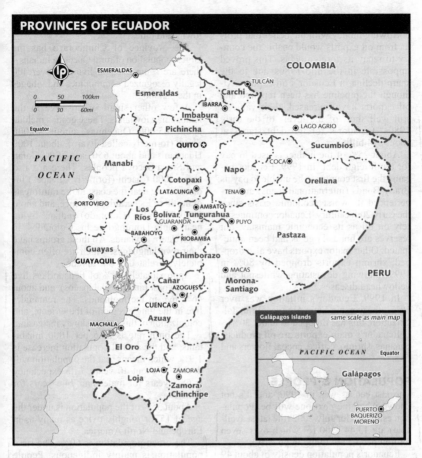

PROVINCES OF ECUADOR

The political parties change often; new ones are formed and old ones are abandoned on a regular basis. They have positions that include left wing, center, populist and right wing; right wing is the most frequently accepted by the voters.

ECONOMY

Until the 1970s, Ecuador was the archetypal 'banana republic,' with bananas the single most important export. This changed with the discovery of oil and petroleum, and exports of these products rose to first place in 1973. By the early 1980s, it accounted for well over half of the total export earnings.

This newfound wealth improved the standards of living to some extent. Nevertheless, Ecuador remains a poor country.

Distribution of wealth has been patchy, and much of the rural population continues to live at the same standard as in the 1970s. About 40% of the national income goes to the richest 5% of the population. However, the country's education and medical services have improved.

Despite the income from oil exports, the 1980s was a difficult decade for the Ecuadorian economy. In 1982–83, El Niño floods caused severe disruptions in agriculture, and this resulted in exports of bananas and coffee being roughly halved. This was followed by a drop in world oil prices in 1986. In 1987, a disastrous earthquake wiped out about 40km of the oil pipeline, severely damaging both the environment and the economy.

After oil was discovered, Ecuador began borrowing money with the belief that profits from oil exports would enable the country to repay its foreign debts. This proved impossible in the mid-1980s due to the sharp decline in Ecuador's oil exports. Although the pipeline has been repaired and oil exports have increased, their value is still well short of the levels of the early 1980s. Ecuador's foreign debt stands at about $14 billion.

About 25% of the budget is used to pay for the foreign debt. In 1999, Ecuador became the first country to be unable to pay its Brady Bonds (international loans) and experienced its worst economic crisis since the early 20th century. Ecuador continues to rely on oil as its economic mainstay, but reserves are not as large as had been anticipated. Other major exports have also dropped; shrimp exports dropped by 80% in 1999 following devastating whitespot and yellowhead diseases.

In 1999, Ecuador's inflation was over 60% – the worst in Latin America. With dollarization, this has dropped to under 20%.

Ecuador's main exports are oil products, bananas, shrimp, coffee, cocoa, flowers and fish.

POPULATION & PEOPLE

The last census was in 1990, and it's not known when the next one will be. Population estimates for July 2002 (the latest available) are 13,447,500 (of which over seven million people are living in poverty).

Ecuador's population density of about 49 people per sq km is the highest of any South American nation. About 25% of this total are Indians, and another 65% are *mestizos*. It is difficult to accurately quantify how many pure-blooded Indians and how many *mestizos* there are – some sources give figures of 40% Indian and 40% *mestizo*. About 7% to 10% of the population are white, and 3% to 10% are black (depending on sources cited), with a small number of people of Asian descent.

The Indian inhabitants of each region have distinctive differences in clothing – it is possible to tell where an Indian is from by the color of their poncho or by the shape of their hat. Most Indians are Quechua. Some of the best-known highland groups include the Otavaleños, Salasacas, Cañaris

and Saraguros. Many Indians now live in towns and cities.

The province of Chimborazo has the largest population of rural Quechua Indians – there are some 270,000 living in over 400 legally recognized communities and villages in the páramo.

A few other small groups live in the Amazonian lowlands. These groups include about 65,000 Quechuas, about 40,000 Shuar (formerly called Jivaro), about 1000 Huaoranis and about 650 each of the Cofan and Siona-Secoya peoples. There are also about 5000 Chachi (formerly Cayapas) Indians living near the coast in the rainforests of northern Esmeraldas Province, and about 1000 Tsachilas (Colorado) Indians living near Santo Domingo de los Colorados, in the western lowlands. All these groups have their own languages, which are often completely unrelated to one another.

Approximately 48% of Ecuadorians live on the coast (and the Galápagos), and about 46% live in the highlands. The remainder live in the jungle region of the Oriente, and colonization of this area is slowly increasing.

The birth rate is 25.5 per 1000 inhabitants, and the annual population increase is 1.9%, which means that the population will double in about 40 years. Life expectancy is 68.8 years for males and 74.6 years for females.

About 35% of the population is under the age of 15, or roughly twice as many as in Europe and North America.

The urban population is 60%. The rural population is mainly indigenous. People living in the country are often referred to as *campesinos* (peasants). An indigenous person is called an *indígena*, but not *indio*, which is considered insulting.

EDUCATION

Elementary education (two years of kindergarten and six grades of school) is mandatory, although about 50% of children drop out of school before completing elementary education. Of those continuing on to the six grades of secondary education, about another 50% drop out. There are about 20 universities and technical colleges in Ecuador.

In the highlands, the school year is from September to June. On the coast, however, the school year is from May to January.

The adult literacy rate is 90%.

ARTS

A visit to any archaeology museum in Ecuador will testify to the artistic excellence of the pre-Columbian peoples. Their pottery shows fine painting and sculpture, and their metallurgy – particularly gold and silver work – was highly developed. Because the names of the artists have long been forgotten, their work is thought of as archaeology rather than fine art.

Colonial Art, Sculpture & Architecture

The Spaniards arriving in the 16th century brought their own artistic concepts, which often revolved around Catholic religious themes. The Spaniards trained local indigenous artists to produce the colonial religious art that is now seen in many churches and art museums. Religious statues were carved, painted, then embellished with gold leaf – sculpture, painting and gold work were all techniques with which the Indians had long been familiar. Paintings, too, had liberal amounts of gold leaf included. And so arose the Escuela Quiteña, or Quito School of Art: Spanish religious concepts as executed and heavily influenced by Indian artists.

The Quito school lasted through the 17th and 18th centuries. Some of the best-known artists of this period include the sculptor Manuel Chili, better known by his nickname, 'Caspicara.' Some of his work can be seen in the Church of San Francisco in Quito. This church also contains a famous sculpture of the Virgin, by Bernardo Legarda. Notable painters include Miguel de Santiago, whose huge canvases grace the walls of Quito's church of San Agustín; and Manuel Samaniego; Nicolás Goríbar; and Bernardo Rodríguez.

Many of Quito's churches were built during this colonial period, and their architects were also somewhat influenced by the Quito school. In addition, churches often had Moorish (Arab) influences (Spain had been under the rule of the Moors for centuries). The overall appearance of the architecture of colonial churches is overpoweringly ornamental and almost cloyingly rich – in short, baroque. In contrast, the houses of the middle and upper classes of that period were elegant and simple, often consisting of rooms with verandas around a central courtyard.

Many of the houses had two stories, the upper floors bearing ornate balconies. The walls were whitewashed and the roofs were of red tile. Quito's colonial architecture has been well preserved, which led to Unesco declaring old Quito a *Patrimonio de la Humanidad* (Patrimony of Humanity) in 1978. Several other towns, notably Cuenca, have attractive colonial architecture.

Post-Colonial Art

The Quito school died out with the coming of independence, and was followed by the 19th-century Republican period. Favorite subjects were heroes of the revolution, important members of high society in the new republic and florid landscapes.

The 20th century saw the rise of the indigenist school, characterized by subject matter rather than by style. The oppression and burdens of Ecuador's indigenous inhabitants are the school's unifying theme. Important indigenist artists include Eduardo Kingman (1913–98), Endara Crow (1936–96), Camilo Egas (1899–1962) and Oswaldo Guayasamín (1919–99). These and other artists have works in modern galleries and museums in Quito.

Music

Traditional Andean music has a distinctive and haunting sound that has been popularized in Western culture by songs such as Simon and Garfunkel's version of 'El Cóndor Pasa' ('If I Could').

Two main reasons contribute to the otherworldly quality of the traditional music of the Andes. The first is the scale: it is pentatonic, or consisting of five notes, as opposed to the seven-note octaves we are used to. The second is the fact that string and brass instruments were imported by the Spanish; pre-Columbian instruments consisted of wind and percussion, which effectively portray the windswept quality of páramo life.

Ancient traditional instruments include the *rondador* (bamboo panpipe); the *quena* and *pingullo* (large and small bamboo flutes); *conchas* (conch shells played like a horn); and a variety of drums, rattles and bells. The Spanish brought stringed instruments (guitars, harps and violins). Some of these were incorporated into Andean music, and others were modified to produce the typical *charango*, a very small instrument with five double strings. The sounding box was often made of an armadillo shell, but fortunately for armadillos, wood is being increasingly used.

Most traditional music today is a blend of pre-Columbian and Spanish influences. It is best heard in a *peña* (bar) or *música folklórica* (folk music) club (see Entertainment in the Facts for the Visitor chapter). Traditional music can be heard on the streets during fiestas, but increasingly often, fiesta ensembles are cacophonous brass bands.

There are occasional symphony concerts, but the more traditional music, with pre-Columbian influences, are of the greatest interest to many visitors.

Crafts

In Ecuador, indeed in much of Latin America, there is a bridge between fine arts and crafts known as *artesanía*. Literally this means 'artisanship' and refers to textile crafts ranging from finely woven ponchos to hammocks, as well as well-made panama hats, basketwork, leatherwork, jewelry, woodcarving and ceramics. These items are discussed in more detail under Shopping in the Facts for the Visitor chapter.

Literature

Ecuador has not produced any writers that have become household names outside the country. Nevertheless, there are several notable literary figures.

Juan Montalvo (1832–89) was a prolific essayist from Ambato who frequently attacked the dictatorial political figures of the time, particularly President Gabriel García Moreno. His best-known work is the book *Siete Tratados* (1882), or 'Seven Treatises,' which includes a comparison between Simón Bolívar and George Washington. Juan León Mera (1832–94), also from Ambato, is famous for his novel *Cumandá* (1891), which describes Indian life in the 19th century. English translations of these two works are hard to track down, but the Spanish originals can be found in Ecuador.

Perhaps the most notable Ecuadorian writer of the 20th century was Jorge Icaza (1906–79), a *quiteño*. Profoundly influenced by the indigenist school, his most famous novel is *Huasipungo* (1934), translated as *The Villagers* (1973). This is a brutal story about Indians, the seizure of their land and the savage massacre of those who protested. The book is made all the more horrifying by the knowledge that this story is based on the real problems facing the Indians. Icaza was also known as a playwright, actor and writer of short stories.

There are many contemporary Ecuadorian writers. A good introduction to Ecuadorian literature is *Diez Cuentistas Ecuatorianos* (1990, Libri Mundi, Quito), a book of short stories by 10 Ecuadorian writers born in the 1940s. The stories are in Spanish with English translations.

Theater

The performing arts are important in Ecuador, although, as with literature, there are no artists whose names are known to most visitors. There are several theaters, especially in Quito, where performances include street theater, mime, political satire and more traditional plays.

SOCIETY & CONDUCT
Social Issues

Legally and morally, everyone is equal in Ecuador, irrespective of race or gender. In reality, blacks and indigenous people are discriminated against and treated as second-class citizens. This is particularly true of indigenous people. The term *indio* (Indian), while having few negative connotations in English, is considered an insult in Spanish.

The Indian population has frequently staged protests about their unfair and inhumane treatment. In 2003, President Lucio Gutiérrez took office – he is clearly in favor of Indian rights and received most of the Indian votes. This is the first time that a pro-Indian candidate has been elected.

Graffiti of the 'Vayase Yanqui' ('Yankee, go home') variety is seen in Ecuador. While many Ecuadorians display some anti-American sentiment, this is directed against the interventionist policy of the USA in Latin America and other parts of the world, and not against the individual US traveler. Indeed, US citizens often remark how friendly the Ecuadorian people are. This is partly because of Ecuadorians' inherent politeness, and partly because US travelers are the second-most frequent visitors (after neighboring Colombians) to Ecuador and thus contribute an important amount to the nation's economy.

Treatment of Animals

Sharing a commonality with most other Latin American countries, bullfighting and cockfighting are considered to be acceptable sporting activities in Ecuador. Most Ecuadorians are either in favor of these traditional activities or will hold no strong opinion for or against them. Few Ecuadorians oppose these blood sports, although most will politely listen to reasonably presented opinions against them.

RELIGION

In common with other Latin American countries, Ecuador's predominant religion is Roman Catholicism. Some of the older towns have splendid 16th- and 17th-century Catholic churches. Although churches of other faiths can be found, they form only a very small minority; about 95% of the population is Catholic. The Indians, while outwardly Roman Catholic, tend to blend Catholicism with their traditional beliefs.

Facts for the Visitor

HIGHLIGHTS

Ecuador is a tiny country, yet it encompasses a huge variety of elevations and environments, from the Pacific coast to glacier-clad Andean highlands, to the Amazonian lowlands, to the Galápagos Islands, 1000km off the coast. So the country's greatest highlight is simply the opportunity to see and experience many different regions in a short time.

Indian Markets

These are often a success story for everyone: gringos go home with beautiful souvenirs; artisans make a living selling their crafts; and local buses, hotels and restaurants benefit from the extra trade as well. There are plenty of great markets; Otavalo is the most famous, but markets at Saquisilí and many other highland towns and villages are also well worth visiting.

Wildlife

Half of the bird species present in South America are found in Ecuador, and little Ecuador has twice as many birds as all of North America. See Books later in this chapter for a list of bird-watching guides. Refugio de Vida Silvestre Pasochoa (near Quito and operated by Fundación Natura) and the Mindo area are among the best places in the highlands to see many species of birds. The Galápagos Islands are fabulous if you want to see frigatebirds, boobies and pelicans, as well as giant tortoises and sea lions, face to face – literally. However, the islands are prohibitively expensive to visit; go if you are really interested, but don't bother if wildlife is not your thing.

Various trips can be taken into the rainforest. Many areas of the Ecuadorian rainforest have been colonized, and you won't see jaguars there (these are, of course, the easiest areas to get to). In the remoter areas, the luxuriant vegetation masks much of the wildlife. Nevertheless, Ecuador is as good a country as any in which to visit the Amazon. See The Oriente chapter for more details.

Finally, don't neglect the wildlife of the highlands. The *páramo* (Andean grasslands) habitats of the Tulcán area, Parque Nacional Cotopaxi and Parque Nacional Las Cajas are all recommended.

Architecture

Many highland towns have Spanish colonial architecture dominating their city centers. Quito's and Cuenca's old towns have been especially well preserved since colonial times and have been designated World Cultural Heritage Sites by Unesco. Many other highland towns have interesting colonial architecture.

Fiestas

From the capital's annual fiesta during the first week in December to local festivities in small towns and villages, fiestas are an excellent chance to mingle with local people and have some fun. The celebrations of All Souls' Day (November 2) is particularly recommended in the highlands; Bolívar's Birthday (July 24) and the Founding of Guayaquil (July 25) are particularly recommended in Guayaquil. Carnaval time (the weekend preceding Ash Wednesday) is celebrated all over Latin America – in Ecuador, it takes the form of water throwing in most areas, and there is a festival of fruit and flowers in Ambato.

Adventures in Transportation

There are numerous interesting, unusual and fun ways to travel, but there's no guarantee of luxurious comfort! Ride on the roof of the train as it zigzags down El Nariz del Diablo (The Devil's Nose) – a dizzying descent from Alausí in the highlands. Voyage along a tropical river in a dugout canoe from Borbón on the coast or Misahuallí in the Oriente. Pack yourself into a bus full of locals and take the high road around Chimborazo. Amble around the Vilcabamba area by horseback.

Adventure Sports

Dedicated mountaineers, hikers, surfers, rafters, kayakers, cyclists and horse riders will find world-class opportunities to practice these pursuits. See Activities later in this chapter.

SUGGESTED ITINERARIES

The following itineraries are suggested for the mainland only and are for the average traveler wanting to get to know Ecuador.

Those who are here to climb or surf etc will probably have their own itineraries.

If you want to add a visit to the Galápagos, remember that the first day of your trip includes flying from the mainland, so you won't begin your cruise until the afternoon. The last day of your trip involves a morning departure by air, so you won't get any cruising in on your last day. Therefore, an eight-day/seven-night tour is recommended because the four-day/three-night options don't allow enough time.

One Week

Allow at least two days in Quito to acclimatize and see the superb colonial architecture. As corny as it might sound, spend a day visiting the Mitad del Mundo monument on the equator; this is the easiest place in the world to stand with your foot in two hemispheres. Spend another day at the bustling Otavalo market, both to shop and visit with the traditional indigenous inhabitants. Then head south, past ice-cream cone-shaped Cotopaxi, to sub-tropical Baños, from where you can have a brief taste of the Oriente.

Two Weeks

Add a three- or four-day tour to the Amazon. The Cuyabeno and Yasuní parks and the lodges along the Río Napo are all popular and worthwhile jungle destinations. Head down to Vilcabamba to relax in the beautiful climate and enjoy the many nearby hikes. Alternatively, spend a couple of days on the coast. Montañita for surfing, Atacames for partying or Guayaquil for excellent museums and superb seafood are all fine choices, depending on your interests. Note that if you depart internationally from Guayaquil, you'll save $15 in departure taxes!

Three Weeks

Choose your favorite area and relax, with an extra day or two in one of the places just described. Spend a couple of days enjoying the quiet architectural marvels of colonial Cuenca, or visit an off-the-beaten-track town such as Guaranda or Macas, traveling with the locals and probably being the only gringo in town. Adventurous and fit travelers may opt for a two-day climb of massive Cotopaxi or a river-rafting excursion. Shoppers will want to visit the lesser-known markets such as the one at Saquisilí.

PLANNING

When to Go

The high seasons are generally considered to be mid-December through January and June through August, as this is when most foreign visitors arrive, but visiting year-round is no problem.

In the Galápagos, peak tourist periods are June to August, December to January and around Easter. The wildlife is always there, and you can see birds courting and young in their nests during any month. The exception are waved albatrosses, which leave en masse in mid-December and stay at sea until late March.

The islands have two seasons: wet from January to about June, and dry from June to December. The rainy season is generally pleasant with many warm, sunny periods interspersed with showers and an occasional downpour. February is the hottest month, when the water is fairly calm and sea temperatures are a balmy 23°C or 24°C, which is great for snorkeling. Sea temperatures drop to around 18°C to 20°C between May and July. The dry season is cooler and often misty, and a warm sweater may be needed at night. The ocean gets choppy in July and is often at its roughest from August to October. Droughts or heavy rains can occur at unpredictable and irregular intervals.

The coast has similar weather; hot and wet from January to May (when rainstorms may make some roads impassable), and drier and cooler during the rest of the year. January to April, although rainy, coincides with coastal school vacations, and so the beaches are crowded. July and August are gray, damp and overcast, but are the best months for whale watching.

The dry season in the highlands is normally June to August or September, which coincides with the wettest months in the Oriente, when roads may be closed.

Maps

The best in-country maps are published by and available at the **Instituto Geográfico Militar** *(IGM; ☎ 254 5090, 222 9075/76)* in Quito (see Maps in the Quito chapter for more details). Few city maps are published, and except for detailed maps of the whole of Quito, Guayaquil and Cuenca, you'll find the city maps in this book are often the best available. The IGM does have some excellent maps of the whole country, ranging from a 1:1,000,000 one-sheet Ecuador map to 1:50,000 topographical maps. These occasionally go out of print, but most maps are freely available for reference, and black-and-white photocopies are available. Some areas, particularly the Oriente and parts of the western lowlands, are inadequately mapped.

Apart from the IGM, the best country map is the 1:1,000,000 Ecuador sheet published by ITMB (Canada).

What to Bring

This is a tough issue. Bring as little as possible...but bring everything that's important to you! If you're a photography buff, you'll only curse every time you see a good shot (if only you'd brought your telephoto lens), and if you're a musician, you won't enjoy the trip if you constantly worry about how out of practice you are getting. But don't bring things you can do without.

A good idea once you're in Quito is to divide your gear. Take what you'll need for the next section of your trip and stash the rest in the storage room at your hotel.

Traveling on buses and trains is bound to make you slightly grubby, so bring one change of dark clothes that don't show the dirt, rather than several changes of nice clothes. Bring clothes that wash and dry easily (jeans take forever to dry).

Clothes can be bought cheaply in Ecuador. T-shirts are popular souvenirs, and heavy wool sweaters and long-sleeved cotton shirts can be bought inexpensively at Indian markets. A shopping mall will yield underwear and socks. You can buy clothes of almost any size, but shoes go up only to size 43 Ecuadorian (and European), which is about 10½ North American and 9½ UK.

Tampons are available in Ecuador, but only in the major cities and in regular sizes, so make sure you stock up before visiting smaller towns, the jungle or the Galápagos. Some tampons are sold without applicators and are relatively expensive – sanitary pads are cheaper. Contraceptives are available in the major cities – condoms are sold, but their quality may be questionable. Spermicidal jelly is hard to find. The choice of oral contraceptives is limited, so if you use a preferred brand, bring it from home.

The highlands are often cold, so bring a windproof jacket and a warm layer to wear beneath it. A hat is indispensable; it'll keep you warm when it's cold, shade your eyes when it's sunny and keep your head dry when it rains (a great deal!). A collapsible umbrella is great protection against sun and rain, too.

In the Galápagos, little is available aboard the boats. You should bring all the film, sunblock, insect repellent, books and medical supplies (including motion-sickness medication) that you need. Sunglasses and a shade hat are also recommended. Snorkelers should bring their own snorkel and mask to ensure a good fit. Likewise, avid bird-watchers should bring binoculars. Shipboard life is casual, so dress accordingly. Be prepared to get wet during landings; shorts are useful. Trails are rocky and the lava is extremely rough; sturdy shoes that can get wet are important. Bring a spare pair of footwear to keep dry and wear on the boat.

The following is a list of small items you will probably need.

- pocket flashlight (torch) with spare bulb and batteries
- travel alarm clock
- Swiss Army-style pocket knife
- sewing and repairs kit (dental floss makes strong, colorless emergency thread)
- a few meters of cord (useful as a clothesline and as spare shoelaces)
- sunglasses
- sealable plastic bags
- toiletries, towel
- toilet paper (rarely found in cheaper hotels and restaurants)
- earplugs for noisy hotels or buses
- insect repellent (containing 30% DEET)
- sunblock (30SPF or higher is recommended but hard to find in Ecuador)
- address book
- notebook, pen
- paperback book (easily exchanged with other travelers)
- water bottle
- first-aid kit

Optional items may include the following:

- camera and film
- Spanish-English dictionary and phrasebook
- small padlock
- large folding nylon bag to leave things in storage
- snorkeling gear (for the Galápagos)
- water-purification tablets or filter
- binoculars and field guides

RESPONSIBLE TOURISM

Ecuador's tourism industry has grown in recent years and is a significant part of the economy. On the surface, international tourists spending money are a positive force. But tourists and travelers need to look deeper than just spending their money. Hundreds of thousands of foreign visitors can create a negative impact on the society and environment of Ecuador.

Problems exist with the dichotomy between rich tourists (and even the most budget-oriented backpacker is rich by local standards) and the locals who work for substandard wages to provide services for tourists. For example, demands by groups of non-Spanish speaking tourists can range from reasonable to rude and obnoxious. Some things that may not seem immediately wrong (taking a person's photograph, demanding toilet paper in a cheap restaurant, expecting the same amenities as you have at home etc) are not as reasonable by local standards.

So what can be done to promote responsible tourism? Here are some suggestions. Start by learning at least enough Spanish to be able to say 'hello,' 'thank you,' 'Ecuador is a beautiful country' and a few more phrases. And don't be afraid to use them! Interact with the local people – don't just take photos and run – and don't make promises you can't keep.

Accept and respect local customs and lifestyles rather than imposing your own. Support local artisans by buying locally made handicrafts and artwork, but don't buy illegal artefacts, such as pre-Columbian pieces, or items made from endangered animals, such as cat skins or jewelry made from sea turtle or black coral.

Read Social Graces, later in this chapter, and act in a locally acceptable way. Remember the old proverb 'When in Rome, do as the Romans do' (but not to the point of littering just because some Ecuadorians do it – use common sense). Use local services as much as possible so as to inject money into the local economy. On outdoor expeditions, don't allow your guides to hunt, cut trees for bonfires, harass wildlife or litter. Try to set a good example, but be sensitive to local customs and beliefs.

TOURIST OFFICES

Ecuador doesn't have an effective system of government-run tourist offices. Some local offices operate in some cities, but their information is not always up to date.

VISAS & DOCUMENTS
Passport

All nationals entering as tourists need a passport that must be valid for at least six months after arrival. You should always carry your passport as there are occasional document checks on public transportation. You can be arrested if you don't have identification. Failure to produce a visa or embarkation card (see Travel Permits later) can result in deportation.

Visas

Most travelers entering Ecuador as tourists do not require visas. Citizens of Cuba, a few Asian countries and some Central American countries currently require a tourist visa.

All travelers who do not wish to enter as tourists require visas. Nonimmigrant visas are available for diplomats, refugees, students, laborers, religious workers, businesspeople, volunteers and cultural-exchange visitors. Various immigrant visas are also available. Obtaining a visa is time consuming, so commence the process as far ahead of your visit as possible. However, visas enable holders to apply for a *censo* (temporary-residence card) and pay resident prices in national parks, as well as on trains and planes, where foreign visitors usually pay more. Visas must be obtained from an Ecuadorian embassy and cannot be arranged within Ecuador. See Embassies & Consulates later in this chapter for a partial list of Ecuadorian embassies.

Visa holders who apply for residency need to get an exit permit from the immigration authorities in Quito before they leave the country. Depending on their status, some residents may have to pay an exit tax.

Travel Permits

Tourists need a passport and a (free) international embarkation card, which is obtainable upon arrival in Ecuador or on your flight if arriving by air. The card needs to be completed with your passport and travel details, and is needed for stay extensions, passport checks and leaving the country. If you should lose it, you can get another at the immigration office in Quito or Guayaquil, or at the point at which you exit the country.

Upon arrival, if you show your outbound ticket, you should get as many days as you need. You are given an identical *entrada* (entrance) stamp on both your passport and embarkation card, which indicates how long you can stay. The maximum is 90 days, but usually less is given. It's easy and quick to get a stay extension in Quito.

Onward Tickets

In addition to your passport and embarkation card, officially you need a ticket out of the country and evidence of sufficient funds for your stay ($20 per day). This is the law, and although it is not regularly enforced, if you turn up at the border stoned or looking as if you haven't washed or eaten for a week, it probably will be.

Airlines flying to Quito require a round-trip or onward ticket or a residence visa. Don't worry about an onward ticket at the land borders; it's very unlikely that the rule will be mentioned if you arrive looking reasonably respectable.

Stay Extensions

There are several immigration offices in Quito, and all are closed on weekends and holidays. **Jefatura Provincial de Migración** (☎ 224 7510; Isla Seymour 1152 near Río Coca; open 8:30am-noon & 3pm-5pm Mon-Fri) is the office to visit for extensions of up to 90 days for tourists who received only 30 or 60 days upon arrival.

Oficina de Migración (☎ 245 6249; Amazonas 2639 near República; open 8am-11:45am & 3pm-5pm Mon-Fri) is in Quito, for tourists who have already stayed 90 days and want 30 more (a process that can be performed only three times, for a maximum of 180 days per year). Normally, this is only done when your time has expired, not in advance, and only at the immigration officer's discretion. Most applicants have been successful.

For stays longer than 180 days, you must obtain a visa from your nearest Ecuadorian embassy. These must be registered within 30 days of arrival at **Dirección de Extranjería** (☎ 256 1010; Carrión & Páez). Visa holders then need to go to Oficina de Migración to purchase an ID called a *censo,* which then enables them to get discounted resident rates on train tickets and airfares and in national parks (see Visas earlier). If visa holders wish

to leave the country and return, they need a *salida* (exit) form from the Jefatura Provincial de Migración, which can be used for multiple exits and re-entries.

Travel Insurance

No matter how you're traveling, make sure you take out travel insurance. This should cover you not only for medical expenses and luggage theft or loss, but also for unavoidable cancellation or delays in your travel arrangements. Everyone should be covered for the worst possible case, such as an accident that requires hospital treatment and a flight home.

Coverage depends on your insurance and type of ticket, so ask both the insurer and the ticket-issuing agency to explain the finer points. Ticket loss is also covered by travel insurance. Make sure you have a separate record of your ticket details or a photocopy of the ticket itself. Also, make copies of your policy in case the original is lost.

Buy travel insurance as early as possible. If you buy it the week before you fly, you may find, for instance, that you're not covered for delays to your flight caused by strikes or other industrial action that may have been in force before you took out the insurance.

Foreign medical insurance, if it covers a hospital visit, normally does not reimburse the hospital. You must pay your own medical fees directly to the hospital or doctor and then bill your insurance company for reimbursement of the covered portions. Doctors and hospitals will normally accept credit-card payments.

Driver's License

If you plan on renting a car, a valid driver's license from your home country is normally accepted if it has a photograph on it. Otherwise, get an international driver's license.

Hostel Cards

Ecuador has a limited hostel system, and hostel cards get you a 10% discount. However, it is not worth getting a hostel card for the trip, because it won't save you much. If you already have one, you might as well bring it.

Student Cards

Students receive small discounts on flights to the Galápagos and pay only 50% of the

$100 Galápagos Islands park-entrance fee. Other discounts may be available, but the savings for the Galápagos are the biggest. International student cards alone are not accepted, because false ones have been issued in Ecuador and officials no longer trust them. Bring both an ISIC card and the student card from your home school, college or university – and make sure that the photo on it looks like you and that it has not expired. Generally, student cards are less useful in Ecuador than in many other countries.

Vaccination Certificates
While these are not required by law, vaccinations are advisable; see Health later in this chapter.

Copies
Before you leave home, you should photocopy all important documents (passport data page and visa page, credit cards, travel insurance policy, air, bus and train tickets, driver's license etc). Leave one copy with someone at home and keep another with you, separate from the originals.

It's also a good idea to store details of your vital travel documents in Lonely Planet's free online Travel Vault in case you lose the photocopies or can't be bothered with them. Your password-protected Travel Vault is accessible online anywhere in the world – create it at **w** www.ekno.lonely planet.com.

EMBASSIES & CONSULATES
Your Own Embassy
It's important to realize what your own embassy – the embassy of the country of which you are a citizen – can and can't do to help you if you get into trouble. Generally speaking, it won't be much help in emergencies if the trouble you're in is remotely your own fault. Remember that you are bound by the laws of the country you are in. Your embassy will not be sympathetic if you end up in jail after committing a crime locally, even if such actions are legal in your own country.

In genuine emergencies, you might get some assistance from your embassy, but only if other channels have been exhausted. If you need to get home urgently, a free ticket home is exceedingly unlikely – the embassy would expect you to have insurance. If all your money and documents are stolen, it might assist you with getting a new passport, but a loan for onward travel would be out of the question.

Some embassies used to keep letters for travelers or have a small reading room with newspapers from your home country, but these days, most of the mail-holding services have been stopped and even newspapers tend to be out of date.

Ecuadorian Embassies & Consulates
Although some countries have Ecuadorian consular representation in several cities, the following are their main offices. Many countries other than the ones listed here have Ecuadorian embassies or consular representation; their addresses and telephone numbers can be found in telephone directories.

Australia & New Zealand (☎ 02-6262 5282, **e** embecu@hotkey.net.au) 1st floor Law Society Bldg, 11 London Circuit, ACT 2601
Canada (☎ 613-563 8206, fax 235 5776; **e** mecuacan@sprint.ca) 50 O'Connor St, Suite 316, Ottawa, Ontario K1P 6L2
France (☎ 331-4561 1021, **e** ambecuad@ wanadoo.fr) 34 Av de Messine 75008 Paris
Germany (☎ 030-238 6217, **e** mecuadoral@ t-online.de, **w** www.embecuador.de) Kaiser-Friedrich Strasse 90, 1 OG,10585 Berlin
Peru (☎ 01-440 9941, fax 422 0711, **e** embj ecuador@terra.com.pe) Las Palmeras 356, San Isidro, Lima 27
UK (☎ 020-7584 1367, fax 823 9701, **e** emba jada@ecuador.freeserve.co.uk) Flat 3B, 3 Hans Crescent, Knightsbridge, London SW1X OLS
USA (☎ 202-234 7200, fax 667 3482, **e** mec uawaa@pop.erols.com) 2535 15th St NW, Washington, DC 20009

Embassies & Consulates in Ecuador
Many countries have embassies in Quito and consulates in Quito or Guayaquil. It is a good idea to register with your embassy, especially if you plan to stay in the country for any extended period of time. Their office hours are short, so it's a good idea call ahead to find out when they are open or if they have recently changed address. There are more embassies and consulates than those mentioned in this section, so check in the yellow pages under 'Consulados' or 'Embajadas.'

Quito Both embassies and consulates are found in Quito. Dial ☎ 02 if calling from outside Pichincha Province.

Canada (☎ 223 2114, 250 6162, fax 250 3108) 6 de Diciembre 2816 & P Rivet, 4th floor
Colombia (☎ 245 8012, fax 246 0054) Atahualpa 955 & República, 3rd floor
France (☎ 254 3101, fax 250 6468) Diego de Almagro 1550 & Pradera
Germany (☎ 297 0820, fax 297 0815) Naciones Unidas & República de El Salvador, Edificio Citiplaza, 14th floor
Ireland (☎ 245 1577, fax 226 9862) Antonio de Ulloa 2651 & Rumipamba
Netherlands (☎ 252 5461, 222 9229, fax 256 7917) 12 de Octubre 1942 & Cordero, World Trade Center, Tower 1, 1st floor
Panama (☎ 256 6449, fax 250 8856) Alpallana 505 & Whymper, Edificio Espro, 6th floor
Peru (☎ 246 8410, 246 8389, fax 246 8411) El Salvador 495 & Irlanda
UK (☎ 297 0800/1, fax 297 0810) Naciones Unidas & República de El Salvador, Edificio Citiplaza, 14th floor
USA (☎ 256 2890, fax 250 2052) Patria & 12 de Octubre

Guayaquil Because Guayaquil is Ecuador's major port and city, there are many consulates here. Travelers heading for Peru may want to visit the Peruvian consulate – its hours were recently 8:30am to 1pm Monday to Friday. Dial ☎ 04 if calling from outside Guayas Province.

Australia (☎ 229 8823, 268 0823) Kennedy Norte, Calle San Roque y Avda. Francisco de Orellana, Edificio Tecniseguros
Canada (☎ 256 3580, 256 6747, fax 231 4562) Córdova 810, 4th floor
Colombia (☎ 263 0674/75) Francisco de Orellana, World Trade Center, Tower B, 11th floor
France (☎ 232 8442) Avenida Mascote 909 & Hurtado
Germany (☎ 220 6867/8, fax 220 6869) Avenidas Las Monjas & CJ Arosemena, Km 2.5, Edificio Berlin
Netherlands (☎ 256 6789/2777/3857, fax 256 3857) Córdova 1004 and P de Icaza
Peru (☎ 228 114, e conperu@gye.satnet.net) Avenida Francisco de Orellana Kennedy Norte, 14th floor, Office 02, Edificio Centrum
UK (☎ 256 0400, 256 3850, fax 256 2641) Córdova 623
USA (☎ 232 3570, fax 232 5286) 9 de Octubre & García Moreno

CUSTOMS

Each traveler is allowed to import a liter of spirits, 300 cigarettes and an unspecified 'reasonable' amount of perfume – all items are duty free. There is no problem with bringing in the usual personal belongings, but if you plan on bringing in something that might not be considered a 'usual personal belonging,' you should check with an Ecuadorian consulate.

Pre-Columbian artefacts are not allowed to be taken out of Ecuador or imported into most other countries. Bringing endangered-animal products home is also illegal.

MONEY
Currency

US dollar bills are the official currency (see the boxed text 'Ecuador's Dollarization' later). New coins of 1, 5, 10, 25 and 50 cents have been minted. These are identical in shape, size and color to their US equivalents, but will bear images of famous Ecuadorians rather than US presidents. Both US and Ecuadorian coins are interchangeable. There are no plans to print Ecuadorian versions of US dollar bills.

Cash bills are likely to be refused if they are worn or have tears in them, so bring a supply of bills in good condition.

Exchanging Money

Banks are generally open from 9am to 1:30pm Monday to Friday. In some cities, banks may stay open later or may be open on Saturday, especially if Saturday happens to be market day. *Casas de cambio* (currency-exchange bureaus) are usually open 9am to 6pm Monday to Friday and until noon on Saturday. There is usually a lunch hour, which varies from place to place.

In Quito and Guayaquil, the international airport and major hotels have exchange facilities that are open past the usual hours.

Cash & Traveler's Checks US dollars are now the accepted Ecuadorian currency. Hard currencies of other nations, and pesos and nuevos soles from neighboring Colombia and Peru, can be exchanged for US dollars in *casas de cambio* and in banks. It is best to change money in the major cities of Quito, Guayaquil and Cuenca. Outside of these cities, traveling with US dollars is advised. Consider bringing US dollars with

Ecuador's Dollarization

During 1999–2000, Ecuador suffered its most severe economic crisis of modern times. Its currency, the sucre, was exchanged at 6000 for $1 in early 1999, but was valued at only 25,000 for $1 in early 2000. At this time, embattled President Jamil Mahuad pinned Ecuador's economic survival on dollarization, a process whereby Ecuador's unstable national currency was replaced by the US dollar. This process has been used successfully in a few other economically hard-hit countries, including nearby Panama (where the US dollar is called a Balboa).

The move met with bitter opposition from various Ecuadorian groups, one of which was the powerful Conaie (Confederation of Indigenous Nationalities of Ecuador). The organization argued that the poorer members of Ecuador's population would not be able to deal with a currency from another country. US dollars, printed in English, would be difficult to read and understand for people who speak Quechua as their first language, Spanish as a second language and English as a distant and rarely encountered third.

Formidable protests by Conaie, supported by a handful of lower-echelon military officials – including Colonel Lucio Gutiérrez, who became president in 2003 – led to the ousting of President Mahuad. He was replaced, after a few hours of political posturing from the protestors, by his constitutional successor, Vice President Gustavo Noboa. The new president vowed to continue with dollarization.

In March 2000, the Ecuadorian parliament approved the law to dollarize the economy, with September 2000 being the final date set for changing sucres to dollars at a rate of 25,000 sucres to $1. Various obstacles had to be overcome: taxi meters and phone booths were reconfigured, $1 bills were needed in great numbers because of Ecuador's low cost of living (ATMs would often run out of popular $1 and $5 dollar bills) and the population had to be educated in the value and use of the new currency.

An immediate effect of dollarization was rounding up. Items which used to cost, for example, 21,000 sucres were sold for $1 because it was easier to deal with than $0.84. The ubiquitous phrase, 'un dolarcito,' a diminutive and endearing reference to the dollar, became heard throughout the country and the cost of living began to climb immediately.

At the time of research, the drastic economic experiment appears to be succeeding. The cost of living has increased, but runaway inflation has been reined in. Even the former opponent to dollarization, President Gutiérrez, was not planning on scrapping the new currency upon his inauguration as president in 2003.

---

you on your trip in case you have trouble exchanging currency from your home country.

Commission for changing traveler's checks ranges from 1% to 4%, with the highest rates charged in small towns. Traveler's checks are much safer because they are refunded if they are lost or stolen. Don't bring all of your money in traveler's checks, however. It's always useful to have a supply of US cash for the occasions when only cash is accepted.

ATMs Ecuadorian ATMs are compatible with foreign credit/debit cards. Holders of Visa cards will find that Banco de Guayaquil and Banco La Previsora have 24-hour ATMs, and holders of MasterCards should use Banco del Pacífico and Banco Popular. Many other banks offer ATM facilities –

look at their logos to see if your credit/debit card is accepted. Make sure that your PIN (Personal Identification Number) is four digits, as Ecuadorian ATMs don't normally recognize longer ones. Occasionally an ATM will swallow a card; try waiting for a few minutes and maybe the card will be released.

It's hard to say whether Visa or MasterCard is better. Generally, ATMs accepting Visa are more widespread, but in the Galápagos, only a MasterCard ATM is available.

To find an ATM anywhere in the world, try the following websites: **w** http://international.visa.com/main.jsp and **w** www.mastercard.com/cardholderservices/atm/.

Credit Cards These can be useful, and most major cards are accepted, particularly

Sorry, No Change!

Don't expect to pay for inexpensive services with large bills because change is often not available. Cab drivers may say they don't have change simply to try to make extra money. It's worth asking drivers, 'Cambio de diez dolares?' ('Do you have change for $10?' – or whatever the size of your bill), to make sure you don't get stuck with this. If traveling to small towns, bring a supply of small-denomination bills·

in first-class restaurants, hotels, gift shops and travel agencies. Cheaper hotels, restaurants and stores don't want to deal with credit cards. Even if an establishment has a credit-card sticker in the window, don't assume that credit cards are accepted. The sticker may be for embellishment only.

Visa, MasterCard and Diners Club are the most widely accepted. American Express is less popular. In Ecuador, merchants accepting credit cards will often add between 4% and 10% to the bill in order to cover the bank transaction fee. Check this carefully – paying cash is often better value.

International Transfers A bank transfer will take at least three business days. Ecuadorian banks that will cooperate with your bank at home include Bank of America, Bank of London & South America and Banco del Pacífico. Contact your family or bank manager to deposit the money in your name at the bank of your choice. Commissions are likely to be charged by the bank sending the money.

Western Union offers a faster and more convenient way of receiving cash, but it is also more expensive. For example, receiving $1000 in Quito costs $85.

Security

Pickpockets prey on easy targets, and unsuspecting tourists are a prime choice. Avoid losing your money by following a few basic precautions. Carry money in inside pockets, money belts or pouches beneath your clothes. Don't carry a wallet in a pocket or a purse, as these are always the first places pickpockets look. Divide your money and carry it in several places – some

in an inside pocket and some in a money pouch, for example – so that if you are pickpocketed you don't lose all your cash.

If you are traveling for many months, it's a good idea to carry an emergency packet somewhere separate from all your other valuables. This emergency packet could be sewn into a jacket (don't lose the jacket!) or even carried in your shoe. Aside from money, it should contain a photocopy of the important pages of your passport in case it is lost or stolen. On the back of the photocopy, list the serial numbers of all your traveler's checks, airline tickets, credit cards and bank accounts, and include any important telephone numbers. Also keep one high-denomination bill in with this emergency stash. You will probably never have to use it, but it's a good idea not to put all your eggs in one basket. In most decent hotels, you can leave money and valuables in a safe-deposit box, although this is not very reliable in the most basic hotels.

Costs

Costs in Ecuador have risen since dollarization, but still remain among the lowest in Latin America.

Ecuador has a two-tier pricing system, in which foreign visitors pay a lot more money than Ecuadorian residents for some services. The few train rides available are $11 for foreigners, compared to $1 for residents. Some flights cost roughly twice as much for foreigners as for residents. National park entrance fees are much higher for foreigners (per person, $10 or $20 on the mainland, $100 in the Galápagos; valid for a week or two weeks). Many top-end hotels charge foreigners double what they charge nationals.

Shoestring travelers staying in the cheapest hotels and eating the meal of the day at restaurants can get by for under $15 per day. Most folks will want to stay in nicer digs, perhaps with private bathroom and hot showers, enjoy more varied meals, take cab rides to museums, and hit a bar for a few beers in the evening, They can expect to be paying $25 to $70 per day.

Saving time and energy by flying back from a remote destination, which required several days of land travel to reach, is also recommended. At present, most internal flights on the Ecuadorian mainland are about $60 or less. First and luxury-class hotels are from $70 to over $200. Even if you demand the very best available, in most parts of Ecuador it will cost much less than it would wherever home may be.

Some typical costs are:

- bus travel per hour – about $1
- small beer – $1
- coffee – $1
- full American breakfast – $3
- quarter chicken and chips – $1.50
- short cab ride in Quito – $2 to $3
- movie – $2 to $4
- bootleg CD – $1 to $3

Tipping & Bargaining

Better restaurants add a 12% tax and a 10% service charge to the bill. If the service has been satisfactory, you can add another 5% for the waiter. Cheaper restaurants don't include a tax or service charge. If you want to tip your server, do so directly – don't just leave the money on the table.

Tip porters at the airport about $0.25 per bag and bellboys at a 1st-class hotel about $0.50 per bag. Hairdressers receive $0.50 or more for special services. Taxi drivers are not normally tipped, but you can leave them the small change from a metered ride.

If you go on a guided tour, a tip is expected. Some Ecuadorian tour companies pay guides low wages, so the guides make more in tips than in wages. If you are in a group, tip a top-notch guide about $2 to $3 per person per day – less for a half-day tour. Tip the driver about half as much as the guide. If you engage a private guide, tip about $10 per day. These suggestions are for professional, bilingual guides – tip more if you feel your guide was exceptional and less if he or she wasn't that great.

If you're going on a long tour that involves guides, cooks and crew (eg, in the Galápagos Islands), tip about $25 to $50 per client per week, and distribute among all the personnel.

If you are driving and decide to park your car on the street, boys or men will offer to look after your car. Give them about $0.20 for several hours, a few cents for a short time.

Bargaining is accepted and expected in markets when buying crafts, and occasionally in other situations. If you're not sure whether bargaining is appropriate, try asking for a *descuento* (discount). These are often given at hotels, tour agencies, gift shops and other places where tourists spend money.

Taxes

A total of 22% (12% tax and 10% service charge) is added to bills in the best hotels and restaurants, although the cheapest hotels and restaurants don't add anything. Ask if you aren't sure. A 12% tax is added to the cost of goods in stores. There is no system of rebates for international travelers.

POST & COMMUNICATIONS
Postal Rates

Since recent privatization, postal rates have shot up, but service has improved. A postcard or letter to North America and Europe costs $0.80/$1.05. Parcels are expensive to send.

Sending Mail

Mail from Ecuador should arrive at its destination, sometimes in as little as a week to the USA or Europe, although closer to two weeks is normal.

Post offices are marked on the maps in this book. In some smaller towns, it is often just part of a building. In larger towns, such as Quito and Guayaquil, there are several post offices around town. Business hours are usually 9am to 5pm Monday to Friday. In the bigger cities, businesses open for half a day on Saturday.

Ecuadorian airmail rates for parcels are expensive. Parcels weighing under 2kg can be sent from most post offices. Heavier parcels should be mailed from the Quito **parcel post office** (*Ulloa 273 near Dávalos*). Regulations change, so check in advance whether the parcel should be sealed or unsealed (for customs inspection) when you bring it to the post office. Sometimes, open parcels need to be sealed up in front of a postal official, so bring tape or strong string. The Quito clubhouse of the **South American Explorers** (*SAE; ☎/fax 222 5228; e quitoclub@saexplorers.org; Jorge Washington 311 & Leonidas Plaza*) is usually up to date on this (see Useful Organizations later in this chapter).

Courier companies in Quito and Guayaquil can send important parcels quickly to major airports around the world, but the addressee must come to the airport to pick up the parcel. This service is fast, reliable, but expensive. For example, FedEx charges about $25 for a 500g envelope to the USA, or $150 for a 10kg box.

Receiving Mail

Incoming mail has become more reliable since privatization. FedEx charges about $50 to send an 8oz document from the USA to Quito. For easy communication, see Email & Internet Access later.

Most travelers use the post office's *lista de correos* (poste restante/general delivery) for receiving mail. Members of the SAE can receive mail at the Quito clubhouse (see Useful Organizations later in this chapter).

Mail sent to the post office is filed alphabetically. If it's addressed to John Gillis Payson, Esq, it could well be filed under 'G' or 'E' instead of 'P.' It should be addressed in the following manner: John PAYSON, Lista de Correos, Correos Central, Quito (or town and province of your choice), Ecuador. Ask your loved ones to print your last name and avoid appending witticisms such as 'World Traveler Extraordinaire.'

Receiving small packages is usually no problem. If the package weighs more than 2kg, however, you will have to go to customs to retrieve it and perhaps pay duty tax.

Telephone

Telephone service in Ecuador is erratic but inexpensive. With patience you can usually place calls to anywhere, although long-distance and international calls from small or remote towns, or from the Galápagos, can be a problem.

Andinatel (mainly in the highlands and Oriente) and Pacifictel (mainly in the coastal lowlands) are the places to go for long-distance and international telephone services. The offices are officially open 8am to 10pm daily, except in small and remote towns, where there may be shorter hours. In addition, the city of Cuenca uses Etapa, a private telephone service.

Calls within Ecuador Public phone booths are many but work in various ways. Some booths use only one of two kinds of phonecards – Porta or BellSouth, which can be bought for various denominations and are usually sold in convenient places. Others accept only coins. For local calls within a city, you can often borrow a phone in a store or use a private phone offered by entrepreneurs on the street – they will dial the call for you (to make sure you are not calling your mum in London) and will charge you a few cents for the call. All but the most basic hotels will allow you to make local city calls.

Intercity calls can be dialed directly or through the operator at Andinatel or Pacifictel offices. Street entrepreneurs will also help you place long-distance calls.

If you need a national operator, dial ☎ 105. For information, dial ☎ 104. In most major cities, the police are on ☎ 101 or ☎ 911; otherwise, follow the instructions given in public phone booths, or ask at your hotel or other off-the-street operator.

Local numbers have six digits, except in Quito and Guayaquil, where there are seven digits. Two-digit area codes beginning with '0' are used; these are provided for each town in this book.

Dial ☎ 09 for cell phones and expect much higher charges for these calls. Area codes are not dialed if calling from within that area code. If dialing from abroad, drop the '0' in the area code.

International Calls The country code for Ecuador is ☎ 593. To call a number in Ecu-

New '2' for Telephone Numbers

An additional '2' has been added to the beginning of all telephone numbers (except cellular numbers) within the province of Pichincha, of which Quito is the capital, and the province of Guayas, of which Guayaquil is the capital. Telephone numbers in Pichincha and Guayas now have seven digits and the first digit is always a '2.' However, business cards, brochures and people still regularly quote only six numbers. If you come across a six-digit number for the province of Pichincha or Guayas, simply add a '2' to the beginning to make it complete. You must still dial the area code (☎ 02 for Pichincha and ☎ 04 for Guayas) when calling from another province. In the future, after all numbers beginning with '2' are taken, new beginning numbers will be used.

ador from abroad, call your international access code, Ecuador's country code, the area code *without* the 0, and the six- or seven-digit local telephone number.

International calls from an Andinatel or Pacifictel office are as cheap as \$0.35 per minute to the USA from major cities, although may be more expensive from remote small towns where you may have to wait for 30 minutes for a connection. Rates are 20% cheaper on Sunday and after 7pm on other days. Internet cafés provide even cheaper 'Net-to-phone' services.

Hotels providing international phone connections often surcharge extremely heavily – ask. Collect (reverse-charge) calls are possible to a few countries that have reciprocal agreements with Ecuador; these agreements vary from year to year, so ask at the nearest telephone office.

International calling cards from your country don't work well in Ecuador, because the local telephone companies don't make any money from them and are reluctant to use them. Buy local cards instead; some have instructions in English.

Email & Internet Access

Internet cafés are everywhere! Quito is the main center, and there are dozens of places competing for your business. Rates are very cheap; about \$1 an hour. Other cities are following suit, but Quito is definitely the place for the best choice and rates.

Some hotels allow you to connect your laptop to their telephone lines; the connections are the same as those used in the USA. Some hotels allow you to use the hotel computer to check your email.

DIGITAL RESOURCES

The Lonely Planet website (w www.lonely planet.com) has succinct summaries on traveling to most places on earth, postcards from other travelers and the Thorn Tree bulletin board, where you can ask questions before you go or dispense advice when you get back. You can also find travel news and alerts, and links to useful travel resources elsewhere on the Web.

If you read Spanish, you can access some of Ecuador's newspapers at the sites listed under Newspapers & Magazines later in this chapter. The University of Texas maintains a site with scores of useful links about everything Ecuadorian at w www.lanic.u texas.edu (search for Ecuador). Ecuador Explorer at w www.ecuadorexplorer.com has general travel and tour information, and a good overview of what the country has to offer. A site containing news, directories, economic developments and historical background is maintained by the Ecuadorian embassy in Washington, DC; check out w www.ecuador.org. The Galápagos Coalition has a website with a comprehensive virtual library that's worth a peek at w www .law.emory.edu/PI/GALAPAGOS/. For news with a strong ecotourism angle, visit w www .planeta.com/ecuador.html.

Many other websites with a more specific focus are listed in appropriate parts of this book.

BOOKS

Most books are published in different editions by different publishers in different countries. As a result, a book might be a hardcover rarity in one country, but readily available in paperback in another. Fortunately, bookstores and libraries can search by title or author, so they are the best place for advice on the availability of the following recommendations. If a book is out of print, you may find it in major city or university libraries – or it may be reprinted soon. For books published in Ecuador, the date and publishers are provided to aid you in tracking the book down.

There are two particularly well-known bookstores in Ecuador that sell a selection of new books in English, French, German and Spanish. In Guayaquil, go to the **Librería Científica** *(Luque 225)*. In Quito, there is **Libri Mundi** *(☎ 223 4791; JL Mera 851; open 8:30am-7pm Mon-Fri, 9am-1:30pm & 3:30-6:30pm Sat)* the best-known bookstore in Ecuador. Some titles listed here can be found only in Ecuador. Check these stores for the latest local guidebooks.

Lonely Planet

Other guidebooks can complement this one, especially if you are visiting South American countries other than Ecuador. *Read This First: Central & South America* is geared toward how to prepare and what to expect on your trip.

Lonely Planet's South American guides include the following titles: *Argentina,*

Uruguay & Paraguay; Bolivia; Chile & Easter Island; Colombia; Brazil; Peru; and *Venezuela.* Budget travelers planning to cover a large part of the continent should consider LP's *South America on a shoestring.* Trekkers will need LP's *Trekking in the Central Andes,* with descriptions of the most memorable and legendary treks in Ecuador, Peru and Bolivia.

LP's *Latin American Spanish phrasebook* is helpful for travelers without a good grasp of the most commonly used language in Ecuador. *Healthy Travel – Central & South America* is an excellent, pocket-sized book for tips on treating common illnesses, coping with high altitudes and avoiding dangerous encounters with wildlife; it has an illustrated guide to medicinal rainforest flora as well.

These and other Lonely Planet products can be found in bookstores worldwide or ordered online at **w** www.lonelyplanet.com.

Guidebooks

Defending Our Rainforest: A Guide to Community-Based Ecotourism in the Ecuadorian Amazon, by Rolf Wesche et al (1999, Acción Amazonia, Quito), is a recommended read. *Guía de Parques Nacionales y Reservas del Ecuador,* created by multiple agencies (1998, Quito), is a glossy book with information in Spanish about the national parks; a separate CD has an English version.

Climbing & Hiking in Ecuador, by Rob Rachowiecki & Mark Thurber, is a detailed guide to climbing Ecuador's mountains, with some hiking descriptions.

Natural History

The Birds of Ecuador, by Robert Ridgely et al, is the only bird-watching guide covering the whole country. There are two heavy volumes – the first has more details for the serious bird-watcher, while the second book has pictures and brief descriptions of the birds. For beginners looking for an introduction, *Common Birds of Amazonian Ecuador,* by Chris Canaday & Lou Jost (1997, Libri Mundi, Quito), is a good choice.

Neotropical Rainforest Mammals – A Field Guide, by Louise H Emmons, is an essential guide for those seriously interested in tropical mammals. The book is detailed and portable, and almost 300 species are described and illustrated. Although some of the mammals included are found only in other neotropical countries, many of Ecuador's mammals, and certainly all the known rainforest inhabitants, are found within the book's pages.

For the layperson interested in rainforest biology, try the entertaining and readable *Tropical Nature,* by Adrian Forsyth & Kenneth Miyata. Another good natural-history book is *A Neotropical Companion,* by John C Kricher.

Ecuador and Its Galápagos Islands: The Ecotraveler's Wildlife Guide, edited by David L Pearson & Les Beletsky, provides a general overview of both mainland and Galápagos wildlife.

The Galápagos Islands

The excellent *A Traveler's Guide to the Galápagos Islands,* by Barry Boyce, is written by an expert tour operator of the islands. It has detailed and lengthy listings of the better boats and tour agencies.

The best general guide to the history, geology, and plant and animal life of these islands is the thorough and highly recommended *Galápagos: A Natural History,* by Michael H Jackson, who is also a Galápagos guide. Other good choices for wildlife are *Identification Guide to the Birds, Mammals, and Reptiles of the Galápagos Islands,* by Andy Swash et al, and *Galápagos Wildlife,* by David Horwell & Pete Oxford.

Avid bird-watchers should enjoy *A Guide to the Birds of the Galápagos Islands,* by Isabel Castro & Antonia Phillips. Jonathan Weiner's *The Beak of the Finch* describes current research on the evolution of Darwin's finches.

The most famous of the visitors to the Galápagos was Charles Darwin, who was there in 1835. You can read his *Origin of Species* or his journal *The Voyage of the Beagle.* These 19th-century texts are rather dated and make heavy reading today. There are numerous modern biographies available, including *Charles Darwin – Voyaging: A Biography,* by Janet Browne. *Floreana,* by Margaret Wittmer (various editions and publishers), describes the life of one of the earliest colonists of the islands (Wittmer arrived in 1932 and lived there till her death in 2000).

No list of books about this fascinating laboratory of evolution is complete without mentioning Kurt Vonnegut's whimsical novel *Galápagos,* in which a group of vacationers are stranded on the islands and become the progenitors for a strange new twist in human evolution. It makes for a good read on the plane ride to the islands.

General

Going back to the arrival of the Spanish conquistadors, the best book is undoubtedly John Hemming's excellent *The Conquest of the Incas.* Although this deals mainly with Peru (the heart of the Inca Empire), there are several sections on Ecuador. Serious students will be enlightened by *Costume and Identity in Highland Ecuador,* by Ann P Rowe et al.

In the Oriente, an eye-opening book about the Huaorani (formerly called the Aucas) is Joe Kane's *Savages.* Another book of great interest is Mike Tidwell's *Amazon Stranger: Rainforest Chief Battles Big Oil,* although the Cofan village chief on whom the book is based, Randy Borman (a son of American missionaries who was raised in the rainforest), says that you should take it all with a pinch of salt.

Living Poor, by Moritz Thomsen, is a classic account of Peace Corps life in coastal Ecuador during the 1960s. Unlike most volunteers, who were in their 20s, Thomsen was 48 when he arrived for a four-year stint in one of Ecuador's poorest areas. He writes with eloquence and humor about the place and people he obviously grew to love.

The Panama Hat Trail, by Tom Miller, is a fascinating book about the author's search for that most quintessential and misnamed of Ecuadorian products, the panama hat.

FILMS

The Lonely Planet *Ecuador* video is a good way to get an understanding of the experience of traveling in Ecuador before actually going there; it's available in stores or on the Lonely Planet website (W www.lonelyplanet .com), under Propaganda. General travel videos about Ecuador, the Amazon and the Galápagos exist in various formats in Ecuador and in many other countries. If buying in Ecuador, make sure the film is compatible with the system in your country (most are compatible only with North American systems). Many libraries lend videos as well as books; check them out.

NEWSPAPERS & MAGAZINES

The two best Spanish newspapers published in Quito are the independent *El Comercio* (W www.elcomercio.com) and the more liberal *Hoy* (W www.hoy.com.ec). Some good Spanish-language newspapers published in Guayaquil are the independent *El Telégrafo* and *El Universo* (W www.eluniverso.com). Ecuador's best-known news magazine is *Vistazo,* which is published every two weeks. It is popular, widely read and covers most of what is going on in Ecuador – politics, sports, economy and so on.

A locally printed, somewhat abbreviated but up-to-date English version of the *Miami Herald* is available in Quito and Ecuador, and costs about $0.50. Other international newspapers are available at **Libri Mundi** (*JL Mera 851*) bookstore in Quito, the reading rooms of the luxury hotels in Quito and Guayaquil, and at the international airports. These tend to be a couple of days old. Latin American editions of *Time* and *Newsweek* are also readily available at about $2 each; they're in English, but they have more space devoted to Latin American news.

PHOTOGRAPHY & VIDEO

Definitely bring everything you think you'll need. Camera gear is expensive in Ecuador, and film choice is limited. Some good films are unavailable, such as Kodachrome slide film. However, you can get Ektachrome and Fujichrome slide films. Ordinary print films, such as Kodacolor and Fujicolor, are the most widely available and reasonably priced (about the same as in the US) and are usually the best buy. Slide film is more expensive. If buying film in small towns, check the expiry date.

Don't have slide film developed in Ecuador if you can help it, as processing is mediocre (although amateur photographers should find print developing to be OK). On the other hand, carrying around exposed film for months is asking for washed-out results. It is best to send it home as soon as possible after it's exposed.

If going to the Galápagos, you'll find that you can get very close to the wildlife and will want to take lots of shots. Film and camera batteries are rarely available on the boats, so make sure you bring enough.

Lonely Planet's *Travel Photography* is full of useful tips.

TIME

The Ecuadorian mainland is five hours behind Greenwich Mean Time, and the Galápagos are six hours behind. Mainland time is equivalent to Eastern Standard Time in North America. Because of Ecuador's location on the equator, days and nights are of equal length year-round, and there is no daylight-saving time.

ELECTRICITY

Ecuador uses 110V, 60 cycles, AC (the same as in North America, but not compatible with Britain and Australia). Plugs have two flat prongs, as in North America.

WEIGHTS & MEASURES

Ecuador uses the metric system and so does this book. For travelers who still use miles, ounces, bushels, leagues, rods, magnums, stones and other quaint and arcane expressions, there is a metric conversion table at the back of this book.

LAUNDRY

There are almost no self-service laundry machines in Ecuador. Almost all *lavanderías* (laundries) only do dry cleaning, although there are a few in Quito, Guayaquil and some other towns popular with travelers where you can have your clothes washed and dried if you leave them for a few hours.

Many hotels will have someone to do your laundry; this can cost very little in the cheaper hotels (about $1 for a change of clothes). The major problem is that you might not see your clothes again for two or three days, particularly if it is raining and they can't be dried. There are faster laundry services in the better hotels, but rates are charged by the piece and are often very expensive.

TOILETS

Ecuadorian plumbing has very low pressure. Putting toilet paper into the bowl may clog the system, so a waste receptacle is provided for paper. A basket of used toilet paper may seem unsanitary, but is much better than clogged bowls and water overflowing onto the floor. A well-run cheap hotel will ensure that the receptacle is emptied and the toilet cleaned daily. The same applies to restaurants and other public toilets. The more expensive hotels have adequate flushing capabilities.

Public toilets are limited mainly to bus terminals, airports and restaurants. Lavatories are called *servicios higiénicos* and are usually marked 'SS.HH.' People needing to use the lavatory often ask to use the *baño* in a restaurant; toilet paper is rarely available, so the experienced traveler always carries a personal supply.

Note that some upscale lavatories provide hand towels. If they are used and damp, you might prefer shaking your hands dry to avoid possible infection.

Because of the lack of public lavatories, men tend to urinate outdoors much more than visitors may be used to, particularly in areas lacking restaurants or similar facilities.

HEALTH

Your health while traveling depends on your pre-departure preparations, your daily health care while traveling and how you handle any medical problem that does develop. While the potential dangers can seem quite frightening, in reality, few travelers experience anything more than an upset stomach.

Pre-departure Planning

Immunizations Plan ahead for getting your vaccinations: some require several injections, and some vaccinations should not be given together or should be avoided during pregnancy and by people with allergies – discuss this with your doctor at least six weeks before travel. Be aware that there is often a greater risk of disease for children and pregnant women.

Although Ecuador does not currently require anyone to have up-to-date vaccinations to enter the country, the following should be considered (for more details about the diseases, themselves, see the individual entries later).

Cholera The current injectable vaccine against cholera is poorly protective and has many side effects, so it is not generally recommended for travelers. However, in some situations, it may be necessary to have a certificate.

Diphtheria & Tetanus Vaccinations for these two diseases are usually combined and are recommended for everyone. After an initial course of three injections (usually given in childhood), boosters are necessary every 10 years.

Hepatitis A The hepatitis A vaccine (eg, Avaxim, Havrix 1440 or VAQTA) provides long-term immunity (possibly for more than 10 years) after an initial injection and a booster at six to 12 months.

Hepatitis B Travelers who should consider vaccination against hepatitis B include those on a long trip in Amazonia, where blood transfusions may not be adequately screened, or anywhere sexual contact or needle sharing is a possibility. Vaccination involves three injections, with a booster at 12 months. More rapid courses are available if necessary.

Polio Everyone should keep up to date with this vaccination, which is normally given in childhood. A booster every 10 years helps you to maintain immunity.

Rabies Although rabies is not common in Ecuador, vaccination should be considered by those who are cycling, handling animals, caving or traveling to remote areas. It should also be considered for children (who may not report a bite or scratch). The pre-travel rabies vaccination involves receiving three injections over 21 to 28 days. If someone who has been vaccinated is bitten or scratched by an animal, they will require two booster injections of vaccine; those not vaccinated require more.

Typhoid Vaccination against typhoid may be required if you are traveling for more than a couple of weeks in most parts of South America. It is now available either as an injection or as capsules to be taken orally.

Yellow Fever A yellow-fever vaccine is recommended for travel in areas where the disease is endemic (parts of South America, including lowland Ecuador). You may have to go to a special yellow-fever vaccination centre.

Alternatively, an injection of gamma globulin can provide short-term protection against hepatitis A – two to six months, depending on the dose given. It is not a vaccine but a ready-made antibody collected from blood donations. It is reasonably effective and, unlike the vaccine, it is protective immediately, but because it is a blood product, there are current concerns about its long-term safety.

The hepatitis A vaccine is also available in a combined form, Twinrix, with the hepatitis B vaccine. Three injections over a six-month period are required, the first two providing substantial protection against hepatitis A.

Malaria Medication Antimalarial drugs do not prevent you from being infected, but they kill the malarial parasites during a critical stage in their development, thus reducing the risk of serious illness or death. Expert advice on medication should be sought, as

there are many factors to consider, including the area to be visited, the risk of exposure to malaria-carrying mosquitoes, the side effects of medication, your medical history and whether you are a child or pregnant. Travelers to isolated areas in high-risk countries may want to carry a treatment dose of medication for use if symptoms occur.

Health Insurance Make sure that you have adequate health insurance. See Travel Insurance under Visas & Documents earlier in this chapter.

Travel-Health Guides Lonely Planet's *Healthy Travel: Central & South America* is described in Books, earlier. *Travel with Children,* by Cathy Lanigan, includes advice on travel health for younger children.

There are some excellent travel-health sites on the Internet. From the Lonely Planet home page, there are links at ⓦ www.lonelyplanet.com/weblinks/wlheal.htm to the World Health Organization and the US Center for Disease Control and Prevention.

Other Preparations Make sure you're healthy before traveling. If going on a long trip, make sure your teeth are OK. If you wear glasses, take a spare pair and your prescription.

If you require a particular medication, take an adequate supply, as it may not be available locally. Know the generic name, as well as the brand, to make getting replacements easier. To avoid problems, have a legible prescription or letter from your doctor to show that you legally use the medication.

Basic Rules

Food Vegetables and fruit should be washed with purified water or peeled when possible. Beware of ice cream that is sold in the street or that might have been melted and refrozen.

If a place looks clean and well run and the vendor also looks clean and healthy, then the food is probably safe. In general, places that are packed with travelers or locals are fine, while empty restaurants are questionable. The food in busy restaurants is cooked and eaten quite quickly and is probably not reheated.

Water The number one rule is *be careful of the water* and especially ice. If you don't know for certain that the water is safe, assume the worst. Reputable brands of bottled water or soft drinks are generally fine. Take care with fruit juice, particularly if water may have been added. Tea or coffee should also be OK, since the water should have been boiled.

Water Purification The simplest way of purifying water is to boil it thoroughly. Vigorous boiling should be satisfactory. At high altitude water boils at a lower temperature, so germs are less likely to be killed. Boil it for longer in these environments.

Consider purchasing a water filter for a long trip. There are two main kinds of filters. Total filters take out all parasites, bacteria and viruses, and make water safe to drink. They are often expensive, but they can be more cost effective than buying bottled water. Simple filters take out dirt and larger foreign bodies from the water so that chemical solutions work much more effectively; if water is dirty, chemical solutions may not work at all. It's important when buying a filter to read the specifications so that you know exactly what it removes from the water and what it doesn't. Simple filtering will not remove all dangerous organisms, so if you cannot boil water, it should be treated chemically. Chlorine tablets will kill many pathogens, but not some parasites, such as Giardia and amoebic cysts. Iodine is more effective for purifying water and is available in tablet form. Follow the directions and remember that too much iodine can also be harmful.

Medical Problems & Treatment

Self-diagnosis and treatment can be risky, so you should always seek medical help. An embassy, consulate or five-star hotel can usually recommend a local doctor or clinic. Although we do give drug dosages in this section, they are for emergency use only. Correct diagnosis is vital. In this section, we have used the generic names for medications – check with a pharmacist for brands available locally.

Note that antibiotics should ideally be administered only under medical supervision. Take only the recommended dose at the prescribed intervals, and use the whole course, even if the illness seems to be cured earlier. Stop immediately if there are any serious reactions, and don't use the antibiotic at all if you are unsure whether you have the correct one. Some people are allergic to commonly prescribed antibiotics such as penicillin; carry this information (eg, on a bracelet) when traveling.

Environmental Hazards

Soroche (Altitude Sickness) Lack of oxygen at high altitudes (over 2500m) affects most people to some extent. The effect may be mild or severe and occurs because less oxygen reaches the muscles and the brain at high altitudes, requiring the heart and lungs to compensate by working harder. Symptoms of Acute Mountain Sickness (AMS) usually develop during the first 24 hours at a high altitude but may be delayed up to three weeks. Mild symptoms include headache, lethargy, dizziness, difficulty sleeping and loss of appetite. AMS may become more severe without warning and it can be fatal. Severe symptoms include breathlessness; a dry, irritative cough (which may progress to the production of pink, frothy sputum); severe headache; lack of coordination and balance; confusion; irrational behaviour; vomiting; drowsiness; and unconsciousness. There is no hard-and-fast rule as to what is too high: AMS has been fatal at 3000m, although 3500m to 4500m is the usual range.

Treat mild symptoms by resting at the same altitude until recovery, usually a day or two. Paracetamol or aspirin can be taken for headaches. If symptoms persist or become worse, however, *immediate descent is necessary;* even 500m can help. Drug treatments should never be used to avoid descent or to enable further ascent.

The drugs acetazolamide and dexamethasone are recommended by some doctors for the prevention of AMS; however, their use is controversial. They can reduce the symptoms, but they may also mask warning signs; severe and fatal AMS has occurred in people taking these drugs. In general, we do not recommend them.

To prevent acute mountain sickness:

- Drink extra fluids. The mountain air is dry and cold, and moisture is lost as you breathe.
- Eat light, high-carbohydrate meals for more energy.
- Avoid alcohol, as it may increase the risk of dehydration.
- Avoid sedatives.

[Continued on page 54]

Galápagos Wildlife Guide

The unique wildlife of the Galápagos is simply astounding. Although the number of species on the islands is relatively small compared to that of the mainland, nowhere else in the world can you see such wild animals at such close range. Because of their lack of natural predators, most animals are literally fearless of human visitors. Not only has the wildlife of this spectacular, barren archipelago been astonishing tourists for years, it has also shaped the course of human history by contributing significantly to Charles Darwin's theory of evolution, which he unfolded during his stay on the islands.

BIRDS

Birds are faithful, ever-present company during a visit to the Galápagos. There are 58 resident bird species on the Galápagos, of which 28 are endemic, and over 30 other migrant species regularly visit the islands. During a week of touring the islands, most careful observers will see a good 40 species of birds.

Seabirds

Boobies Although boobies are not endemic to the Galápagos, they are among the most popular with visitors, thanks to their amusing appearance and the ease with which visitors can approach their colonies. You can often get within a meter of an active nest, which means great photographs. Three species of boobies breed on the islands. Punta Pitt, on San Cristóbal, is the only visitor site where the three species can be seen together. All boobies are fast fliers and exceptional plunge divers.

The **blue-footed booby** is perhaps the most famous Galápagos seabird and is often the first booby seen by visitors. This big, whitish-brown seabird really does have bright-blue feet, which it picks up in a slow, dignified fashion when performing a courtship display. Bowing, wing-spreading and sky-pointing are all part of the booby's enchanting courtship display – watching this rather clownish behavior is one of the highlights of any visit.

The **masked booby** is pure white with a black band at the edges of its wings and the end of its tail. A blackish area of bare skin surrounds its bill, giving the appearance of a face mask. It's the biggest of the Galápagos boobies and is found on most of the islands. They often nest near cliff tops to give themselves an advantage when taking off.

The **red-footed booby** is the smallest of the Galápagos boobies and is readily distinguished by its red feet and its blue bill. Although it's the most numerous of the Galápagos boobies, it is found only on the outer islands and is therefore infrequently seen.

Frigatebirds With the largest wingspan-to-weight ratio of any bird, frigatebirds are dazzling fliers. Both species of frigatebirds found in the archipelago – the **magnificent frigatebird** and the **great frigatebird** – make their acrobatic living by aerial piracy, often harassing smaller birds into dropping or regurgitating their catch and then swooping to catch the booty in midair. Frigatebirds do this because they cannot secrete enough oils to waterproof their feathers and therefore

Title page: Masked boobies. (Photo by Ralph Lee Hopkins)

Greater flamingos and Galápagos sea lion

WES WALKER

Blue-footed booby

RALPH LEE HOPKINS

Red-footed booby

RALPH LEE HOPKINS

Frigatebird during the mating season

RICHARD I'ANSON

Flightless cormorants

RALPH LEE HOPKINS

Albatrosses

RALPH LEE HOPKINS

Masked boobies

RALPH LEE HOPKINS

Galápagos penguin

RALPH LEE HOPKINS

Darwin's finch

Marine iguana

Giant (Galápagos) tortoise

Pacific green sea turtle

Lava lizard

Galápagos land iguana

Galápagos sea lion and snorkelers

Galápagos sea lion pup

Sally Lightfoot crab

School of dolphins

cannot dive underwater to catch prey. Their dinosaurian wingspan, however, reaches up to 2.3m! The males have bright-red flaps of skin hanging under their necks that they inflate into impressive, football-sized balloons to attract females.

Cormorants Other than the penguin, the **flightless cormorant** is the only flightless seabird in the world, and it is endemic to the Galápagos. Its ancestors were almost certainly able to fly, but when they reached the Galápagos, they found no predators in the rocky shallows where they fed. Therefore, they didn't need wings to flee, and the cormorants that survived best were the streamlined ones that could swim and dive strongly in the surf. Thus, birds with small wings and strong legs had an advantage, and through natural selection, the flightless cormorant evolved.

There are only about 700 to 800 pairs in the Galápagos, and to see them you should plan on a two-week tour that takes you to the coasts of Isabel and Fernandina islands.

Penguins The most northerly penguin in the world is the **Galápagos penguin** and it can survive on the islands thanks to the cool Humboldt current flowing from Antarctica. They normally breed in the western parts of Isabela and Fernandina, although a small colony is often seen at Isla Bartolomé. The clumsiness of penguins on land belies their skill and speed underwater. The best way to appreciate this, of course, is to jump in and snorkel with them.

Albatrosses One of the world's most magnificently graceful birds the **waved albatross** is the only species of albatross on the islands. It can spend years at sea without touching land. It's the largest bird in the archipelago, with an average weight of 5kg and a wingspan as long as 2.4m. Apart from a few pairs that have bred on Isla de la Plata, the entire world population of some 12,000 pairs nests and breeds on Isla Española between April and December. The rest of the year they're at sea.

The waved albatross engages in one of the most spectacular courtship displays of any bird. It involves perfectly choreographed bowing, bill clicking, bill circling, swaying and freezing, honking and whistling – one of the most memorable sights of the Galápagos.

Other Seabirds The unmistakable **red-billed tropicbird** is one of the most spectacular Galápagos seabirds. The most noticeable feature of this splendid white bird is its pair of tail streamers – two feathers which are often as long as its body. They nest in cliff crevices or rock piles on most of the islands.

The lovely, endemic **swallow-tailed gull** is gray and white, with bright-red feet and legs, and a crimson eye ring. It's the only nocturnal gull in the world and is frequently seen perched on cliff tops during the day. The second of the islands' two gull species, the **lava gull**, is the rarest gull in the world, and only about 400 pairs exist. Despite this, you have a fairly good chance of seeing them, as they are widely distributed around the islands.

Gliding extraordinaires, the **brown pelican** is often the first bird visitors spot, and is instantly recognizable by its huge pouched bill and large size. The little **brown noddy tern** is often seen feeding with pelicans, sometimes even perching on the pelican's head to scavenge food scraps.

The small **dark-rumped petrel** and the even smaller **Audubon's shearwater** are regularly seen, as are the three species of **storm petrels**, the smallest of all Galápagos seabirds.

Shore & Wetland Birds

The largest heron in the islands, with a wingspan approaching 2m, is the **great blue heron**, easily recognizable by its long legs and neck, and by the way it stands and flies with its head hunched into its shoulders. It's found along the rocky coasts of most of the islands. The all-white **cattle egret** is found in similar habitats. The small **lava heron** is the only endemic heron in the islands. It lives and hunts in the lava shorelines on most of the islands, but its dark-green plumage camouflages it against the rock, making it difficult to spot. The **striated heron** and the nocturnal **yellow-crowned night heron** are both common.

Few people have trouble identifying the **greater flamingo**, that grand, pink bird with black wing feathers and long legs, often seen poking around salty lagoons, feeding on insects, shrimp and other crustaceans. Flamingos are nervous birds, particularly when nesting, and visitors should be quiet when viewing them or the birds may desert their nests.

The black-and-white **American oystercatcher** and the **black-necked stilt** are regularly seen along the rocky coasts and salty lagoons of most islands. Other small shorebirds include the **semi-palmated plover**, the **ruddy turnstone** and four members of the **sandpiper** family.

Land Birds

Finches The most famous birds of the Galápagos are the 13 species of **Darwin's finches**. Although these little flappers are nothing spectacular to look at, they helped changed the world. All 13 species are thought to have descended from a common ancestor, and their present differences in distribution, body size, plumage, beak size and shape, and feeding habits helped Darwin formulate his evolutionary theories.

Darwin's finches include the **warbler finch**, the **small ground finch** and the **large cactus finch**. The **wood-pecker finch** and the **mangrove finch** sometimes grasp twigs in their bills and poke them into holes and cracks in dead trees to extract a grub or other prey – a remarkable example of tool use that is very rare among birds.

Raptors The endemic **Galápagos hawk** has no natural enemies and is quite fearless, often allowing curious visitors to approach within a meter. Unfortunately, their fearlessness has led to their extinction from hunting on several islands. Just over a hundred pairs remain on the islands. Islas Santiago, Bartolomé, Española, Santa Fe, Fernandina and Isabela are the best islands on which to see them.

The **barn owl**, with its striking off-white, heart-shaped facial disk, is most common on Isla Fernandina, but is rarely glimpsed because of its nocturnal habits. The much larger **short-eared owl** is darker than the barn owl, and, because it's diurnal, is spotted much more frequently.

Other Land Birds Widespread in the highlands, the resident adult male **vermilion flycatcher** is tiny but unmistakable with its bright-red crown and chest. Females are brown above and yellowish beneath. The endemic **large-billed (Galápagos) flycatcher** is seen more frequently.

The fearless **mockingbirds** of the Galápagos (of which there are four species) are all endemic to the islands. The tiny **yellow warbler** is the only bright-yellow bird in the Galápagos and is found throughout the islands. The **dark-billed cuckoo** is also common, but difficult to see.

REPTILES

The Galápagos are crawling with prehistoric-looking reptiles that are easily approached and observed. Over two-dozen species belonging to five families have been recorded and most of them are endemic.

Tortoises

The most famous reptile is the **giant tortoise**, or **Galápagos**, for which the islands are named. This species has been divided into 14 subspecies, three of which are extinct. The differences in the subspecies' carapaces (shells) contributed to Darwin's development of his theory of evolution.

Whalers and sealers killed many thousands of tortoises, particularly in the 18th and 19th centuries. Now, only some 15,000 remain. The easiest way to see both tiny yearlings and full-grown adults is at the breeding project at the Charles Darwin Research Station in Puerto Ayora, Santa Cruz. To see these majestic creatures in the wild, visit the tortoise reserve on Santa Cruz or the Los Galápagos visitor site on San Cristóbal, or climb Volcán Alcedo on Isabela.

Giant tortoises can reach a weight of 250kg – 3000 times the weight of a newborn hatchling! They are vegetarians, and scientists estimate their lifespan to be about 150 years.

The tortoises usually mate toward the end of the rainy season, when the males posture and shove other males in contests of dominance before seeking out a mate. Unsuccessful males have been known to attempt to mate with other males, or even with appropriately shaped boulders! The females, once mated, look for dry, sandy areas to make a nest.

Marine Turtles

Leatherback and hawksbill turtles have occasionally been recorded in the Galápagos, but only the **Pacific green sea turtle** is a resident breeder. Adults are huge and can reach 150kg. Snorkelers sometimes see them flapping serenely by underwater, a truly emotional sight.

The turtles mate in the water near the shore, and between December and June, the females crawl ashore at night to lay dozens of eggs in pockets they dig into the sand. After about 60 days, the eggs hatch almost simultaneously and the newborns emerge from the sand and wriggle toward the sea. Those that aren't gobbled up by predators on that fateful first crawl swim out to a sea full of hungry fish and stay away for years. They have exceptional navigational skills, and those that survive return to mate near the same beach where they were hatched.

Iguanas

There are three species of iguanas in the **Galápagos**, the most frequently seen reptiles on the islands. All of them are endemic.

The **marine iguana** is the only seagoing lizard in the world and is found on the rocky shores of most islands. It has blackish skin, which in males can change to startling blues and reds during the breeding season. The row of spines along their backs, their scaly skins, their habit of snorting little puffs of salt spray into the air and their length of nearly 1m make them look like veritable little dragons.

Marine iguanas feed mainly on intertidal seaweed, although mature males have been recorded offshore at depths of up to 12m and can remain submerged for over an hour.

The two species of land iguanas look almost alike, and their preferred food is the succulent pads and yellow flowers of the prickly pear cactus. They're both yellowish in color and bigger than their marine relatives, sometimes weighing up to 6kg. The **Galápagos land iguana** is found on Islas Isabela, Santa Cruz, Fernandina, Seymour and – most of all – South Plaza. The similar but slightly bigger **Santa Fe land iguana** is found only on that island and can exceed 1m in length.

Other Reptiles

The seven **Galápagos** species of **lava lizard** are frequently seen scurrying across rocks throughout the islands. Another lizard you might spot (especially in hotels) is the **gecko**, a small, harmless nocturnal lizard with adhesive pads on its digits which allow it to climb vertical walls and walk upside down on ceilings. Finally, you may see the **Galápagos snake**, which is small, drab and nonpoisonous.

MAMMALS

There are few mammals in the Galápagos because of the difficulty of surviving a long ocean crossing. There are only six native mammals – two are **seals**, two are **bats** and two are **rice rats**.

Seals

The native mammal you'll see the most is the **Galápagos sea lion**, of which there are an estimated 50,000 throughout the islands. The territorial bulls, which can reach 250kg, are aggressive and sometimes chase swimmers out of the water. They have been known to bite if harassed, so don't approach them too closely. The females and young, however, are extremely playful, and you can often snorkel very close to them – they'll often be as curious about you as you are about them.

Dominant males control particularly attractive beaches that can contain up to 30 females. The dominant male has mating access to these females, but only for as long as he's able to keep other males away, which may mean that he goes for days without much food or sleep.

Pups (generally one per mother) are usually born around the beginning of the dry season. The mother nurses it for five or six months, at which point it begins to fish for itself.

The endemic **Galápagos fur seal** is less commonly seen. Its fur is very dense and luxuriant, qualities which attracted sealers who decimated the population in the 19th century.

Whales & Dolphins

Other marine mammals you may see when cruising the islands are whales and dolphins. The seven whale species regularly recorded in the archipelago are the **finback**, **sei**, **humpback**, **minke**, **sperm**, **killer** and **pilot** whales.

Bottle-nosed dolphins are often seen surfing the bow waves of boats. At night, the dolphins cause the ocean to glow around them with bioluminescence as they stir up thousands of tiny phosphorescent creatures that light up when disturbed.

FISH

Over 400 species of fish have been recorded in the Galápagos, of which about 50 are endemic. Snorkeling in the Galápagos is a wonderful experience, and schools containing thousands of tropical fish are routinely seen. To name but a few, you might see **blue-eyed damselfish**, **white-banded angelfish**, **yellow-tailed surgeonfish**, **Moorish idols**, **blue parrotfish**, **concentric puffer fish**, **yellow-bellied triggerfish** and **hieroglyphic hawkfish**.

The **sharks** of the Galápagos have never been known to attack a human swimmer. Snorkelers and divers frequently see them, and their speed and grace underwater is almost unworldly. In fact, one of the best reasons to snorkel or dive in the Galápagos is for the chance to see these magnificent animals in reasonable safety. The most common species are the **white-tipped reef shark** and the **Galápagos shark**. Scuba divers who head out to the dive site Rocks Gordon (easily arranged through a dive center in Puerto Ayora) have a good chance of seeing **hammerheads**.

Rays are also thrilling to see underwater. **Stingrays** sometimes bask on the sandy bottoms of the shallows and can inflict an extremely painful wound to waders and paddlers. It's a good idea to enter the water by shuffling your feet along the sandy bottom, giving the stingray the chance to swim away before you step on it.

Other rays found in deeper waters are the **spotted eagle ray**, the beautiful, golden **mustard ray** and the less frequently seen giant **manta ray**. The latter is most often spotted when it leaps out of the water – with a maximum spread of 6m from the tip of one fin to the other, they make a huge splash when they land.

INVERTEBRATES

Many invertebrates are encountered in the Galápagos. Water invertebrates include **barnacles**, **crabs** (such as **Sally Lightfoot**, **ghost** and **hermit crabs**), **lobsters**, **jellyfish**, **sea anemones**, **starfish**, **sea urchins**, **sea cucumbers** and **sand dollars** – all great fun to search for in tide pools or while snorkeling.

[Continued from page 46]

Heat Exhaustion Dehydration and salt deficiency can cause heat exhaustion. Take time to acclimatize to high temperatures, drink sufficient liquids, and do not do anything too physically demanding.

Salt deficiency is characterized by fatigue, lethargy, headaches, giddiness and muscle cramps; salt tablets may help, but adding extra salt to your food is better.

Anhidrotic heat exhaustion is a rare form of heat exhaustion, which is caused by an inability to sweat. It tends to affect people who have been in a hot climate for some time more than newcomers. It can progress to heatstroke. Treatment involves moving to a cooler climate.

Heatstroke This serious, occasionally fatal, condition can occur if the body's heat-regulating mechanism breaks down and the body temperature rises to dangerous levels. Long, continuous periods of exposure to high temperatures and insufficient fluids can leave you vulnerable to heatstroke.

The symptoms are feeling unwell, not sweating very much (or at all) and a high body temperature (39°C to 41°C or 102°F to 106°F). Where sweating has ceased, the skin becomes flushed and red. Severe, throbbing headaches and a lack of coordination will also occur, and the sufferer may become confused or aggressive. Eventually, the victim will become delirious or convulse. Hospitalization is essential, but in the interim, get victims out of the sun, remove their clothing, cover them with a wet sheet or towel, and then fan them continuously. Give them fluids if they are conscious.

Hypothermia Too much cold can be just as dangerous as too much heat. If you are trekking at high altitudes or simply taking a long bus trip over mountains, particularly at night, be prepared.

Hypothermia occurs when the body loses heat faster than it can produce it, causing the core temperature of the body to fall. It is surprisingly easy to progress from very cold to dangerously cold due to a combination of wind, wet clothing, fatigue and hunger, even if the air temperature is above freezing. It is best to dress in layers; silk, wool and some of the new artificial fibers are all good insulating materials. A hat is important, as a lot of heat is lost through the head. A strong, waterproof outer layer is essential.

Symptoms of hypothermia are exhaustion, numb skin (particularly toes and fingers), shivering, slurred speech, irrational or violent behaviour, lethargy, stumbling, dizzy spells, muscle cramps and violent bursts of energy. Irrationality may take the form of sufferers' claiming they are warm and trying to take off their clothes.

To treat mild hypothermia, first get the victims out of the wind and/or rain, remove their clothing if it's wet and replace it with dry, warm clothing. Give them hot liquids – not alcohol – and some high-energy, easily digestible food. Do not rub victims; instead, allow them to slowly warm themselves. This should be enough to treat the early stages of hypothermia. The early recognition and treatment of mild hypothermia is the only way to prevent severe hypothermia, which is a critical condition.

Jet Lag This is experienced when a person travels by air across more than three time zones (each time zone usually represents a one-hour time difference). It occurs because many of the functions of the human body (such as temperature, pulse rate and the emptying of the bladder and bowels) are regulated by internal 24-hour cycles. When we travel long distances rapidly, our bodies take time to adjust to the 'new time' of our destination, and we may experience fatigue, disorientation, insomnia, anxiety, impaired concentration and a loss of appetite. These effects will usually be gone within three days after arrival, but to minimize the impact of jet lag, do the following:

- Rest for a couple of days prior to departure.
- Try to select flight schedules that minimize sleep deprivation; arriving late in the day means you can go to sleep soon after you arrive. For very long flights, try to organize a stopover.
- Avoid excessive eating (which bloats the stomach) and alcohol (which causes dehydration) during the flight. Instead, drink plenty of non-carbonated, nonalcoholic drinks, such as fruit juice or water.
- Avoid smoking.
- Make yourself comfortable by wearing loose-fitting clothes and by bringing an eye mask and ear plugs to help you sleep.
- Try to sleep at the appropriate time for the time zone you are traveling to.

Motion Sickness Eating lightly before and during a trip will reduce the chances of motion sickness. If you are prone to motion sickness, try to find a place that minimizes movement – near the wing on aircraft, close to midships on boats, near the center on buses. Fresh air usually helps; reading and cigarette smoke hurt. Commercial motion-sickness preparations, which can cause drowsiness, have to be taken before the trip commences. Ginger (available in capsule form) and peppermint (including mint-flavoured sweets) are natural preventatives.

Prickly Heat This condition is an itchy rash that's caused by excessive perspiration trapped under the skin. It usually strikes people who have just arrived in a hot climate. Keeping cool, bathing often, drying the skin and using a mild talcum or prickly heat powder may help (or you could resort to air-conditioning if possible).

Sunburn In the tropics or at high altitudes you can get sunburned surprisingly quickly, even through cloud cover. Use sunscreen, a hat and a barrier cream for your nose and lips. Calamine lotion or a commercial after-sun preparation are good for mild sunburn. Protect your eyes with good-quality sunglasses, particularly if you will be near water, sand or snow.

Infectious Diseases

Diarrhea Simple things – such as a change of water, food or climate – can cause a mild bout of diarrhea, but a few rushed toilet trips with no other symptoms is not indicative of a major problem.

Dehydration is the main danger with any diarrhea – particularly for children or the elderly, as dehydration can occur in them quite quickly. Under all circumstances, *fluid replacement* (at least equal to the volume being lost) is the most important thing to remember. Soda water, weak black tea with a little sugar, or soft drinks allowed to go flat and diluted 50% with clean water are all good. With severe diarrhea, a rehydrating solution is preferable to replace lost minerals and salts. Commercially available oral rehydration salts (ORS) are very useful; add them to boiled or bottled water. In an emergency, you can make up a solution of six teaspoons of sugar and a half teaspoon of salt per liter of boiled or bottled water. You need to drink at least the same volume of fluid that you are losing through bowel movements and vomiting. Urine is the best guide to the adequacy of replacement – if you have small amounts of concentrated urine, you need to drink more. Keep drinking small amounts often. Stick to a bland diet as you recover.

Gut-paralysing drugs, such as loperamide or diphenoxylate, can be used to bring relief from the symptoms, although they do not actually cure the problem. Only use these drugs if you do not have access to toilets, eg, if you *must* travel. Note that these drugs are not recommended for children under the age of 12 years.

Antibiotics may be required in certain situations: diarrhea with blood or mucus (dysentery), diarrhea with fever, profuse watery diarrhea, persistent diarrhea not improving after 48 hours and severe diarrhea. These suggest a more serious cause of diarrhea, and in these situations, gut-paralysing drugs should be avoided.

In these situations, a stool test may be necessary to diagnose what bug is causing your diarrhea, so you should seek medical help urgently. Where this is not possible, the recommended drugs for bacterial diarrhea (the most likely cause of severe diarrhea in travelers) are norfloxacin (400mg twice daily for three days) or ciprofloxacin (500mg twice daily for five days). These are not recommended for children or pregnant women. The drug of choice for children would be co-trimoxazole (dosage is dependent on weight; a five-day course is given). Ampicillin or amoxicillin may be given during pregnancy, but medical care is necessary.

Two other causes of persistent diarrhea in travelers are giardiasis and amoebic dysentery. Giardiasis is caused by a common parasite, *Giardia lamblia*. Symptoms include stomach cramps, nausea, a bloated stomach, watery and foul-smelling diarrhea, and frequent gas. Giardiasis can appear several weeks after you have been exposed to the parasite. The symptoms may disappear for a few days and then return; this can go on for several weeks.

Amoebic dysentery is caused by the protozoan *Entamoeba histolytica* and it is characterized by a gradual onset of low-grade diarrhea, often with blood and mucus.

Cramping abdominal pain and vomiting are less likely to occur than in other types of diarrhea, and fever may not be present. It will persist until treated and can recur and cause other health problems.

You should seek medical advice if you think you have giardiasis or amoebic dysentery, but where this is not possible, tinidazole or metronidazole is the recommended drug. Treatment is a 2g single dose of tinidazole or a 250mg dose of metronidazole three times daily for five to 10 days.

Fungal Infections These infections occur more commonly in hot weather and are usually found on the scalp, between the toes (athlete's foot) or fingers, in the groin and on the body (ringworm). You get ringworm (which is a fungal infection, not a worm) from infected animals or other people. Moisture encourages these infections.

To prevent fungal infections, wear loose, comfortable clothes, avoid artificial fibers, wash frequently, and dry yourself carefully. If you do get an infection, wash the infected area at least daily with a disinfectant or medicated soap and water, and rinse and dry well. Apply an antifungal cream or powder, such as tolnaftate. Try to expose the infected area to air or sunlight as much as possible. Change all towels and underwear often, wash them in hot water, and let them dry in the sun.

Hepatitis The general term for inflammation of the liver is hepatitis. Several different viruses cause hepatitis, and they differ in the way that they are transmitted. The symptoms are similar in all forms of the illness and include fever, chills, headache, fatigue, feelings of weakness, and aches and pains; these are followed by loss of appetite, nausea, vomiting, abdominal pain, dark urine, light-colored faeces, jaundiced (yellow) skin, and yellowing of the whites of the eyes. People who have had hepatitis should avoid alcohol for some time after the illness, as the liver needs time to recover.

Hepatitis A is transmitted by contaminated food and drinking water. You should seek medical advice, but there is not much you can do apart from resting, drinking lots of fluids, eating lightly and avoiding fatty foods. Hepatitis E is transmitted in the same way as hepatitis A; it can be very serious in pregnant women.

There are almost 300 million chronic carriers of hepatitis B in the world. It is spread through contact with infected blood, blood products or body fluids – for example, through sexual contact, unsterilized needles and blood transfusions – or through contact with blood via small breaks in the skin. Other risk situations include shaving or having a tattoo or body piercing done with contaminated equipment. The symptoms of hepatitis B may be more severe than type A, and the disease can lead to long-term problems, such as chronic liver damage, liver cancer or a long-term carrier state.

Hepatitis C and D are spread in the same way as hepatitis B and can also lead to long-term complications.

There are vaccines against hepatitis A and B, but there are currently no vaccines against the other types of hepatitis. Following the basic rules about food and water (hepatitis A and E) and avoiding risk situations (hepatitis B, C and D) are important preventative measures.

HIV & AIDS Infection with the human immunodeficiency virus (HIV) may lead to acquired immune deficiency syndrome (AIDS), which is a fatal disease. Any exposure to contaminated blood, blood products or body fluids may put the individual at risk. The disease is often transmitted through sexual contact or dirty needles – vaccinations, acupuncture, tattooing and body piercing can be potentially as dangerous as intravenous drug use. HIV/AIDS can also be spread through infected blood transfusions; Ecuador's best clinics screen their blood supply. If you do need an injection, ask to see the syringe unwrapped in front of you, or take a needle and syringe pack with you.

Intestinal Worms These parasites are most common in rural, tropical areas. The different worms have different ways of infecting people. Some worms, such as tapeworms, may be ingested by eating food such as undercooked meat, and some, such as hookworms, enter through your skin. Infestations may not show up for some time, and although they are generally not serious, if left untreated, some can cause severe health problems later. Consider having a stool test when you return home to check for these.

Sexually Transmitted Infections (STIs)
HIV/AIDS and hepatitis B can be transmitted through sexual contact – see the relevant sections earlier for more details. Other STIs include gonorrhoea, herpes and syphilis: sores, blisters or rashes around the genitals and discharges or pain when urinating are common symptoms. In some STIs, such as wart virus or Chlamydia, symptoms may be less marked or not observed at all, especially in women. Chlamydia infection can cause infertility in both men and women before any symptoms have been noticed. Syphilis symptoms eventually disappear completely, but the disease continues and can cause severe problems in later years. While abstinence from sexual contact is the only 100% effective prevention, using condoms is a significant deterrent. The treatment of gonorrhoea and syphilis is done with antibiotics. Each sexually transmitted infection requires specific antibiotics.

Typhoid A dangerous gut infection, typhoid fever is caused by contaminated water and food. Medical help must be sought.

In its early stages, sufferers may feel they have a bad cold or flu on the way, as initial symptoms are a headache, body aches and a fever that rises a little each day until it is around 40°C (104°F) or more. The victim's pulse is often slow relative to the degree of fever present – unlike a normal fever, during which the pulse increases. There may also be vomiting, abdominal pain, diarrhea or constipation.

In the second week, the high fever and slow pulse continue, and a few pink spots may appear on the body; trembling, delirium, weakness, weight loss and dehydration may occur. Complications such as pneumonia or perforated bowel may occur.

Insect-Borne Diseases
Chagas' disease, leishmaniasis, typhus and yellow fever are all insect-borne diseases, but they don't pose a great risk to travelers. For more information on them, see Less-Common Diseases later.

Malaria This serious and potentially fatal disease is spread by mosquito bites. If you are traveling in endemic areas, it is extremely important to avoid mosquito bites and to take tablets to prevent this disease. Symptoms range from fever, chills and sweating, headache, diarrhea and abdominal pains to a vague feeling of ill health. Seek medical help immediately if malaria is suspected. Without treatment, malaria can rapidly become more serious and can be fatal.

If medical care is not available, malaria tablets can be used for treatment. You need to use a malaria tablet that is different from the one you were taking when you contracted malaria. The standard treatment dose of mefloquine is two 250mg tablets and another two tablets six hours later. For Fansidar, it's a single dose of three tablets. If you were previously taking mefloquine and cannot obtain Fansidar, then other alternatives are Malarone (atovaquone-proguanil; four tablets once daily for three days), halofantrine (three doses of two 250mg tablets every six hours) or quinine sulphate (600mg every six hours). There is a greater risk of side effects with these dosages than with normal use if used with mefloquine, so medical advice is preferable. Be aware also that, because of side effects, halofantrine is no longer recommended by the WHO as an emergency standby treatment; it should only be used if no other drugs are available.

Travelers are advised to prevent mosquito bites at all times. The following are some preventative measures.

- Wear light-colored clothing.
- Wear long trousers and long-sleeved shirts.
- Use mosquito repellents containing the compound DEET on all exposed areas (be aware that the prolonged overuse of DEET may be harmful, especially to children, but its use is considered preferable to being bitten by disease-transmitting mosquitoes. Strengths over 30% do not increase effectiveness).
- Avoid perfumes or aftershave.
- Use a mosquito net impregnated with mosquito repellent – it may be worth taking your own.
- Impregnate clothes with repellent to effectively deter mosquitoes and other insects.
- Sleep under a fan; mosquitoes don't like wind.

Dengue Fever This viral disease is transmitted by mosquitoes and is fast becoming one of the top public-health problems in the tropical world. Unlike the malaria mosquito, the *Aedes aegypti* mosquito, which transmits the dengue virus, is most active during the day and is found mainly in urban areas, in and around human dwellings.

Signs and symptoms of dengue fever include a sudden onset of high fever, headache, joint and muscle pains (hence its old name, 'breakbone fever'), and nausea and vomiting. A rash of small red spots sometimes appears three to four days after the onset of fever. In the early phase of illness, dengue fever may be mistaken for other infectious diseases, including malaria and influenza. Minor bleeding such as nose bleeds may occur during the course of the illness. Recovery may be prolonged, with fatigue lasting for several weeks.

You should seek medical attention as soon as possible if you think you may be infected. A blood test can exclude malaria and indicate the possibility of dengue fever. There is no specific treatment for dengue. Aspirin should be avoided, as it increases the risk of haemorrhaging. There is no vaccine against dengue fever. The best prevention is to avoid mosquito bites – see Malaria, previous, for advice.

Cuts, Bites & Stings
See Less-Common Diseases for details on rabies, which is passed through animal bites and scratches.

Cuts & Scratches Wash well and treat any cut with an antiseptic. Where possible, avoid bandages and Band-Aids, which can keep wounds wet. Coral cuts are notoriously slow to heal, and if they are not adequately cleaned, small pieces of coral can become embedded in the wound.

Bedbugs & Lice Bedbugs live in various places, but particularly in dirty mattresses and bedding, evidenced by spots of blood on bedclothes or on the wall. Bedbugs leave itchy bites in neat rows. Calamine lotion or a sting-relief spray may help.

All lice cause itching and discomfort. They make themselves at home in your hair (head lice), your clothing (body lice) or in your pubic hair (crabs). You catch lice through direct contact with infected people or by sharing combs, clothing and the like. Powder or shampoo treatment will kill the lice, and infected clothing should then be washed in very hot, soapy water and left in the sun to dry.

Bites & Stings Bee and wasp stings are usually more painful than dangerous. However, in people who are allergic to them, severe breathing difficulties may occur, requiring urgent medical care. Calamine lotion or a sting-relief spray will give relief, and ice packs will reduce the pain and swelling. There are some spiders with dangerous bites, but antivenins are usually available. Scorpion stings are notoriously painful; scorpions often hide in shoes or clothing.

Jellyfish Avoid contact with these sea creatures, which have stinging tentacles and can be painful. Dousing in vinegar will deactivate any stingers that have not 'fired.' Calamine lotion, antihistamines and analgesics may reduce the reaction and relieve the pain.

Ticks You should always check all over your body if you have been walking through a potentially tick-infested area, as ticks can cause skin infections and other, more serious, diseases. If a tick is found attached, press down around the tick's head with tweezers, grab the head, and gently pull upward. Avoid pulling the rear of the body, as this may squeeze the tick's gut contents through the attached mouth parts into the skin, increasing the risk of infection and disease. Smearing chemicals on the tick will not make it let go and is not recommended.

Snakes To minimize your chances of being bitten, always wear boots, socks and long trousers when walking through undergrowth where snakes may be present. Don't put your hands into holes and crevices, and be careful when collecting firewood.

Snakebites do not cause instantaneous death, and antivenins are usually available. Immediately wrap the bitten limb tightly, as you would for a sprained ankle, and then attach a splint to immobilize it. Keep the victim still and seek medical help, bringing the dead snake, if possible, for identification. Don't attempt to catch the snake if there is a possibility of being bitten again. Tourniquets and sucking out the poison are now comprehensively discredited.

Women's Health
Gynaecological Problems Antibiotics, synthetic underwear, sweating and contraceptive pills can lead to fungal vaginal infections, especially when traveling in hot climates. Fungal infections are characterized

by a rash, itch and discharge and can be treated with a vinegar or lemon-juice douche, or with yogurt. Nystatin, miconazole or clotrimazole pessaries or vaginal cream are the usual treatment. Maintaining good personal hygiene and wearing loose-fitting clothes and cotton underwear may help prevent these infections.

Sexually transmitted infections are a major cause of vaginal problems. Symptoms include a pungent discharge, pain during intercourse and sometimes a burning sensation when urinating. Medical attention should be sought, and sexual partners must also be treated. For more information, see Sexually Transmitted Infections earlier.

Pregnancy It is not advisable to travel to some places while pregnant, as some vaccinations that are normally used to prevent serious diseases are not advisable during pregnancy (eg, yellow fever). In addition, some diseases are much more serious in pregnant women (and may increase the risk of problems with the pregnancy).

Most miscarriages occur during the first three months of pregnancy. Miscarriage is not uncommon and can occasionally lead to severe bleeding. The last three months of pregnancy should be spent within reasonable distance of good medical care. A baby born as prematurely as 24 weeks early stands a chance of survival, but only in a good, modern hospital. Pregnant women should avoid all unnecessary medication, although vaccinations and malarial prophylactics should still be taken where needed. Additional care should be taken to prevent illness, and particular attention should be paid to diet and nutrition. Alcohol and nicotine, for example, should be avoided.

Less-Common Diseases

The following diseases pose a small risk to travelers, and so are only mentioned in passing. Seek medical advice if you think you may have any of these diseases.

Chagas' Disease In remote rural areas of South America, this parasitic disease is transmitted by a bug that hides in crevices in the walls, in the thatched roofs of mud huts and on palm fronds. It bites at night, and a hard, violet-colored swelling appears in about a week. Chagas' disease can be treated in its early stages, but when untreated, infection can lead to death some years later.

Cholera This is the worst of the watery diarrheas, and medical help should be sought. Outbreaks of cholera are generally widely reported, so you can avoid such problem areas. Fluid replacement is the most vital treatment – the risk of dehydration is severe, as you may lose up to 20L a day. If there is a delay in getting to a hospital, then begin taking tetracycline. The adult dose is 250mg four times daily. Tetracycline is not recommended for children under the age of nine or for pregnant women. Tetracycline may help shorten the illness, but adequate fluids are required to save lives.

Leishmaniasis This is a group of parasitic diseases transmitted by sandflies. Cutaneous leishmaniasis affects the skin tissue, causing ulceration and disfigurement, and visceral leishmaniasis affects the internal organs. Seek medical advice, as laboratory testing is required for diagnosis and correct treatment. Avoiding sandfly bites is the best precaution. Bites are usually painless but itchy. Cover up and use protection.

Rabies This viral infection is fatal. Many animals can be infected (such as dogs, cats, bats and monkeys), and it is their saliva that is infectious. Any bite, scratch or even lick from an animal should be cleaned immediately and thoroughly. Scrub with soap and running water, and then apply alcohol or iodine solution. Medical help should be sought promptly to receive a course of injections to prevent the onset of symptoms and/or death.

Tetanus This disease is caused by a germ that lives in soil and in the faeces of horses and other animals. It enters the body via breaks in the skin. The first symptom may be discomfort in swallowing, or a stiffening of the jaw and neck; this is followed by painful convulsions of the jaw and whole body. The disease can be fatal. It can be prevented by vaccination.

Tuberculosis (TB) This is a bacterial infection usually transmitted from person to person by coughing, but it may also be transmitted through the consumption of unpasteurized milk. Milk that has been boiled is safe to drink, and the souring of milk to make yogurt or cheese also kills the bacilli. Travelers are usually not at great risk, as close household contact with the infected person is usually required before the disease is passed on. You may need to have a TB test before you travel, as this can help diagnose the disease later if you become ill.

Typhus This disease is spread by ticks, mites or lice. It begins with fever, chills, headache and muscle pains, followed a few days later by a body rash. There is often a large painful sore at the site of the bite, and nearby lymph nodes are swollen and painful. Typhus can be treated under medical supervision. Seek local advice in areas where ticks pose a danger, and always check your skin carefully for ticks after walking in a danger area, such as a tropical forest. An insect repellent can help, and people walking in tick-infested areas should consider having their boots and trousers impregnated with benzyl benzoate and dibutylphthalate.

Yellow Fever This viral disease is endemic in South America and is transmitted by mosquitoes. The initial symptoms are fever, headache, abdominal pain and vomiting. Seek medical care urgently and drink lots of fluids.

SOCIAL GRACES

Greetings are important to Ecuadorians, especially in the highland areas. Strangers conducting business will, at the very least, exchange a cordial 'Buenos días, cómo está?' before launching into whatever they are doing. Male friends and casual acquaintances meeting one another in the street shake hands at the beginning and end of even a short meeting. Women will kiss one another on the cheek in greeting and farewell. Men often kiss women decorously on the cheek as well, except in a business setting, where a handshake is deemed more appropriate. Close male friends hug one another in the traditional *abrazo*. Indians, on the other hand, rarely kiss; and their handshakes, when they're offered, are a light touch rather than a firm grip. In all situations, politeness is a valued habit. It is appropriate to mention here that punctuality is not one of the things Latin Americans are famous for.

Ecuadorians are used to less personal space than North Americans and Europeans. Conversations tend to take place face to face; streets and public transportation are very crowded, and homes have little individual space. Frequent kissing and hugging on a nonsexual basis, such as that described above, is an example of this. Noise seems to be part of the way of life. Radios and TVs in cheaper hotel rooms are turned on early in the morning and late at night without thought as to whether guests in neighboring rooms can hear; using earplugs is a solution.

Clothing is important to Ecuadorians, and even poor people will try to dress their best. The casually unkempt look (except among teenagers) is out; the well-pressed suit or attractive skirt and blouse are in. That is not to say that Ecuadorians don't like to dress informally – they do – but a neat and conservative turnout is preferred, especially in the highlands. Shorts are rarely worn in the highlands, except by athletes and gauche travelers. Wear long pants or a skirt.

Spitting is commonplace, particularly in the lower socio-economic classes; however, belching or burping in public is considered the absolute height of bad manners by everyone.

The concept of smoking being a health hazard is not very big in Ecuador. Nonsmoking areas are rare, and most restaurants allow diners to smoke wherever they please. The same applies to public transportation, including airplanes.

When calling someone over to you, don't crook your finger up and beckon, as people do in North America or Europe. This is rude. A better way to call someone over from a distance is to give a flat, downward swipe of the open hand. Body language using hands and facial expressions is hard to describe, but is an important part of interpersonal communications. Watch to see how Ecuadorians do things.

Begging is a fact of life in Ecuador. If you drive on the back roads in the highlands at certain times, you may see *campesinos* (peasants) lined up along the roads with their hands out in supplication. This is particularly true on Sundays and around Christmas. At those times, it's considered OK to give the people something, but please do so in a manner that shows some basic human respect. This author once saw a busload of tourists throw candy through the windows of the bus and onto the ground. They then filmed the ensuing scramble and roared off without any interaction with the people begging. It is difficult to say which were the more pathetic – the tourists or the beggars.

Begging children are becoming more common in the cities. Particularly sad is the sight of little girls, four or five years old, walking through the main streets of Quito, trying to sell roses to tourists at all hours of the night. These kids are often forced to work the streets until the early hours of the morning. While giving them money may help them on an immediate level, the long-term problem of homeless kids working the streets and not receiving an education is exacerbated. Donations to one of the many charities (such as Save the Children) that help homeless children all over the world is a good alternative – you can specify that you wish the money to be spent in Ecuador. In Quito, ask at the SAE clubhouse about donating time or money to worthwhile causes.

Photographing People

The Ecuadorian people make wonderful subjects for photos. From an Indian child to the handsomely uniformed presidential guard, the possibilities of 'people pictures' are endless. However, most people resent having a camera thrust in their faces, and people in markets will often proudly turn their backs on pushy photographers. Ask for permission with a smile or a joke, and if this is refused, don't become offended. Some people believe that bad luck can be brought upon them by the eye of the camera. Others are just fed up with seeing their pictures used in books, magazines and postcards; somebody is making money at their expense. Sometimes a 'tip' is asked. Be aware and sensitive of people's feelings – it is not worth upsetting someone to get a photograph.

It is worth bringing some photographs from home – of your family and the places where you live, work or go to school. They will be of interest to the Ecuadorian friends you make, and they're a great icebreaker if your Spanish is limited.

WOMEN TRAVELERS

Generally, women travelers will find Ecuador safe and pleasant to visit, despite the fact that machismo is very much alive and prac-

tised. Ecuadorian men generally consider gringas to be more liberated (and therefore easier sexual conquests) than their Ecuadorian counterparts. Local men often make flirtatious comments, whistle and hiss at single women – both Ecuadorian and foreign. Women traveling together are not exempt from this attention. Ecuadorian women usually deal with this by looking away and completely ignoring the man, which works reasonably well for gringas, too. Women who firmly ignore unwanted verbal advances are often treated with respect.

Women who speak Spanish find that it is easier to deal with traveling and with the persistent (and often well-meant) questions: 'Where are you from?' 'How old are you?' 'What do you study/do for work?' 'Are you married/do you have a boyfriend?' The pattern is always the same. Some single women claim to be married or have steady boyfriends. Some wear a wedding ring and carry a photo of their 'husband.' A useful phrase in Spanish is *No, me molestes!* ('Don't bother me!').

Many solo women travelers have made friends with Ecuadorian men and found them charming and friendly. However, unless you are attracted to a local man, you should avoid going somewhere with him alone, as that indicates that you are interested in sleeping with him, and you will be pressured to do so. Friendships are best developed in public group settings.

Occasional reports have been received of women being harassed by hotel owners or employees, especially in the cheaper hotels. Try to rent a room with a secure lock which can be closed from the inside.

GAY & LESBIAN TRAVELERS

Gay rights in a political or legal context don't even exist as an issue for most Ecuadorians. Gays were not legally considered equal until an antidiscrimination law was passed in late 1998 and there is still much antigay bias. As in most Latin countries, sexuality is more stereotyped than it is in Europe or North America, with the man playing a dominant macho role and the woman tagging along with that. This attitude spills over into the perception of homosexuality. A straight-acting macho man will seldom be considered gay, even if he is, while an effeminate man, regardless of his sexual orientation, will be called a *maricón,* a mildly derogatory term for a homosexual man. Relatively few gay men in Ecuador are exclusively homosexual; bisexuality is more common.

Ecuadorian gay and lesbian groups seldom promote themselves as such in order to avoid any organized backlash. Lesbians, often unwilling to associate themselves with larger, less politically compromised activist groups, are an almost ignored segment of the population. Same-sex couples traveling in Ecuador should be wary of showing affection in public. There is a small gay scene (see the organizations later in this section).

Several fiestas in Ecuador have parades with men cross-dressing as women. This is all meant in fun, rather than as an open acceptance of sexual alternatives, but it does provide the public at large (both gay and straight) a popular cultural situation in which to enjoy themselves in an accepting environment. On New Year's Eve, puppets representing the old year are burned at midnight. Meanwhile, men dressed as women (posing as the puppets' widows) walk the streets, asking passers-by for spare change that will later be used for the year-end party. More entertaining still, Latacunga's incredible Mama Negra festival, in late September, features cross-dressing men brandishing whips!

In Quito, you can see roaming bands of transvestites on the streets of the tourist district. Some of these are dangerous prostitutes; others are out for fun.

The best website about gay Quito is the incredibly detailed **w** http://gayquitoec.tripod.com/. There is a community center for lesbian, gay, bi-sexual and transsexual people, as well as an AIDS-activist organization called **FEDAEPS** (*☎ 02-222 3298; e admin@fedaeps.ecuanex.net.ec; Baquerizo Moreno 166 & Tamayo, Quito).* It's open to the public on Thursday at 3pm; gay and lesbian literature is available, and there are often discussions held at 6:30pm.

Zenith Travel (*☎ 02-252 9993; w www.galapagosgay.com; Juan Leon Mera 453 & Roca, Edificio Chiriboga No 202, Quito)* specializes in gay and lesbian tours.

DISABLED TRAVELERS

Unfortunately, Ecuador's infrastructure for disabled travelers is virtually nonexistent. Wheelchair ramps are few and far between,

and sidewalks are often badly potholed and cracked. Bathrooms and toilets are often too small for wheelchairs. Signs in Braille or telephones for the hearing impaired are practically unheard of.

Nevertheless, disabled Ecuadorians get around, mainly through the help of others. It's not particularly unusual to see disabled travelers being carried onto a bus, for example. Buses are (legally) supposed to carry disabled travelers for free. Local city buses, which are already overcrowded, won't do that, but long-distance city buses sometimes do. Disabled travelers are also eligible for 50% discounts on domestic airfares.

SENIOR TRAVELERS

Seniors may be able to arrange discounts for flying into Ecuador, but once there, options are limited. People over 65 are legally allowed to travel at half price on buses, but this is mainly for locals; foreign travelers can ask about it. Also ask about 50% discounts on domestic airfares; these should be available.

TRAVEL WITH CHILDREN

Children pay full fare on buses if they occupy a seat, but they often ride for free if they sit on a parent's knee. The fare for children under 12 is halved for domestic flights (and they get a seat), while infants under two cost 10% of the fare (but they don't get a seat). In hotels, the general rule is simply to bargain. The charge for children should never be as much as that for an adult, but whether they stay for half price or free is open to discussion. While 'kids' meals' (small portions at small prices) are not normally offered in restaurants, it is perfectly acceptable to order a meal to split between two children or an adult and a child. Foreigners traveling with children are still a curiosity in Ecuador (especially if they are gringos) and will meet with extra (generally friendly) attention and interest.

USEFUL ORGANIZATIONS

The South American Explorers (SAE) has clubhouses in Quito; Lima, Peru; Cuzco, Peru; and a head office in Ithaca, New York. The clubhouses function as information centers for travelers, adventurers, scientific expeditions etc, and provide a wealth of advice about traveling anywhere in Latin America. The **SAE Quito clubhouse** (*☎/fax 222 5228;*

e *quitoclub@saexplorers.org; Jorge Washington 311 & Leonidas Plaza)* is open 9:30am to 5pm Monday to Friday (until 8pm on Thursday), and 9am to noon on Saturday.

The SAE is an entirely member-supported, nonprofit organization. Annual membership is $50/80 per individual/couple and includes four quarterly issues of the informative and enjoyable *South American Explorer* magazine. (Memberships are tax deductible in the USA. Members from other countries must add $10 for postage.)

Members are entitled to use the Quito, Lima and Cuzco clubhouses, and this includes the use of an information service and library of books, maps and trip reports left by other travelers; storage of luggage (any size); storage of mail addressed to you at the club; a relaxing place to read and research, or just to have a cup of tea and a chat with the friendly staff and other members; current advice about travel conditions, currency regulations, weather conditions and so on; a book exchange; the buying and selling of used equipment; a noticeboard; discounts on books, maps and gear sold at the club; extra activities, such as the Thursday-night talks presented in Quito; and other services. One area of the clubhouse is dedicated to volunteer programmes within Ecuador. Services for nonmembers are limited – the staff are happy to answer a few quick questions about Ecuador and show you around the clubhouse, but they are volunteers and members' needs come first. Much of the clubhouse is designated for members only, although there is a room for visitors with a limited amount of free handouts and information about volunteer opportunities; you are encouraged to join. Paid-up members can stay all day.

Further information is available at **w** www .samexplo.org.

DANGERS & ANNOYANCES
Theft

Armed robbery is still rare in Ecuador, although parts of Quito and some coastal areas do have a reputation for being dangerous (specific information is given in the appropriate regional chapters of this book). Sneak theft is more common, and you should remember that crowded places are the haunts of pickpockets. This means poorly lit bus stations, crowded city streets or bustling markets.

Thieves look for easy targets. Tourists who carry a wallet or passport in a hip pocket are asking for trouble. Apart from your daily spending money, keep your money well hidden. Always use at least an inside pocket – or preferably, a body pouch, money belt or leg pouch – to protect your money and passport. Leaving money in hotel safe deposit boxes is usually reliable, but make sure that it is in a sealed, taped envelope – don't just turn over a money belt or wallet. A few readers have reported a loss of money from deposit boxes in the cheaper hotels. Separate your money into different places so that if you are robbed, you won't lose it all.

Thieves often work in pairs or groups. While one distracts you, another is robbing you. This can happen in a variety of ways: a bunch of kids fighting in front of you, an old lady 'accidentally' bumping into you, someone dropping something in your path or spilling something on your clothes, several people closing in around you on a crowded city bus – the possibilities go on and on. The only thing you can do is try, as much as possible, to avoid very tight crowds and stay alert, especially when something out of the ordinary happens.

Razor-blade artists slit open your luggage when you're not looking. This includes a pack on your back or luggage in the rack of a bus or train – or even your trouser pocket. Many travelers carry their day packs in front of them and others buy large grain sacks from hardware stores or markets and put their packs or luggage in them when they travel. This makes their bag look less obviously like a tourist's bag – many locals use grain sacks to transport their belongings. Also, the sacks will keep your luggage clean and more protected.

When walking with a large pack, move fast and avoid stopping – this makes it difficult for anyone intent on cutting the pack. If you have to stop (at a street crossing, for example), gently swing from side to side and stay alert. Taking a taxi from the bus station to a hotel is a safer alternative in some cities (this is mentioned in the text under the appropriate city). Never put your bag down unless you have your foot firmly on it.

One of the best solutions to avoid theft is to travel with a friend and watch out for one another.

Drugs

Definitely avoid any conversation with someone who offers you drugs. In fact, talking to any stranger on the street can hold risks. In some instances travelers who have talked to strangers have been stopped soon after by plainclothed 'police officers' accusing them of talking to a drug dealer. In this situation, never get into a vehicle with the 'police,' but insist on going to a bona fide police station on foot.

Scams

Be wary of false or crooked police who prey on tourists. Plainclothes 'policemen' may produce official-looking documents – always treat these with suspicion, or simply walk away with a smile and a shrug. On the other hand, a uniformed official who asks to see your passport in broad daylight in the middle of a busy street is probably just doing a job.

Don't accept food from strangers. Occasional reports surface of travelers eating adulterated cookies offered by some smooth-talking 'friends' on a bus and waking up two days later in an alley with everything robbed.

Robbery

Every year or so, you hear of a couple of long-distance, night-time bus robberies. Night buses are simply held up at a road block and robbed by a group of armed men. It happens to one bus in many thousands, so don't get too paranoid if your schedule demands a night bus.

If you are driving a car, never park it unattended. Never leave any valuables in sight in the car – even attended cars will have their windows smashed by hit-and-run merchants.

There has been a rash of robberies for climbers and hikers. Armed gangs have robbed tourists hiking up Quito's backyard volcano, Pichincha. Never leave your gear unattended in a mountain hut while you are hiking. Some huts, eg, on Cotopaxi or Chimborazo, have guardians and a place to lock up your gear when you climb, and these are relatively safe. Inquire at the South American Explorers clubhouse (see Useful Organizations earlier in this chapter) for more up-to-date information on these problems. Also, climb and hike in a sizable group in questionable areas.

Take out traveler's insurance if you're carrying valuable gear. But don't get too paranoid – Ecuador is not an extremely dangerous country; there are people who have made dozens of trips to Ecuador without ever being robbed.

If you are robbed, you should file a police report as soon as possible. This is a requirement for any insurance claim, although it is unlikely that the police will be able to recover the property. Normally, only the main police station in a town will deal with this.

Hotel Security

Theft from your hotel room is not frequent. Once in a while, you'll find that a budget room doesn't look very secure – perhaps there's a window that doesn't close, or the wall doesn't reach the ceiling and can be climbed over. It's worth finding another room. Some travelers carry their own padlock for the cheapest rooms.

Don't leave valuables lying around the room. It's just too tempting for a maid who earns only $2 a day for her work. Money and passports should be kept in a secure body pouch; valuables can usually be kept in the hotel strongbox. Keep your stuff in your locked luggage when you are out of the room.

Drowning

Much of the coast suffers from riptides, especially during the highest tides and biggest waves. In one weekend alone in February 2003, 11 people drowned along various parts of the coast. Some beaches use flags – red indicates dangerous conditions while yellow indicates that it's OK to swim. Many beaches don't have flags, so be aware of riptides.

EMERGENCIES

The telephone system is improving, but there is no nationwide emergency system. In major cities, dialing ☎ 101 or ☎ 911 will get you the police. Otherwise, follow instructions given in public phone booths or ask at your hotel or other operator.

LEGAL MATTERS

If you get into legal trouble and are jailed, your embassy can offer only limited assistance. This may include an occasional visit from an embassy staff member to make sure that your human rights haven't been violated, letting your family know where you are and putting you in contact with an Ecuadorian lawyer (whom you must pay yourself). Embassy officials will not bail you out, and you are subject to the laws of Ecuador, not to the laws of your home country.

Drug penalties in Ecuador for possession of even small amounts of illegal drugs are much stricter than in the USA or Europe. Defendants often spend many months in jail before they are brought to trial, and if convicted (as is usually the case), they can expect several years in jail.

Businesspeople should be aware that a legal dispute that may be of a civil nature in their home country may be handled as a criminal proceeding in Ecuador. This may mean that you are not allowed to leave Ecuador while your dispute is being settled, and that it could possibly lead to your arrest and jailing until the case is settled.

Drivers should carry their passport, as well as their driver's license. In the event of an accident, unless extremely minor, the vehicles should stay where they are until the police arrive and make a report. This is essential for all insurance claims. If the accident results in injury and you are unhurt, you should take the victim to obtain medical help, particularly in the case of a pedestrian accident. You are legally responsible for the pedestrian's injuries and will be jailed unless you pay, even if the accident was not your fault. Drive defensively.

BUSINESS HOURS

Banks are open 9am to 1:30pm Monday to Friday. Many stay open later, but money-changing facilities stop at around 1:30pm.

In Quito and Guayaquil, most stores, businesses, exchange houses and government offices are open from about 9am to 5:30pm Monday to Friday, with an hour off for lunch. In smaller towns, lunch breaks of two hours are not uncommon. On Saturday, many stores and some businesses are open 9am to noon. Stores in major shopping malls are open until about 8pm.

Restaurants tend to remain open late in the big cities, where 10pm is not an unusual time to eat an evening meal. In smaller towns, restaurants often close by 9pm; in villages, much earlier. Restaurants are often closed on Sunday, so the selection of eating places can be quite limited then.

PUBLIC HOLIDAYS & SPECIAL EVENTS

Many major festivals are oriented toward the Roman Catholic liturgical calendar. They are often celebrated with great pageantry, especially in highland Indian villages, where a Catholic feast day is often the excuse for a traditional Indian fiesta, which includes drinking, dancing, rituals and processions. Other holidays are of historical or political interest. On major holidays, banks, offices and other services are closed, and transportation is often very crowded, so book ahead if possible.

The major holidays may well be celebrated for several days around the actual date. Those marked by an asterisk (*) are official public holidays, when banks and businesses are closed; others are more local holidays. If an official public holiday falls on a weekend, offices may be closed on the nearest Friday or Monday. If an official holiday falls midweek, it may be moved to the nearest Friday or Monday to create a long weekend.

New Year's Day* January 1

Epiphany* January 6

National Community Spirit Day February 27

Carnaval* February, March or April – Held on the last few days before Lent, Carnaval is celebrated with water fights. Ambato has a fruit and flowers festival.

Easter* March or April – Palm Sunday, Holy Thursday, Good Friday, Holy Saturday and Easter Sunday are celebrated with religious processions. Holy Saturday is a public holiday, but many businesses close earlier in the week.

Labor Day* May 1 – This day is celebrated with workers' parades.

Battle of Pichincha* May 24 – This honors the decisive battle of independence from the Spanish in 1822.

Corpus Christi June – This religious feast day, falling on the ninth Thursday after Easter, combines with a traditional harvest fiesta in many highland towns and features processions and street dancing.

St John the Baptist June 24 – In the Otavalo area, this day is celebrated with a fiesta.

Sts Peter and Paul June 29 – In the Otavalo area and other northern highland towns, this day is celebrated with a fiesta.

Simón Bolívar's Birthday* July 24

Founding of Guayaquil July 25 – This major festival for the city of Guayaquil combines with the national holiday of July 24, and the city closes down and parties.

Quito Independence Day* August 10

Fiesta del Yamor September 1–15 – This is Otavalo's annual festival.

Guayaquil Independence Day* October 9 – This combines with the October 12 national holiday and is an important festival in Guayaquil.

Columbus Day* October 12 – This national holiday to celebrate the 'discovery' of America is also known as *Día de la Raza*.

All Saints' Day* November 1

All Souls' Day* November 2 – Celebrated by flower-laying ceremonies in cemeteries, it's especially colorful in rural areas, where entire Indian families show up at cemeteries to eat, drink and leave offerings in memory of the departed.

Cuenca Independence Day* November 3 – Combines with the national holidays of November 1 and 2 to give Cuenca its most important fiesta of the year.

Founding of Quito* December 6 – Celebrated in Quito throughout the first week of December with bullfights, parades and street dances.

Christmas Eve* December 24

Christmas Day* December 25

End-of-year celebrations December 28–31 – Parades and dances culminate in the burning of life-size effigies in the streets on New Year's Eve.

In addition to these major festivals, there are many smaller ones. Most towns and villages have their own special day, as well as a weekly market day (see Shopping later in this chapter).

ACTIVITIES

Where to begin? There are so many exciting activities to experience in Ecuador that any list of suggestions will certainly be inadequate. The following are the main outdoor activities that are possible. Also see the regional and city chapters for more information about specific activities.

Bird-Watching

Ecuador boasts some of the world's best bird-watching. The Galápagos Islands have 28 endemic species; a Guayaquil ornithologist claims that within 50km of that city, you can find over 50 Ecuadorian mainland endemic species. Serious bird-watchers with a good guide can certainly rack up their life lists in Ecuador.

Hiking & Mountaineering

Guided treks and climbs are available, and tents, sleeping bags and other gear can be rented in Quito and some other towns. Many hikes and climbs are briefly described in this book. In the Central Highlands chapter read about adventures in Parque Nacional Cotopaxi, on the Ilinizas mountains, around Chimborazo (Ecuador's highest mountain), around the Baños area and around Laguna Quilotoa. Hiking around Lagunas de Mojanda is described in the Northern Highlands chapter. The Cuenca & the Southern Highlands chapter takes you to hikes in the national parks of Las Cajas and Podocarpus, as well as the Vilcabamba area and trekking to the Inca site of Ingapirca.

Topographical maps are available from the **Instituto Geográfico Militar** *(IGM;* ☎ *254 5090, 222 9075/76)* in Quito. Trekkers will find four multinight trips described in detail in Lonely Planet's *Trekking in the Central Andes*. Climbers can refer to *Climbing & Hiking in Ecuador* (see Books earlier in this chapter). A useful website is **w** www.cotopaxi.com.

Ecuador's two highest peaks, those of Chimborazo (6310m) and Cotopaxi (5897m), make ideal destinations for travelers who want to get some real high-altitude experience. Both can be climbed in one long day from their respective climbers' refuges, usually leaving at midnight to avoid soft-snow conditions in the late afternoon. Climbers *must* acclimatize before attempting an ascent – several days in Quito or another highland town is a minimum. Cotopaxi is the most frequently climbed high peak in Ecuador.

Mountaineers will require standard snow and ice gear: a rope, crampons, ice axe, high-altitude sun protection and cold-weather clothing as a minimum. Unless you are very experienced, hiring a guide from Quito or Riobamba is recommended. Several agencies offer both rental gear and guides: very roughly expect to pay $150 per person to climb a major peak. If you are inexperienced, find a guide who will teach you how to use your equipment. This will cost extra.

The weather can turn bad quickly in the Andes, and even experienced climbers have been killed. Some 'guides' have climbed a mountain a couple of times and then offer their services for very low prices – these people are not listed in this book. Hire an experienced climbing guide and climb in safety. Good guides should have a card accrediting them to the Ecuadorian Mountain Guides Association (ASEGUIM).

You can climb year-round, but the best months are considered to be June to August and December to February.

Horse Riding

Unfortunately, the standards of care for horses used for tourist trails has been very low over the years, and several travelers have written in to say that the horses are old, overworked, underfed and have sores. There are, however, some agencies that do look after the animals, but they charge more for tours. Those travelers looking for the cheapest rates are going to get a hack and contribute to its misery. Go with a reputable company, even if it costs more.

An expensive but fully reputable company is **RideAndes** (☎ 09-738 221, ☎/fax 02-437 644, UK ☎/fax 1780-740 220; w www.ride andes.com). Day tours from Quito are $50 and seven-day tours featuring either a combination of hotels and camping or stays in rural haciendas and riding between them are offered for experienced riders. Costs start at $945. Custom-made tours for both experienced and inexperienced riders are available. Horses and guides are top notch.

Mountain Biking

Mountain biking is still a relatively new sport, although a couple of outfitters in Quito have been around for years and offer adequate bikes and knowledgeable guides – see Travel Agencies & Tour Operators in the Quito chapter. Most outfitters will prefer to send a guide with you, as riders of rental bikes are notorious for trashing the bike. The guides know all the best routes, and in the mountains, van support takes riders to the tops of spectacular long rides down the Andes.

River-Rafting & Kayaking

Both rafters and kayakers will find superb white water in Ecuador. Rafting is done year-round, and even beginners can enjoy the activity, as rafts are captained by seasoned and qualified experts. Kayakers tend to be more experienced, and often will bring their own state-of-the-art kayak with them to enjoy a few weeks of world-class kayaking.

The Río Blanco, 2½ hours west of Quito, is a year-round possibility as a day trip from the capital (for outfitters see the Quito chapter), with wildest conditions from February to about June.

On the eastern side of the Andes, Ríos Napo and Misahuallí, near Tena, are the best known, with the latter including an exciting portage round a waterfall (see The Oriente chapter). Multiday trips on the Río Upano, near Macas, are good from about September to February, with camping on the beach or in Indian villages (see The Oriente chapter). Río Pastaza and Río Patate, near Baños, have also been run commercially, but the Patate is very polluted (see the Central Highlands chapter). Other rivers are being discovered, although they are rarely run commercially for kayaking or rafting.

Many good companies raft rivers accompanied by a kayaker experienced in river rescue and travelers should always check a guide's credentials. The river-guide association is called Asociación de Guías de Aguas Rapidas del Ecuador (AGAR; Ecuadorian White-Water Guides Association). Only a few river guides have passed AGAR testing, and only reputable companies are listed in this book.

A good river-raft operator will have insurance and highly experienced guides with certified first-aid training. They will carry a well-stocked and up-to-date medical kit (especially on multiday trips), serve hygienically prepared food and provide top-notch equipment, including self-bailing rafts, US Coast Guard-approved life jackets, first-class helmets, dry bags in good condition, rain- and insect-proof tents, splash jackets or wetsuits for the colder rivers, and high-quality lightweight paddles and spares.

Surfing

Not yet a well-developed sport in Ecuador, surfing nevertheless has its aficionados. The best spot in Ecuador for meeting a few other surfers and swapping stories is Montañita; it's not unduly crowded.

Snorkeling

If you're going to the Galápagos, snorkeling will expose you to a completely new world. Baby sea lions may come up and stare at you through your mask, various species of rays come slowly undulating by, and penguins dart past you in a stream of bubbles. The hundreds of species of fish are spectacularly colorful, and you can watch the round, flapping shapes of sea turtles as they circle you.

You may be able to buy a mask and snorkel in sporting goods stores in Quito or Guayaquil, and they can sometimes be borrowed or rented in the Galápagos, but it's recommended that you bring a mask from home to ensure a good fit. The water temperature is around 22°C from January to April and about 18°C during the rest of the year, so you may want to bring a 'shorty' wetsuit with you, too.

Scuba Diving

This activity is becoming increasingly popular in the Galápagos, although diving conditions are difficult for beginners. Don't plan on flying for at least 12 hours after your last dive.

Diving in the islands provides excellent opportunities for seeing some really dramatic underwater wildlife – hammerhead and other sharks, a variety of rays (occasionally a manta ray will appear), turtles, penguins, sea lions, moray eels, huge numbers of fish of many kinds and, if you're very lucky, dolphins or even whales.

See The Galápagos Islands chapter for information on dive centers.

Diving is also offered out of Puerto López (see the North Coast & Lowlands chapter).

COURSES

Many travelers want to learn Spanish, and there is a plethora of schools to help them at any level. Courses are both one-on-one and group classes, and are usually several hours a day. Accommodations with local families can be arranged, and costs are among the cheapest in Latin America. Most schools are found in Quito, but there are also schools in Cuenca, Otavalo, Baños and other towns; these are listed under the specific towns in the regional chapters.

There is a dance school (see Dancing Lessons in the Quito chapter) that teaches salsa. Other cultural activities (eg, music and weaving) can also be learned, but not usually from a school. Ask around for artists who would like to tutor you.

WORK

Officially, you need a worker's visa to be allowed to work in Ecuador.

Teaching

Tourists can obtain jobs teaching English in language schools, usually in Quito. Schools advertise for teachers on the bulletin boards of hotels and restaurants. You are expected to be a native English speaker or the equivalent. Pay is just enough to live on.

If you have a bona-fide teaching credential, so much the better. Schools such as the American School in Quito will often hire teachers of mathematics, biology and other subjects, and may help you get a work visa if you want to stay on. They also pay much better than the language schools. Check ads in local hotels and newspapers.

If you want to look in advance, a useful website is w www.teachabroad.com/search .cfm, which lists both paying and voluntary positions.

Volunteer Work

Numerous organizations look for volunteers. Most want a minimum commitment of several weeks or months, and many charge a small amount to cover board and lodging (this may be as high as $10 a day, but it's often less). Volunteers can work in conservation programmes, help street kids, teach, build nature trails, construct websites, do medical or agricultural work – possibilities are varied.

The clubhouse of the **South American Explorers** (SAE; ☎/fax 222 5228; e quito club@saexplorers.org; Jorge Washington 311 & Leonidas Plaza) in Quito has a volunteer desk where current offerings are posted. Contact the clubhouse for a listing in advance. The clubhouse itself often needs volunteers.

It's also worth searching the Internet for voluntary work. An organization that can provide you with long lists of voluntary positions in Ecuador (and elsewhere) for a fee is **Working Abroad** (☎ 1273-711 406; w www .workingabroad.com; 59 Lansdowne Place, Hove, BN3 1FL, East Sussex, UK).

Finally, if you are already in Ecuador, ask around. Word-of-mouth contacts are often the best.

ACCOMMODATIONS

It is virtually unheard of to arrive in a town and not be able to find somewhere to sleep, but during major fiestas or on the night before market day, accommodations can be rather tight.

Reservations

The telephone numbers for many hotels are included in this book, but the cheaper ones may not accept phone reservations, or may not honor them if you arrive late in the day. It's best to call from the bus station to see if the hotel has a room available; if you then intend to stay, head over right away. Better hotels will tell you what time you have to arrive by; others may want a prepayment by means of a deposit to their bank account.

Also included where appropriate are the hotel's email address or website. These are convenient tools, but expect to pay for them. Rates secured by email are guaranteed, but walk-in rates off the streets can be much lower, as long as rooms are available.

Camping

Camping in tents is allowed on the grounds of a few rural hotels, in the countryside and in some national parks. There are no camping grounds in towns; the constant availability of cheap hotels makes them superfluous.

There are climbers' *refugios* (refuges) on some of the major mountains; you need to bring your own sleeping bag.

Hostels

The youth-hostel system in Ecuador is limited, and holders of youth-hostel cards often get a small 10% discount. The cheapest hostels start at around $5 per person in dorms, but they are clean and well run. Most hostels have more expensive private rooms as well. Cheaper hotels can, however, be found, and so hostels aren't necessarily a better deal. See Places to Stay under the individual towns in the regional and city chapters for details.

Budget

Budget hotels are the cheapest, but not necessarily the worst accommodation option. Although rooms are usually basic, with just a bed and four walls, they can nevertheless be well looked after, very clean and amazing value. These hotels are often good places to meet other travelers, both Ecuadorian and foreign. Prices in this category range from $2 to $15 per person. Every town has hotels in this price range, and in smaller towns, that's all there is. Although you'll usually have to use communal bathrooms in the cheapest hotels, you can sometimes find rooms with a private bathroom for as little as $5 per person.

Lodging Vocabulary

Hotels go by a variety of names. A *pensión* or a *hospedaje* is usually an inexpensive boarding house or place of lodging that's often family run. A *hostal* (as opposed to a youth hostel) can vary from inexpensive to moderately priced, depending on whether the owner thinks of the place as a cheap hostel or an upmarket inn.

A *hostería* tends to be a mid-priced, comfortable country inn. Cabañas are cabins found both on the coast and in the Oriente. They range from basic and cheap little boxes to pleasant, mid-priced bungalows. Hotel is a catch-all phrase for anything from a flea-ridden brothel to the most luxurious place in town.

A lodge tends to be in remote rural areas and usually provides complete service (meals, guides and transportation arrangements), as well as lodging, which is often rustic, but comfortable enough if kerosene lanterns and cold showers aren't a deterrent.

Couples sharing one bed (*cama matrimonial*) are sometimes charged less than two people in a room with two beds.

Sometimes it's difficult to find single rooms, and you may get a room with two or more beds. In most cases, however, you are only charged for one bed and won't have to share unless the hotel is full. Some of the cheapest hotels have 'dormitory-style' accommodations; don't leave your valuables unattended, and don't assume that every traveler is honest.

Never rent a room without looking at it first. In most hotels, even the cheapest, the person working there will be happy to let you see the room. Also ask to see the bathroom, and make sure that the water runs if you want a wash.

Mid-Range

Rooms in mid-range hotels usually cost from about $10 to $50 per person (depending on the city), but the cheapest are not always better than the best hotels in the budget price range. On the whole, however, you can find some very good bargains here. Many mid-range hotels advertise cable TV. This is usually Spanish language; only a few of the better places have international cable with CNN or similar English-language channels.

Look around the hotel if possible. The same prices are often charged for rooms of different quality. You may be amazed at the results.

Top End

First-class hotels are absent from many towns. In the major cities, hotels in this price category may be luxurious and may have a two-tiered pricing system. In Guayaquil and Quito, for example, a luxury hotel might charge a foreigner over $100 for a double, but an Ecuadorian might get the room for half the price or less. This system stinks, but is legal, and there's not much you can do about it other than avoid staying in luxury hotels. Apart from the expensive luxury hotels, included in this category are some nice hotels with rates that are still very cheap by Western standards – about $75 a double and up.

Homestays

Homestays are normally organized by Spanish schools to enable the traveler to practise Spanish in a home environment and eat meals with the family. However, remember that if you are staying at someone's house that you might not get to sample many of the local restaurants, and young women may find that the family they stay with are overly concerned about their going out alone at night.

FOOD

In Ecuador 'mains' refer to the cost of an average single main course, without appetizers, desserts or drinks.

For breakfast, the usual eggs and bread rolls or toast are available in restaurants. *Huevos fritos* are fried eggs, *revueltos* are scrambled, and *pasados* or *a la copa* are boiled or poached. These last two are usually runny, so ask to have them *bien cocidos* (well cooked) or *duros* (hard) if you don't like your eggs that way. *Tostadas* are toast and *panes* are bread rolls, which go well with *mantequilla y mermelada* (butter and jam). A good, local change from eggs is sweet-corn tamales, called *humitas,* which are often served for breakfast with coffee (mainly in the highlands). If you want inexpensive luxury, have breakfast at the fanciest hotel in town (assuming it has a restaurant or cafeteria). You can relax with coffee, rolls and the morning paper, or get a window seat and watch the world go by. Despite the elegant surroundings and the bow-tied waiter, you are only charged an extra few cents for your coffee. It makes a nice change, and the coffee is often very good.

Lunch is the biggest meal of the day for many Ecuadorians. If you walk into a cheap restaurant and ask for the *almuerzo,* or set lunch of the day, you'll get a decent meal for under $2. An almuerzo always consists of a *sopa* (soup) and a *segundo* (second dish), which is usually a *seco* (stew) with plenty of rice. Sometimes, the *segundo* is *pescado* (fish) or a kind of lentil or pea stew *(lenteja, arveja),* but there's nearly always rice. Many, but not all, restaurants will give you a salad (often cooked), juice and a *postre* (dessert) in addition to the two main courses.

The supper of the day is usually similar to lunch. Ask for the *merienda.* If you don't want the almuerzo or *merienda,* you can choose from the menu, but this is always more expensive. However, the set meals do tend to get repetitious, and most people like to try other dishes.

Local Food

The following is a list of local dishes worth trying at markets, street stands and restaurants. Only the adventurous should eat at markets, and then they should stick to food which is freshly cooked and thoroughly hot.

Caldos These soups are very popular and are often served in markets for breakfasts. Soups are known as *caldos*, *sopas* or *locros*. Chicken soup, or *caldo de gallina*, is the most popular. *Caldo de patas* is soup made by boiling cattle hooves; it's as bad as it sounds.

Cuy This is a whole-roasted guinea pig and is a traditional food dating back to Inca times. It tastes rather like a cross between rabbit and chicken. The sight of the little paws and teeth sticking out and eyes tightly closed is a little unnerving, but *cuy* is supposed to be a delicacy, and some people love it.

Lechón This is suckling pig; they are often roasted whole and are a common sight at Ecuadorian food markets. Pork is also called *chancho*.

Llapingachos These fried potato-and-cheese pancakes are often served with *fritada* – scraps of fried or roasted pork.

Locro This is a thick soup, usually made of potatoes and corn and with an avocado or cheese topping.

Seco This is meat stew and is usually served with rice. It can be *seco de gallina* (chicken stew), *de res* (beef), *de chivo* (goat) or *de cordero* (lamb). The word literally means 'dry' (as opposed to a 'wet' soup).

Tortillas de maíz Tasty fried corn pancakes.

Yaguarlocro Potato soup with chunks of barely congealed blood sausage floating in it. If you happen to like blood sausage, you'll find this soup very tasty.

A *churrasco* is a hearty plate that comes with a slice of fried beef, one or two fried eggs, vegetables (usually boiled beet slices, carrots and beans), fried potatoes, a slice of avocado and tomato and the inevitable rice. If you get *arroz con pollo*, you'll be served a mountain of rice with little bits of chicken mixed in. If you're fed up with rice, go to a *Pollo a la Brasa* restaurant, where you can get fried chicken, often with fried potatoes on the side. *Gallina* is chicken that has usually been boiled, as in soups, while *pollo* is more often spit-roasted or fried. *Pollo* tends to be underdone, but you can always send it back to have it cooked longer.

Parrilladas are steak houses or grills. These are recommended if you like meat and are a complete loss if you don't. Steaks, pork chops, chicken breasts, blood sausages, liver and tripe are all served on a grill, which is placed on the table. If you order a *parrillada* for two people, you might find there's enough for three (or you can get a plastic bag for the leftovers). If you don't

want the whole thing, choose just a chop or a steak. Although *parrilladas* aren't particularly cheap, they are reasonably priced and very good value.

Seafood in Ecuador is very good, even in the highlands, as it is brought in fresh from the coast and iced. The most common types of fish are *corvina*, a white sea bass, and *trucha*, which is trout. *Ceviche* is popular throughout Ecuador. This is a dish of uncooked seafood marinated in lemon and served with popcorn and sliced onions – it's delicious. Unfortunately, improperly prepared *ceviche* has recently been identified as a source of the cholera bacteria. However, most restaurants in Ecuador are aware of this and prepare the *ceviche* under sanitary conditions, so if the restaurant is popular and looks clean, the *ceviche* will most likely be both delicious and safe. *Ceviche* can be *de pescado* (fish), *de camarones* (shrimp) or *de concha* (shellfish).

Most Ecuadorian meals come with *arroz* (rice), and some travelers get fed up with it. Surprisingly, one of the best places to go for a change from rice is a Chinese restaurant. These are known as *chifas* and are generally

Food Safety

The worst culprits for making you sick are salads and unpeeled fruit. With fruit, stick to bananas, oranges, pineapples and other fruit that you can peel yourself. With unpeeled fruit or salads, wash them yourself in water that you can trust (see Health earlier in this chapter). As long as you take heed of the salad warning, you'll find plenty of good things to eat at reasonable prices. You certainly don't have to eat in a fancy restaurant; the kitchen facilities there may not be as clean as the white tablecloths. A good sign for any restaurant is if the locals eat there – restaurants aren't empty if the food is delicious and healthy.

Drinking tap water is not recommended. *Agua potable* means that the water comes from the tap, but it's not necessarily healthy. You can buy bottled water very cheaply in almost any grocery store. It comes in various-sized plastic bottles and is either *con gas* (carbonated) or *sin gas* (noncarbonated).

inexpensive and good value. Apart from rice, they serve *tallarines,* which are noodles mixed with your choice of pork, chicken, beef, or *legumbres* or *verduras* (which both mean vegetables). Portions tend to be filling.

Vegetarian

Vegetarians shouldn't have major problems in Ecuador. Some towns have vegetarian restaurants, and in other places, something can easily be found. *Chifas* are found in most towns and usually can do a noodle and vegetables dish or something similar. Note that telling the wait staff that you don't want meat doesn't always get the right message across – meat usually refers to red meat, so chicken-noodle soup might be suggested as a vegetarian choice! Pizza is also popular – it doesn't have to have meat on it – or you can go to a *cevichería* (seafood restaurant) if you don't consider seafood to be meat. If you are a vegan, you may need to exercise a little more imagination, but dedicated vegans have said that they have gotten by OK.

DRINKS
Nonalcoholic Drinks

Soft drinks are collectively known as *colas,* and the local brands are very sweet. Most international flavors are available, including diet soft drinks. Ask for your drink *helada* if you want it out of the refrigerator or *al clima* if you don't. Remember to say *sin hielo* (without ice) unless you really trust the water supply.

Jugos (juices) are available everywhere, and cost more than soft drinks. Most juices are either *puro* (with no water) or made with *agua purificada* (boiled or bottled water), although you may want to avoid juices from roadside stands or cheap restaurants, where the water quality is questionable. The most common kinds of juice are *mora* (blackberry), *naranja* (orange), *toronja* (grapefruit), *piña* (pineapple), *maracuya* (passion fruit), *sandía* (watermelon), *naranjilla* (a local fruit that tastes like a bitter orange) or papaya.

Coffee is available almost everywhere, but may be disappointing. Coffee beans may be roasted and finely ground, then compacted into a small perforated metal cup over which boiling water is slowly poured. The result is a thick syrup, which is then poured into cruets and diluted with hot milk or water. Sometimes it tastes OK, but

sometimes it's poor. It looks very much like soy sauce, so always check before pouring it into your milk (or over your rice)! Instant coffee is also served. 'Real' filtered coffee is becoming more available. Espresso is available only in the better restaurants. *Café con leche* is coffee with milk, and *café negro* is black coffee.

Tea, or *té,* is served black with lemon and sugar. Herb teas and hot chocolate are also popular.

Alcoholic Drinks

Finally, we come to those beverages that can loosely be labeled 'libations.' The selection of beers is limited, but they are quite palatable and inexpensive. Pilsner usually comes in large 650ml bottles, while Club comes in small 330ml bottles. Other beers are imported and available only in the more expensive restaurants or at some speciality liquor stores.

Local wines are truly terrible and should not be experimented with. Imported wines from Chile, Argentina or Peru are good, but cost much more than they do in their country of origin – nevertheless, they are the best deals for wine drinkers.

Spirits are expensive if imported and not very good if made locally, with some notable exceptions. Rum is cheap and good. The local firewater, *aguardiente,* or sugarcane alcohol, is an acquired taste but is also good. It's very cheap; you can get a half bottle of Cristal *aguardiente* for about $1. A popular fiesta drink that is made and sold on the streets is a *canelita,* or *canelazo* – a hot toddy made with hot water, *aguardiente,* lemon and *canela* (cinnamon).

ENTERTAINMENT

The most typical nightlife is a *peña* or Ecuadorian *música folklórica* club – bars and clubs playing traditional folk music; see Music in the Facts about Ecuador chapter for a description of floric music. This is a popular form of entertainment for all Ecuadorians, from cabinet ministers to campesinos. Concerts are informal affairs that are usually held late on a weekend night and are accompanied by plenty of drinking. They are not held everywhere – Quito and Otavalo often have good ones.

Apart from *peñas,* there are the usual nighttime activities in Quito and Guayaquil, but they are limited elsewhere. Cinemas are popular and cheap, but they are losing their audience to the world of video rental. There are theater productions and symphonies in the main cities. Discos and dance clubs are popular in the main cities, too. Some of these are great fun if you like dancing to Latin rhythms such as salsa or merengue. In many smaller towns, there isn't much to do. On the whole, Ecuador is not a major destination for those who seek entertainment of the nightlife variety.

SPECTATOR SPORTS

The national sport is *fútbol* (soccer), which is played in every city, town and village. Major-league games are played in Quito and Guayaquil on Saturday afternoons and Sunday mornings. People in Ecuador, as in all of Latin America, can be quite passionate about soccer, and going to a game is usually exciting. The entire nation celebrated when Ecuador was one of the 32 nations to qualify for the soccer World Cup in 2002 for the first time ever.

Volleyball is popular, but more as an amateur game played in parks and parking lots than as a professional sport. Golf and tennis are becoming ever more popular, and Ecuadorian tennis players are becoming increasingly known worldwide. Ecuadorian tennis player Andres Gómez gained fame in the 1980s and was followed by Nicolás Lapentti, who was ranked No 8 in the world by the ATP (Association of Tennis Professionals) during 1999 and is consistently in the world's top 50 players. Another notable sporting achievement was Jefferson Perez' gold medal in the 20km walk during the 1996 Atlanta Olympics.

Typically, Latin American activities such as bullfighting and cockfighting are popular here. The main bullfighting season is during the first week in December in Quito, when bullfighters from Mexico and Spain may take part. Other highland towns have occasional bullfights where the sport is popular. Bullfighting is less popular in the lowlands. Cockfighting is popular nationwide, and most towns of any size will have a *coliseo de gallos* (cockfighting arena). A variety of strange ball games are also played. One of these is a sort of paddleball called *pelota de guante,* where players hit a rubber ball with large, spiked paddles.

Main Market Days

Ambato – Monday
Latacunga – Saturday
Machachi – Sunday
Otavalo – Saturday
Pujilí – Sunday
Riobamba – Saturday
Sangolquí – Sunday
Saquisilí – Thursday

SHOPPING

Souvenirs are good, varied and cheap. Although going to village markets is fun, you won't necessarily save a great deal of money. Similar items for sale in the main cities are often not much more expensive, so if you're limited on time, you can shop in Quito or Guayaquil. If you only have the time or inclination to go on one big shopping expedition, you'll find that the Saturday market at Otavalo is one of the largest in South America, has a wide variety and is convenient, which makes it very popular. Many other markets are colorful events for locals rather than tourists.

In markets and smaller stores, bargaining is acceptable, indeed expected, but don't expect to reduce the price by more than about 20%, unless you are buying in quantity. In 'tourist stores' in Quito, prices are usually fixed. Some of the best stores are quite expensive; on the other hand, the quality of their products is often superior. Shopping in markets is more traditional and fun – but remember to watch your pockets.

Clothing

Woolen goods are popular and are often made of a pleasantly coarse homespun wool. Otavalo is good for sweaters, scarves, hats, gloves and vests. The price of a thick sweater will begin under $10, depending on size and quality; fashionable boutique sweaters can fetch $50. Wool is also spun into a much finer and tighter textile for making ponchos: Otavaleño Indian ponchos are among the best anywhere.

Hand-embroidered clothes are also attractive, but it's worth getting them from a reputable shop; otherwise they may shrink or run. Cotton blouses, shirts, skirts, dresses and shawls are available.

Ecuadorian T-shirts with designs featuring Galápagos animals are very popular; many other bold and distinctive motifs are available. If you're a T-shirt collector, you'll find all sizes and colors to choose from.

Panama hats are worth buying. A good panama is so finely made that reputedly it can be rolled up and passed through a man's ring, but it's unlikely that you'll find many of that quality. They are made from *toquilla,* a palm that grows abundantly near the coast. See the boxed text 'It's Not a Panama, It's a Montecristi!' in the North Coast & Lowlands chapter, and Shopping in Cuenca in the Cuenca & Southern Highlands chapter for more information about panama hats.

Weavings

A large variety of mainly woolen weavings range from square-foot pieces that can be sewn together to make throw cushions or shoulder bags, to weavings large enough to be used as floor rugs or wall hangings. Designs range from traditional to modern; MC Escher styles are popular.

Bags

Apart from bags made from two small weavings stitched together, you can buy *shigras,* or shoulder bags made from agave fibre, that are strong, colorful and eminently practical. They come in a variety of sizes and are expandable. Agave fibre is also used to make macramé bags.

Leather

A famous center for leatherwork is Cotacachi, north of Otavalo. Prices are cheap in comparison to those in more developed countries, but quality varies, so examine possible purchases carefully. Although the best leatherwork in Ecuador is supposedly done in the Ambato area, it's much easier to find leather goods for sale in Cotacachi. Leatherwork items range from full suits to coin purses and from wide-brimmed hats to luggage.

Products from Trees

The major woodworking center of Ecuador is San Antonio de Ibarra, and many items bought elsewhere are likely to have been carved there. Items range from the utilitarian (bowls, salad utensils, chess sets, candlesticks) to the decorative (crucifixes, statues, wall plaques). Again, the prices are low, but quality varies.

Balsa-wood models are popular. They are made in the Oriente and are sold in many of Quito's gift stores. Brightly painted birds are the most frequently seen, but other animals and boxes are also sold.

Tagua-nut carvings are common souvenirs. (See the boxed text 'Riches from the Rainforest' in the North Coast & Lowlands chapter.)

Jewelry

Ecuador isn't famous for its gemstones, but it does have good silverwork. Chordeleg, near Cuenca, has beautifully filigreed silver items. The Amazon area produces necklaces made from nuts and other rainforest products.

Bread Figures

Painted and varnished ornaments made of bread dough are unique to Ecuador and are best obtained in Calderón, a village just north of Quito. Some are designed as great Christmas tree ornaments and are cheap, imaginative and fun: Christmas stockings with a mouse peeking out, giant green cacti vaguely suggestive of a Christmas tree, animals, candles etc.

Other Items

Baskets made of straw, reeds or agave fibres are common everywhere. Onyx (a pale, translucent quartz with parallel layers of different colors) is carved into chess sets and other objects. Miniature blowpipes modeled after those used by Amazonian Indians are also popular, and you'll find plenty of other choices as well.

Getting There & Away

There are three ways of getting to Ecuador: by air from anywhere in the world, by land (from either Colombia or Peru) and by sea. However, very few people even consider the ocean route these days, as it is more expensive and less convenient than flying.

AIR
Tickets
The high season for air travel to and within Ecuador is mid-June through early September and December through mid-January. Lower fares may be offered at other times.

The ordinary tourist- or economy-class fare is not the most economical way to go. However, it is convenient because it enables you to fly on the next plane out, and is valid for 12 months, which isn't the case when you buy an advance purchase excursion (APEX) ticket.

It is essential to reconfirm your round-trip flights 72 hours in advance or you may well get bumped off the list. If you are going to be in the boonies, have a travel agency do this for you.

Airlines
Currently no Ecuadorian airlines provide long-distance international flights. Most international flights are provided by **American Airlines** (**W** *www.aa.com*), **Aero Continente** (**W** *www.aerocontinente.com*), Aerolíneas Argentinas, Avianca, Alitalia, **Continental** (**W** *www.continental.com*), Copa, Iberia, KLM, **LanChile** (**W** *www.lanchile.com*), Lufthansa, Lacsa and Varig.

Two major international airports serve Ecuador: Guayaquil and Quito. A flight between these two cities costs $58 if you buy the ticket in Ecuador, but about $100 when bought in other countries. See the Getting There & Away sections in the Quito and Guayaquil & the South Coast chapters for contact details of international airlines in those cities.

Departure Tax
A $25 departure tax for international flights is charged in Quito; $10 is charged in Guayaquil. These taxes are not included in ticket prices and must be paid at the airport. Taxes are payable in cash only – sorry, no

Warning

The information in this chapter is particularly vulnerable to change: Prices for international travel are volatile, routes are introduced and canceled, schedules change, special deals come and go, and rules and visa requirements are amended. Airlines and governments seem to take a perverse pleasure in making price structures and regulations as complicated as possible. You should check directly with the airline or a travel agency to make sure you understand how a fare (and the ticket you may buy) works. In addition, the travel industry is highly competitive and there are many lurks and perks.

The upshot of this is that you should get opinions, quotes and advice from as many airlines and travel agencies as possible before you part with your hard-earned cash. The details given in this chapter should be regarded as pointers and are not a substitute for your own careful, up-to-date research.

plastic. Short cross-border hops, such as Tulcán-Cali (Colombia), are not taxed.

Special Deals
Discount ticket agencies, also known as consolidators (in the USA) and bucket shops (in the UK), can often provide you with much cheaper fares than the APEX fare. See under The USA and The UK for agencies.

Students with an international student ID card and those under 26 can get discounts with most airlines. Students fares may also be eligible for a free stopover and are often valid for a year.

If you're flexible with dates and can manage with only carry-on luggage, you can fly to Ecuador as a courier. This is most practical from major US gateways. Some of the largest US-based courier operators are the **Air Courier Association** (☎ *800-282 1202;* **W** *www.aircourier.org*), **Air Courier International** (☎ *800-682 6593*) and the **International Association of Air Travel Couriers** (☎ *308-632 3273;* **W** *www.courier.org*).

Travelers with Special Needs
Most airlines can accommodate travelers with special needs, but only if these needs

Volcanic Activity

Since late 1999, Volcán Pichincha has been erupting on a regular basis. So far, these eruptions have been confined to huge clouds of gas, steam and ash shooting several kilometers into the air – major lava flows have not yet occurred. Pichincha is close to Quito, but because of the geographical lay of the land, it would be impossible for lava flows to reach the capital. However, occasional eruptions have covered Quito with a light sprinkling of volcanic ash, and this has forced the international airport to close several times for periods ranging from a few hours to a few days.

In addition, Volcán Reventador erupted several times in late 2002, again covering the capital with ash and closing the airport for days (see the boxed text 'El Reventador Lives Up to Its Name' in The Oriente chapter). Arriving international flights have been diverted to Guayaquil, from where passengers are either bussed to Quito, which takes about seven hours, or flown there the next day if conditions have improved. Domestic flights could be diverted to Latacunga, a 1½-hour drive from the capital.

are requested several days in advance. A variety of cuisine can be ordered in advance at no extra charge. Wheelchairs designed to fit in aircraft aisles, plus an employee to push the chair if necessary, are also available if you give notice. Passengers can check in their own wheelchairs as luggage. Visually impaired passengers can request to have an employee take them through the check-in procedure and all the way to their seats.

The USA

From the USA, you can get a direct flight nonstop to Quito or Guayaquil from the gateways of New York, Houston and Miami. American Airlines and Continental are the US carriers, and some Latin American airlines, especially LanChile and Aero Continente, will also stop in Ecuador en route to another destination. Flights from other cities or with any of the other airlines require an aircraft change in the US gateways listed above, or in another Latin American capital.

Consolidators (discount ticket agencies) advertise in the Sunday travel sections in many newspapers.

A good place for students to start is **STA Travel** (☎ 800-329 9537; e go@statravel.com; w www.statravel.com), which has offices in many towns. The 800 number automatically connects you to the nearest office, or you can surf their website.

Another excellent source for cheap tickets is **eXito Latin America Travel Specialists** (☎ 800-655 4053, fax 510-868 8306; e info@exitotravel.com; w www.exitotravel.com). It specializes in Latin America trips only and can do both short- and long-term tickets with multiple stopovers if desired, as well as tours.

Canada

From Canada, American Airlines and Continental have connections from Toronto and Montreal via New York or Miami and on to Guayaquil or Quito. Air Canada flies to US gateways and connects with other carriers. **Travel CUTS** (☎ 866-246 9762, 800-667 2887; w www.travelcuts.com) has about 60 offices nationwide and is a good choice for student, youth and budget airfares.

See The USA, previous, for other companies that can arrange discounted fares from Canada to Ecuador. Also check out the Sunday travel sections of major newspapers for advertising by consolidators offering cheap fares.

The UK

There are no direct flights from the UK to Ecuador. Discount ticket agencies generally provide the cheapest fares from the UK to South America. Fares from London are often cheaper than those from other European cities, even though your flight route may take you from London through a European city!

In London, competition is fierce. Discount flights are often advertised in the classifieds. **Journey Latin America** (JLA; ☎ 0208-747 3108, fax 0208-742 1312; e adventure@journeylatinamerica.co.uk; w www.journeylatinamerica.co.uk) receives consistently good reports. JLA specializes in cheap fares to South America, in addition to arranging itineraries (by phone or fax) for both independent and escorted travel; ask for the free magazine, *Papagaio*. **Flightbookers** (☎ 0870-010 7000; w www.flightbookers.net) recently had some of the cheapest flights from the

UK. Another good, recommended agency is **Trailfinders** (☎ 020-7983-3939; 194 Kensington High St, London W8 7RG).

Specializing in flights for students and people under 26 is **STA Travel** (☎ 020-7361 6099; w www.statravel.com), which has offices throughout the UK.

The cheapest fares from London may start at under £600 – an incredible deal considering the distance. Restrictions usually apply: flights may leave only on certain days, tickets may be valid for only 90 days and there may be penalties for changing your return date. A £10 departure tax is added.

Continental Europe

There are few direct flights from Europe to Ecuador; most involve a change of plane and airline in Miami or in a South American capital other than Quito. Iberia has a nonstop flight to Quito or Guayaquil from Madrid, and KLM has a flight from Amsterdam to Quito or Guayaquil via Curacao in the Caribbean (no change of planes is required).

Across Europe, many travel agencies have ties with **STA Travel** (w www.statravel .com), where cheap tickets can be purchased and STA-issued tickets can be altered (usually for a $25 fee). Visit the website for information on STA worldwide partners.

Many European (especially Scandinavian) budget travelers buy from London ticket agencies, as cheap fares are difficult to find in their own country. Although the discounted tickets sold by these ticket agencies are often several hundred dollars cheaper than official fares, they usually carry certain restrictions – but they are valid and legal; see The UK previous.

France has a network of student travel agencies that can supply discount tickets to travelers of all ages. **OTU Voyages** (w www .otu.fr) has 28 offices around the country.

Also in France, **Nouvelles Frontières** (☎ 08 03 33 33 33; w www.nouvelles-fron tieres.com) has additional offices throughout Europe.

Belgium, Switzerland, the Netherlands and Greece are also good places for buying discount air tickets, using STA and Nouvelles Frontières.

In the Netherlands, **NBBS Reizen** (☎ 0900-10 20 300; w www.nbbs.nl) is the official student travel agency. There's a branch in Amsterdam, and several other agencies around the city. There's several discount travel agencies along Rokin in Amsterdam.

In Athens, check the many travel agencies in the back streets between Syntagma and Omonia Squares.

Australia & New Zealand

There is no real choice of routes between Australia/New Zealand and South America, and there are certainly no bargain fares available. Using the airline combinations of Qantas, Air New Zealand and Aerolíneas Argentinas, you can fly from Sydney, Melbourne, Brisbane or Auckland to Buenos Aires, from where there are connections to Ecuador. Alternatively, fly with Qantas or Air New Zealand to Papeete, Tahiti, and then connect with a LanChile flight to Santiago, continuing north to Ecuador. Or you can combine your South American trip with a visit to the USA – there are daily flights to Los Angeles. Finally, a round-the-world (RTW) ticket may be an option worth considering if you have the time and inclination.

Students should check with **STA Travel** (Australia ☎ 1300 733 035, New Zealand ☎ 09-309 9723; w www.statravel.com.au), which has dozens of offices in Australia and New Zealand. Also try the **Flight Centre** (Australia ☎ 133 133, New Zealand ☎ 0800 24 35 44; w www.flightcentre.com.au); there are many branches in both countries.

Check the ads in the travel pages of newspapers such as *The Age* in Melbourne or the *Sydney Morning Herald*.

Latin America

Flights from Latin American countries are usually subject to high tax, and good deals are not that easy to come by.

Many Latin American airlines fly to Ecuador, including Aerolíneas Argentinas; Avensa and Servivensa (Venezuela); Avianca (Colombia); Copa (Panama); Cubana de Aviación (Cuba); TAME (Ecuador); Grupo Taca (Central America); LanChile; and Varig (Brazil). In addition, several US companies have flights between some Latin American cities and Lima, Peru.

LAND

If you live in the Americas, it is possible to travel overland by bus. However, if you want to start from North or Central America, the Carretera Panamericana stops in Panama and begins again in Colombia, leaving a 200km roadless section of jungle known as the Darien Gap. This takes about a week to cross on foot and by canoe in the dry season (January to mid-April), but is much heavier going in the wet season. This overland route has become increasingly dangerous because of banditry and drug-related problems, especially on the Colombian side. Most overland travelers fly over or take a boat round the Darien Gap.

Once in South America, it is relatively straightforward to travel by public bus from the neighboring Andean countries (Colombia and Peru), although this is a fairly slow option. See the Lonely Planet guidebooks to those countries for full details. There is no departure tax for leaving Ecuador overland.

Border Crossings

If you are entering or leaving Ecuador, border formalities are straightforward if your documents are in order. All tourists entering Ecuador need an international embarkation card, which is available free at the office. Exit tickets from Ecuador and sufficient funds ($20 per day for the length of your stay) are legally required, but are very rarely asked for. You will receive an identical stamp on both your embarkation card (keep it for when you leave) and in your passport allowing you up to a 90-day stay. Instead of 90 days, 30 or 60 days are sometimes given, but it is easy to obtain a renewal in Quito or Guayaquil.

When leaving Ecuador, present your passport and international embarkation card (the small document you filled out on arrival). You will receive a *salida* (exit) stamp in your passport, and the immigration authorities will keep your embarkation card. You must have an exit stamp to legally leave (and later re-enter) Ecuador. There are no costs involved. If you have lost your embarkation card, you should be able to get a free replacement at the border, assuming that the stamp in your passport has not expired. If your documents aren't in order, several things might happen. If you've merely overstayed the allowed time by a few days, you can pay a fine which is usually about $10 – this really is a fine, not a bribe. If you've overstayed by several months, you may have to pay a hefty fine or

you will be sent back to Quito. And if you don't have an *entrada* (entrance) stamp, you will also be sent back.

Travelers who are not tourists and are traveling on a visa may need to get an exit permit from the immigration authority in Quito before they leave the country. Depending on their status, some residents may have to pay an exit tax.

Peru

There are two border posts to cross into Ecuador from Peru and vice versa.

Huaquillas The main border is that of **Río Zarumilla** *(open 24 hr)*, which is crossed by an international bridge in the village of Huaquillas (called Aguas Verdes on the Peruvian side; see the Guayaquil & the South Coast chapter). Many travelers report that crossing at night is much easier – it allows you to avoid the crowds, touts and overzealous immigration officials (as opposed to the sleeping immigration officials who, in the middle of the night, simply want the stamping over with and you on your way).

The **Ecuadorian migraciones office** *(immigrations office; open 24 hr)* is inconveniently about 3km north of the bridge; all entrance and exit formalities are carried out here. The Peruvian immigration office is about 2km south of the border.

If you are leaving Peru and entering Ecuador, first obtain an exit stamp in your passport from the Peruvian authorities. After walking across the international bridge, you'll find yourself on the main road, which is crowded with market stalls and stretches out through Huaquillas. Take a taxi (about $1.50) or a Machala-bound bus to the Ecuadorian *migraciones* office.

If you are leaving Ecuador, stop at the Ecuadorian *migraciones* office, 3km before the border. If you're traveling by bus from Machala, the driver usually does not wait for you. You must save your ticket and board the next Machala–Huaquillas bus (they pass every 20 minutes or so) or continue on to the border by taxi.

As you cross the international bridge, you will be asked to show the exit stamp in your passport to the Ecuadorian bridge guard. On the Peruvian side (Aguas Verdes), you normally have to show your passport to the bridge guard, but full entrance formalities are carried out in the immigration building about 2km from the border. Taxis are available for about $0.50 per person.

Most European nationalities, North Americans, Australians and New Zealanders don't need a visa to enter Peru. They, and many other nationalities, too, normally just need a tourist card (also called an Andean Immigration Card), which is available at the Peruvian immigration office. If you do need a visa, you have to go back to the Peruvian consulate in Machala.

Although an exit ticket out of Peru is officially required, gringo travelers are rarely asked for this unless they look thoroughly disreputable. Other Latin American travelers are often asked for an exit ticket, however. If necessary, there is a bus office in Aguas Verdes that sells (nonrefundable) bus tickets out of Peru. The immigration official will tell you where it is.

From the immigration building in Peru, *colectivos* (shared taxis; about $1.50 per person) go to Tumbes – beware of overcharging. Tumbes has plenty of hotels, as well as transportation to take you further into Peru. See Lonely Planet's *Peru* for more information.

Macará About 3km from the border at Río Macará is the town of Macará (see the Cuenca & the Southern Highlands chapter). Ecuadorian immigration offices are by the market plaza, and you need to get your exit stamp here before heading to Peru (arriving travelers come here to get entry stamps). Pickup trucks leave the market plaza once or twice an hour and charge about $0.50 (or the Peruvian equivalent). You can take a taxi for $1. Vehicles wait at the border to pick up passengers from Peru.

Facilities for accommodations, transportation and food are inferior on the Peruvian side; it is best to stay in Macará, if possible. Peruvian buses and shared taxis leave the border for the Peruvian town of Sullana (two hours) on a paved road. Sullana has hotels and connections to nearby Piura, a major city. It is difficult to get transportation into Peru later in the afternoon and evening; crossing the border in the morning is therefore advisable.

Colombia The Panamericana, north of Tulcán (see the Northern Highlands chapter), is currently the only safe place to cross into Colombia. You don't need to obtain an exit or entry stamp in the town of Tulcán. All formalities are taken care of at the Ecuador-Colombia border crossing known as Rumichaca, which is 6km away. Fourteen-seat minibuses to the border leave as soon as they are full, between 6am and 7pm, from Tulcán's Parque Isidro Ayora. The fare is about $0.60 (Colombian currency or dollars).

Round-trip buses from the border will charge the same to the town center, but you can usually persuade the driver to charge you double and take you to the Tulcán bus terminal some 1.5km away if you are in a hurry to head south. Taxis between the bus terminal and the border are about $4.

The border is open 24 hours a day, every day. Entrance formalities into Ecuador are usually no problem, but be absolutely certain that your papers are in order. With the conflict in Colombia, drug and weapons searches on the Ecuadorian side have been stepped up.

On the Colombian side, entrance formalities are straightforward, as long as your passport and visa are in order. Check with a Colombian consulate to make sure your nationality doesn't require a visa. From the border, there is frequent transportation to Ipiales, the first town in Colombia, 2km away. There you'll find plenty of hotels and onward connections; see Lonely Planet's *Colombia* or *South America on a shoestring* for more information.

In the Oriente, the Colombian border is less than 20km north of Lago Agrio (see The Oriente chapter). However, the area is notorious for smugglers, and in early 2000, FARC (Revolutionary Armed Forces of Colombia) rebels crossed the border and kidnapped a group of tourists and local oil workers, who were then released over a period of weeks. Another FARC incursion later that year resulted in a deadly fire fight with Ecuadorian soldiers. The Colombian border area is dangerous, and you should avoid it unless local information indicates that relative safety has returned. If you must go this way, expect numerous passport and baggage checks by the Ecuadorian and Colombian military. Check with immigration authorities in Lago Agrio about where to get an exit stamp in your passport, as border-crossing posts may not be functioning.

The most frequently used route from Lago Agrio is to La Punta (about 1½ hours away), on Río San Miguel. Taxi-trucks leave Lago Agrio from the corner of Alfaro and Colombia and go to La Punta during the day. From La Punta you cross to Puerto Colón, on the Colombian side of the river, and then get a bus to Puerto Asís (about six hours by unpaved road), where there are places to stay and transportation by road, air and river to other parts of Colombia. There are other routes from Lago Agrio into Colombia, but they are rarely used.

SEA

Occasionally you can find a ship going to Guayaquil, Ecuador's main port, although this is a very unusual way to arrive in Ecuador. It's certainly cheaper and more convenient to fly, but the 'romance' of crossing the world the old way is still a draw to some.

Very few cruise ships use Guayaquil as a port of call as they head down the Pacific coast of South America. A few cargo lines will carry passengers.

The standard reference for passenger ships is the *OAG Cruise & Ferry Guide*, published by **Reed Travel Group** (☎ 0158-2600 111; *Church St, Dunstable, Beds LU5 4HB, UK*). A useful website is **w** www.travel-library.com/rtw/html/rtwfreighters.html.

It is possible to arrive in Ecuador on your own sailing boat or, if you don't happen to have one, as a crew member. Crew members don't necessarily have to be experienced because many long ocean passages involve standing watch and keeping your eyes open. You should be able to get along with people in close quarters for extended periods of time, as this is the most difficult aspect of the trip. If you get fed up with someone, there is nowhere else to go. Crew members are often (but not always) asked to contribute toward expenses, especially food. Still, this form of transportation is usually much cheaper than traveling overland. Check the noticeboards around marinas for vessels looking for additional crew members. In Ecuador, Salinas is the port most frequented by international yachts. For further information, read the *World Cruising Handbook* by Jimmy Cornell.

RIVER

Since 1998, when the long-awaited Peace Treaty was signed with Peru, it has been possible to travel down Río Napo from Ecuador to Peru, joining the Amazon near Iquitos. The border facilities are minimal, and the boats doing the journey are infrequent, but it is possible to do the trip – see the Coca and Nueva Rocafuerte sections in The Oriente chapter.

Neotropic Turis (☎ *252 1212, fax 255 4902;* **w** *www.neotropicturis.com; Pinto N4-340 & Amazonas Ave*) does river tours from Macas to the Río Marañón and to Iquitos in Peru (see Travel Agencies & Tour Operators in the Quito chapter).

It is also geographically possible to travel down Río Putumayo into Colombia and Peru, but this is a dangerous region because of drug smuggling and terrorism, and is not recommended.

Child in market, Saquisilí

Otavaleña woman, Otavalo

Boy and hens, Santo Domingo de los Colorados

Shopping, Saquisilí

JOHN MAIER JR

Barbecuing pig, Quito

JEFF GREENBERG

Food vendor, Saquisilí

RICHARD I'ANSON

Fruit and vegetable stall, Otavalo

ERIC L WHEATER

Selling grain, Saquisilí

Getting Around

Ecuador has a more efficient transportation system than most Andean countries. Also, because of its small size, you can usually get anywhere and everywhere quickly, easily and enjoyably. Bus is the most frequently used method of transportation; for example, you can take a bus from Tulcán, on the Colombian border, to Huaquillas, on the Peruvian border, and the journey takes only 18 hours. Airplanes and boats (especially in the Oriente and in the Galápagos) are also frequently used, but trains are limited to a couple of short tourist routes.

Whichever form of transportation you use, remember to have your passport with you – do not leave it in the hotel safe or packed in your luggage. To board many planes and boats, you need to show it. Buses may go through a transit police check upon entering any town, and although your passport is not frequently asked for, it's good to have it handy for those times when you are asked to show it. Passport controls are more frequent when traveling by bus in the Oriente. If it's in order, these procedures are cursory.

AIR
With the exception of flying to the Galápagos Islands, internal flights are comparatively cheap. There is a two-tier pricing system on flights to and from the Oriente and to the Galápagos, on which foreigners pay more than Ecuadorians.

Most flights originate or terminate in Quito or Guayaquil, so a useful way for the traveler to utilize these services is by taking a long overland journey from one of these cities and then returning quickly by air. Apart from the many flights a day between Quito and Guayaquil, and a few a day between Cuenca and Quito or Guayaquil, most destinations are served with only one flight per day or a few flights per week. Details of frequency and costs are given under the appropriate cities in the relevant chapters.

Ecuador's most important domestic airline is TAME, which flies to almost all destinations in the country. Other, smaller airlines include AeroGal, Aerolitoral, Aeropacifico, Austro Aeréo and Icaro. Some flights are in light aircraft carrying five to nine passengers. Chartered flights can be arranged.

Flights from Quito go to Baltra (Galápagos), Coca, Cuenca, Esmeraldas, Guayaquil, Lago Agrio, Loja, Macas, Machala (with a change in Guayaquil), Manta, Portoviejo, San Cristóbal (Galápagos) and Tulcán.

Flights from Guayaquil go to Baltra, Cuenca, Esmeraldas (via Quito), Lago Agrio (via Quito), Loja, Macas (via Quito), Machala, Quito, San Cristóbal and Tulcán (via Quito).

Flights departing in the morning are likely to be on time, but by the afternoon, things tend to slide half an hour behind schedule. You should show up about an hour early for domestic flights, as baggage handling and check-in procedures can be chaotic. Some major towns now offer advance check-in for travelers with carry-on luggage.

If you show up early for your flight between Quito and Guayaquil, you can often get on an earlier flight if there is room.

On most domestic flights you select your seat once aboard, on a first-come, first-served basis. Many flights give extraordinary views of the snowcapped Andes; it's worth getting a window seat even in bad weather, as the planes often rise above the clouds, allowing spectacular views of volcanoes riding on a sea of cloud.

If you can't get a ticket, go to the airport early and get on a waiting list – passengers often don't show up. If you do have a reservation, reconfirm flights both 72 and 24 hours in advance.

BUS
Long-Distance Buses
Hundreds of different bus companies exist, serving specific routes. Ecuador has a system of central bus terminals (often called *terminal terrestre*) in major cities, where all buses arrive and depart. Some towns still haven't completed their main bus terminals and may have several bus stations.

Watch your luggage carefully in bus terminals. See Dangers & Annoyances in the Facts for the Visitor chapter for more information on playing it safe.

On average, bus journeys cost about $1 per hour of travel. Exact schedules are not given; they change often and may not be adhered to. If a bus is full, it might leave early.

Conversely, an almost empty bus, especially in smaller towns, may spend half an hour giving *vueltas* (cruises of the major streets), with the driver's assistant yelling out of the door in the hope of attracting more passengers.

Various buses are used, roughly grouped into two types. *Busetas* (small buses) usually hold 22 passengers and are fast and efficient. Although standing passengers are not normally allowed, the seats can be rather cramped. Larger coaches, called *autobuses* or *buses grandes,* have more space but often allow standing passengers and they can get rather crowded. These coaches are generally slower than the *busetas,* because they drop off and pick up so many standing passengers. Increasing numbers of buses have installed video players, and so if the passing countryside is not enough to entertain you, you might be able to watch a film.

If you're traveling light, it's best to keep your luggage inside the bus with you. For a short trip, store excess luggage and travel with a small bag. Local people take fairly large pieces of luggage aboard, so you don't have to put yours on the outside luggage rack, even if the driver tells you to.

If your luggage has to go on top or in a luggage compartment, pack your gear in large plastic bags (garbage bags are good) in case of rain. The luggage compartment is sometimes filthy, so using a large protective sack is a good idea. Many locals use grain sacks as luggage; you can buy them for a few cents in general stores or markets. There are a few stories of theft from luggage inside luggage compartments, and even of whole pieces of luggage being stolen. This is not a frequent occurrence, but minimize the risk by securely locking checked luggage and keeping your eye on it as it is loaded into the luggage compartment. Check on it during stops.

Long-distance buses usually stop for a 20-minute meal break at the appropriate times. The food in terminal restaurants may be somewhat basic, so if you're a picky eater you should bring food with you.

On remote routes, full buses allow passengers to travel on the roof. This can be fun, with great views but minimal comfort!

Reservations If you go to the terminal the day before your bus trip, you can usually buy tickets in advance. This means you can choose your approximate time of departure, and often your seat number, too. If you're tall, especially if you're over 6ft (180cm), you can avoid being squished in the tiny back seat of a bus by reserving a seat. Try to avoid those rows over the wheels – usually the third row from the front and the third from the back in the *busetas,* and the fourth or fifth rows from the front and back in larger buses. Ask about the position of the wheels when buying your ticket. Also remember that the suspension at the back of a bus is usually far worse than anywhere else, so try to avoid the back rows altogether.

Some bus companies don't sell tickets in advance. This is usually when they have frequent departures (twice an hour or more). You just arrive and get on the next bus that's going your way. If the next bus out has only uncomfortable seats, you can miss it and be first on the one following.

If traveling during long-holiday weekends or special fiestas, you may find that buses are booked up for several days in advance, so book early if you can.

The larger terminals often have traveler information booths that can advise you about routes, fares and times.

Trucks In remote areas, trucks often double as buses. Sometimes these are flatbed trucks with a tin roof, open sides and uncomfortable wooden-plank seats. These curious-looking buses are called *rancheras* or *chivas,* and are seen on the coast and in the Oriente.

In the remote parts of the highlands, *camionetas* (ordinary trucks or pickups) are used to carry passengers; you just climb in the back. If the weather is OK, you get fabulous views and can feel the refreshing wind (dress warmly). If the weather is bad, you bunker down underneath a dark tarpaulin with the other passengers. It certainly isn't the height of luxury, but it may be the only way of getting to some remote rural areas, and if you're open minded about the minor discomforts, you may find that these rides are among the most interesting you have in Ecuador.

Payment for these rides is usually determined by the driver and is a standard fare depending on the distance. You can ask other passengers how much they are paying; usually you'll find that the trucks double as buses and charge almost as much.

Local Buses

Local buses are usually slow and crowded, but they are also very cheap. You can get around most towns for $0.10 to $0.20. Local buses often travel to nearby villages, and riding along is a good, inexpensive way to see the area.

When you want to get off a local bus, yell '¡Baja!,' which means 'Down!' (as in 'The passenger is getting down'). Telling the driver to stop will make him think you're trying to be a backseat driver, and you will be ignored. He's only interested if you're getting off the bus. Another way of getting him to stop is to yell '¡Esquina!,' which literally means 'corner.' He'll stop at the next one. Adding por favor (please) doesn't hurt and makes everyone think you speak excellent Spanish. If you don't actually speak Spanish and someone tries to converse with you after your display of linguistic brilliance, a smile and a sage nod should suffice until you get down from the bus.

TRAIN

Ecuador's rail system is now extremely limited and consists mainly of the dramatic descent from Alausí along El Nariz del Diablo (The Devil's Nose; see the boxed text in the Central Highlands chapter), a spectacular section of train track made famous by a British TV series about the world's greatest train journeys.

There is also a weekend excursion train between Quito and the Area de Recreación El Boliche, near Cotopaxi (see the Quito chapter). Passengers are allowed to ride on the roof of some carriages, and these are very popular trips.

CAR & MOTORCYCLE
Road Rules

Driving is on the right side of the road. Ecuador's system of road signs is very poor: A sign may point to your destination several kilometers before the turnoff, then when you reach the turnoff there may be no sign at all. Large potholes, narrow roads and drivers passing on curves, speeding or going too slow are all part of the adventure. Even so, a car does allow you the freedom to choose where you go if you can figure out how to get there!

Because of generally poor road conditions and dangerously fast local drivers, driving in Ecuador is not recommended – unless you are a confident and experienced driver.

Rental

Renting a car in Ecuador is more expensive than car rental in Europe or the USA. Cheap car rentals just aren't found. If the price seems reasonable, check to see what extras you may have to pay, as often there is a per-kilometer charge and you have to buy insurance. Some cars are not in good condition.

It is difficult to find car-rental agencies outside of Guayaquil, Quito and Cuenca. You need a credit card to rent, as a cash deposit is not accepted. Renters normally have to be 25 years old (a few companies may accept younger drivers). A valid driver's license from your home country is usually accepted if it has your photograph on it, otherwise an international driver's license is needed.

Typical rates start at around $40 per day for a subcompact car, but can go over $100 for a 4WD vehicle. It's worth shopping around for the best price, but if the price is low beware of getting a poor car. Budget, Ecuacar and Localiza have received mainly favorable reports.

Automobile insurance policies carry a hefty deductible – at least $1000, depending on the company. Some international rental agencies will make reservations for you from your home country.

To avoid confusion or misunderstanding, your written rental agreement should include prices, kilometraje (distance allowances), any applicable discounts, taxes or surcharges, and the place and time of vehicle return. Make sure any existing damage to the vehicle (scratches etc) are noted on the rental form. Rental cars are often rather old and beat-up, but reasonably well serviced. Make sure there is a spare tyre and a jack.

Rental cars are targets for thieves. Don't leave your car parked with bags or other valuables in sight. When leaving your car for any period, especially overnight, park it in a guarded lot.

Ecuador is an oil-producing country and it keeps down the price of gasoline (petrol) for domestic consumption. Depending on the grade, gas is approximately $1.12 per gallon.

Motorcycle rental is hard to find in Ecuador. Riders with their own machines will find an endless amount of information at w www.horizonsunlimited.com/.

TAXI

Ecuadorian taxis come in a variety of shapes and sizes, but they are all yellow. Most taxis have a lit sign on top reading 'taxi,' while those that don't have a 'taxi' sticker in the windshield. Taxis often belong to cooperatives; the name and telephone number of the cooperative is usually printed on the door.

Always ask the fare beforehand, or you'll be overcharged more often than not. Meters are rarely seen, except in Quito, where they are obligatory. Even if there is a meter, the driver may not want to use it. This can be to your advantage, because with the meter off the driver can avoid interminable downtown traffic jams by taking a longer route. A long ride in a large city (Quito or Guayaquil) shouldn't go over $3 and short hops cost well under $1. In smaller towns fares vary from about $0.50 to $2. Fares from international airports (Quito and Guayaquil) can be exorbitantly high – see those towns for tips on how to avoid getting burned. On weekends and at night, fares are always about 25% to 50% higher. Taxis can be hard to flag down during rush hours.

You can hire a taxi for half a day for about $15 if you bargain. You can also hire pickup trucks that act as taxis to take you to remote areas (such as a climbing hut or a refuge). If you hire a taxi to take you to another town, a rough rule of thumb is about $1 for every 10km. Remember to count the driver's return trip, even if you're not returning. Hiring a taxi for a few days is comparable to renting a car, except that you don't have to drive, and you have to pay for the driver's food and room. Some tour companies in Quito rent 4WD vehicles with experienced drivers.

BICYCLE

Each year a handful of cyclists attempt to ride from Alaska to Argentina, or any number of shorter long-distance rides, and manage to get through Ecuador OK. They report that coastal areas are flat and relatively boring, while cycling in the Andes is more fun and visually rewarding, although strenuous. Mountain bikes are recommended, as road bikes don't stand up to the poor road quality.

Renting bikes has only recently become an option in Ecuador, and is mainly for short tours (see Travel Agencies & Tour Operators in the Quito chapter for information on mountain-biking tours). Otherwise, rental is uncommon and the quality of bikes is poor. Bikes for sale tend to be of the one-speed variety, so dedicated bike riders are probably better off bringing their own. Most airlines will allow bikes to be checked at no extra cost if they're in boxes. However, boxes give baggage handlers little clue as to the contents, and the box is liable to be roughly handled, possibly damaging the bike. An alternative is wrapping your bike in heavy-duty plastic. The bike-carrying policies of the various airlines differ, so shop around.

Bike shops are scarce in Ecuador and their selection of parts is often inadequate. Bring important spare parts from home.

HITCHHIKING

Hitchhiking is never entirely safe in any country in the world, and we don't recommend it. Travelers who decide to hitchhike should understand that they are taking a small but potentially serious risk. People who do choose to hitchhike will be safer if they travel in pairs and let someone know where they are planning to go.

Hitching is not very practical in Ecuador for three reasons: There are few private cars, public transportation is relatively cheap and trucks are used as public transportation in remote areas, so trying to hitch a free ride on one is the same as trying to hitch a free ride on a bus. Many drivers of *any* vehicle will pick you up but will also expect payment. If the driver is stopping to drop off and pick up other passengers, ask them what the going rate is. If you are the only passenger, the driver may have picked you up just to talk with a foreigner, and he may wave aside your offer to pay. If you do decide to try hitching, make sure that you and the driver agree on the subject of payment in advance of your ride.

WALKING

Ecuador has several options for adventurous treks in the Andes, although the trails are not as well known as those in Peru. Some excellent hiking and climbing guidebooks have been published specifically for those travelers wanting to see Ecuador on foot.

Walking around cities is generally safe, even at night, if you stick to well-lit areas. Parts of Quito are unsafe at night and taxis are recommended for even short distances. Always be on the alert for pickpockets, though, and make inquiries before venturing into an area you don't know.

BOAT

Boat transportation is common in Ecuador and can be divided into four types. The most common is the motorized dugout canoe, which acts as a water taxi or bus along the major rivers of the Oriente and parts of the coast. In the Galápagos, there are medium-sized motor cruisers and sailboats that are used by small groups to move between the islands of the archipelago. Third, there are large vessels, which are used either for carrying cargo and a few passengers, or as cruise ships for many passengers.

Finally, many rivers are crossed by ferries that vary from a paddled dugout taking one passenger at a time, to a car ferry capable of moving half a dozen vehicles. These are sometimes makeshift transportation to replace a bridge that has been washed out, is being repaired or is still in the planning stages.

Dugout Canoes

Motorized dugout canoes often carry as many as three dozen passengers and are the only way to get around many roadless areas. If you hire one as a personal taxi, it is expensive. However, taking a regularly scheduled ride with other passengers is quite affordable, although not as cheap as a bus for a similar distance. An outboard engine uses more fuel per kilometer than a bus engine, and dugouts travel more slowly than a bus.

The only places in which you are likely to travel any distance in dugouts are on jungle tours in the Oriente and on a few parts of the northwest coast.

Most of these boats are literally dugouts, with a splashboard sometimes added to the gunwales. These are long in shape and short on comfort. Seating is normally on hard, low, uncomfortable wooden benches which accommodate two people each. Luggage is stashed forward under a tarpaulin, so carry hand baggage containing essentials for the journey. You will be miserable for hours if you don't take the following advice, which alone is worth the cost of this book: *Bring seat padding*. A folded sweater or towel will make a world of difference on the trip.

On the smaller boats, the front seats give better forward views but are the narrowest;

the middle seats are wider and more comfortable; and the back seats are closest to the noise and fumes of the engine.

Pelting rain and glaring sun are major hazards, and an umbrella is excellent defense against both. Bring suntan lotion or wear long sleeves, long pants and a sun hat – people have been literally unable to walk because of second-degree burns on their legs after six hours of exposure to the tropical sun. The breeze as the boat motors along tends to keep insects away and cool you, so that you are not likely to notice the burning effect of the sun. If the sun should disappear or the rain begin, you can become quite chilly, so bring a light jacket.

Insect repellent is useful during stops along the river. Bottled water and something to snack on will complete your hand baggage. Don't forget to stash your spare clothes in plastic bags, or they'll get soaked by rain or spray.

A final word about dugout canoes: They feel very unstable! Until you get used to the rocking motion, you might worry about the whole thing just rolling over and tipping everybody into the shark-, piranha- or boa constrictor–infested waters. Desperately gripping the side of the canoe and wondering what madness possessed you to board in the first place doesn't seem to help. Dugouts are much more stable than they feel, so don't worry about a dunking.

Yachts

The idea of sailing your own yacht to the Galápagos sounds romantic. Unfortunately, to sail around the Galápagos you need a license, and licenses are all limited to Galápagos boats. If you arrive at the islands in your own boat, you will have to moor the boat in Puerto Ayora and hire one of the local boats to take you around. The Ecuadorian authorities give transit permits of seven days for sailors on their own boats. Longer stays may be possible if you are moored and not sailing.

Other Boats

In the Galápagos, you have a choice of traveling in anything from a small sailboat to a cruise ship complete with air-conditioned cabins and private bathrooms. More information on these boats is given in The Galápagos Islands chapter.

In addition to the dugout canoes of the Oriente, one cruise ship, *Amazon Manatee Explorer*, makes relatively luxurious passages down Río Napo; see **Nuevo Mundo Expeditions** (w *www.nuevomundotravel.com*) under Travel Agencies & Tour Operators in the Quito chapter.

A few boats travel between the Galápagos and Guayaquil, but it's easier to fly there and sail between the islands once you arrive. Again, there is more information under the appropriate coastal towns.

ORGANIZED TOURS

Many kinds of tours can be arranged within Ecuador and are described in the main body of this book under the appropriate cities, especially in Quito where the majority of travel agencies and tour operators are found.

Most of the travel agencies in Quito will sell you both domestic and international airline tickets (adding the obligatory 12% tax), make hotel reservations and arrange guided trips to hike in the mountains, climb volcanoes, explore the jungle or visit the Galápagos. But be warned: most guide services are not cheap. It is usually better to deal directly with the operator supplying the services you want.

Note that it is often cheapest (although not easiest) to book a tour close to where you will be touring. Therefore, some travelers try to arrange a tour in the Galápagos or in the Oriente upon arrival in these destinations. This works, but there are several problems. During the Galápagos' high seasons, many boats are full and it may be difficult to find one available. During the low seasons (and at any time in the Oriente), it may take several days to get a group of people together who are interested in doing the same thing. This is OK if you have a week or two to kill, but if you want to be sure of leaving on a trip soon after you arrive, you should book in advance.

If you're a budget traveler who's not limited by time and you want to take a trip to the Oriente, a good tactic is to gather a group of budget travelers by advertising in your hotel or at the **South American Explorers** (SAE; ☎ 222 5228; e *quitoclub@saexplorers.org*; w *www.samexplo.org*; Jorge Washington 311 & Leonidas Plaza Gutiérrez) clubhouse in Quito. Then go to the Oriente together, as a group, to find a guide. If you are on a short trip, by all means book a tour in Quito. Good guides and tours are available, and you can leave quickly, although you'll pay a bit more for this convenience.

Tour costs vary tremendously depending on what your requirements are. The cheapest camping jungle tour can be as low as $20 per person, per day, while the most expensive lodges can be $200 per person, per night, including all meals and tours. Climbs of the volcanoes are usually about $150 per person for a two-day climb. Galápagos boat cruises range from $1000 to almost $3000 per week, including air fare, taxes and entrance fees. Day tours out of Quito range from $25 to $80 per person per day.

See The Galápagos Islands and The Oriente chapters for more general information on tours in those areas. A useful website for Galápagos travel is w *www.igtoa.org*.

Quito

☎ 02 • pop 1,400,000 • elevation 2850m

When it comes to setting, Quito has it made. Tucked amid a high Andean valley, Quito is flanked by majestic mountains, and on a clear day, several snowcapped volcanoes are visible in the distance. Despite the fact that it's only 22km south of the equator, Quito's elevation gives it a wonderful springlike climate year-round.

Quito's colonial center, declared a World Cultural Heritage site by Unesco, is equally splendid. Strictly controlled development has kept it wonderfully preserved, and its bustling street life is an exciting contradiction of tradition and chaotic modernity jammed together in one of South America's most spectacular colonial centers. To walk down colonial Quito's streets on Sunday, when traffic is reduced, is to step into a bygone era.

Only a 20-minute walk from the old town, Quito's 'new town' (as its modern area is called) is a different world entirely, a mixture of multistory hotels, mirrored commercial high-rises and drab government complexes. For travelers, its heart is the colorful Mariscal (Field Marshal) Sucre, which has block after block of trendy cafés, international restaurants, travel agencies, sophisticated cybercafés, raucous bars and imaginative, small hotels. The area definitely lives up to its nickname *gringolandia* (gringo land), but *quiteños* (people from Quito) dig it too, so it keeps its Ecuadorian flair.

However, the country's fledgling economy has given Quito its problems: increased poverty and immigration into the city have put crime on the rise, giving the city an edge of uncertainty, especially at night. Armed rent-a-cops with beefy dogs guard business entrances throughout the Mariscal Sucre, and people walk quickly or take cabs to bars. But once they're inside, wham! The party takes over, the dance floor gets sweaty and the world outside disappears.

HISTORY

The site of the capital dates from pre-Columbian times. Early inhabitants of the area were the peaceful Quitu people, who gave their name to the city. The Quitus integrated with the coastal Caras, giving rise to the Indian group known as the Shyris.

Highlights

- Wandering the colonial streets of the old town – the Plaza and Monastery of San Francisco shouldn't be missed

- Shakin' your groove-thing all night long in the Mariscal's crowded, sweaty nightclubs

- Dining on fabulous national and international cuisine in one of the city's countless restaurants

- Taking salsa dancing lessons and practicing your new moves at the *salsotecas* (salsa nightclubs)

- Being a total tourist and straddling the hemispheres at La Mitad del Mundo monument on the equator

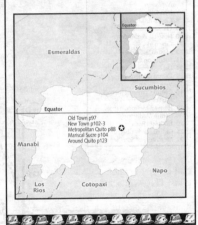

Old Town p97
New Town p102-3
Metropolitan Quito p88 ✪
Mariscal Sucre p104
Around Quito p123

Around AD 1300, the Shyris joined with the Puruhás through marriage, and their descendants fought against the Incas in the late 15th century.

By the time the Spanish arrived in Ecuador in 1526, Quito was a major Inca city. Rather than allowing it to fall into the hands of the Spanish conquerors, Rumiñahui, a general of Atahualpa, razed the city shortly before their arrival. There are no Inca remains. The present capital was founded atop the ruins by Spanish lieutenant Sebastián de Benalcázar on December 6, 1534. Many colonial-era buildings survive in the old town.

METROPOLITAN QUITO

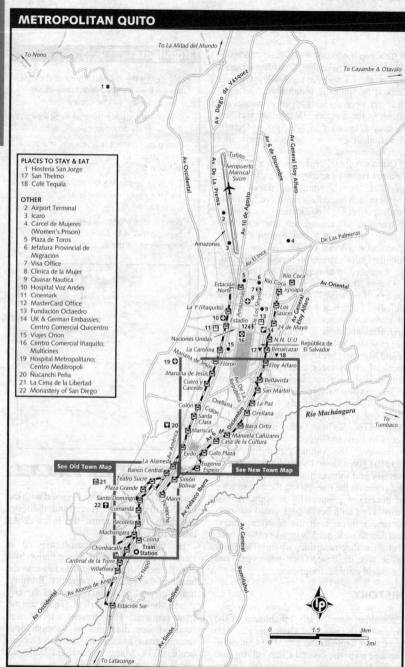

To Nono

To La Mitad del Mundo

To Cayambe & Otavalo

Av Occidental

Av Diego de Vásquez

Av De La Prensa

Av 10 de Agosto

Av 6 de Diciembre

Av General Eloy Alfaro

Tufiño

Aeropuerto
Mariscal
Sucre

Amazonas

De Las Palmeras

Av El Inca

PLACES TO STAY & EAT
1 Hostería San Jorge
17 San Thelmo
18 Café Tequila

OTHER
2 Airport Terminal
3 Icaro
4 Carcel de Mujeres
   (Women's Prison)
5 Plaza de Toros
6 Jefatura Provincial de
   Migración
7 Visa Office
8 Clínica de la Mujer
9 Quasar Nautica
10 Hospital Voz Andes
11 Cinemark
12 MasterCard Office
13 Fundación Octaedro
14 UK & German Embassies;
   Centro Comercial Quicentro
15 Viajes Orion
16 Centro Comercial Iñaquito;
   Multicines
19 Hospital Metropolitano;
   Centro Meditropoli
20 Ñucanchi Peña
21 La Cima de la Libertad
22 Monastery of San Diego

Río Coca

Río Coca

Jipijapa

Av Oriental

Av General Eloy Alfaro

Estación
Norte

La Y (Iñaquito)

Estadio

Los
Sauces

24 de Mayo

Av Amazonas

De Los Shyris

Naciones Unidas

N.N. U.U

República de
El Salvador

Benalcazar

La Carolina

Mariana de Jesús

Floron

Eloy Alfaro

Mariana de Jesús

Bellavista

Cuero y
Caicedo

San Martín

Colón

Colón

Orellana

La Paz

Av De La República

Santa
Clara

Orellana

Río Machángara

To
Tumbaco

Mariscal

Baca Ortiz

Av 6 de Diciembre

Manuela Cañizares

Av América

Casa de la Cultura

Ejido

Galo Plaza

La Alameda

Eugenio
Espejo

See Old Town Map

See New Town Map

Banco Central

Teatro Sucre

Simón
Bolívar

Plaza Grande

Santo Domingo

Marín

Cumandá

Pichincha

Recoleta

Machángara

Colina

Chimbacalle

Train
Station

Cardinal de la Torre

Villaflora

Av Velasco Ibarra

Av General

Rumiñahui

Av Napo

Bolívar

Av Occidental

Av Alonso de Angulo

Estación Sur

Av Simón

To Latacunga

0   1.5   3km
0   1   2mi

ORIENTATION

Quito's population of over 1,400,000 makes it the second-largest city in Ecuador (Guayaquil is the largest). It lies along the central valley in a roughly north–south direction and is approximately 17km long and 4km wide. It can conveniently be divided into three segments.

The center (El Centro) is the site of the old town, with its whitewashed, red-tiled houses and colonial churches. This is the area of greatest historical interest to travelers, but it is also a poor area with few good hotels (although travelers can stay here comfortably).

The north is modern Quito, the new town, with its major businesses, airline offices, embassies, shopping centers and banks. Most hotels and restaurants are found here, especially in the Mariscal Sucre neighborhood, where most travelers eat, sleep and drink. The northern end of the city contains the airport and the middle- and upper-class residential areas. Amazonas is the best-known street, although Avenida 10 de Agosto and Avenida 6 de Diciembre are the most important thoroughfares.

The south of Quito consists mainly of working-class residential areas.

Maps

Excellent topographical maps ($2 each) and various tourist highlight maps are available from the Instituto Geográfico Militar (IGM; ☎ 254 5090, 222 9075/76; map sales room open 8am-1pm & 1:30pm-4:30pm Mon-Thur, 7am-3pm Fri) located on top of a hill, southeast of Parque El Ejido, in the new town. There are no buses, so you have to walk or take a taxi. You need to leave your passport at the gate. Aside from the giant map of Quito for sale, city maps are limited.

The most useful maps of Quito are the blue-covered ones by Nelson Gómez, available at most bookstores. The Empresa del Centro Histórico (see Tourist Offices following) publishes free walking maps with detailed information on the sights of Quito's old town.

INFORMATION
Tourist Offices

The helpful Cámara Provincial de Turismo de Pichincha (Captur; w www.captur.com) provides tourist information about Quito and Pichincha Province at its Mariscal information office (☎ 255 1566; Reina Victoria & Cordero; open 9am-5pm Mon-Fri) and old town information office (☎ 295 4044; Venezuela & Chile; open 9am-5pm Mon-Sat). Both are staffed by friendly, helpful folks. The Captur administration office (☎ 222 4074; Avenida 6 de Diciembre N22-02 & Jeronim Carrión; open 8am-6pm Mon-Fri) stocks some maps, but offers little tourist information.

The Empresa del Centro Histórico (ECH; ☎/fax 258 3827; Venezuela 976 & Mejía; open 8:30am-5pm Mon-Fri) is the company responsible for the restoration and promotion of Quito's historical center. Its tourist information office (Palacio Arzobispal, Local 3), on the Plaza de la Independencia, is staffed with friendly cop-cum-tourist guides who have lots of information and advice to offer. They also organize various two- to three-hour guided 'cultural walks' of the old town for $10 per person.

South American Explorers

The South American Explorers clubhouse (SAE; ☎ 222 5228; w www.samexplo.org; Jorge Washington 311 & Leonidas Plaza Gutiérrez; open 9:30am-5pm Mon-Fri, 9:30am-8pm Thur, 9am-noon Sat) is in the new town, one block south of Avenida 6 de Diciembre. The mailing address is: Apartado 17-21-431, Quito. See Useful Organizations in the Facts for the Visitor chapter for more details on the organization.

Addresses in Quito

Quito's addresses are given by placing the building number after the street name, eg, Jorge Washington 311. At time of writing, Quito was changing to a new address system based on N, S, W and E quadrants, so an address might be Amazonas N22-62. Some buildings have the old address, some have both and some have just the new address, which can be confusing to the traveler. Both are used in this chapter, depending on the information received from each place.

Taxi drivers know locations more by cross streets than the numbered street address. If you provide your driver with both, you should have no problem arriving at your destination.

QUITO

Money

There are several banks in the new town along Amazonas between Avenida Patria and Orellana, and there are dozens more throughout town. Banks can receive money wired from your bank at home and pay you in US dollars. Many banks also have 24-hour ATMs. The following banks have ATMs and change traveler's checks:

Banco de Guayaquil (☎ 256 4324) Amazonas N22-147 at General Veintimilla in the new town. Open 9am to 4pm Monday to Friday. There's also a branch at Avenida Cristóbal Colón and Reina Victoria.

Banco del Pacífico (☎ 250 1218) 12 de Octubre & Cordero in the new town; (☎ 228 8138) cnr Guayaquil & Chile in the old town. Both open 8:30am to 4pm Monday to Friday.

Banco del Pichincha (☎ 258 4149) Guayaquil at Manabí in the old town. Open 8am to 3:30pm Monday to Friday. Go to window No 1 or 2.

You can also change traveler's checks at *casas de cambio* (currency-exchange bureaus) on Amazonas and a few other parts of town. They are usually open until 6pm Monday to Friday and on Saturday mornings.

When you need a *casa de cambio* on the weekend the Multicambios office at the airport is open for all flight arrivals in the international arrival area. If you aren't an arriving passenger, try **Producambios** (*open 6am-9pm daily*) in the domestic lounge. In the new town, try **Producambios** (☎ 256 3900; *Amazonas 350; open 8:30am-6pm Mon-Fri, 9am-2pm Sat*) or the **casa de cambio** (*Centro Comercial El Jardín, Amazonas & Avenida de la República; open 10am-6pm daily*).

Credit cards are widely accepted in 1st-class restaurants, hotels, travel agencies and stores. Watch the exchange rate. Some places charge a 4% to 10% commission to cover their banking costs; ask before signing. Visa is the most widely accepted card, followed by MasterCard. The main credit-card offices are:

American Express (☎ 256 0488) Amazonas 339, 5th floor. Open 8am to 5pm Monday to Friday, 9am to 1pm Saturday.

Diners Club (☎ 298 1300) Amazonas 4560 at Pereira. Open 8:30am to 6:30 pm Monday to Friday, 9am to 1:30pm Saturday.

MasterCard (☎ 226 2770) Naciones Unidas 8771 at De Los Shyris. Open 8:30am to 5pm Monday to Friday, 9am to 1pm Saturday.

Visa (☎ 245 9303) De Los Shyris 3147

For money transfers, **Western Union** (☎ 256 5059; *Avenida de la República 433 near Diego de Almagro; open 8am-7pm daily* • ☎ 290 1505; *Avenida Cristobal Colón 1333*) charges $85 for a $1000 transfer from the USA.

Post

The **central post office** (☎ 228 2175; *Espejo 935; open 8am-5:40pm Mon-Fri, 8am-noon Sat*) is in the old town. Currently, this is where you pick up your *lista de correos* (general delivery) mail. There's also a **branch post office** (☎ 250 8890; *cnr Avenida Cristobal Colón & Reina Victoria; open 8am-5:40pm Mon-Fri, 8am-noon Sat*). If you are mailing a package over 2kg, use the **parcel post office** (☎ 252 1730; *Ulloa 273 near Dávalos; open 8am-5:40pm Mon-Fri, 8am-noon Sat*).

At **American Express** (☎ 256 0488; *Amazonas 339, 5th floor; open 8am-5pm Mon-Fri*) clients can receive mail sent to them c/o American Express, Apartado 17-01-02-605, Quito, Ecuador.

There are several air-courier services: **DHL** (☎ 290 1505; *Avenida Cristobal Colón 1333 at Foch; open 8am-7pm Mon-Fri, 9am-5pm Sat*); **FedEx** (☎ 290 9209; *Amazonas 517 near Santa María; open 8am-7pm Mon-Fri, 10am-2pm Sat*); and **UPS** (☎ 225 6790, 246 0469; *Iñaquito N35-155 near Santa María de Vela; open 8:30am-6:30pm Mon-Fri*). Rates are high: A package weighing 1kg costs about $71 to send to the USA and $83 to send to Europe; it's about $30 for 500g.

Telephone

For information on the province's new seven-digit telephone numbers, see Telephone in the Facts for the Visitor chapter. The main office of **Andinatel** (☎ 297 7100; *Eloy Alfaro 333 near 9 de Octubre; open 8am-10pm Mon-Fri, 8am-noon Sat*) is in the new town. There are two convenient **branch offices** (☎ 290 2756; *JL Mera 741 at General Baquedano* • *Reina Victoria near J Calamá; both open 8am-10pm Mon-Fri, 9am-9pm Sat & Sun*) in the Mariscal area. There is an **old town office** (☎ 261 2112; *Benalcázar at Mejía; open 8am-10pm Mon-Fri, 9am-9pm Sat & Sun*) and offices at the main bus terminal and at the airport. See Email & Internet Access for cheaper options.

Email & Internet Access

The Mariscal area (especially along J Calamá) is bursting with cybercafés, where you can read or send emails, surf the Web or use net-to-phone services. Cybercafés are trickier to find in the old town, but they exist. Rates vary little from place to place (about $0.60 per hour in the new town and from $0.90 to $1.20 in the old town). Computer quality and modem speeds vary widely, so try a few places if you're around for a while. Atmosphere ranges from smoky dens serving beer, coffee and snacks to sharp office-like places where the computer is king. The following are a few of the more popular choices:

Cybercafé (☎ 257 1059) Sucre 350, Galería Sucre in the old town. Open 9am to 7pm Monday to Saturday. The sharpest café in the old town.

Kapikua 3 Venezuela near Bolívar in the old town. Open 9am to 7pm Monday to Saturday, 10am to 4pm Sunday.

La Sala (☎ 254 6086) Reina Victoria 1137 at J Calamá in the new town. Open 9am to midnight daily. A bright café with espresso drinks and fast computers.

Papaya Net (☎ 255 6574) J Calamá 469 at JL Mera in the new town. Open 9am to midnight daily. The most popular cybercafé in the Mariscal with groovin' music, alcohol, espresso drinks, snacks and lots of crook-necked email freaks.

Sambo.net (☎ 290 1315) JL Mera at J Pinto in the new town. A comfy place with a fast connection.

Travel Agencies & Tour Operators

The agencies mentioned here can generally be found in the new town. The prices quoted below do not include park fees or transportation costs to the tour departure point.

Andísimo (☎ 250 8347, W www.andisimo.com) 9 de Octubre 479 at Vicente Ramón Roca. German-owned operator using Asociación Ecuatoriana de Guias de Montaña (ASEGUIM) guides, specializing in trekking and climbing. Several languages are spoken.

Arie's Bike Company (☎/fax 290 6052, W www.ariesbikecompany.com) Wilson 578 at Reina Victoria. Arie's offers one- to three-day mountain-bike excursions to or around Otavalo, Mitad del Mundo, Cotopaxi, Chimborazo and Laguna Quilatoa. The popular (and thrilling) down-hill day trips cost $45 per person.

Biking Dutchman (☎ 256 8323, 254 2806, W www.bikingdutchman.com) Foch 714 at JL Mera. Ecuador's pioneer mountain biking operator has good bikes and guides and offers one- to 12-day tours. A one-day ride through the *páramo* (Andean grasslands) of Parque Nacional Cotopaxi costs $45. Two-day tours costs about $100 and five-day tours about $540.

Compañía de Guías de Montaña (☎ 290 1551, 255 6210, W www.companiadeguias.com) Jorge Washington 425 at Avenida 6 de Diciembre. A top-notch mountain climbing operator whose guides are all ASEGUIM instructors and speak several languages. All climbing tours are tailor-made for the client.

Cultura Reservation Center (☎/fax 255 8889, ☎ 222 4271, W www.cafecultura.com) Francisco Robles 513. Located in the hotel Café Cultura (see Places to Stay later in this chapter). Makes reservations for a dozen attractive hotels and lodges around the country.

Dracaena (☎ 290 6644) J Pinto E4-453. Offers four- to eight-day tours of Cuyabeno that have received excellent reviews from our readers. A five-day tour costs $200 per person.

Ecuadorian Tours (☎ 256 0488, W www.ecuadoriantours.com) Amazonas 339 near Jorge Washington. Affiliated with American Express, this is a good all-purpose travel agency.

Emerald Forest Expeditions (☎ 254 1278, ☎/fax 254 1543, W www.emeraldexpeditions.com) J Pinto E4-244 at Amazonas. Owned by Luís García, one of the best guides in the northern Oriente, Emerald Forest consistently gets outstanding reports from travelers. Luis is part Cofan and bases his trips in Pañacocha just off the Río Napo (see also Coca in The Oriente chapter). Prices average $60 per person per day. Tailor-made trips cost about $80 per day. All trips are best arranged in Quito.

Enchanted Expeditions (☎ 256 9960, fax 256 9956, W www.enchantedexpeditions.com) Foch 769 between JL Mera & Amazonas. Formerly known as Angermeyer's Enchanted Expeditions, this operator runs some of the best small boats in the Galápagos. Eight-day tours start at around $1375 per person. There is sometimes a discount of several hundred dollars for passengers booking less than a week before a cruise. Enchanted Expeditions also arranges excursions to the Oriente and the Andes.

Etnotur (☎ 256 4565, 223 0552) Cordero 1313 at JL Mera. Another agency with mainland and Galápagos tours. English, German, French and Spanish are spoken.

Fundación Golondrinas (☎ 222 6602, W www.ecuadorexplorer.com/golondrinas) Isabel La Católica N24-679. Located inside La Casa de Eliza (see Places to Stay later in this chapter). This conservation project arranges four-day walking tours ($222 to $248, depending on the number of people) in the *páramo* and forests west of Tulcán (see the boxed text 'The Cerro Golondrinas Project' in the Northern Highlands chapter).

Galasam (☎ 250 7079/080, W www.galasam
.com) Amazonas 1354 at Cordero. Galasam is
known for its economical to mid-range Galápagos cruises, but reports from customers have
been mixed; complaints are frequent. That said,
last-minute prices on more expensive boats
(where service is better) are sometimes unbeatable, especially if you have a small group and
bargain ferociously. The head office is in
Guayaquil.

Kem Pery Tours (☎ 222 6583, 222 6715, W www
.kempery.com) J Pinto 539. Kem Pery does trips
to Bataboro Lodge, on the edge of Huaorani
territory (see Coca in The Oriente chapter).

Metropolitan Touring (W www.metropolitan-tour
ing.com) main office (☎ 298 8200) República de
El Salvador N36-84; branch office (☎ 250 6650
/51, fax 256 0807) Amazonas 329 near 18 de
Septiembre; . This is Ecuador's biggest and best
known travel agency, specializing in medium-
priced to luxury tours in the Galápagos on both
yachts and cruise ships. Metropolitan also operates expensive but luxurious train trips and can
set up tours and stays at haciendas throughout
the country (see the boxed text 'Hacienda
Hualilagua' later). Metropolitan's preset itineraries are good, but the company is not as good
at customized, tailor-made travel. Service can be
brusque.

Native Life (☎ 250 5158, 255 0836, 250 5158,
e natlife1@natlife.com.ec) Foch E4-167 at Amazonas. Offers five-day tours ($210 per person)
based at its new lodge on the Río Aguarico in
the southern Cuyabeno in the Oriente. Eight-
day tours deeper along the Aguarico cost $410
per person.

Neotropic Turis (☎ 252 1212, 09-980 3395, fax 255
4902, e info@neotropicturis.com, W www.cuya
benolodge.com) J Pinto E4-340 near Amazonas.
Neotropic runs the comfortable Cuyabeno Lodge
in the Reserva Producción Faunística Cuyabeno
(see Organized Tours in The Oriente chapter). A
four-day trip costs $220 to $250 per person depending on the number of travelers and the type
of accommodations requested. They also offer an
eight-day river tour from Macas to Iquitos in
Peru, for $750 per person.

Nuevo Mundo Expeditions (☎ 256 4448, 255
3818, W www.nuevomundotravel.com) Coruña
N26-207 at Orellana. A small but very professional outfit with strong conservation interests
(English-speaking owner Oswaldo Muñoz is a
founding member and past president of the
Ecuadorian Ecotourism Association). The company has top-end prices, but it also has top-end
tours and guides. Nuevo Mundo organizes Galápagos tours; arranges visits to Reserva Producción Faunística Cuyabeno (see The Oriente
chapter); offers four- to five-day cruises on the
Río Napo and into Parque Nacional Yasuní on

their *Amazon Manatee Explorer*, which has nine
double and four triple cabins, all with private hot
showers and air-conditioning ($461 to $613 per
person); and offers a variety of Andean horse
riding and trekking trips. Of particular interest
are the company's cultural tours, one of which
features shamanism and natural healing.

Pamir (☎ 222 0892, fax 254 7576, e info@
pamirtravels.com.ec) JL Mera 721 near General
Veintimilla. Slick operators with very experienced climbing and trekking guides. Also sells
Galápagos cruises.

Quasar Nautica (☎ 244 1550, 244 6996, W www
.quasarnautica.com) Carlos Montúfar E14-15 at
La Cumbre. Offers expensive but excellent luxury
yacht trips in the Galápagos.

Rainforestur (☎/fax 223 9822, W www.rain
forestur.com) Amazonas 420 at Francisco Robles. Readers have consistently recommended
this jungle outfitter which offers excellent rafting trips on the Río Pastaza near Baños, as well
as trips to Cuyabeno and elsewhere (for details,
see Baños in the Central Highlands chapter).
The staff arranges trekking and Indian-market
tours in the Quito area.

Safari Tours (☎ 255 2505, 222 3381, e admin@
safari.com.ec) J Calamá 380 at JL Mera. Open
9am to 7pm daily. This operator/agency has an
excellent reputation. It offers in-depth information and services ranging from volcano climbs and
jungle trips to local jeep tours and personalized
off-the-beaten-track expeditions. Day tours cost
$40 per person, and there are plenty of multiday
tours to choose from. The agency's mountain
guides are among the best in Quito, and the
owner, Jean Brown, is a walking encyclopedia of
travel information. Safari Tours provides 4WD
transportation to just about anywhere and has a
database of available Galápagos trips, as well as
contacts at a host of hotels and lodges. There is a
paperback book exchange, too.

Sangay Touring (☎ 255 0176, 255 0180, W www
.sangay.com) Amazonas N24-196 at Cordero.
Offers a variety of day tours in the Quito area
aimed at the budget traveler. Jeep trips, hiking
excursions and visits to cloud forests and erupting volcanoes are among the day tours offered,
at rates ranging from $25 to $60 per person depending on the distance covered. The staff also
arranges economically priced Galápagos tours
and excursions to the Oriente.

Scuba Iguana (☎ 290 6666, 290 7704, W www
.scubaiguana.com) Amazonas 1004 at Wilson.
One of the best dive operators for the Galápagos, offering four- to eight- day dive cruises
among the islands (see Puerto Ayora in The
Galápagos Islands chapter). It also offers PADI
dive courses (theory and pool classes) in Quito.

Sierra Nevada Expeditions (☎ 255 3658, fax 255
4936, W www.hotelsierranevada.com) J Pinto

637 near Cordero. This company offers climbing, river-rafting and mountain-biking trips.

Surtrek (☎ 223 1534, 256 1129, **W** www.surtrek .com) Amazonas 897. Surtrek has years of experience doing trekking and climbing excursions, and they offer mountain biking as well.

Tropic Ecological Adventures (☎ 222 5907, **W** www.tropiceco.com) Avenida de la República E7-320 at Diego de Almagro. This operator works closely with Indian communities in the northern Oriente. The company offers a monthly six-day tour to the Huaorani territory ($700 to $1300 per person, depending on the number of people) which includes kayaking, canoeing and hiking. Plenty of other excursions are offered as well.

Viajes Orion (☎ 246 2004/05/07, **W** www.vo rion.com) Iñaquito 300, Edifico Milmad at Atahualpa. A top-end ecotourism company that also features cultural tours and bird-watching expeditions. The general manager, Myriam Burneo, speaks English and French fluently.

Yacu Amu Rafting/Ríos Ecuador (☎ 223 6844, 290 4054, **W** www.yacuamu.com) Foch 746 between JL Mera and Amazonas. Yacu Amu has some of the most experienced river-rafting guides and top-class equipment around. There are daily departures for the 'Lo...ng Run,' which has 42 rapids (Class III-IV) in 27km of river – supposedly the longest one-day rafting trip in Ecuador. Rates are $60 per person, which includes a three-hour bus ride from Quito down the western slopes of the Andes, several hours of rafting, and lunch and beverages waiting for you when the fun is done. Other trips range from two to eight days. There is also a four-day kayaking school for beginners, costing $250 to $330 per person depending on the number of students. Owner Steve Nomchong has competed and worked as a judge and safety inspector on the international circuit, so you're in good hands. He now owns the recommended Ríos Ecuador, based in Tena (see River-Rafting under Tena in The Oriente chapter for details).

Bookstores

Libri Mundi (☎ 223 4791; JL Mera 851; open 8:30am-7pm Mon-Fri, 9am-1:30pm & 3:30pm-6:30pm Sat) is Quito's best bookstore, with a good selection of titles in English, German, French and Spanish. It has books about Ecuador, as well as those of a more general nature.

Libro Express (☎/fax 254 8113; Amazonas 816 & General Veintimilla; open 9:30am-7:30pm Mon-Fri, 10am-2pm Sat) is good for maps, magazines and Ecuador-related books.

Abya Yala Bookstore (☎ 250 6247, 256 2633; Avenida 12 de Octubre 1430 & Wilson; open 8am-6:15pm Mon-Fri, 9am-1pm Sat) has books on Indian culture and anthropology (mainly in Spanish).

Confederate Books (☎ 252 7890; J Calamá 410; open 10am-5:30pm daily) has Ecuador's best selection of second-hand books in English and several other languages. If all you want is a novel for that long bus trip or flight home this is your best bet. Everything is less than the cover price, and you can sell books there too. Sometimes the store stays open later.

Cultural Centers

Alianza Francesa (☎ 224 9345/50; Avenida Eloy Alfaro N32-468 near Belgica & Avenida 6 de Diciembre; open 8:30am-2:30pm & 3:30pm-6:30pm) is the French cultural center.

Asociación Humboldt (☎ 254 8480; Vancouver at Polonia) is the German cultural center, hosting lectures, exhibitions and films.

Centro Cultural Afro-Ecuatoriano (☎ 252 2318; JL Tamayo 985) is a good information source for black Ecuadorian culture and events in Quito.

Centro Cultural Mexicano (☎ 225 5149; Suiza 343 & República de El Salvador) sometimes features the artworks of Ecuadorian and Latin American artists.

Laundry

At the following places you can have your clothes washed, dried and folded within 24 hours (often within five hours), and all charge between $0.75 and $1 per kilogram of clothing:

Opera de Jabón (☎ 254 3995) J Pinto 325 near Reina Victoria

Rainbow Laundry (☎ 223 7128) JL Mera 1337 at Cordero

Sun City Laundry (☎ 255 3066) cnr JL Mera & Foch

Wash & Go (☎ 223 0993) J Pinto 340 at JL Mera

Most hotels will wash and dry your clothes, but this gets quite expensive, especially in the 1st-class hotels. The cheaper hotels will often provide facilities for hand-washing laundry.

Photography

Cameras are expensive in Quito. If yours breaks, a recommended repairer is **Gustavo Gómez** (☎ 223 0855; Edificio Molino, Asunción

130 & 10 de Agosto, Office 1; open 8am-4pm Mon-Fri).

There are several places along Amazonas in the new town and around Plaza Santo Domingo in the old town where print film is processed within a day. The results are usually satisfactory but not top quality. See Photography & Video in the Facts for the Visitor chapter for more information.

Medical Services

An American-run hospital with an outpatient department and emergency room is **Hospital Voz Andes** (☎ 226 2142; Juan Villalengua 267), which is near the Iñaquito trolley stop. Fees start at about $15 for an office visit. The best hospital in town is probably the **Hospital Metropolitano** (☎ 226 1520, 226 9030, emergency ☎ 226 5020; Mariana de Jesús & Avenida Occidental).

A private clinic specializing in women's medical problems is **Clínica de la Mujer** (☎ 245 8000; Amazonas 4826 & Gaspar de Villarroel).

In the new town, **Clínica Pichincha** (☎ 256 2408, 256 2296; General Veintimilla 1259 & U Páez) does lab analysis for parasites, dysentery etc.

The following individual doctors have been recommended, many of whom have offices in the Centro Meditropoli near the Hospital Metropolitano: **Dr Alfredo Jijon** (☎ 245 6259, 246 6314; Centro Meditropoli, office 215, Mariana de Jesús & Avenida Occidental) is a gynecologist; **Dr John Rosenberg** (☎ 252 1104, ext ☎ 310, 222 7777, 09-973 9734, pager ☎ 222 7777; Foch 476 & Diego de Almagro), an internist who specializes in tropical medicine, speaks English and German, makes house calls and is available for emergencies nearly anytime; **Dr José A Pitarque** (☎ 226 8173; Centro Meditropoli, office 211) is an ophthalmologist who speaks English. Your embassy or the SAE can recommend others.

There are many dentists in Quito. Recommended ones include: English-speaking **Dr Jorge Cobo Avedaño** (☎ 225 6589, 246 3361, ext ☎ 222; Centro Meditropoli, office 004); English- and German-speaking **Dr Roberto Mema** (☎ 256 9149; Coruña E24-865 & Isabel La Católica); and orthodontists **Sixto and Silvia Altamirano** (☎ 244 119; Amazonas 2689 & Avenida de la República).

See also Health in the Facts for the Visitor chapter.

Women Travelers

La Casa de Mujer (☎ 254 6155; Los Ríos 2238 & Gándara near La Parque Alameda) provides support and can recommend shelters for women who are victims of domestic violence. It's geared toward Ecuadorian women, but it might be of some assistance to other women in an emergency. The **Carcel de Mujeres** (Women's Prison; Calle de Las Toronjas off Avenida El Inca) has several foreign women imprisoned for drug offenses, who have all requested visitors to chat with. Inexpensive care packages – shampoo, tampons (which are especially hard to get in prison), fruit, audio cassettes, magazines etc – are welcomed. Visiting hours are 10am to 3pm (last entry at 2:30pm and no entry or exit from noon to 1pm) Wednesday, Saturday and Sunday.

Emergency

Some helpful numbers to have in an emergency include:

Police	☎ 101
Fire department	☎ 102
Red Cross ambulance	☎ 131

Dangers & Annoyances

Unfortunately, crime in Quito has been on the rise over the last few years. Be aware that pickpockets work crowded areas, such as buses, markets and plazas. See also Dangers & Annoyances in the Facts for the Visitor chapter.

The old town, where there are plenty of camera-laden tourists, has a reputation for being a prime stomping ground for thieves, especially the Ipiales market area. If you dress inconspicuously and don't carry a valuable camera, you're likely to be fine.

Definitely avoid the steps of García Moreno heading from Ambato to the top of El Panecillo – there have been repeated reports of armed thieves there. Take a taxi or a tour to the top, and once there, stay within the paved area around the statue of the Virgin. You won't have any problem there, and you can take good photos of Quito and the surrounding mountains.

Unfortunately, the most dangerous area in the new town is the Mariscal Sucre, which is where most of the budget hotels, bars, cybercafés and restaurants are. Knife and gun holdups are regular occurrences at

High on Altitude

Did the hotel stairs make you breathless? Is your head spinning or achy? Have you got cotton mouth? If so, you're probably suffering the mild symptoms of altitude sickness, which will disappear after a day or two. Quito's elevation of about 2850m can certainly have this affect if you've just arrived from sea level. To minimize symptoms, take things easy upon arrival, eat light and lay off the smokes and alcohol.

night. The easiest way to avoid getting mugged is to always take a taxi after dark, even if it's only for a block. Do not walk around any parks after sunset.

Should you be unfortunate enough to be robbed, you should file a police report, particularly if you wish to make an insurance claim. The place to go is the **police station** (*Mideros & Cuenca*), in the old town, between 9am and noon. In the new town, you can report a robbery at the **police station** (*cnr Reina Victoria & Vicente Ramón Roca*). For insurance purposes, the report should be filed within 48 hours of the theft.

Despite these warnings, if you avoid attracting undue attention and take taxis at night, it's unlikely you'll have any problems in Quito at all.

WALKING TOUR

Stroll along the old-town streets, and you'll pass an interesting sight on almost every block. It's a bustling area, full of yelling street vendors, ambling pedestrians, tooting taxis, belching buses, and whistle-blowing policemen trying to direct traffic in the narrow, congested one-way streets. It is well worth spending several hours walking around this historic area, if not several days. Sunday, when there is little traffic and fewer people, is a good day to walk around the old town. The easiest way to the old town from the north is aboard the *trole* (trolley); catch it on 10 de Agosto and get off at the Plaza Grande stop. From there it's one block northwest to the Plaza de la Independencia.

See Things to See & Do, following, for more details about the places described in this tour. The **Empresa del Centro Histórico** (*ECH; ☎/fax 258 3827; Venezuela 976 & Mejía; open 8:30am-5pm Mon-Fri*) publishes

free or nominally priced maps of walks in the old town with detailed information on the sights seen; the staff offer interesting guided walks as well.

The area of the old town bounded by Calles Flores, Rocafuerte, Cuenca and Manabí has most of the colonial churches and major plazas. The **Plaza de la Independencia** (also known as Plaza Grande) is a good starting point; after checking out the **Palacio del Gobierno** and the **cathedral**, continue southwest on García Moreno and turn right on Sucre to see **La Compañía de Jesús**. From here, walk one block northwest along Sucre to the impressive **Plaza and Monastery of San Francisco**. From the plaza, backtrack to García Moreno and head southwest (right) for three blocks, under the arch at Rocafuerte, to the **Museo de la Ciudad**. If you continue past the museum on García Moreno, you'll hit the historic street Juan Dios Morales. Turn southeast (left) and after two blocks you'll be on the historic alley of **La Ronda** whose colonial balconied houses are some of the oldest in Quito. The street is notorious for bag snatchers. However, the Empresa del Centro Histórico is restoring many of the buildings along this street (and relocating the brothels), which may make it safer; ask at the office on the Plaza Grande. From La Ronda walk up to Guayaquil and turn northeast (left) and you'll pass the **Iglesia and Plaza de Santo Domingo** on your right.

From the Plaza de Santo Domingo, head northeast along Calle Guayaquil toward the new town. Between Mejía and Chile you'll pass the hole-in-the-wall **Heladería San Agustín** (see Places to Eat later), a 140-year-old ice-cream parlor well worth a stop for a couple of scoops of nourishment before leaving the old town.

Continue north on Guayaquil merging with Avenida 10 de Agosto. Bear north (left), and you'll pass the **Banco Central** on your left and, on your right, the southernmost point of the triangular **Parque La Alameda** with its impressive **Simón Bolívar monument**. As you head north through the park, you'll pass the **Quito Observatory**, the oldest European astronomical observatory in South America.

As you leave the park, continue north on Avenida 6 de Diciembre. After three blocks, you'll pass the modern **Palacio Legislativo** (Legislative Congress Building) on your right. Continuing on Avenida 6 de Diciembre takes you past the popular **Parque El Ejido** on your left and the huge, circular, mirror-walled **Casa de la Cultura Ecuatoriana** on your right. Turn left past the Casa de la Cultura and walk three blocks along Avenida Patria, with Parque El Ejido to your left, until you reach the small stone arch marking the beginning of Quito's most famous modern street, **Amazonas Avenidas**.

It is about 3km from the heart of the old town to the beginning of Amazonas, a one-way street with banks, boutiques, souvenir stands and sidewalk cafés.

THINGS TO SEE & DO

With its interesting museums, bustling street markets and enchanting colonial architecture, Quito has plenty to keep the curious busy for days. If you're short on time, be sure to at least see the Plaza de la Independencia and the Plaza and Monastery of San Francisco in the old town. You really shouldn't miss the Church of La Compañia either.

The old town has most of Quito's wealth of churches, chapels, convents, monasteries, cathedrals and basilicas. We've highlighted just a selection of the most interesting and frequently visited. Flash photography is usually prohibited in churches. Slides and postcards can be bought at the post office in the old town. Churches are open every day but are crowded with worshippers on Sunday; early morning is usually a good time to visit. Churches often remain open until around 6pm, but they regularly close for parts of the day. There are signs asking tourists not to wander around during religious services – at such times, you can enter and sit in a pew.

Deciding which museums to visit depends on your interests. Quito's most notable are those within the Casa de la Cultura Ecuatoriana, the Museo de Arte Colonial and the Museo Guayasamín. Hit these and you'll get a healthy dose of archaeology, religious history and colonial, modern and contemporary art. For good measure, throw the interesting Museo de la Ciudad into the mix for more down-to-earth local history. Museums are generally closed on Mondays.

The opening hours listed below are prone to change (like everything in Ecuador).

Old Town
Plaza de la Independencia While wandering around colonial Quito, you'll probably pass through the Plaza de la Independencia several times. The low white building on the northwest side of the plaza with the national flag flying atop is the **Palacio del Gobierno** (Presidential Palace). The president carrys out business in this building, so sightseeing is limited to the entrance area. Inside, you can see a mural depicting Francisco de Orellana's descent of the Amazon. The guard at the gate may allow you in to view the mural.

On the southwest side of the plaza stands Quito's recently painted **cathedral** (*admission $1, Sunday services free; open 10am-4pm Mon-Sat, Sunday services hourly 6am-noon & 5pm-7pm*). Although not as rich in decoration as some of the other churches, it has several points of historical interest. Plaques on the outside walls commemorate Quito's founders, and Mariscal Sucre, the leading figure of Quito's independence, is buried in the cathedral. To the left of the main altar is a statue of Juan José Flores, Ecuador's first president. Behind the main altar is the smaller altar of Nuestra Señora de los Dolores; the plaque there shows where President Gabriel García Moreno died on August 6, 1875. He was shot outside the Palacio del Gobierno (just across the plaza) and was carried, dying, to the cathedral. The cathedral contains religious paintings by several notable artists of the Quito school.

The **Archbishop's Palace** (Palacio Arzobispal), now a colonnaded row of small shops, can be seen on the northeast side of the plaza. The interior patios can be visited and a couple of restaurants were recently opened inside.

Just off the plaza, and a bit difficult to find because the sign is not very obvious, is the museum **Antiguo Cuartel de la Real Audencia** (☎ 221 4018, 221 0863; *Espejo 1147 & Benalcázar*). It used to be a Jesuit house until 1767, when it became a *cuartel* (army barracks). It contains a wealth of early colonial art dating from the 16th and 17th centuries, as well as more modern art. The basement has gory waxworks showing the assassination of local patriots by royalist forces in 1810, over a decade before independence was achieved.

North of Plaza de la Independencia
Two blocks northwest of the Plaza de la Independencia you'll find one of colonial Quito's most recently built churches, **La**

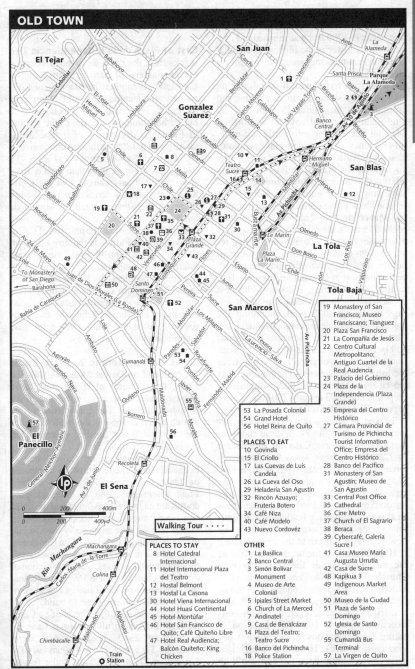

OLD TOWN

El Tejar

San Juan

Gonzalez Suarez

Banco Central

San Blas

San Blas

Teatro Sucre

Hermano Miguel

Le Marín

La Tola

Plaza La Marín

Santo Domingo

Tola Baja

San Marcos

Av Pichincha

To Monastery of San Diego

El Panecillo

El Sena

Río Machangara

Machangara

Colina

Chimbacalle

Train Station

0   200   400m
0   200   400yd

Walking Tour · · · ·

PLACES TO STAY
- 8 Hotel Catedral Internacional
- 11 Hotel Internacional Plaza del Teatro
- 12 Hostal Belmont
- 13 Hostal La Casona
- 30 Hotel Viena Internacional
- 44 Hotel Huasi Continental
- 45 Hotel Montúfar
- 46 Hotel San Francisco de Quito; Café Quiteño Libre
- 47 Hotel Real Audiencia; Balcón Quiteño; King Chicken
- 53 La Posada Colonial
- 54 Grand Hotel
- 56 Hotel Reina de Quito

PLACES TO EAT
- 10 Govinda
- 15 El Criollo
- 17 Las Cuevas de Luis Candela
- 26 La Cueva del Oso
- 29 Heladería San Agustín
- 32 Rincón Azuayo; Frutería Botero
- 34 Café Niza
- 40 Café Modelo
- 43 Nuevo Cordovéz

OTHER
- 1 La Basílica
- 2 Banco Central
- 3 Simón Bolívar Monument
- 4 Museo de Arte Colonial
- 5 Ipiales Street Market
- 6 Church of La Merced
- 7 Andinatel
- 9 Casa de Benalcázar
- 14 Plaza del Teatro; Teatro Sucre
- 16 Banco del Pichincha
- 18 Police Station
- 19 Monastery of San Francisco; Museo Franciscano; Tianguez
- 20 Plaza San Francisco
- 21 La Compañía de Jesús
- 22 Centro Cultural Metropolitano; Antiguo Cuartel de la Real Audiencia
- 23 Palacio del Gobierno
- 24 Plaza de la Independencia (Plaza Grande)
- 25 Empresa del Centro Histórico
- 27 Cámara Provincial de Turismo de Pichincha Tourist Information Office; Empresa del Centro Histórico
- 28 Banco del Pacífico
- 31 Monastery of San Agustín; Museo de San Agustín
- 33 Central Post Office
- 35 Cathedral
- 36 Cine Metro
- 37 Church of El Sagrario
- 38 Beraca
- 39 Cybercafé; Galería Sucre I
- 41 Casa Museo María Augusta Urrutia
- 42 Casa de Sucre
- 48 Kapikua 3
- 49 Indigenous Market Area
- 50 Museo de la Ciudad
- 51 Plaza de Santo Domingo
- 52 Iglesia de Santo Domingo
- 55 Cumandá Bus Terminal
- 57 La Virgen de Quito

Merced *(cnr Cuenca & Chile; admission free; open 6am-noon & 3pm-6pm daily)*. Construction began in 1700 and was finished in 1742. At 47m, its tower is the highest in colonial Quito and contains the largest bell of Quito's churches.

La Merced has a wealth of fascinating art – paintings show volcanoes glowing and erupting over the church roofs of colonial Quito and the capital covered with ashes, Marshal Sucre going into battle and many other scenes. The stained-glass windows also show various scenes of colonial life, such as early priests and conquistadors among the Indians of the Oriente. It is a surprising and intriguing collection.

One block to the northeast is the fascinating **Museo de Arte Colonial** *(☎ 221 2297; Mejía 915 at Cuenca; admission $0.50; open 10am-6pm Tues-Fri, 10am-2pm Sat)*. In a restored 17th-century building, the museum houses what many consider to be Ecuador's best collection of colonial art from the 16th to the 18th centuries. It's surely the best place to see the famous sculptures and paintings of the Quito School, including the works of Miguel de Santiago, Manuel Chili (the indigenous artist known as Caspicara) and Bernardo de Legarda. The small collection of period furniture offers respite from the lofty religious works. The museum was closed for restoration in 2002, with plans to reopen in late 2003 or early 2004; call or ask at one of the tourist offices.

Tucked in among other colonial buildings northeast of the Plaza de la Independencia, the historic **Casa de Benalcázar** *(☎ 228 8102; Olmedo 968 & Benalcázar; admission free; open 9am-1pm & 2pm-6pm Mon-Fri)* is worth a peek if you're in the area. The building dates from 1534 and was restored by Spain in 1967. Sometimes classical piano recitals are held here, a delightful site for such entertainment; check the newspapers or inquire at the *casa* (house).

High on a hill in the northeastern part of the old town stands the relatively new **Church of La Basílica** *(Venezuela; admission $1; open 9:30am-5:30pm daily)*. With minor details still unfinished, it's technically still a work in progress, even although construction began in 1926 (the tradition of taking decades to construct a church is obviously still alive). The church's highlight is its **tower**; climb to the top and you'll be rewarded by one of the best views of old Quito anywhere.

East of Plaza de la Independencia Two blocks from the Plaza de la Independencia, the **Monastery of San Agustín** *(Chile & Guayaquil)*, is another fine example of 17th-century architecture. Many of the heroes of the battles for Ecuador's independence are buried here, and it is the site of the signing of Ecuador's declaration of independence on August 10, 1809. In the church's convent, the **Museo de San Agustín** *(☎ 251 5525, 258 0263; Chile & Flores; open 9am-1pm & 3pm-6pm)* houses many canvases of the Quito School, including a series depicting the life of Saint Augustine, painted by Miguel de Santiago.

Further northeast, at the junction of Calles Guayaquil and Flores, is the tiny **Plaza del Teatro**, where you'll find, along with microphone-toting preachers and hollering newspaper peddlers, the **Teatro Sucre**. Built in 1878, it is Quito's most sophisticated theater. Unfortunately, performances have been suspended indefinitely while the theater is restored, an under-funded project whose completion looks years away.

Calles García Moreno & Sucre Beside the cathedral on García Moreno stands the 17th-century **Church of El Sagrario** *(García Moreno; admission free; open 6am-noon & 3pm-6pm daily)*. The construction of the church began in 1657 as the main chapel of the cathedral; it was finished 49 years later, but is now a separate church.

Around the corner on Calle Sucre is Ecuador's most ornate church, **La Compañía de Jesús** *(admission $2.50; open 9:30am-11am & 4pm-6pm daily)*. Its green-and-gold domes are an impressive sight from the Plaza San Francisco just two blocks away. Seven tonnes of gold were supposedly used to gild the walls, ceilings and altars of La Compañia, and *quiteños* proudly call it the most beautiful church in the country. The construction of this Jesuit church began in 1605, the year that the Monastery of San Francisco was completed, and it took 163 years to build.

A block-and-a-half southeast of La Compañía is the beautifully restored **Casa de Sucre** *(☎ 295 2860; Venezuela 573 & Sucre; admission $1; open 8:30am-4:30pm Tues-Fri, 10am-4pm Sat & Sun)*. This is the former home of Mariscal Antonio José de Sucre, the hero of Ecuadorian independence (and the man after whom the former Ecuadorian currency was named). It is now a small museum, full of early 19th-century furniture. It also has a small gift shop with books about Ecuador.

Back on Calle García Moreno, just southwest of Calle Sucre, you'll find the **Casa Museo María Augusta Urrutía** (☎ 258 0107; *García Moreno 760 near Sucre; admission $2.50; open 9am-5pm Tues-Sun*). This restored house was once the home of the distinguished philanthropist María Augusta Urrutía. With plenty of period furnishings, it is a good example of a late-19th-century aristocrat's house.

Occupying a beautifully restored building dating from 1563, the **Museo de la Ciudad** (☎ 228 3882; *García Moreno & Rocafuerte; admission $3; open 9:30am-5:30pm Tues-Sun*) is two blocks southwest of the Casa Museo María Augusta Urrutía. The building itself housed the San Juan de Dios hospital until 1973, and is now a fascinating museum with well-conceived exhibits depicting daily life in Quito through the centuries. There are also temporary exhibits of contemporary Ecuadorian and foreign art. Guides are available for an additional $2 in Spanish or for $4 in English.

Plaza & Monastery of San Francisco

Walking from the narrow colonial streets of the old town into the openness of Plaza San Francisco reveals one of the finest sites in all of Ecuador – a sweeping cobblestone plaza backed by the long whitewashed walls and twin bell towers of Ecuador's oldest church, the Monastery of San Francisco (*admission free; open 7am-11am daily, 3pm-6pm Mon-Thur*). With its giant plaza, its mountainous backdrop of Volcán Pichincha, and the bustling street market flanking its northeastern side, the church (both inside and out) is surely one of Quito's highlights.

Construction of the monastery began only a few weeks after the founding of Quito in 1534, but the building was not finished until 70 years later. It is the city's largest colonial structure. The founder was the Franciscan missionary Joedco Ricke, who is credited with being the first man to sow wheat in Ecuador. He is commemorated by a **statue** at the far right of the raised terrace in front of the church.

Although much of the church has been rebuilt because of earthquake damage, some of it is original. The **chapel of Señor Jesús del Gran Poder**, to the right of the main altar, has original tilework. The **main altar** itself is a spectacular example of baroque carving, while much of the roof shows Moorish influences.

The church contains excellent examples of early religious art and sculpture, although it is often too dark to see them clearly. The bells are rung every hour, often on the quarter hour, and you can see the bell ringer at work in his cubbyhole just to the right of the main door.

To the right of the main entrance of the monastery is the **Museo Franciscano** (☎ 228 2545; *admission $2.50; open 9am-6pm Mon-Sat, 9am-noon Sun*), which contains some of the church's finest artwork. Here you can see paintings, sculpture and furniture dating to the 16th century. One of the oldest signed paintings is a Mateo Mejía canvas that is dated 1615. Some of the furniture is fantastically wrought and inlaid with literally thousands of pieces of mother-of-pearl. The admission fee includes a guided tour, which is usually in Spanish, but is occasionally in English if you ask.

To the left of the monastery is the **Cantuña** chapel, which houses an excellent art collection from the Quito School. To the right of the monastery begins the sprawling **Ipiales street market**, which heads up the hill toward Calles Imbabura and Chile. The market has grown with Quito over the years, and more streets succumb to the blue overhead tarps and vendors selling everything from pirate CDs to underwear. This is a fascinating area to visit, but watch for pickpockets and bag and camera snatchers.

Plaza & Church of Santo Domingo

Near the southwest end of Guayaquil, Plaza Santo Domingo, is a regular haunt for street performers, and crowds of neighborhood *quiteños* fill the plaza to watch pouting clowns and half-cocked magicians do their stuff. The plaza is especially attractive in the evening when the domes of the 17th-century Church of Santo Domingo, on the southeast side of the plaza, are floodlit (but don't hang out here alone after dark when muggings are frequent). In front of the church stands a **statue of Mariscal Sucre**, depicting the marshal pointing toward Pichincha where he won the decisive battle for independence on May 24, 1822.

The interior of the church (Flores & Rocafuerte; admission free; open 7am-1pm & 4:30pm-7:30pm daily), even during the day, is almost spooky; giant hardwood boards creak beneath your feet as you approach the dramatic Gothic-like altar toward the front. An exquisite **statue of the Virgen del Rosario**, a gift from King Charles V of Spain, is now one of the church's main showpieces – you can find it in an ornately carved baroque-style side chapel. Construction of the church began in 1581 and continued until 1650.

El Panecillo The small, ever-present hill to the south of the old town is called **El Panecillo** ('The Little Bread Loaf') and is a major Quito landmark. It is topped by a huge statue of **La Virgen de Quito**, with a crown of stars, eagle's wings and a chained dragon atop the world. Reading the Bible (Revelations 12) will give you some ideas about why the Virgin was built as she is.

From the summit, there are marvelous **views** of the whole city stretching out below, as well as views of the surrounding volcanoes. The best time for volcano views (particularly in the rainy season) is early morning, before the clouds roll in. Definitely don't climb the stairs at the end of Calle García Moreno on the way to the statue – there have been numerous reports of travelers being robbed on the climb. A taxi from the old town costs about $10 to $20, including wait time and round trip.

At the bottom of El Panecillo is the intersection of Avenida 24 de Mayo and Cuenca, an area that was once a major open-air **indigenous market**. An indoor market was opened in 1981 at the upper end of Avenida 24 de Mayo, impacting on the outdoor affair. Nonetheless, some outdoor selling still takes place, especially around the intersection and on the streets northwest of Cuenca. Saturday and Wednesday are the main market days, but the area is busy on other days as well.

West of the Old Town

Northwest of El Panecillo, the **Monastery of San Diego** (Calicuchima 117 & Farfán; admission $2; open 9:30am-1pm & 2:30pm-5:30pm daily) is an excellent example of 17th-century colonial architecture. There is a treasure of colonial art, including a **pulpit** (considered one of the country's finest) by the notable Indian woodcarver Juan Bautista Menacho. The **cemetery**, with its numerous tombs, mausoleums and other memorials, is also worth a peek. Visits are guided and include a walk through the monks' living quarters and a stop at the onsite **museum** (☎ 295 2516). You may have to ring the doorbell if the building is closed. The best way there is by taxi.

On the flanks of Volcán Pichincha, northwest of the monastery of San Diego, **La Cima de la Libertad** (☎ 228 8733; Av de los Libertadores s/n; admission $0.50; open 8:30am-4pm Tues-Fri, 10am-3pm Sat & Sun) is a museum housing a collection of historical and military artefacts and a huge and impressive mural by Eduardo Kingman. The museum is a modern building, built on the hill where Marshal Sucre fought the decisive battle for independence on May 24, 1822. Upon surrender of your passport, a soldier will guide you around. Photography is prohibited inside the museum. Outside, however, photography is recommended – there are great views of the city below. It is best reached by taxi.

New Town

Parques La Alameda & El Ejido From the northeast edge of the old town the long, triangular Parque La Alameda begins its grassy crawl toward the new town. At the southern apex of the park stands the **Simón Bolívar monument**, and on the southeast side there is a **relief map of Ecuador**. Toward the middle of the park are **statues** of the members of the 1736–44 French Académie des Sciences expedition that surveyed Ecuador and made the equatorial measurements that gave rise to the metric system of weights and measures.

In the center of the park is the **Quito Observatory** (☎ 257 0765; admission $0.20, night viewings $0.40; open 8am-noon & 3pm-5pm Mon-Fri, 8am-noon Sat), which was opened by President García Moreno in 1864 and is the oldest in the continent. It is still used both for meteorology and astronomy. You can visit during opening hours. On very clear nights the observatory opens for gazing at stars and planets; call ahead of time if the weather looks promising.

At the north end of La Alameda – an area popular with picnickers on weekends – are a pair of ornamental **lakes**, where rowboats can be hired. Nearby is a small monument with a spiral staircase and a view of the **Church of El Belén**, which was built on the site of the first Catholic mass to be held in Quito.

Northeast of La Alameda, the pleasant, tree-filled Parque El Ejido is the biggest park in downtown Quito. It's a popular spot for impromptu games of soccer and volleyball. Occasionally you might spot people playing a strange, giant marbles game (played with steel balls the size of golf balls) typical to Ecuador. The north end of the park teems with activity on weekends, when open-air **art shows** are held along Avenida Patria. Just inside the north end of the park, artisans and crafts vendors set up stalls and turn the sidewalks into what's probably Quito's largest handicrafts market.

Between Parque Alameda and Parque El Ejido is the **legislative palace** (Montalvo near Avenida 6 de Diciembre), the equivalent of the houses of parliament or congress, where elected members carry out the nation's affairs. A huge sculpted panel stretching across the north side of the building represents the history of Ecuador and is worth a quick look.

Casa de la Cultura Ecuatoriana This landmark, circular, glass building across from Parque El Ejido houses two important museums: the Museo de Arte Ecuatoriano and the Museo del Banco Central.

The **Museo de Arte Ecuatoriano** (☎ 222 3392; cnr Avenidas Patria & 12 de Octubre; admission $1; open 9am-5pm Tues-Fri, 10am-3pm Sat & Sun) boasts a large collection of contemporary, modern and 19th-century Ecuadorian art. The exhibits include canvases by Ecuador's most famous artists, including Oswaldo Guayasamín, Eduardo Kingman and Camilo Egas. There is also an exhibit dedicated to musical instruments.

Quito's best archaeology museum, the **Museo del Banco Central** (☎ 222 3259; cnr Avenidas Patria & 12 de Octubre; admission $1; open 9am-5pm Tues-Sun, 10am-3pm Sat & Sun) is a maze of well-displayed artefacts. Allow at least a couple hours to eyeball all the goods, including pottery, gold ornaments, the gold mask that is the symbol of

Museo del Banco Central, skulls showing deformities and early surgical methods, a mummy and much more.

Within the Casa de la Cultura complex there is also a movie theater that often shows international movies of note, as well as an auditorium where classical and other kinds of music are performed. Check newspapers, the posters on the front of the building, or the Casa de la Cultura website at [W] www.cce.org.ec for information about events.

Amazonas A solitary stone archway at the north end of Parque El Ejido marks the beginning of modern Quito's showpiece street, Avenida Amazonas. It rolls as far north as the airport, although the strip you're likely to become most familiar with lies between Parque El Ejido and the busy Avenida Cristobal Colón. It's the main artery of the **Mariscal Sucre** area, lined with modern hotels, airline offices, travel agencies, banks and restaurants. There's plenty of room for pedestrians, and the outdoor restaurants near the intersection of Vicente Ramón Roca are favorite spots for espresso, newspapers, sandwiches and ice-cold Pilsener.

Mariscal Sucre & Around The Mariscal Sucre area, known simply as the 'Mariscal,' is the neighborhood loosely bound by Avenidas 10 de Agosto, Cristobal Colón, 12 de Octubre and Patria. All the travel-related services you could possibly need can be found in this area.

On Avenida 12 de Octubre, just south of the Mariscal, are two worthwhile museums.

The **Museo Amazónico** (☎ 256 2663; Avenida 12 de Octubre 1436; admission $1; open 8am-4pm Mon-Fri, 9am-1pm Sat & Sun) is run by the Salesian Mission and has a small display of indigenous artefacts collected by the missionaries in the jungle.

The **Museo de Jacinto Jijón y Caamaño** (☎ 257 5727/1317, 252 1834; Avenida 12 de Octubre & Vicente Ramón Roca; admission $0.60; open 8:30am-4pm Mon-Fri) houses an interesting private archaeology collection and an exhibit of colonial art featuring some of the masters of the Quito School. This museum is on the 3rd floor of the library in the **Universidad Católica**, across the traffic circle from the Casa de la Cultura Ecuatoriana. Admission includes a guided tour (in English if you call in advance).

QUITO

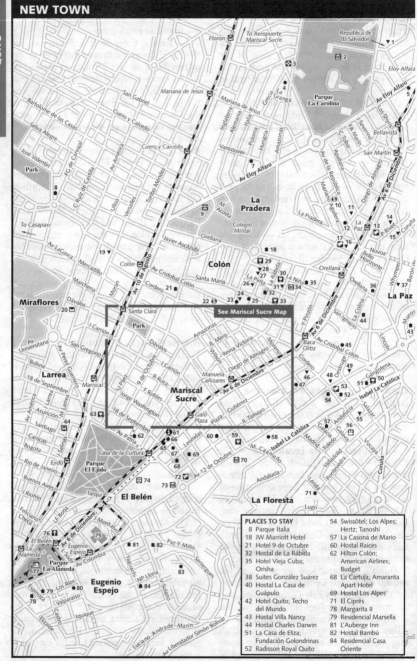

NEW TOWN

See Mariscal Sucre Map

Anyone interested in reptiles and amphibians should check out the **Vivarium** (☎ 223 0988, 221 0863; Reina Victoria 1576 & Santa María; admission $1; open 9:30am-12:45pm & 2:30pm-5:45pm Tues-Sat, noon-6pm Sun) on the northeast edge of the Mariscal. This herpetological research and education center is home to a number of live animals, including the highly poisonous fer-de-lance snake, boa constrictors, iguanas, turtles and tortoises. Call ahead to arrange a tour.

About two blocks north of the Vivarium is a small museum run by **Fundación Sinchi Sacha** (☎ 223 0609; W www.sinchisacha.org; Reina Victoria N26-166 & La Niña; open 8am-8pm daily), a nonprofit organization supporting Amazonian cultures. The **museum** (open 8am-6:30pm Mon-Fri, 10am-6pm Sat) exhibits the artwork and utensils of the peoples of the Oriente and sells a variety of related literature. Sinchi sacha is Quechua for 'powerful forest.' There is also a gift shop (see Shopping later in the chapter).

Museo de Ciencias Naturales North of the Mariscal, in Parque La Carolina, you'll find the country's best natural-history museum, the Museo de Ciencias Naturales (☎ 244 9824; adult/student $1/0.20; open 8:30am-4pm Mon-Fri, 9am-1pm Sat, 9am-2pm Sun). It is well worth a visit if you want to acquaint yourself with the country's flora and fauna, or simply freak yourself out looking at the thousands of dead insects and arachnids on display. It's on the De Los Shyris side of the park, opposite República de El Salvador.

Museo Guayasamín In the former home of the world-famous indigenous painter Oswaldo Guayasamín (1919–99), this museum (☎ 246 5265, 245 2938; Calle Bosmediano 543; admission $2; open 9am-1:30pm & 3pm-6:30pm Mon-Fri) houses the most complete collection of his work. It also houses Guayasamín's collection of pre-Columbian and colonial pieces, and a jewelry workshop with plenty of original pieces for sale. You can also buy original paintings or posters.

The museum is in the residential district of Bellavista, northeast of downtown. You can walk uphill, or take a bus along Avenida 6 de Diciembre to Avenida Eloy Alfaro and then a Bellavista bus up the hill.

QUITO

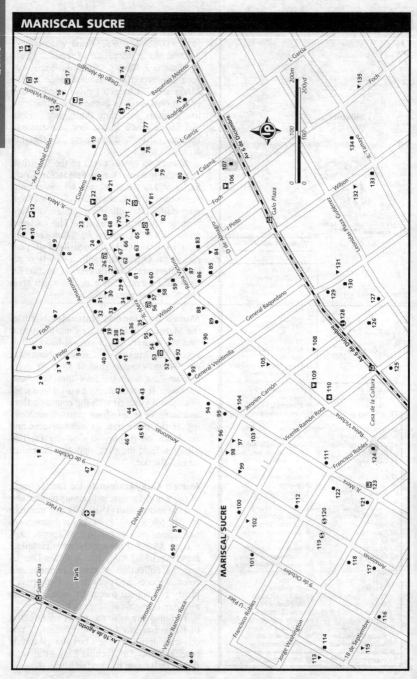

MARISCAL SUCRE

PLACES TO STAY

1 Hostal Palm Garten
6 Albergue El Taxo
19 El Cafecito
20 Hostal Alcalá
21 Alberto's House
28 Orange Guesthouse;
    Enchanted Expeditions; Yacu
    Amu Rafting/Ríos Ecuador
31 Hostal Vamara; Tropical
    Dancing School
34 Tortuga Verde
36 Hotel Pickett
37 Mansión del Ángel
39 Hostal Amazonas Inn
51 Hostal Dé jà vu
58 Hostelling International
    Ecuador; Opera de Jabón
59 Hostal Mundo Net
61 Magic Bean
63 Crossroads
74 Hotel Sebastián
76 Posada del Maple
77 Antinea Apart Hotel
78 Loro Verde
79 El Centro del Mundo
83 Hostal Alpa Aligu
85 El Vagabundo
107 La Casa Sol
114 Rincón de Bavaria
124 Café Cultura; Cultura
    Reservation Center
126 Villa Nancy B&B
130 Casa Helbling
133 Hostal Fuente de Piedra
134 Hotel Viena

PLACES TO EAT

3 Café Colibri
16 La Jaiba Mariscos
25 El Marqués
30 Red Hot Chili Peppers;
    Mango Tree Café
35 Sugar Mammas
44 La Terraza del Tartaro; Las
    Redes
46 El Hornero
47 Cevichería Viejo José
52 Super Papa
55 El Español
62 Texas Ranch
65 Adam's Rib

66 Siam
67 El Maple; Shogún; Zócalo
69 Su Cebiche
70 Café Sutra; Safari Tours
71 La Creperie; Dagui's
80 Shorton Grill
81 Boca del Lobo
82 Mama Clorindas
84 Il Risotto
88 Tex Mex
90 Grain de Café; Le Arcate
91 Art Forum Café
96 Fast Food Restaurants
97 La Guarida del Coyote
98 Sakti
99 Pavement Cafes
102 Rincón de Francia
103 Fried Bananas
105 El Arabe
108 Chifa Mayflower
113 Mágico Oriental
115 Costa Vasca
131 Churrascaría Tropeiro
132 Chifa Hong Kong
135 Mare Nostrum

OTHER

2 Sierra Nevada Expeditions
4 Emerald Forest Expeditions
5 Kem Pery Tours
7 Native Life
8 Sangay Touring
9 Galasam
10 Yuturi Jungle Adventure
11 TAME Office
12 Colombian Embassy
13 Banco de Guayaquil
14 Vivarium
15 Papillon
17 Panamericana
18 Branch Post Office
22 Mayo 68
23 Etnotur; Rainbow Laundry
24 Confederate Books
26 Papaya Net
27 Biking Dutchman
29 Sun City Laundry
32 Beraca
33 Dracaena
38 Patatu's Bar
40 Neotropic Turis
41 Scuba Iguana

42 Surtrek
43 Libro Express
45 Banco de Guayaquil
48 Clínica Pichincha
49 Ritmo Tropical
50 Dirección de Extranjería
53 Andinatel (Branch)
54 Libri Mundi; Galería
    Latina
56 Sambo.net
57 Atahualpa
60 Matrioshka; Wash & Go
64 La Sala
68 No Bar
72 Andinatel (Branch)
73 Cámara Provincial de Turismo
    de Pichincha Tourist Informa-
    tion Office
75 Productos Andinos
86 Arie's Bike Company
87 The Explorer
89 Los Alpes
92 Centro Artesanal
93 ekeko
94 Pamir
95 The Altar
100 Sani Lodge Office
101 Andísimo
104 La Bodega; Ag
106 La Cascada Mágica; Dr
    Rosenberg
109 La Reina Victoria
110 Police Station
111 MCCH
112 Rainforestur
116 Patio de Comedías
117 Metropolitan Touring Branch
    Office
118 Amazonas Spanish School
119 American Express; Ecuadorian
    Tours
120 Producambios
121 El Aborigen
122 Ecuafolklore
123 Transportes Ecuador
125 Mercado Artesanal La
    Mariscal
127 Bipo & Toni's
128 Cámara Provincial de Turismo
    de Pichincha Administration
    Office
129 Localiza

Guápulo

If you follow Avenida 12 de Octubre up the hill from the Mariscal, you'll reach the Hotel Quito at the top. Behind the hotel, stairs lead steeply down the other side of the hill to the neighborhood of El Guápulo, which is set in a precipitous valley. At the center of this small neighborhood stands the **sanctuary of El Guápulo** (*open 9am-noon daily*), built between 1644 and 1693. The church has an excellent collection of colonial art and sculpture of the Quito School, and the pulpit, carved by Juan Bautista Menacho in the early 18th century, is particularly noteworthy.

The best views of this delightful colonial church are from the lookout behind the Hotel

Quito, at the **statue of Francisco de Orellana** (*Calle Larrea near González Suárez*). The statue depicts Francisco de Orellana looking down into the valley that was the beginning of his epic journey from Quito to the Atlantic – the first descent of the Amazon by a European. The footpath down to Guápulo makes for a pleasant walk, although its somewhat strenuous coming back. You can also take the local No 21 Santo Domingo–Guápulo bus.

DANCING LESSONS
Learn to dance salsa or you'll spend a lot of time shoe-gazing anytime you hit one of Ecuador's many *salsotecas* (salsa nightclubs). Salsa is the dance of choice for most students, although merengue, cumbia and other Latin dances are taught. The following schools in the new town are both excellent:

Ritmo Tropical (☎ 222 7051, **e** ritmotropical5@ hotmail.com) Avenida 10 de Agosto 1792, Office 108. One-on-one lessons cost $5 per hour, group lessons $4 per hour. Classes are held 9am to 8pm Monday to Friday.
Tropical Dancing School (☎ 222 4713, **e** tropical dancing@hotmail.com) Foch E4-256 at Amazonas. One-on-one lessons cost $4 per hour, group lessons $3 per hour. Classes are held 10am to 7pm Monday to Friday.

LANGUAGE COURSES
Studying Spanish is the perfect excuse for a prolonged stay in Quito. There are dozens of Spanish schools with classes taught at all levels. Courses can last anywhere from a couple days to months or more. Most schools offer one-on-one instruction and can arrange accommodations with local families. Make sure you get what you want by visiting several schools before deciding. The SAE is a good source for further recommendations – see Information earlier in this chapter. Rates vary from about $4 to $10 per hour.

Amazonas Spanish School (☎ 252 7509, **w** www .eduamazonas.com) Jorge Washington 718 at Amazonas
Atahualpa (☎ 254 5914, 225 1229, **w** www .atahualpa.com) J Pinto 375 at JL Mera
Beraca (old town ☎ 228 8092) García Moreno 858; (new town ☎ 290 6642) Amazonas 1114; **e** beraca@interactive.net.ec
Bipo & Toni's (☎ 255 6614, 256 3309, **w** www .bipo.net) Jeronim Carrión E8-183 at Leonidas Plaza Gutiérrez

Instituto Superior de Español (☎ 222 3242, **w** www.instituto-superior.net) Darquea Terán 1650 near 10 de Agosto

SPECIAL EVENTS
As is the case throughout the rest of Ecuador, people celebrate New Year's Eve in Quito by burning elaborate, life-sized puppets (often representing politicians) in the streets at midnight. Carnaval, held the weekend before Ash Wednesday in February, is celebrated by intense water fights – no one is spared. Colorful religious processions are held during Semana Santa (Easter Week).

Throughout the first week of December, the founding of Quito is celebrated with bullfights at the Plaza de Toros, just beyond the intersection of Avenidas América and 10 de Agosto. The fiesta reaches its height on the night of December 6, when there is lots of dancing in the streets.

PLACES TO STAY
Fewer people stay in the old town these days, opting instead for the new town's more comfortable hotels, with their proximity to international restaurants, cybercafés, travel agencies and Quito's best nightlife. If you'd like a more traditional slice of Quito, and don't mind the absence of granola-and-cappuccino breakfasts around every corner, the old town might be for you. The lowest rates are in the old town, but there are plenty of cheap options in the new town too. In both areas you should always take a taxi anywhere you go after dark.

Many *hostales* (smaller, economically priced inns or hotels) offer discounts for stays of more than five days or so, but you have to ask. The more expensive hotels add a 12% or 22% tax – the rates given here include taxes, but ask at the better hotels.

December is a busy month in Quito, and things don't quiet down until after the Christmas/New Year period. Try not to arrive in the evening without a reservation if you wish to stay in a particular hotel during this time. July and August are busy with vacationers from North America and Europe – hotel prices may go up a bit then.

Old Town
Many cheap hotels (a couple of them are quite good value) are at the south end of the old town, on the streets heading toward the

bus terminal. Some travelers, particularly single women, may not feel comfortable staying in this area. It's fine during the daytime, but the area north of the Plaza Santo Domingo is safer.

Grand Hotel (☎ 228 0192; w www.geoci ties.com/grandhotelquito; Rocafuerte 1001; singles/doubles with shared bath $3.50/6, with private bath $5.50/10) is a large and secure, family-run place popular with backpackers. Rooms are simple, but they're clean and have hot showers.

La Posada Colonial (☎ 228 2859, fax 250 5240; Paredes 188; singles/doubles $5/10) is another of the old town's better hotels. It's a simple place with saggy beds, but it's very friendly, clean and safe (and a bit more personal than the Grand Hotel). The showers are hot, too.

Hotel Reina de Quito (☎/fax 295 0347; Maldonado 2648; rooms with bath per person $5), south of the bus terminal, boasts a Jacuzzi and sauna (which aren't always on), as well as a restaurant and a guest kitchen.

Hotel Huasi Continental (☎ 295 7327; Flores 332; singles/doubles with shared bath $4/7, with private bath $6/11) is a friendly place with spartan but clean modernish rooms. Beds are firm.

Hotel Montúfar (☎ 228 4644; Sucre 160; singles/doubles with shared warm bath $3/4, with warm bath & TV $5/6) has three floors of small, dark rooms around an empty interior courtyard.

Hostal Belmont (☎/fax 295 6235; e hbel monte@waccom.net.ec; Antepara 413; singles/ doubles $3/6) is cheap and offers kitchen privileges, but the rooms are boxy, dark and stuffy.

Hostal La Casona (☎ 258 8809; Manabí 255; singles/doubles $6/9) occupies an interesting colonial building with three floors of dark, clean rooms with hot baths, opening onto a dimly lit, covered courtyard.

Hotel Catedral Internacional (☎ 295 5438; Mejía 638; singles/doubles with private showers & TV $7/12) is a decent hotel with dark, spacious and slightly musty rooms.

Hotel Internacional Plaza del Teatro (☎ 295 9462, 295 4293; Guayaquil N8-75; singles/ doubles $8/14), across from the Plaza del Teatro, maintains some of its old elegance with its marble staircase, wide hallways and balconied rooms with hot baths. The off-street rooms lack balconies but are much quieter.

Hotel Viena Internacional (☎ 295 4860; Flores 600; singles/doubles with bath $12/24) offers a touch of comfort in the old town. Large carpeted rooms all have telephones, TV, bathrooms and hot water, and some have balconies.

Hotel San Francisco de Quito (☎ 228 7758; e hsfquito@andinanet.net; Sucre 217; singles/doubles with private bath $14/24, miniapartments with kitchenettes $18/25) is the most attractive hotel in the old town. Its spotless rooms (some with lofts) have a telephone, TV, private baths and constant hot water. Because it's a colonial building, rooms lack windows but open onto a lovely flowery courtyard. There's a good restaurant below, and breakfast is included in the price. Use of the sauna and Jacuzzi costs $1.50 extra.

Hotel Real Audiencia (☎ 295 2711; w www .realaudiencia.com; Bolívar Oe-3-18; singles/ doubles $26/37), near the northern corner of Plaza Santo Domingo, is the priciest hotel in the old town. It has large clean rooms with bath, phone and TV. Many rooms have views, and the service is excellent. The price includes breakfast in the top-floor restaurant, which has unbeatable views over the Plaza Santo Domingo.

Between the Old & New Towns

L'Auberge Inn (☎ 255 2912; w www.ioda .net/auberge-inn; Avenida Colombia N12-200; singles/doubles with shared bath $6/12, with private bath $9/15) is a comfortable hostal with spotless rooms, a small garden area, an onsite travel agency, a common room with a fireplace, a games room and an excellent pizzeria. You can arrange to be picked up from the airport.

Hostal Bambú (☎ 222 6738; G Solano 1758 near Avenida Colombia; rooms per person $5-10) is a gem of a hostal, with spacious rooms and a welcoming atmosphere. It boasts a guest kitchen, a small library, laundry facilities and outstanding views from the hammocks on the roof.

Residencial Marsella (☎/fax 295 5884; Los Ríos 2035; rooms per person $4-6), about a block south of Parque La Alameda, has an empty rooftop terrace and 35 clean rooms (which vary widely in quality) with shared baths and thin mattresses.

Margarita II (☎ 295 0441; Los Ríos 1995; singles/doubles with bath $5/8), just east of

Parque La Alameda, is a popular, no-frills hotel with four floors of clean, simple rooms with private bath and TV.

New Town

Budget The friendly and popular **Hostal Vamara** (☎ 222 6425; e hostalvamara@yahoo.com; Foch 753 & Amazonas; dorm beds $3, private rooms with shared bath per person $6, with private bath & TV per person $8) has some of the cheapest dorm beds in town and is well run and clean.

El Centro del Mundo (☎/fax 222 9050; e centrodelmundo@hotmail.com; L García 569, E7-22; dorm beds $5, singles/doubles with private bath $9/16) is run by travelers (an Ecuadorian and French-Canadian couple) for travelers and features cable TV, home cooking, kitchen privileges, lots of information and a party reputation. Rooms come with breakfast.

Tortuga Verde (☎ 556 829, fax 227 882; cnr JL Mera & J Pinto; dorm beds per person $5) is a busy little place that some love and others prefer to leave. It's worth a look. The clean dorm rooms sleep six and have lockers. There's a TV lounge and a travel agency below.

El Cafecito (☎ 223 4862; e cafecito@ecuadorexplorer.com; Cordero E6-43; dorm beds $6, singles/doubles $9/14), over the café of the same name, is popular with budget travelers. Rooms are clean, the place has a mellow vibe and the excellent café below is very convenient (see Cafés under Places to Eat later). There are a few doubles and several rooms with four or six beds; bathrooms are shared.

Albergue El Taxo (☎/fax 222 5593; e acordova@ramt.com; Foch E4-116; dorm beds $5, singles/doubles with shared bath $10/14) is a converted house with hammocks and a bar out front (and a small stage for music on its way). Rooms are a bit shabby (which goes with the relaxed atmosphere) and have shared baths. The common area, adorned with funky art, is dimly lit and has a fireplace.

Hostelling International Ecuador (☎ 254 3995; J Pinto 325, E16-12; dorm beds $6-7, singles/doubles with private bath $11/18) is Quito's only HI-affiliated youth hostel. It's impersonal but spotless, with four floors of usually empty rooms. There's a guest kitchen, and breakfast is included.

Magic Bean (☎ 256 6181; w www.ecuadorexplorer.com/magic/home; Foch E5-08; dorm beds $7, singles/doubles/triples with bath $25/29/36), above the popular restaurant of the same name (see Cafés under Places to Eat later), has two private rooms and one dorm room. The place is clean, popular, and smack in the middle of the Mariscal. Prices include breakfast. It also has mid-range rooms available.

Hostal Amazonas Inn (☎ 222 5723, 222 2666; J Pinto E4-324 & Amazonas; singles/doubles/triples $9/18/27) is excellent value. The rooms are straightforward and spotless, with private baths, constant hot water and cable TV; those on the 1st floor have windows. The staff are friendly, the location is central and there's a café connected to the hotel. It's a tough one to beat.

Crossroads (☎/fax 223 4735; w www.crossroadshostal.com; Foch E5-23; dorm beds $5.50-6.60, doubles with shared bath $24.50, singles/doubles with private bath $15.50/27) is a well-kept, popular hotel in a converted house. Facilities include a good café, cable TV, kitchen and a patio with a fireplace.

Posada del Maple (☎ 254 4507; w www.posadadelmaple.com; Rodríguez E8-49; dorm beds $6.50, singles/doubles with shared bath $12/20.50, singles with private bath $14.50-18.50, doubles with private bath $22.50-33) is a comfortable, friendly hotel in a lovely little historic house. The street is quiet and tree-lined.

Hostal Alcalá (☎ 222 7396; w www.alcalahostal.com; Cordero E5-48; dorm beds $6.50, singles $15-18, doubles $27) is owned by the same folks as the Maple and provides similarly comfortable accommodations and friendly service. Prices for both places include a buffet breakfast. Ask about their minisuites with kitchenettes.

Loro Verde (☎ 222 6173; Rodríguez E7-66; singles/doubles $8/14) boasts spacious rooms with baths and a great location on a leafy street in the Mariscal.

El Vagabundo (☎ 222 6376; e vagabundo ecuador@hotmail.com; Wilson E7-45; rooms per person $8) offers clean but dull rooms that have private bath and hot water. It's a good deal, and people like it for its friendly owners and attached pizzeria.

Hostal Raices (☎ 223 4355, 223 6432; JL Tamayo N21-255; singles/doubles $12/20) is a small, attractively decorated hotel with a cable TV lounge. Most rooms have private bath, and breakfast is included.

Villa Nancy B&B (☎ 256 3084; e villa_nancy@yahoo.com; Jeronim Carrión 335; singles/doubles $18/25) is a Ecuadorian/Swiss-owned B&B in a quiet area. The building has a sort of simple schoolhouse feel, but it's quite comfortable, and the rooms (all but one with shared bath) are spacious. It has a grassy garden, and the friendly, multilingual owners offer airport pickup. A buffet breakfast is included.

La Casa de Eliza (☎ 222 6602; e manteca@uio.satnet.net; Isabel La Católica N24-679; dorm beds $5, doubles $10) is a homey place (it's a converted house after all) with a big guest kitchen, a sociable common area and modest, comfortable rooms. Breakfast is available for $1 extra. Eliza, the owner, arranges excellent treks through northern Ecuador in association with the Cerro Golondrinas Cloud Forest Conservation Project (see the boxed text 'The Cerro Golondrinas Project' in the Northern Highlands chapter).

La Casona de Mario (☎ 254 4036, 223 0129; e lacasona@punto.net.ec; Andalucía N24-115; rooms per person $7) is in an attractive old house with a garden and TV lounge. Guests have laundry and kitchen privileges.

El Ciprés (☎/fax 254 9558, 254 9561; e elcipres@hotmail.com; Lérida 381; rooms per person without bath $7, singles/doubles with private bath $14/18) is in the quiet neighborhood of La Floresta. It has a big garden, friendly owners, spotless rooms, good beds, a TV lounge, Internet access and complimentary continental breakfast. You can be picked up at the airport if you plan to stay a few nights.

Parque Italia (☎ 462 823, fax 224 393; w www.ecuador-travel.net/B&B.htm; Narvaez Oe5-12; rooms per person with shared/private bath $8/12) is a pleasant B&B, in a quiet area, operated by an Ecuadorian/Austrian couple. It has a good café and pleasant rooms, some of them with terraces. Weekly rates are available.

Hostal La Casa de Guápulo (☎ 222 0473; w www.ecuasearch.com/lacasadeguapulo; Leonidas Plaza Gutiérrez 257; rooms per person without/with bath $9/11) is in the historical residential district of Guápulo, east of the new town. It makes for a lovely stay in a colonial neighborhood away from the hustle and bustle of the rest of the city. French, English and Spanish are spoken. Rates include breakfast.

Other hotels offering good value in the new town include: **Hostal Alpa Aligu** (☎ 256 4012; e alpaaligu@yahoo.com; J Pinto 240; dorm beds per person $4); **Hostal Mundo Net** (☎ 223 0411; e mundonet@netscape.net; J Pinto E6-32; dorm beds/private rooms $3.50/5); **Dagui's** (☎ 222 8151; e davidcando@hotmail.com; J Calamá E6-05; shared rooms per person $5); **Hotel Pickett** (☎/fax 541 453, 551 205; Wilson 712; singles/doubles $12/16); **Hostal Dé jà vu** (☎ 222 4483; e dejavu_hostal@hotmail.com; 9 de Octubre 599; dorm beds $5, singles/doubles $8/12, with private bath $10/15); **Hotel Viena** (☎ 235 418; JL Tamayo 879; singles/doubles with private bath $8/16); and **Hotel 9 de Octubre** (☎ 255 2424/2524; 9 de Octubre 1047; singles/doubles $9/12).

Mid-Range If you want to stay near but not in Quito, see Around Quito later in this chapter for several other mid-range suggestions.

Casa Helbling (☎ 222 6013; w www.casahelbling.de; General Veintimilla E18-166; singles/doubles with shared bath $10/16, with private bath $14/24) is in a homey, colonial-style house in the Mariscal. It's clean, relaxed, friendly and has a guest kitchen, laundry facilities and plenty of common areas for chilling out.

Rincón de Bavaria (☎ 250 9401; e atrios@ramt.com; U Páez 232; singles/doubles with private bath $15/25) is a small, family-run hotel with carpeted rooms that have private hot baths and TV. It's a bit tattered around the edges, but comfortable, and breakfast comes included in the price.

La Casa Sol (☎ 223 0798; w www.lacasasol.com; J Calamá E8-66; singles/doubles $18/31; suites with kitchen $26/44) is an immaculate, bright-orange B&B with two floors of small rooms opening onto a tiny courtyard. Guests rave about the place, and the staff are helpful. Rates include breakfast.

Hostal Charles Darwin (☎ 223 4323; e chdarwin@ecuanex.net.ec; La Colina 304; singles/doubles $26/36) is an intimate hotel in a stylish modern house (think 1960s) on a quiet street. Rooms are dark but comfortable and have private bath and cable TV. Extras include a small garden, Internet access, kitchen facilities, laundry service, friendly owners and the company of two big dogs. Rates include breakfast.

Hostal Palm Garten (☎ 252 3960, 252 6263; 9 de Octubre 923; singles/doubles $25/ 37), in a converted mansion, is small and pleasant and has comfortable and attractive rooms with TV and telephone.

Orange Guesthouse (☎ 255 6960; e info@ enchantedexpeditions.com; Foch 726; singles/ doubles $27.50/34) has eight pleasant rooms, each with private bath. Rates include breakfast.

Hostal Fuente de Piedra (☎ 252 5314; w www.ecuahotel.com; Wilson 211 & JL Tamayo; singles/doubles $25/35) is an attractive 19-room hostal in an older building. Rooms are heavy on the floral decor, but they're comfy.

Hostal de La Rábida (☎ 222 2169; w www.hostalrabida.com; La Rábida 227; singles/doubles $46/59) is in a lovely converted house with an immaculate white-wall interior and fresh, carpeted rooms. There's a tiny bar/lounge and a restaurant serving delicacies such as filet chateaubriand and crepes suzette (for guests only). The 10 rooms have private hot baths and cable TV. Parking and a laundry service are available.

La Cartuja (☎ 252 3577; Leonidas Plaza Gutiérrez 170; singles/doubles with bath $43/ 57) is a small hotel in an older mansion with a dozen crisp yellow rooms, each of them unique. The highlight is the grassy interior garden with lounge chairs and plenty of sun. Breakfast is included.

Hotel Vieja Cuba (☎ 252 0738; e vieja cuba@andinanet.net; Diego de Almagro 1212; singles/doubles $47/57, suites $67) is a stunning new hotel with masterfully designed, refreshing rooms. Two rooms have fireplaces, and the two tower suites are delightfully comfortable. The theme is colonial Cuba, and the entire hotel has a colorful feel. A bank of additional rooms were still being finished in back when we stopped in. The attached Cuban restaurant is outstanding (see Places to Eat later in this chapter).

Hostal Los Alpes (☎ 256 1110; e alpes@ accessinter.net; JL Tamayo 223; singles/doubles $40/50) is a real beauty. The common area and restaurant of this restored house are filled with art and artefacts, giving the whole place an artsy Latin American feel. The comfortable carpeted rooms have spotless bathrooms and a telephone. The rates

include an American breakfast. The restaurant is excellent. Reservations are advised.

Café Cultura (☎/fax 222 4271; w www .cafecultura.com; Francisco Robles 513; singles/ doubles $55/66) is another charming hotel in a converted mansion with a garden. It is above the restaurant of the same name (see Cafés under Places to Eat later). The beautifully painted public areas feature three fireplaces. The rooms are very comfortable and are attractively and individually decorated. The onsite travel office makes reservations for a dozen other unique hotels throughout Ecuador. Travelers love this place and reservations are advised.

Suites González Suárez (☎ 223 2003, 222 4417; w www.sgshotel.com; San Ignacio 2750 & González Suárez; singles/doubles $48/72) is a sophisticated little hotel perched on the hill overlooking Guápulo. Views from many of the rooms are excellent. It's a quiet place, and the price includes a buffet breakfast and airport pickup.

Hostal Villa Nancy (☎ 550 839, 562 473, fax 562 483; e npelaez@pi.pro.ec; Muros 146; singles $40-50, doubles $70), in a mid- to upper-class residential area east of Mariscal Sucre, is an excellent choice if you don't mind being a bit removed from the action. The place has superb staff and there is always a helpful, English-speaking person on duty. The hotel features a sundeck, a Scandinavian sauna, a small garden, a lobby bar with free coffee and a breakfast room. The 13 rooms are spotless and have plenty of hot water and private showers, a hair-dryer, minifridge, writing desk, phone, cable TV and a morning newspaper. Rates include airport transfers and a self-serve buffet continental breakfast. The friendly owner, Nancy, speaks impeccable French and English and is normally around during breakfast, chatting with guests and making sure everyone is happy.

Hostería San Jorge (☎/fax 256 5964, 223 9287; w www.hostsanjorge.com.ec; singles/ doubles $50/60, suites $85) is the place to choose if you want to stay in an old hacienda on a mountain overlooking Quito. The 25-room hostería (small hotel), once owned by 19th-century Ecuadorian President Eloy Alfaro, is 4km west of Avenida Occidental, on the road to Nono. It's situated at an altitude of 3200m and is on the flanks of Rucu Pichincha. The hacienda has over 30 hectares and is suitable for hiking, horse riding, bird-watching and mountain biking – all of which can be arranged for a fee. The hiking is good acclimatization for folks wanting to climb Ecuador's major peaks. There is an indoor heated pool, sauna, whirlpool and steam room, as well as pleasant gardens. A restaurant serves local and international food, and a bar features a pool table, darts and other games for relaxing after an active day. All rooms have rustic fireplaces and hot showers. Airport pickup costs $10 and all meals are available at moderate rates.

Top End All top-end hotels are in the new town. Hotels in this category compare with 1st-class hotels anywhere in the world. Although luxury hotels are popular with businesspeople and tour groups, their inflated rates place them beyond the price range of most independent travelers. Most of Quito's luxury hotels offer cheaper rates to walk-in guests than they do when booked from abroad (provided, of course, there are rooms). It's worth popping in if you're out for a splurge – you might find a decent deal.

Hotel Sebastián (☎ 222 2300/400/500; **e** hsebast1@hsebastian.com.ec; Diego de Almagro 822; singles/doubles $59/69, suites $74/84) has about 50 good-sized rooms and seven suites – many with balconies and some with great views. Rooms all feature cable TV, direct-dial phones, room service, desks and attractive furnishings. The fruits and vegetables served in the coffee shop and restaurant are organically grown. There is a cozy bar with a fireplace and two meeting rooms.

Hotel Quito (☎ 254 4600; **e** hotelquito@ orotels.com; González Suárez N27-142; standard singles/doubles $73/85, business class singles/doubles $85/110) is a Quito landmark, set high on the hill above Guápulo, northeast of the Mariscal. Although its heyday was in the 1960s (as its minimalist design makes clear), it's still a classy place and the views from its rooms (and from the bar, the restaurant, the lobby and the outdoor swimming pool) are unbeatable. It's a modern hotel, but it has a nostalgic romance that other luxury hotels lack.

Mansión del Ángel (☎ 255 7721, fax 223 7819; USA & Canada toll free ☎ 1-800-327-3573; Wilson E5-29; singles/doubles $65/105)

is an intimate and attractive boutique hotel in a refurbished colonial-style home. Rooms are elegantly furnished with curtained four-poster brass beds, and there is a rooftop garden. Rates include continental breakfast.

Hilton Colón (☎ 256 1333, 256 0666; **w** www.hiltoncolon.com; Amazonas & Avenida Patria; singles/doubles low season from $158/183; high season from $193/220) is Quito's premier luxury hotel. Besides its fabulous location, it has everything you might need for a luxurious stay – a pool, sauna, massage parlor, exercise room, discotheque, casino, salons, a small shopping mall, a 24-hour coffee shop, several cafés and restaurants, two bars and numerous meeting rooms. The Colón is one of the capital's main social centers and this is where many visiting dignitaries stay. Its central location also makes it one of upper-class Quito's most lively meeting places. Almost all of the 450 rooms have good views of Quito – head up to the 20th floor and walk out onto the roof for a great view. The rooms here vary in size, but all have cable TVs, telephones, desks and spacious bathrooms.

Swissôtel (☎ 256 7600, 256 6497; **w** www.swissotel.com; Avenida 12 de Octubre 1820; rooms from $115) is a 240-room luxury hotel with all the amenities you could possibly want (including pool, gym, excellent restaurants and a casino). More expensive suites are available.

Radisson Royal Quito (☎ 223 3333; **w** www.radisson.com/quitoec; Cordero 444; rooms from $120) is directly across from the Swissôtel and next door to the World Trade Center. It caters primarily, although not exclusively, to the business crowd. The rooms are large and pristine, but the restaurants aren't as interesting as those in other luxury hotels.

JW Marriott Hotel (☎/fax 297 2000; **e** anamarriott@hotmail.com; **w** www.marriott.com; Orellana 1172 & Amazonas; rooms from $150) stands out – architecturally anyway – more than any other hotel in town. It's the monstrous, modern, pyramid-like structure on Amazonas. It's the priciest in town and everything is tops.

Apartments & Homestays

Visitors wanting to stay for a longer time may want to rent a room, apartment or suite with a kitchen. Many apartments require a one-month minimum stay, although we've listed some here that can be rented daily or weekly as well. The SAE has a noticeboard full of shared-housing advertisements (see Information earlier in this chapter).

Residencial Casa Oriente (☎ 254 6157; *Yaguachi 824; singles/doubles per month $100/125)* has simple rooms with kitchen privileges and a rooftop terrace overlooking the city.

Alberto's House (☎ 222 4603; e *alberto house@hotmail.com; L García 648; rooms per week/month $35/100)* has facilities that include shared hot showers, a laundry room, kitchen privileges, a TV lounge, a pool table and a garden with a barbecue area. It's a popular place.

The following apartments offer daily rates.

Amaranta Apart Hotel (☎ 254 3619, fax 256 0586; e *amaranta@interactive.net; Leonidas Plaza Gutiérrez N20-32; singles/ doubles $41/52)* has well-equipped but small apartments that come with breakfast.

Antinea Apart Hotel (☎ 250 6838, fax 250 4404; e *hotelant@access.net.ec; Rodríguez 175; singles/doubles $48/54)* has lovely furnished apartments.

Hotel San Francisco de Quito (☎ 228 7758; e *hsfquito@andinanet.net; Sucre 217; singles/doubles/triples $18/25/45)* rents a few modern apartments over their hotel near Plaza Santo Domingo in the old town. See the Old Town under Places to Stay earlier in this chapter.

If you'd like to stay in a local home, stop by the SAE for their long list of families interested in hosting travelers (see Information earlier). The local classifieds are also helpful in finding homestays. If you are taking Spanish courses, ask at your school. Prices average between $5 and $15 per person per day, and sometimes include meals and laundry service. English is not always spoken.

PLACES TO EAT

If you're pinching your pennies, always ask about *almuerzos* and *meriendas* (set lunch and dinner menus, respectively) that are sold in most restaurants, particularly those used by locals. These set meals usually cost $1 to $3 and are often not shown on the menu. Almuerzos and *meriendas* are more difficult to find on weekends because they're aimed at working people. Many restaurants are closed Sunday.

In the most expensive restaurants, two people can dine well for about $30 or $40 (not including wine, which would add at least $10 per bottle).

Old Town

There are few restaurants of note in the old town, although this is where the cheapest places are found.

Café Quiteño Libre *(Sucre 217; almuerzos $1.30, mains $2-3; open 8am-5pm Mon-Sat),* in the brick-wall cellar of the Hotel San Francisco de Quito (see Places to Stay earlier), does a booming lunchtime business. Almuerzos are cheap, tasty and fresh.

Nuevo Cordovéz (☎ 295 5200; *Guayaquil 774; almuerzos $1.40-1.75, mains $2-3; open 8am-8pm Mon-Sat),* is a downtown family eatery with colorful booths and a bullfighting theme. The set meals are good and menu items include the usual Ecuadorian standards.

King Chicken (☎ 295 6655; *Bolívar 236; mains $2-4; open 10am-9:30pm Mon-Sat)* measures up to its name, serving good fried chicken to hungry families in a diner-like atmosphere complete with an organ player. There are plenty of other dishes on the menu too, including big ice-cream sundaes.

El Criollo (☎ 228 9828; *Flores N7-31; mains $2-3.50; open 8am-9pm daily)* is another good, clean place for Ecuadorian standards. *Yaguarlocro* (potato and blood-sausage soup) is served on Saturdays and *caldo de patas* (cow-foot soup) on Sundays – two classic dishes.

Tianguez *(Plaza San Francisco; mains $3-5; open 9am-6pm daily),* under the Monastery of San Francisco, is run by the Fundación Sinchi Sacha (see Mariscal & Around under Things to See & Do earlier). It serves snacks, juices and well-prepared Ecuadorian specialties. In good weather, there are tables outside – an unbeatable location for lunch.

Govinda (☎ 295 1083; *Esmeraldas 853; mains $1-3; open 8am-4pm Mon-Sat),* run by the Hare Krishnas, serves delicious vegetarian meals. They whip out everything from soy-egg breakfasts to vegie lasagne. There's no sign; look for the blue paint job and the Vaisnava Academy bookstore.

La Cueva del Oso (☎ 258 3826; *Chile 1046; mains $5-10; open noon-midnight Mon-Sat,*

Palacio del Gobierno, Quito

Monastery of San Francisco, Quito

Plaza de la Independencia, Quito

Inside the Monastery of San Francisco, Quito

Entertaining the crowds, Quito old town

Dressing up for a fiesta, Quito

La Virgen de Quito, El Panecillo, Quito

Selling flowers, Quito

noon-4pm Sun) is the most elegant, and arguably the best, restaurant in the old town, serving exquisitely prepared Ecuadorian specialties. The high, old-fashioned, pressed-tin ceilings and photos of old Quito add a touch of the past to your repast.

Las Cuevas de Luís Candela *(☎ 228 7710; Benalcázar 713 & Chile; mains $6-10; open 11am-6:30pm Mon-Sat)* is an atmospheric old Spanish restaurant built in the vaulted cellar of an old building. It's been around since 1963. The bullfighters Manolo and Manolete both ate here, and the toilet (the first of its kind in the old town) was inaugurated by President Arosemena (be sure to take a…look).

Balcón Quiteño *(☎ 251 2711; mains $4-8),* above the Hotel Real Audiencia, is worth a try for decent dining and good views over the Plaza Santo Domingo.

Heladería San Agustín *(☎ 228 5082; Guayaquil 1053; open 9am-5:30pm Mon-Sat)* is an absolute must for ice cream fans. The Alvarez Andino family has been making *helados de paila* (ice cream that's been handmade in big copper bowls) here for over 140 years. Try the *leche y mora* (cream and blackberry).

If you just need to fill the belly with something wholesome, try **Rincón Azuayo** *(Espejo 812; open 8am-6pm daily)* for standard dishes, or **Frutería Botero** *(Espejo 832; open 8am-8pm Mon-Sat)* for light meals and juices. For breakfast, coffee, ice cream and light eats, try the popular **Café Modelo** *(cnr Sucre & García Moreno; open 8am-8pm daily).* **Café Niza** *(Venezuela near Sucre)* opens at 7:30am and is always busy for its good, cheap breakfasts – share a table.

New Town

If you're willing to splash out a bit, you can have a lot of fun feeding your face in the new town. If you're on a budget, look for little eateries tucked away on side streets and offering set meals – the food is usually unexciting but good value. If you want inexpensive fast food, walk down Jeronim Carrión, east of Amazonas; several places there whip out burgers and other artery-blockers such as *papi pollo* (fried chicken and French fries) and *salchipapas* (sausage and fries). Make sure that your burger is thoroughly cooked and hot – the hygiene is questionable in these joints.

Traditional Ecuadorian A modest, friendly restaurant serving good national specialties at reasonable prices is **Mama Clorindas** *(☎ 254 4362; Reina Victoria 1144; meals $2-3).* The almuerzos cost about $5 so you're just as well off ordering from the menu. It's a great choice for lunch. *Cuy* (roast guinea pig) is on the menu, too.

La Choza *(☎ 223 0839; Avenida 12 de Octubre 1821; mains $4-7; open noon-4pm & 7pm-10pm Mon-Fri, noon-4pm Sat & Sun)* serves delicious Ecuadorian food in colorful, elegant surroundings. Expect to pay about $15 for a complete meal.

Rincón La Ronda *(☎ 245 0459; Bello Horizonte 400; open noon-11pm daily)* offers quality food and excellent service in a beautifully decorated dining room.

Seafood Ecuador is justly famous for its *ceviche* (marinated, uncooked seafood).

Las Redes *(☎ 252 5691; Amazonas 845; mains $5-13)* is one of the city's best cevicherías. Try the *ceviche mixta* (mixed uncooked seafood); it's huge and delicious and costs about $10.

Su Cebiche *(☎ 252 6380; JL Mera N24-200; mains $4-7; open 9am-5pm daily)* serves excellent coastal specialties. Try the *sopa marinera,* a delicious mixed-seafood soup, or one of seven types of ceviches. It's best for lunch.

Mare Nostrum *(☎ 223 7236, 256 3639; Foch 172; mains $7-15; open noon-10pm Tues-Sat),* in a rather Gothic castle-like building, is popular, pricey and delicious.

Cevicheria y Marisquería 7 Mares *(La Niña 525; mains $1-5; open 7:45am-5:30pm daily)* is the place to go for cheap *encebollado* (a tasty seafood, onion and yucca soup). Bowls – served cafeteria-style – are only $1 and make an excellent breakfast or lunch.

La Jaiba Mariscos *(☎ 254 3887; Avenida Cristobal Colón 870)* is another excellent upscale seafood restaurant.

Cevichería Viejo José *(☎ 254 0187; General Veintimilla 1254; meals around $3; open daily),* run by folks from Manabí Province, serves good-quality coastal dishes at comfortable prices.

Latin American With its wooden tables and graffiti-covered walls, **La Bodeguita de Cuba** *(☎ 254 2476; Reina Victoria 1721; mains $3-5; open noon-4pm & 7pm-10pm*

Tues-Fri, noon-midnight Sat & Sun) is a superb place for Cuban food and lots of fun. The bar comes alive at night, especially on Thursdays, when Cuban musicians perform to a standing-room-only crowd, and the bar stays open till 2am.

Varadero (☎ 254 2575; *Reina Victoria 1721; mains $3-4; open noon-2am Mon-Sat)*, owned by the same folks as La Bodeguita, serves Cuban sandwiches and light meals and has live music on Wednesday, Friday and Saturday nights.

Orisha (☎ 252 0738; *Diego de Almagro 1212; mains $4-7; open noon-4pm & 7pm-midnight Tues-Sun)* is a cozy little Cuban restaurant with Yoruba crafts adorning the walls and excellent food on the menu.

La Guarida del Coyote (☎ 250 3293; *Jeronim Carrión 619; mains $3-6; open noon-11pm Mon-Sat)* prepares excellent Mexican food, and probably has the most authentic – or at least diverse – Mexican menu in town. The tavern-like atmosphere is great, too.

Red Hot Chili Peppers (☎ 255 7575; *Foch 713; mains $4-6; open noon-10:30pm Mon-Sat, noon-3pm Sun)* serves some delicious Mexican dishes, especially the fajitas. Wash it all down with their famous daiquiris. Skip the enchiladas.

Tex Mex (☎ 252 7689; *Reina Victoria 847; mains $3-6; open 12:30pm-11:30pm daily)* is a colorful place serving tasty plates of 'Americanized' Mexican cuisine – that is, food from the Texas–Mexican border. It's good stuff.

Café Tequila (☎ 244 6288; *Avenida Eloy Alfaro 2897)* is another trendy Tex-Mex restaurant and bar.

Churrascaría Tropeiro (☎ 254 8012; *General Veintimilla 546; mains $4-8)* is Brazilian and is a good place to go if you are hungry – especially for meat.

Chinese *Chifas* (Chinese restaurants) are popular in Ecuador, and Quito has several good ones. The following are only a sample.

Mágico Oriental (☎ 222 6767; *U Páez 243; mains $3-10; open noon-3:30pm & 6pm-10:30pm daily)* is elegant, classy and authentic, serving delicious dishes that average around $6.50 each.

Pekin (☎ 223 5273; *Whymper N28-42; mains $4.50-8; open noon-3pm & 7pm-10:30pm Mon-Sat, noon-8:30pm Sun)* has a slightly conservative air, but the owners are friendly and the food is good. The menu includes three types of frogs' legs.

Two other Chinese restaurants are **Chifa Mayflower** (☎ 254 0510; *Jeronim Carrión 442; meals from $3)* and **Casa China** (☎ 252 2115; *Cordero 613; mains about $4; open 11am-3pm & 6:30pm-10:30pm daily)*, which are both good and reasonably priced. **Chifa Hong Kong** (☎ 222 3313; *Wilson 246)* is a little more expensive, but the food's delicious.

French & Swiss These restaurants are pricey but they're excellent. Tourists are fine in their travel wear, but expect the locals to be dressed to the nines. Reservations are recommended.

Rincón de Francia (☎ 222 5053; *Vicente Ramón Roca 779)* is one of the best-known French restaurants in town and has been for decades. A full meal will cost at least $20 and twice that if you dip into the wine.

Ile de France (☎ 255 3292; *Reina Victoria 1747; mains $8-15; open 12:30pm-3pm & 6pm-midnight daily)* is the place for fondues, with over a dozen variations on the menu. It also has six types of raclette. Expensive but worth it.

Los Alpes (*Avenida 12 de Octubre 1820; mains $7-15; open noon-3pm & 7pm-11pm daily; tea buffet 4pm-6:30pm Mon-Fri)* serves delicious fondues ($8 to $10), as well as main courses such as veal and poached salmon. The weekday tea buffet ($8) is a perfect opportunity to stuff yourself with chocolate fondue, cakes, cookies, truffles, coffee and tea.

La Creperie (☎ 222 6780; *J Calamá 362; mains about $6)*, a casual café, specializes in both dinner and dessert crepes, but also serves other dishes such as goulash and steak.

Italian You'll be hard-pressed to find better Italian food than you'll find at **La Briciola** (☎ 254 7138; *Toledo 1255; mains $6-10; open 12:30pm-3pm & 7:30pm-11pm Mon-Sat)*. It's a longtime favorite, with an outstanding and varied menu and friendly waiters with thick Italian accents. The portions are large and the wine is fairly priced. Make a reservation if you hope to eat before 9:30pm.

Trattoria Sole e Luna (☎ 223 5865; *Whymper N31-29 & Coruña; mains $6-8; open noon-4pm & 7pm-10:30pm Mon-Sat)* is an excellent new restaurant with a delightful nouveau-Italian atmosphere and friendly service. It's great for lunch, and the risotto is tops.

Il Risotto (☎ 222 0400; J Pinto 209; mains $5-15; open noon-3pm & 6pm-11pm Tues-Sun) has a small, elegant dining room (but the kind of atmosphere that makes you want to linger for hours after your meal) and delicious food. It's probably the best in the Mariscal.

Pavarotti (☎ 256 6668; Avenida 12 de Octubre N24-551; mains $5-11; open noon-3:30pm & 7pm-midnight Mon-Sat) is more formal and subdued than the previous two places, serving sophisticated Italian dishes aimed at business diners and well-heeled tourists.

Le Arcate (☎ 223 7659; General Baquedano 358; mains $4-6; open 11am-3pm & 6pm-11pm Tues-Sun) bakes over 50 kinds of pizza (likely the best around) in a wood-fired oven and serves reasonably priced lasagne, steak and seafood.

Art Forum Café (☎ 252 3756; JL Mera 870; mains $3-5; open 9am-8pm Mon-Sat, 9am-4pm Sun) is good for unpretentious pasta lunches served at outdoor tables.

El Hornero (☎ 542 518; General Veintimilla 1149; pizza per person $2.50-4; open noon-11pm daily) is a popular national chain whipping out tasty, cheap wood-oven pizzas.

Japanese There are several excellent Japanese restaurants in town.

Sake (☎ 252 4818; P Rivet N30-166; open 12:30pm-3pm & 6:30pm-11pm Mon-Sat, 6:30-9pm Sun) is Quito's premier (and most expensive) sushi restaurant. It's a trendy, slightly upscale place, and the food is absolutely sublime. Reservations are a must on weekends.

Shogún (☎ 290 6200; JL Mera E5-134; complete meal about $15-20 per person; open 12:30pm-4pm & 6pm-late Mon-Sat) serves delicious sushi and other Japanese specialties. It's convenient and fun, the food is always fresh, and the stylish atmosphere (and big squishy chairs) suck you right in.

Tanoshi (☎ 256 7600; Avenida 12 de Octubre 1820; mains $15-25; open noon-3pm & 7pm-midnight daily) has a long, expensive menu and a reputation for excellent quality.

Spanish Spanish restaurants tend to be elegant, pricey and popular with the upper class and smartly dressed businesspeople. The food is high quality.

La Vieja Castilla (☎ 256 6979; La Pinta 435; mains $7-18; open 12:30pm-3pm Mon-Fri year-round) has an unusual flowery dining room, but it serves some of the best Spanish food in town. Call ahead for dinner, which is by reservation only from January to June and October and November – you can just walk in off the street during the other months.

Costa Vasca (☎ 252 3827; 18 de Septiembre 553; mains $7-20; open noon-3pm & 6pm-10:30pm Mon-Sat) is excellent, formal and expensive.

La Paella Valenciana (☎ 222 8681; Diego de Almagro 1727; mains $8-20) serves knockout Spanish seafood plates, including excellent paella (hence the name). Portions are gigantic.

Steakhouses & Grills For the highest-quality, imported Argentinean beef, try **San Thelmo** (☎ 243 4128, 225 6739; Portugal 570). It's expensive, but it has the best steaks in town. Other meat and fish dishes are also served.

La Casa de Mi Abuela (☎ 256 5667; JL Mera 1649; meat dishes $6-8; open noon-3pm & 4:30pm-10pm Mon-Sat) has an odd dining room but great steaks.

Shorton Grill (☎ 252 3645; J Calamá E7-73; mains $8-22; open noon-11pm daily) is excellent and serves everything (meat, seafood, poultry) a la brasa (grilled).

Texas Ranch (☎ 290 6199; JL Mera 1140; mains $3-6; open 1pm-midnight daily) serves up whopping burgers (that's the Texas part) and Argentinean-style grilled meats.

Adam's Rib (☎ 256 3196; J Calamá 329; open noon-11pm Mon-Fri, noon-9pm Sun) is great for barbecued meats – especially ribs and steaks – and has a bar, pool table and satellite TV, all well-used by its faithful stream of American expats.

Vegetarian Quito is probably the best place in Ecuador for a choice of vegetarian food. Many of the cafés listed later – especially Grain de Café, Sugar Mammas and El Cafecito – offer a variety of vegetarian dishes as well.

El Maple (☎ 225 1503; J Calamá 369; mains $3-5; open 7am-11pm daily) is organic as well as vegetarian and, although some of the food can be a bit on the bland side, it's wholesome. The soy burgers are huge and delicious.

Sakti (☎ 252 0466; *Jeronim Carrión 641; almuerzos $1.50, mains $2-3; open 8am-6pm Mon-Fri*) serves cheap, wholesome soups, vegies, fruit salad, pastas and lasagne. It's a cafeteria-type place popular with the local lunch crowd.

Other good places for reasonably priced, set lunches include **Windmill Vegetarian Restaurant** (☎ 222 2575; *Avenida Cristobal Colón 2245*) and **El Marqués** (*J Calamá 443*).

International Quito's luxury hotels have excellent international restaurants. The **Hilton Colón** (*Amazonas & Avenida Patria*) serves a delicious all-you-can-eat lunch buffet in the lobby every Sunday from noon until 2:30pm. It costs $15 and is well worth it if you are looking for a luxurious splurge. See Places to Stay earlier for more details about the hotel.

Fried Bananas (☎ 223 1810; *JL Mera 539; mains $3.50-4.50; open noon-9pm Mon-Sat*) has a varied menu of steak, seafood, trout, chicken, soups and salads, all creatively prepared. It's a cute little place with good prices.

Boca del Lobo (☎ 223 4083; *J Calamá 284; mains $6-10; open 4pm-1am Mon-Sat*) is an ultra-stylish restaurant with a mind-boggling menu. Beneath the sonic ooze of ambient grooves, smartly dressed diners struggle to choose from delicacies such as rosemary sea bass, Salmon Ishpungo (made with an Amazonian cinnamon-like spice), stuffed plantain tortillas, raclette, focaccias, pizzas and excellent desserts.

La Terraza del Tartaro (☎ 252 7987; *General Veintimilla 1106*), on the top floor of the Edificio Amazonas, is a classy place serving a variety of international food. The highlight, however, is the beautiful view. It's expensive but the setting is unbeatable. An elevator at the back of the ground-floor lobby takes you up.

Zócalo (☎ 223 3929; *cnr JL Mera & J Calamá; mains $4-6; open 10am-2am daily*) is a popular restaurant-cum-bar with a prime, 2nd-floor location right in the hub of the Mariscal Sucre – hence its popularity. The atmosphere is fun and the food (snacks, Mexican-style dishes, etc) is decent, varied and filling.

Cafés The popular **pavement cafés** (*Amazonas near Vicente Ramón Roca*) are great places to watch the world go by. They serve a decent cup of coffee and good, straightforward sandwiches and the waiters don't hassle you if you sit there for hours.

Sugar Mammas (☎ 09-990 3788; *JL Mera 921 & Wilson; mains $2-4, juices $1-2.50; open 8am-8pm Mon-Fri, 9am-1pm Sat*) is a cozy little juice-bar and café with some of the most imaginative and tasty juice and smoothie combinations you'll find in Ecuador. They're all fresh and pure. The three-course almuerzos (served with juice of course) are excellent value. Breakfasts are delicious and plenty of vegetarian items grace the menu.

Magic Bean (☎ 256 6181; *Foch E5-08; mains $4-7; open 7am-10pm daily*) has a variety of well-prepared, although expensive, meals and snacks for the ever-present crowd of hungry travelers. The place serves excellent coffee, dozens of juices and good breakfasts. See also Places to Stay earlier.

Mango Tree Café (☎ 222 6847; *Foch 721; mains $3-6; open 8am-8:30pm Mon-Sat*) is a friendly, comfortable café with good prices and tasty food (which includes pastas, vegetarian dishes, bagels and soup).

Café Cultura (*cnr Francisco Robles & Reina Victoria; mains $4-8; open 7am-9pm daily*) is a lovely British-run café with excellent breakfasts. Lunch and English afternoon tea are also served. See also Places to Stay earlier for more details.

El Español (☎ 255 3995; *cnr JL Mera & Wilson; open 8am-8:30pm Mon-Sat, 9am-8:30pm Sun*) is a Spanish delicatessen and a good place to stock up for picnic lunches.

Super Papa (☎ 222 2721; *JL Mera N23-41; mains $2.50-3.50; open 7am-9:30pm Mon-Fri, 7am-8pm Sat & Sun*) serves breakfast and baked potatoes stuffed with hot or cold fillings. It has one of the best noticeboards in town.

Café Sutra (☎ 250 9106; *J Calamá 380; snacks $2-6; open noon-2am Mon-Sat, 3pm-2am Sun*), with its dim lighting, mellow music and cool crowd, is a great place for a snack and a beer before a night out. The free bowls of popcorn are neverending, and goodies such as falafel, hummus and fried cheese balls hit the spot.

El Cafecito (☎ 234 862; *Cordero 1124*) serves inexpensive, mainly vegetarian meals and snacks all day long. There is also a cozy bar with a fireplace. See also Places to Stay earlier.

Grain de Café (☎ 256 5975; General Baquedano 332; mains $3-5; open 7am-11pm Mon-Sat) is a café/restaurant where you can kick back over coffee or order a full meal. It's a laid-back place in the best sense, and there are lots of vegetarian options.

Café Galleti (☎ 223 7881; Amazonas 1494; open 8am-8pm) is classy little espresso bar with checker-board tables (bring your own checkers) and good coffee drinks.

Mirador de Guápulo (☎ 256 0364; Rafael León Larrea y Pasaje Stübel; mains $4-6; open 9:30am-10:30pm Sun-Tues, 9:30am-1am Wed-Sat), run by Fundación Sinchi Sacha (see Things to See & Do earlier), is a comfy café behind the Hotel Quito, on the cliffside overlooking the Sanctuary of Guápulo. The views are great, and the food – much of it Ecuadorian specialties – is tasty.

Sató (☎ 225 6172; República de El Salvador N34-51 at Suisa; open 9am-9pm Mon-Sat) is a gourmet café and art gallery. A hairdressing salon occupies the same building, so you can get your hair done, browse the art, and then enjoy a special meal, such as a smoked trout salad. Everything is freshly prepared. It's slightly expensive for a café, but worth it.

Other For hearty portions of German food – including goulash, rösti (sautéed shredded potatoes) and käsespätzle (egg noodles with cheese) – visit the German-owned **Café Colibri** (☎ 256 4011; J Pinto 619; mains $2.50-5; open 7am-9pm daily). Breakfasts, too, are delicious, and there are tables both indoors and out.

El Arabe (☎ 254 9414; Reina Victoria 627; open 11am-midnight Mon-Sat) is the place to go for a quick, inexpensive meal of falafel and hummus or shawermas.

Siam (☎ 223 9404; J Calamá E5-10; mains $5-8; open 12:30pm-4pm & 6:30pm-11pm daily) does great Thai food. There are several vegetarian options on the menu.

ENTERTAINMENT
There are plenty of places to let loose on the dance floor (or on the bar top) in Quito. The line between a 'bar' and a 'dance club' is a blurry one though, as many bars become sweaty dance halls as the night rolls on. Bars with dancing often charge admission, which usually includes a drink.

Most of Quito's nightlife is concentrated in and around the Mariscal area. For movie listings and other events, check the local newspapers *El Comercio* and *Hoy*.

Bars & Pubs
If your idea of a night out is a drink and a chat in a pleasant bar, you'll find plenty of good places in Quito.

La Reina Victoria (☎ 223 3369; Reina Victoria 530), a British pub managed by a friendly Aussie couple, is a real home away from home for the homesick British traveler. There is a fireplace, dartboard, bumper pool and excellent pub ambience suitable for all ages. Good food and a couple of microbrews are available.

Other comfortable British or American bars which have a publike atmosphere include **Patatu's Bar** (Wilson E4-229 near Amazonas), **The Turtle's Head** (☎ 256 5544; La Niña 626) and **King's Cross** (☎ 252 3597; Reina Victoria 1781; open 5:30pm-late Mon-Fri, 6:30pm-late Sat). All have pool tables and serve good British and bar meals. **Ghoz Bar** (La Niña 425) is another choice for bar games and drinking.

Mumbai (Isabel La Católica N24-685) is Quito's only martini bar, with a hip, moneyed crowd and a stylish, modern atmosphere.

La Cascada Mágica (☎ 252 7190; Foch 476) features pool, foosball, hockey and snacks, along with the drinks.

Techo del Mundo (González Suárez N27-142) is a swanky lounge on the top floor of the Hotel Quito with fabulous views and expensive drinks.

Nightclubs
On Reina Victoria, around Santa María and Pinta, there are several wildly popular bars with packed weekend dance floors. The area is flooded with bar-hoppers, taxis and hot-dog vendors on weekend nights, but it's a dangerous area after dark, so don't wander far from the club entrances. Inside you're fine. Two favourites near here are **Tijuana** (cnr Reina Victoria & Santa María; admission $3) and **Papillon** (cnr Santa María & Diego de Almagro; admission $3). Both blast out a broad mix of international dance music.

No Bar (J Calamá 380 & JL Mera; admission $3; open 6pm-3am daily) is a Quito standby. Four small, dark dance floors surround a chaotic bar (always with dancing on top), and beer-bongs and the spraying of Pilsener are a common sight. It's mobbed on weekends. Expect high-energy dance pop and lots of pick-up lines.

Matrioshka (☎ 255 2669; J Pinto 376; admission $5; open Tues-Sat) is possibly the best *discoteca* in town and is one of Quito's more openly gay nightclubs.

Beer House Café Concert (☎ 244 5979; Avenida de los Granados E14-605 & Eloy Alfaro; admission $3; open 7pm-3am Tues-Sat) is one of the newer dance crazes in Quito, featuring more packed dance floors and pop-dance mixes.

Hitting the dance floor of one of Quito's *salsotecas* is a must. If you don't know how to salsa, try a few classes first – see Dancing Lessons earlier.

Seseribó (General Veintimilla & Avenida 12 de Octubre, Edificio Girón) is Quito's best-known *salsoteca*. It's small, the music is tops and the atmosphere is superb. You must consume a minimum of $6 in drinks, or pay the cover charge. The devoted *salseros* (salsa dancers) turn up on Thursdays – a great night to go. Fridays and Saturdays are packed – and still great nights to go.

Mayo 68 (García 662) is smaller (and some say, for that reason, better) than Seseribó.

Live Music
Peñas are usually bars that have traditional *música folklórica* (folk music) shows.

Ñucanchi Peña (☎ 254 0967; Universitaria 496; admission $5; open 8pm-2am or 3am Thur-Sat) in the new town is a fairly inexpensive place. It's popular with students and families and is probably the best choice for travelers wanting to see a *peña* show. There are performances Thursday through Saturday starting at 9:30pm.

La Taberna del Duende (☎ 254 4970; U Páez 141) is a cozy local bar with traditional music Thursday through Saturday.

La Bodeguita de Cuba (Reina Victoria 172) features excellent live Cuban music on Thursday nights from about 9pm to 2am. Get there early. See Places to Eat earlier for more information about La Bodeguita.

Theater & Dance
Metropolitan Touring, along with Ministerio de Turismo, has organized the spectacular

Ballet Folklórico Nacional Jacchigua. It is presented at Teatro Aeropuerto at 7:30pm Wednesday and Friday. Contact any travel agency for tickets or buy them at the door (where they might be cheaper). Admission is $15.

Teatro Prometeo (☎ 222 6116; Avenida 6 de Diciembre 794), across from Parque El Ejido in the new town, is affiliated with the Casa de La Cultura Ecuatoriana. It's inexpensive and sometimes has modern-dance performances and mime shows that anyone can understand.

Patio de Comedías (☎ 256 1902; 18 de Septiembre 457) presents plays and performances Thursday through Sunday nights, usually at 8pm.

Humanizarte (☎ 222 6116; Leonidas Plaza Gutiérrez N24-226) presents both contemporary and Andean dance. Call to check what's on and watch out for their posters in the Mariscal.

Cinemas
Most cinemas in Quito show popular English-language films with Spanish subtitles, while cheaper places resort to kung-fu and porn.

Cinemark (☎ 226 0301; Naciones Unidas & Avenida América; admission $4) and the **Multicines** (☎ 225 9677; Centro Comercial Iñaquito; admission $4) are the biggest cinemas. They are multiscreen, state-of-the-art cinemas which show recent Hollywood blockbusters.

Ocho y Medio (☎ 290 4720/21/22; w www.ochoymedio.net; Valloldolid N24-353 & Vizcaya; café open 11am-10:30pm) is a new film house that shows some great art films (often in English) and has occasional dance, theater and live music. There's a small café attached. The Ocho y Medio website has lots of information about Quito's nightlife.

Casa de la Cultura Ecuatoriana (cnr Avenidas Patria & 12 de Octubre) and the **Fundación Octaedro** (☎ 246 9170, 246 4261; El Zuriaga E-28) also show independent and arty movies.

SHOPPING
Arts & Crafts
There are many good stores for crafts hunters in the new town along and near Avenida Amazonas. If buying from street

stalls, you should bargain. In the fancier stores, prices are normally fixed, although bargaining is not out of the question. Note that souvenirs are a little cheaper outside Quito if you have the time and inclination to search them out – but it is more convenient to shop in the capital.

The following is a list of stores that sell a wide selection of goods at a variety of prices. There are many other stores in the area.

Folklore Olga Fisch (☎ 254 1315; Avenida Cristobal Colón 260; open 9am-7pm Mon-Fri, 9am-1pm & 3pm-7pm Sat) is the store of legendary designer Olga Fisch (who died in 1991). This is the place to go for the very best and the most expensive items.

Productos Andinos (☎ 222 4565; Urbina 111; open 9am-7pm Mon-Fri, 9am-1pm Sat) is an artisans' cooperative with reasonably priced crafts.

Galería Latina (☎ 254 0380; JL Mera N23-69; open 10:30am-8:30pm Mon-Sat, 11am-6pm Sun) has superb Andean textiles at high prices.

Centro Artesanal (☎ 254 8235; JL Mera E5-11; open 10am-2pm & 3pm-7pm Mon-Fri) is known for canvases painted by local Indian artists and other products.

La Bodega (☎ 222 5844; JL Mera N22-24; open 10am-1:30pm & 2:30pm-7:30pm Mon-Fri, 9:30am-1:30pm & 4pm-6pm Sat, 11am-5pm Sun) has a wide and wonderful selection of high-quality crafts. Attached is **Ag**, which sells some of the best silver jewelry around.

MCCH (JL Mera & Francisco Robles) is a women's artisan cooperative with a fine selection of crafts.

El Aborigen (☎ 250 8953; Jorge Washington 614; open 9am-2pm & 3pm-7:30pm Mon-Sat), **Ecuafolklore** (☎ 252 4315; Francisco Robles 609) and **ekeko** (☎ 256 4752; cnr JL Mera & General Baquedano; open 10am-1:30pm & 3pm-7pm Mon-Sat) are good for mid-range prices and wide selections.

Fundación Sinchi Sacha (☎ 223 0609; w www.sinchisacha.org; Reina Victoria N26-166 & La Niña; open 8am-8pm daily) sells excellent Amazonian crafts. Profits benefit indigenous groups. See Things to See & Do earlier in this chapter.

Markets
On Saturday and Sunday, the north end of **Parque El Ejido** turns into Quito's biggest crafts market and sidewalk art show.

Two blocks north, on JL Mera between Jorge Washington and 18 de Septiembre, the **Mercado Artesanal La Mariscal** (open daily) is an entire block filled with craft stalls.

The vast **Ipiales street market** begins on Calle Cuenca, beside the Monastery of San Francisco, and works its way uphill to its chaotic center near Calle Imbabura; it's quite a scene as the crowds browse everything from knock-off designer jeans to bootleg CDs, cheap shoes and kitchen gadgetry. Definitely watch your pockets.

Mercado Santa Clara (Ulloa & Versalles), just south of Avenida Cristobal Colón, is the main produce market in the new town.

Outdoor Supplies
The following stores sell and rent camping and mountaineering equipment.

Alta Montaña (☎ 255 8380) Jorge Washington 425
The Altar (☎ 290 6029) JL Mera 615
Andísimo (☎ 250 8347) 9 de Octubre 479 at Vicente Ramón Roca
The Explorer (☎ 255 0911) Reina Victoria 928
Los Alpes (☎ 223 2362) Reina Victoria N23-45
Moggely Climbing (☎ 255 4984) J Pinto E4-225 at Amazonas

Shopping Centers
Shopping centers are nearly identical to North American shopping malls and usually called *centros comerciales* (CC). Most stores are closed Sunday, but the following malls are open every day. They all have fast-food restaurants inside.

Centro Comercial El Jardín (☎ 298 0928) Amazonas & Avenida de la República
Centro Comercial Iñaquito (CCI; ☎ 225 9444) Amazonas & Naciones Unidas
Centro Comercial Quicentro (☎ 246 4512) Avenida 6 de Diciembre & Naciones Unidas

GETTING THERE & AWAY
Air
Quito has one airport, Aeropuerto Mariscal Sucre, with its domestic and international terminals side by side. It's located about 10km north of the city center. See Getting Around later for bus and taxi information.

Services at the terminal include tourist information, money exchange, ATMs, a post office, a cafeteria/bar, an **Andinatel office** (*open 8am-10pm*) and gift shops.

Domestic There is no departure tax for domestic flights, which are fairly inexpensive (except to the Galápagos). Prices vary little, if at all, between domestic airlines. South of the airport are several companies that charter small planes. The following are Ecuador's principal domestic airlines, with the widest choice provided by TAME.

AeroGal (☎ 225 7301/8087/8086) Amazonas 7797, near the airport
Icaro (☎ 245 0928, 245 1499, **w** www.icaro.com.ec) Palora 124 at Amazonas, across from the airport
TAME (☎ 250 9375/76/77/78, 290 9900, **w** www.tame.com.ec) Amazonas 1354 at Avenida Cristobal Colón

The following price information and schedule are all subject to change. Most travel agencies will also sell domestic airline tickets for usually the same price as the airline offices. The prices quoted in this section are one way.

Cuenca $58; twice daily Monday through Friday, once daily Saturday and Sunday with Icaro; three times daily Monday through Friday, twice daily Saturday and Sunday with TAME
Esmeraldas $37; once daily Monday, Wednesday, Thursday, Friday and Sunday with TAME
Guayaquil $58; once daily on AeroGal; three times daily Monday through Friday, once Saturday and Sunday with Icaro; 10 to 12 times daily with TAME. Flights on TAME are rarely full and last-minute tickets can usually be purchased at the airport on the day of the flight.
Lago Agrio $56; once daily Monday through Saturday with Icaro; twice daily Monday, Thursday and Friday, and once daily Tuesday, Wednesday and Saturday with TAME
Loja $55; twice daily Monday through Friday, once daily Saturday and Sunday with Icaro; twice daily Monday through Saturday with TAME
Macas $57; once daily Monday through Thursday with TAME
Machala $66, via Guayaquil only; once daily Monday through Friday with TAME
Manta $50; once daily with TAME
Portoviejo $50; once daily Monday, Wednesday and Friday with TAME
Tulcán $33; once daily Monday, Wednesday and Friday with TAME

TAME has two morning flights to Isla Baltra in the Galápagos, the main destination for anyone heading to the islands for a cruise. The round-trip fare is $389 for non-Ecuadorian residents ($333 in the low season). TAME also has morning flights to Isla San Cristóbal (for the same price as to Isla Baltra) on Monday, Wednesday, and Saturday. AeroGal flies to San Cristóbal on Wednesday and Saturday. All flights have a 45-minute layover (without changing planes) in Guayaquil.

International Several international airlines have offices in Quito. There is an international departure tax of $25 payable in cash only; check in first. If you are flying internationally, confirm 72 hours in advance; flights are frequently overbooked, so if you don't confirm, you might get bumped. Arrive at the airport three hours before your flight.

The following major airlines fly into Ecuador and have offices in Quito; there are others.

Air France (☎ 222 4818, 222 1605, **w** www.airfrance.com) Avenida 12 de Octubre N24-562, office 710, World Trade Center
American Airlines (☎ 226 0900, **w** www.aa.com) Amazonas 4545 at Pereira; also at the Hilton Colón (☎ 226 0900) Avenida Patria & Amazonas
Avianca/Alianza Summa (☎ 223 2015/16/20, **w** www.summa.aero) Coruña 1311, No 3, at San Ignacio
Continental Airlines (☎ 255 7170/64/65/66, **w** www.continental.com) Avenida 12 de Octubre 1942, office 1108, World Trade Center
Iberia (☎ 255 6009, **w** www.iberia.com) Edificio Finandes, Avenida Eloy Alfaro 939, 5th floor
KLM (☎ 298 6828, **w** www.klm.com) Edificio Torre, Avenida 12 de Octubre 1492, office 1103
Lacsa/Grupo Taca (☎ 292 3170/69/68/67, **w** www.grupotaca.com) República de El Salvador N35-67 at Portugal
LanChile (☎ 250 8396; 250 8400, **w** www.lanchile.com) 18 de Septiembre 238 at Reina Victoria
Lufthansa (☎ 254 1300, 250 8396, **w** www.lufthansa.com) 18 de Septiembre 238 at Reina Victoria
Varig (☎ 225 0126, 225 0131, **w** www.varig.com) Portugal 79 at Republica de El Salvador

Bus

Quito's bus terminal, the Terminal Terrestre de Cumandá, is a few hundred meters south of Plaza Santo Domingo, in the old town. It can be reached by walking down the steps from Maldonado, or by taking *el trole* to the nearby Cumandá stop. Taxi drivers often take an alternate route that enters the terminal from the south side.

The terminal contains the offices of several dozen bus companies which, together, serve most of the country. You can often be on your way within minutes of arriving. If you plan on traveling during vacation periods, it's best to go to the terminal and book in advance. On Fridays arrive early. The terminal has a post office, an Andinatel office, ATMs, restaurants and small stores.

Approximate fares and travel times are shown in the following table. There are daily departures for each destination and several departures per day to most. There may be several buses per hour to popular places such as Ambato or Otavalo. There is a $0.20 departure tax from the bus terminal.

destination	cost (US$)	duration (hrs)
Ambato	2	2½
Atacames	8	6 to 8
Bahía de Caráquez	7	8
Baños	3	3½
Coca	8	10
Cuenca	10	9
Esmeraldas	7	6
Guayaquil	7	8
Ibarra	2	2½
Lago Agrio	8	8
Latacunga	1.50	1½
Loja	12	14
Machala	9	10
Manta	6 to 8	8 to 10
Otavalo	1.80	2¼
Portoviejo	6	8 to 9
Puerto López	8	11
Puyo	4	5½
Riobamba	3	4
San Lorenzo	6	6
Santo Domingo	2	3
Tena	5	6
Tulcán	4	5½

For comfortable buses to Guayaquil from the new town, which avoid the trip to the terminal, you can go with **Panamericana** (☎ 255 3690, 255 1839; *Avenida Cristobal Colón & Reina Victoria*), or with **Transportes Ecuador** (☎ 222 5315; *JL Mera N21-44 near Jorge Washington*). Panamericana also has long-distance buses to several other towns, including Machala, Loja, Cuenca, Manta and Esmeraldas. Its prices are higher than companies at the bus terminal, but the buses are good and the service is convenient.

A few buses leave from other places for some destinations in the Pichincha Province. **Cooperativa Flor de Valle** (☎ 252 7495) goes to Mindo ($2, 2½ hours) daily at 3:20pm and also at 8am Friday, Saturday and Sunday. The bus leaves from Larrea just west of Ascunción, near Parque El Ejido. Get there early, as the bus fills up.

Train

Although most of Ecuador's train system is in shambles, you can still ride the rails if you're determined. A weekend tourist train leaves Quito and heads south for about 3½ hours to the Area Nacional de Recreación El Boliche, adjoining Parque Nacional Cotopaxi (see the Central Highlands chapter). These trains are old-fashioned and uncomfortable with primitive bathroom facilities (all part of the fun), and many passengers ride on the roof – a unique experience with great views, but very cold. The train leaves at 8am on Saturday and Sunday and arrives in El Boliche at about 11:30am. Passengers have about 2½ hours to hike or picnic before the train leaves El Boliche at 2pm for the return to Quito.

The **Quito train station** (☎ 265 6142; *Sincholagua & Vicente Maldonado*) is about 2km south of the old town. The train station booking office is open the day before trains depart, but there is normally no problem obtaining tickets from 7am onward on travel days ($4.60 one way).

GETTING AROUND
To/From the Airport

The airport is at the north end of Avenida Amazonas, about 10km north of the old town. Many of the northbound buses on Amazonas and Avenida 10 de Agosto go to the airport. Some have *Aeropuerto* placards, and others say *Quito Norte*. If you are going from the airport into town, you will find bus stops on Avenida 10 de Agosto, about 150m away from the front entrance of the terminal.

A taxi from the new town should cost $3 to $4 (more from the old town). From the

QUITO

airport into town, taxi drivers will invariably charge you more if you hail them within the airport driveway. To save a couple of dollars, walk across the taxi cab/passenger pick-up area and catch a cab just outside the airport on either side of Amazonas. Bargain hard, unless your cab has a meter.

Bus

The crowded local buses have a flat fare that you pay as you board. They are safe enough and rather fun, but watch your bags and pockets. Generally speaking, buses run north-south and have a fixed route. There are various bus types, each identified by the color of their stripe. *Popular* (light-blue) buses are the cheapest and most crowded. The *ejecutivo* (dark-blue) and *selectivo* (red) buses are less crowded, and some don't allow standing passengers. Fares vary from about $0.10 to $0.20. Pink-striped buses go out of Quito into nearby towns (but they are not long distance), and green-striped buses are feeders into the trolley (see following). Buses have destination placards in their windows, and drivers are usually helpful and will tell you which bus to take if they are not going to your destination. Traffic in the old town is very heavy, and you may often find it's faster to walk than to take a bus, especially during rush hours.

The narrow streets of downtown are usually one way. Calles Guayaquil and Venezuela are one way into the old town toward El Panecillo, and Calles García Moreno and Flores are one way out of the old town and away from El Panecillo. There are about 40 different bus routes. If you have a specific place you want to get to by local bus, ask your hotel's staff, bus drivers or passersby. The locals know where the buses go. It's not difficult to get around if you ask and are prepared to put up with very crowded buses.

Trolley

El Trole (the trolley) is Quito's most comfortable and useful transportation system. Trolleys run along Avenida 10 de Agosto, through the old town to the north end of the southern suburbs. The trolleys have designated stations and car-free lanes along the streets they travel, so they are both speedy and efficient. They also are modern and designed to minimize pollution. The line runs between the Estación Sur, on Maldonado south of Villaflora, and the Estación Norte, on Avenida 10 de Agosto just north of Avenida de la Prensa. Trolleys run along Maldonado and Avenida 10 de Agosto about every 10 minutes from 6am to 12:30am (more often in rush hours), and the fare is $0.20. In the old town, southbound trolleys take the west route (along Guayaquil), while northbound trolleys take the east route (along Montúfar and Pichincha).

A new system, called the Ecovía, runs along Avenida 6 de Diciembre between Río Coca in the north and La Marin in the south.

Car

Car rental in Quito, as with elsewhere in Ecuador, is expensive – taxis and buses are much cheaper and more convenient than renting a car. Rental vehicles are useful for visiting some out-of-the-way areas that don't have frequent bus connections (in which case, a more expensive 4WD vehicle is a good idea).

The following companies are found in Quito. Ecuacar and Localiza have been recommended as particularly reliable and competitively priced. See the Getting Around chapter for more car-rental information.

Avis (☎ 244 0270) at the airport
Budget (☎ 223 7026) Amazonas 1408 near Avenida Cristobal Colón; (☎ 252 5328) Hilton Colón; (☎ 224 0763, 245 9052) at the airport
Ecuacar (☎ 252 9781, 254 0000) Avenida Cristobal Colón 1280 near Amazonas; (☎ 224 7298) at the airport
Hertz (☎ 256 9130) Swissôtel; (☎ 225 4257) at the airport
Localiza (☎ 250 5974, 250 5986) Avenida 6 de Diciembre 1570 near Wilson

Taxi

Cabs are all yellow and have red 'taxi' stickers in the window. Usually there are plenty available, but rush hour, Sundays and rainy days can leave you waiting 10 or 15 minutes for an empty cab.

Cabs are legally required to have meters, and almost all drivers now use them, although occasionally cab drivers will ask to arrange a price with you beforehand. Sometimes this is to your advantage, as it enables the driver to take a roundabout route to avoid traffic, thus saving both of you time. But generally you should have the driver use the meter. Late at night and on Sundays, drivers will ask for a higher fare, but it shouldn't be more than twice the metered rate. Some drivers will tell you that the meter is broken – you can always flag down another cab.

Short journeys around town start at about $1 and climb to about $4 for a longer trip. The minimum charge is $0.80. Between the old and new town, expect to pay $2 to $3. From Amazonas to the top of El Panecillo costs about $20, including a one-hour wait and the round trip.

Taxis can be hired for several hours or for a day. If you bargain hard and don't plan on going very far, you could hire a cab for a day for about $60. Cabs hired from the better hotels have set rates for long trips and are a bit more expensive but they are more reliable.

Unless you are visiting a well-known landmark, you will probably have to tell the cab driver the nearest cross street of your destination.

Around Quito

☎ 02

Many excursions can be made from Quito, using the city as a base. The destinations here are meant for day trips rather than as part of an overnight tour. In addition, the thermal baths of **Papallacta** can be a day trip from Quito (see From Quito to Lago Agrio in The Oriente chapter).

POMASQUI

This village is about 16km from Quito on the way to La Mitad del Mundo. Two churches on Plaza Yerovi (the main plaza), two blocks east of the gas station on the main highway, are worth a look.

On the plaza's south side, the **Church of El Señor del Árbol** (the Lord of the Tree) has a noted sculpture of Christ in a tree – the branches of the tree look like Christ's arms raised above His head in a boxing champion's salute. Various miracles have been ascribed to this image by devotees.

On the plaza's east side, the **parish church** contains religious paintings – some of which are slightly bizarre (eg, the miraculous intervention of the Virgin to save a believer from certain death) – as well as various statues, including a carved and

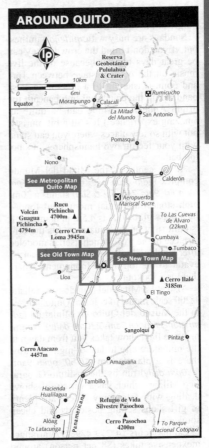

polychromed Santa Clara, who is the patron saint of Pomasqui.

The fiesta of El Señor del Árbol is normally the first Sunday in July. Día de Santa Clara is July 27, and so the whole month is a busy one for the citizens of Pomasqui, who have processions, games, bullfights etc.

LA MITAD DEL MUNDO

The most famous local excursion is to the equator at La Mitad del Mundo ('The Middle of the World'), near the village of San Antonio, about 22km north of Quito. This is the place where, in 1736, Charles-Marie de La Condamine's expedition made the measurements that showed that this was indeed the equator. These measurements gave rise to the metric system and proved that the

QUITO

world is not perfectly round, but that it bulges at the equator.

Sundays are busy with *quiteño* families, but, if you don't mind the crowds, they can be great days to visit because of the live music on the outdoor stage between 1pm and 6pm. (Listening to a nine-piece salsa band rip up the equatorial line beneath the bright Andean sunshine can be quite an amazing experience.) It's all a bit touristy, but with so few places where you can stand with your feet in two hemispheres, it's not too bad.

At the center of the Mitad del Mundo complex (*admission $0.50; open 9am-6pm Mon-Fri, 9am-7pm Sat & Sun*) stands a 30m-high stone trapezoidal **monument** topped by a brass globe that is 4.5m in diameter. It is built right on the equator and is the center-piece of the park, which itself is modeled after a colonial village. You can take an elevator to the top of the monument, where there is a lookout.

Also at La Mitad del Mundo is a realistic 1:200 scale model of colonial Quito, housed in the **Museo del Quito en Miniatura** (*admission $1; open 9am-5:30pm daily*). An impressive light show takes you from dawn in the miniature city to late at night. Nearby, there is a **planetarium** (*$0.50; open 9am-5:30pm daily*) run by the Instituto Geográfico Militar, which has a variety of shows dealing with astronomy. There are plenty of gift shops selling postcards and cheap souvenirs.

Calima Tours (☎ 239 4796/97) arranges inexpensive hikes ($8 per person) around the crater rim of nearby Pululahua. It's a good price, considering it includes the $5 park entrance fee. It also goes to Rumicucho ruins (see Rumicucho later).

Outside and a few hundred meters east of the Mitad del Mundo complex is the **Museo Solar Inti Ñan** (☎ 239 5122; admission $1), a tiny, red-brick construction with fascinating exhibits of astronomical geography and interesting explanations of the importance of Ecuador's geographical location. One of the highlights is the 'solar chronometer,' a unique instrument made in 1865 that shows precise astronomical and conventional time, as well as the month, day and season – all by using the rays of the sun. There are also some fun demonstrations of tasks that can only be performed at the equator.

Places to Stay & Eat

Hostería Alemán (☎ 239 4243; doubles about $16) is on the west side of the highway from Quito, almost 1km south of La Mitad del Mundo. It has pleasant gardens, 11 rooms with hot showers and balconies, and a good restaurant.

Mitad del Mundo Hostal (*rooms per person $5*), southeast of the monument on the road to San Antonio, is pretty basic. **Hostal Sol y Luna** (☎ 239 4979), opposite Mitad del Mundo, is better.

Rancho Alegre (☎ 239 5552; rooms $30), in San Antonio, about 1.5km from the monument, has a pool, sauna, Jacuzzi and café, in addition to 10 clean rooms with hot showers and TV.

There are plenty of restaurants inside the complex's faux village area, although many close midweek. Good ones include the well known and pricey **Equinoccio** (☎ 239 4741), near the entrance, and **Cafetería Calima** (☎ 239 4105; mains $2-5; open 9am-6pm daily). There are *comedores* (cheap restaurants) outside the complex.

Getting There & Away

In Quito, catch a pink-striped bus ($0.35, 45 minutes) signed 'Mitad del Mundo' from anywhere along Avenida América; the intersection with Avenida Cristobal Colón is a good spot to wait. The buses run several times an hour, but they tend to be crowded on Sunday.

Depending on how well you bargain, a taxi will cost about $30 round trip, including waiting time at the monument.

Tours with bilingual guides (about $20 per person) are available from most of the major travel agencies.

RUMICUCHO

About 5km north of La Mitad del Mundo, this small, pre-Columbian **archaeological site** (*admission $1; open 9am-3pm Mon-Fri, 8am-4pm Sat & Sun*) was built around 500 BC by the Quitu-Cara culture and used principally as a ceremonial site during the equinoxes. The site is officially open during the hours listed above, but you can walk in at anytime. It's not Ecuador's most impressive site, but there are good views of Quito in the distance, and there probably won't be anyone else there so you can have the spot to yourself. Walk all the way through; the best views are from the side furthest from the entrance.

Taxis to Rumicucho are available in San Antonio; the round-trip fare, including waiting time, should be about $4.

RESERVA GEOBOTÁNICA PULULAHUA

This small, 3383-hectare reserve lies about 4km northwest of Mitad del Mundo. The most interesting part of the reserve is the **volcanic crater** of the extinct Pululahua. This was apparently formed in ancient times, when the cone of the volcano collapsed, leaving a huge crater some 400m deep and 5km across. The crater's flat and fertile bottom is used for agriculture. Within the crater there are two small cones – the larger Loma Pondoña (2975m) and the smaller Loma El Chivo.

The crater is open to the west side, through which moisture-laden winds from the Pacific Ocean blow dramatically. It is sometimes difficult to see the crater because of the swirling clouds and mist. The moist winds, combined with the crater's steep walls, create a variety of microclimates, and the vegetation on the fertile volcanic slopes is both rampant and diverse. Because the walls are much too steep to farm, the vegetation grows undisturbed and protected. There are many flowers and a variety of bird species.

The crater can be entered on foot by a steep trail from the **Mirador de Ventanillas** viewpoint on its southeast side (easily reached by bus from La Mitad del Mundo). The steep trail is the best way to see the birds and plants, because most of the flat bottom is farmed. There is also an unpaved road on the southwest side via Moraspungo.

Information

The official entrance fee for the reserve is $5 which you must pay before you hike down into the crater or as you enter by car via Moraspungo; there are no charges for viewing from the Ventanillas viewpoint.

See Calima Tours under La Mitad del Mundo earlier for information on inexpensive tours from there.

Near Moraspungo are some **cabins** in the upper-budget price range. Near the Ventanillas viewpoint, perched on the crater's edge, is **El Crater Restaurant** (☎ 243 9254;

open weekends only), which has good food and superb views.

The Texaco station near the village of **Calacalí** is the last place for gas before Los Bancos if you are heading west. In the colorful village of Calacalí itself, the (much smaller) **original equatorial monument** can be seen; it was moved there after being replaced by the enlarged replica now at La Mitad del Mundo.

Getting There & Away

From La Mitad del Mundo, a paved road continues to the village of Calacalí, about 7.5km away. There are occasional buses from San Antonio to Calacalí, particularly on weekends. About 4km beyond La Mitad del Mundo on the road to Calacalí is the first paved road to the right. Ask the driver to drop you off there. About 1km along this road, there is a small parking area at the viewpoint.

Alternatively, continue on the road to Calacalí for 3km, which brings you to a sign for Moraspungo to the right. From the turnoff, it's 3km to Moraspungo and about 12km more into the crater. You pay the entry fee of $5 per person at Moraspungo.

Las Cuevas de Alvaro

About 32km east of Quito, just off the road to the Oriente, are Alvaro's caves. Created by Ecuadorian eccentric Alvaro Bustamente, these caves were excavated by hand from a grassy hill in the middle of nowhere. Eventually, they became a series of caves joined by underground passageways. It isn't clear why Alvaro built this structure – something about 'man's ties and dependence on the land.'

Now the caves have been turned into a seven-room underground hotel with shared hot showers and a restaurant serving homemade food. Day-trippers can check the place out for a small fee or eat lunch underground. A children's play area, an artificial lake with a rowboat, and lookout towers are on the grounds around the hotel, and horse riding and hiking are ideal activities. **Cuevas del Alvaro Lodge** (Quito ☎/fax 222 8902; **e** birdecua@hoy.net; Jeronim Carrión 555-C) has an office in Quito. Rates are about $60 per person, including three meals and a horse-riding trip.

QUITO

Taxis from San Antonio or Quito will take you to the rim, and tours can be arranged from Quito in combination with a visit to La Mitad del Mundo.

CALDERÓN

This village is about 10km northeast of Quito on the Panamericana (not the road to Mitad del Mundo). Calderón is a famous center of unique Ecuadorian folk art: The people make bread-dough decorations, ranging from small statuettes to colorful Christmas tree ornaments such as stars, parrots, Santas, tortoises, candles and tropical fish. The ornaments make practical gifts as they are small, unusual and cheap (buy a handful for $1). These decorative figures are inedible – preservatives are added so that they'll last many years. There are many stores selling the crafts on the main street.

Buses heading to Cayambe or Otavalo can take you there from Quito; flag one down on Avenida 10 de Agosto or at a main intersection, such as Avenida Cristobal Colón.

SANGOLQUÍ

The Indian market nearest the capital is Sangolquí's Sunday-morning market. There is a smaller market there on Thursday. Local buses go there frequently from Plaza Marín, also known as 'La Marín,' in Quito's old town. Sangolquí is about 20km southeast of Quito's old town.

Sangolquí itself has a number of cheap local places. However, the following recommended places lie just out of town.

Hostería Sommergarten (☎/fax 233 2761, 233 0315; e rsommer@uio.satnet.net; Chimborazo 248; singles/doubles $61/74) is a quiet, 20-room hotel with a pool, sauna, steam bath and whirlpool (these facilities can be used by nonguests on weekends for $4). Rates include an American breakfast.

Hostería La Carriona (☎ 233 1974, 233 2004; w www.lacarriona.com; singles/doubles $74/85) is 2.5km southwest of Sangolquí on the road to Amaguaña. This 200-year-old colonial hacienda is a delightful place to stay and is just a 30-minute drive from Quito. The old architecture is fronted by a cobbled courtyard and is surrounded by flower-filled gardens. It has a pool, sauna, steam bath, Jacuzzi, games area and a large restaurant. The 30 units vary distinctly in character, from cozy rural rooms to lavish ornate suites. All have private bath, TV and phone.

El Viejo Roble (☎ 233 4036; Vía Amaguaña, Km2.5, Avenida Rumiñahui; open 9am-6pm daily) is not very far from Hostería La Carriona and is the area's best restaurant, with Ecuadorian and international cuisine.

REFUGIO DE VIDA SILVESTRE PASOCHOA

Formerly a private reserve operated by Fundación Natura (see Information following) this refuge became part of the Ecuadorian system of protected areas in 1996, although Fundación Natura still plays a part. The refuge is roughly 30km southeast of Quito and has one of the last remaining stands of undisturbed humid Andean forest left in the central valley. Over 100 species of birds have been recorded there.

Hacienda Hualilagua

Hualilagua de Jijón was built in 1718 on a hill with fabulous views of the central valley some 30km south of Quito. One of its outstanding features is a small stand of original Andean forest, which originally covered much of the sides of the central valley. The hospitable owners delight in showing you around the elegant hacienda and talking about the period furniture and artwork found throughout.

Normally, it is open Thursday and Sunday, when a breakfast ($12) or lunch ($23) of organic food is offered, thus making this a stopping point on the day trip to the Thursday Saquisilí market (see the Central Highlands chapter for more details) or Sunday Machachi market. Reservations at the hacienda can be made with **Metropolitan Touring** (☎ 298 8200, w www.metropolitan-touring.com), which offers a 'Hacienda, Chagras and Rodeo' package for $104 – an all-day affair including the market, lunch at the hacienda, horse riding and transportation (see Travel Agencies & Tour Operators under Quito earlier). 'Chagra' is the Ecuadorian term for a typical Andean cowboy, dressed in a heavy wool poncho, sheepskin chaps and a fedora to protect against the cold. During a short rodeo, they show off their riding abilities and their skills with a lasso – a photogenic spectacle.

The forest is luxuriant and contains a wide range of highland trees and shrubs. These include the Podocarpaceae, which are the only conifers native to the Ecuadorian Andes (the pines seen elsewhere are introduced); various species of mountain palm trees; the Andean laurel; and the huge-leaved *Gunnera* plant (nicknamed 'the poor folks' umbrella'). Orchids, bromeliads, ferns, lichens and other epiphytic plants contribute to the forest's attractions. The prolific birdlife includes hummingbirds, of which at least 11 species are present. Various other tropical birds – such as furnarids, tapaculos, honeycreepers and tanagers – may be seen along the nature trails. Mammals such as rabbits, squirrels and deer are sometimes observed; foxes, and even pumas, more rarely so.

The reserve is a small one (only 500 hectares) and is on the northern flanks of the extinct volcano of Pasochoa, at elevations of 2900m to 4200m. The area is within the collapsed volcanic caldera (crater), and there are good views of other peaks. There are several trails, from easy half-hour loops to fairly strenuous all-day hikes. The shorter trails are self-guided; guides are available for the longer walks. One trail leads out of the reserve and to the summit of Pasochoa (4200m) – this hike takes about eight hours.

Information

Foreigners pay an entrance fee of $7. The park ranger will give you a small trail map.

Overnight **camping** *(per person $0.75)* is permitted in designated areas. There are latrines, picnic areas, barbecue grills and water. There is also a simple **hostal** *(beds per person $3)* with 20 bunk beds – bring your own sleeping bag. Hot showers and kitchen facilities are available. On weekends, when the place is usually crowded with locals, a small restaurant is open; otherwise, bring your own food. The reserve is open every day from dawn to dusk and it is usually quiet midweek.

Fundación Natura *(☎ 250 3385/86/87, 250 3394/202/203; Av República 481 & Diego de Almagro; open 9am-1pm & 2pm-5pm Mon-Fri)* in Quito has trail maps and information and can make overnight reservations.

Getting There & Away

Buses leave from Plaza La Marín in Quito's old town about twice an hour for the village of Amaguaña ($0.35, 1 hour). Ask the driver to let you off near El Ejido. From the church nearby, there is a signed cobblestone road to the reserve, which is about 7km away. You have to walk. Alternately, you can go all the way into Amaguaña (about 1km beyond El Ejido) and hire a truck to the reserve's entrance and information center for about $7 (the truck can take several people).

Taxis from Quito will take you for about $40 round trip, but make sure they know the way. Arrange a driver on the day before you visit to get there early – the best bird-watching is in the early hours. **Safari Tours** *(☎ 255 2505, 222 3381, e admin@safari .com.ec)* arranges tours as well (see Travel Agencies & Tour Operators under Quito earlier).

VOLCÁN PICHINCHA

Quito's closest volcano is Pichincha, looming over the western side of the city. The volcano has two main summits – the closer, dormant Rucu Pichincha (about 4700m) and the higher Guagua Pichincha (4794m), which is currently very active and is monitored by volcanologists. A major eruption in 1660 covered Quito in 40cm of ash; there were three minor eruptions in the 19th century. A few puffs of smoke occurred in 1981, but in 1999 the volcano rumbled into serious action (see the boxed text 'Volcanic Activity' in the Getting There & Away chapter).

Climbing either of the summits is strenuous but technically straightforward, and no special equipment is required.

Climbing the smoking **Guagua Pichincha** is a longer trip, but less beset with non-mountainous hazards, although reaching the crater is currently not permitted. Again, check with the SAE or with a climbing guide for the latest information before you go. The climbing guides listed earlier under Travel Agencies & Tour Operators in Quito can also be of assistance. Guides will usually have a jeep available to drive you past all the problem areas and to a point high up on the mountains. Most avoid Rucu Pichincha all together.

Dangers & Annoyances

You are advised not to climb Rucu Pichincha. Unfortunately the access routes to Rucu Pichincha have been plagued with violent attacks on hikers. The main access street, Avenida 24 de Mayo, has been the scene of frequent attacks, robberies and rapes. Once out of the city, the route goes past the TV antennas on the hill named Cruz Loma – several attacks, robberies and rapes

have been reported in this area as well. Do not take these warnings lightly – even large groups have been attacked at gunpoint. The staff of the SAE are always an excellent source of up-to-date information.

Northern Highlands

The Andean highlands, north of Quito, are one of the most popular travel destinations in Ecuador. Few people spend any time in the country without visiting the famous Indian market in the small town of Otavalo, where you can buy a wide variety of weavings, clothing and handicrafts. Although many travelers limit their visit to just Otavalo, there is much more to see in this region.

The dramatic mountain scenery is dotted with shining white churches set in tiny villages and includes views of Volcán Cayambe, the third-highest peak in the country, as well as a beautiful lake district. Several small towns are noted for handicrafts, such as woodcarving or leatherwork.

Ibarra is a small, charmingly somnolent colonial city worth visiting, both in its own right and as the beginning of the Ibarra–San Lorenzo route to the north coast. Further north, the town of Tulcán is the safest border crossing to Colombia, but you should check locally about safety in Colombia before heading north of the border. Tulcán is safe, but, due to the conflict in Colombia, travel in the remoter border regions on either side of the border was not advised at the time of writing.

The spectacular and unique cloud forests of the western Andean slopes, descending toward the lowlands, are easily accessible from Quito – in only 2½ hours you can get to the lovely village of Mindo, where there are several outstanding lodges and some of the country's best bird-watching. Nearby there are several other cloud-forest reserves, lodges and villages worth visiting to explore some of Ecuador's most endangered types of forest. The road via Mindo makes a great route to the coast.

NORTH TO CAYAMBE
☎ 02

About 10km north of Quito on the Panamericana is the village of Calderón (see Around Quito in the Quito chapter). Beyond Calderón, the road descends in a series of magnificent sweeps toward the village of **Guayllabamba**, set in a fertile river valley of the same name that is famous for its produce. Road-side stalls offer huge avocados and that strangely reptilian-looking

Highlights

• Haggling in Otavalo, home of the most famous crafts market in South America

• Eating and sleeping in style at one of the many upscale colonial haciendas near Otavalo

• Hiking around the spectacular lakes of Lagunas de Mojanda or across the fog-bound *páramo* (high Andean grasslands) in the Páramos de El Ángel

• Bird-watching, hiking and relaxing in the cloud forests of Mindo on the western Andean slopes

NORTHERN HIGHLANDS

Andean fruit, the *chirimoya;* it's comparable to the sweetsop. The knobbly green skin is discarded, and the custardlike white pulp inside is eaten. The *chirimoya* definitely tastes better than it looks or sounds.

Guayllabamba is the site of the new **Quito Zoo** (☎ 236 8900, 236 8898; admission $2; open 9am-5pm Tues-Sun). It's actually about 3km before (southwest of) Guayllabamba, but bus drivers to Otavalo know where to drop you off. From the zoo, pickups charge about $0.30 to go to Guayllabamba and leave whenever they have a load; of course, you can opt to hike the 3km. Most exhibits are Ecuadorian animals, although there are a few African and Asian species.

Some 3km beyond Guayllabamba, the road forks, and both routes end at Cayambe.

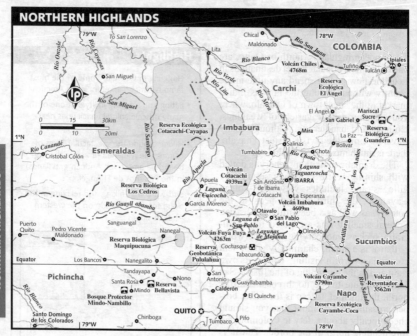

NORTHERN HIGHLANDS

About 10km along the right fork, you pass a turnoff that leads back to Quito via **El Quinche**, known for its statue of the Virgin of El Quinche and for the paintings inside its impressive church. The road continues through pretty countryside and tiny hamlets to the town of **Pifo**. Here, you can turn west and return to Quito via the town of **Tumbaco**.

The left fork, although a little shorter, is somewhat more twisting and slower than the right-hand route, and therefore, some drivers avoid it. The region is generally less inhabited and has more barren countryside than the other road. Some prefer it for the exciting drive and wild scenery. The only village of any size on this road is **Tabacundo**.

COCHASQUÍ RUINS

Heading toward Tabacundo from Quito (along the left fork), you'll find a turnoff to the left, a few kilometers before Tabacundo, which leads to the ruins of Cochasquí. These ruins were built by the Cara Indians before the Inca conquest and had been largely forgotten until recently. The area was declared a national archaeological site in 1977 and is currently being excavated and investigated.

Fifteen low, truncated, grass-covered pyramids (some of which are almost 100m long) and about 30 other mounds are visible. The remarkable panoramic view from the site (you can see the Quito hill El Panecillo if you have good binoculars) has led archaeologists to assume that Cochasquí was built for strategic purposes. Additionally, the alignment of the pyramids and some of the structures associated with them seem to indicate they had ceremonial and astronomical uses. The site is interesting but not dramatic – some readers have been disappointed by it.

There is a small on-site museum, and local Spanish-speaking guides give tours of the **museum and site** (both open 9am-4pm Tues-Sun). If you are pressed for time, ask for a short tour – longer tours last a couple of hours. Although entrance to the site and tours are officially free, visitors should tip guides, because their wages are inadequate.

The guides can also show you life-sized houses that were modeled after indigenous architectural styles and using ancient methods. Inside, you'll see indigenous furnishings and cooking utensils, while guinea pigs (a traditional delicacy of the Incas) scurry around. Outside, a garden teems with a cornucopia of Andean plants that were used for food, medicinal, ceremonial and utilitarian purposes.

There is no public transportation. Some buses (try Transportes Lagos) between Quito and Otavalo take the Tabacundo road and can drop you off at the turnoff (there is a sign). From there, a cobbled road climbs about 9km to the site. The site workers and guides usually drive up to the ruins at about 9am and can give you a lift, but otherwise you have to walk. Hitching opportunities are few due to the lack of traffic. Taxis can be hired from Cayambe and will do the round trip, including waiting time, for about $13.

CAYAMBE
☎ 02 • pop 15,000

Cayambe, about 64km north of Quito along the Panamericana, is the most important town on the way to Otavalo. It is famous for its dairy industry, and there are many stores and restaurants selling a variety of local cheeses and cheese products. Salt crackers called *bizcochos* are also produced here. The local Salesian monastery reportedly has an excellent library on indigenous cultures. Any bus between Quito and Otavalo can drop you in Cayambe.

Although this is the only town of any size so close to the equator, few people stay here, preferring instead to buy some cheese and continue on to Otavalo.

Youth Hostal Cayambe (☎ 236 0007; *Bolívar 23; bunks per person $5)* is centrally located and the cheapest place to stay.

Hostería Mitad del Mundo (☎ 236 0226; *beds per person $6)*, at the south end of town, is clean.

Hostería Napoles (☎ 236 0231; *singles/doubles $10/15)*, about 1km north of town on the Panamericana, has cabins with private bath, hot water and TV. Cheese products are sold, and it has one of the best restaurants in Cayambe.

Hacienda Guachala (☎ 236 3042; w *www .haciendaguachala.com; singles/doubles $31/37)* was founded in 1580 and is said to be the oldest hacienda in Ecuador. The place has housed Ecuadorian presidents and visiting luminaries during its four centuries in existence. In 1993, it opened as a hotel and it now offers 14 comfortable rooms with

private bath. Horse riding, hiking and jeep tours are available, and there's a swimming pool, restaurant and bar. Seven kilometers south of Cayambe is the turnoff to the Cangahua road, which heads southeast from the Panamericana. Another 1.5km along this road is the hacienda. Several readers have recommended this place.

FROM CAYAMBE TO OTAVALO
From Cayambe, it is 31km along the Panamericana to Otavalo. The snowcapped mountain east of the road is the extinct **Volcán Cayambe**. At 5790m, it is Ecuador's third-highest peak. Trivia buffs: it is also the highest point in the world through which the equator directly passes – at about 4600m on the south side. There is a **climbing refuge** (per person $10), but you need a 4WD to reach it. From the refuge, the climb is more difficult than the more frequently ascended peak of Cotopaxi but climbing guides in Quito can get you up there.

The Panamericana climbs from Pichincha Province to Imbabura Province, a region known for its indigenous inhabitants and pretty lake district. Soon you see the largest of these lakes, **Laguna de San Pablo**, stretching away to your right, with the high peak of **Volcán Imbabura** (4609m) behind it. The area is dotted with villages inhabited by the Otavaleño Indians.

OTAVALO
☎ 06 • pop 26,000 • elevation 2550m

This small town is justly famous for its friendly people and their Saturday market. The market dates back to pre-Inca times, when jungle products were brought up from the eastern lowlands and traded for highland goods. Today's market serves two different groups: locals who buy and barter animals, food and other essentials; and tourists looking for crafts.

The goods sold at the market are undeniably oriented toward the tourist market, and this has led to complaints from travelers. But it's important to keep in mind the well-being of the weavers – their prosperity in this ever-changing and difficult world is quite a feat.

But an even truer measure of their success is their continuing sense of tribal identity and tradition. One of the most evident features of the Otavaleños' cultural integrity is their

OTAVALO

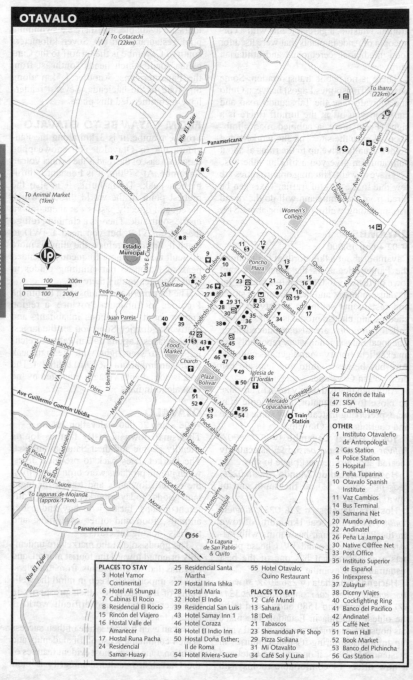

To Cotacachi (22km)
To Ibarra (22km)
Rio El Tejar
Panamericana
To Animal Market (1km)
Women's College
Estadio Municipal
Poncho Plaza
Staircase
Food Market
Church
Plaza Bolívar
Iglesia de El Jordán
Mercado Copacabana
Train Station
To Laguna de San Pablo & Quito
To Lagunas de Mojanda (approx 17km)
Panamericana
Rio El Tejar

0   100   200m
0   100   200yd

PLACES TO STAY		44 Rincón de Italia
25 Residencial Santa Martha		47 SISA
3 Hotel Yamor Continental		49 Camba Huasy
27 Hostal Irina Ishka		**OTHER**
6 Hotel Ali Shungu	28 Hostal María	1 Instituto Otavaleño de Antropologia
7 Cabinas El Rocío	32 Hotel El Indio	2 Gas Station
8 Residencial El Rocío	39 Residencial San Luis	4 Police Station
15 Rincón del Viajero	43 Hotel Samay Inn 1	5 Hospital
16 Hostal Valle del Amanecer	46 Hotel Coraza	9 Peña Tuparina
17 Hostal Runa Pacha	48 Hotel El Indio Inn	10 Otavalo Spanish Institute
24 Residencial Samar-Huasy	50 Hostal Doña Esther; Il de Roma	11 Vaz Cambios
	54 Hotel Riviera-Sucre	14 Bus Terminal
	55 Hotel Otavalo; Quino Restaurant	19 Samarina Net
		20 Mundo Andino
	PLACES TO EAT	22 Andinatel
	12 Café Mundi	26 Peña La Jampa
	13 Sahara	30 Native C@ffee Net
	18 Deli	33 Post Office
	21 Tabascos	35 Instituto Superior de Español
	23 Shenandoah Pie Shop	36 Intiexpress
	29 Pizza Siciliana	37 Zulaytur
	31 Mi Otavalito	38 Diceny Viajes
	34 Café Sol y Luna	40 Cockfighting Ring
		41 Banco del Pacífico
		42 Andinatel
		45 Caffé Net
		51 Town Hall
		52 Book Market
		53 Banco del Pichincha
		56 Gas Station

Otavalo's Weavings – A Phenomenal Success

The story of the phenomenal success of the *otavaleño* (people from Otavalo) weavers is an intriguing one. The backstrap loom has been used in the area for some 4000 years. The Indians' proficiency as weavers was harshly exploited by the colonialists beginning in 1555, and later by Ecuadorian landowners, who forced them to labor in *obrajes* (sweatshops), often for 14 or more hours a day. Miserable though this was, it did have the effect of instilling a great knowledge of weaving in the *otavaleño* people.

In 1917, a local weaver had the idea of copying the Scottish tweeds that were then in vogue, and this was so successful that it again led to recognition of the skill of the *otavaleño* weavers. This ability, combined with the Agrarian Reform of 1964 and the people's shrewd business sense, has made the *otavaleños* the most prosperous Indian group in Ecuador – perhaps on the continent. It is difficult to find a town of any size that does not have an *otavaleño* store. The *otavaleños* also make frequent business trips to neighboring countries, and even to North America and Europe.

dress. Traditional attire is worn on normal workdays in homes, villages and fields – what you see them wearing is not just for tourists at the Saturday market. Otavaleño men are immediately distinctive with their long ponytails, calf-length white pants, rope sandals, reversible gray or blue ponchos and dark felt hats. The women, too, are very striking in their beautifully embroidered blouses, long black skirts and shawls and interesting folded head cloths. The women also wear bright jewels, the most obvious being the many strings of golden blown-glass beads around their necks and the long strands of red beads around their wrists and arms.

Most of the inhabitants of Otavalo are whites or *mestizos* (persons of mixed Spanish and indigenous descent). Of the 40,000 Indians in the area, most live in the many nearby villages and come into Otavalo for market day. However, quite a few Indians own stores in Otavalo, where you can buy most items if you are unable to come for the market.

For detailed cultural information about the people of Otavalo, read Lynn Meisch's *Otavalo: Weaving, Costume and the Market* (Libri Mundi, Quito, 1987), available only in Ecuador.

Information

On Poncho Plaza, **Vaz Cambios** (cnr Modesto Jaramillo & Saona) gives good exchange rates and changes traveler's checks. **Banco del Pacífico** (Modesto Jaramillo near Calderón; open 8:30am-3pm Mon-Fri) and **Banco del Pichincha** (Bolívar at García Moreno) change traveler's checks and have ATMs.

The **post office** (Sucre at Salinas, 2nd floor) is just off Pancho Plaza. Make calls at the two **Andinatel** branches (Calderón near Modesto Jaramillo; open 8am-8pm daily • Salinas 509; open 8am-9pm daily). Internet access is available for $1.20 per hour at **Caffé Net** (☎ 920 193; Sucre near Colón), **Native C@ffee Net** (☎ 923 540; Sucre near Colón; open 8:30am-9:30pm Mon-Sat) and **Samarina Net** (☎ 921 468; Bolívar near Salinas Quiroga; open 8am-9pm daily).

Run by the English-speaking, knowledgeable, Señor Rodrigo Mora, **Zulaytur** (☎ 921 176; w www.geocities.com/zulaytur; cnr Sucre & Colón, 2nd floor) has had many recommendations from readers. A variety of inexpensive guided tours enable you to visit local Indian homes, learn about the entire weaving process, buy products off the loom and take photographs. You can go horse-riding too. Señor Mora's emphasis on anthropology and sociology makes his tours very worthwhile. Tours cost about $16 per person with a maximum of 10 passengers. Don't mistake other similarly named operations for Zulaytur.

Diceny Viajes (☎ 921 217; Sucre 10-11) offers warmly recommended hiking trips up Volcán Cotacachi with indigenous guides who explain the cultural and natural history of the area. **Intiexpress** (☎ 921 436; Sucre 11-06) is a reliable, friendly outfit offering horse-riding trips.

You can buy, sell and trade books in English, German, French and other languages at **Book Market** (Bolívar at García Moreno; open Mon-Sat).

The following doctors have been locally recommended: **Dr Patricio Buitrón** (☎ 921

159, 921 678; Roca near Quiroga) speaks some English and **Dr Klaus Fay** *(☎ 921 203; Sucre near Morales; open Tues-Sat)* speaks German and English. The **hospital** *(☎ 920 444, 923 566; Sucre)* is about 400m north of downtown.

The **police station** *(Avenida Luis Ponce de Leon)* is at the northeastern end of town.

Markets

The main market day is Saturday. There are three main plazas, with the overflow spilling out on to the streets linking them. Poncho Plaza is the **crafts market** *(open daily year-round)*, where the items of most appeal to tourists are sold. Here, you can purchase woolen goods such as ponchos, blankets, scarves, sweaters, tapestries and gloves, as well as a variety of embroidered blouses and shirts, shawls, string bags, rope sandals, jewelry etc.

Bargaining for each purchase is normal. Some people are not good at it and feel uncomfortable trying to knock a few cents off an already cheaply priced item. Just remember that it is expected and make an offer a little below the first asking price.

This market gets under way in the early morning and continues until mid-afternoon. You are advised to spend Friday night in Otavalo and get to the market early. It can get rather crowded by mid-morning, when the big tour groups arrive and prices are higher. If you come in the early morning, you'll find a greater selection at better prices. Note that there are increasing numbers of pickpockets and bag snatchers at the market – keep your eyes open and your valuables hidden. Some stalls stay open on Poncho Plaza every day (especially during the June-to-August high season), others are only open on Saturday, while stores around town selling crafts are open daily year-round. Travelers wanting to avoid crowds may opt to come on a day other than Saturday – the shopping is still good.

The **food market** *(cnr Modesto Jaramill & Montalvo)* sells produce and household goods for the locals, and there is an **animal market** *(open 6am-10am)* that begins in the predawn hours on the outskirts of town. These are not oriented toward tourists, but many people find the sight of poncho-clad *indígenas* (indigenous people) quietly bartering for a string of screaming piglets much more interesting than the scene at Poncho Plaza. The animal market is over by early morning, so plan on an early arrival. It lies over a kilometer out of town; cross the bridge at the end of Colón and follow the crowds to get there.

Instituto Otaveleño de Antropología

The Instituto Otavaleño de Antropología *(admission free; open 8:30am-noon & 2:30pm-6pm Tues-Fri, 8:30am-noon Sat)*, just off the Panamericana north of town, houses a small archaeological and ethnographical museum of the area, a library, and a bookstore selling books (in Spanish) about the anthropology and culture of Otavalo.

Language Courses

Mundo Andino *(☎ 921 864;* e *espanol@ interactive.net.ec; Salinas 4-04)* has been warmly recommended for its personable service and good teachers. The charge is about $4 per hour for individual tuition, and homestays with local families can be arranged. Mundo Andino also arranges hikes, dinners and other activities for students, including long-term volunteer activities.

Otavalo Spanish Institute *(☎ 925 475;* w *www.otavalospanish.com; 31 de Octubre 4-76)* offers two- to four-week intensive Spanish courses packed with outdoor and cultural activities. You can combine these with classes in Baños. The owner is very enthusiastic, and students speak highly of the school.

The Quito-based **Instituto Superior de Español** *(☎ 922 414;* w *www.instituto-super ior.net; Sucre 11-10)* also offers quality Spanish lessons at its Otavalo branch.

Special Events

Otavalo's best-known fiesta, the Fiesta del Yamor, is held in the first two weeks of September. There's plenty of music, processions and dancing, as well as fireworks displays, cockfights and an election of the Queen of the Fiesta – and, of course, lots of *yamor* (a delicious nonalcoholic corn drink made with seven varieties of corn).

June 24 is St John the Baptist Day (which is especially celebrated in the San Juan suburb, around the intersection of Cisneros with the Panamericana) and June 29 is the Day of St Peter and St Paul. These and the intervening days are an important fiesta for

Otavalo and the surrounding villages. There is a bullfight in Otavalo and a boating regatta on Laguna de San Pablo, as well as celebrations in nearby Ilumán.

Some small village fiestas date back to pre-Columbian rituals and can last as long as two weeks. Drinking and dancing are a big part of the festivities. They are not much visited by outsiders and, in some cases, it would be dangerous for tourists just to show up. One little-known annual event involves a ritual battle between rival villages at which locals are sometimes killed. The authorities turn a blind eye and outsiders are not tolerated.

A few kilometers southeast of Otavalo, on the southern shores of Laguna de San Pablo, in the villages around San Rafael, there is a fiesta called Corazas on August 19. Also in some of the south-shore villages is the Pendoneros Fiesta on October 15.

The precise dates of these celebrations vary from year to year, but they are usually well publicized, and you can find out what's going on from posters in the area.

Places to Stay

Otavalo's popularity with visitors has led to a proliferation of comfortable, good-value hotels. Still, hotels fill up on Friday night for the Saturday market, so arrive early for the best selection. If you arrive midweek and plan to stay a few days, you'll probably have time to check out several places to find the best deal for you, and you can often negotiate a cheaper price since you're staying longer.

Note that the best hotels are in the countryside outside of town (see Places to Stay under Around Otavalo later). A car or taxi is the most convenient way to get to these and, although they're outside of Otavalo proper, they're wonderful places to base yourself for visits to town.

Budget One of the most relaxing hotels in town is the **Hostal Valle del Amanecer** (☎ 920 990, fax 921 159; e amanecer@uio .satnet.net; cnr Roca & Quiroga; rooms per person with shared/private bath $7/9). The place resembles an old, walled hacienda and the rustic wooden rooms open on to a cobbled, hammock-strewn patio. There are lots of tables and comfy chairs around (and plenty of travelers sprawled out in them) and a fire pit, too. Breakfast is included in the price.

Volcano Folklore

Two extinct volcanoes can be seen from Otavalo on clear days: the massive bulk of Volcán Imbabura (4609m) to the east and the sharper, more jagged Volcán Cotacachi (at 4939m it's Ecuador's 11th-highest mountain) to the northwest. The locals refer to these peaks as Taita ('Daddy') Imbabura and Mama Cotacachi. Legend has it that when it's raining in Otavalo, Taita Imbabura is pissing in the valley. Another legend suggests that when Mama Cotacachi awakes with a fresh covering of snow, she has been visited by Taita Imbabura during the night.

Hotel Riviera-Sucre (☎ 920 241; e riviera sucre@hotmail.com; García Moreno 3-80; rooms per person with shared/private bath $5/8) is a Belgian-owned hotel in a lovely converted old house with large colorful rooms, a small courtyard, laundry facilities and a small café. It's an outstanding deal. There's plenty of hot water, too.

Residencial El Rocío (☎ 920 584; Morales 11-70; rooms per person with shared/private bath $4/5) is clean, plain, friendly and quiet. Hot water is available and the view from the roof is good. The owner has a vehicle, arranges lake tours, and owns **Cabinas El Rocío** (rooms per person $6), a quiet place in the San Juan neighborhood, just beyond the Panamericana; it has good views and a pleasant garden. The rooms are comfortable, clean and worth the price if you want to get away from the town center.

Rincón del Viajero (☎/fax 921 741; e rincondelviajero@hotmail.com; Roca 11-07; rooms per person with shared/private bath $6/8) offers clean, well-lit rooms which are small but comfortable. There's parking, hot water and a rooftop terrace with hammocks. Breakfast is included.

Hostal Runa Pacha (☎ 921 730; Roca 10-02; rooms per person $7-9) has a brightly painted facade and is convenient to both the bus terminal and Poncho Plaza. A hard-working staff provides good service. Rooms vary in price, depending on the season and whether or not you want a TV.

Residencial San Luis (☎ 920 614; Calderón 6-02) is run by a wonderfully friendly woman who keeps her three floors of tiny rooms impeccably clean. There's a washbasin and rooftop clothes line.

Residencial Samar-Huasy (*Modesto Jaramillo 6-11; rooms per person $2*) has clean, small rooms with shared baths. Hot water is unpredictable.

Hotel El Indio (☎ 920 060; *Sucre 12-14*) is similarly priced, centrally located and often full by Wednesday afternoon; the guests stay for the rest of the week. It also has rooms with TV, private hot showers and a restaurant. Don't confuse this place with Hotel El Indio Inn, which is listed under the midrange accommodations section following.

Other reliable, inexpensive hotels include **Hostal Irina Ishka** (☎ 920 684; *Modesto Jaramillo 5-69; rooms per person with shared/private bath $3/4*); **Hostal María** (☎ 920 672; *Modesto Jaramillo near Colón; rooms per person $3*), which has private baths; **Residencial Santa Martha** (☎ 920 147; *Colón & 31 de Octubre; rooms per person $3*); and **Hotel Samay Inn 1** (☎/fax 922 871; *Calderón 10-05; rooms per person $3*).

Mid-Range Occupying a beautifully refurbished old building, **Hotel Otavalo** (☎ 923 712, 924 999; *Roca 5-04; singles/doubles $18/26*) offers spotless rooms with TV and hot bath. Some rooms have balconies and private baths, while the interior rooms are quiet and dark. There's a classy restaurant upstairs, an espresso bar below and a well-lit, covered courtyard for sitting.

Hostal Doña Esther (☎/fax 920 739; *Montalvo 4-44; singles/doubles $21/29*) is a lovely colonial-style hotel with lots of plants hanging over the balustrades, a little patio and pleasant attractively furnished rooms. It's small and personable and has a good Italian restaurant.

Hotel El Indio Inn (☎ 920 325, ☎/fax 922 922; *Bolívar 9-04; singles/doubles $22/37*) is a tasteful modern hotel with two interior patios and a game room. It has 40 large rooms with TV and telephone as well as a good restaurant downstairs. Don't confuse this place with the budget Hotel El Indio, mentioned earlier.

Hotel Coraza (☎ 921 225; **e** h.coraza@ uio.satnet.net; *cnr Sucre & Calderón; rooms per person $13*) has over 50 modern carpeted rooms with TV and telephone. There is a decent restaurant, bar, coffee shop, gift shop and parking garage. It's good value.

Hotel Yamor Continental (☎ 920 451; *Avenida Luis Ponce de Leon; rooms $15*) has clean and spacious rooms in a hacienda-like building set in flower-filled gardens at the northeast end of town. There is a pool, restaurant and bar. Rooms have private bath, TV and phone.

Hotel Ali Shungu (☎ 920 750; **w** www.ali shungu.com; *singles/doubles $37/49, apartments $98-134*), at the northwest end of Quito, is the prettiest hotel in town. This non-smoking hotel has a giant, flowery garden with fine views of Volcán Imbabura. The 16 rooms are appealingly decorated with local crafts and flowers, and have private bath and plenty of hot water. There are also two apartments, complete with VCR and stereo system, for two to six people. The American owners require a two-night minimum during weekends, especially in the high season.

Places to Eat

With so many travelers rolling into town for the market, Otavalo's restaurants are varied and abundant.

Shenandoah Pie Shop (☎ 921 465; *Salinas 5-15; pie slices $1; open 7:30am-9pm daily*) is perennially popular for its knockout homemade pies.

Café Mundi (☎ 921 729; *Quiroga 6-08; mains $2-4; open 8am-10pm daily*) has been turning out good, cheap, wholesome food for years. The menu includes 16 types of pancakes, nachos, hummus, seven vegetarian plates and several traditional Ecuadorian dishes.

Tabascos (☎ 922 476; *cnr Salinas & Sucre; mains $3-5; open daily*), just off the Poncho Plaza, has slightly pricey Mexican and Italian food, decent breakfasts and a 2nd-floor patio overlooking the plaza, which is perhaps the best reason to eat there.

Sahara (☎ 922 212; *Quiroga at Sucre; mains $2-4; open noon-11pm daily*) serves good Middle Eastern food such as falafel, hummus and shawermas. When you finish you can lay back on a straw floor-mat and smoke a big bowl of fruit-flavored tobacco from a giant hookah.

Café Sol y Luna (*Bolívar 11-10; mains $2-3; open 8:30am-10pm Tues-Sun*) is a friendly American-owned café serving good portions of well-prepared organic food, including hearty soups, vegie burgers and tofu sandwiches.

Mi Otavalito (☎ 920 176; Sucre 11-19; mains $2-4; open 8am-11pm daily) is great for Ecuadorian dishes and the family atmosphere. The almuerzos and meriendas (set lunches and dinners, respectively) are excellent value.

Pizza Siciliana (☎ 925 999; Morales 5-10; pizzas per person around $5; open noon-10:30pm daily) bakes decent pizzas at rather steep prices. It's at its best on Friday and Saturday nights when the traditional música folklórica (Andean folk music) bands take to the floor and play to a packed house.

Rincón de Italia (☎ 922 555; Sucre 919; pizzas per person around $3.50; open 9am-11pm Mon-Sat, 4pm-11pm Sun) is a small place serving good thin-crust pizzas, as well as spaghetti, cannelloni and lasagne.

Il de Roma (Montalvo 4-44) in the Hostal Doña Esther, has good wood-oven pizzas and Italian food (see Places to Stay earlier).

SISA (☎ 920 154; Calderón 409; mains $2-5; open 7am-10pm daily), on the 2nd floor of the arts complex of the same name, has a wide variety of dishes. Good coffee is sold in the café downstairs.

Camba Huasay (☎ 920 359; Bolívar near Calderón; mains $1.50-3; open 8am-4pm daily) is a tiny family-run place serving a filling $2 almuerzo. $1 will get you a whopping plate of lentils and rice, and there's good fried chicken, too.

Deli (☎ 921 558; Quiroga at Bolívar; mains $3-4; open 8am-6pm Mon-Thur, 8am-10pm Fri & Sat, 8am to 8pm Sun) puts an odd twist on Mexican food, but it turns out OK. The vegetarian nachos ($4) with cheese, eggplant, mushrooms, beans and a mountain of other vegetables are delicious.

Quino Restaurant (Roca near García Moreno), by Hotel Otavalo, is very popular and serves good, if pricey, food.

Hotel Ali Shungu (Quito; open 7:30am-8:30pm) has some of the best food in town, and it's worth the extra few dollars. There are both vegetarian and meat dishes on the menu, and there's live música folklórica on weekends (when a donation is requested).

Entertainment

Otavalo is quiet during the week, but it livens up on weekends.

Peña La Jampa (☎ 922 988; cnr Jaramillo & Morales; admission $2-3 open 10pm-3am Fri & Sat) showcases live salsa, merengue, rock en español (Spanish rock) and folklórica. It can be hit or miss, but when it's good it's great. There's plenty of room to dance and lots of little tables for tucking away.

Peña Tuparina (Morales near 31 de Octubre; admission $1; open 9am-2am Fri & Sat July & Aug) is a mainstay of the local music scene. It has live bands ranging from salsa to folklórica.

Pizza Siciliana (Morales 5-10) has live folklórica on weekend nights and it's always packed.

There's a weekly cockfight (admission $0.50) held every Saturday starting about 6pm in the ring at the southwest end of 31 de Octubre.

Getting There & Away

Bus Getting from Quito to Otavalo is straightforward. Buses leave Quito's main terminal every 20 minutes or so and all charge under $2 for the two- to three-hour ride. Transportes Otavalo and Transportes Los Lagos are the only ones allowed into Otavalo's bus terminal. Other companies will drop you off on the Panamericana, forcing you to walk into town.

From the northern towns of Ibarra ($0.35, 35 minutes) or Tulcán ($2.50, three hours), you'll find buses leaving for Otavalo every hour or so from their respective terminals. Buses from Tulcán drop you on the Panamericana.

In Otavalo, the main bus terminal (Atahualpa) is at the north end of town, from where you can take a taxi to most hotels for $1. From this terminal, Transportes Otavalo or Transportes Los Lagos will take you to Quito or Ibarra.

Transportes Otavalo also has buses to the towns of Apuela and García Moreno. You can also catch old local buses to some of the villages south of Otavalo, such as San Pablo del Lago. Cooperativa Imbaburapac has buses from Otavalo to Ilumán, Agato, San Pablo del Lago and Cayambe every hour or so. Transportes Cotacachi goes to Cotacachi via the longer route (through Quiroga), and Transportes 6 de Junio takes the shorter route ($0.20, 25 minutes), via the Panamericana. Transportes Cotacachi has some buses continuing on to Apuela and García Moreno. Transportes 8 de Septiembre is a local bus that also goes to Ilumán. There is no strict schedule for services to any of these towns and prices are low. Adventurous travelers might just want to get on board and see what happens, but leave enough time to get back to a hotel, as most of the small villages have no formal accommodations.

For the villages of Calderón, Guayllabamba and Cayambe, take an Otavalo–Quito bus (they're busy Saturday afternoons). You'll be dropped off at the turnoff from the main road and will have to walk several hundred meters to the village.

Taxi & Shuttle You can always hire a taxi from Quito for the day for around $60.

For door-to-door van service contact **Hotel Ali Shungu** (☎ 920 7500); their shuttle goes back and forth between Quito and your hotel for $17 per person one way (see Places to Stay earlier).

AROUND OTAVALO
☎ 06

The spectacular countryside surrounding Otavalo is scattered with lakes, indigenous villages, hacienda-hotels and hiking trails. It's all easily accessible to anyone who has the slightest inkling to beat the Otavalo market scene and take to the hills. You can stay at any of the places listed in this section and from where it's easy to get to the Saturday market in Otavalo by taxi (about $5) or bus.

In the mountains southwest of Otavalo are the spectacular páramo lakes of **Lagunas de Mojanda**. Southeast of Otavalo, the giant Laguna de San Pablo has several *hosterías* (small hotels) along its shore and the village of San Pablo del Lago at its southeast end.

The Panamericana heads northeast out of Otavalo and the indigenous villages of **Peguche**, **Agato** and **Ilumán** are loosely strung together along its side, just a few kilometers outside Otavalo. They can be reached by bus or taxi, on foot or with a tour.

There are several other *otavaleño* villages in the area, and a visit to the tourist agencies in Otavalo will yield much information. The villages southwest of Laguna de San Pablo are known for the manufacture of fireworks, as well as for *totora* mats and other reed products.

Although people are generally friendly, bear in mind that on Saturday afternoon after the market, as well as on Sunday, some of the Indian men get blind drunk (as happens throughout the Andes). You may, therefore, find this an inopportune time to visit these villages.

Occasional reports of robberies trickle in, but they are not frequent. Many travelers enjoy walking around the area. When hiking around the region, ask locally for advice.

Lagunas de Mojanda
These beautiful lakes are set in high páramo scenery about 17km south of Otavalo. They acquired protected status (primarily through the hard work of Casa Mojanda) in 2002. Camping is possible on the south side of the biggest lake, **Laguna Grande**, and there is a basic stone refuge (bring a sleeping bag and food). **Fuya Fuya**, a jagged, extinct volcano (4263m), is nearby. You can walk to the lakes or get there by taxi (about $8 each way plus $6 per hour to wait); there is a dirt road from Otavalo. You can make a good day trip by taking a taxi first thing in the morning and hiking back. Both Casa Mojanda and Zulaytur (see Information under Otavalo) offer guided day-hikes of the area, which include transportation, for about $25. For information about the lakes, stop at the Mojanda Foundation/Pachamama Association directly across from Casa Mojanda on the road to the park.

From the lakes, it is possible to hike across the páramo about 20km due south to the ruins of Cochasquí. The views are fantastic on clear days. A useful 1:50,000 topographical map of the Mojanda area, numbered NII-F1, 3994-III, is available from the IGM in Quito (see Maps in the Facts for the Visitor and Quito chapters).

In years past, several attacks were reported in the Lagunas de Mojanda area. With its new park status, however, it is now reportedly perfectly safe. It never hurts to ask locally before heading out.

The lovely country inn and organic farm of **Casa Mojanda** (☎/fax 09-973 1737, fax 970 3843; w www.casamojanda.com; singles low/high season $75/90, doubles year-round $120) lies about 4km south of Otavalo on the road to Lagunas de Mojanda; the setting is spectacular. The Ecuadorian and American owners speak perfect English and are enthusiastic about their projects, which include low-impact tourism to benefit education, and cultural and health awareness in the local indigenous communities. Casa

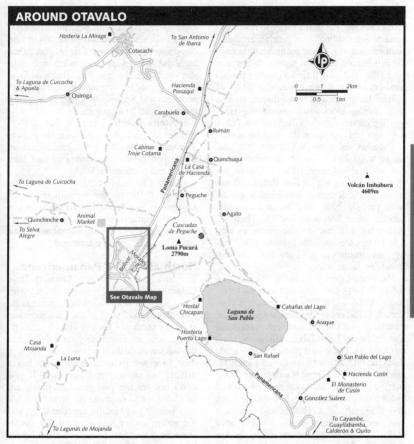

AROUND OTAVALO

Hostería La Mirage
To San Antonio de Ibarra
Cotacachi
To Laguna de Cuicocha & Apuela
Quiroga
Hacienda Pinsaquí
Carabuela
Ilumán
Cabinas Troje Cotama
Quinchuquí
La Casa de Hacienda
Volcán Imbabura 4609m
To Laguna de Cuicocha
Peguche
Agato
Quinchinche
Animal Market
To Selva Alegre
Cascadas de Peguche
Loma Pucará 2790m
See Otavalo Map
Bolívar Morales
Hostal Chicapan
Laguna de San Pablo
Cabañas del Lago
Araque
Hostería Puerto Lago
San Rafael
San Pablo del Lago
Casa Mojanda
La Luna
Hacienda Cusín
El Monasterio de Cusín
González Suárez
Panamericana
To Cayambe, Guayllabamba, Calderón & Quito
To Lagunas de Mojanda

0   1   2km
0   0.5   1mi

Mojanda consists of eight individual guest cottages, each built using rammed-earth construction (similar to adobe) and natural building materials. Some have fireplaces and all have sweeping views of the stunning Andean countryside. Rates include breakfast and lunch made entirely of ingredients from the organic farm; they also include use of the hot tub, video library with over 400 movies and big screen TV, a library, and short guided hike to nearby waterfalls. Rentals of mountain bikes, kayaks and horses can be arranged with advance notice. There is also one cottage for groups with rates of $30 per person.

La Luna *(☎/fax 09-973 7415; camp sites $2, dorm beds with/without breakfast $4.50/3, rooms per person with shared bath $6,* *doubles with private bath $16)* is 4.5km south of Otavalo on the way to Lagunas de Mojanda. Run by two friendly Argentineans who speak English, this quiet place with a kitchen, dining room and fireplace has been recommended by several readers. There is a dorm with 12 bunks, three shared toilets and two hot showers. For two or three people, there are four smaller rooms with shared bath. Two other doubles have a private bath and fireplace. If you camp, you can make use of hot showers and the dining/bar area with videos and games. The owners can arrange mountain-bike and hiking tours and will make packed lunches or dinners with advance notice. Call them to ask about the bus schedule or to get picked up in Otavalo. A taxi will cost about $4.

Laguna de San Pablo

From Otavalo, the easiest way to reach Laguna de San Pablo on foot is to head roughly southeast on any of the paths heading over the hill behind the train station. When you get to the lake, you'll find a (mostly paved) road encircling it, with beautiful views of Volcán Imbabura to the northeast; on this road, going clockwise around the lake, you'll pass through the village of **San Pablo del Lago** and end up on the Panamericana.

Cabañas del Lago (☎ *918 001, 918 108, Quito* ☎ *02-243 5936;* e *cablago@uio.sat net.net; doubles/cabañas $55/147)* is on the east side of Laguna de San Pablo and has some 15 modern and comfortable cabins with private bath. The more expensive cabañas have fireplaces and TV. There's a restaurant and bar on the premises and small boats are available for hire. Horse riding and miniature golf are also offered. Breakfast is included.

Hacienda Cusín (☎ *918 013, 918 316, USA* ☎ *800-683-8148;* w *www.haciendacusin.com; single/doubles $75/105)* is a beautiful converted 17th-century hacienda with all the trimmings – it's on the southern outskirts of San Pablo del Lago (about 10km southeast of Otavalo). The oldest part of the hacienda dates to 1602, although it was completely remodeled in 1990. There is a cozy bar with a roaring fireplace, games room, well-stocked video room, reading room, beautiful gardens and a squash court. Horses and mountain bikes are available for guests. Two exclusive craft shops, including the one run by the Andrango family from Agato (see Agato later), are on the premises. The hacienda is usually booked well in advance for weekends, but it is less busy midweek. Complete packages, including three delicious homemade meals and two hours of horse riding or mountain biking, are available. Lunches are especially good – the traditional soups and local dishes attract day-trippers from Quito. Discounts can be negotiated for extended stays or if booked online.

El Monasterio de Cusín, nearby, is under the same ownership as the hacienda. Reservations are made through the hacienda, although the monastery is used mostly for overflow accommodations and conferences. There are 20 large rooms or cottages with fireplaces and beamed ceilings set around two attractive courtyards. A tower reading room offers lovely views, and the extensive gardens are filled with perennial flowers. The Cusín also has information about and can make reservations for several other highland haciendas. Extended hacienda stays and special trips – including weddings and honeymoons, overnight horse-riding expeditions and Spanish-language or weaving courses – can be arranged.

Hostería Puerto Lago (☎ *921 901/2; doubles $79)* is right on the lake, about 5km southeast of Otavalo on the Panamericana. There is a good restaurant with fine lake views, and boats are available.

Hostal Chicapan (☎ *920 331; rooms per person $10-15)*, on the western shores of Laguna de San Pablo, has rooms with hot showers. Some rooms have balcony views of the lake. There is a restaurant and horse and bike rentals can be arranged.

North along the Panamericana

The lovely, down-to-earth **Cabañas Troje Cotama** (☎/fax *946 119; rooms without/with meals $32/35)* is a refurbished hacienda on an unpaved road west of the Panamericana and 4km north of Otavalo. The 10 comfortable rooms are completely remodeled, but the adobe buildings themselves maintain their time-worn charm. Each room has a private hot shower and fireplace. If you don't opt for the full package, meals are available for $7 each ($3 for breakfast). It's very relaxing and totally unpretentious, and the young owner sets up multiday excursions so you can hacienda-hop by horseback, sleeping in a different hacienda each night. There are mountain bikes for rent. Best of all, the price is manageable.

Hacienda Pinsaquí (☎ *946 116/17;* w *www .haciendapinsaqui.com; rooms $72-120, suites $144)* is an elegant country home with 16 lovely guest rooms and a renowned horse stable. It was built in 1790 as a textile workshop, although it later outgrew its humble origins. Simón Bolívar overnighted here during trips between Ecuador and Colombia. A photo in the hotel shows the owner leading his favorite stallion through the French doors of the lounge to meet the guests! (He doesn't do that any more.) The common areas include a reading room with a fireplace, chapel and cozy bar. The man-made lake and the 200-year-old gardens are very pretty and relaxing. Both horses and mountain bikes are available for hire. Rooms and suites, some of which have a Jacuzzi, accommodate one to four people and include an American breakfast. Lunch or dinner is $15. The hacienda is near the turn to Cotacachi, just off the Panamericana.

Peguche

A good walk heads out of Otavalo to the north and then east off the main highway, landing you in Peguche in about an hour. Another way of reaching Peguche from Otavalo is simply by walking northeast along the train tracks for about 3km; from Peguche you can continue to Ilumán or Agato. Some people visit Peguche with hopes of being invited into indigenous homes and buying the best weavings direct from the loom at bargain prices. That's wishful thinking. Prices aren't much (if at all) lower than in Otavalo and the people have better things to do than invite curious gringos into their houses. On the other hand, the locals are friendly and you might be lucky – especially if you speak Spanish (or better, Quechua). Cooperativa Imbaburapac has some buses that go through Peguche en route to Agato.

One place that may allow visits is **Tejidos Mimahuasi**, which is the home of weavers José María Cotacachi and Luz María Fichabamba – they also sell their wares there. On the central plaza of Peguche, the **Centro Pachakutik** will sometimes have *folklórica* concerts.

From the railway line in Peguche, a trail leads about 2km southeast to the waterfalls known as **Cascada de Peguche**. Near the falls are some pre-Columbian ruins in poor condition. A small entrance fee may be charged on weekends. Ask locals in town for directions and advice.

Hostal Aya Huma (☎ 922 663; w www .ayahuma.com; singles/doubles with shared bath $8/12, with private bath $14/20,) is a well-liked place near the train tracks. It has 24-hour hot water, a laundry service, fireplace, gardens with hammocks and parking. Hiking maps are available. It is run by a Dutch-Ecuadorian couple who serve vegetarian food and meat dishes (and pancakes!). There's live Andean music on Saturday nights beginning at 8pm. The hotel's **Casa Aya Huma** (singles/doubles $5/8), also on the premises, has a few bedrooms with shared

bath, kitchen and dining room. Reservations are suggested for Friday and Saturday.

Hostería Peguche Tío (☎ 922 619; e peg uchetio@mail.com; rooms per person $10) is a newer, attractive hotel closer to the village center. There are 12 rooms with private bath and fireplace, a restaurant, bar, music on weekends and locally made crafts for sale.

La Casa de Hacienda (☎ 946 336; e hos teriacasadehacienda@hotmail.com; doubles/ quads $40/60), about a kilometer north of Peguche, is a modern but peaceful and rustic-looking small hotel. The rooms all have fireplaces, and there are pleasant mountain views and a restaurant.

Agato

Another interesting village to visit is Agato, about 3km north of Laguna de San Pablo or 2km east of Peguche. Here you can find the **Tahuantinsuyo Weaving Workshop** which is run by master weaver Miguel Andrango in his own house. An excursion to Tahuantinsuyo is highly recommended for people with knowledge of or an interest in weaving. Señor Andrango is assisted by his daughter, Luz María, who is an expert in embroidery and designs, and by his son-in-law, Licenciado Humberto Romero, who is a specialist in the study of the traditional significance of the various designs used in *otavaleño* weaving.

The family make traditional weavings on backstrap looms using handspun wool and natural dyes and products. Almost all other weavers use the upright Spanish loom and/or chemical dyes. Tahuantinsuyo's work is more expensive than the market weavings, however, and is mainly for those seriously interested in textiles. Weavings are not normally sold in the Saturday market but can be bought directly from the weavers at the workshop. They have an outlet at the Hacienda Cusín on weekends (see Laguna de San Pablo earlier), and orders can be placed by mail at PO Box 53, Otavalo. Visitors to the workshop can often see a demonstration of the weaving process.

You can get to Agato from Otavalo by bus using Cooperativa Imbaburapac. There are two routes – the northern one through Peguche passes by the workshop, the southern one doesn't. The workshop has a sign. A taxi will cost about $3 from Otavalo, or you can walk (about 7km via Peguche), but it is easier to take a bus there and walk back.

Ilumán

This village, just off the Panamericana about 7km northeast of Otavalo, is another good place to see weavers at work. The Conterón family runs a handicrafts store, **Artesanías Inti Chumbi**, on the 2nd floor of their house on Parque Central. Apart from weavings and embroidered work, one of their specialties are very attractive *otavaleño* dolls. Weaving demonstrations can be arranged. *Cuy* (roast guinea pig) is prepared here if you order it a day in advance.

The easiest way to get to Ilumán from Otavalo is to take the Transportes 8 de Septiembre bus. You can also walk along the Panamericana or along the train tracks past Peguche.

Cotacachi

☎ 06

This small village, some 15km north of Otavalo and just west of the Panamericana, is famous for its leatherwork. Stores are strung out all along the main street of 10 de Agosto, and you can find almost anything you might want in the way of leather goods. Market day is Sunday. Most tourists just pay a quick visit to the stores and return to Ibarra or Otavalo, but if you wander around to the right of the main street, you'll find an attractive main plaza.

The small **Museo Etnográfico Tamaño Natural** (*García Moreno; admission $1; open 9am-12:30pm & 3pm-6pm Mon-Fri, 9am-noon & 3pm-5pm Sat, 9am-2pm Sun*) is worth a quick peek.

Information For information about local ecotourism try **Organicafe-net** (*☎ 916 525; Modesto Penaherrera 15-78; open 11am-7pm Wed-Sun*). It also provides Internet access and serves organic coffee.

Places to Stay & Eat The best budget hotel in town is **Hostal Plaza Bolívar** (*☎ 915 755; e cotacachi@turismoaventura.net; Bolívar 12-26 at 10 de Agosto; rooms per person with shared/private bath $4/6*). It's on the 3rd floor and rooms (many with private hot showers) are simple and spotless. The owners are friendly and helpful.

El Mesón de las Flores (*☎ 915 264; García Moreno & Sucre; singles/doubles $30/39*) is in a lovely colonial building, decorated inside with antique musical instruments and lots of plants. It has a good bar and delightful courtyard **restaurant** (*mains $4-6; open 7am-8pm daily*).

Hostería La Mirage (*☎ 915 237, 915 077, USA ☎ 800-327 3573, fax 915 065; e mirage1@mirage.com.ec; doubles $268-342*) is elegant and romantic and set in pleasant gardens almost a kilometer out of town. This lovely country hotel has antique furniture, a bar, restaurant, fireplace, spa amenities, sauna, an indoor swimming pool, a massage center, tennis court, horse riding and tame birds. The hotel restaurant is the only one in Ecuador to achieve membership in the exclusive Relais & Chateaux association. These features have attracted various distinguished guests, among them the Queen of Spain. Twenty-three spacious rooms and suites all have a fireplace and attractively carved furniture. Rates include taxes, dinners and breakfasts (served in bed, if you wish). The hotel is often full on weekends, so reservations are recommended. The renowned restaurant is packed for lunch on Saturday with shoppers from the Otavalo market.

La Casa de Pablo (*10 de Agosto & Pedro Moncayo*) is a recommended restaurant.

Getting There & Away From Otavalo's bus terminal there are buses at least every hour ($0.20, 25 minutes). In Cotacachi, *camionetas* (pickups or light trucks) can be hired from the bus terminal by the market at the far end of town to take you to various local destinations, such as Laguna de Cuicocha ($6 to $8 round trip, including half-hour waiting time). A taxi to/from Otavalo costs about $4.

RESERVA ECOLÓGICA COTACACHI-CAYAPAS

This huge reserve (*admission $1*) protects western Andean habitats ranging from Volcán Cotacachi down to the northwestern coastal lowlands. One cannot travel from the highland to lowland part of the reserve except by very difficult bushwhacking. Most visitors either visit the lowlands from San Miguel on Río Cayapas (see the North Coast & Lowlands chapter) or the highlands around Laguna de Cuicocha, which are described here. From Cotacachi, just before arriving Laguna de Cuicocha, you will pass the rangers' booth and entrance to the Reserva Ecológica Cotacachi-Cayapas.

Laguna de Cuicocha

Driving west some 18km from the town of Cotacachi, you reach an ancient, eroded volcanic crater famous for the deep lake found within. The crater is on the lower southern flanks of Volcán Cotacachi, and the sight of the 3km-wide lake, with Cotacachi behind it, is quite impressive. At the lake, boats can take you on a cheap half-hour trip ($1.25) around the islands in the middle. There is a pleasant restaurant here, but nowhere to stay.

A path follows the edge of the lake, sometimes along the shore and sometimes inland because of cliffs. A profusion of flowers, including orchids, attract hummingbirds. Views of the lake and the mountains surrounding it are excellent when the weather is good. The trail begins near the reserve's entrance booth and circles the lake counterclockwise. Ask the guards at the booth for details. Allow about six slow hours for the complete circuit, and bear in mind that the path becomes faint in places, particularly on the far side of the lake. Consider going as far as the trail is easy to follow and backtracking.

There have been occasional reports of hikers being robbed on this walk and the guards at the park entrance claim the far side of the lake is risky. Ask at the park entrance; they're up to date on this.

Getting There & Away

A group can hire a taxi or pickup from Cotacachi for under $10, including a short waiting time at the lake and the round trip. One-way fares by taxi or truck cost about $4 from Cotacachi.

You can avoid the main roads (the Panamericana from Otavalo to the Cotacachi turnoff and then the paved road through Cotacachi to the lake) either by hiking along the more direct, unpaved road between the lake and Cotacachi or by taking the old road between the lake and Otavalo (a long day hike). The 1:50,000 Otavalo map numbered ÑII-F1, 3994-IV is recommended for this region; this map should be available at IGM in Quito.

APUELA
☎ 06

West of Laguna de Cuicocha, the road reaches its highest point and begins to drop down the western slopes of the Andes. The scenery is splendidly rugged and this is an opportunity to see some of the remoter, less-visited parts of the highlands. Some 40km (by road) west of Cuicocha, you reach the village of Apuela, set in subtropical forests at about 2000m above sea level. The people in Apuela are very friendly and will direct you to the **thermal springs** (admission $0.50), about an hour's walk away from the village along the main road to the west. The three pools are about 35°C and one is 18°C; it's a quiet, relaxing place.

Accommodations are basic in town. Hostal Veritas is on the plaza, and the clean and friendly Residencial Don Luis is a couple of blocks away up the hill – both have cold showers and charge about $3 per person. There is a simple restaurant across the street from Residencial Don Luis.

Outside town there are better places to stay. **Cabañas Río Grande** (Otavalo ☎ 920 548, 920 442; rooms per person $4) has rustic but clean cabins that sleep four. Private hot showers are available and it's about an hour's hike to the springs. Get off the bus before Apuela – ask the driver. Zulaytur in Otavalo can make a reservation (see Information under Otavalo earlier).

There are several buses a day from Otavalo (four hours), more on Saturdays, and they are often crowded. Try Transportes Otavalo and Transportes Cotacachi. Beyond Apuela, there are remoter villages, including Santa Rosa; inquire in Apuela about transportation between them.

SAN ANTONIO DE IBARRA
☎ 06

This village is on the Panamericana about 20km north of Otavalo, just before the town of Ibarra (see following). Although this place is famous for woodcarving, there's little wood found in the Ibarra area – most of it comes from the Ecuadorian jungles. Cedar and walnut are among the more frequently used woods. The village has a pleasant main square (called the 'Parque Central,' not to be confused with the large, empty 'Plaza Central' two blocks downhill), around which stands a number of stores that are poorly disguised as 'workshops' or 'factories.' Carvings depict various subjects, but the favorites seem to be beggars, religious statues and nude women.

The most famous gallery is the **Galería Luis Potosí** *(☎ 932 056; Parque Central; admission free; open 8am-6pm daily)* which has some of the best carvings. Señor Potosí is famous throughout Ecuador, and his work sells all over the world.

Hostal Los Nogales *(☎ 932 000; Sucre 3-64; rooms per person with shared bath $3, singles/doubles with private bath $5/7)* is the only hotel in town and has basic rooms. Most visitors stay in Ibarra or Otavalo.

There are few restaurants in San Antonio de Ibarra; one place, **Andi Burger** *(mains $1-2; open 8am-3pm daily)*, a block off the Plaza Central, serves greasy hamburgers and hot dogs, and simple almuerzos.

Transportation from Ibarra ($0.15, 15 minutes) is frequent during daylight hours; buses drop you off at the main plaza. Alternately, you can walk the few kilometers or so south on the Panamericana from Ibarra. A taxi costs around $4.

IBARRA
☎ 06 • pop 140,000 • elevation 2225m
The charming colonial town of Ibarra, 22km northeast of Otavalo, is the provincial capital of Imbabura. There's not much to do in Ibarra besides letting your mind float back to the 19th century. Horse-drawn carts clatter along cobbled streets flanked by colonial buildings and dark-suited old gentlemen sit in the shady parks discussing the day's events. It's a relaxing sort of place. Many of Ibarra's houses are built in the colonial style and their red-tiled roofs and whitewashed walls have given Ibarra the nickname of *la ciudad blanca* (the white city).

Ibarra has a unique blend of students, *mestizos*, highland Indians and Afro-Ecuadorians from the nearby Valle de Chota, a combination that gives the city an exciting multicultural edge. When you're through relaxing in its leafy plazas, take a stroll around the train station and market area which is always abuzz with interesting activity.

Market day, a bustling local affair, is Saturday. Afterwards, the local men play *pelota de guante*, a strange Ecuadorian paddleball game played with a small, soft ball and large, spiked paddles that look like medieval torture implements.

Ibarra's annual fiesta (when hotels fill up quickly) is held during the last weekend in September.

Orientation
Ibarra can be roughly divided into two areas. The southeast area around the train station is the busiest and has many cheap hotels, while to the north are the main plazas and the older buildings – it's a generally quieter and more pleasant area.

Streets in Ibarra are both numbered and named. Roughly, north–south streets are numbered *carreteras*, and east–west streets are numbered *calles*. Both numbers and names appear on the street signs, but names seem to be more widely in use. Names are used in the text of this section.

Information
The **tourist office** *(☎ 955 711, 958 547; García Moreno 7-44; open 8:30am-1pm & 2pm-5pm Mon-Fri)* is slim on handouts, but the staff is helpful.

The only place in town that changes traveler's checks is **Banco del Pacífico** *(☎ 957 714; cnr Olmedo & Moncayo; open 8:30am-4pm Mon-Fri)*; it has an ATM, too. There's a **Produbanco ATM** *(cnr Sucre & Flores)* and several other ATMs around town.

For mail, try the **post office** *(☎ 643 135; Salinas 6-64; open 8am-7pm Mon-Fri, 8am-1pm Sat)*. Make phone calls at **Andinatel** *(Sucre 4-48; open 8am-10pm daily)*. You can get online for $1 per hour at **Zonanet** *(☎ 258 858; Moncayo 5-74; open 8:30am-9pm daily)*. There is also an Internet café below **Hostal El Ejecutivo** *(Bolívar 9-69; open 7am-late daily)*.

A reliable, all-purpose travel agency is **Metropolitan Touring** *(☎ 956 239; Flores near Sucre; open 8:30am-6:30pm Mon-Fri, 9am-noon Sat)*.

You can have your clothes washed and dried in about six hours at **Lava Fácil** *(Sucre near Grijalva)*.

Things to See & Do
Also known as Peñaherrera, **Parque La Merced** has a church topped with a huge statue of the Virgin – Virgin de La Merced. Inside the church, there is an ornate altar. The larger and tree-filled **Parque Pedro Moncayo** is dominated by the nearby **cathedral**. Pedro Moncayo (1807–88) was an Ibarra-born journalist and diplomat.

Out at the north end of Bolívar is the quaint little **Parque Santo Domingo**. Behind this small park, the modern concrete-block

Blanket seller, Otavalo

Bag seller, Otavalo

Woman crocheting, Poncho Plaza, Otavalo

ERIC L WHEATER

Río Chota valley, near Ibarra

LEE FOSTER

Mother and daughter, Otavalo

LEE FOSTER

Traditional woven rugs, Otavalo

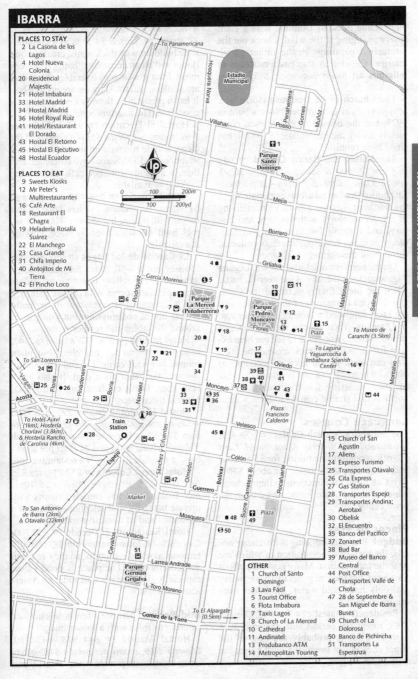

IBARRA

PLACES TO STAY
2 La Casona de los Lagos
4 Hotel Nueva Colonia
20 Residencial Majestic
21 Hotel Imbabura
33 Hotel Madrid
34 Hostal Madrid
36 Hotel Royal Ruíz
41 Hotel/Restaurant El Dorado
43 Hostal El Retorno
45 Hostal El Ejecutivo
48 Hostal Ecuador

PLACES TO EAT
9 Sweets Kiosks
12 Mr Peter's Multirestaurantes
16 Café Arte
18 Restaurant El Chagra
19 Heladería Rosalía Suárez
22 El Manchego
23 Casa Grande
31 Chifa Imperio
40 Antojitos de Mi Tierra
42 El Pincho Loco

OTHER
1 Church of Santo Domingo
3 Lava Fácil
5 Tourist Office
6 Flota Imbabura
7 Taxis Lagos
8 Church of La Merced
10 Cathedral
11 Andinatel
13 Produbanco ATM
14 Metropolitan Touring
15 Church of San Agustín
17 Aliens
24 Expreso Turismo
25 Transportes Otavalo
26 Cita Express
27 Gas Station
28 Transportes Espejo
29 Transportes Andina; Aerotaxi
30 Obelisk
32 El Encuentro
35 Banco del Pacifico
37 Zonanet
38 Bud Bar
39 Museo del Banco Central
44 Post Office
46 Transportes Valle de Chota
47 28 de Septiembre & San Miguel de Ibarra Buses
49 Church of La Dolorosa
50 Banco de Pichincha
51 Transportes La Esperanza

To Panamericana
Estadio Municipal
Parque Santo Domingo
Parque La Merced (Peñaherrera)
Parque Pedro Moncayo
Plaza
Train Station
Market
Parque Germán Grijalva
Plaza Francisco Calderón

To San Lorenzo
To Hotel Ajaví (1km), Hostería Chorlaví (3.8km), & Hostería Rancho de Carolina (4km)
To San Antonio de Ibarra (2km) & Otavalo (22km)
To El Alpargate (0.5km)
To Museo de Caranchi (3.5km)
To Laguna Yaguarcocha & Imbabura Spanish Center

Hosquera Nerva
Villahar
Penaherrera
Gomes
Muñoz
Posso
Troya
Mejía
Borrero
Grijalva
Garcia Moreno
Rodriguez
Oviedo
Maldonado
Salinas
Montalvo
Moncayo
Velasco
Colón
Bolívar
Sucre (Carretera 8)
Rocafuerte
Guerrero
Mosquera
Villacis
Larrea Andrade
L-Toro Moreno
Gomez de la Torre
Vargas
Flores
Acosta
Rivadeneira
Boria
Narvaez
Sánchez y Cifuentes
Olmedo
Espejo
Cevallos

0 100 200m
0 100 200yd

NORTHERN HIGHLANDS

Church of Santo Domingo is topped by a huge statue of Saint Dominic with a giant rosary swinging in the wind. Check out the interesting paintings in the rather garish interior. The church also has a **museum of religious art** *(open 9am-noon & 3pm-6pm Mon-Sat)*.

The **Church of La Dolorosa** *(Sucre near Mosquera)* is also of interest. It was built in 1928, but the domed roof collapsed completely during the earthquake of 1987. It has since been rebuilt.

The **Museo del Banco Central** *(☎ 644 087; cnr Oviedo & Sucre; admission $0.50; open 8:30am-1:30pm & 2:30pm-4:30pm Mon-Sat)* houses historical archives pertaining to the northern Sierras, a library specializing in art, archaeology, anthropology and history, and a small but interesting archaeology museum featuring artefacts collected throughout the northern highlands.

On the northern outskirts of town, **Laguna Yaguarcocha** is the site of the horrific battle when the Incas finally defeated the Caras and dumped thousands of their bodies into the lake, supposedly turning the water red. In Quechua, Yaguarcocha means 'Lake of Blood.' There's not much to see out here except for an auto racetrack around the lake. You can walk to the lake in a couple of hours by heading east on Oviedo to the edge of town, crossing the river and heading north. A taxi should cost $3 to $4.

Language Courses
The **Imbabura Spanish Center** *(☎ 959 429; Urbanización La Victoria, Manzana 33, Casa 10)* offers one-on-one tuition for $5 an hour and homestays with meals for about $15 a day. Call them for directions to their school, which is in a private house away from the town center.

Places to Stay
Budget Ibarra is bursting with cheap hotels, the highest concentration of which are near the train station. Many cost only about $3 a head, but they're generally basic, noisy and only have cold water; the better ones are listed here.

Residencial Majestic *(☎ 950 052; Olmedo 7-63; rooms per person with shared/private bath $2/2.50)* is probably the best of the super cheapies in town. It's bare-bones but will do for a night.

Hotel Imbabura *(☎ 950 155, 958 522; e hotel_imbabura@hotmail.com; Oviedo 9-33; rooms per person $4-5)* is in a colonial-style building with thick walls, creaky wood floors and clean communal baths. The beds range from concave to tolerable, the toilets are seatless, and the showers are usually hot. It has a pretty little flowery courtyard and a good café. The interior rooms are dark.

Hostal El Ejecutivo *(☎ 956 575; Bolívar 9-69; rooms per person $5)* is a good deal for clean, simple rooms with private hot baths, telephone and TV. Some have balconies, and there's a handy Internet café downstairs. Parking is available.

Hostal Ecuador *(☎ 956 425; Mosquera 5-54; rooms per person $5)* has large, clean rooms with private hot shower. The beds are rock hard, but it's a friendly place. Parking is available.

La Casona de los Lagos *(☎ 957 844, fax 951 629; Sucre 3-50; rooms per person $6)*, a member of Hostelling International, offers clean, pleasant rooms with private bath, TV and telephone. The restaurant in the patio area is out of commission, but you can sit around the tables and read or write.

Hotel Madrid *(☎ 956 177; Moncayo 7-41; rooms per person $7)* has clean but plain rooms, but with cable TV and private hot showers they're a good deal. It also has a restaurant. Don't confuse this with Hostal Madrid listed later.

Hostal El Retorno *(☎ 957 722; Moncayo 4-32; rooms per person with shared/private bath $4/5)* has fair-size rooms (some with TV and private bath) and 24-hour hot showers – a good deal. There's a restaurant, too.

Hotel Nueva Colonia *(☎ 952 918, fax 955 543; Olmedo 5-19; singles/doubles $6/10)* is nice looking and has carpeted rooms with private bath, TV and telephone. There is a restaurant and an attractive roofed patio.

Hotel/Restaurant El Dorado *(☎ 958 700; Oviedo 5-74; rooms per person $8)* recently remodeled six of its rooms, so they're clean and comfortable. The place is good value, especially since the price includes an American breakfast.

Mid-Range There are a few hotels in town catering to folks with a looser budget.

Hostal Madrid *(☎ 644 918, 643 110; Olmedo 8-69; rooms per person $10)* offers sharp rooms with private bath, cable TV and telephone. Don't confuse this with Hotel Madrid listed earlier.

Hotel Royal Ruíz (☎/fax 644 644/653; **e** hroyalruiz@andinet.net; Olmedo 9-40; rooms per person $10) is a modern hotel with cheery rooms that come with cable TV, telephone and private bath. There's off-street parking and breakfast is available for an additional $2.

The best hotels are west of town, on or just off the Panamericana and south toward Otavalo. They often booked well in advance, particularly on weekends. Make reservations if possible.

Hotel Ajaví (☎ 955 221/787/555, fax 952 485; singles/doubles $39/46) is 1st class (by Ibarra standards) and is just under 1km west of the town center. The hotel is modern and boasts a restaurant, bar, big swimming pool and sauna ($5 extra). Rooms are clean and spacious but unexciting. Doubles have TV, telephone and minifridge.

Hostería Chorlaví (☎ 955 777; singles/ doubles about $35/41) is almost 4km west of Ibarra and is the best hotel in the area. This converted hacienda, with plenty of old world charm, has pretty gardens, a (cold) swimming pool and an excellent restaurant/bar. It also has a famous buffet brunch ($7 for nonguests) on weekends, which is very popular with well-off Ecuadorians and tour groups after the Otavalo market – making it perhaps a bit too touristy for some travelers' tastes. Meals are about $8 and a buffet breakfast is included in the room rates.

Hostería Rancho de Carolina (☎ 953 215; **e** rancho@andinanet.net; singles/doubles $21/ 34), almost next door to Chorlaví, is clean and comfortable and a good choice if Chorlaví is full. The price includes breakfast.

Places to Eat

Ibarra is known for its tasty nogadas (nougat), usually made with walnuts or mixed nuts. It's also famous for it's sweet arrope de mora, a thick blackberry syrup that goes wonderfully with fruit, yogurt or pancakes. You can purchase both these at the sweets kiosks outside the old military barracks, across from Parque La Merced.

El Alpargate (☎ 644 062; Barrio El Alpargate 1-59; set meals $4; open noon-6pm daily) is famous in Ibarra for serving the best plato típico (traditional meal) in town. There's only one plate on the menu: marinated,

---

Rosalía's Famous Ice Cream

People eat a lot of ice cream in Ibarra, but not just any old ice cream. The town is famous for its helados de paila, sorbets made by hand in a large copper pail (the paila), which is spun on a bed of straw and ice and stirred with a wooden spoon. The most famous shop in town – indeed, the most famous ice cream shop in Ecuador – is **Heladería Rosalía Suárez** (☎ 958 722; Oviedo 7-82), founded by Rosalía Suárez who began experimenting with helados de paila in 1897 when she was 17. She used ice carried down from Volcán Imbabura (the only ice around back then) and the pure juice of local tropical fruits such as guanábana, (similar to sour sop), maracuyá (passionfruit) and mora (blackberry). Doña Rosalía is credited with perfecting helados de paila and she reportedly lived till she was 104. It was all that ice cream.

Doña Rosalía's shop is now run by her grandson and the ice cream is still made by hand. Visit the source – it's an Ibarra tradition.

---

cubed beef with sausage, fresh cheese, avocado, mote (similar to hominy), potatoes and empanadas. It's excellent. The restaurant is in the oldest part of town, Barrio El Alpargate, and is most easily reached by taxi ($1). To walk (allow about 20 minutes), head east on Gomez de la Torre to the end, turn right and look for the sign.

Café Arte (☎ 950 806; Salinas 5-43; mains $2-3; open 9am-midnight Mon-Thur, 9am-2am Fri & Sat) specializes in art, music and Mexican snacks. Tacos, enchiladas and burritos grace the artsy menu along side other inexpensive treats like such as personalized pizzas, sandwiches and expresso drinks. There's live music every Friday and Saturday night, and the atmosphere (warmed up by photography and painting exhibits) is welcoming.

Restaurant El Chagra (Olmedo 7-48; mains about $2; open 8am-10pm daily) is worth a visit for large helpings at small prices. It's popular with locals and has a large-screen TV and comfy wooden booths. The almuerzo is a deal for $1.20.

Mr Peter's Multirestaurantes (☎ 955 539; Sucre 5-36; mains $2-4; open 10am-midnight *daily*) is best for the $2 almuerzo or set dinner. Vegetarians can dig into big, cheap plates of *menestra* (lentils or beans) and rice. Breakfasts are a good deal, too.

El Pincho Loco (☎ 953 881; *Moncayo 4-61; mains $2-3; open 11am-11pm daily*) whips out cheap *asados* (grilled meats) to the sonic onslaught of a blaring TV – and everyone seems to love it.

Antojitos de Mi Tierra (☎ 950 592; *Plaza Francisco Calderón; open noon-10pm Tues-Sun*) is run by historian, chef and local TV-show host Marta Jduregi. She makes some of Ibarra's most traditional treats, including *chicha de arroz* (a sweetened rice drink) and *tamales, humitas* and *quimbolitos* (all variations of corn dumplings steamed in corn husks or leaves). It's a great place for a snack.

Chifa Imperio (☎ 959 405; *Olmedo 9-79; mains $2-4; open 11am-10pm daily*) is good for Chinese food.

Casa Grande (☎ 643 085; *Narvaez 6-97; almuerzos $1.70; open lunch only Mon-Sat*) serves hearty almuerzos in a down-home dining room in an old house that takes up an entire traffic circle.

El Manchego (☎ 950 905; *cnr Narvaez & Oviedo; mains about $3; open 7am-5pm daily*) and **Hotel/Restaurant El Dorado** (*Oviedo 5-74*) are other good choices for cheap almuerzos and reliable, standard lunch fare.

Entertainment

Ibarra is a quiet city, but it has a few places worth popping into for a mellow evening.

El Encuentro (☎ 959 520; *Olmedo 9-35*) is an eclectic little hideaway bar with saw-horse barstools, low ceilings and lots of saddles, antiques and oddities. It's a great (and popular) place to tuck into.

Café Arte (*Salinas 5-43*) has live music every Friday and Saturday night, as well as occasional dance performances and poetry readings.

Aliens (*Oviedo at Bolívar; open 9pm-late Mon-Sat*) draws the weekend crowds to its packed dance floor. It's your best bet for dancing downtown.

Bud Bar (*Plaza Francisco Calderón; open 4pm-midnight Wed-Sat, 10am-4pm Sun*) is a small, pleasant, modern bar.

Getting There & Away

Bus Ibarra has no main bus terminal. Rather, buses leave from various private terminals,

most of which are within a few blocks of the old train station and walking distance from most hotels.

Aerotaxi (☎ 955 200; *cnr Velasco & Boria*) goes to Quito ($2, 2½ hours), Guayaquil ($8, 10 hours), Esmeraldas ($8, eight to nine hours), Atacames ($9, nine hours) and San Lorenzo ($4, 3½ to four hours). **Transportes Andina** (☎ 950 833), at the same terminal, goes to Quito and Santo Domingo ($4, six hours).

Flota Imbabura (☎ 951 094; *Flores at Imbabura*) goes to Quito ($2, 2½ hours), Tulcán ($2, 2½ hours) Guayaquil ($10, 11 hours), Cuenca ($14, 12 hours) and Manta ($10, 12 hours).

Expreso Turismo (☎ 955 730; *cnr Moncayo & Flores*) goes to Tulcán and Quito ($2, 2½ hours).

Transportes Otavalo (☎ 955 593; *Vargas near Acosta*) heads regularly to Otavalo ($0.35, 35 minutes).

Transportes Valle de Chota (☎ 643 864; *Espejo & Colón*) goes four times daily to San Lorenzo ($2, 2½ hours).

Transportes Espejo (☎ 959 917) serves Quito, San Lorenzo and El Ángel ($1.10, 1½ hours).

Cita Express (☎ 955 627; *Flores 13-70*) goes to Ambato ($4, five hours) via El Quinche.

Transportes La Esperanza (*Larea Andrade near Sanchez y Cifuentes*) goes to the village of La Esperanza ($0.20, 20 minutes; see later in this chapter).

For San Antonio de Ibarra, see Getting Around later.

Train Since the road opened to the coastal town of San Lorenzo, train service on the Ibarra–San Lorenzo line has been suspended. There are, *autoferros* (buses mounted on a train chassis) that go as far as the point known as Primer Paso ($3.80 one way, 1¾ hours), less than a quarter of the way from Ibarra to San Lorenzo. The short ride is now essentially a round-trip tourist attraction. Alternately, you can get off at Primer Paso and wait for a passing bus to San Lorenzo.

At the time of writing, the *autoferro* would not leave Ibarra without a minimum of 16 passengers (or the minimum fare of $60.80, which one person could pay and be on their way). It left Ibarra at 7am Monday through Friday and at 8am on Saturday and

Sunday. The return ride departed Primer Paso at 2pm daily. Outside the tourist high season there are rarely enough passengers, so cancelled departures are the norm.

Always call the **train station** (☎ 950 390) for the latest information.

Taxi If you're in a real hurry to get back to Quito, try **Taxis Lagos** (☎ 955 150; Flores 9-24). Six passengers are crammed into a large taxi and dropped off wherever they want in Quito ($6, 2¼ hours).

Getting Around

Local buses with the companies 28 de Septiembre and San Miguel de Ibarra provide service around town and some continue to San Antonio de Ibarra. The best place to catch a San Antonio de Ibarra bus is on Sanchez y Cifuentes near Guerrero. Different buses leave from near the same intersection for several other local destinations.

LA ESPERANZA
☎ 06

This is a pretty little village in the country, about 7km due south of Ibarra. It is a good place for budget travelers looking for peace and quiet. There's nothing to do except talk to the locals and take walks in the surrounding countryside.

Volcán Imbabura (4609m) is about 9km to the southwest as the crow flies. It is easier to climb this mountain from La Esperanza than from the Laguna de San Pablo side. From La Esperanza, the volcano looks deceptively close – remember that you are not a flying crow and that the summit is about 2000m higher than La Esperanza. There is a maze of tracks heading toward the summit, but you'll have to scramble the last bit – ask the locals for directions. Allow about 10 hours for the round trip, including time at the top for photographs of Laguna de San Pablo way below you.

If Imbabura seems like too ambitious a climb, try **Loma Cubilche** (3836m). This hill is about 8km due south of La Esperanza. It's an easier climb and also offers good views. If climbing doesn't appeal to you at all, you can take the cobbled road through pretty countryside to the south – buses go along there occasionally.

Casa Aida (☎ 642 020; Calle Gallo Plaza s/n; rooms per person $3-4) is a friendly hostal run by the amiable Aida and her two daughters. It's the only place reliably open. Aida is famous for her pancake breakfasts ($2), which she serves in a cozy little dining room, and is a great source of information about the area. Most of the nine shared bathrooms have hot water and rooms are small and basic.

Buses from Ibarra ($0.20, 20 minutes) serve the village frequently along a cobbled country road and irregularly continue further south through Olmedo to Cayambe. You can walk from Ibarra.

RÍO BLANCO AREA
☎ 06

This rural area is home to many of Ecuador's Afro-Ecuadorian farmers. The elevation is a subtropical 1000m and the people are friendly. In the village of **Limonal**, you can stay at **Hostería Martyz** (☎ 648 693; rooms per person $7) where all but two of its rooms have shared bath. The slightly cheaper **Hostal Limonal** (☎ 648 688; singles/doubles $5/10) has private baths. Both places have a swimming pool. The village can be reached by taking one of the several buses a day between Ibarra and San Lorenzo.

Bospas Forest Farm (e bospas@hotmail.com), on the outskirts of Limonal, is run by Piet Sabbe, a Belgian. It's an example of a sustainable farm in an area that has suffered substantial deforestation. His idea is to teach the locals by example and he accepts volunteer assistants who have a basic knowledge of Spanish and who are familiar with the fields of permaculture, agroforestry, erosion control, organic-pest control, fruit-tree grafting and related fields. Assistants are required to contribute about $150 per month for meals and accommodations (there are showers, but there is no electricity and the nearest phone is in Limonal) and a two-month minimum stay is suggested. Piet can arrange interesting hikes and horse rides in the hills.

NORTH OF IBARRA
☎ 06

After passing Laguna Yaguarcocha (see Things to See & Do under Ibarra), the Panamericana soon drops quite steeply to the **Río Chota valley**, at about 1565m, before beginning the long climb to San Gabriel, at almost 2900m. In the valley, the warm and dusty town of **Chota** is inhabited by reserved but friendly Afro-Ecuadorians whose ancestors were originally brought in to Ecuador as slaves in the 17th century. They now make their living growing fruit. Chota is less than an hour from Ibarra and can be visited as a day trip. Fiestas and concerts there may occasionally be advertised in Ibarra. The music is a weird and wonderful mix of plaintive Andean and driving African sounds and is worth hearing if you get the chance.

After leaving Chota, the Panamericana crosses the provincial line from Imbabura into Carchi. The road passes the little town of **Bolívar**, capital of the canton of the same name, and a few kilometers further on the village of **La Paz**. Near La Paz are **thermal springs** and waterfalls, as well as a grotto containing stalactites and a famous statue of the Virgin. There are buses to the springs from Tulcán, or you can walk about 5km southeast of the Panamericana from La Paz on a road signed for 'Las Grutas.' The complex (thermal springs, pool and grotto) is open Thursday to Sunday. The road in this

area is steep, winding and rather slow and the scenery is wild.

About 90km north of Ibarra and 38km south of Tulcán is the small town of **San Gabriel**, which has a couple of basic hotels with cold water only. Five kilometers east is **Bosque de los Arreyanes** (open 8:30am-4:30pm daily), which has many huge myrtle and other trees; it's a good place for bird-watching. Take a taxi or walk. There are two waterfalls – **Las Cascadas de Paluz** – on Río San Gabriel 3km and 4km north of San Gabriel (head north on Calle Bolívar and keep going). One of the falls is about 60m high.

EL ÁNGEL
☎ 06

This village is about 20km west of San Gabriel, and is the entrance point to the **Páramos de El Ángel**, a wild area of highland vegetation and mists. Among the most notable plants in the páramo are the *frailejones*, a giant member of the daisy family that can grow to 2m in height – an amazing

The Cerro Golondrinas Project

The Cerro Golondrinas area lies west of the Reserva Ecológica El Ángel and encompasses various ecosystems, including páramo and, in its lower elevations, temperate and subtropical montane cloud forest. Similar forests on the western slopes of the Ecuadorian and Colombian Andes have been deforested at an alarming rate. The Cerro Golondrinas Project aims to conserve some of the remaining forests while improving the living standards of the farmers who reside in the area.

The project is one of the more successful grassroots conservation undertakings in Ecuador. It involves the cooperation of local *campesinos* (peasants) and a small local nongovernment organization (NGO) called Fundación Golondrinas, headquartered in a popular budget travelers' *hostal* in Quito, La Casa de Eliza (see Places to Stay in the Quito chapter).

Fundación Golondrinas promotes sustainable agricultural techniques – including (but not limited to) tree nurseries, orchid farms, beekeeping, reforestation projects and seed banks – as an alternative to the prevalent and highly destructive logging/cattle-ranch cycles (see Ecology & Environment in the Facts about Ecuador chapter). Tourists are encouraged to trek through the area, enjoy the plants and animals and visit with local families. The local families, in turn, work in sustainable agriculture and as hosts, guides and interpreters for visitors. This form of tourism benefits the locals, protects the forests and provides visitors with an in-depth immersion into this remote region of Ecuador.

Travelers can become involved both as tourists and as volunteers or researchers. Four-day treks on foot or horseback led by local guides traverse a cross-section of Andean habitats and offer excellent opportunities for bird-watching and nature study, as well as interaction with local families. A four-day trek costs $222 to $248, depending on the number of people, and includes all food, accommodations and guiding services. During the wet months of October to May, the trails can get very muddy; the best time to go is during the dry season, when departures occur weekly.

More information is available through **Fundación Golondrinas** (☎ 02-222 6602; **W** www.ecuador explorer.com/golondrinas; Isabel La Católica N24-679) in Quito.

sight. The páramo is one of the few areas in Ecuador where Andean condors are seen and there are many other intriguing plants and animals. In 1992, this area became protected by the formation of the **Reserva Ecológica El Ángel**, which covers almost 16,000 hectares of páramo. Day tours (about $10 per person, depending on the group's size) reportedly can be arranged at Grijalva 04-26 in El Ángel. The best way to visit the páramo is with the Cerro Golondrinas Project (see the boxed text).

Market day, on Monday, enlivens El Ángel, which is otherwise a very quiet little town.

Ofelia López Peñaherrera (*Grijalva 02-59*) rents basic rooms; there are no showers and the water is cold, but the family is friendly.

Residencial Viña del Mar, on the main plaza, is basic but also worth a try; rooms are OK, but the bathrooms are grubby.

Restaurant Los Faroles (☎ *937 144; rooms per person $2*), nearby, serves food and offers basic rooms.

Transportes Espejo, on the main plaza, goes to Quito ($3.50, four hours) via Ibarra ($1.20, 1½ hours) about once an hour during the day. Buses to Tulcán leave only in the early morning.

RESERVA BIOLÓGICA GUANDERA

This 1000-hectare, tropical, wet, montane forest reserve was founded in 1994 by Fundación Jatun Sacha (see The Oriente chapter). The reserve lies between 3100m and 3600m on a transitional ridge (forest to paramo) about 11km east of San Gabriel, near the village of Mariscal Sucre (which is not found on most maps). Andean spectacled bears (rarely glimpsed) and high-altitude parrots and toucans are among the attractions. Jatun Sacha operates a **refuge** (*bunk beds per person $15*) up here with three meals included in the nightly price. Reservations are required and fees must be paid in advance at the **Jatun Sacha office** (☎ *243 2240/46, 243 2173; **w** www.jatun sacha.org; Pasaje Eugenio de Santillán N34-248 & Maurián, Urbanización Rumipamba; PO Box 17-12-867*) in Quito. There is a research station and volunteers (who must pay $300 a month for food and accommodations) are needed.

From the village of San Gabriel it is 90 minutes on foot to the reserve. The only bus (the school bus) goes to Mariscal Sucre from San Gabriel's main plaza, leaving the plaza at 1pm Monday through Friday when school is in session. Otherwise, there are Saturday morning buses and cars leaving San Gabriel for the Mariscal Sucre Saturday market. You can take a taxi from San Gabriel for about $10 one way.

TULCÁN
☎ 06 • pop 53,000 • elevation 3000m

Tulcán is the provincial capital of Carchi, the northernmost province of the Ecuadorian highlands. Driving north, you see plenty of farms and ranches, particularly as you get close to Tulcán, which is an important market town. For most travelers, its main importance is as the gateway into Ecuador from Colombia, some 6km away. Tulcán is not a particularly interesting town, but there are some interesting trips in the vicinity, described at the end of this chapter.

Tulcán is popular for Colombian weekend bargain hunters. There is a Sunday street market (with few tourist items), and the hotels are often filled with Colombian shoppers on Saturday night.

Tulcán has a cold climate and is the highest provincial capital and town of its size in the country.

Orientation
The town is long and narrow, with most activity happening on or near the parallel streets of Bolívar and Sucre. A new numbering system for addresses has been developed, but many places still have or use the old numbers. To avoid confusion, the nearest intersections, rather than the numbers, are used here.

Information
The only tourist office in Túlcan is the **Ministerio de Turismo** (☎ *984 184; open 8:30am-5pm Mon-Fri*), which is at the Rumichaca border crossing.

The **Colombian consulate** (☎ *980 559; Bolívar 3-68 & Junín; open 8am-1pm*) is near the post office.

Exchanging money (between US dollars and Colombian pesos) is only slightly better in Tulcán than at the border. The bus running between Tulcán and the border accepts both

TULCÁN

To Airport (2km)
Border (6km) &
Ipiales (Colombia; 6km)

Cemetery

Parque
Isidro
Ayora

Central
Plaza

Market

Parque
Julio
Andrade

0   100   200m
0   100   200yd

PLACES TO STAY
6   Hotel San Francisco
7   Hotel Azteca
    Internacional
12 Hotel Sara
    Espindola; Crazy
    Residencial Quito
15 Hotel Machado
17 Hotel Lumar
25 Hotel Unicornio;
26 Chifa Pack Choy
27 Hotel Alejandra
30 Hotel las Acacias;
    Restaurant Acacias
31 Hotel Los Alpes;
    Restaurant Los Alpes

PLACES TO EAT
3   Fruit & Vegetable
    Market
10 Mi Casita
16 Los Arrieros
18 Asadero La Brasa
21 El Patio
22 La Fonda Paisa

OTHER
1   Cemetery Entrance
2   Minibuses to
    Airport & Border
4   Clínica
    Metropolitana
5   Cooperativa
    Transportes Norte
8   Colombian
    Consulate
9   Post Office
11 Andinatel
13 TAME Airline
14 Casa de Cambio
19 Ecctur
20 Teatro Sucre
23 Banco del Pichincha
24 Cathedral
28 Transportes Velotaxi
29 Bus Terminal

Colombian currency and US dollars. Street changers with little black attaché cases full of money hang out around the border and in front of the banks in town. Because there is no real black market, you won't get better rates from them than from the exchange houses, but they are useful when the other places are closed. Watch for trick calculators and do your own math.

Banco del Pichincha (*cnr 10 de Agosto & Sucre*) will change currency and traveler's checks on weekdays only; it has a Visa ATM. There are other banks nearby, or you could try the **casa de cambio** (*currency-exchange bureau; ☎ 985 731; Ayacucho at Sucre; open 7am-6pm daily*).

The **post office** (*☎ 980 552; Bolívar near Junín; open 8am-6pm Mon-Fri, 9am-noon Sat*) is centrally located. Make phone calls at **Andinatel** (*Olmedo near Junín; open 8am-10pm daily*); there are branches at the bus terminal and at the border.

When the TAME office is closed you can purchase tickets to Quito or Cali at **Ecctur** (*☎ 980 468/368; Sucre at 10 de Agosto*). Ecctur also arranges tours.

The **Clínica Metropolitana** (*Bolívar & Panamá*) is open 24 hours. There is a better hospital in Ipiales, 2km north of the border.

Things to See & Do

The big tourist attraction in town is the cemetery **topiary garden**. It's the most striking example in Ecuador of topiary gardening, in which bushes and trees are trimmed and sculpted into animal or geometrical shapes; it is also one of the best in Latin America.

Behind the cemetery, the locals play a strange Ecuadorian paddleball game on weekends called **pelota de guante**, which is played with a soft ball and large, spiked paddles.

On weekends, Cooperativa 11 de Abril buses make day trips to nearby thermal springs, departing from in front of the cathedral. At 8am on Saturday they go to **La Paz thermal springs**, 5km from the village of that name (see North of Ibarra earlier).

At 7am on Sunday they go to **Aguas Hediondas** (literally 'stinking waters') thermal baths, beyond the village of Tufiño near the Colombian border. Many of the pools are on the Colombian side; you can cross the border on a day pass to soak in the

Abdón Calderón – A Bloody Good Hero

Parque Isidro Ayora has a rather striking white statue of Abdón Calderón riding a horse. Calderón, a battle-hardened 18-year-old lieutenant, fought against the Spanish Royalists at the decisive Battle of Pichincha, which cemented Ecuador's independence on May 24, 1822. Abdón Calderón is famous not only for his youth, but also for his tenacity during the battle. Historians report that he was shot in the right arm, causing him to wield his sword with his left hand. A second bullet in the left arm made him drop his sword, but he continued fighting after having one of his soldiers tie the sword to his arm. A third shot in the left leg didn't stop him either. Finally, a bullet tore apart his right leg just as the battle was ending victoriously. He died the next day and was promoted to captain posthumously.

pools, but you are sent back to Tulcán if you want to enter Colombia properly. Be sure to inquire locally about the safety of travel in this remote border region – due to the conflict in Colombia, it may not be advised.

During the rest of the week, Cooperativa Transportes Norte buses bound for Maldonado can drop you at the turnoff to Aguas Hediondas. These trips are subject to seasonal changes (see Getting There & Away later).

Places to Stay

Tulcán's hotels are a dismal lot, but there are plenty to choose from, thanks to the once steady stream of Colombians rolling into town to shop at Ecuadorian prices. Since Ecuador's dollarization (and subsequent inflation), fewer Colombians shop in Tulcán, meaning hotels are cheaper and often nearly empty. Shoppers still hit Tulcán on weekends, however, and you should avoid showing up late Saturday afternoon without a reservation.

There are two good hotels across the street from the bus terminal. They are **Hotel Las Acacias** (☎ 982 501; JR Arellano near Bolívar; rooms per person $4) and **Hotel Los Alpes** (☎ 982 235; JR Arellano near Bolívar; rooms per person $4). Both offer plain, clean rooms with private baths, hot water and TV and both have restaurants.

Residencial Quito (☎ 980 541; Ayacucho at Bolívar; rooms per person $2) is very basic but reasonably clean and is one of the better cheap hotels. Bring your own toilet paper.

Hotel San Francisco (☎ 980 760; Bolívar near Atahualpa; rooms per person $3.50) is one of the best in its price range. Rooms have private baths, hot water and TV.

Hotel Alejandra (☎ 981 784; cnr Sucre & Quito; rooms per person $4) has clean rooms with bath, hot water and TV. It's a few blocks

south of the hustle and bustle, so it's quieter than most. There's a parking garage, too. Try for a room with an off-street window.

Hotel Unicornio (☎ 980 638; cnr Pichincha & Sucre; rooms per person $6) is conveniently located over a good Chinese restaurant and has carpeted rooms with private bath, TV and telephone. Choose your room carefully as they vary widely in quality. Parking is available.

Hotel Azteca Internacional (☎ 980 481, 981 447; Bolívar near Atahualpa; singles/doubles $6/10), near García Moreno, has a restaurant and downstairs disco and bar. The clean rooms have firm beds, TV and phone, but the disco can be loud on weekends.

Hotel Lumar (☎ 980 402, 987 137; Sucre near Pichincha; rooms per person $8.50) is friendly, modern and comfortable. There's a parking garage and rooms have carpet, cable TV, telephone, good beds and private, hot baths. It's good value.

Hotel Machado (☎ 984 221, 984 810; cnr Ayacucho & Bolívar; rooms per person $13) has 14 clean, bright rooms (mostly doubles) with cable TV, telephone and hot showers. Breakfast is included.

Hotel Sara Espindola (☎ 985 925; cnr Sucre & Ayacucho; rooms per person $13.50), on the central plaza, is the town's best hotel. It has cable TV, a restaurant, sauna, an elevator, uniformed staff, off-street parking, a small casino and a weekend disco.

Places to Eat

Tulcán has plenty of Colombian restaurants, so it's a good place to put a twist on your Ecuadorian diet. Most Colombian restaurants serve the ever-popular *bandeja paisa*, a hearty plate of beans, rice, salad, egg, avocado, fried pork skin, a piece of beef and fried banana.

La Fonda Paisa (☎ 987 153; *Bolívar at Pichincha; mains $1-2; open 8am-9pm Mon-Sat, 8am-5pm Sun)* and **Los Arrieros** (☎ 987 213; *Bolívar near Ayacucho; mains $1-2; open 9am-9pm daily)* are both good for *bandeja paisa* and cheap filling almuerzos for about $1.20.

Mi Casita *(Sucre near Boyacá; mains $1-2.50; open 7am-9pm daily)* is a reliable family-run place where the owner swears there's not a Colombian item on the menu.

El Patio (☎ 984 872; *Bolívar near 10 de Agosto; mains $1-2; open 8am-9pm Mon-Sat, 8am-5pm Sun)* has large portions and good breakfasts.

Chifa Pack Choy *(cnr Pichincha & Sucre; mains $2-3; open noon-11:30pm daily)*, beneath Hotel Unicornio, serves the town's best Chinese food.

Asadero La Brasa (☎ 980 968; *Ayacucho near Bolívar; mains $1.50; open 8am-9pm daily)* is the spot for grilled chicken with French fries.

Both **Restaurant Acacias** *(JR Arellano near Bolívar)* in the Hotel Acacias, and **Restaurant Los Alpes** *(JR Arellano near Bolívar)* in the Hotel Los Alpes, are simple, inexpensive restaurants near the bus terminal.

Check out the **fruit and vegetable market** *(Panamá & Sucre)* where horse-drawn carts unload produce every day.

Out by the border, there are plenty of snack stalls and fast-food carts.

Entertainment

You can shake your money-maker at **Crazy** *(cnr Sucre & Ayacucho; open Thur-Sat)*, the *discoteca* in Hotel Sara Espindola (see Places to Stay earlier).

Getting There & Away

Air The airport is 2km northeast of the center. **TAME** (☎ 980 675; *Sucre near Junín; open 8:30am-9:30am, 11:30am-2:30pm & 3pm-5pm Mon, Wed & Fri, 8:30am-1:30pm & 3pm-6pm Tues & Thur)* has an office downtown and another at the **airport** (☎ 982 850). TAME flies from Quito to Tulcán at 9:30am Monday, Wednesday and Friday and returns to Quito at 2:15pm on the same days. The half-hour flight saves you five hours on the bus and costs about $32. There are also flights to Cali in Colombia at 11am on Monday, Wednesday and Friday, returning from Cali at 12:30pm ($78 one way, plus a

$25 international departure tax). Note that flights from Tulcán to Quito are often full.

Bus There are buses traveling to and from Ibarra ($2.20, 2½ hours) and Quito ($4, five hours) which leave and arrive via the bus terminal, at the southwestern end of town. There are frequent departures, but the selection of times is better in the mornings. There are long-haul buses to Cuenca ($16, 17 hours, once a day), Guayaquil ($13, 13 hours) Ambato ($6, eight hours), Riobamba ($7, 10 hours), and San Lorenzo ($6, six hours).

Transportes Velotaxi, two blocks north of the bus terminal, has small, fast buses to Quito at least every hour from 2:25am to 10:30pm.

Note that there can be a very thorough customs/immigration check between Tulcán and Ibarra even though they are in the same country.

If you wish to travel west of Tulcán along the border to Tufiño, Maldonado and Chical, take a **Cooperativa Transportes Norte** (☎ 980 675) bus leaving from Sierra between Cuenca and Cotopaxi. There is a bus to Tufiño ($0.40, one hour) every couple of hours until mid-afternoon. At least one bus departs daily around 11am to Maldonado ($2.50, 4½ hours) and Chical ($2.75, five hours) via Tufiño.

Cooperativa 11 de Abril buses leave from a stop in front of the cathedral – these buses go to the thermal springs (see Things to See & Do earlier) as well as many other nearby destinations.

Getting Around

To get to the airport, take the bus crossing the border, which will leave you by the entrance of the airport for the same price as going to the border (see Land in the Getting There & Away chapter). A taxi will cost about $2.50, or it's a 2km walk from the city center. If flying into Tulcán, you have to take a taxi or walk, because there are no buses to take you from the airport into town.

The bus terminal is inconveniently located 2.5km southwest of the town center. City buses ($0.10) run southwest from the center along Bolívar and will deposit you at the terminal. If arriving at Tulcán, cross the street in front of the terminal and take the bus to get to the town center.

Western Andean Slopes

The old road to Santo Domingo via the popular village of Mindo offers access to some of the last remaining stands of cloud forest on the western Andean slopes. The lodges, reserves and villages listed in this section allow you to explore this unique and spectacular region, often in style. The area is especially popular with bird-watching fanatics. Many of these places are only a few hours' bus ride from Quito.

NANEGALITO
☎ 02

This village, a couple of hours northwest of Quito, marks the road junction with a choice of heading southwest to Bosque Protector Mindo-Nambillo and Reserva Bellavista or north to Reserva Biológica Maquipucuna, all described in this section. Buses to these places pass through Nanegalito. There is an Andinatel office in the village.

Pensión Don Fabara (☎ 286 5187; *rooms per person $2*), in Nanegalito, has six basic rooms sharing a hot shower.

About 1km past Nanegalito toward Mindo is a sign for **La Sigcha** (*day-use fee $2, beds $4, meals $3*), a small, rustic cloud-forest lodge owned by Patricio Ruales, who can be contacted in **Restaurant Sabrozón** in Nanegalito (the best restaurant in town). From La Sigcha's sign, it's a steep 1.5km downhill (4WD is essential) to the lodge, where there is a cabin sleeping six and another sleeping 16. (The last 400m is down a muddy trail and over a suspension footbridge; it must be hiked.) Cold showers, home cooking, solitude, a tiny pool, bird life, views, cloud-forest foot and horse trails (horses available) that lead to waterfalls and no electricity are the attractions here.

TANDAYAPA
☎ 02

From Km 32, 400m past the Café Tiepolo, a road branches south (left) to Tandayapa, a village 6km away. Here you'll find the **Tandayapa Bird Lodge** (☎ 222 5180, 09-973 5536; w www.tandayapa.com; *singles/doubles including 3 meals $85/140*), which offers multilingual bird-watching guides, a comfortable lodge in the cloud forest and a canopy platform for bird-watching. Packages can be arranged.

RESERVA BIOLÓGICA MAQUIPUCUNA

This reserve, which covers over 3000 hectares on the western slopes of the Andes, is only about 30km northwest of Quito as the condor flies. It protects a variety of premontane and montane cloud forests in the headwaters of Río Guayllabamba at elevations ranging from about 1200m to 2800m. In 1987, the reserve was purchased by The Nature Conservancy and is administered by Fundación Maquipucuna, a nonprofit conservation organization. About 80% of the reserve is undisturbed primary forest – the remainder is secondary growth and includes a research station and ecotourism lodge. In the reserve, almost 350 species of bird (a bird list is available), 240 species of butterfly, 45 species of mammal and thousands of plants have been documented, and more are being inventoried.

There is a research station and a rustic **lodge** (w www.arches.uga.edu/~maqui; *rooms per person $50*). The lodge has four quadruple rooms with double bunks and one room with a double bed. There are shared bathrooms with hot showers, restful decks and balconies with forest views and a simple restaurant serving nourishing meals. Accommodations include three meals. Day guests pay a $5 entry fee and can hire a guide for $10. There are seven trails, ranging from an easy 1km walk to a demanding 5.5km hike.

More information on the lodge is available from **Fundación Maquipucuna** (☎ 02-250 7200; e root@maqui.ecx.ec; Baquerizo 238 y Tamayo, La Floresta, Quito). The foundation's education, inventory and research work is urgently in need of financial support – contributions are welcomed at the address above. In the UK, the contact is **Rainforest Concern** (☎ 020-7229 2093, fax 7221 4094; e rainforest@gn.apc.org). In the USA, write to **The Choco-Andean Rainforest Corridor** (☎ 706-542-2968; Institute of Ecology, University of Georgia, Athens, GA 30602-2202).

A Transportes San José de Minas bus from Anteparra and Plaza San Blas (near El Ejido) in Quito leaves at 1pm, and a Transportes Alóag bus from Quito's Terminal Terrestre leaves at 2pm daily for Nanegal, with round trip buses leaving at 4am and

9am (there may be another bus on Sunday). About 12km beyond Nanegalito (shortly before Nanegal), at a place that is locally called La Delicia, you get off the bus and walk along the road to your right for about 7km to the reserve. At La Delicia, there is a country store and a sign that reads 'Departamento Forestal.' Fundación Maquipucuna can provide updated bus information or arrange a private vehicle from Quito (about $75 total for one to four visitors).

If you are driving, a 4WD is recommended from La Delicia to the reserve, although high-clearance 2WDs can make it in the dry season.

RESERVA BIOLÓGICA LOS CEDROS

This remote area covers 6400 hectares of cloud forest to the north of Maquipucuna. Several new species of insects, frogs and orchids have been discovered here, and anyone who has spent any length of time out here claims it's the one of the most relaxing places they've been. Facilities include a scientific research station, dining and cooking facilities, accommodations in dorms or private rooms, hot water and electricity.

Transportes San José de Minas (see Getting There & Away under Reserva Biológica Maquipucuna previous) has a daily 8am bus from Quito to **Sanguangal** (six hours), where there are a couple of pensiones, or ask for Gringo Pepe's Hacienda. From Sanguangal, it's a six-hour hike. You can also get there from the nearby village of Chontal (from where it's a three-hour hike), due west of García Moreno. For more information on this route, and to arrange a visit, contact **Centro de Investigaciones de Bosques Tropicales** (CIBT; ☎ 02-223 1768; e cibt@ecuanex.net.ec; Jonas Guerrero 138 near Larrea, 4th floor). It's best to set up a visit in advance so the caretaker can arrange for mules to pack your stuff up.

Rates are $30 a day, including meals. Volunteer positions may be arranged (there is a charge of $250 per month, one month minimum) and most visitors are either researchers (who must have their projects planned and approved in advance) or bird-watchers, although anyone can visit. You won't be disappointed.

Safari Tours (☎ 02-255 2505, 222 3381; e admin@safari.com.ec) also has information

on getting there and can arrange transportation (see Information in the Quito chapter).

RESERVA BELLAVISTA

This 700-hectare reserve is in the same western Andean slopes as Maquipucuna (see earlier), at about 2000m above sea level. About 25% is primary forest and the rest has been selectively or completely logged but is being allowed to regenerate. Various conservation projects are under way. There are 8km of well-marked trails and the area is highly recommended by bird-watchers (320 species of birds have been recorded).

The main **lodge** (communal rooms per person $44, singles/doubles/triples with private bath $79/134/194) is a wooden geodesic dome with a library/restaurant/bar on the ground floor, over which are five small rooms, topped by a two-story dormitory area with a shared bath, a restaurant and a balcony with 360° views of the surrounding cloud forest – quite a magnificent place to wake up. These are wonderful sleeping spots if you like to share with others. There are also larger, private cabins nestled into the forest a short walk from the main lodge. About a kilometer from the main lodge is a research station with a kitchen and hostal-type accommodations.

Accommodations rates all include three meals and tax. Prices are cheaper without food. Variously priced packages including transportation from Quito and guided hikes are offered, as well as multiday packages combining rafting and mountain biking in other areas. For more information, contact **Richard or Gloria Parsons** (☎ 02-211 6380, 09-949 0891, Quito ☎/fax 02-223 2313, 290 3166; e info@bellavistacloudforest.com; Jorge Washington E7-23 & Reina Victoria).

Reaching the lodge is fairly straightforward. Take a bus to Nanegalito ($2), then hire a pickup truck opposite the bus stop to take you the last 16km. Otherwise, get off the bus at Km 52 (about 4km before Nanegalito) and hike up a steep 12km dirt road. If driving, you can also reach Bellavista using unpaved 12km roads from Km 62 or from Km 77. These roads are fine for standard-drive cars most of the year.

MINDO
☎ 02 • elevation 1250m
This small village, about a three- or four-hour drive west of Quito, is a popular destination

for bird-watchers and nature lovers who want to see some of Ecuador's western forests at a reasonable cost. Mindo has an area of premontane cloud forest nearby called the **Bosque Protector Mindo-Nambillo**. Between local community activism, ecotourism and the work of private groups, much of Mindo's forests are being preserved or are regenerating. Locals say it's the only place in Ecuador that is *gaining* forest. It's a beautiful area and, with over 400 species of birds recorded, the bird-watching is hard to beat.

Information

Amigos de la Naturaleza-Mindo (☎ 276 5463; e amigosmindo@hotmail.com) is a local conservation organization with an office in Mindo. It has information about the area and can provide details on hiking. The office is a short walk up a dirt road from the plaza.

British bird-watcher Simon Allen has written *A Birder's Guide to Mindo*. You can contact him by emailing him at e spm _allen@hotmail.com or writing to 63 Goldstone Crescent, Hove, BN3 6LR, UK.

Bird-Watching Guides

Many of the following bird-watching guides have telephone contacts only through Quito, but you can often find these particular guides in Mindo simply by asking around. Although many speak only Spanish, they all know the bird names in English and have spent many a day guiding non-Spanish speakers. Most charge between $70 and $140 per day.

Irman Arias (*Quito* ☎ 02-229 9475) is an excellent guide and Irman's brother **Marcelo Arias** comes highly recommended as well; both can be contacted at Irman's number in Quito or at the Andinatel office in Mindo. Both speak enough bird-watching-English for folks who don't speak Spanish.

Julia Patiño (☎ 276 5459) is one of the few (if only) women guides in the area, and she comes well recommended.

Pablo Leon is a biologist and owner of Séptimo Paraíso (see Places to Stay later); he speaks English, charges about $70 per day and is reportedly very good.

Hugolino Oñate (contact him at Armonía Orchid Gardin, see Things to See & Do following) is the curator of a nearby **cock-of-the-rock lek** (*admission $8*), and he will guide you there and around for $15 per day.

He's also an expert on local orchids. **Juan Carlos Calvachi** (☎ 09-966 4503, 286 5213; e calvachi@uio.satnet.net) speaks perfect English, is a top guide and charges about $130 to guide two people for a day (including transportation).

Another local guide to search out is **Efraín Toapanta**, who speaks perfect German and English.

Things to See & Do

Do your best to pop into **Armonía Orchid Garden** (☎ 276 5471; *admission $1; open 7am-6pm daily rain permitting*) where owner Hugoloín Oñate will guide you through his collection of over 200 orchids. It's behind the soccer field.

Caligo Butterfly Farm (☎ 244 0360; *admission $3; open 9am-3pm daily*), which is about 3km south of town, is also worth a visit; get there early to see the cocoons hatching. It's a pleasant walk out here along the Río Mindo.

You'll see **inner-tubes** for rent up and down the main drag in town; it's cheap to rent one and hire a guide to take you splashing down the feisty little rapids of the Río Mindo.

See Getting Around later for jeep transportation to areas around Mindo.

Places to Stay & Eat

There are basic but friendly places to stay and eat in the village and more comfortable and expensive places in the surroundings. Hotel owners are hip to bird-watchers' inability to sleep past 3am and will usually serve crack-of-dawn breakfasts on request (if they have a restaurant).

In Town Just as you roll into Mindo you'll pass **Hostal Bijao** (*Quito* ☎ 02-276 5740; *rooms per person with shared/private bath $4/7.50*), a clean, friendly, thatch-roof place with six rooms with private bath and three more sharing a bath. There is hot water and an excellent, family-run **restaurant** (*mains $3-4.50*) that is also open to nonguests. Rates include breakfast.

Hostal Arco Iris (☎ 276 5445; e albert mind@yahoo.com.ar; main plaza; *rooms per person with shared/private bath $5/6*) is a friendly, run-of-the-mill hotel with clean small rooms and electric hot showers.

La Casa de Cecilia (☎ 276 5453; e casa dececilia@yahoo.com; *rooms per person $5*) is in a private house 1½ blocks behind the plaza. Quarters are cramped but it's clean and welcoming, thanks to Cecilia's friendliness. Kitchen use is an extra one-time fee of $2 per group.

Cabañas Armonía (☎ 276 5471; cabins per person $14) is tucked into Armonía Orchid Garden (see Things to See & Do earlier); it's great if you like orchids. There are four cozy little wood cabañas with private hot baths and breakfast is included.

El Descanso (☎ 276 5383; w www.eldescanso.net; dorm beds $10, private rooms per person $15) is an attractive new place behind the soccer field with excellent rooms, a hammock-strewn terrace and backyard. Think comfortable.

Hostal Flor del Valle (☎ 276 5452; rooms per person $3), just off the main drag, has tiny wooden rooms with shared bath.

There are several restaurants along the main street leading up to the plaza. On weekends, **Café El Monte** (☎ 276 5472), just off the main drag, serves delicious pizzas, pastas, pastries and sandwiches.

Outside of Town About 4km south of Mindo along a winding dirt road is **El Monte Sustainable Lodge** (☎/fax 276 5472; e info@ecuadortravel.com; w www.ecuadorcloudforest.com; rooms per person $61). Run by a warmhearted and knowledgeable young US/Ecuadorian couple, this place is a real find. From a tiny parking area, it's reached by a *tarabita* (hand-powered cable car) over Río Mindo. El Monte has three lovely private cabins, as well as a communal lodge. The cozy, two-story, A-frame, river-side cabins all sleep up to four people and have hot showers, good beds and a sitting room. The lodge has a restaurant with a library, bar and games. Rates include all meals (vegetarian, fish, poultry, there's no red meat) and guided activities (bird-watching, hiking, tubing, horse riding); a two-night minimum is suggested. Reservations are recommended to ensure that the owners can guide you (they'll meet you in Mindo) and that you have a cabin to yourself (sharing is unnecessary). They also own the **Mindo Biostation** (researchers/nonresearchers per person $10/61), a hike-in research station and lodge set in primary forest within the buffer zone of Mindo-Nambillo reserve. There's hot water, a kitchen, eating area,

six rooms with shared bath and one room with a private bath (and hammocks out on the porch).

Mindo Gardens Lodge (Quito ☎ 02-225 2489/90; e casablan@uio.satnet.net; rooms per person $62) is about a kilometer north of El Monte Sustainable Lodge and is reached by car or a 45-minute walk from town. Set in nicely landscaped gardens, the lodge has four main buildings. The central building has an elegant dining room with an international menu (open to the public), as well as a games room (with a pool table and cable TV) and bar. Outside, there is a barbecue and pizza oven, which is used as needed. The three cabins all have three bedrooms, each with a private hot bath and all sharing a sitting room. The rooms sleep two to four people. Two cabins are by the river and the third is surrounded by forest. The lodge can arrange local tours and is run well. Rates include all meals.

Centro de Educación Ambiental (CEA; dorm beds/private rooms per person $5/8, with three meals $17/18) is run by Amigos de la Naturaleza-Mindo (see Information earlier) and is between the two lodges listed previously, but it is reached by foot – the road doesn't go there. Ask how to get there in Mindo. Accommodations are rustic but well constructed and attractive. A dorm with 15 mattresses (bring a sleeping bag) plus four private double rooms share bathroom facilities. If you don't choose to have your meals included, you can use the kitchen to prepare your own.

Séptimo Paraíso (☎ 09-993 4133, Quito ☎ 02-289 3512; w www.septimoparaiso.com; standard/superior rooms $61/73, suites $88), just off the road down to Mindo (2km below the 'Y'), has room for 72 people between its wooden main lodge and its annexe lodge, both set within a private 300-hectare reserve with great bird-watching. Both lodges have rooms with private bath and hot water and some have excellent views into the forest. It's a slick place that feels rustic (lots of wood) yet upscale (shiny brass bed frames and flowery spreads). Rates include breakfast. The **restaurant** (mains $5-9), which is open to the public, is excellent – try the trout.

Getting There & Away

From Quito, **Cooperativa Flor de Valle** (☎ 527 495) goes to Mindo ($2, 2½ hours) daily at 3:20pm and also at 8am on Friday, Saturday and Sunday. The bus leaves from M Larrea just west of Ascunción, near Parque El Ejido. Get there early as the bus fills up. The bus returns from Mindo to Quito daily at 6:30am and 2pm on Friday, Saturday and Sunday.

There is also a Mindo bus from the Santo Domingo de los Colorados bus terminal at 2pm daily with Cooperativa Kennedy (five hours). There are buses from Mindo to Santo Domingo at 7am and 1pm (five hours).

Getting Around

For jeep transportation just about anywhere you want to go around Mindo, ask for Raul Narvaez; he drives a blue Nissan Patrol, charges fairly, and can usually be found around the plaza.

WEST OF MINDO

Beyond Mindo, the road drops to **Los Bancos** (also known as San Miguel de los Bancos), shortly beyond which the road improves and continues through Puerto Quito and on to intersect with the main road between Santo Domingo de los Colorados and the north-coast port of Esmeraldas (see the North Coast & Lowlands chapter). This is an infrequently used and beautiful route from Quito to the western lowlands.

Puerto Quito

About 2km before Puerto Quito, at Km 140, a sign points to **Aldea Salamandra** (e aldea salamandra@yahoo.com; beds per person $8), about 500m away on the banks of Río Caoni. This is a very tranquil, rustic hideaway where you can swim and canoe in the river; it's also an excellent place to go bird-watching or to just relax. There are no showers (you can wash in the river) or flushing toilets. Packages that include three meals and guided excursions are $21 a day or $120 a week. The place is gaining popularity among young budget travelers, but it is far from 'discovered.'

Cabañas del Río (☎ 02-223 8712; rooms per person $45), also on Río Caoni, has rustic, clean cabañas with private, cold showers. They sleep two to eight and rates include meals and guided walks.

Although Puerto Quito is only 300m above sea level, there is no malaria reported in this area.

Puerto Quito is reached by frequent buses from Quito's bus terminal (use Transportes Kennedy, San Pedrito or Alóag) and by less-frequent buses from Santo Domingo.

Pedro Vicente Maldonado

Arashá Rainforest Resort & Spa (☎ 02-276 5348/49, Quito ☎ 02-226 5757, 224 9881; e arasharv@interactive.net.ec; w www.arasha 1spa.com; rooms around $100) is the most luxurious hotel in the biodiverse forests of Ecuador's western slopes. In addition to bird-watching, hiking and wildlife-watching excursions, the resort offers a pool, whirlpool, waterfalls, a kid's swimming area, rafting, two international restaurants, a bar, games and video room, conference room and beautiful grounds. There are 26 cottages with a total of 47 rooms, all with private bath.

The hotel lies 3km outside the village of Pedro Vicente Maldonado at Km 120 and about 200m off the main road to Puerto Quito.

Central Highlands

The Panamericana heads almost due south of Quito through a long valley flanked by two parallel ranges of high mountains. These two ranges consist for the most part of volcanoes, and several of them are still active. It was this feature that prompted Alexander von Humboldt, the German explorer who visited the country in 1802, to name Ecuador's central valley 'The Avenue of the Volcanoes' – a name that is still used today.

The central valley is only a tiny fraction of Ecuador's land surface, yet it contains almost half of its population. Traditionally, Ecuador's Andean Indians farmed the valley's rich volcanic soils, and after the conquest, the Spanish found that the central valley made a good communication route between the north and south. Today, the same route is used for the Panamericana, and a string of towns stretches south from the capital to Cuenca, 442km away.

In between lies some of Ecuador's wildest scenery, including nine of the country's 10 highest peaks and scores of tiny villages of indigenous Andeans leading lives that have changed little in centuries. Many of these villages are so remote that access is only possible on foot; some are easier to get to, however, and provide a fascinating glimpse of Andean life. The further south one goes, the larger and remoter the Indian populations. Most indigenous villages have minor differences in dress that are immediately recognizable to the local people – the pattern, color or shape of a poncho, hat, dress, blouse, trousers or waistband can all indicate where someone is from.

Ecuador's most popular mountain climbs take place in this region, and a handful of local climbers and visiting mountaineers make attempts at scaling these giants year-round. In terms of weather and snow conditions, December and January are considered the best months to visit, and March to May the worst. Some climbing and hiking information is given in this chapter for the most important peaks and trails. More details can be found in the books listed under Books in the Facts for the Visitor chapter, at the South American Explorers (SAE) in Quito or through the climbing guides and outfitters mentioned in the Quito chapter.

Highlights

- Watching the lively sale of livestock, produce, pig heads and much, much more at the indigenous market at Saquisilí
- Roaming the Quilotoa loop, a spectacular high-Andean road with indigenous villages, great hiking and a magnificent crater lake
- Riding on the roof of the train down the hair-raising switchbacks of El Nariz del Diablo (The Devil's Nose)
- Barreling by on mountain bike from Baños down to Puyo, past one of Ecuador's greatest waterfalls, El Pailón del Diablo
- Ascending toward the most distant point from the center of the Earth – the peak of Volcán Chimborazo
- Taking mind-altering bus rides to Guaranda and Salinas, where there's nothing to do but eat chocolate and cheese
- Peering at the pyrotechnics of the active Volcán Tungurahua from one of several villages in the Baños area
- Exploring the spectacular Andean scenery surrounding Volcán Cotopaxi, Ecuador's second-highest peak

Central Highlands p161

Most travelers, however, visit the larger towns, which are well connected with one another by road, and travel is generally easy and accompanied by superb views. Villagers generally come into the larger towns

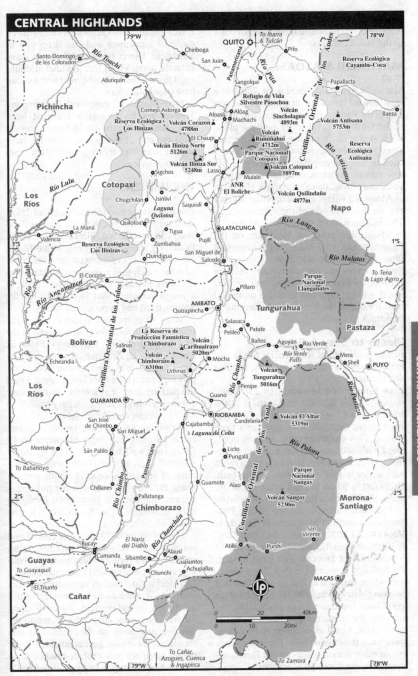

To Ibarra & Tulcán

QUITO

Chiriboga
San Juan
Pifo

Santo Domingo de los Colorados

Río Toachi

Alluriquín

Reserva Ecológica Cayambe-Coca

Papallacta

Pichincha

Cornejó Astorga

Reserva Ecológica Los Ilinizas

Volcán Corazón 4788m

Aloasí
Machachi

Refugio de Vida Silvestre Pasochoa

Alóag

Volcán Sincholagua 4893m

Volcán Antisana 5753m

Baeza

Río Pita

Sangolquí

El Chaupi

Volcán Iliniza Norte 5126m

Volcán Iliniza Sur 5248m

Sigchos

Lasso

Volcán Rumiñahui 4712m

Parque Nacional Cotopaxi

Volcán Cotopaxi 5897m

Reserva Ecológica Antisana

Río Antisana

Cordillera Oriental de los Andes

Mulaló

Cotopaxi

Chugchilán

Isinliví

Laguna Quilotoa

Quilotoa

Saquisilí

ANR El Boliche

Volcán Quilindaña 4877m

Napo

Río Langoa

Río Lulu

Los Ríos

La Maná

Valencia

Tigua

Zumbahua

Pujilí

LATACUNGA

San Miguel de Salcedo

Río Mulatos

To Tena & Lago Agrio

Reserva Ecológica Los Ilinizas

Quindigua

El Corazón

Río Angamarca

Río Calabí

Pillaro

AMBATO

Quizapincha

Parque Nacional Llanganates

Tungurahua

Pastaza

Salasaca
Pelileo

Patate

Baños

Agoyán
Río Verde

Mera
Shell

PUYO

Bolívar

Salinas

Echeandía

La Reserva de Producciòn Faunística Chimborazo

Volcán Carihuairazo 5020m

Volcán Chimborazo 6310m

Mocha

Urbinas

Río Verde Falls

Volcán Tungurahua 5016m

Río Pastaza

Cordillera Occidental de los Andes

Los Ríos

Guano

Penipe

San José de Chimbo

San Miguel

GUARANDA

RIOBAMBA

Candelaria

Volcán El Altar 5319m

Río Palora

Montalvo

San Pablo

Cajabamba

Laguna de Colta

To Babahoyo

Chillanes

Pallatanga

Chimborazo

Guamote

Licto
Pungalá

Alao

Río Chambo

Cordillera Oriental de los Andes

Parque Nacional Sangay

Volcán Sangay 5230m

Morona-Santiago

Río Chimbo

Río Chanchán

El Nariz del Diablo

Bucay

Guayas

Cumanda

Alausí

Sibambe

Huigra

Guasuntos

Chunchi

Achupallas

San Vicente

Atillo

Purshí

MACAS

To Guayaquil

El Triunfo

Cañar

LP

0   20   40km
0 10   20mi

To Cañar, Azogues, Cuenca & Ingapirca

To Zamora

on market days, and their traditional and brightly dyed clothing adds splashes of color to the market scenes.

MACHACHI & ALOASÍ
☎ 02

Machachi, with a population of 7000, is a small town 35km south of Quito, on the east side of the Panamericana. Its main attraction is the Güitig mineral-water bottling plant. It's a 4km walk from town, or you can take a taxi; everyone knows where it is. You'll need to leave your passport at the gate before you can enter. Apart from a cold pool you can swim in, there's not much else here.

Aloasí is a village almost opposite Machachi, on the west side of the Panamericana. The Machachi train station is in Aloasí.

About 6km north of Machachi on the Panamericana, near Alóag, is the important junction with the road to Santo Domingo de los Colorados and the coast. Here, you can get food 24 hours a day, have your car serviced, and get off a bus from the south and wait for one to the coast without having to backtrack to Quito.

Places to Stay & Eat
In Machachi, **Hotel Residencial Mejía** and **Hotel Miravalle** are both a bit dirty, but also dirt cheap.

La Estación de Machachi (☎ 230 9246; singles/doubles $20/22), in Aloasí, is at the train station (don't worry about the noise from trains; there are very few trains from Quito). This charming little hotel is decorated with antiques and has a pleasant garden, a good restaurant, 10 rooms and a cabin which sleeps four – all with private bath. Breakfast is $4 to $5, and other meals are about $8. There is a lunch buffet on Sunday.

The best places to eat are on the Panamericana south of Machachi. **El Café de la Vaca** (☎ 231 5012; almuerzo $4; open 8am-5:30pm Wed-Sun), about 3km south of Machachi, is a favorite. You can't miss it; the building is painted to look like a black-and-white dairy cow, and in fact, this is a working dairy farm. The restaurant serves good local food, as well as sandwiches and burgers; the almuerzo (set-lunch menu) is good value. Local information and roadside assistance is available here. There are a couple of other decent places on the Panamericana between here and Machachi.

Getting There & Away
Buses depart from Quito's bus terminal en route to Latacunga and can drop you in Machachi. Direct buses to Machachi leave from the small Villa Flora terminal in southern Quito, which can be reached by city buses for Villa Flora.

From Machachi, buses with the company Transportes La Dolorosa leave at least every hour during the day to Aloasí. Stay on until the end of the line to reach the train station, which is approximately 3km from the Panamericana.

THE ILINIZAS
☎ 02

The Ilinizas are two mountains about 25km southwest of Machachi as the condor flies. Both can be climbed. **Iliniza Sur** (5248m), Ecuador's sixth-highest peak, is a difficult ice climb for experienced mountaineers who have technical equipment. **Iliniza Norte** (5126m), Ecuador's eighth-highest peak, is a rough scramble that is suitable for fit, acclimatized and experienced hikers.

Many climbers elect to stay in one of the several simple *hostales* (small hotels) in the El Chaupi area (see following). From El Chaupi you can continue on foot (or try to hire a truck to take you) another 9km to the parking area where the climb begins. From the parking area, it is a three- to four-hour climb to a **refuge** (bunk beds per person $10) where you can spend the night.

Fit hikers could leave Quito at dawn, catch an early bus from Machachi to El Chaupi and walk hard to reach the refuge by nightfall. Part of the climb is up a steep ramp of volcanic scoria. The bulls you see along the way are bred for the bullring – imagine the strength they attain living up here at 4200m! The locals all tell you '¡cuidado!' (beware).

The refuge is at 4650m, just east of and below a saddle between the two mountains, and has bunks (bring a sleeping bag), cooking facilities, a fireplace (although not much fuel) and a caretaker. A generator provides lighting. Water has to be carried from a nearby stream and purified. You could camp for free, but camp sites are exposed to the weather and have no facilities, and you should not leave your gear unattended. From the refuge, it is a two- or three-hour climb to Iliniza Norte along a fairly well-defined –

but at times narrow, steep and slippery – trail.

El Chaupi Area

Most folks who come to El Chaupi, a tiny village about 7km southwest off the Panamericana, are on their way to climb the Ilinizas. There are several hostales in the area. El Chaupi itself has a phone and a store with minimal supplies.

Places to Stay & Eat

Hostal Llovizna (☎ 09-699 068; beds per person $10), about 500m from El Chaupi, on the road to Ilinizas, is owned by Vladimir Gallo, the manager of the Ilinizas climbers refuge. It has several beds and a kitchen, and rates include breakfast.

Hostería Papagayo (☎ 231 0002, 09-990 3524; Panamericana Sur Km 43; rates per person $5-9, camping $3) is a pretty, converted farmhouse with both dorm beds and private rooms. It's Israeli owned with simple but colorful rooms and a restaurant, bar and disco. Hiking information is available and tours, guides and horse riding can be arranged. It's 500m west off the Panamericana and about 2km north of the El Chaupi turn-off.

Hacienda Nieves (☎ 231 5092; cabins per person $8) is about 3km from El Chaupi on the road to the Ilinizas and offers day trips from Quito (which include horse riding) for $45. There is a six-bed cabin with a kitchen; call ahead to arrange accommodations.

Hacienda San José (☎ 09-973 7986, Quito ☎ 02-289 1547; bunks per person $10) is 3km from El Chaupi by another road. Owned by Rodrigo Peralva, who is friendly and helpful, this farm has two cabins with bunks, fireplaces and hot showers. In the main house, there's a kitchen and a sitting room. Maps are available, and the climbers refuge can be reached in a few hours of walking. Very fit hikers could reach Iliniza Norte and return in one long day. When Rodrigo is gone (usually on weekends), he leaves a key with the caretaker behind the house. Rates include breakfast when Rodrigo is there. This place has been recommended by climbers.

Getting There & Away

To get to El Chaupi from Machachi, take one of the blue-and-white buses signed 'El Chaupi,' which leave about every hour during the day. If you're driving, take the unsigned turn-off from the Panamericana about 7km south of Machachi (taxi drivers know it) and continue along a cobbled road another 7km to El Chaupi. From El Chaupi the road turns to dirt and continues another 9km to the parking area, identified by a small shrine to the Virgin. You can also hire a pickup in Machachi (ask around the plaza) to take you directly to the parking area for about $30. Don't drive a rental car and leave it here, as break-ins are frequent.

PARQUE NACIONAL COTOPAXI
☎ 03

Established in 1975, the 33,393-hectare Parque Nacional Cotopaxi (admission $10) is mainland Ecuador's most popular and frequently visited national park. That is not to say it is crowded – indeed, it can be almost deserted midweek. Weekends are busier.

The park gives you a good look at the páramo (Andean grasslands). The pine forests on the lower slopes are not Ecuadorian; they are imported trees grown for forestry purposes.

The park's centerpiece is the beautifully cone-shaped, snowcapped volcano **Cotopaxi** (5897m), Ecuador's second-highest peak. Present volcanic activity is limited to a few gently smoking fumaroles (the highest in the world) that cannot be seen except by mountaineers who climb up to the icy crater and peer within. There have, however, been many violent eruptions in the past few centuries – three of them have wiped out the town of Latacunga. There are also several other peaks within the park, of which **Rumiñahui** (4712m) is the most important.

The wildlife is unusual and interesting. The Andean condor is present, although rarely seen. More frequently spotted birds include the caruncolated caracara (a falcon with a distinctive orange face), the Andean lapwing, the Andean gull, highland hummingbirds, the great thrush, a number of species of duck and shorebird, as well as many others.

The most frequently seen mammals in the park are white-tailed deer and rabbits. Little red brocket deer are also present; they are only about 35cm high at the shoulder. With luck, you may catch a glimpse of the colpeo (Andean fox) or puma. The rare Andean spectacled bear lives on the remote and infrequently visited eastern slopes of the park.

CENTRAL HIGHLANDS

PARQUE NACIONAL COTOPAXI AREA

Although Cotopaxi park has the most well-developed infrastructure of the mainland parks – there are rangers, a small museum and information center, a climbers refuge, and camping and picnicking areas – facilities are basic, and most nonmountaineering visitors come on day trips.

The park-entrance fee doesn't include the overnight refuge fees ($10, cash only) or camping fees (about $2). **Area Nacional de Recreación El Boliche**, an area which abuts the national park to the west, also charges $10, but the ticket is valid for both Cotopaxi and El Boliche, and it remains valid until you leave. The main problems facing the park are litter, poaching and inadequate staff.

The main entrance gate is officially open 7am to 3pm, but you can get out until about 6:30pm. Hikers can get in or out at anytime. Drivers can usually find a park guard who is happy to let them through at odd hours for a tip.

Altitude sickness is a very real danger – acclimatize for several days in Quito before attempting to walk in. Do not attempt to visit the park immediately after arriving in the highlands from a low elevation.

Hiking & Climbing

There are excellent hiking and mountaineering possibilities within the park. You can camp for a night, or bring plenty of food and hike all the way around Cotopaxi – this takes about a week. Information is available at the entrance booth, and finding these information places is straightforward. A popular place to hike is around **Laguna de Limpiopungo**, a large Andean lake at 3880m above sea level; a few kilometers beyond the lake is the small **Museo Nacional Mariscal Sucre** and **information center**.

Mountaineers and the curious like to go up to **Refugio José Rivas** (bunks $10) at about 4800m on the northern slopes of the mountain. Bunk beds and cooking facilities are available, but bring a warm sleeping bag. There is a guardian on duty who can show you where you can leave your gear if you need to do so; bring a padlock. Climbing beyond the refuge requires stamina, experience and snow- and ice-climbing gear; it's not a climb for beginners, although it is a relatively straightforward climb for those who know what they are doing. See Organized Tours under Riobamba and Baños, respectively, later in this chapter, for information on hiring mountaineering guides.

The Limpiopungo area for camping and picnicking is about 4km beyond the park museum, and the refuge is 12km further. The lake is at 3880m, and the refuge is almost 1000m higher – a hard walk at this altitude if you aren't acclimatized.

Places to Stay

Some camping places in the area have simple shelters (a roof and walls, but no facilities). Another popular camping place is in the Area Nacional de Recreación El Boliche.

The following are comfortable accommodations in the area surrounding the park.

Hacienda San Agustín de Callo (☎ 719 160, 719 510, Quito ☎ 02-290 6157/58; W www.incahacienda.com; singles/doubles $232/278) is a wonderful place a few kilometers west of the park and east of the Panamericana, via signed dirt roads. Within the hacienda, the buildings have well-preserved Inca walls; the dining room and the private chapel are almost entirely Inca. These are the most northerly and well-preserved remains of the Inca empire (others, further north, are poorly maintained). After the conquest, the Augustine friars of Quito built a country house here, and the chapel is attributed to them. Several famous expeditions used San Agustín de Callo as a base, including the French Geodesic mission to measure the equator in 1748, and the expeditions of Alexander von Humboldt in 1802 and Edward Whymper in 1880.

In 1921, the hacienda was sold to the Plaza family, who, at one time, owned most of the land between Quito and Cotopaxi. Today, the owner is the warm-hearted Mignon Plaza, whose grandfather and uncle were once presidents of Ecuador. She relates interesting stories about the history of the hacienda, and you can eat dinner in the same dining room where Peruvian President Fujimori and Ecuadorian President Mahuad were entertained. In 1998, *National Geographic* funded research on the site, and excavations and investigations are slowly ongoing.

There are five double rooms and two suites, and three of the bedrooms have some Inca walls. All the rooms have at least two fireplaces, one in the bedroom and one in the bathroom. Rates include breakfast and dinner and guided activities such as fishing, trekking and mountain biking. Horse-riding trips and day tours can be arranged for an additional cost.

The hacienda can arrange transportation from Quito, or travel agencies can drop you off after a Cotopaxi visit. If you're driving or busing, look for signs on the north side of Lasso; the hacienda is about 5km northeast of the Panamericana on unpaved roads. A truck from Lasso can be hired for about $2.

Cuello de Luna (☎ 09-970 0330, Quito ☎ 02-224 2744; W www.cuellodeluna.com; dorm beds from $11, singles/doubles/triples without bath $20/26/36, singles/doubles/triples/quads with bath $23/34/45/53) is a good budget choice almost 2km west of the

Where Have All the Frogs Gone?

In the 1980s, *Atelopus* frogs, which have a distinctive orange belly and black back, were frequently seen around Limpiopungo. In the 1990s, sightings were few and far between. Herpetologists (scientists who study reptiles and amphibians) have been puzzling the loss of frog and toad species all over the world during the past decade. Amphibians that once were common are now severely depleted in number or are simply no longer found at all. Scientists have been unable to agree upon an explanation for the sudden demise of so many amphibian species in so many different habitats.

One of several theories holds that worldwide air quality has degenerated to the extent that amphibians, which breathe both with primitive lungs and through their perpetually moist skin, are exposed to lethal doses of airborne toxins because of the gas exchange through their skin. Another theory is that frog skin gives little protection against UV light, and that the increasing UV-light levels of recent years has proven deadly to amphibians. Perhaps frogs are the modern-day canaries in the coalmine – when the canary keeled over it was time for the miners to get out! Are our dying frogs and toads a symptom of a planet that is becoming too polluted?

Panamericana opposite the Clirsen entrance to the national park. At 3125m, it is a good place to acclimatize and hike before heading into Cotopaxi. There are dorm beds, a few rooms with shared hot showers and 16 rooms with private hot showers (many with fireplaces). Breakfast ($4) and other meals ($6.50 to $11) are available. Several of our readers have recommended this pleasant and friendly place.

Hostería La Ciénega (☎ 719 052, 719 093, Quito ☎ 02-254 9126, 254 1337; **e** hcie nega@uio.satnet.net; singles/doubles/triples $38/50/57, suites $89) is some 30km south of Machachi or 20km north of Latacunga. This 400-year-old hacienda was converted into a hotel in 1982 and has 16 old rooms with walls several feet thick and colonial or 19th-century furnishings. The annexe with 18 modern rooms is less attractive, although it's priced the same. The restaurant/bar is a popular stopping place for lunch and is often crowded with tour groups. Lunch reservations are advised. Try to confirm that your reservation is in the original house, and get there early to avoid losing your space. The hostería (small hotel) is 1.5km west of the Panamericana and a short distance south of the village of Lasso; there is a sign. Bus drivers will drop you at the sign and from there you can walk.

La Posada del Rey (☎ 719 319; singles/ doubles $24/31) is a newer place just before La Ciénega with a swimming pool and perfectly adequate modern rooms with private bath, fireplace and TV.

Hostería San Mateo (☎ 719 015; **w** www .hosteriasanmateo.com; singles/doubles $36/ 44), further south near Km 75 on the Panamericana, is a centuries-old place in attractive rural surroundings with distant views of Cotopaxi. There are five comfortable doubles with private hot bath, and a private cottage (which costs a little more). The owners are hospitable and run a good restaurant.

Hacienda Yanahurco (Quito ☎ 02-254 5472; 2-day packages per person $295) is a remote place beyond the far east side of the park. It has seven rooms with private bath and affords you the opportunity to visit some of the lesser-known eastern slopes of the Andes. Rates include all meals, horse riding, fishing, rain gear and rubber boots. Longer stays are also available.

Getting There & Away

You can drive, walk or hitchhike into the park. There are two main roads that lead in from the Panamericana, about 16km and 22km south of Machachi (or roughly 36km and 30km north of Latacunga), respectively. You can ask any Quito–Latacunga bus driver to let you off at either entrance.

The more northerly entrance is shortly after the Panamericana crests its highest point between Quito and Latacunga (at about 3500m). The entrance road has a sign for the park and another for the Clirsen Satellite Tracking Station. The road is paved as far as Clirsen, which was previously operated by NASA, about 2km from the Panamericana. Nearby is a llama-breeding facility and the Cotopaxi train station, where the Sunday train excursion from Quito stops. From here, the road then becomes dirt and soon passes the Río Daule camp site in Area Nacional de Recreación El Boliche, eventually reaching the entrance station to Cotopaxi. This dirt road is reportedly closed to vehicles, but it makes a good walk. It is about 3km shorter than driving along the road from the more important southerly entrance, which also has a national-park sign. Follow the main dirt roads (also signed) through the entrance point (about 8km or 10km from the Panamericana) to the **Museo Nacional Mariscal Sucre** (about 15km from the Panamericana).

On weekends, local tourists visit the park, and there is a good chance of getting a lift. Midweek the park is almost deserted and you'll probably end up walking.

Rides in pickups from Latacunga cost about $20 to $30, but you should bargain. Mountaineers wishing to reach Refugio José Rivas must clearly specify that they want to go up the steep dirt road to the parking lot under the refuge at the end of the road. You can arrange for the pickup to return for you on a particular day for another $20 to $30. It is almost an hour's walk uphill (at 4800m) from the parking lot to the refuge, which looks as if it's about a 10-minute stroll away. Any car will get you into the park to visit the museum, see the llamas and picnic by Limpiopungo (about $10 from Lasso), where excellent views of the mountain are possible if the weather permits. You could camp here and continue on foot.

It is possible to reach the park from the north, such as from Machachi or Sangolqui, but you need to hire a vehicle and a guide who knows the route.

Many of the major travel agencies in Quito can arrange tours to Cotopaxi, normally via the Panamericana. Bicycle tours can be arranged in Quito (see Travel Agencies & Tour Operators in the Quito chapter) and in Latacunga (see Organized Tours under Latacunga following).

The weekend tourist train from Quito (see Getting There & Away under Quito) can drop you at the Area Nacional de Recreación El Boliche, after which it turns around and heads back to Quito.

LATACUNGA
☎ 03 ● pop 54,000 ● elevation 2800m
The drive from Quito to Latacunga is magnificent in clear weather. Like a mammoth ice-cream cone, Cotopaxi looms to the left of the Panamericana as you travel south, and the two Ilinizas, also snowcapped, are on your right. Several other peaks are visible during the 90km drive, including distant Chimborazo if you are lucky. On exceptionally clear days, nine of Ecuador's 10 highest peaks can be seen.

Latacunga is the capital of Cotopaxi Province. Although not an exciting town, it has an interesting history and is a good base for several excellent excursions. The town's name originates from the Indian words *llacta cunani*, which translate rather charmingly into 'land of my choice.' Latacunga became an important colonial center immediately after the conquest, but today, there is little evidence of its long and varied history.

Cotopaxi, which dominates the town on a clear day, erupted violently in 1742 and destroyed the town, which was rebuilt. Another eruption 26 years later wiped it out again, but the indomitable (or foolhardy) survivors rebuilt it a second time. An immense eruption in 1877 destroyed it a third time, and yet again it was rebuilt on the same site. At present, the volcano's activity is minor, and it is unlikely that an eruption will occur within the next several years.

Information
There is no tourist office in Latacunga.

Banco de Guayaquil (*Maldonado 7-20; open 8am-3:30pm Mon-Fri*) changes traveler's checks and has an ATM. **Banco del**

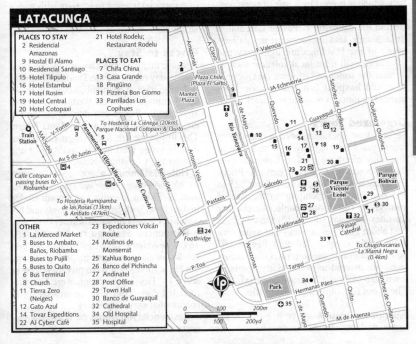

LATACUNGA

PLACES TO STAY
2 Residencial Amazonas
9 Hostal El Alamo
10 Residencial Santiago
15 Hotel Tilipulo
16 Hotel Estambul
17 Hotel Rosim
19 Hotel Central
20 Hotel Cotopaxi
21 Hotel Rodelu; Restaurant Rodelu

PLACES TO EAT
7 Chifa China
13 Casa Grande
18 Pingüino
31 Pizzería Bon Giorno
33 Parrilladas Los Copihues

OTHER
1 La Merced Market
3 Buses to Ambato, Baños, Riobamba
4 Buses to Pujilí
5 Buses to Quito
6 Bus Terminal
8 Church
11 Tierra Zero (Neiges)
12 Gato Azul
14 Tovar Expeditions
22 AJ Cyber Café
23 Expediciones Volcán Route
24 Molinos de Monserrat
25 Kahlua Bongo
26 Banco del Pichincha
27 Andinatel
28 Post Office
29 Town Hall
30 Banco de Guayaquil
32 Cathedral
34 Old Hospital
35 Hospital

Pichincha *(Quito near Salcedo)* and other banks around town have ATMs.

Both **Andinatel** *(open 8am-10pm daily)* and the **post office** *(open 8am-6pm Mon-Fri, 8am-1pm Sat)* are on Quevedo, which is near Maldonado.

Internet access is available at **Gato Azul** *(Guayaquil 6-14)* and **AJ Cyber Café** *(Quito 16-19)*; both places charge $1 per hour.

Things to See & Do

Latacunga is a good center for excursions to Cotopaxi (see earlier) and to the nearby villages that are described at the end of this section. It's also the main point from which to visit the Thursday morning market in Saquisilí. In the town itself, there is little to see, partly because most of the historic buildings have been wiped out by volcanic eruptions. A small ethnography and art museum, **Molinos de Monserrat** *(Vela 3-49; admission $0.30; open Tues-Sat)*, near Salcedo, is run by the Casa de la Cultura Ecuatoriana.

There are several plazas, of which **Parque Vicente León** is the most attractive, with its well-tended garden and topiary work. At the southeast corner of this plaza is the **town hall**, which is topped by a pair of stone condors, and on the south side is the **cathedral**. Behind the cathedral is **Pasaje Catedral**, a little arcade that includes an art gallery. Many of the buildings are light gray and have been built from local volcanic rock.

Near the south end of town on Quevedo is an **old hospital** that is a historic landmark. The modern hospital is a block away.

Organized Tours

Several tour operators have sprung up in recent years offering day trips and two- to three-day climbing trips to Cotopaxi (see Parque Nacional Cotopaxi earlier). Prices for a day trip to Cotopaxi are about $25 to $35 per person, depending on the size of your group (the more people, the cheaper the rate). Two-day summit trips to Cotopaxi cost about $120 per person – but make sure your guide is qualified and licensed if you're attempting the summit. Other excursions are offered as well. Many hotels in town also offer day trips to Cotopaxi, too. Check out the following local outfits.

Expediciones Volcán Route (☎ 812 452, ⓔ volcanroute@hotmail.com) Salcedo 4-55

Tierra Zero (Neiges; ☎ 801 170, 804 327, ⓔ guillermoneiges@latinmail.com) Guayaquil 5-13. A professional outfitter offering trips to the Ilinizas and Chimborazo and a two-day trip to Quilotoa.

Tovar Expeditions (☎ 811 333) Guayaquil 5-38. Offers a Cotopaxi day trip along a less-traveled southern route. Also offers downhill-mountain biking, extended trekking, horse riding and paragliding.

Special Events

Latacunga's major annual fiesta is La Virgen de las Mercedes, more popularly known as the Fiesta de La Mamá Negra. Held on September 23 and 24, the celebration involves processions, costumes, street dancing, Andean music and fireworks. This is one of those festivals that, although outwardly Christian, has much pagan Indian influence and is worth seeing. A big parade in honor of La Mamá Negra is held during the Independence of Latacunga, which is celebrated on November 11 with parades and a bullfight.

There is also a weekly market on Saturday and a smaller one on Tuesday – both are held in the market areas at Vela and Echeverria. The markets are colorful and fun but of no special interest to tourists, although a few crafts are sold, especially the small string bags known as *shigras*.

Places to Stay

Because many people stay in Latacunga on Wednesday nights for the Thursday-morning Indian market at Saquisilí, hotels often fill up by midafternoon on Wednesday. Try to arrive early. Prices can double during the hugely popular Fiesta de La Mamá Negra. The following are low-season prices that usually go up a bit in July and August and around the Christmas–New Year holidays.

Hotel Estambul *(☎ 800 354; Quevedo 73-40; rooms per person with shared/private bath $6/8)* is a friendly and recommended budget hotel with large clean rooms and hot water in clean communal showers.

Residencial Santiago *(☎ 800 899, 802 164; 2 de Mayo & Guayaquil; rooms per person $8)* is also good and helpful with large but basic rooms that have private hot baths and a TV. Downstairs rooms were being remodeled during our visit, promising spiffy rooms (that may be pricier).

Residencial Amazonas *(☎ 812 673; F Valencia 47-36; rooms per person with shared/*

private bath $3/5), on the north side of the market, has small, basic, dark rooms. It's clean enough and good for the price.

Hostal El Alamo *(☎ 810 656, 812 042; e alamo@andinanet.net; JA Echeverria; rooms per person $8)* has spartan but spotless tile-floor rooms with TV, telephone and private hot showers.

Hotel Cotopaxi *(☎ 801 310; Salcedo 5-61; rooms per person $7)* offers spacious, comfortable rooms with TV, private bath and hot water. Some rooms have giant windows and pretty views of the park, although they can be a little noisy. It's a friendly place, popular with climbers and an excellent deal. There is a simple restaurant.

Hotel Central *(☎ 802 912; Sanchez de Orellana at Salcedo; rooms per person $7)*, around the corner from Hotel Cotopaxi, is nearly identical (it's the same building) to its neighbor, sans the views of the park. It's equally friendly and sometimes a dollar or so cheaper.

Hotel Tilipulo *(☎ 810 611; e hoteltilipulo@hotmail.com; Guayaquil & Quevedo; singles/doubles $9/16)* has clean, good-sized rooms with hot water, TV and telephone. The owner is very helpful with organizing tours and providing local information (including bus schedules). There is a restaurant.

Hotel Rosim *(☎ 802 172, 813 200; Quito 16-49; rooms per person $10)* offers comfortable rooms that vary from plain to over-furnished but cozy. They all have private baths with hot water.

Hotel Rodelu *(☎ 800 956, 811 264; e rodelu@uio.telconet.net; Quito 16-31; singles/doubles $14/23, suites singles/doubles $28/36)*, just off the Parque Vicente León, is the fanciest hotel in town. The rooms are comfy, with lots of wood paneling, TV, telephone and private hot baths. There's a pleasant restaurant downstairs, too.

People looking for more comfort often stay at **Hostería La Ciénega**, about 20km to the north (see Parque Nacional Cotopaxi earlier), or **Hostería Rumipamba de las Rosas**, about 13km south of Latacunga, near San Miguel de Salcedo.

Places to Eat

The classic dish of Latacunga is the *chugchucara*, a tasty, heart-attack-inducing plate consisting of fritada (fried chunks of pork); *mote* (hominy) with *chicharrón* (fried bits of pork skin); potatoes; fried banana; *tostada* (toasted corn); popcorn; and cheese empanadas. There are several *chugchucara* restaurants on Quijano y Ordoñez, a few blocks south of the center. They're busiest on weekends, when families fill the tables and musicians stroll door to door. One of the best is **Chugchucaras La Mamá Negra** *(☎ 805 401; Quijano y Ordoñez 1-67; chugchucara $4; open 10am-7pm Tues-Sun)*.

Parrilladas Los Copihues *(Quito 14-25; mains $3-6)* is good for steaks and meat dishes and is popular with the business crowd.

Restaurant Rodelu *(Quito 16-31)*, in the hotel of the same name, serves darn good pizza, good breakfasts and espresso drinks.

Pizzería Bon Giorno *(☎ 804 924; cnr Sanchez de Orellana & Maldonado; mains $4-7; open noon-10pm daily)* has the best pizzas and Italian food in town.

Chifa China *(Antonio Vela near 5 de Junio; mains $2.50-4)* is one of the better Chinese restaurants.

Casa Grande *(cnr Quito & Guayaquil; almuerzos $1; open 9am-3pm daily)* is a little family-run place serving cheap almuerzos.

Pingüino *(Quito)* serves the best cup of coffee in town. It's also the place to go for ice cream.

The Latacunga area is also famous for its *allullas* (pronounced 'azhiuzhia'), dry biscuits made of flour, pork fat and a local un-pasteurized cheese – they taste no better than they sound. Women sell them at every bus stop or checkpoint.

Entertainment

Latacunga is pretty quiet, but if you're itchin' for a drink, try the friendly bar **Kahlua Bongo** *(Salcedo near Quevedo; open from 7pm daily)*.

Getting There & Away

Bus From Quito ($1.50, two hours) buses will drop you at the bus terminal if Latacunga is their final destination. If you're taking a bus that's continuing to Ambato or Riobamba the bus will either drop you on the Panamericana at Avenida 5 de Junio, or at the corner of Avenida 5 de Junio and Cotopaxi, about five blocks west of the Panamericana. Buses to Ambato ($0.80, one hour) leave from the bus terminal. If you're heading south to Riobamba, it's easiest to catch a passing bus from the corner of

CENTRAL HIGHLANDS

5 de Junio and Cotopaxi, although these are often full during vacations. Otherwise, bus it to Ambato and change there.

Slower Quito-bound buses leave the terminal, while faster long-distance buses can be flagged on the Panamericana near Avenida 5 de Junio.

Transportes Cotopaxi has hourly buses to Quevedo ($3, five hours) in the western lowlands. The road is paved as far as Pujilí, beyond which it deteriorates. This is one of the roughest, least-traveled and perhaps most spectacular bus routes joining the highlands with the western lowlands. The bus climbs to Zumbahua, at 3500m, and then drops to Quevedo at only 150m above sea level.

For buses to villages along the Quilotoa loop, see the boxed text 'Transportation on the Quilotoa Loop,' later.

Taxi Plaza Chile (Plaza El Salto) is the place to go to hire taxis and pickup trucks for visits to Parque Nacional Cotopaxi and remote villages (pickups double as taxis on many of the rough roads in the highlands). Rates depend on your bargaining ability.

THE QUILOTOA LOOP
☎ 03

The Quilotoa loop gives the adventurous traveler a close look at Andean life in some of the remote villages west of Latacunga. The scenery around this area is splendid. The area's indigenous inhabitants are somewhat withdrawn, although they are friendly and helpful once the ice has been broken, especially if you speak Spanish (or, even better, Quechua). Transportation is infrequent, and you may have to walk for long distances or wait for hours, so always carry warm clothes, a water bottle, some snacks and maybe even a sleeping bag. The area is photogenic, but people are often not keen on being photographed by strangers. All these places have basic accommodations.

The loop is explained heading clockwise from Latacunga, although you can do this circuit in reverse with no problem. Public transportation (see the boxed text 'Transportation on the Quilotoa Loop') is infrequent but available – be prepared for extremely crowded buses (or you can ride on the roof if the weather permits). Hiring a car is an option, but it limits your contact with the locals.

Pujilí
elevation 2900m

This village is 10km west of Latacunga and is easily visited by frequent public buses. It has a basic cheap hotel just off the main plaza and a couple of simple restaurants. The main market day is Sunday and there is a smaller market on Wednesday. All Souls' Day festivities (November 2) are quite traditional, as are the Corpus Christi celebrations (a movable date in June), when the colorful El Danzante festival takes place and costumed dancers parade around on stilts.

Zumbahua & Tigua

Some 57km further west, the tiny village of Zumbahua, with an elevation of 3500m, has an unspoiled, interesting local market on Saturday. Inhabitants often use llamas to transport goods to and from the market. There is traditional Andean music, dancing and heavy drinking on Friday night, which spills over to market day – this is not a tourist event. There are a few small and very basic *residenciales* (cheap hotels) that fill up fast on Fridays, so get there early. **Condor Matzi** *(rooms per person $4)* is the best.

Some 15km east of Zumbahua is Tigua, a community that's known for the bright paintings of Andean life that are locally made on sheepskin canvases mounted on wooden frames. Originally used to decorate drum skins, this indigenous art form is now known beyond the Tigua region but still takes its name from the village. At Km 53 on the Latacunga–Zumbahua road, you'll find the paintings of Alfredo Toaquiza, whose father, Julio, was a progenitor of the Tigua art form. Several other family members are involved in Tigua art, as is Humberto Latacunga (see Laguna Quilotoa following). The paintings are also sold in Quito, but prices are better in Tigua and in the village of Quilotoa. There are no hotels or restaurants in Tigua.

Laguna Quilotoa
elevation 3854m

About 14km north of Zumbahua is the famous volcanic-crater lake of Quilotoa. From the top of the crater, there are beautiful views of the green lake below and the snow-capped Cotopaxi and Iliniza Sur (5248m) in the distance. The lake has no inflow or outlet, and the water is very alkaline and

Hiking from Laguna Quilotoa to Chugchilán

It takes about four to five hours to hike around the rim of Laguna Quilotoa, which is about 3850m above sea level. The lake itself is about 400m below the rim, and steep trails will take you down to the water in about 30 minutes – allow an hour to climb back up. From the parking area by the village, look for a precipitous cut to the left, which leads down to these trails.

A good hike is from Quilotoa to Chugchilán, which takes five hours with breaks. From the parking area, look left across the crater for the lowest, widest and biggest sandy spot, about a quarter of the way around. You will walk 45 to 60 minutes to reach that spot. As you walk around the rim, it is the third low sandy spot. The most common mistake is to leave the crater's rim too early, which is why you should identify the low sandy spot before starting the hike.

From the low sandy spot, looking just west of north, you can see the village of Huayama and, across a canyon, Chugchilán beyond. Follow a row of eucalyptus trees down and head toward Huayama. Eventually, you'll walk along or cross the road to Huayama (go to Huayama and not Huayama Grande, which is actually smaller). In Huayama, you may be able to buy a drink if you ask.

Huayama to Chugchilán is about two more hours. Leaving Huayama, walk past the cemetery. The first right is next to the cemetery. The second right goes to a small house. The third right follows the top of a gully. Don't drop into the gully; follow the path above it. After 15 to 20 minutes, you'll reach the edge of the canyon. A tunnel-like trail leads all the way to Chugchilán. You'll cross two footbridges as you drop down a narrow switchback trail. Cross a cement footbridge over the Río Sihui and then climb to Chugchilán for about an hour.

Directions courtesy of Black Sheep Inn

impossible to drink. A recent expedition measured it at 250m deep, and although evaporation is slowly exceeding precipitation, the lake won't dry up anytime soon. You can hire a mule or guide to visit the lake or other areas.

On the southwest side of the crater lake is the tiny village of Quilotoa, where accommodation can be found in ramshackle little places run by local indigenous folks. Accommodations are extremely basic, but they're also unique and friendly. Be sure to bring warm clothes and a sleeping bag, as these places can be freezing at night. All prices quoted here (which change frequently) include a simple breakfast and dinner.

Hostal Cabañas Quilotoa (☎ 814 625; rates per person $5-7), operated by artist Humberto Latacunga, is the biggest (although not necessarily best) place here, sleeping up to 40 people in basic dorm or private rooms. Blankets are provided, but not linen. There's a fireplace, latrines and an electric shower. Performances of Andean music and dancing can be arranged for groups, and Humberto's Tigua landscapes can be purchased at reasonable prices.

The smaller places tend to be slightly more personal and homey, yet also more basic. They all have smoky fireplaces, communal sleeping areas and charge about $5 per person. They include Hostal Quilotoa, Hostal Chosita, Hostal Sol and Refugio Quilotoa.

Chugchilán
elevation 3200m

Continuing another 22km north of the lake on a terrible road, you reach the small village of Chugchilán, which is surrounded by wild Andean scenery. This is an excellent place to base yourself for the numerous day hikes in the area. Besides a basic place in the village, there are three good places to stay on the northern edge of town on the road to Sigchos. All three will arrange horse-riding trips and provide local hiking information.

Hostal Mama Hilda (☎ 814 814, Quito ☎ 02-258 2957; e mama_hilda@hotmail.com; dorm beds per person $8, private rooms per person $9) is an attractive place with a few cozy private rooms with lofts and a dorm room. Bathrooms are shared and spotless, but the hot water supply is sporadic. It's popular with budget travelers and very friendly. Rates include breakfast and dinner.

Hostal Cloud Forest (☎ 814 808; rooms per person $6) is also clean and friendly, with a warm common room, and plain bed-rooms with shared baths and hot water. Rates include breakfast and dinner.

Black Sheep Inn (☎ 814 587; **w** www .blacksheepinn.com; bunk beds $20-22.50, singles $40-42.50, doubles $49-53.50, triples $70.50-77, quads $89.50-98.50), barely 1km north of town, is a special place to unwind for a few days in a tranquil Andean setting. It is especially good if you're interested in ecotourism. Owned by a North American couple who have lived at the inn since 1994, it's a friendly place that practices high-altitude permaculture and participates in community projects. It has self-composting toilets (that are bedecked with lovely flowers), an organic vegetable garden and a combination chicken/greenhouse for fresh eggs and salads. The inn provides detailed hiking

information for its guests and arranges horse-riding and jeep trips. There is a good music collection, a lending library and free purified water, coffee and tea. Cold beer, cheese, brownies and cookies are always on hand for you to munch on. Outside there's a zipline and a beautiful wooden sauna ($10 extra per group).

The cozy bunkhouse sleeps eight, and the private rooms sleep up to four. Each private room has a loft, a wood-burning stove, comfy beds and a homey feel. All bathrooms are shared and have blazing-hot showers. The views from the bunkhouse are excellent and rates include delicious, whole-some vegetarian breakfasts and dinners. Small discounts for longer stays, students, seniors and SAE members are given, but credit cards are not accepted.

Transportation on the Quilotoa Loop

Most people get around the Quilotoa loop by public transportation, which is fun, but it takes patience. No buses go all the way around the loop. From Latacunga, they only go as far as Chugchilán, and they either go clockwise (via Zumbahua and Quilotoa) or counterclockwise (via Saquisilí and Sigchos).

If you don't wish to take public transport, you could hire a taxi in Latacunga. They'll do the whole route in a long day starting at around $40. The road is the worst between Quilotoa and Sigchos. The section between Zumbahua and Quilotoa is slowly being paved.

The following schedule lists public transport going both directions on the loop. The times listed here are rough (like the road) so always be ready a little early.

Latacunga–Chugchilán

The bus **via Zumbahua** departs daily from Latacunga at noon, passing Zumbahua at around 1:30pm, Laguna Quilotoa at around 2pm and arriving in Chugchilán at about 4pm. The bus via **Sigchos** departs daily at 11:30am, passing Saquisilí just before noon and Sigchos at around 2pm, arriving in Chugchilán around 3:30pm. This bus leaves Latacunga's bus terminal an hour earlier (10:30am) on Saturdays.

Chugchilán–Latacunga

Good morning! Buses returning to Latacunga via **Zumbahua** leave Chugchilán Monday through Friday at 4am, passing Quilotoa (two hours) at around 6am, Zumbahua (about 2½ hours) at around 6:30am and arriving in Latacunga (about four hours) around 8am. On Saturday this bus leaves at 3am, and on Sunday it leaves at 6am and 10am. Buses via **Sigchos** leave Monday through Friday at 3am, passing Sigchos at around 4am, Saquisilí at around 7am and arriving in Latacunga around 8am. On Saturday this bus departs at 7am. On Sunday you must switch buses in Sigchos.

Latacunga–Zumbahua

Transportes Cotopaxi buses ($1.80, two hours) bound for Quevedo depart hourly from Latacunga's bus terminal, and drop passengers a short walk from Zumbahua.

Zumbahua–Laguna Quilotoa

Trucks can be hired for anywhere between $3 and $8 per person (there's usually a $10 minimum per truck), depending on the number of people in you group and your bargaining skills. The

Sigchos
elevation 2800m

From Chugchilán, it's 23 muddy, bumpy kilometers to the town of Sigchos, which has a small Sunday market, and...that's about it. You can hike here in about five hours from Chugchilán via the Toachi canyon, and then get the 2pm bus back or the bus east toward Saquisilí and Latacunga. It's 52km from here to Saquisilí. There are a couple of basic places to stay and a small Sunday market.

Restaurant y Hotel La Posada (☎ 714 224; cnr Galo Atiaga & Las Ilinizas; rooms per person $3) is a good choice. It has private bathrooms, and the rooms are small but they're respectable. It has a good **restaurant** (almuerzos $1.40; open 6am-9pm daily) downstairs. Also try the three-story **Hostal**

Tungurahua (Calle Tungurahua; rooms per person $4) or the smaller **Pensión Sigchos** (rooms per person $3).

Saquisilí

Ecuadorian economists consider Saquisilí's **Thursday morning market** the most important Indian village market in the country, and many travelers rate it as the best they've seen in Ecuador. It's not a tourist-oriented market, although there are the usual few otavaleños (people from Otavalo) selling their sweaters and weavings. This market is for the inhabitants of remote Indian villages who flood into town to buy or sell everything from bananas to homemade shotguns and from herbal remedies to strings of piglets. The majority of the Indians from the area wear little felt porkpie hats and red ponchos.

Transportation on the Quilotoa Loop

Latacunga–Chugchilán bus passes around 1:30pm and the trip from Zumbahua to Laguna Quilotoa takes approximately 45 minutes.

Laguna Quilotoa–Chugchilán
To get from Laguna Quilotoa to Chugchilán take the Latacunga–Chugchilán bus between 2pm and 2:30pm.

Chugchilán–Sigchos
A daily milk truck leaves Chugchilán between 9am and 10am taking about one hour to reach Sigchos, allowing you to avoid the 3am Chugchilán–Latacunga bus. Two other buses go to Sigchos on Thursday afternoon. Sunday departures are at 4am, 5am, noon and between 1pm to 3pm and 7pm to 9pm.

Sigchos–Latacunga
The bus for Sigchos to Latacunga ($1.40, 2½ hours) departs daily at 2:30pm from beside the church. Additional buses leave on Sunday at noon and 4pm. Otherwise catch the passing bus from Chugchilán at around 7am. Both stop in Saquisilí.

Saquisilí–Latacunga
Buses ($0.25, 20 minutes) depart Plaza Concordia in Saquisilí every 10 minutes.

Latacunga–Saquisilí
Buses ($0.25, 20 minutes) depart from Latacunga's bus terminal every 10 minutes.

Latacunga–Sigchos
Transportes Nacional Saquisilí buses leave Latacunga's bus terminal at 9am daily Friday to Wednesday. On Sunday, an additional bus (2½ hours) leaves at 3:30am.

Sigchos–Chugchilán
Take the passing bus from Latacunga or the daily milk truck which leaves Sigchos around 8am; the trip takes about one hour.

There are eight different plazas, each of which sell specific goods. Especially interesting is the **animal market**, a cacophonous affair, with screaming pigs playing a major role. It's almost 1km out of town – go early and ask for directions.

The bus from Latacunga drops you off near the Plaza La Concordia, with its many trees surrounded by an iron railing. On Thursday, this becomes a market plaza. As for all busy markets, watch for pickpockets.

Most travelers find it best to stay in Latacunga; the bus service begins at dawn, so you won't miss anything. You can stay at **Pensión Chavela** *(Plaza La Concordia)* although it's pretty run down and likely to be full the night before the market.

Hostería Rancho Muller *(☎ 721 103; rooms from $15)* is on the outskirts of town and is German run. Rooms are clean, plain and have a bath, and the owner helps with your local arrangements. There is also a slightly pricey international restaurant, which has the best food in town.

There are plenty of hole-in-the-wall places to eat. One plaza seems to be nothing but food stalls – if you stick to cooked food and don't have a delicate stomach, you'll enjoy it.

Numerous tour companies in Quito organize one- or two-day tours to Saquisilí; see Travel Agencies & Tour Operators in the Quito chapter for more information.

ISINLIVÍ
elevation 3000m

Some 14km southeast of Sigchos, just off the main Quilotoa loop, is the village of Isinliví. You can hike here from either Sigchos or Chugchilán. There's an interesting woodworking/cabinetry shop in the village, a small handicrafts center and nearby *pucarás* (pre-Incan hill fortresses). A popular day hike is to the Monday market at nearby Guantualo.

You will find good accommodation at **Llullu Llama** *(☎ 814 790/570; dorm beds $5, private rooms per person $7-8)*, a renovated, old adobe farmhouse with meter-thick walls and a wood-burning stove. There's a sauna (fired up for an additional cost), and food is available (including vegie options) for $2 to $3 per meal. The place is owned by Jean Brown of Safari Tours (see Travel Agencies & Tour Operators in the Quito chapter).

There are direct buses to Isinliví from Latacunga's bus terminal at 1pm on Monday,

Tuesday, Wednesday and Friday, and at 10:30am or 11am on Saturday and Sunday. Buses leave Saquisilí to Isinliví on Thursday between 10:30am and 11am. There are two daily buses from Sigchos.

SAN MIGUEL DE SALCEDO
☎ 03

This small town, usually just called Salcedo, is 14km south of Latacunga on the Panamericana. It has a Sunday market and a lesser market on Thursday. In mid-March, it hosts the important Agricultural and Industrial Fair, and there's a big Mamá Negra fiesta around November 1. There are a couple of basic hotels in the town center.

Hostería Rumibamba de las Rosas *(☎ 726 128, 726 306, 727 309; doubles $50)* is on the northern outskirts of town and is a fairly modern hotel with comfortable 'log cabin' bungalows furnished with antiques. It has a popular restaurant and bar, a small private zoo, a duck pond, pony and llama rides, a swimming pool, tennis courts and game rooms. The whole place has a Disneyland atmosphere, but it's clean and well run.

AMBATO
☎ 03 • pop 174,261 • elevation 2800m

Some 47km south of Latacunga (136km south of Quito) is the important town of Ambato, the capital of Tungurahua Province. It was badly damaged in a 1949 earthquake, but a modern city was soon rebuilt. It is prosperous and growing, and the downtown streets and market areas are lively.

The city is proud of its cultural heritage, and nicknames itself 'Tierra de Los Tres Juanes' (Land of the Three Juans). The 'three Juans' were the writers Juan Montalvo and Juan León Mera (see Arts in the Facts about Ecuador chapter), and lawyer/ journalist Juan Benigno Malo. All three are immortalized in Ambato's parks, museums and buildings.

Apart from the festivals described under Special Events, later, most travelers just pass through Ambato on their way to Baños.

The Monday market is a huge affair – the biggest in Ecuador.

Information

The **tourist office** *(☎ 821 800; Guayaquil & Rocafuerte; open 9am-3pm Mon-Fri)* is by Hotel Ambato.

Cambiato (☎ 821 008; Calle Bolívar 686) changes traveler's checks. **Banco del Pacífico** (cnr Lalama & Cevallos), **Banco de Guayaquil** (cnr Mera & Sucre) and **Banco del Pichincha** (Lalama near Sucre) will all change foreign currency and have ATMs.

Andinatel (open 8am-10pm daily) and the **post office** (open 8am-6pm Mon-Fri, 8am-noon Sat) are both on Castillo by Parque Juan Montalvo.

For Internet access try **Net Place** (Juan Montalvo & Cevallos), which charges $1 per hour or **Catedral Internet** (Bolívar 16-49), which costs $1.20 per hour. Or try the cyber-café inside the **Casa de Cultura** (Calle Bolívar), which also charges $1.20 per hour.

Travel and 1st-class tour arrangements can be made at **Metropolitan Touring** (☎/fax 824 084; Rocafuerte 1401).

Las Quintas

Most of the buildings in the center are new and of no great interest because of reconstruction since the 1949 earthquake. A recommended walk is along Calle Bolívar, southwest of the center, to the pleasant modern suburb of Miraflores, on the banks of Río Ambato (note that Calle Bolívar changes into Avenida Miraflores). The river can be crossed about 2km away from town on Avenida Los Guaytambos, which soon leads to **La Quinta de Juan Montalvo** (open 9am-noon & 2pm-6pm daily), where that writer's villa stands (quinta means country house). It's in the suburb of Ficoa and can be visited.

Several other famous ambateños (people from Ambato) had country houses that survived the earthquake and are worth visiting. **La Quinta de Juan León Mera** (Avenida Los Capulíes; open 9am-noon & 2pm-6pm) is set in an attractive botanical garden in the suburb of Atocha. Close by is **La Quinta de la Liria**, the country home of the mountaineer Nicolás Martínez; this quinta is also set in a pleasant garden. Next to this home, **Centro Cultural de la Liria** was built in 1995 and contains an art museum and photography gallery of old and new photographs of Ambato.

The suburb of Atocha is on the far side of Río Ambato, about 2km northeast of the city center. It can be reached on foot by walking northwest out of town on Montalvo, which soon crosses the river, and then by turning right on Capulíes, about 200m beyond the river. La Quinta de Juan León Mera is about 1.5km to the northeast, and La Quinta de la Liria just beyond it. Local buses and taxis go to all these places.

Museo de Ciencias Naturales

This natural-history museum (☎ 821 958; Sucre & Lalama; admission $2; open 8:30am-12:30pm & 2:30pm-5:30pm Mon-Fri, 9am-5pm Sat) is in the Colegio Bolívar, on the northwest side of the Parque Cevallos. There are hundreds of stuffed birds, mammals and reptiles. In the absence of comprehensive field guides to Ecuadorian wildlife, this is a good museum to visit if you wish to identify species you may have seen in the wild. There's also a rather gruesome display of freaks, such as two-headed calves and six-legged lambs, an archaeological collection with Inca pieces, traditional Ecuadorian clothing, a coin collection and other displays.

Parque Juan Montalvo

This attractive park features a statue of Montalvo and is Ambato's most important plaza. On the northwest side of the plaza, you can visit his house, **Casa de Montalvo** (☎ 824 248; admission $0.40; open 9am-noon & 2pm-6pm Mon-Sat), which has some of Montalvo's original manuscripts, as well as photos of old Ambato. Next door is **Casa de Cultura** (☎ 820 338, 824 248; admission free; open 9am-noon & 3pm-6pm Mon-Fri), which has an art gallery and an Internet café. On the northeast side of this plaza is the modern and rather bleak **cathedral**, which has some good stained-glass windows.

Markets

The huge weekly market is held on Monday, and there are smaller ones on Wednesday and Friday. Established in 1861, the Monday market is the largest city market in the country. Although it has been modernized (it takes place in buildings rather than outdoors), it is still a huge, bustling affair, attracting Indians from many nearby communities. The main spot for produce is the modern Mercado Central, at the southeastern end of Lalama, but there are many other markets scattered around town and in the suburbs (these are generally not aimed at tourists). Walking along Cevallos will bring you past Mercado Colombia (also called Modelo), and as you go further northeast along Cevallos, you will pass some stalls

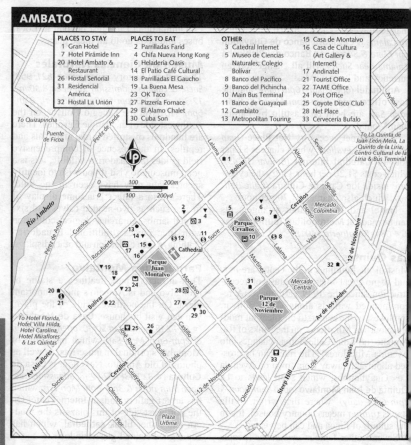

AMBATO

PLACES TO STAY	PLACES TO EAT	OTHER	15 Casa de Montalvo
1 Gran Hotel	2 Parrilladas Farid	3 Catedral Internet	16 Casa de Cultura
7 Hotel Pirámide Inn	4 Chifa Nueva Hong Kong	5 Museo de Ciencias	(Art Gallery &
20 Hotel Ambato &	6 Heladería Oasis	Naturales; Colegio	Internet)
Restaurant	14 El Patio Café Cultural	Bolívar	17 Andinatel
26 Hostal Señorial	18 Parrilladas El Gaucho	8 Banco del Pacífico	21 Tourist Office
31 Residencial	19 La Buena Mesa	9 Banco del Pichincha	22 TAME Office
América	23 OK Taco	10 Main Bus Terminal	24 Post Office
32 Hostal La Unión	27 Pizzería Fornace	11 Banco de Guayaquil	25 Coyote Disco Club
	29 El Alamo Chalet	12 Cambiato	28 Net Place
	30 Cuba Son	13 Metropolitan Touring	33 Cervecería Bufalo

selling local handicrafts – the best area is about 10 blocks from the center. As always, watch for pickpockets.

Special Events

Ambato is famous for its Fiesta de Frutas y Flores (Festival of Fruit and Flowers), which is an annual festival that's supposed to coincide with Carnaval but is usually held during the last two weeks in February. Apart from fruit and flower shows, the festivities include bullfights, parades, late-night street dancing and general fun.

Places to Stay

Residencial América (Vela 737; rooms per person $3) is probably the best of the super-budget hotels. Baths are shared and the beds are saggy, but the bedside lamps give this friendly place a hint of hominess.

Hostal La Union (☎ 822 375; cnr Espejo & 12 de Noviembre; rooms per person $3) is also OK. Baths are shared, the water's hot, the beds are saggy, but it's secure.

Hotel Pirámide Inn (☎ 842 092, fax 854 358; cnr Cevallos & Egüez; singles/doubles $10/18) has comfortable rooms with carpet, bath, telephone and cable TV. It's good value.

Gran Hotel (☎ 825 915; Lalama & Rocafuerte; singles/doubles $13/20) has carpeted rooms with private hot bath, telephone and TV. A restaurant and parking are available.

Hostal Señorial (☎ 825 124, 826 249; cnr Cevallos & Quito; singles/doubles $12/24) has spacious, clean, carpeted rooms with bath, telephone, cable TV and big windows.

Animal market, Saquisilí

Shepherding, Parque Nacional Cotopaxi

Volcán Cotopaxi, Parque Nacional Cotopaxi

Musicians and spectators, Chimborazo

Basilica de Nuestra Señora de Agua Santa,

Young girl, Saquisilí

Hotel Ambato (☎ 412 004/05/06; e hotel
_ambato@andinanet.net; Guayaquil 0108;
singles/doubles $37/49) is by far the best
hotel in the town center. There is a casino;
a good restaurant and bar (room service is
available); and cozy rooms with private
bath and hot water, telephone and cable TV.
A café and terrace allow you to enjoy a
snack outside.

Out on Avenida Miraflores, in the suburb
of the same name, are four quiet and pleasant hotels, all of which have been recommended. They all have restaurants (with
limited menus or set meals) and double
rooms with private baths and hot water. The
closest to town is **Hotel Florida** (☎ 843
040/74; Avenida Miraflores 1131; singles/
doubles $20/30); followed by the German-
run **Hotel Villa Hilda** (☎ 845 014, 840 700;
Avenida Miraflores; singles/doubles $24/42);
then the cheaper **Hotel Carolina** (☎ 821 539;
Avenida Miraflores; singles $18-20, doubles
$36-40); and, finally, the clean and modern
Hotel Miraflores (☎ 843 224, fax 844 395;
w www.hmiraflores.com.ec; Avenida Miraflores 227; singles/doubles $36/48).

Places to Eat
There are plenty of places to eat cheaply
around the Mercado Central.

Chifa Nueva Hong Kong (☎ 823 796;
Calle Bolívar 768; mains $2-3) serves good,
albeit standard, Chinese food.

El Patio Café Cultural is almost next to
Casa de Montalvo and – apart from serving
light meals and coffee – features cultural
events, including poetry readings, musical
evenings and art openings. Stop by and see
what's happening.

Heladería Oasis (Sucre) serves delicious
helados de paila (ice cream handmade in
large copper bowls).

Parrilladas El Gaucho (☎ 828 969; Calle
Bolívar near Quito; mains $6-8; open noon-
11pm Mon-Sat, noon-4pm Sun) does delicious Argentinean-style parrillada (grills),
serving fat juicy steaks or combo plates
brought sizzling on a grill to the table.

Parrilladas Farid (☎ 824 664; Calle Bolívar
16-74; mains $5-7; open 11am-11pm Mon-
Sat, 11am-9pm Sun) is similar to El Gaucho,
but slightly cheaper and a bit more down-home.

Pizzería Fornace (☎ 823 244; Cevallos 17-
28; mains $4-7; open noon-10pm Mon-Wed,
noon-11pm Thur-Sun) serves some of the

best food in town. Pizzas are baked in a
roaring wood oven and tables are dimly lit
with candles. Plenty of pasta dishes adorn
the menu as well.

El Alamo Chalet (☎ 824 704; Cevallos 17-
19; mains $3-6; open 8am-11pm daily), spot-
ted by the giant wooden flowers outside,
serves good diner-style comfort-food all day
long: sandwiches, pastas, meat and chicken
dishes, llapingachos (fried pancakes made
of mashed potatoes and cheese), milkshakes,
espresso drinks and more.

Hotel Ambato (Guayaquil 0108) has the
best hotel restaurant – some argue it's the
best restaurant in town.

La Buena Mesa (☎ 822 330; Quito 924;
mains $5-8; open 10am-4pm & 7pm-10pm
Mon-Sat), nearby, is Hotel Ambato's most
obvious competitor. This is a good French
restaurant recommended for its slightly
kitschy but pleasant, 1960s atmosphere.

Cuba Son (cnr Cevallos & Montalvo; mains
$2-4; open 1pm-2am daily) is a cool little bar
that serves Cuban snacks and light meals
such as ropa vieja (a classic Cuban stew of
shredded beef) and fried yucca.

OK Taco (☎ 827 958; cnr Calle Bolívar &
Quito; mains $2-4; open noon-10pm daily)
serves very un-Mexican Mexican food, but
it's still a nice change from the usual fare.

Entertainment
There is some nightlife in Ambato, but not
much. **Coyote Disco Club** (Calle Bolívar near
Quito) has dancing in the evenings. It's popular with young people and a bit more upscale than the funkier **Cervecería Bufalo**
(Olmedo & Mera), where there is beer and
dancing. Also check out **El Patio Café Cultural** (see Places to Eat earlier) for somewhat more intellectual pursuits. There is a
casino at Hotel Ambato. The pleasant bar at
Cuba Son (see Places to Eat earlier) is a
good place for a beer.

Getting There & Away
Air There is a small airstrip near Ambato
for emergency and military use only. **TAME**
(☎ 826 601, 820 322, 822 595; Calle Bolívar
20-17) only makes reservations for flights
from other cities.

Bus The main bus terminal (☎ 821 481) is
2km away from the town center and buses
to all destinations leave from there. Get

there by heading north on 12 de Noviembre to the traffic circle and then turn right on Avenida de las Américas.

destination	cost (US$)	duration (hrs)
Baños	1	1
Cuenca	7	7
Esmeraldas	6	8
Guaranda	1.60	2
Guayaquil	4.80	6
Ibarra	4	5
Lago Agrio	6	11
Loja	9	12
Machala	6	8
Manta	6	10
Otavalo	3.50	4½
Portoviejo	6	9½
Puyo	2	3
Quito	2	2½
Riobamba	1	1
Santo Domingo	3	4
Tena	4	6

For destinations north of Quito, you can easily take a bus to Quito and change at the terminal there.

Getting Around

The most important local bus service for travelers is the route between the bus terminal and the town center. From the terminal, climb the exit ramp to Avenida de las Américas, which crosses the train tracks on a bridge. On this bridge is a bus stop, where a westbound (to your right) bus, usually signed 'Centro,' will take you to Parque Cevallos for $0.14.

Buses marked 'Terminal' leave from the Martínez side of Parque Cevallos – if in doubt, ask. Buses to the suburb of Ficoa also leave from this park. A block away is Bolívar, which has buses to the suburb of Miraflores running along it. Buses to the Atocha suburb (more *quintas*) leave from 12 de Noviembre and Sevilla or Espejo. Buses for several surrounding villages also depart from the Parque Cevallos area.

AROUND AMBATO
☎ 03

Salasaca and Pelileo are the most frequently visited villages near Ambato because they lie on the good main road to Baños. Other villages are off the main road but are interesting to visit on day trips. With the exception of Patate, none of these villages off the road to Baños have accommodations and travelers are a rarity. In Ambato, ask at the bus terminal or at Parque Cevallos about buses to these places.

Quizapincha & Píllaro

Quizapincha, about 10km west of Ambato, is known for its leatherwork. It can be reached by buses crossing the Puente de Ficoa (*puente* means 'bridge'), at the northwest end of Montalvo.

Píllaro, some 20km to the northeast, is in a cereal- and fruit-growing area. July to August are big months for fiestas celebrated with bullfights, highland food and parades. On July 15 is the fiesta of Apostolo Santiago (St James), and July 25 is Cantonization Day. Quito's Independence Day, on August 10, is also vigorously celebrated with a bullfight and a bull run, in which the bulls charge through the streets; everybody participates.

Píllaro is the entry point for **Parque Nacional Llanganates**, a very remote and difficult-to-reach mountain range in which Atahualpa's treasure is supposedly buried. Many bona-fide expeditions have searched for the treasure using ancient maps and documents from the time of the conquest, but nobody has found it yet!

Salasaca

As you head southeast from Ambato on the Baños road, the first place of interest is Salasaca, about 14km away. The village and its environs are inhabited by some 2000 indigenous Salasaca, who are famous for their tapestries. They are less well known for their history, which is particularly interesting. Originally, the Salasaca came from Bolivia, but they were conquered by the Incas in the 15th century.

One of the ways in which the Incas controlled the peoples they had conquered was to move them en masse to an area that the Incas had long dominated, and where there was less chance of an uprising. Apparently this is what happened to the Salasacas, who were moved from Bolivia. After the Spanish conquest they remained where they were, but retained an unusually high degree of independence and were almost unknown by outsiders until the middle of the 20th century.

The villagers are recognizable by their typical dress – especially the men, who will normally wear broad-brimmed white hats, black ponchos and white shirts and trousers. Traditionally a farming community, the Salasacas raise their own sheep to obtain wool for their weavings, which are a secondary source of income. Their tapestries are all handmade and are different from the work done by other Indian groups (although it's difficult to see the difference unless you have spent time examining Ecuadorian weaving).

There is a **craft market** held every Sunday morning near the church on the Ambato–Baños road. Also along this road are several craft stores that are open daily. One of these is a women artisans' cooperative. Nearby is **Alonso Pilla's house** (☎ 09-984 0125; open 7am-6pm daily). As you arrive from Baños, it's on the left, about 100m past the Evangelical church in the center of the village. Pilla's house is open and he gives weaving demonstrations on a backstrap loom using traditional techniques – his work has been highly recommended. Salasacan tapestries are also sold in craft stores in Quito and Cuenca.

The many Indian fiestas in the Salasaca area are worth looking out for. May and June are good months for fiestas all over the highlands. On the Sunday after Easter, there is a street dance between Salasaca and the town of Pelileo. On June 15, the Salasacas dress up in animal costumes for Santo Vintio. Corpus Christi (which takes place on a movable date in June) is celebrated in Salasaca and Pelileo. The feast of St Anthony is celebrated at the end of November. All the usual annual holidays (Christmas, Easter etc) also offer interesting fiesta possibilities.

Pelileo

Some 6km beyond Salasaca on the Baños road is the larger village of Pelileo. Despite its 400-year history, the Pelileo of today is a very modern village. It was founded by the colonialist Antonio Clavijo in 1570 but was destroyed by earthquakes in 1698, 1797, 1840 and 1949. The present site is about 2km away from the ruins of the old town. It was among the places evacuated in 1999 following Tungurahua's eruptions, and although residents have returned now, it is still likely that ashfall could affect the town in the event of a major eruption. Pelileo is the market town for nearby villages, including Salasaca (Saturday is market day). Pelileo

could be dubbed the 'Blue Jeans Capital of Ecuador' – there is an amazing variety of brands and sizes of jeans for sale, especially on market day.

Pelileo celebrates its cantonization on July 22 with the usual highland festivities: bullfights, parades and plenty of food and drink.

Baños is only 24km away, but the road drops some 850m from Pelileo. The descent along the Río Pastaza gorge is spectacular, and some of the best views of the erupting Tungurahua are to be seen on this drive. At 5016m (pre-eruption height), Tungurahua is Ecuador's 10th-highest peak and gives its name to the province.

Patate & Around

Patate, 25km from Ambato and 5km northeast of Pelileo, is a pretty village known for its picturesque locale on Río Patate, for its grapes and for its *aguardiente* (sugarcane alcohol), which is allegedly some of the best in the highlands. There are buses from Pelileo to Patate. Although it may suffer from light ashfall in the event of a major eruption, Patate is considered safer than Pelileo and Baños.

Hotel Turístico Patate (☎ 870 214; doubles $12) offers 15 double rooms with private bath and hot water. There is a restaurant, bar and recreation area, and the management can arrange tours to the Llanganates and local ruins.

Viña del Mar Hotel (☎/fax 870 139) is cheaper than Hotel Turístico Patate and is the current favorite for volcano watchers hoping to see a Tungurahua eruption.

Hacienda Manteles (☎/fax 859 474, 870 123, Quito ☎ 02-250 4902, 255 0791; W www .haciendamantelesecuador.com; singles/doubles/triples/quads $57/69/81/93) is at 2900m in the mountains northeast of Patate, about 15km away by road. This family farm was converted into a delightful country inn in 1992. From the hacienda, there are pretty views of the Río Patate valley below and Volcán Tungurahua and other mountains in the distance. Above the inn is an area of cloud forest that can be explored on foot or by horse ($5 per hour). Bird-watching, hiking and fishing are other possible activities.

There are seven good-sized rooms, and fresh homemade meals are served buffet style and are all-you-can-eat. Breakfast is $6, and lunch or dinner is $13. The restaurant/bar has a fireplace and is attractively decorated with Salasacan weavings. Guests with reservations can arrange to be picked up from the bus station in Patate at no extra charge.

BAÑOS
☎ 03 • elevation 1800m

The idyllically set town of Baños has long been popular with Ecuadorians and foreigners alike. Although Baños suffered a major setback in 1999 due to the erupting Tungurahua (see the boxed text 'Tungurahua Comes Back to Life'), volcanic activity had decreased significantly by early 2003, and the town was well on its way back to being one of the most important tourist spots in the country. It is, however, an unpredictable area and you must keep yourself appraised of potential dangers.

Baños means 'baths,' which is precisely what the town is famous for. Some of them are fed by thermal springs from the base of the active Volcán Tungurahua, which means 'little hell' in Quechua. Other baths have meltwater running into them from Tungurahua's icy flanks. Locals swear that the baths are great for your health. While that is a debatable point, it is true that the casual atmosphere of this pretty resort town has made it a place to unwind after some hard traveling. Baños' elevation gives it an agreeable climate, and the surroundings are green and attractive.

For a while there, the attraction of watching the erupting Tungurahua practically dwarfed the baths. Although not as dramatic as it was, the volcano still puffs smoke and ash. Ironically, the crater cannot be seen from the town itself, but all the tour companies will take you to good vantage spots, or you can walk to ones nearby.

Baños is also the gateway town into the jungle via Puyo and Misahuallí. East of Baños, the road drops spectacularly, and there are exceptional views of the upper Amazon Basin stretching before you. In the town itself, there are more attractions: an interesting basilica, a small museum, a little nightlife and restaurants with local cuisine.

Information

The **municipal tourist office** (☎ 740 483; **e** mun_banos@andinanet.net; Espejo & Reyes; open 8am-5pm Mon-Fri) can be found at the bus terminal; a guidebook to Baños is sold here and maps are provided, but information beyond that is slim.

You can change traveler's checks at **Banco del Pacífico** (cnr Halflants & Rocafuerte; open 8:30am-4pm Mon-Fri) and **Banco del Pichincha** (cnr Ambato & Halflants; open 8am-1pm & 2:30pm-5pm Mon-Fri). Both have ATMs.

The **post office** (☎ 740 901; open 8am-noon & 2pm-6pm daily) and **Andinatel** (☎ 740 411; open 8am-10pm daily) are both on Parque Central.

Baños has lots of cybercafés, but they appear and disappear frequently. Try **Linknet** (☎ 16 de Diciembre; open 8am-10pm Mon-Sat, 9am-10pm Sun) or **Direct Connect** (Martínez near Alfaro; open 9am-10pm daily); both charge $2 per hour.

The small, local **hospital** (☎ 740 443/301) is on Montalvo near Pastaza. You will find several pharmacies along Ambato.

The **police station** (☎ 740 251, 101) is on Oriente near Mera. Visitors should ask at their hotels about emergency-evacuation procedures in the event of an eruption. Familiarize yourself with the street layout and where to go if an emergency evacuation is announced.

Baths

There are three baths – two are in Baños (only one is hot), and the third is out of town. All have changing rooms and clothing storage. Towels and bathing suits may be available for rent, and soap is for sale. Everyone is supposed to shower and put on a bathing suit before entering the pools. The pools look murky because of the mineral content of the water, which is touted for its restorative and healthful properties. Chlorates, sulfates and magnesium are among the principal chemicals found in the baths.

The best-known bath in Baños is **La Piscina de La Virgen** (Montalvo; admission $2; open 4:30am-5pm & 6pm-10pm daily), which has hot showers and three concrete pools of different temperatures reaching over 50°C. You can't miss them – they're right under the waterfall.

Piscinas Santa Clara (admission $2; open 8am-5pm Fri-Sun) has two cooler pools (about 22°C). Several of the better hotels have swimming pools or saunas.

If you walk up the hill and past the cemetery on Martínez, you'll end up on a track that crosses a stream (Quebrada de Nagu-asco) on a small wooden footbridge. The trail continues on the other side to a road in front of Cabañas Bascun, where you turn left to reach the **Piscina El Salado**, which also opens at 4:30am. (There are buses, too, that take a different, longer route.) Piscina El Salado has hot and cold showers, several concrete pools of varying temperatures (up to 50°C) and an ice-cold waterfall to stand under if you're the masochistic sort. Because it is 2km or 3km out of town, this place is not quite so crowded.

Basilica de Nuestra Señora de Agua Santa

Within the town itself, the Basilica de Nuestra Señora de Agua Santa is worth seeing. The church is dedicated to the Virgin of the Holy Water, who is credited with several miracles in the Baños area. Inside the church, paintings depict her miracles and have explanations in Spanish along the lines of 'On January 30, 1904, Señor X fell off his horse as he was crossing the Río Pastaza bridge. As he fell 70m to the torrents below, he yelled 'Holy Mother of the Holy Water' and

---

Tungurahua Comes Back to Life

Baños, an idyllically placed small town of about 18,000 inhabitants living in a lush green valley on the slopes of Volcán Tungurahua, has for decades been synonymous with relaxation and tourism. Several dozen small hotels catered to Ecuadorian and foreign tourists alike, offering them vacations ranging from relaxing dips in hot springs after a night of dancing to strenuous climbs to peer into the gently active crater of the snowcapped volcano – which at 5016m is the 10th-highest peak in the country.

Although the volcano erupted in 1918, it was afterward considered semidormant and unthreatening. This suddenly changed in 1998, when increased seismic activity was detected. The volcano was placed on yellow alert – using a scale running from white to yellow to orange to red – meaning that the volcano was being monitored and showing signs of activity, but that dangers of a major eruption were not imminent. This was changed to an orange alert after an Australian climber and his Ecuadorian guide were burned by a gaseous eruption on October 5, 1999. (An orange alert means that there is a 90% chance of a major eruption over the coming weeks or months, and that minor eruptions could occur at any time.)

Over the next two weeks, Tungurahua pumped clouds of steam and ash into aerial columns many kilometers in height, and ashfall was a regular occurrence in the surrounding area. At night, streams of glowing lava could be seen cascading down the sides of the volcano. By October 17, the authorities ordered the evacuation of over 20,000 inhabitants of Baños and nearby villages, saying that a major eruption could pose a deadly threat to the population. The roads between Ambato and Puyo and between Riobamba and Puyo were also closed. With the volcano erupting almost daily, tour operators in Quito and Ambato began offering trips to see the volcanic wonders from a safe distance.

Weeks turned into months, and by January 2000, there still had not been an eruption large enough to cause substantial damage to Baños. The inhabitants, desperate to return to their homes and their livelihoods, defied government orders and clashed with troops at a military checkpoint, resulting in several injuries and the death of one woman. Soon afterward, an agreement was reached, and about 3000 people were allowed back into Baños, and the road between Ambato and Puyo was reopened.

Slowly, curious day-trippers and tourists began to trickle into Baños, and week after week, more residents began to return and reopen their tourism businesses. By July 2000, an estimated 60% to 70% of businesses were operating in Baños. The town was kept on orange alert until September 5, 2002, when it was demoted to yellow alert.

At the time of research, the volcano was still active, burping ash and steam, but the threat of an eruption was no longer considered imminent, and tourism and daily life were pretty much back to normal. The road between Baños and Riobamba, however, was still closed.

To keep the public apprised of the situation *El Comercio* (**W** www.elçomercio.com) posts updates, in Spanish, on its website and in its newspaper. Spanish-speakers can also visit the website of the **Instituto Geofísico** (**W** www.igepn.edu.ec/). The **University of North Dakota's** site *(Volcano World;* **W** http://volcano.und.nodak.edu)* has an updated Tungurahua information page in English.

BAÑOS

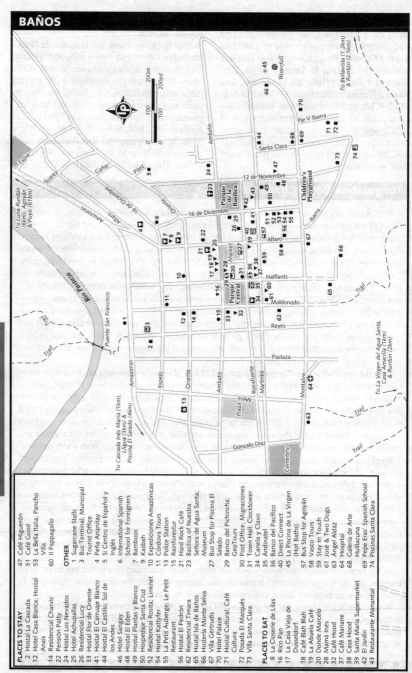

PLACES TO STAY
2   Hostal La Cascada
12 Hotel Casa Blanca; Hostal
    Anaïs
14 Residencial Charvic
22 Pensión Patty
24 Hostal Los Nevados
25 Hotel Achupallas
33 Hostal Flor de Oriente
41 Hostal El Carruaje Blanco
44 Hostal El Castillo; Sol de
    los Andes
46 Hotel Sangay
48 Hostal El Edén
49 Hostal Plantas y Blanco
50 Hospedaje Santa Cruz
52 Residencial Rosita; Linknet
54 Hostal Kattyfer
55 La Petit Auberge; Le Petit
    Restaurant
56 Hostal El Pedrón
62 Residencial Timara
65 Hostal Isla de Baños
66 Hostería Monte Selva
67 Villa Gertrudis
70 Hotel Palace
71 Hostal Cultural; Café
    Cultura
72 Posada El Marqués
73 Villa Santa Clara

PLACES TO EAT
8   La Closerie de Lilas
16 Rico Pan
17 Casa Vieja de
    Dusseldorf
18 Café Blah Blah
19 La Abuela Café
20 Donde Marcelo
28 Mama Inés
32 Café Hood
37 Café Mariane
38 Casa Hood
39 Santa María Supermarket
    El Jardín
43 Restaurante Manantial

47 Café Higuerón
51 Café Good
53 La Bella Italia; Pancho
    Villa
60 Il Pappagallo

OTHER
1   Sugarcane Stalls
3   Bus Terminal; Municipal
    Tourist Office
4   Peña Ananitay
5   Si Centro de Español y
    Inglés
6   International Spanish
    School for Foreigners
7   Bamboos
9   Kasbah
10 Expediciones Amazónicas
11 Córdova Tours
13 Police Station
15 Rainforestur
21 Hard Rock Café
23 Basilica of Nuestra
    Señora de Agua Santa;
    Museum
27 Bus Stop for Piscina El
    Salado
29 Banco del Pichincha;
    GeoTours
30 Post Office; Migraciones
34 Town Hall; Clocktower
35 Canela y Clavo
35 Andinatel
36 Banco del Pacífico
40 Direct Connect
45 La Piscina de La Virgen
    (Hot Baths)
57 Bus Stop for Agoyán
58 Vasco Tours
59 Stay In Touch
61 José & Two Dogs
63 Ángel Aldaz
64 Hospital
68 Galería de Arte
    Huillacuna
69 Pepe Eras' Spanish School
74 Piscinas Santa Clara

was miraculously saved!' Other paintings show people being miraculously saved from exploding volcanoes, burning hotels, transit accidents and other misfortunes. Reading the explanations is amusing and a great way to practice your Spanish.

Just above the church is a **museum** with an eclectic display of taxidermic animals, religious paintings, church vestments and local handicrafts.

Other Sights

You can browse, and buy if you want, the exhibits at the **Galería de Arte Huillacuna** (☎ 740 187; cnr Santa Clara & Montalvo; open 8:30am-7pm daily).

There is a big **waterfall** (admission $0.75; open from 4:30am) at the southeastern end of town. You can see the falls from most parts of Baños.

Massages

For excellent full-body massages and herbal facials, make an appointment or drop by **Stay In Touch** (☎ 09-920 8000, 09-920 8360; Martínez), which is the massage practice of a friendly and skilled US/Ecuadorian couple. Massages are $20 and facials are $12.

Hiking

Once you've visited all the pools, there are many walks to take. Plenty of information about walks is available in Baños. The following are some suggestions.

The walk down to Río Pastaza is easy and popular. Just behind the **sugarcane stalls** by the bus station is a short trail that leads to the **Puente San Francisco**, the bridge which crosses the river. You can continue on trails up the other side as far as you want.

Going south on Maldonado takes you to a footpath that climbs to **Bellavista**, where there is a building with a white cross high over Baños (visible from the town). The path then continues on to the tiny settlement of **Runtún**, some two hours away. The views are outstanding.

West of town, turn right by a religious shrine and walk down to Puente San Martín and visit the impressive falls of **Cascada Inés María**, a few hundred meters to the right of the bridge. You can also cross the bridge and continue to the village of **Lligua**, about three hours away. From this road, trails climb up the hills to your right.

Jungle Trips

Loads of jungle trips from Baños are advertized, but not all guides are experienced. Guides should have licenses. For more information on jungle tours, see the boxed text 'Preparing For a Jungle Trip' in The Oriente chapter.

Three- to seven-day jungle tours cost about $30 to $45 per person per day, depending on the destination (there is usually a three- or four-person minimum). Some focus more on Indian culture and plants; others focus more on wildlife. Don't expect to see many animals in the rainforest – it takes patience and luck. June to September is the busy season, and reservations are a good idea if you want to go on a specific date during that season – but if you just show up and don't mind waiting around, you can usually hook up with a tour. Baños is always full of travelers and is a good town in which to organize a group if you are not already with one.

Rainforestur (☎/fax 740 743; e rainfor@ interactive.net.ec; w www.rainforestur.com; Ambato 800) has received several recommendations for its tours to Reserva Producción Faunística Cuyabeno (see The Oriente chapter for details on this reserve). Other areas of both primary and secondary jungle can also be visited on different tours. Tours last three days to a week. Some of the agency's guides speak English, German or French, as well as Spanish. Rainforestur also has a Quito office (see Travel Agencies & Tour Operators in the Quito chapter).

Vasco Tours (☎ 740 017; Alfaro near Martínez) is run by the Vasco brothers, and their guide Juan Medina is recommended.

Climbing & Trekking

Climbers are advised not to ascend the currently erupting Volcán Tungurahua (5016m). The refuge on that volcano has been destroyed, and, although some people still climb up to it, it is not recommended. Check with local climbing operators for current conditions as they change regularly. Many local agencies arrange tours to good spots for watching the eruptions.

Climbs of Cotopaxi and Chimborazo can also be arranged. A reputable climbing outfitter is **Expediciones Amazónicas** (☎ 740 506; e amazonicas2002@yahoo.com; Oriente 11-68 near Halflants). It has rental equipment and can arrange licensed guides. **Willie Navarette** is also recommended; contact him at Café Higuerón (see Places to Eat later). **Rainforestur** has rental equipment and licensed climbing guides and can tailor your itinerary to include acclimatization (see Jungle Trips earlier). The going rate for climbs with a minimum of two people is $60 to $80 per person per day, plus park fees.

The jagged and extinct Volcán El Altar (5319m) is hard to climb, but the wild páramo surrounding it is a good area for backpacking and camping. The active but remote Volcán Sangay (5230m) can also be explored on week-long trekking expeditions.

For detailed information about these volcanoes see under Parque Nacional Sangay, later in this chapter.

Mountain Biking

Several companies rent mountain bikes starting at about $5 per day. Check the equipment carefully as maintenance is sometimes poor. The most popular ride is the dramatic descent to Puyo (see From Baños to Puyo later in this chapter), which is about 60km east, on the edge of the Oriente. You pass the spectacular Pailón del Diablo waterfall on the way. Parts of the road are unpaved, and there is a passport control at Shell, so carry your documents. From Puyo (or earlier), you can simply take a bus back to Baños, putting your bike on the roof. Various other mountain-biking options are available, and the outfitters will be happy to tell you about them.

Horse Riding

You can rent horses for about $10 per half day through **Ángel Aldáz** (☎ 740 175; Montalvo & Mera); the price is higher if you also want a guide. Christián, at **Hostal Isla de Baños** (see Places to Stay later), arranges guided horse-riding trips that last a half day, a full day, or from two to nine days. Christián speaks English and German. **José & Two Dogs** (☎ 740 746; e josebalu_99@yahoo.com; Maldonado & Martínez) is reportedly also quite good.

Horses can be rented by the hour, but by the time you saddle up and get out of town, it's hardly worth going for such a short period. Many half- or full-day trips start with a long jeep ride out of town, and the actual riding time is short – inquire carefully to get what you want.

River-Rafting

The best professional white-water guides should be certified by AGAR. **GeoTours** (☎ 741 344; w www.ecuadorexplorer.com/geotours; Ambato at Halflants) is run by an Ecuadorian/Swiss couple. Half-day trips to Río Patate are offered for $30 and leave on demand. Trips last four hours (two hours is spent on the river) and a snack is included. Also available is a full-day trip to Río Pastaza for $100, leaving at 8:30am. This trip is 10 hours, with four hours on the river, and lunch is included. Transportation, a guide, raft, paddles, life jackets, wet suits and helmets are all provided. Experience is not necessary, although you should know how to swim.

Rainforestur (see Jungle Trips earlier) also offers excellent rafting trips.

Language Courses

One-on-one or small-group Spanish classes are offered at **International Spanish School for Foreigners** (☎ 740 612; 16 de Diciembre & Espejo); at **Si Centro de Español y Inglés** (☎/fax 740 360), at the end of Páez; and also at **Pepe Eras' Spanish School** (☎ 740 232; Montalvo 5-26).

Organized Tours

For a tour of the town, contact **Córdova Tours** (☎ 740 923, 09-965 4365; e cordova tours@hotmail.com) by the bus terminal. The company arranges 'party tours' in *chivas* (open-sided buses) at night and regular tours during the day. Tours average $5 per person. Car and jeep rentals are available through this company.

Special Events

Baños became the seat of its canton on December 16, 1944, and an annual fiesta is celebrated on this and the preceding days. There are the usual processions, fireworks, music and a great deal of street dancing and drinking at night. Fun! Also, there are processions and fireworks during the entire month of October as the various *barrios* (neighborhoods) of Baños take turns to pay homage to the local icon, Nuestra Señora de Agua Santa.

Places to Stay

There are scores of hotels in Baños, and competition is stiff, so prices are low. That said, rates are highest Friday evenings, and holiday weekends when every hotel in town can fill up. You can often negotiate lower rates if you stay more than two nights.

Hotels in Baños can be noisy – it is a vacation town, after all. For some quieter accommodations, see Around Baños later under Places to Stay.

Budget One of the cheapest places to stay is **Pensión Patty** (☎ 740 202; Alfaro 556; rooms per person $2). It's a well-known, family-run place which has friendly management and information on trekking, climbing and horse riding in the area. Most of the rooms are pretty dark and funky, but the price is right. There is one hot and several cold communal showers, as well as a guest kitchen.

Residencial Timara (☎ 740 599; Maldonado; rooms per person $3) is friendly and has hot water and kitchen facilities.

Villa Santa Clara (☎ 740 349; 12 de Noviembre; rooms per person $6) is a great deal for motel-style rooms opening on to a sparse patio area. You get private hot shower and kitchen privileges, and there's a restaurant to boot. Rooms in the old house are slightly cheaper than those in the newer sector.

Residencial Lucy (☎ 740 466; Rocafuerte 2-40; rooms per person with shared/private bath $3/4) is a friendly, motel-like place with three floors of simple rooms whose doors all open to the outside. Some rooms have hot water.

Hostal La Cascada (☎ 740 946; rooms per person $3) and **Hostal Anais** (☎ 741 068; rooms per person $4) are right next to the bus terminal – good for early departures.

Hostal Los Nevados (☎ 740 673; rooms per person $4), a block east of Parque de la Basílica, is excellent value. Spacious rooms come with private hot showers.

Hotel Casa Blanca (☎/fax 740 092; e hcasablanca@latinmail.com; Maldonado & Oriente; rooms per person $5) is clean and modern and has rooms with private hot showers and cable TV. Some rooms are a bit cramped.

Hostal Plantas y Blanco (☎/fax 740 044; e option3@hotmail.com; Martínez at 12 de Noviembre; rooms per person with shared/private bath $6/7) is very popular and is attractively decorated with plants and has a pleasant rooftop terrace (for breakfast) and a steam bath. There are laundry and Internet facilities, and the place is often full. The single rooms, however, are very cramped.

Hospedaje Santa Cruz (☎ 740 648; e santa_cruz@bacan.com; 16 de Diciembre; rooms per person $4), around the corner from Hostal Plantas y Blanco, is excellent value for spacious rooms with bath and hot water.

Residencial Rosita (☎ 740 396; 16 de Diciembre near Martínez; rooms per person $3, apartment per person $4) offers plain, clean rooms with shared bath. There's also a large apartment that sleeps six to eight people and has a kitchen.

Hostal Kattyfer (☎ 740 856; 16 de Diciembre near Martínez; rooms per person with shared/private bath $3/4) has large, simple rooms and a guest kitchen.

Hotel Achupallas (☎ 740 389; 16 de Diciembre; rooms per person with bath $4), on Parque de la Basílica, is a good deal if you get a window over the plaza (and don't mind a bit of street noise).

Hostal El Castillo (☎ 740 285; Martínez 255; rooms per person $5) offers clean, run-of-the-mill rooms with private bath and TV. The attached restaurant offers good cheap meals at discounts to guests.

Hostal El Pedrón (☎ 740 701, 824 390; Eloy Alfaro; rooms per person with shared/private bath $3/5, with TV $8) offers clean, straightforward rooms in an old building. The highlight is the large tree-filled garden with hammocks and chairs – there's no other hotel garden this size in town.

Hostal El Carruaje Blanco (☎ 740 913; e hostalelcarruajeblanco@yahoo.com.mx; Martínez; rooms per person $6) is a small, family-run place with comfortable rooms and kitchen privileges. Rooms have private bath and hot water.

Residencial Charvic (☎ 740 298/113; Maldonado & Oriente; singles/doubles with shared bath $3/6, with private bath $8/10) is a large, modern, nondescript place, with decent deals for the cheaper rooms. Rooms all have TV.

Mid-Range At the end of a quiet street, the comfortable and friendly **Posada El Marqués** (☎ 740 053; Pje V Ibarra; e posada_marques@yahoo.com; rooms per person $8.50) offers spacious, colorfully painted rooms.

Hostal El Eden (☎ 740 616; 12 de Noviembre; rooms per person $8) has clean, pleasant, motel-like rooms with private baths and TV. There's a good restaurant attached.

Hostal Flor de Oriente (☎ 740 418, 740 717; e flordeoriente@yahoo.es; cnr Ambato &

Maldonado; rooms per person $8) has spotless rooms with private bath, hot water, telephone and cable TV. There is a decent restaurant downstairs, and parking is available.

La Petit Auberge (☎ 740 936; e lepetit banos@yahoo.com; 16 de Diciembre; rooms per person $12-16) is a lovely rustic place with cozy rooms with private hot showers. The pricier rooms have a fireplace, as does the open-air common area.

Hostal Isla de Baños (☎/fax 740 609; e isla banos@andinanet.net; Halflants 1-31; rooms per person $7-10) is a German-run hostal set in attractive gardens with cheerful, clean rooms with private bath and hot water. The pricier rooms have balconies. The owner offers horse and jeep tours, and there's lots of good travel information around.

Hostal Cultural (☎/fax 740 083; e hostal cultural@yahoo.com; Pje V Ibarra; rooms per person $10-15) is small but pretty and has seven comfortable rooms with private bath; the mid-range rooms have views, as do the priciest rooms, which also have fireplaces. A terrace gives views of the waterfall, and a restaurant serves delicious, wholesome, traveler-friendly meals.

Hostería Monte Selva (☎ 740 566, 740 244; e hmonteselva@andinanet.net; singles/doubles $31/34) has attractive wooden cabins set on a lush hillside just above Baños. The plant-filled gardens have a pool and a sauna. Rooms include a continental breakfast, and there is a bar and restaurant.

Hotel Palace (☎ 740 470; e hotelpalace@hotmail.com; Montalvo 20-03; singles/doubles $24/32), by the waterfall, is clean and pleasant and has a good attached restaurant. There is a garden, a small swimming pool, a sauna, a spa, a Turkish bath and a games room (darts and table tennis). Rooms have private bath, TV and telephone.

Hotel Sangay (☎ 740 490/917; e sangay spa@hotmail.com; Montalvo near Martínez; standard singles/doubles $18/27, cabins $27/37; executive rooms $39/51) is just opposite the Piscina de La Virgen baths. There are squash and tennis courts, a swimming pool, a Jacuzzi and sauna, and a restaurant and bar. All rooms have private bath, hot water, telephone and cable TV. The hotel is popular with Ecuadorian tour groups, but it is gloomy when there aren't groups to fill up the 72 rooms. All rates include continental breakfast and use of the facilities.

Villa Gertrudis (☎ 740 441; Montalvo 20-75; singles/doubles $16/29) is low-key and much quieter than Hotel Sangay. It is also set in pretty gardens and has a big indoor pool across the street. The rate includes two meals. Nonguests can use the swimming pool for $1.50.

Around Baños About 2km from town by footpath or 4km by road is the Piscina El Salado, with four nearby hotels that are quieter than most of the places in Baños. There are two basic residenciales right by the baths that have good views of Tungurahua – **El Salado** and **Puerto del Salado**. Rates are about $3.50 per person.

Cabañas Bascún (☎/fax 740 334; singles/doubles $37/49) is about 10 minutes away from the baths. It has a hot and a cold pool, a water slide, a sauna, a tennis court and a restaurant. The pool facilities are open only on weekends and holidays, but the hotel rooms and restaurant are open all week. The place is popular as a family weekend getaway. Nonguests can use the pool and sauna for about $4.

Casa Nahuazo (☎ 740 315; singles/doubles about $12/24) is a B&B between the Bascún and the Piscina El Salado. It is very quiet, and the five clean and pleasant double rooms have private bath, hot water, fresh fruit and flowers. Rates include continental breakfast.

Luna Runtún (☎ 740 882/83, 740 835; w www.lunaruntun.com; standard singles/doubles $100/150, superior doubles $195, presidential suite $240) is high above Baños, is Swiss-managed, and is the town's most exclusive hotel. By road, it's 6km beyond Baños; follow the signs east of town on the road to Puyo. Luna Runtún can be reached on foot by climbing up from Baños for about 3km along either of the main trails. Most guests do not carry their suitcases up a steep trail but prefer to drive in. The trails are better for a downhill hike back into Baños. Horse riding and guided hiking can be arranged. The views are gorgeous, especially when Volcán Tungurahua is exploding. The 32 rooms and one suite are spacious and comfortable, all with large bathrooms and views. Rates include an American breakfast and a complete à la carte dinner. The superior rooms have a private terrace overlooking Baños.

Places to Eat

Ambato, Baños' busy pedestrian street, is lined with restaurants. Some are expensive, some are cheap and none are exceptional. Their best features are the outdoor tables that make for good people-watching. The best restaurants are on side streets.

La Abuela Café (☎ 09-983 8681; Ambato; mains $2-4; open 7:30am-10:30pm daily) is a friendly little place good for sandwiches, dessert or a light meal. Next door, **Café Blah Blah** (☎ 740 263; Ambato; mains $1-3; open 8am-8pm daily) is a tiny place serving good breakfasts and freshly brewed coffee.

Mamá Inés (☎ 740 538; Ambato; mains $2-5; open 9:30am-10pm daily), also on the pedestrian section of Ambato, has a few Mexican dishes and other international food items.

La Casa Vieja de Dusseldorf (☎ 740 430; Ambato; mains $3-6), opposite Mamá Inés, is also quite good and reasonably priced, although the menu is more local than German.

Rico Pan (☎ 740 387; open 7am-8pm Mon-Sat, 7am-noon Sun), on the next block of Ambato, is good for breakfast (including granola and yogurt), juices and snacks. It sells some of the best bread in town – wholegrain, of course.

Donde Marcelo (☎ 740 427; Ambato; mains $4-7) has Ecuadorian food and a very popular bar upstairs. The service is friendly and efficient, and the food is quite good, but slightly pricey.

El Jardín (Parque de la Basílica; mains $3-6) is a popular hang-out and has a variety of meat and fish dishes and sandwiches that can be enjoyed on the leafy outdoor patio.

Café Cultural (Pje V Ibarra; mains $2-4; open 7:15am-10pm daily) is in Hostal Cultural and serves homemade breads, vegie burgers, Swedish meatballs, fruit pies, fresh fish, pastries, fruit juices and various other delectable items.

The following three places have such similar names it's easy to get them confused.

Café Good (☎ 740 592; 16 de Diciembre; mains $2-4; open 8am-10pm daily) serves vegetarian food, curries, pastas and chicken dishes. It has a small book exchange and a nightly 8pm movie. The $1.20 almuerzos are a good deal.

Casa Hood (☎ 740 425; Martínez; mains $2-4.50; open 8am-10:30pm Wed-Mon) also has nightly 8pm movies. The book exchange

here is probably the best in town. The food (much of it vegetarian) is equally good, in a wholesome, comforting sort of way.

Café Hood (☎ 740 573; Maldonado; mains $3-6; open 8am-midnight) is on the Parque Central. It also has a good book exchange. Some of the dishes, such as the chickpeas and spinach in curry sauce with yogurt and cucumbers, are simply excellent. There are several Mexican and Thai dishes as well.

Café Higuerón (☎ 740 910; 12 de Noviembre 2-70; open 8am-10pm Thur-Tues) has a good variety of meat and vegetarian plates, teas and yummy desserts.

Restaurante Manantial (☎ 740 306; Martínez; mains $2-6; open noon-midnight daily) has an absurdly diverse menu with plates from over a dozen different countries. Italy is well represented with good pizza and lasagne.

La Closerie de Lilas (☎ 741 430; Alfaro 6-20; mains $3-5; open 9am-10pm daily) is a great little family-run place (kids included) serving steaks, delicious trout dishes and pastas. Some dishes have a French flair. The $5 set-menu trout lunch is a good deal.

Le Petit Restaurant (16 de Diciembre; open 8am-10am, noon-3pm & 6pm-10pm daily; mains $2-8) at La Petit Auberge (see Places to Stay earlier), serves modest portions of delicious French food (by non-French standards anyway). There's lots of hors d'oeuvres, crepes, soups and fondues. It's a relaxing place to hang out.

Café Mariane (Halflants & Rocafuerte; mains $3-6; 6pm-10pm daily) serves excellent French-Mediterranean cuisine at reasonable prices. Try the fondue Provençal ($6).

Il Pappagallo (☎ 740 750; Martínez; mains $4-5; open noon-10pm daily) is a welcoming little Italian place with good food and a smart but casual dining room.

La Bella Italia (☎ 741 559; 16 de Diciembre; mains $3-6) is small but friendly and is especially tasty.

Pancho Villa (16 de Diciembre; mains $2-3; open 12:30pm-9:30pm daily) serves good, cheap Mexican standbys, such as tacos, burritos, nachos and fajitas. The atmosphere is festive and the prices are good.

Sol de Los Andes (☎ 740 514; mains $2-3), adjoining Hostal El Castillo, serves economical Ecuadorian food and will prepare cuy (roast guinea pig) with advance notice. Good, hearty almuerzos cost about $2.50.

On certain days (particularly during fiestas), you can buy cuy at some of the market restaurants or along Ambato. They are normally roasted whole, and some people find the sight of their little roasted feet sticking up and their tiny teeth poking out a bit disconcerting. Surprisingly, they taste quite good – a little like a cross between chicken and rabbit.

Another local food popular in Baños is *melcocha*, a delicious chewy toffee. You can see people swinging it onto wooden pegs in the doorways of many of the town's shops in order to blend and soften the toffee. *Caña de azucar* (sugarcane) is sold everywhere, but especially at the stands across from the bus terminal. Pieces of whole cane are sliced and chewed.

To stock up on picnic supplies and the like, visit the large, modern **Santa María Supermarket** (☎ 741 641; cnr Alfaro & Rocafuerte; open 8:30am-8:30pm daily).

Entertainment

Nightlife in Baños means dancing in local *peñas* (small venues featuring live folk music), hanging out in bars or simply winding down the night in a restaurant with friends after a day's mountain biking and soaking in the pools.

Barhopping is easy on Alfaro on the two blocks north of Ambato, where several bars draw international and Ecuadorian tourists. The knock-off **Hard Rock Café** and **Donde Marcelo** (see Places to Eat earlier) are both Baños standbys with rock, reggae and a bit of dancing. **Kasbah**, just up the street, is a cool new place dropping some stiff competition on its neighbors. There are several other bars on Alfaro worth checking out, too.

Bamboos (cnr Alfaro & Espejo) was once the hottest salsa club in town, but after relocating to its present location it's a little more subdued – but still worthy of a night out. **Canela y Clavo** (☎ 741 566; cnr Rocafuerte & Maldonado; open 6pm-2am nightly) is a great new *peña* with dim lighting and a low stage. The *folklórica* (Andean folk music) kicks in every night around 9pm.

Peña Ananitay (16 de Diciembre) has live *folklórica* late on weekend nights. It gets very crowded, but it's one of the best places in town to hear Andean music.

All of these are suitable for solo women travelers (less suitable are the many small pool halls, especially on the back streets, which are frequented mainly by men).

Getting There & Away

Buses from Ambato's bus terminal leave about every half-hour for Baños. The fare is under $1 and the ride is about an hour. To and from Quito and many other towns, it's sometimes quicker to catch a bus to Ambato and change rather than wait for the less frequent direct buses.

The Baños bus terminal is within walking distance of most hotels – it's a small town. Buses for Quito ($3, 3½ hours) leave almost every hour. The road to Riobamba is currently closed so buses go via Ambato. To the Oriente, buses depart regularly for Puyo ($1.50, two hours) and Tena ($3.50, five hours).

Getting Around

Westbound buses leave from Rocafuerte, behind the market. They are marked 'El Salado' and go to the baths of that name. The fare is about $0.14. Eastbound buses that go as far as the dam at Agoyán leave from Alfaro at Martínez.

FROM BAÑOS TO PUYO
☎ 03

When it comes to incredible views of the upper Amazon Basin, it just doesn't get much better than the stretch of road from Baños to Puyo. The bus ride is great, but taking in the views from the seat of a mountain bike is even better. It's mostly downhill, but there are some definite climbs, so ready those legs (it's about 60km if you do the whole thing). Some people go only as far as the spectacular Pailón del Diablo waterfalls, about 20km from Baños. To get back to Baños grab a bus and throw the bike on the roof. For information on mountain-bike rentals, see Baños, earlier.

The road follows the Río Pastaza canyon as it drops steadily from Baños, at 1800m, to Puyo, at 950m. Just beyond the Agoyán hydroelectric project, the road passes through a tunnel. A few kilometers further, a waterfall splashes from the overhanging cliff onto the road – quite refreshing if you're zipping by on a bike.

One of the most impressive sights along the way is the **Río Verde waterfalls**, which are near the village of Río Verde, about 20km east of Baños. You have to walk down a short trail to a suspension bridge to appreciate the waterfall properly. There is a sign at the beginning of the trail that reads '**Pailón del Diablo**.' If you're traveling by bus (wimp), ask the driver for 'El Pailón del Diablo' – all drivers know it.

Next to the sign for Pailón del Diablo is another sign for the guest farm **El Otro Lado** (*rooms per person about $25*), which literally means 'The Other Side.' The trail to the waterfall continues by footbridge across Río Pastaza to El Otro Lado, which is about a 20-minute walk from the road. The place is tranquil and has bungalows, private hot showers and good views. Rates include breakfast and dinner. You can make reservations at the **Cultura Reservation Center** (☎/fax 02-255 8889, ☎ 02-222 4271; **w** www .cafecultura.com) – see Travel Agencies & Tour Operators in the Quito chapter.

As the road drops beyond Río Verde, the vegetation rapidly becomes more tropical, and the walls of the Río Pastaza canyon are covered with bromeliads, giant tree ferns, orchids and flowering trees. The village of Río Negro is passed some 15km beyond Río Verde, and several kilometers beyond Río Negro is a bus stop known as La Penal (a few kilometers before the village of Mera). From La Penal, a trail goes down to Río Pastaza and crosses it on a suspension footbridge, continuing on to **El Monasterio de Cumandá**, almost an hour from the road. It's not a monastery but a simple guesthouse with tropical forest and waterfalls nearby; more information is available from **Safari Tours** (☎ 255 0176, 255 0180; **w** www.san gay.com) – see Travel Agencies & Tour Operators in the Quito chapter.

PARQUE NACIONAL SANGAY

Stretching for about 70km south and southeast of Baños, the 517,765-hectare Parque Nacional Sangay contains some of the remotest and most inaccessible areas in Ecuador. The park was established in 1979 and became a World Heritage Site in 1983, protecting an incredible variety of terrain. Its western boundary is marked by the Cordillera Oriental, and three of Ecuador's highest volcanoes are within the park. The northernmost, Tungurahua, used to be accessed easily from Baños (although it is currently not accessible because of eruptions), while the

more southerly volcanoes, El Altar and Sangay, require a much greater effort. The area around the park's namesake Volcán Sangay in particular is very rugged and remote, and relatively few people have penetrated it. Nevertheless, the routes to the three volcanoes provide the most frequently used ways to access the park.

From the park's western areas, which climb to over 5000m around each of the three volcanoes, the terrain plunges from the high páramos down the eastern slopes of the Andes to elevations barely above 1000m at the park's eastern boundaries. In between is terrain so steep, rugged and wet (over 400cm of rain annually in some eastern areas) that it remains a wilderness in the truest sense. A few small and remote Andean communities (not large enough to be graced by the title of 'village') dot the páramos, but the thickly vegetated slopes east of the mountains are the haunts of very rarely seen mammals, such as Andean spectacled bears, mountain tapirs, pumas, ocelots, jaguarondis and porcupines. Nobody lives in these parts.

Only one road of any importance enters this national park, going from Riobamba to Alao (the main access point to Volcán Sangay) and petering out in the páramos to the east. Another road is still under construction. When this dirt road is completed, it will link Guamote (in the highlands) with Macas (in the southern Oriente), passing through the southern extremities of the park. Since construction began, Unesco has placed Parque Nacional Sangay on its 'National Parks in Peril' list, because 8km of the road will pass through the park, and a much longer section will form the park's southern boundary. Local authorities say that the road's construction has destroyed 20 lakes and has contributed to erosion, deforestation, loss of habitat, damage to water-drainage basins and the cutting of wildlife corridors. Colonization, which is sure to follow in the wake of this road, is the greatest future threat to the park.

Volcán Tungurahua

With a (pre-eruption) elevation of 5016m, Tungurahua is Ecuador's 10th-highest peak. It was a beautiful, cone-shaped volcano with a small cap of snow perched jauntily atop its lush, green slopes. Since the many eruptions beginning in late 1999, much of the snow has melted, and the cone and crater have changed in shape.

Until 1999, many travelers liked to walk part of the way up the volcano, perhaps as far as the village of Pondoa, or to the (now destroyed) refuge, at 3800m. Beyond the refuge, it gets steep, but the mountain was considered one of Ecuador's easier 5000m peaks to climb. It will probably be many months before it becomes stable enough to climb again. As of early 2003 people were ascending as far as the refuge, although this is risky at best and therefore not advised. Ask in Baños about the current situation.

Volcán El Altar

At 5319m, this jagged and long-extinct volcano is the fifth-highest mountain in Ecuador. It is considered the most technically difficult of Ecuador's peaks and was not climbed until 1963. The wild páramo surrounding the mountain and the greenish lake (Laguna Amarilla, or 'Yellow Lagoon') within the blown-away crater are targets for adventurous backpackers with complete camping gear. Although the area looks almost uninhabited, do not leave any gear unattended, or it may disappear.

To get to El Altar, take a bus from Riobamba to **Penipe** (if possible), a village halfway between Riobamba and Baños. Penipe was evacuated in 1999, and the road between Penipe and Baños, considered to be in the most dangerous zone, is closed. However, buses from Riobamba may go as far as Penipe. From Penipe, go to **Candelaria**, about 15km to the southeast. There is supposedly a daily bus between Penipe and Candelaria; trucks go there occasionally, or you can hire a pickup truck in Penipe. From Candelaria (which has a very simple store), it is about 2km to Hacienda Releche (not a place to stay), near which there is a Parque Nacional Sangay station. You pay the park fee of $10 there and can stay the night for another $2. The station has cooking and washing facilities. To see if the station is open, check with the climbing guides in Baños or Riobamba.

From Candelaria, it is a full-day hike to the crater. Guides and mules can be hired in Candelaria. There are many trails in the area, and it is worth having a guide to show you the beginning of the main trail to El Altar, which is less than an hour away from the station. Once you're on the main trail, the going is fairly obvious.

The best times to go are December to March. The wettest months in the Oriente are July and August, which means that El Altar is frequently clouded in at that time. El Altar is far enough south of Tungurahua that even a massive explosion should not affect hikers in the area.

Volcán Sangay

This 5230m volcano is one of the most active in the Andes – it is constantly spewing out rocks, smoke and ash. The volcanological situation changes from hour to hour and year to year. The mountain is not technically difficult to climb, but people attempting it run the risk of being killed by explosions, so climbing attempts are rare. You can hike to the base if you wish, although the approach is long and tedious, and the best views are from afar.

To get there, take a bus southeast from Riobamba to the villages of **Licto** or **Pungalá**, which are next to one another (you can ask in Riobamba's bus terminal about these buses). From there, occasional trucks (which leave early in the morning on most days) go another 20km (one hour) to the village of **Alao**, where there is a national-park ranger station. There, you pay the park fee, get information and are allowed to sleep for a nominal fee. There are a couple of simple stores in Alao, and guides are available there for the three- or four-day hike to base camp – you'll probably get hopelessly lost without a guide so it's worth getting one. Rates are about $15 to $25 per day plus food and shelter. Most guides will watch you climb the mountain from the base camp – very few will go up with you! One that does is Carlos Caz, and he charges a higher rate for climbing up there.

Another approach is to take the incomplete highway from Guamote to Macas. The road goes southeast as far as the village of **Atillo** and then becomes a mule trail dropping down through the eastern Andes to the village of **San Vicente**, about two or three days away. En route, you pass through the southernmost extremity of the national park (see The Oriente chapter). This long and ambitious hike, as well as the approaches and climbs of Sangay and El Altar, are described in the guidebooks mentioned under

Books in the Facts for the Visitor chapter. South American Explorers, in Quito, has some recent expedition reports on file.

GUARANDA

☎ 03 • pop 20,474 • elevation 2670m

Guaranda is a quiet, dignified, provincial town surrounded by pretty hills in the mountains of Bolívar Province. Although it's the capital of this agricultural province, it's nevertheless a small town. Its name derives from that of the Indian chief Guarango. Seven hills surround Guaranda, which inspires locals to call their town 'the Rome of the Andes.' It certainly can't be described as exciting, and the main reasons to visit are probably the bus rides (they're spectacular from both Riobamba and Ambato), to walk the streets, relax and perhaps explore the surrounding countryside.

Information

Banco del Pichincha (Azuay; open 9am-2pm Mon-Fri) has an ATM but does not change traveler's checks.

Make phone calls at **Andinatel** (Rocafuerte near Pichincha; open 8am-10pm daily) and send mail from the **post office** (Azuay near Pichincha).

Several clinics, including **Clínica Bolívar** (☎ 981 278), and pharmacies are found near Plaza Roja, south of the hospital.

Things to See & Do

The main **market day** is Saturday, and there's a smaller market on Wednesday. The best place for the market is Plaza 15 de Mayo, which is worth visiting even on ordinary days for its pleasantly quiet, forgotten colonial air. The market at Mercado 10 de Noviembre is held in a modern, ugly, concrete building.

A traditional local activity is the evening *paseo* (stroll) around Parque Simón Bolívar, from about 6pm to 9pm nightly.

About 3km out of town is a hill with a 5m-high monument, **El Indio de Guarango**, from which you get a good view of Guaranda, Volcán Chimborazo and the surrounding countryside. There is a tiny **museum** near the monument. A taxi will take you for about $1.50. The monument is clearly visible from the northwest end of town and you can walk there – ask the locals for directions.

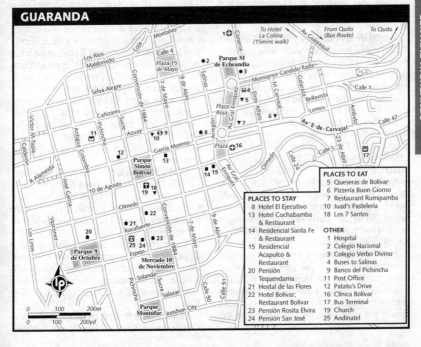

GUARANDA

PLACES TO STAY
8 Hotel El Ejecutivo
13 Hotel Cochabamba & Restaurant
14 Residencial Santa Fe & Restaurant
15 Residencial Acapulco & Restaurant
20 Pensión Tequendama
21 Hostal de las Flores
22 Hotel Bolívar; Restaurant Bolívar
23 Pensión Rosita Elvira
24 Pensión San José

PLACES TO EAT
5 Queseras de Bolivar
6 Pizzería Buon Giorno
7 Restaurant Rumipamba
10 Juad's Pastelería
18 Los 7 Santos

OTHER
1 Hospital
2 Colegio Nacional
3 Colegio Verbo Divino
4 Buses to Salinas
9 Banco del Pichincha
11 Post Office
12 Patatu's Drive
16 Clínica Bolívar
17 Bus Terminal
19 Church
25 Andinatel

CENTRAL HIGHLANDS

Special Events

Carnaval is very popular – people stream in from all over the province and beyond for such rural festivities as water fights, dances and parades. Groups of local amateur musicians stroll from house to house playing music and getting invited in for a drink or snack. The local drink of choice is 'Pájaro Azul' (Blue Bird), an *aguardiente* flavored with local herbs (one *guarandeño* said chicken is used to flavor this drink!). Many consider this to be one of Ecuador's best Carnavales.

Places to Stay

The cheapest hotels in town are pretty ratty and include **Pensión San José** *(Sucre near Rocafuerte; rooms per person $2)* and the basic **Pensión Rosita Elvira** *(Sucre; rooms per person $2)*, a malodorous, thin-walled dump. **Pensión Tequendama** *(Rocafuerte near José García; rooms per person $2)* is equally basic, but much cleaner.

Hotel Bolívar *(☎ 980 547; Sucre 7-04; rooms per person with shared/private bath $5/7)* is pleasant and has simple but clean rooms around a flowery courtyard, and a reception area jammed with archaeological artefacts. It's a clean, friendly place with hot water.

Hostal de las Flores *(☎ 980 644; Pichincha 4-02; rooms per person with shared/private bath $7/8)* is a lovely new hostal in a beautifully refurbished old building. The rooms are cheerful and open onto a small interior courtyard and have private baths, hot water, cable TV, firm beds and telephones.

Residencial Acapulco *(☎ 981 953; 10 de Agosto 8-06; rooms per person with shared/private bath $3/5)* has hot showers but is otherwise quite basic. There's a restaurant attached.

Residencial Santa Fé *(☎ 981 526; 10 de Agosto; rooms per person with shared/private bath $4/6)* has rooms in varying states of disrepair. Some are stuffy and boxlike, others have windows and are tolerable. There's a decent restaurant downstairs.

Hotel El Ejecutivo *(☎/fax 982 044; García Moreno 8-03; rooms per person $7)* offers stark, coldly tiled but clean rooms with TV. Each room shares a hot-water bathroom with one other room (which may mean you'll get it to yourself if no one's in the room next door).

Hotel Cochabamba *(☎ 981 958, 981 124; e vviteri@gu.pro.ec; García Moreno; singles/doubles $15/22)*, near 7 de Mayo, is the town's most traditionally upscale hotel.

Hotel La Colina *(☎/fax 980 666, 981 954; Avenida Guayaquil; singles/doubles $21/28)* is a 15-minute walk out of town and is a tourist complex that is often empty midweek. Located on a hill, it features some rooms with good views, a restaurant, a bar, a small indoor swimming pool and a Jacuzzi. Rooms are comfortable and have private bath and hot water.

Places to Eat

There are few restaurants in Guaranda, and they usually close early – many by 7:30pm. Several of the best places to eat are in hotels. **Restaurant Cochabamba** *(García Moreno; open Tues-Sun until 10pm)*, at the hotel of that name, is the slickest restaurant in town, and although it's comfortable and very friendly, and the food's good, it's quite overpriced.

Restaurant Bolívar *(Sucre 7-04; mains $1.50-3)* has a reasonable selection of food, cheap almuerzos and a friendly atmosphere.

Los 7 Santos *(☎ 980 612; Convención de 1884 near 10 de Agosto; mains $1-3; open 9am-11pm or midnight Mon-Sat)* is a gem of a café/bar in an old converted house with lots of art around. It's run by a local family and has a few cheery well-lit tables near the windows and lots of cozy tables tucked into the back room by the fireplace. The food is mostly snacks, light meals and breakfast.

Pizzería Buon Giorno *(García Moreno; pizzas $3.50-7; open noon-11pm Tues-Sun)* is a nice little pizza parlor serving fluffy-crust pizzas, pasta and lasagne. It's downhill from the center on the way to the bus terminal.

Juad's Pastelería *(☎ 982 312; cnr Convención de 1884 & Azuay; open 8:30am-1pm & 3pm-8pm Mon-Sat)* serves delicious pastries, chocolate cake, tiramisu, coffee, cappuccino and more. The selection is best in the morning.

There are several eateries around Plaza Roja, of which **Restaurant** *(☎ 980 754; open 7am-9pm Mon-Sat)* is the best (although still simple), serving things like *secos* (stews), *caldo de gallina* (chicken soup) and fried fish.

Queseras de Bolívar *(☎ 982 205; Avenida Gral Enriquez; open 8:30am-1pm & 2:30pm-*

6:30pm daily) sells cheeses of the province (one of the joys of Bolívar), cheese sandwiches, and has information about visiting the nearby village of Salinas, where cheese production is an important part of the economy. It stocks excellent chocolate from Salinas as well.

Entertainment

You can bump softly into midnight at **Los 7 Santos**, a groovy little café/bar (see Places to Eat earlier) with a fireplace in the back. If you fancy something livelier, try **Patatu's Drive** *(García Moreno near Sucre)* where there's dancing Thursday through Saturday nights.

Getting There & Away

Most buses leaving from the bus terminal head east on García Moreno and Avenida E de Carvajal – you can't miss it. Buses depart from about 4am to 7pm daily. Afternoon buses can get booked up in advance, so plan ahead.

Buses depart hourly for Ambato ($1.60, two hours) and Quito ($3.60, five hours). Almost as frequently, there are buses for Babahoyo ($2.25, four hours) and Guayaquil ($3.60, five hours). There are five daily buses on the spectacular road to Riobamba ($1.65, two hours), and buses at 7:45am and 2pm via the less-populated El Arenal route (two hours), which is best for reaching the turn-off to the Chimborazo mountain refuges.

Buses for Salinas leave from the north end of Plaza Roja at 6am and 7am. Trucks for Salinas leave from near here on Saturday

(to coincide with Guaranda's market) and occasionally on other days as well. The fare is about $1.

There are also several buses a day to Chillanes, a small town some 50km (or three hours) south of Guaranda. There is reportedly a basic pensión there. It certainly would be getting off the beaten track if that's what you want. The Chillanes area produces coffee and *aguardiente*. En route to both Babahoyo and Chillanes, you pass through the old town of San Miguel, which still has wooden colonial buildings with carved balconies. Buses for San José de Chimbo and San Miguel leave several times an hour. There are also several buses a day to other villages, such as San Luis, Caluma and Echeandia, if you want to explore an even remoter area.

SALINAS

☎ 03

About 35km north of Guaranda, in wild and beautiful countryside, is the peaceful community of Salinas. The town is known for its excellent cheeses, homemade salamis, chocolate, dried mushrooms and rough-spun sweaters, and you can visit the small cooperative factories that produce them. The people are very friendly and not much used to seeing travelers. It's an interesting destination for people who enjoy venturing off the beaten track and wish to see how people live in a remote rural Ecuadorian community. Market day is Tuesday. The countryside around offers pleasant walks. It is definitely very *tranquilo*.

Bus Rides to Blow Your Mind

The bus rides to and from Guaranda are some of the most spectacular in the country. The 99km road from Ambato to Guaranda is the highest-paved road in Ecuador, climbing to well over 4000m in the bleak *páramo* (Andean grasslands) before dropping down to Guaranda, at 2650m. The road passes within 10km of Volcanes Chimborazo (6310m) and Carihuairazo (5020m), affording mind-boggling views of these snowcapped giants. If going to Guaranda, sit on the left side for the best views. In addition to the mountains, you get a good look at the harsh and inhospitable páramo.

From Guaranda you can head due east to Riobamba on a dizzying 61km dirt road that skirts the southern flanks of Chimborazo and provides fantastic views that are not for the faint of heart (sit on the left side of the bus). A new road to Riobamba via El Arenal gets you even closer to Chimborazo and avoids the steep drop-offs of the older route.

Finally, you can head down the western slopes of the Andes to Babahoyo and the coast – a spectacular route that was once the most important connection between Quito and Guayaquil, although it is now infrequently used.

There is a small store on the Salinas plaza that sells naturally dyed, rough-spun sweaters for well under $12. Prices are fixed, and other woolen goods are available. There is also a small restaurant, and you can buy cheese in 31kg balls!

Places to Stay

El Refugio (☎ 981 253, 981 574, 981 266; e fugjs@ecnet.ec; dorm beds $6, private rooms with bath per person $10), on the outskirts of town, is a clean, comfortable, recommended place run by the local youth group. Simple dinners cost a couple of dollars and hot showers are available. The managers can arrange for local youths to guide you around the various cooperatives and give suggestions for hikes in the local countryside. Also ask at the store on the plaza about a cheap hostel run by the cheese-making cooperative.

Getting There & Away

Queseras de Bolívar cheese shop in Guaranda (see Places to Eat under Guaranda earlier) has information about getting to Salinas.

Otherwise, take a bus from near the Plaza Roja in Guaranda; they leave at 6am and 7am daily. You can also take a bus to Cuatro Esquinas, about 10km north of Guaranda on the road to Ambato. From here, it's about 25km to Salinas; wait for a passing truck to give you a ride (expect to pay).

To get back to Guaranda, hang out in Salinas' main plaza and flag down any vehicle. Most vehicles leaving town are going to Guaranda. The drive is spectacular.

RIOBAMBA

☎ 03 • pop 126,101 • elevation 2750m

'All roads lead to Riobamba,' proclaims a road sign as you enter this city, and it is indeed true that Riobamba is at the heart of an extensive and scenic road network. Whichever way you arrive or leave, try to plan your journey for daylight hours so you don't miss the great views.

From Ambato, 52km to the north, the Panamericana climbs over a 3600m pass that affords great views of Volcanes Chimborazo (6310m) and Carihuairazo (5020m) before dropping to Riobamba, at 2750m. An even more spectacular route is the dirt road arriving from Guaranda. The road

from Baños, which follows the Río Chambo valley, is currently closed due to mudslides from the erupting Volcán Tungurahua.

Riobamba is the main departure point for the spectacular train ride to Sibambe (see Getting There & Away, and the boxed text 'El Nariz del Diablo' later) and the city's proximity to Chimborazo, Ecuador's highest peak, has made the city a hub of climbing activity and an excellent place to hire climbing guides. Agencies in town, as well as most hotels, can also arrange day trips to refuges on Chimborazo for nonclimbers who wish to take in the spectacular views from the shoulder of the peak.

Deemed the 'Sultan of the Andes,' the city itself is sedate yet handsome, built in a regular chessboard pattern with wide avenues and imposing 18th- and 19th-century stone buildings. It is set on a large plain surrounded by several snowcapped peaks, which are visible from the city on clear days. An important commercial center for the central highlands, it's always alive with activity, and indigenous people pour in, especially on Saturdays, to buy and sell along the streets and in the markets.

Information

Traveler's checks can be cashed at Banco de Pichincha (cnr García Moreno & Primera Constituyente; open 8am-2pm Mon-Fri) or next door at Banco de Guayaquil (Primera Constituyente; open 8:30am-4:30pm Mon-Fri). You can also change foreign currency at the casa de cambio (10 de Agosto 25-41) in Hostal Montecarlo. Other banks with ATMs are around town.

The post office (Espejo & 10 de Agosto; open 8am-6pm Mon-Fri, 8am-1pm Sat) is in an old-fashioned building. Andinatel (Tarqui at Veloz; open 8am-10pm daily) has an office downtown and another at the main bus terminal.

Internet access is available for $0.60 per hour at Bambario Net (Rocafuerte near 10 de Agosto; open 9am-10pm Mon-Sat).

You can have your clothes washed and dried for $0.80 per kilogram, usually within three hours, at Lavandería Donini (Villaroel near Larrea; open 9am-1pm & 3pm-6pm Mon-Sat).

Riobamba's Hospital Policlínico (☎ 961 705, 965 725, 968 232; Olmedo 11-01) is at the eastern end of town. Locals recommend

RIOBAMBA

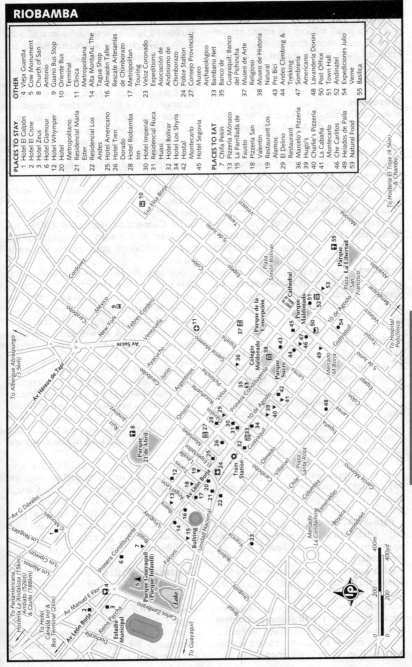

Clínica Metropolitana (☎ 941 930; Junín 25-28), between España and García Moreno. There is a small but central **police station** (Avenida León Borja), near the train station, while the **main police station** (☎ 961 913, 969 300, 911; Primera Constituyente) is at the southeastern end of this street.

Museums

In the old Church of La Concepción, is the renowned **Museo de Arte Religioso** (☎ 965 212; Argentinos; admission $2; open 9am-noon & 3pm-6pm Tues-Sat). The building has been beautifully restored, and there are many rooms with a good variety of paintings, sculptures and religious artefacts. The major piece is a huge, gem-encrusted gold monstrance said to be priceless.

At Primera Constituyente and Carabobo is the **Consejo Provincial** (Provincial Counsel Office), which has a **Museo Archaeológico** that's open only occasionally. The **Colegio Maldonado** (Primera Constituyente & Larrea) has a small, but unremarkable **Museo de Historia Natural** (Natural History Museum; admission $0.30) that is also occasionally open.

Parks

There is an observation platform at **Parque 21 de Abril** from where the city and surrounding countryside can be appreciated. There is also a tile-work representation of the history of Ecuador. The view of Volcán Tungurahua rising behind the Church of San Antonio is especially impressive.

Parque La Libertad is a quiet plaza. Its basilica is famous as the only round church in Ecuador. Begun in 1883, it took over 30 years to complete and was designed, built and decorated mainly by locals – a source of civic pride. It's often closed; try Sundays and evenings after 6pm.

Parque Maldonado is a pleasant park that's alive with trees, flowers and (at sunset) birds. Riobamba's **cathedral** is on the northeastern side.

Also known as Parque Infantil, **Parque Guayaquil** boasts swings and slides for the kids, as well as a small lake, where rowboats can be rented. It's popular for family weekend picnics. The tiled **cow monument** at the park's north end, sculpted by Endara Crow, is one of the more unusual statues that you'll see in an Ecuadorian town.

Markets

The Saturday market brings the streets of Riobamba to life – especially around 5 de Junio and Argentinos, although almost every plaza and park in the city seems to be busy. The market is a colorful affair, with thousands of people from surrounding villages flocking to barter, buy and sell. It's rather incongruous to see a barefoot indigenous woman leading a squealing piglet on a string through the streets of a major town.

The newer market buildings detract somewhat from the *ambiente*, and many market areas sell mainly food items and plastic consumer goods. Nevertheless, it is the shoppers, rather than the shopping, who are of interest to travelers. One plaza, however, has plenty of crafts for sale – this is **Parque de la Concepción** (Orozco & Colón), the only part of the market oriented toward tourists (although other plazas are worth visiting).

An interesting *riobambeño* handicraft is *tagua*-nut carving. These 'nuts' are actually seeds from a type of rainforest palm that grows in many lowland areas (see the 'Riches from the Rainforest' boxed text in the North Coast & Lowlands chapter), but highland Riobamba has traditionally been a carving center.

Another interesting handicraft from the Riobamba area is the *shigra*, a tough woven bag made from *cabuya* (agave, or century plant) fibers. Their durability and practicality make *shigras* very popular souvenirs for many travelers, who often use them as day bags. *Cabuya* is also used to make rope and rope sandals.

There are also baskets and mats that have been woven by the Colta Indians from the reeds lining the shores of Laguna de Colta, a few kilometers south of Riobamba. Many clothing items, such as woven belts, fine ponchos and embroidered shawls, are also sold.

Sunday, the day after market day, is dead in Riobamba – definitely a day of rest!

Organized Tours

Riobamba is an excellent base for climbing Chimborazo and is home to numerous excellent mountain guides. Make sure you get a good guide, as your life depends on it. Most of the trips described here are not recommended for beginning mountaineers. Enrique Veloz, of Riobamba, is the veteran advisor of the Asociación de Andinismo de Chimborazo and owner of **Veloz Coronado Expeditions** (☎ 960 916; e velozexpedici ones@hotmail.com; Chile 33-21 at Francia). He has climbed Chimborazo and the other peaks many times and can either guide himself or set you up with other ASEGUIM guides registered with the association.

Expediciones Julio Verne (☎ 963 436, after 6pm ☎ 960 398; w www.julioverne-travel .com; 5 de Junio 21-46) is a recommended Ecuadorian/Dutch-owned operator offering two-day summit trips to Chimborazo ($140 per person), Cotopaxi ($150 per person) and other peaks. The company arranges guided treks, rents climbing and trekking gear and mountain bikes ($10 per day, including gear), and offers transfers to trailheads for climbers going without guides. It's also a good place to set up tours to the Oriente (the owner has been arranging tours to the jungle for years).

Alta Montaña (☎ 950 651; e aventurag@ laserinter.net; Avenida León Borja 35-17) is run by friendly Rodrigo Donoso, an accomplished mountaineer and photographer who speaks English. Apart from arranging guided climbs of the highest mountains in Ecuador, Alta Montaña manages three mountain refuges on Volcán Chimborazo (see later); arranges acclimatization and training days before ascents; organizes treks along the Inca Trail to Ingapirca, around Chimborazo and to Sangay; offers horse-riding and bicycle tours and various other adventures; and has an excellent gift shop. Rates for a two-day Chimborazo ascent start at $145 per person (six climbers) to $200 (two climbers), including experienced guides, climbing gear, transportation, meals and use of the refuge. Keep in mind that there is no guarantee that the summit will be reached.

Two other excellent guides are Marcelo Puruncajas and his son Pablo, who speak Spanish, English and German. Both guides can be found at Marcelo's **Andes Climbing & Trekking** (☎ 940 963/64; w www.andes -trek.com; Colón 22-25). Rates are about $300 to take two climbers to the summits of Cotopaxi or Chimborazo, with everything provided. They can also be hired for trekking trips anywhere in Ecuador.

The best known (and most expensive) guide is **Marco Cruz** (☎ 940 818). His Riobamba office is at the Albergue Abraspungo

(see Places to Stay later). He runs his own very comfortable hostal for acclimatization and works with international groups most of the time.

Pro Bici (☎ 942 468, 961 877, fax 961 923; Primera Constituyente 23-51) offers mountain-bike rentals and tours. The owner, Galo Brito, speaks English. The bikes are in good shape and the guided tours have received several recommendations.

Both Pro Bici and Expediciones Julio Verne offer downhill tours from the refuge on Chimborazo – an exhilarating way to take in the views!

For standard tour arrangements, the local office of **Metropolitan Touring** (☎/fax 969 600/601; e mtrioopr@andinanet.net; cnr Avenida León Borja & Francia) is one of the best known.

Special Events
Riobamba's annual fiesta celebrates the Independence Battle of Tapi on April 21, 1822. On and around that date, there is a large agricultural fair with the usual highland events – street parades, dancing and plenty of traditional food and drink. The city and hotels can be particularly crowded then.

Places to Stay
Budget Most hotels are in the town center, 2km from the bus terminal; those near the terminal are pretty run down. **Hotel Canada Inn** (☎/fax 946 677; Avenida de la Prensa 23-31; rooms per person about $9), catty corner from the bus terminal, is one exception; rooms have private hot baths and TV, and there's a restaurant.

Residencial Ñuca Huasi (☎ 966 669; 10 de Agosto 10-24; rooms per person with shared/ private bath $2/3) is a very basic place once popular with backpackers. Rooms are grimy, but hot water is available from 7am to 9am and 7pm to 9pm.

Hotel Bolívar (☎ 968 294; cnr Carabobo & Guayaquil; rooms per person $3) offers dark no-frills rooms and hot water. It's dull but it's clean. If that place is full, travelers watching their pennies can try the more basic **Hotel Americano** (cnr Montalvo & Avenida León Borja), **Residencial María Ester** (Unidad Nacional) and **Residencial Los Andes** (Unidad Nacional).

Hotel Imperial (☎ 960 429; Rocafuerte 22-15; rooms per person with shared/private bath

$5/6$) is a clean and friendly (albeit noisy) place with hot water. The manager will arrange trips to Chimborazo.

Hotel Tren Dorado (☎/fax 964 890; e htren dorado@hotmail.com; Carabobo 22-35; rooms per person $7) is right near the train station and has spotless, comfortable rooms with private hot baths. There's a good restaurant attached which opens at 5:30am on days the train runs. It's excellent value.

Hotel Segovia (☎ 961 269; Primera Constituyente 22-26; rooms per person $7) is drab and impersonal but secure and clean. All rooms have shared baths.

Hotel Metropolitano (☎ 961 714; Avenida León Borja & Lavalle; rooms per person $5) charges less than Segovia for adequate rooms with TV, bath and hot water.

Hotel Los Shyris (☎ 960 323; Rocafuerte & 10 de Agosto; singles/doubles $8/14) is large and friendly and recommended for its central location and clean rooms with TV and hot showers.

Hotel Whymper (☎ 964 575, fax 968 575; Ángel León 23-10; rooms per person $8) has received mixed reviews from readers. Certainly, rooms vary considerably (some have better views of the town), but more readers seem satisfied than not. Breakfast is available at an extra cost, and tours and transportation to Chimborazo can be arranged there.

Mid-Range & Top End The comfortable **Hotel Riobamba Inn** (☎ 961 696, 940 958; Carabobo 23-20; singles/doubles $12/22) has spacious rooms with private bath, hot water, TV and telephone, and there is a restaurant with limited hours.

Hostal Montecarlo (☎/fax 960 557, 961 577; 10 de Agosto 25-41; singles/doubles $15/29) is the best hotel in the center. Inside an attractively restored, turn-of-the-20th-century house, it has 18 comfortable rooms with TV, a restaurant and a café. Breakfast is available from 5am on train days.

Hotel Glamour (☎ 944 406; Primera Constituyente 37-85; singles/doubles $12/17) is in a relatively quiet area, has a restaurant, and offers clean rooms with cable TV, heat and private hot baths.

Hotel Zeus (☎ 968 036/37/38; e hotel zeus@ecuabox.com; Avenida León Borja 41-29; singles/doubles $24/37, executive rooms $37/49, suites $55-80), between the bus terminal and downtown, is a seven-story hotel

with varying rooms. The standards are pretty worn out, but the pricier rooms are excellent, and some have great views. The 6th-floor presidential suites have stunning views from the giant bathtubs! The 7th-floor bar boasts the best views in Riobamba. There's a restaurant, too.

Hotel El Galpón (☎/fax 960 981/2/3; e gal pon@ch.pro.ec; Argentinos & Zambrano; singles/doubles $15/24) is about 1km west of the center in a quiet area. It has a restaurant and pool and 44 slightly worn rooms with hot showers and TV.

Hotel El Cisne (☎ 964 573, 941 980, fax 941 982; e elcisne@ch.pro.ec; Avenida León Borja near Duchicela; singles/doubles $14/22) is modern and pleasant and has rooms with bath and TV.

Hostería El Troje (☎/fax 964 572; w www .eltroje.com; singles/doubles $37/43) is 4.5km southeast of town on the minor road to Chambo. It has a pool, tennis court, restaurant and bar. Many of the rooms also have fireplaces.

Albergue Abraspungo (☎ 940 820, fax 940 819; w www.abraspungo.com; singles/doubles $37/49) is 3.5km northeast of town on the road to Guano. It is quite attractive and is built around a traditional hacienda. Spacious rooms, a restaurant and bar, and horse riding are all available here. Climbing expeditions can also be arranged.

Hostería La Andaluza (☎ 904 223, 904 248; w www.hosteria-andaluza.com; singles $45-61, doubles $55-73) is about 15km north of Riobamba on the Panamericana. This colonial hacienda has been attractively restored and is now perhaps the best hotel in Chimborazo Province. There are two restaurants, a small exercise room and sauna, and a bar with a fireplace. Nearly all the antique-furnished rooms have fireplaces, as well as cable TV and telephones. If you take a chance and just arrive, much lower rates can be negotiated than those listed above.

Places to Eat
Riobamba's many restaurants are fairly basic and cheap. **Restaurant Los Alamos** (Lavalle & Avenida León Borja) and several other inexpensive places near the train station are good for cheap meals.

Pizzería San Valentín (☎ 963 137; León Borja & Torres; mains $3-5; open Mon-Sat) is a lively place in the evenings and a favorite place for both young locals and tourists. You have to order pizza at the counter and Mexican food is also available. It's sometimes closed on Monday.

Marcelo's Pizzería (*García Moreno 24-42; mains $3-4; open evenings Mon-Sat*) is more of a traditional pizza parlor than San Valentin. **Pizzería Mónaco** (*☎ 947 342; Ibarra 22-46; mains $3-4; open daily*) and **Charlie's Pizzería** (*☎ 968 231; García Moreno & 10 de Agosto; mains $2-5; open daily*) both have good pizzas and lasagnes.

Natural Food (*☎ 09-800 8816; Tarqui near Primera Constituyente; almuerzos $1.50; open 8:30am-3pm daily*) does hearty vegetarian or seafood almuerzos (your choice). It's so popular the owner may be open for dinner by the time this book is out.

Chifa Pekin (*☎ 960 325; Avenida León Borja near Brasil; mains $2-3; open 10am-10pm daily*) has a rather odd-smelling dining room but the food is good.

La Cabaña Montecarlo (*☎ 962 844; García Moreno 24-10; mains $4-6; open noon-9pm Tues-Sat, noon-3:30pm Sun*) is pricey by Riobamba standards, but both the service and food are good. Dishes include seafood, trout, soups, filet mignon and various other meat dishes. It's owned by Hostal Montecarlo, which also has a good **café** (*open 7am-10pm daily*) next to its hotel. It serves breakfast, lunch and dinner and opens at 5am on days the train runs.

El Delirio Restaurant (*☎ 966 441, 967 502; Primera Constituyente 28-16; mains $5-9; open 2:30pm-10pm daily*) is Riobamba's most atmospheric eatery, although the food and service can be hit or miss. When it's good, however, it's great. The restaurant is in a historic house where Simón Bolívar stayed and, on July 5, 1822, wrote his epic poem *El Delirio* about his attempted ascent of Chimborazo (he reached the snowline). Part of the restaurant is in an outdoor patio, and there's often live *folklórica*.

La Parrillada de Fausto (*☎ 967 876; Uruguay 20-38; mains $4-5; open 10am-3pm & 6pm-11pm Mon-Sat*) serves great grilled steaks, trout and chicken. The dark wood tables give it a ranch-style atmosphere. The steaks at **Che Carlitos** (*☎ 963 769; Colón 22-44; mains $4-6; open 10am-9pm Mon-Sat*) are a far cry from those at Fausto's, but it's cheap and central. It's best on weekend evenings.

Hugo's (*Pichincha near Guayaquil; sandwiches $1-3; open 9am-9pm*) is a cool old-school sandwich shop with a fridge full of cold beer and lots of submarine-style sandwiches prepared by a tie-clad barman.

Helados de Paila (*Espejo 21-43; open 9am-7pm daily*) serves probably the best handmade ice cream in town.

The restaurants at **Hostería La Andaluza** and **Albergue Abraspungo** (see Places to Stay earlier) are popular weekend lunch destinations for locals.

Entertainment

Nightlife, limited as it is, centers around the intersection of Avenida León Borja and Torres and northwest along León Borja toward Duchicela. **Pizzería San Valentin** (see Places to Eat earlier) is an eternally popular hangout in the area. Further up, **Vieja Guardia** (*Avenida Manuel E Flor 40-43*) is a decent *discoteca*.

Shopping

The Tagua Shop (*Avenida León Borja 35-17; open 9am-7pm Mon-Sat, 10am-5pm Sun*) has an excellent selection of tagua carvings, as well as the best selection of maps and travel books in town. Several other places nearby sell tagua carvings, too. A block away on León Borja is the **Almacén Taller Rescate Artesanías de Chimborazo** ('Workshop to Rescue the Crafts of Chimborazo'), where tagua and various local products are sold.

For high-quality, felt porkpie hats (the type you see many indigenous folks wearing in the area) stop into the old **Sombrería Americano** (*Espejo near 10 de Agosto; open 8am-noon & 2pm-6pm Mon-Sat*).

Getting There & Away

Bus Riobamba has two bus terminals. The **main bus terminal** (*Avenida León Borja*) is almost 2km northwest of the center. Buses bound for Quito ($3, four hours) and intermediate points are frequent, as are the buses for Guayaquil ($3.60, 4½ hours). Transportes Patria has a Machala bus at 9:45am ($5, six to seven hours). There are several buses a day for Cuenca ($5, six hours). Buses for Alausí leave 20 times a day between 5am and 8pm with CTA ($1.20, two hours). Flota Bolívar has seven daily buses to Guaranda ($1.65, two hours). Some continue on to Babahoyo, most go via the

CENTRAL HIGHLANDS

rougher southern route, and the 8:45am and 2pm buses go via El Arenal for access to Chimborazo. Buses for local towns leave from a smaller terminal to the south (see Getting Around, later).

For buses to Baños and the Oriente, you have to go to the **Oriente bus terminal** (*Espejo & Luz Elisa Borja*). However, the road to Baños from Riobamba was still closed at the time of writing because of falling ash from Tungurahua – buses were therefore going via Ambato (but still leaving from this terminal).

Train The schedules for trains from Riobamba change regularly and you should inquire locally for the latest information. South American Explorers (SAE) in Quito (see Information in the Quito chapter) is usually up to date on this. Your best bet is to call the **train station** (☎ 961 909).

The only service out of Riobamba is the famous ride down **El Nariz del Diablo** (see the boxed text 'El Nariz del Diablo' later this chapter). It leaves Riobamba at 7am Wednesday, Friday and Sunday ($11). It picks up more passengers in Alausí and goes only as far as Sibambe, immediately below El Nariz del Diablo, where there are no services. From Sibambe, the train ascends El Nariz del Diablo and returns to Alausí, where passengers can spend the night, continue on to Cuenca by bus or return to Riobamba by bus. Riding on the roof is, of course, allowed.

Getting Around

North of the main bus terminal, behind the Church of Santa Faz (the one with a blue dome), is a local bus stop with buses to the city center, nearly 2km away. These buses run along Avenida León Borja, which turns into 10 de Agosto near the train station. To return to the bus terminal, take any bus marked 'Terminal' on Primera Constituyente; the fare is $0.14.

Three long blocks south of the main bus terminal (turn left out of the front entrance), off Unidad Nacional, is a smaller terminal with frequent local buses for Cajabamba, Laguna de Colta and the chapel of La Balbanera; the fare is $0.25. Buses for Guamote also leave from there.

To visit the villages of Guano and Santa Teresita, take a $0.20 local bus ride from the stop at Pichincha and New York.

SOUTHWEST OF RIOBAMBA
☎ 03

The southbound Panamericana heads west out of Riobamba until it reaches a cement factory 10km away. There the road forks; the right branch continues on to Guaranda, and the main highway heads southwest to **Cajabamba**, about 7km further on.

Founded in 1534, Cajabamba was historically important until it was devastated by the 1797 earthquake, which killed several thousand inhabitants. Most of those who survived founded nearby Riobamba, but a few remained, and their descendants still live there. As you arrive, look up to your right and you'll see a huge scar on the hillside. This is the only sign of the landslide that caused much of the damage over two centuries ago.

Right around Cajabamba, the Panamericana splits – the easternmost branch is the **Ecuadorian Panamericana**, which becomes a regular road when it hits the border with Peru, and the westernmost branch is the **international Panamericana**, which is still referred to as such once it hits the Peruvian border. Throughout the rest of this chapter, references to the Panamericana should be understood as the Ecuadorian, not international, Panamericana.

Most of the buses from Riobamba continue down the Panamericana beyond Cajabamba; if you want to see some of the old town, get off at the junction of the main highway and Avenida 2 de Agosto on the right. Most bus drivers stop here.

Just south of town on the Panamericana, you'll see a few food stalls and very basic restaurants, and soon pass the open fields that are the site of the interesting Sunday market. There are no permanent buildings; the Indians just lay out their wares in neat rows. Every Sunday morning, the bare fields are transformed by a bustling but surprisingly orderly throng of people who buy, sell and barter produce. Quechua, rather than Spanish, is spoken, and there are no tourist items; this is one of the more traditional markets in the Ecuadorian highlands. Amazingly, it takes place right by the side of the Panamericana – a measure of just how rural this part of Ecuador is.

Most buses from Riobamba continue about 4km beyond Cajabamba to Laguna de Colta. On the way, the road gently climbs to a notch in the hill to the south and the little chapel of **La Balbanera**. It is built on the site of the earliest church in Ecuador, which dates from August 15, 1534, although only a few stones at the front survived the devastating earthquake of 1797. The church has been almost completely rebuilt, and the curious traveler can enter to inspect its simple interior and look at the usual disaster paintings.

Next to the chapel are a few simple restaurants where you can sample local dishes. A little to the south of the chapel, there is a fork in the road. You can either continue south on the Panamericana or take the 100km detour to the right, via the junction of El Triunfo, and then return to the Panamericana at Cañar. Occasional road closures caused by landslides might make the detour impossible to avoid.

Opposite the fork in the road is **Laguna de Colta**. Its blue expanse is often choked up by reeds, which form an important crop for the local Colta Indians. Sometimes you can see the Coltas' rafts on the lake; the Indians cut the reeds for use as cattle fodder or to make the reed mats and baskets for which they are famous.

Some of the more traditional Colta Indian women can be easily identified, as they dye the fringes of their hair a startling golden color. If you have the time or inclination, you could walk around the lake in a couple of hours.

You can visit this area on a day excursion from Riobamba by taking local buses or by hiring a taxi. The views of the volcanoes, especially Chimborazo, are particularly good as you return from Laguna de Colta to Riobamba along the Panamericana – try to sit near the front of the bus.

VOLCÁN CHIMBORAZO

Not only is the extinct Volcán Chimborazo the highest mountain in Ecuador, but its peak (6310m) is also the furthest point from the center of the earth (due to the earth's equatorial bulge). For insatiable trivia buffs, it is higher than any mountain in the Americas north of it. Nearby is the ninth-highest mountain in Ecuador, the 5020m **Volcán Carihuairazo**. Climbing either mountain is an adventure only for experienced mountaineers with snow- and ice-climbing gear (contact the guides listed under Riobamba, Baños or Quito), but reaching the refuge on Chimborazo is as simple as hiring a car.

Chimborazo and Carihuairazo are both within **La Reserva de Producción Faunística Chimborazo** *(admission $10)*. It's called a 'fauna-production reserve' because hundreds of vicuñas (a wild relative of the llama) live and breed here. Sharp-eyed travelers can even catch sight of them on the bus from Guaranda to Riobamba (via El Arenal), or sometimes on other routes. Hikers are likely to see these lovely animals.

Climbing

Most climbers acclimatize at a lower elevation (Riobamba or Quito are just adequate; higher lodges are a better choice) and arrive at Chimborazo's climbing refuges ready to climb. After a short sleep (more like a restless nap), climbers set out around midnight, when the snow is hard. There are several routes, but most parties these days take the **Normal Route**, which takes eight to 10 hours to the summit and two to four to return (although fit, acclimatized climbers will be faster, one group took 20 hours for the round trip!).

The previously popular **Whymper Route** is currently unsafe. Just below the summit is a large bowl of snow that must be crossed; this gets notoriously soft during the day and is the main reason climbers leave the refuge at midnight. Because many parties climb this route, wands marking the way are often found. The sunrise high up on the mountain is unforgettable.

There are no proper refuges on Carihuairazo (although there is a dilapidated hut that could collapse any year now), so climbers usually set up a base camp on the south side of the mountain. When climbing, do not leave anything unattended, as it could get stolen. The climb is fairly straightforward for experienced climbers, but the usual ice-climbing gear is needed. Skiers and snowboarders have made some descents on this mountain. **Quebrada Sachahaicu**, a river valley on the southeast side of the mountain, has one of the biggest stands of undisturbed Polylepis forests in the country.

Hiking

The area around these mountains is also suitable for backpacking trips – the walk from Mocha (on the Panamericana north of Riobamba) or Urbina (see Places to Stay following) over the pass between the two

CENTRAL HIGHLANDS

mountains and emerging at the Ambato–Guaranda road is as good a choice as any. Allow three days for this hike and bring plenty of warm clothes. June to September is the dry season in this region. Maps are available at the Instituto Geográfico Militar (see Maps in the Quito chapter), or from the Tagua Shop, in Riobamba (see Shopping, under Riobamba, earlier).

Places to Stay

There are three small lodges on the lower slopes of Chimborazo, which are suitable for acclimatization, and two high climbing refuges, suitable as bases for climbing the volcano. Note that all of these places are very cold at night, so bring appropriate clothing. Blankets are provided in the lower lodges, but many people use their sleeping bags as well.

The cheapest place to stay is **La Casa del Condor** *(beds $2)*, named after the shape of the building, in the small indigenous community of Pulingue San Pablo, on the left, just after crossing over the boundary into the reserve on the Riobamba–El Arenal road. The community, although within the reserve, owns the surrounding land, and the ecotourism project **Proyecto El Cóndor** *(Condor Project;* **w** *www.interconnection.org/condor)* is helping them to improve their livelihoods in this harsh environment. Families still live in the small, rounded, thatched-roof huts typical of the area, but La Casa del Condor is a stone building with rooms for a weaving cooperative and two bedrooms, each with two bunk beds for travelers. Electricity reached the village in late 1999, and there is a gas-heated shower for guests. Basic kitchen facilities are available. The altitude here is over 3900m – perfect for acclimatization. Locals are being trained to provide basic guiding services, and there are fine hikes in the area, which is a few kilometers south of Chimborazo. This is ecotourism at its most grassroots level, and the money goes directly to the *campesino* (peasant) villagers. Be patient when you arrive; it can take a while for the locals to find the person who has the key to the rooms. Information can be obtained from Riobamba resident **Tom Walsh** *(☎ 03-941 481, fax 940 955;* **e** *twalsh@ch.pro.ec)*, who has been instrumental in helping the villagers set up the project.

A few hundred meters beyond Pulingue San Pablo, to the right of the road, is **La Posada**, which is where Marco Cruz (see Organized Tours under Riobamba earlier) brings his groups for acclimatization. This is a fairly comfortable but much more expensive lodge, and it may not be available if a group has booked it.

Just outside the reserve's boundary, southeast of Chimborazo, is Urbina, which at 3618m consists of nothing more than a train station that was built in 1905. This historic building has been turned into **Posada La Estación** *(beds $7)*, a simple but comfortable hostal operated by Alta Montaña (see Organized Tours under Riobamba earlier). There are eight rooms that can sleep a total of 20 people, a hot shower, a fully equipped kitchen and meals. Good acclimatization, or simply scenic hikes, can be achieved from here as well.

Alta Montaña also operates the two climbers refuges. The lower one is **Refugio Hermanos Carrel** *(beds $10)*, at 4860m, and the upper one is **Refugio Whymper** *(beds $10)*, at 5000m. The latter was named after Edward Whymper, the British climber who in 1880 made the first ascent of Chimborazo with the Swiss Carrel brothers as guides. The lower refuge has 14 beds, while the upper one has 70 and is the best suited for a summit attempt. Both have caretakers, equipped kitchens, storage facilities and limited food supplies (soups and sandwiches). At 5000m, Refugio Whymper is Ecuador's highest, and altitude sickness is a very real danger. It is essential to spend several days acclimatizing at the elevation of Riobamba or even higher before going on to the refuge.

Getting There & Away

At least two buses a day go from Riobamba to Guaranda via El Arenal (ensure that the bus goes via El Arenal). This road is paved up to a short distance beyond Pulingue San Pablo (see Places to Stay earlier), which is reached in less than an hour. Another 7km on this road (now unpaved, although paving is planned) brings you to the signed turn-off for the Chimborazo refuges. The elevation here is 4370m. This is the cheapest access route. From the turn-off it is 8km by road to the parking lot at Refugio Hermanos Carrel; you have to walk this road (or hitchhike if you are lucky). Because of the altitude, allow several hours for this walk. Refugio

Whymper is almost 1km further, and you have to walk (allow another hour if you are carrying a heavy pack).

Most hotels in Riobamba can arrange a taxi service to Refugio Hermanos Carrel via this route. You'll probably need a pickup or similar vehicle to negotiate the final 8km from the road. Rates have been falling as the road to El Arenal becomes paved, but expect to pay about $25 for a taxi to take you there, wait while you look around and take you back to Riobamba.

Another approach, for mountaineers prepared to go cross-country, is to take the same Riobamba–Guaranda road via El Arenal and continue about 5km beyond the refuge-bound road to a hairpin bend, from where you climb a gully east to the lower refuge, about 5km away. The hairpin bend is approximately 5km south of the Ambato–Guaranda road if you are arriving from the opposite direction.

To reach Posada La Estación (see Places to Stay earlier) take a bus along the Panamericana and ask the driver for the Urbina road, almost 30km north of Riobamba. It's about 1km from the Panamericana by road to Urbina. When the train ran between Quito and Riobamba you could just jump off at the *posada*.

GUANO & SANTA TERESITA
☎ 03

These small villages are a few kilometers north of Riobamba and are easily reached by bus. Guano is an important carpet-making center, and although most travelers won't have room in their luggage for a couple of souvenir carpets, it's interesting to see this cottage industry. To see some carpet stores, get off the bus in Guano's central plaza, and then walk down Avenida García Moreno. There are no hotels and only a few restaurants. Look for the topiary garden with El Altar rising in the background – a pretty sight.

From the main plaza, you can continue by bus to Santa Teresita, a few kilometers away. At the end of the bus ride, turn right and head down the hill for about 20 minutes to the *balneario* (spa), where swimming pools are fed by natural springs. The water is quite cool (22°C), but the views of Tungurahua and El Altar are marvelous. There is a basic cafeteria and camping is permitted.

GUAMOTE
☎ 03

From Riobamba, the southbound Panamericana roughly follows the train tracks and crosses them quite often. Some 47km beyond Riobamba, you reach the village of Guamote, which has an interesting and unspoiled Thursday market – one of the largest rural markets in Ecuador. There is a basic pensión near the train tracks.

Note that Guamote is located in a valley almost 1km off the Panamericana. Unless your bus is actually going to Guamote (usually only on Thursdays), you will be dropped off on the Panamericana and will have to walk in.

ALAUSÍ
☎ 03

Alausí, near the head of the Río Chanchán valley, is about 97km south of Riobamba and is the last town the train passes through before its descent down the famous Nariz del Diablo. There is a busy Sunday market and a smaller one on Thursday. The feast of St Peter and St Paul (June 28) is one of Alausí's major fiestas, and the town is very crowded then.

Orientation & Information
The main street is Avenida 5 de Junio, which is about six blocks long. Buses arrive and depart from this street, and most of the hotels are located along it. The train station is at the north end of 5 de Junio. There is an **Andinatel** office one block to the west of 5 de Junio, behind the fire station and near the train station. From the train station, head east and wander around to find a plaza, church, cobbled streets and balconied buildings – *tranquilísimo*.

Places to Stay & Eat
Hotels are often full on Saturday nights for the Sunday market and Ecuadorian weekend visitors. There are no 1st-class hotels, and most accommodations are along 5 de Junio.

Hotel Tequendama (☎ 930 123; *rooms per person $4*) is clean, family run and has hot water. Breakfast is available.

Other possibilities are the friendly **Hotel Panamericano** (☎ 930 156; *rooms per person $5*), which has private baths with hot water and a basic restaurant; **Hotel Europa**, which also has a restaurant; and **Residencial Alausí**

El Nariz del Diablo

The most exciting part of the train ride south of Riobamba is the hair-raising descent from Alausí to Sibambe, down a death-defying stretch of track called El Nariz del Diablo (The Devil's Nose). The run is the only section of track still functioning of the once spectacular Ferrocarril Transandino (Trans-Andean Railway), which ran from Guayaquil to Quito.

Construction of this historic line began in Guayaquil in 1899 and made it as far as Sibambe, where it met a steep Andean slope of nearly solid rock, no less intimidating than the devil's nose itself. To reach Alausí a series of switchbacks were carved into the rock (and many lives were lost in the process) that would allow the train, by advancing and reversing, to ascend nearly 1000m to Alausí at 2607m. The completion and first ascent of the Nariz del Diablo in 1902 was the most incredible feat of railway engineering the world had seen.

The Ferrocarril Transandino reached Riobamba in 1905, later crossed its highest point at Urbina (3618m) and finally reached Quito, after its magnificent wind through the Avenue of the Volcanoes, in 1908.

Landslides caused by the torrential rains of the 1982–83 El Niño, and further damage during the 1997–98 El Niño effectively closed the entire run, and only the stretch from Riobamba to Sibambe has been repaired.

The steep descent after Alausí is still accomplished by a series of switchbacks down the steep mountainside. Occasional rickety-looking bridges cross steep ravines, and daredevils ride on the flat roof of the train, with nothing but empty space between them and the valleys far below. The local machos stand up on the roof, especially when going through tunnels, where there is barely enough clearance for the sombrero jammed jauntily on their heads. Actually, the greatest hazard is probably the train's emission of steam, soot and cinders during the ride, so wear clothes you don't mind getting dirty.

(☎ 930 361; Estaban Orozco; rooms per person with private bath $4), just off the south end of 5 de Junio, which has nice rooms.

Hotel Gampala (☎ 930 138; rooms per person $6) has erratic hot water and a restaurant (which tends to overcharge).

Hotel Americano (☎ 930 159; García Moreno 159; rooms per person $4), a block east of 5 de Junio, near the train station, is your best bet. Good, clean doubles come with private hot bath.

Apart from the hotel restaurants, there are a couple of basic restaurants along the main street, mostly serving *meriendas* (set dinners). There's really not much choice, but the food is quite adequate.

Getting There & Away

Bus The buses from Riobamba ($1.20, 1½ hours) arrive every hour or so. Buses turn off the Panamericana and drop down into town, where they normally stop near Hotel Panamericano. Buses for Cuenca ($3, five hours) also leave from here several times a day, but less often on Sunday. Buses between Riobamba and Cuenca don't normally enter town, but they leave passengers on the Panamericana, from which it is almost a 1km walk down into town.

Old buses (or pickup trucks acting as buses) leave from 5 de Junio for nearby destinations. Some of the rides can be quite spectacular, especially the one to Achupallas (see later), about 23km by road to the southeast. Make sure that any sightseeing ride you take is coming back to Alausí, as there are few if any places to stay in these villages.

There are also buses and trucks to the village of Chunchi, about 25km further south on the Panamericana. Here you'll find a local Sunday market and a few places to stay.

Train Alausí used to be a major railroad junction, but services are now limited to the Riobamba–Sibambe run (see Getting There & Away under Riobamba earlier for more details) and are subject to occasional cancellation. The train leaves Alausí daily at 9:30am, and tickets go on sale at 8am. This train usually arrives from Riobamba and is often quite full, but ticket sales are orderly. The fare is $11. The trip takes around two hours to go over the famous Nariz del Diablo (see the boxed text 'El Nariz del Diablo').

Roof-riding is allowed, but the roof is often full with riders from Riobamba or tour groups who pile on while their guide stands in line to buy tickets.

ACHUPALLAS
☎ 03

This village is the starting point for a three-day hike south along the old Inca road to Ingapirca, the most important Inca ruins in Ecuador (see the Cuenca & the Southern Highlands chapter). Occasional trucks leave Alausí for Achupallas, or you can hire a taxi (pickup) for about $9 one way. Alternatively, there is transportation from Alausí to **Guasuntos** (also known as La Moya), from where you can wait for trucks to Achupallas. It is about 10km from Alausí to La

Moya and another 15km to Achupallas. There is nowhere to stay at either place.

The hike from Achupallas to Ingapirca is a good one (see the hiking guides that are recommended under Books in the Facts for the Visitor chapter). The Inca road is faint in places, but you could probably find your way to Ingapirca with a compass and map, asking the locals for directions if you don't have a hiking book. Head south, and pack some extra food in case you get lost. The area is remote but inhabited, so don't leave your stuff lying around outside your tent, and be prepared for persistent begging from children. The area is covered by three 1:50,000 topographical maps available from the IGM in Quito. These are the Alausí CT-ÑV-A3, Juncal CT-ÑV-C1 and Cañar CT-ÑV-C3 sheets.

Cuenca & the Southern Highlands

As you roll down the Panamericana into the southern highland provinces of Cañar, Azuay and Loja, the giant snowcapped peaks of the central highlands fade from the rearview mirror. The climate gets a bit warmer, distances between towns become greater, and the decades clunk down by the wayside. Although few peaks top 4000m here, the topography is rugged – so rugged in fact that not until the 1960s did the first paved road reach Cuenca, Ecuador's third-largest city and the southern highland's main urban center. The only other town with a population over 100,000 is the attractive colonial town of Loja, 205km further south, where the locals will tell you how odd it was to see a car roll past the main plaza as little as 20 years ago.

Cars are plentiful in the area these days, but the region's isolation, until relatively recently, has given the southern highlands a rich and tangible history. Many villages have cobbled streets and old houses with balconies, and the tradition of handicrafts, ranging from jewelry-making to weaving, is still very strong.

Although you won't be out scaling glaciered volcanoes in the southern highlands, there are some excellent opportunities for a wide range of outdoor activities. The misty, lake-studded Parque Nacional Cajas (whose rocky moors have drawn comparisons to the Scottish highlands) has some great hiking trails, as well as superb trout fishing. Parque Nacional Podocarpus, which stretches from the highlands near Loja down to the cloud forests of the Oriente, is easily accessible from either Loja or the delightful Oriente town of Zamora, which is only two hours east from Loja. From the laid-back gringo hang-out of Vilcabamba you can spend days walking or horse riding through the mysterious mountainside.

If the southern highland colonial towns don't take you far enough into the past, there's always Ingapirca, the site of Ecuador's most important and best known Inca ruins, and a two-hour bus ride (an easy day trip) north of Cuenca.

Highlights

- Indulging in a shopping spree for panama hats and filigreed jewelry in Cuenca
- Hiking and camping in Parque Nacional Cajas
- Visiting Ecuador's best Inca ruins at Ingapirca
- Exploring the unique cloud forests of Parque Nacional Podocarpus
- Hiking around and chilling out in the gringo mountain hang-out of Vilcabamba
- Savoring whole-roasted *cuy* (roast guinea pig) in Loja while contemplating your sibling's favorite pet

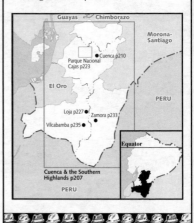

History

The southern highlands had a colorful history even before the Spanish conquest. These were the lands of the Cañari Indians, an independent culture with exceptional skill in producing ceramics, fine weavings, and gold jewelry and other metalwork.

In the late 15th century the Cañaris were conquered by the Incas, who built several major centers. These included the city of Tomebamba, near present-day Cuenca, and the fortress of Ingapirca, the best-preserved pre-colonial ruin found in Ecuador today.

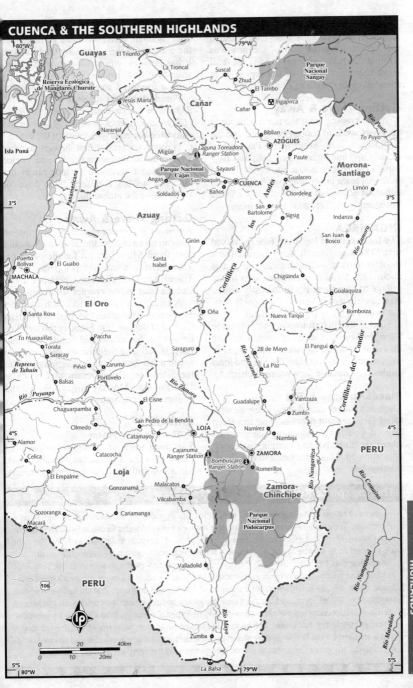

CUENCA & THE SOUTHERN HIGHLANDS

The Inca influence was short lived, however, and the Spanish conquistadors under Pizarro took control by the 1530s. Cuenca was (re)founded relatively late, in 1557. Several other important towns of the region were founded earlier, such as Loja in 1548.

Getting There & Away

If you're coming from the north, Cuenca is six hours south of Riobamba by bus and the first logical stop. From there, Parque Nacional Cajas and Ingapirga are both easy daytrips. Loja is four hours further south, and from this town buses head regularly to Peru, either via Macará or via Vilcabamba and the infrequently used crossing near Zumba.

INGAPIRCA

The Incan ruins of Ingapirca (see the boxed text 'The Ingapirca Ruins') is Ecuador's most important archaeological site and is about 1km away from the bus stop in the village of Ingapirca. It's most easily visited on a day trip from Cuenca. The weekly market is on Friday in Ingapirca village.

Next to the archaeological site *(admission $6; open 8am-6pm daily)* is a small, on-site **museum**, near the entrance. A few signs in English and French explain the site, and local guides are available for a nominal charge.

Places to Stay & Eat

There is a shelter near the site entrance with toilet facilities and benches. You can sleep there if you have a sleeping bag and mat (there are no beds), and camping is reportedly allowed. This is included in the $6 admission fee.

Inti Huasi *(☎ 290 767; doubles with bath $5)* is a small, clean hotel and restaurant at the entrance to the village, by the bus stop. It has doubles with hot water; rooms with shared bath are cheaper. The owner is Mama Julia, a friendly Cañari woman.

Posada Ingapirca *(Cuenca ☎ 07-831 120, 838 508; e santa@etapaonline.net.ec; Cordóva at Borrero; singles/doubles $37/43)* is an old converted hacienda with views of the site and cozy rooms with private hot showers, minibar and heater. Its restaurant is a favorite choice for some tour groups; it's a little pricey but OK. The building is a steep 500m drive (or walk) above the archaeological site.

Getting There & Away

Agencies in Cuenca organize day trips, or you can rent a taxi for the day, which should cost about $40 – bargain for the best rate. Tours start at about $35 per person – see Travel Agencies & Tour Operators under Cuenca later in this chapter for details.

A cheaper option is to catch a direct Transportes Cañar bus ($2, two hours) from Cuenca at 9am or 1pm Monday through Friday, or on Saturdays and Sundays at 9am only. If you take the morning bus, you can spend a few hours at the ruins and return in the afternoon. Buses return to Cuenca at 1pm and 4pm Monday through Friday and at 9am and 1pm Saturday and Sunday.

CAÑAR
☎ 07 • elevation 3104m

The small town of Cañar, 66km north of Cuenca on the Ecuadorian Panamericana, has a colorful local market every Sunday,

---

The Ingapirca Ruins

Ingapirca (3230m) is the major Inca site in Ecuador, but opinions are mixed about the significance of the ruins. They have never been 'lost,' as were the Inca ruins at Machu Picchu in Peru. The Frenchman Charles-Marie de La Condamine drew accurate plans of Ingapirca as far back as 1739. The ruins are referred to as a fortress, but its garrison – if there was one – must have been quite small.

Archaeologists think that the main structure, an *usnu* (elliptical platform) known as the Temple of the Sun, had religious and ceremonial purposes. This building boasts some of the Inca's finest mortarless stonework, including several of the trapezoidal niches and doorways that are hallmarks of Inca construction. The less-preserved buildings were probably storehouses, and the complex may have been used as a *tambo* (stopping place) for runners carrying imperial messages from Quito to Tomebamba.

Unfortunately, the ruins were well known and lacked protection, so many of the dressed stones that were used for the buildings were stolen over the centuries for use in colonial and modern building projects. Ingapirca's importance is now recognized, and the ruins are officially protected.

which is visited by indigenous Cañari who come down from the remote villages in the surrounding mountains.

Cañari men wear distinctive belts made by an unusual weaving method that gives rise to designs and motifs appearing on both sides of the belt. These may be available in the market – they are also woven by the local prisoners and if you head down to the jail, you will be allowed in to make purchases.

Hostal Ingapirca (☎ 235 201; Calle Sucre at 5 de Junio; singles/doubles $4/6) has decent rooms with TV; most of them have shared baths and all the showers are hot.

Residencial Monica is on the corner of the main plaza and charges a little less than Hostal Ingapirca.

If these are all full, you can find accommodations in unsigned private houses – ask around.

There are adequate simple restaurants serving standard Ecuadorian fare. There are frequent buses to Cañar from Cuenca's bus terminal (around $1, 1½ hours).

AZOGUES
☎ 07 • pop 33,321

This bustling town is the capital of Cañar Province and an important producer of panama hats, although these are finished and sold in Cuenca. Saturday is market day. Azogues lies about 35km north of Cuenca on the Ecuadorian Panamericana.

The Pacifictel and post office are on the main plaza.

Things to See & Do
The **Church of San Francisco** dominates the town from a hill to the southeast, reached by a half-hour climb or a short taxi ride. The original church dates from colonial times, but it was completely rebuilt in the 1940s, and only parts of the altar retain the colonial style. Outside, sweeping views of the town and the surrounding countryside make the climb worthwhile. The building is sometimes illuminated at night – sitting on the dark hill, it looks almost as if it were floating in mid-air. Part of the Saturday market is held below the church.

Biblián, a village 9km north of Azogues on the Ecuadorian Panamericana, is the home of **Santuario de la Virgen del Rocío** (Sanctuary of the Virgin of the Dew). This church is highly visible to the east of the main highway on a steep hill dominating Biblián and looks more like a fairy-tale princess's palace than it does a church.

It was originally a small colonial shrine built into a cliff, but in the 1940s, it was enlarged into a church with the altar built into the rock where the shrine was. There is a huge pilgrimage here on September 8 (see Special Events under Loja later in this chapter) and a lesser one on Good Friday.

Places to Stay & Eat
Hotel Santa María (☎ 241 883; cnr Serrano & Emilio Abad; singles/doubles $8/12), near the main plaza, is clean and has rooms with private hot showers.

Hotel Chicago (☎ 241 040; 3 de Noviembre & 24 de Mayo; rooms per person $4) is OK. Its restaurant has good, cheap set lunches and is one of the best in town.

Hostal Rivera (☎ 248 113, fax 244 275; 24 de Mayo & 10 de Agosto; singles/doubles $13/20) is the best hotel. It has a restaurant and 24 clean rooms with TV, telephone and private hot shower.

Several other inexpensive places to eat are found in town.

Getting There & Away
The main bus-stop area is just off the Ecuadorian Panamericana, which is renamed 24 de Mayo as it goes through Azogues. There are many daily departures for Quito, Guayaquil and Machala from here; for other destinations, it's best to go to Cuenca and change buses.

For buses to Cañar, it may be best to stand on the highway outside the bus plaza and wait for one to come by – often, Cuenca–Cañar buses don't pull into the bus plaza.

For Cuenca, there is a local bus terminal on Rivera about three blocks south of the main market. Buses for Cuenca leave as soon as they are full – several times an hour from dawn until about 7pm. Later on, you can catch buses to Cuenca by waiting on the Panamericana outside the main bus plaza. The fare to either Cuenca or Cañar should be about $0.50.

CUENCA
☎ 07 • pop 417,000 • elevation 2530m

When it comes to colonial charm, Cuenca arguably reigns supreme in Ecuador. Its narrow cobblestone streets and whitewashed

CUENCA

CUENCA

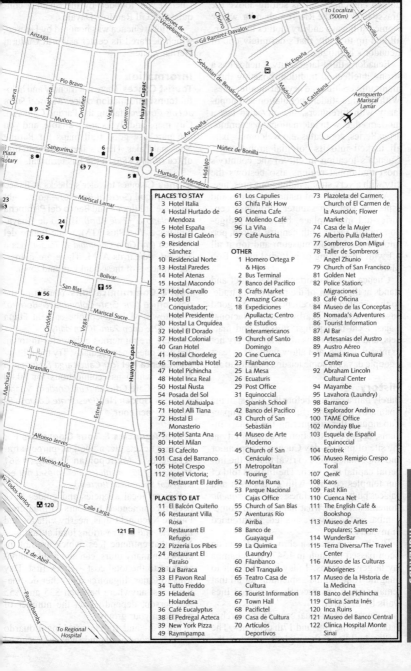

PLACES TO STAY
3 Hotel Italia
4 Hostal Hurtado de Mendoza
5 Hotel España
6 Hostal El Galeón
9 Residencial Sánchez
10 Residencial Norte
13 Hostal Paredes
14 Hotel Atenas
15 Hostal Macondo
21 Hotel Carvallo
27 Hotel El Conquistador; Hotel Presidente
30 Hostal La Orquídea
32 Hotel El Dorado
37 Hostal Colonial
40 Gran Hotel
41 Hostal Chordeleg
46 Tomebamba Hotel
47 Hotel Pichincha
48 Hotel Inca Real
50 Posada del Sol
54 Hotel Ñusta
56 Hotel Atahualpa
71 Hotel Alli Tiana
72 Hostal El Monasterio
75 Hotel Santa Ana
80 Hotel Milan
93 El Cafecito
101 Casa del Barranco
105 Hotel Crespo
112 Hotel Victoria; Restaurant El Jardín

PLACES TO EAT
11 El Balcón Quiteño
16 Restaurant Villa Rosa
17 Restaurant El Refugio
22 Pizzería Los Pibes
24 Restaurant El Paraíso
28 La Barraca
33 El Pavon Real
34 Tutto Freddo
35 Heladería Holandesa
36 Café Eucalyptus
38 El Pedregal Azteca
39 New York Pizza
49 Raymipampa

61 Los Capulíes
63 Chifa Pak How
64 Cinema Cafe
90 Moliendo Café
96 La Viña
97 Café Austria

OTHER
1 Homero Ortega P & Hijos
2 Bus Terminal
7 Banco del Pacífico
8 Crafts Market
12 Amazing Grace
18 Expediciones Apullacta; Centro de Estudios Interamericanos
19 Church of Santo Domingo
20 Cine Cuenca
23 Filanbanco
25 La Mesa
26 Ecuaturis
29 Post Office
31 Equinoccial Spanish School
42 Banco del Pacífico
43 Church of San Sebastián
44 Museo de Arte Moderno
45 Church of San Cenáculo
51 Metropolitan Touring
52 Monta Runa
53 Parque Nacional Cajas Office
55 Church of San Blas
57 Aventuras Río Arriba
58 Banco de Guayaquil
59 La Quimica (Laundry)
60 Filanbanco
62 Del Tranquilo
65 Teatro Casa de Cultura
66 Tourist Information
67 Town Hall
68 Pacifictel
69 Casa de Cultura
70 Artículos Deportivos

73 Plazoleta del Carmen; Church of El Carmen de la Asunción; Flower Market
74 Casa de la Mujer
76 Alberto Pulla (Hatter)
77 Sombreros Don Migui
78 Taller de Sombreros Angel Zhunio
79 Church of San Francisco
81 Golden Net
82 Police Station; Migraciones
83 Café Oficina
84 Museo de las Conceptas
86 Tourist Information
87 Al Bar
88 Artesanías del Austro
89 Austro Aéreo
91 Mamá Kinua Cultural Center
92 Abraham Lincoln Cultural Center
94 Mayambe
95 Lavahora (Laundry)
98 Barranco
99 Explorador Andino
100 TAME Office
102 Monday Blue
103 Esquela de Español Equinoccial
104 Ecotrek
106 Museo Remigio Crespo Toral
107 QenK
108 Kaos
109 Fast Klin
110 Cuenca Net
111 The English Café & Bookshop
113 Museo de Artes Populares; Sampere
114 WunderBar
115 Terra Diversa/The Travel Center
116 Museo de las Culturas Aborígenes
117 Museo de la Historia de la Medicina
118 Banco del Pichincha
119 Clínica Santa Inés
120 Inca Ruins
121 Museo del Banco Central
122 Clínica Hospital Monte Sinai

red-tiled buildings, handsome plazas and domed churches, and its setting above the grassy banks of the Río Tomebamba, where women still wash and dry clothes in the sun, all add up to a city that's definitely one of Ecuador's highlights.

Ecuador's third-largest city, Cuenca has a strong intellectual tradition, boasting three major universities and several smaller ones. With its large student population and popularity with foreigners, the city also has a modern edge, with international restaurants, art galleries, cool cafés and welcoming bars all tucked into its colonial architecture. Cuenca's location in one of the country's most traditional regions also bestows the city with a very strong indigenous presence.

After a breakfast of mandarin crepes and espresso, you can saunter through a centuries-old marketplace, barter for indigenous crafts, visit a 16th-century church, pop into the modern-art museum and top it all off with an evening of butt-shaking to Bob Marley at the bar.

Cuenca is an important crafts outlet and stands at the center of the panama hat trade, so the shopping is excellent. It's also a good base for visiting nearby Parque Nacional Cajas, local hot springs, villages and markets, and the Inca ruins of Ingapirca. Try not to miss the place, and allow yourself at least a couple days for some leisurely exploration.

History

Barely half a century before the arrival of the Spaniards, the powerful Inca tribe Tupac-Yupanqui, after conquering the Cañari Indians, began construction of a major city at the site of present-day Cuenca. Its splendor and importance were to rival that of the imperial capital of Cuzco. The Indians told of sun temples covered with gold sheets and palaces built using the finest skill of *cuzqueño* stonemasons, but what happened to Tomebamba, as the city was called, is shrouded in mystery.

By the time Spanish chronicler Cieza de León passed through in 1547, Tomebamba lay largely in ruins. Today it is difficult to imagine Tomebamba's splendor, for all that remains are a few recently excavated Inca walls by the river.

Cuenca's old colonial center has churches dating from the 16th and 17th centuries. The earliest building is the original cathedral, the construction of which began in 1557, the year Cuenca was founded by the Spanish conquistador Gil Ramírez Dávalos.

In 1999, Cuenca was honored by Unesco, which declared its center a World Cultural Heritage Site.

Information

Tourist Offices There is a friendly and helpful **tourist information office** (*Mariscal Sucre at Luís Cordero*) facing the Parque Calderón. City maps and flyers are available, and you can purchase good trail maps for Parque Nacional Cajas. There's also an **information office** (☎ 843 888) in the bus terminal.

Money Changes traveler's checks at **Banco de Guayaquil** (*Sucre at Borrero*) – go straight up to the 3rd floor – and **Banco del Pichincha** (*cnr Solano & 12 de Abril*). Banco de Guayaquil has a Visa/Plus ATM, while **Banco del Pacífico** (*cnr Gran Colombia & Tarqui*) has a MasterCard/Cirrus ATM. There are numerous branches of these banks around town.

Post & Communications You'll find the **post office** (*cnr Gran Colombia & Borrero*) downtown. Make telephone calls at **Etapa** (*Malo 726; open 7am-10pm daily*).

There are numerous cybercafés in town, and new ones open regularly. Try the following: **Cuenca Net** (*cnr Calle Larga & Hermano Miguel*), which has connections for $0.80 per hour; **Café Oficina** (*Luís Cordero & Jaramillo*); or **Golden Net** (*Presidente Córdova 9-21*) at $1 per hour.

Travel Agencies & Tour Operators For airplane tickets etc, a good all-purpose travel agency is **Metropolitan Touring** (☎ 861 463, 831 185; e *metrocue@impsat.net.ec; Mariscal Sucre near Borrero*).

Several local agencies and guides have been recommended for tours to Ingapirca, Parque Nacional Cajas, nearby villages and markets, and other various local attractions. Note that entrance fees, which are not included in many tours, can add a substantial amount to the total cost – check first. Day trips to Cajas, Ingapirca and other destinations cost anywhere between $35 and $55 per person, depending on the number of people in your group.

English- and Italian-speaking Eduardo Quito is a good local guide who has received several recommendations. Eduardo works with **Ecuaturis** (☎ 823 018; e equito@az.pro.ec; Hermano Miguel 9-56) and can take you to Ingapirca, Cajas or a host of other local destinations.

Expediciones Apullacta (☎ 837 681; Gran Colombia 11-02) also offers day tours to Ingapirca, Cajas and other places. These tours are competitively priced and popular.

Ecotrek (☎ 841 927, 834 677; e ecotrek@az.pro.ec; Calle Larga 7-108) is recommended for trekking, mountaineering (rock and ice) and Amazon travel – especially to the Miazal area, in the southern Oriente. It is run by well-known local adventurer Juan Gabriel Carrasco, who speaks English.

English-speaking naturalist guide Edgar 'Negro' Aguirre, at **Aventuras Río Arriba** (☎ 830 116, fax 840 031; e negro@az.pro.ec; Hermano Miguel 7-14), is another good choice for a variety of tours.

English-speaking **Humberto Chica**, at Cabañas Yanuncay (see Places to Stay, Mid-Range), organizes day trips and overnight tours to Cajas (three days; $100 per person), the southern Oriente (five days; around $250 per person) and other areas. Tours are small and personal and include food, accommodations and transportation.

Terra Diversa/The Travel Center (☎ 823 782; w www.terradiversa.com; Hermano Miguel 4-46) is an alliance between Monta Runa, a company which offers well-received

horse-riding trips, and Biketa, which offers mountain-biking trips. Both cost about $48 per person per day, including guide, transportation, lunch and your bike or horse. They offer two- to four-day horse-riding trips, overnighting in haciendas. The office has a small library, maps to look at, luggage storage and a noticeboard.

Mamá Kinua Cultural Center (see the boxed text 'Mamá Kinua's Cultural Tours') is a company offering some very interesting cultural tours.

Bookstores For second-hand books, check out **The English Café & Bookshop** (Calle Larga near Hermano Miguel), which works mostly by exchange.

Laundry For same-day laundry service, take your clothes to **Lavahora** (☎ 823 042; Honorato Vásquez 6-76; open 9am-1pm & 3pm-6:30pm Mon-Sat) where up to 5kg costs $3 to wash, or **Fast Klín** (Hermano Miguel 4-21; open 8am-7pm Mon-Sat) which charges $1 per kilo.

Medical Services Of the several hospitals and clinics, **Clínica Santa Inés** (☎ 817 888; Daniel Córdova 2-113) has had several recommendations. **Clínica Hospital Monte Sinai** (☎ 885 595; Miguel Cordero 6-111) is also well recommended. These clinics have some English-speaking staff.

Mamá Kinua's Cultural Tours

Mamá Kinua Cultural Center (Jaramillo 6-35; open 9am-7pm Mon-Fri, 9am-2pm Sat) is a Quechua-run café, bookstore, gift shop, cultural center and community-tourist project all rolled into one. Not only can you get some of the best, healthiest, down-home Quechua cooking around, but you can set yourself up on one of Cuenca's most interesting tours.

Two Saturdays each month, the center offers guided visits to a Cañari-Quechua village outside of Cuenca. The locals throw a large, traditional pampa mesa (community feast), show crafts and give demonstrations. The price is $20 per person. Every Wednesday, guided horse rides are offered with a guide from the community who explains local traditional forest uses and medicinal plants along the way. The ride costs $30 per person.

The center also has plans to offer short family-stays in indigenous homes, where guests help out with daily chores, eat with the family and learn about life in a small Ecuadorian community.

The best part about these trips is that every penny you spend here goes directly to the Quechua community of Tarqui, about 20km south of Cuenca. The money helps fund a recently built health center and provide economic alternatives to migration (which has been extremely high since the economic crisis in 1999). The health center was created by the international nonprofit Medicos del Mundo (Doctors of the World) and will be managed by the community. Stop by the cultural center for more information (and a bite to eat!).

Emergency If you have an emergency, dial ☎ 911. There is a **police station** (☎ 101, 810 068; Luís Cordero near Presidente Córdova). The migraciones (immigration office) is also here.

Things to See & Do

Río Tomebamba is attractively lined with old colonial buildings, and washerwomen still lay out clothes to dry on its grassy banks. Avenida 3 de Noviembre follows the river's northern bank and makes for a pleasant walk.

Parque Calderón The main plaza, or Parque Calderón, is dominated by the new **Catedral de la Inmaculada Concepción**, with its huge blue domes. It is particularly attractive when illuminated, although the lighting hours are unpredictable. Inside, the marbled interior is rather stark. Construction began in 1885, and the cathedral was supposed to be much taller than it is – an error in design meant that the tall bell towers could not be supported by the building.

Almost unnoticed on the other side of the park is the squat **old cathedral** (also known as El Sagrario), which was renovated for the 1985 visit of Pope John Paul II to Ecuador. Construction of this building began in 1557, the year that Cuenca was founded. In 1739, it was used as a triangulation point by La Condamine's expedition to measure the shape of the earth. It is currently being restored and will reportedly be used for cultural events rather than religious services.

Plaza de San Sebastián Continuing west along Sucre brings you to this plaza, also known as Parque Miguel León. This is a quiet and pleasant park with the interesting 17th-century **Church of San Sebastián** at the north end and the **Museo de Arte Moderno** (see later) at the south end. In 1739, the Frenchman Juan Seniergues, a member of La Condamine's geodesic expedition, was killed in this plaza during a fiesta, apparently because of an affair with a local woman.

Plazoleta del Carmen A block from Parque Calderón, at the corner of Sucre and Aguirre, is this small plaza and the **Church of El Carmen de la Asunción**, founded in 1682. Although the church itself is open infrequently, there is a colorful and attractive daily **flower market** in front of the church –

a pretty sight. Turning left down Aguirre brings you to the 19th-century **San Francisco church and market**, a block away.

Casa de Cultura On the southwest corner of Parque Calderón, the Casa de Cultura (☎ 832 639; open 9am-1pm & 3pm-6:30pm Mon-Fri, 9am-1pm Sat) has a good art gallery with frequently changing exhibits. Most paintings are by local artists and are for sale, but there is absolutely no pressure to buy. In fact, it's sometimes hard to find a salesperson if you happen to see a work that you're seriously interested in. There's also a bookstore of art-oriented books in Spanish.

Churches Four blocks east of Museo de las Conceptas is where colonial Cuenca's boundary used to lie, marked by the **Church and Plaza of San Blas**. Originally built in the late 16th century, the small colonial church has since been replaced by an early 20th-century building. The modern church is one of the city's largest and is the only one in Cuenca built in the form of a Latin cross.

The republican **Church of San Cenáculo** (cnr Bolívar & Montalvo) looks very bare in contrast to the opulent churches of Quito. After San Cenáculo, head north for one block and continue into the center along Gran Colombia, the main handicraft and shopping street in Cuenca. Soon, you pass the **Church of Santo Domingo** (cnr Gran Colombia & Padre Aguirre) on your left, which has some fine carved wooden doors and colonial paintings inside. Although it looks older, the church was built in the early 20th century. In the next few blocks, you pass several stores selling a variety of handicrafts. Parque Calderón is only a block to the south.

Inca Ruins Walking down Calle Larga along the river, you come to some small Inca ruins (Avenida Todos Santos; admission free) beside the Río Tomebamba. There are some fine niches and walls, but most of the stonework was destroyed to build colonial buildings. There are a few explanatory signs in Spanish. On the Calle Larga side of the ruins is a small **museum**, which costs a few cents to visit.

Markets Thursday is the main market day and there's a smaller market on Saturday. There are two main market areas: one around the Church of San Francisco and the other at the Plaza Rotary, by Mariscal Lamar and Hermano Miguel. The San Francisco market is mainly for locals rather than tourists, and craft shoppers will do better to visit the Plaza Rotary market or along Gran Colombia. The markets are lively and interesting and continue on a smaller scale on other days of the week.

Museo del Banco Central This museum (*Calle Larga near Huayna Capac; admission $0.50; open 9am-5pm Mon-Fri, 9am-1pm Sat*), in the southeast part of town near Río Tomebamba, is considered Cuenca's best.

There is a permanent collection of old black-and-white photographs of Cuenca, a small exhibit of ancient musical instruments and the usual small displays of art and archaeology. Its changing exhibits are often very good, and it has occasional slide shows and cultural movies.

The guard at the gate may ask to see your passport.

Behind the museum is an Inca archaeological site, **Pumapungo**.

Museo de Artes Populares This small but worthwhile museum (*☎ 840 919, 829 451; Hermano Miguel 3-23; admission free; open 9:30am-1pm & 2:30pm-6pm Mon-Fri, 10am-1pm Sat*) is run by the Centro Interamericano de Artesanías y Artes Populares (Cidap). There is a small exhibit of traditional native and regional costumes and various handicrafts. There is also a changing exhibition that can feature anything from Chinese porcelains to *cuencano* (from Cuenca) pottery. The museum is below the steps leading down to the river from Hermano Miguel.

Museo Remigio Crespo Toral This museum (*Calle Larga 7-07*), near Borrero, is also known as Museo Municipal, and has been under restoration for some years. The collection contains religious sculptures, colonial furniture and paintings, and a fine selection of Indian artefacts. It was scheduled to reopen in late 2003.

Museo de las Conceptas Considered to be Cuenca's best religious museum, Museo de las Conceptas (*☎ 830 625; Hermano Miguel 6-33; admission $1; open 9am-5pm Tues-Fri, 10am-1pm Sat*) is housed in the Convent of the Immaculate Conception, three blocks up from the river. The museum is in what used to be the old infirmary of the convent, which was founded in 1599. Parts of the building date to the 17th century. The chapel of the infirmary has a display of crucifixes by the noted 19th-century local sculptor Gaspar Sangurima. Other parts of the building display a variety of religious art: paintings, carvings, statuettes, nativity scenes etc.

Museo de Arte Moderno This museum (*☎ 831 027; Mariscal Sucre & Talbot; admission free, donations requested; open 9am-1pm & 3pm-6pm Mon-Fri*) is sometimes open on weekends. There is a small permanent collection and changing shows of (mainly) local artists and sculptors.

Museo de las Culturas Aborígenes This private museum (*☎ 839 181; Calle Larga 5-24; admission $2; open 9am-6pm Mon-Sat*) houses an outstanding collection of about 5000 archaeological pieces representing some 20 pre-Columbian cultures of Ecuador and reaching as far back as 13,000 BC. It easily rivals that of the Banco Central, and a guidebook is provided in several languages so you can read about each exhibit. The layout is very attractive, and there's a small gift shop and bookstore.

Mirador de Turi For a lovely view of Cuenca, take a taxi south of town along Avenida Fray Vicente Solano to the white Church of Turi perched high on a hillside in the southern suburb of Turi. The views are especially splendid on weekend evenings when all of the churches' steeples and domes are lit throughout town. It's about 4km from the center, and a taxi ride should cost you around $3.

Language Courses

Centro de Estudios Interamericanos (*Cedei; ☎ 839 003, 823 452; e info@cedei.org; Gran Colombia 11-02*) is a nonprofit school offering drop-in and/or long-term courses in Spanish, Quechua, Portuguese, Latin American literature and indigenous culture. Students who already speak Spanish can take semester-long internships (for credits) in areas ranging from ethnomusicology to trade export.

Other good language schools include: **Amazing Grace** (*☎ 835 003; Mariscal Lamar*

6-56), especially for advanced students; **Sampere** (☎ 823 960; w www.sampere.com/cuenca; Hermano Miguel 3-43); **Esquela de Español Equinoccial** (☎ 884 353; e ece@cue.satnet.net; Calle Larga near Malo), which is a school also offering salsa-dancing lessons; and the lively **Abraham Lincoln Cultural Center** (☎ 823 898; e rboroto@cena.or.ec; Borrero 5-18).

Most schools charge $5 to $6 per hour for one-to-one classes. Both Cedei and the Abraham Lincoln Cultural Center often have teaching opportunities for native English speakers with a college degree.

Special Events

Cuenca's Independence Day is November 3, which combines with November 1 and 2 (All Saints' Day and All Souls' Day) to form an important vacation period for the city. The markets are in full swing, and there is music, dancing, parades and drinking. Hotel rooms are difficult to find at this time and prices rise. April 12 is the anniversary of the foundation of Cuenca and is similarly celebrated for several days around that date.

Carnaval, as in other parts of Ecuador, is celebrated with boisterous water fights. No one is spared – one author witnessed a whole bucket of water poured from a balcony over an old nun's head! Cuenca seems to be more enamored of these soggy celebrations than the rest of the country; Easter and New Year's are also popular with waterthrowers. Protect your camera gear.

There is a colorful parade on Christmas Eve, starting in the suburbs in late morning and emerging, finally, near the cathedral in the afternoon. It may be held on the Saturday before Christmas. Corpus Christi (usually the ninth Thursday after Easter) is also colorfully celebrated for several days.

Places to Stay

Hotels are pricier in Cuenca than in other cities – try bargaining. Note that the first week in November and mid-April are vacation periods, and hotel rooms are more difficult to find.

Budget Of the several cheap hotels in the market area near Mariscal Lamar and Cueva, **Residencial Norte** (☎ 827 881; Cueva 11-63; rooms per person with shared/private bath

$3/5) is probably the best. The interior is bright yellow and the rooms are unimpressive but large, and there's plenty of hot water. Hotels around here get hectic on market days, but it's an interesting area.

Residencial Sánchez (☎ 831 519; Muñoz 4-32; rooms per person with shared/private bath $4/7) has an odd faux-brick interior and dark rooms with private bath. Rooms with shared bath have windows. It's friendly, but don't expect much.

Hotel Pichincha (☎ 823 868; e karolina7a@hotmail.com; Torres 8-82; rooms per person $4.50) is a big, impersonal 60-room hotel, but it's good value, clean and popular with backpackers. All bathrooms are shared and have hot water.

Hostal El Monasterio (☎ 824 457; Padre Aguirre 7-24; rooms per person with shared/private bath $5/6) is a unique hostal (small, reasonably priced hotel) on the 6th floor of a building across from the San Francisco market. Views from the communal kitchen and eating area are absolutely stunning, and the rooms are comfy and clean. There's lots of travel information around, and the friendly owners plan to expand beyond the dozen or so rooms now available.

Hostal Paredes (☎ 835 674; Luís Cordero 11-29; rooms per person with shared/private bath $4/6) is a friendly place in an early 20th-century building and is reputedly one of Cuenca's oldest hotels. The spacious rooms have colonial-style furniture, and there are many flowers. In rooms that have a private shower, the hot water may be erratic. Beds are saggy but it's a great deal.

Hotel Milan (☎/fax 831 104, 835 351; Presidente Córdova 9-89; rooms per person $8) has friendly staff and good, comfortable rooms with private showers telephone and cable TV. Some rooms have balconies with good views, and there's a pool table and a 4th-floor café serving breakfast (included in the price).

El Cafecito (☎ 832 337; e elcafec@cue.satnet.net; Honorato Vásquez 7-36; dorm beds $4; private rooms with bath per person $7) has a popular restaurant and bar, which are often overflowing, and is a favorite with young international travelers. Behind is a garden, and rooms with shared and private showers. This hotel may be a useful source of travel information, and live music and happy hours (5pm to 7pm) are other attractions.

Hostal Ñusta (☎ 830 862; *Borrero 8-44; rooms per person $9*) is another favorite with backpackers and has about eight oversized rooms sleeping one to six people. Rates include breakfast. Private baths and a TV lounge are featured.

Casa del Barranco (☎ 839 763; *Calle Larga 8-41; rooms per person $9*) is better for its location near the river than it is for its dark rooms, although they're just fine if you don't mind the lack of windows.

Gran Hotel (☎ 831 934, 835 154; *Torres 9-70; singles/doubles $10/14*) is friendly and has rooms with bath and TV. There is a restaurant and an attractive courtyard, although rooms near it can be noisy. Rates include breakfast.

Hostal Macondo (☎ 840 697, 830 836; e *macondo@cedei.org; Tarqui 11-64; singles/doubles with shared bath $11/17, with private bath $16/22*) is attractive and friendly and offers kitchen privileges, a sunny plant-filled courtyard and several indoor sitting areas. A continental breakfast is included in the price, but if you spend a little extra, you can gorge yourself on the cook's knock-out cornmeal pancakes (or other wholesome breakfasts). It's in a converted old house with spacious rooms. Reservations are recommended for the high season. This place is affiliated with Hostelling International.

Between downtown and the bus terminal, **Hostal El Galeón** (☎ 831 827; *Sangurima 2-42; rooms per person $8*), **Hotel España** (☎ 831 351; *Sangurima 1-17; singles/doubles $9/13*) and **Hostal Hurtado de Mendoza** (☎ 831 909; *Huayna Capac & Sangurima; singles/doubles $15/25*) are all clean and have private hot baths and TV.

Mid-Range In a beautifully refurbished colonial building, **Hostal La Orquídea** (☎ 824 511, 835 844; *Borrero 9-31; singles/doubles low season $12/18, high season $19/25, apartments $40-60*) has comfortable, immaculate rooms with cable TV, bathroom, and telephone. One apartment, with a kitchen, sleeps up to eight.

Cabañas Yanuncay (☎ 883 716, ☎/fax 819 681; e *yanuncay@etapa.com.ec; Calle Canton Gualaceo 2-149; rooms per person $12*) offers rooms in a private house or in two cabins in the owner's garden. It's a quiet place just outside downtown, and there are good walks in the area. Rooms have private bath,

and rates include breakfast, kitchen privileges and the use of a sauna and whirlpool. Dinners cost $6 and are made with organic products from the owner's farm. The owner, Humberto, speaks English and German and arranges local tours. The place is just under 3km southwest of the center. Take a taxi or bus (they run frequently) out along Avenida Loja and take the first right after 'Arco de la Luz,' 200m along the river.

Hostal Colonial (☎ 823 793; e *hcolonia@cue.satnet.net; Gran Colombia 10-13; singles/doubles $14/23*) offers cozy modern rooms with bath, cable TV, telephone and a complimentary breakfast. Rooms are a tad musty, but comfortable, and there's a small covered courtyard and a restaurant.

Hotel Atenas (☎ 825 338; *Luis Cordero 11-89; singles/doubles $15/25*) offers 20 spacious, newly remodeled rooms with cable TV and large baths. It's a friendly unassuming place with an attached bar/café.

Hotel Alli Tiana (☎ 831 844, 821 955; *Presidente Córdova & Padre Aguirre; singles/doubles about $16/21*) has modern rooms with TV and telephone. Some rooms have balconies, and the 6th-floor restaurant has excellent views.

Hotel Atahualpa (☎ 831 841, fax 842 345; *Mariscal Sucre 3-50; singles/doubles $15/19*) is friendly and clean and good value. Rates include breakfast.

Hostal Chordeleg (☎ 822 536, ☎/fax 824 611; e *hostalfm@etapa.com.ec; Gran Colombia 11-15; singles/doubles $16/24*) is very attractive and has a decent restaurant and rooms with TV and telephone in a refurbished older building with a nice patio. Rates include breakfast.

Tomebamba Hotel (☎ 823 797, 831 589; *Bolívar 11-19; singles/doubles $20/30*) is a modern hotel, with pleasant, clean rooms that have telephone, TV and minifridge. The rooftop terrace is a draw.

Hotel Santa Ana (☎ 848 138, 847 530; *Presidente Córdova 11-49; singles/doubles $23/46*) is a slick new place with slightly stuffy but spotless rooms. It has a studied business-class feel and an indoor pool, sauna, Jacuzzi and whirlpool. Breakfast is included.

Posada del Sol (☎ 838 695; e *pdelsol@impsat.net.ec; Bolívar 5-03; singles/doubles around $25/32*) is a small hotel in an attractive 18th-century house that features local artwork. Comfortable rooms have telephone and plenty of hot water and rates include continental breakfast; some rooms have balconies. There's a vegetarian restaurant as well. Local tours and transfers can be arranged.

Hotel Italia (☎ 840 060, 842 884; *Avenida España at Huayna Capac; singles/doubles $30/ 37*) on the unattractive traffic circle near the bus terminal, is a very polished little hotel boasting 68 channels of cable TV and room service. It also has a restaurant.

Hotel Inca Real (☎ 823 636; e *incareal@ cue.satnet.net; Torres 8-40; singles/doubles $37/45*) has been charmingly renovated and has cozy carpeted rooms with TV and telephone. Rates include breakfast, and there is a nice restaurant and bar.

Hotel Presidente (☎ 831 979/066/341, fax 824 704; *Gran Colombia 6-59; singles/ doubles about $30/39*) is a well-run, modern hotel with good-sized, very clean rooms, which seem like fair value. Apart from all the usual amenities, it has a 9th-floor bar with a great view of the city.

Hotel Victoria (☎ 827 401, 845 887; *Calle Larga 6-93; singles/doubles $37/43*) is a 23-room hotel in an exquisitely remodeled building overlooking the river. The rooms are immaculate and have white walls and wood finishing. Two suites have giant terraces over the river and everything smells fresh. It also has a cozy, dimly lit bar and an excellent restaurant.

Hotel Carvallo (☎ 832 063; *Gran Colombia 9-52;* e *carvallo@etapaonline.net.ec; singles/ doubles $43/53, suites $80-90*) is a new hotel in a splendidly refurbished, century-old three-story building. The 30 carpeted rooms are all immaculate and have a mini-bar and cable TV. They open on to balconies over an open interior, and some still have their original pressed-tin ceilings. It's quite a place.

Hotel El Conquistador (☎ 831 788, 841 703; w *www.hotelconquistador.com; Gran Colombia 6-65; singles/doubles $43/51*) is a modern, comfortable, five-story hotel with a coffee shop, restaurant and bar. Rates include breakfast, room service is available, and it has a weekend disco.

See also Baños later in this chapter.

Top End The most worthwhile of the top-end hotels is **Hotel Crespo** (☎ 842 571; *Calle Larga 7-93; singles/doubles with river views*

$73/85). It's in a lovely, century-old building overlooking Río Tomebamba. Of the 31 rooms, 12 have lovely river views. The rooms are spacious and have high, molded ceilings, wood-paneled walls and classical furnishings. There's an elegant restaurant and room service, and prices include breakfast.

Hotel El Dorado (☎ 831 390; e *eldorado@ cue.satnet.net; Gran Colombia 7-87; singles/ doubles about $85/98*) is the fanciest hotel downtown. It's modern and has a good restaurant and piano bar with views from the 7th floor. It also has a coffee shop and lobby bar downstairs, a disco and a sauna/exercise room. The 92 rooms are modern and spacious and rates include a buffet breakfast. An airport shuttle is available.

Hotel Oro Verde (☎ 831 200, fax 832 849; e *ecovc@gye.satmet.net; Avenida Ordóñez Lazo; doubles $128, suites $177*) is at the northwestern edge of Cuenca, just over 3km from the city center, and is the most expensive place to stay. It's popular with North Americans (US embassy staff stay here on their jaunts down to Cuenca) and is set in pleasant gardens with a small pool, a little lake with boats and a playground. There's an expensive restaurant with room service, as well as a sauna and exercise room.

Places to Eat

If you're leaving town – or arriving, for that matter – you can eat at the bus terminal, where 24-hour snack bars and daytime restaurants serve adequate food.

Many restaurants close on Sunday. The best hotels have good restaurants that are often among the first to open in the morning.

The coffee shop at Hotel El Conquistador has decent coffee, and the one at El Dorado serves breakfast at 6:30am. Both have top-floor restaurant/bars with good city views.

El Cafecito (*Honorato Vásquez 7-36*), in the hotel of that name, is usually crowded, noisy and fun (see Places to Stay earlier). The food is reasonably priced and tends toward pizza and hamburgers.

Restaurant El Refugio (*Gran Colombia 11-24*) is quite elegant and good value for lunch. It serves Ecuadorian food.

Restaurant El Paraíso (*Ordóñez 10-19*) is an inexpensive vegetarian place where a tasty set lunch is just $1.

El Balcón Quiteño (☎ 824 281; *Sangurima 6-49; mains $2-4; open Mon-Sat*) serves tasty

Ecuadorian food in a bright and plastic environment.

Chifa Pak How (☎ 844 295; *Presidente Córdova 7-72; mains $2-4; open daily*) is among the best of the several *chifas* (Chinese restaurants) in town.

El Pavon Real (☎ 846 678; *Gran Colombia 8-33; mains $2-4*) serves huge, American-style breakfasts, inexpensive but filling lunch specials, and Ecuadorian meat-and-rice dinners.

Moliendo Café (☎ 828 710; *Honorato Vásquez 6-24; light meals $1-2; open 9am-9pm Mon-Sat*) is an excellent little café serving Colombian *antojitos* (appetizers). The *arepa mixta* (a sort of corn pancake smothered with seasoned beans, chicken, peas and beef) is a delicious meal in itself – and you can't beat it for $1.50.

Heladería Holandesa (☎ 831 449; *Malo 9-55; snacks $1-2*) serves up excellent coffee, ice cream, cakes, yogurt and fruit salads.

Tutto Freddo (☎ 840 295; *Malo 9-60; ice cream $1-2; open 8:30am-11pm daily*), across the street from Heladería Holandesa, easily rivals its neighbor for Cuenca's best ice cream – better try them both.

Café Austria (☎ 840 899; *Malo 5-45; $1-3; open 9am-7pm Tues-Sun*) serves Austrian-style cakes and coffee and sandwiches on whole-grain bread.

Cinema Café (☎ 822 446; *Cordero 7-42; light eats $1-3; open 9:30am-9:30pm Mon-Sat, 2pm-9pm Sun*), upstairs in the Casa de Cultura, is named for the movie posters it displays, but it doesn't show films. It's a quiet place for sandwiches, desserts and coffee.

Mamá Kinua Cultural Center (*Jaramillo 6-35; set lunch $1.80; open 9am-7pm Mon-Fri, 9am-2pm Sat*) serves one of the tastiest *almuerzos* (set-lunch menu) around. It's mostly vegetarian, but always wholesome and filling. It's Quechua-run so the food is often typically Quechua (such as quinoa soup and fried yucca). For $1.80, you can't go wrong. It's a cute place inside a bookstore and cultural center (see the boxed text 'Mamá Kinua's Cultural Tours' earlier).

Raymipampa (☎ 834 159; *Malo 8-59; mains $3-5; open 8:30am-11pm Mon-Sat, 9:30am-10pm Sun*), next to the new cathedral, is a good place to hang out. It's very popular with both locals and travelers, who enjoy the large portions, although the service and food get mixed reviews.

Lovers of Italian food will find plenty to choose from.

Pizzería Los Pibes (☎ 826 979; *Gran Colombia 7-66; pizzas $1.50-6*) is a dimly lit pizza joint serving slices and whole pies as well as pastas.

New York Pizza (☎ 842 792, 825 674; *Gran Colombia 10-43; mains $1.50-3.50*) is yet another pizza parlor serving slices, whole pizzas, big empanadas, calzones, and, for good measure, Ecuadorian *chifa* standards such as *chaulafán* (fried rice). They'll deliver, too.

La Viña (☎ 843 434; *Jaramillo 7-79; mains $3-6; open 6pm-midnight Mon-Sat*) is a cozy Italian-owned restaurant serving tasty homemade spaghetti, tortellini, lasagne, gnocchi, risotto, fresh salads and other Italian favorites (avoid the pesto, however, unless you just *love* salt). It's a cool place.

El Pedregal Azteca (☎ 823 652; *Gran Colombia 10-33; mains $5-9; open 6pm-11pm Mon, 12:30pm-3pm & 6pm-11pm Tues- Fri*) serves excellent Mexican food (probably because it's Mexican-run). The portions can be a bit small, however, so fill up on the free corn chips. There's live music on Friday nights.

La Barraca (☎ 842 967, 825 094; *Borrero 9-68; mains $3-8*) is in a pleasant building with a nice atmosphere and serves good, reasonably priced local dishes, as well as rather more expensive international food. It's popular with locals and travelers alike, and board games are provided for entertainment.

Café Eucalyptus (☎ 849 157; *Gran Colombia 9-41; small plates $1-5; open daily*) is in a remodeled old building with two fireplaces, a bar, 30 wines, microbrews and 100 small-plate dishes (international tapas) from around the world – plates such as buffalo wings, Pad Thai, Cuban Mojo, eggplant caviar etc. It hadn't yet opened for business on our visit, but the menu made us drool. The British/American owners know the restaurant business, so it should be good. The bar has Direct TV, too.

Los Capulíes (☎ 832 339; *cnr Presidente Córdova & Borrero; mains $4-6; open noon-midnight daily*) has a pleasant, elegant patio; delicious, reasonably priced, traditional Ecuadorian meals; and live entertainment on weekends. The cantina out back provides after-dinner fun. Tour groups dig the place, so be ready.

Restaurant El Jardín (*Calle Larga 6-93; open noon-3pm & 7pm-11pm daily*), in Hotel Victoria, is reputed to be one of the best in town (see Places to Stay earlier). It's certainly spiffy, and a full meal with tax, tip and a modest wine will cost about $35 to $45 for two. The subdued lighting is either romantic or too dark to read the menu, depending on your mood. The menu tends toward continental and French.

Restaurant Villa Rosa (*☎ 837 944; Gran Colombia 12-22; mains $7-13; open Mon-Fri*) gives El Jardín competition for 'best in town.' It's in a pretty, covered courtyard within a colonial house and serves both local and international dishes, with an emphasis on elegant Ecuadorian dining. It's an excellent place to splurge.

On Gran Colombia, about 1km west off the map, is an area of midpriced restaurants and bars that are popular with more affluent young locals and any travelers who find their way there.

Entertainment

Bars & Discos Cuenca is Ecuador's third-largest city, so you'll always find something to do on the weekend. Midweek, however, the place can be as dead as Pizarro. Discos are open Thursday through Saturday nights and they generally open around 10pm but don't really get moving until around midnight. Bars are generally open nightly, often as early as 5pm.

Mayambe (*Honorato Vásquez 7-46*) is a decent, small *salsoteca* (salsa club) and one of several bars on Honorato Vásquez, near El Cafecito (see Places to Stay earlier). All these bars are small, friendly and popular with travelers. If you really want to salsa, however, you should hit **La Mesa** (*Gran Colombia 3-55*).

Del Tranquilo (*☎ 843 418; Borrero near Mariscal Sucre*) is a fun but tame bar in an old converted house. People go for the live music Thursday through Saturday nights.

WunderBar (*☎ 831 274; Hermano Miguel at Calle Larga*) is a hip, hoppin' hang-out over the river; food is served. Nearby, **QenK** (*Calle Larga*) is good for beer and playing pool. **Monday Blue** (*cnr Calle Larga & Luís Cordero*), two blocks west, is a friendly low-key bar with a young crowd; snacks are served.

Along Presidente Córdova, east of Hermano Miguel, are several popular bars with dance floors. They're all tucked into old buildings in a dark area so they're pretty cool. One favorite is the trendy **Al Bar** (*drink minimum $2*), which has vintage motorcycles on the walls. The table-talk stops after midnight when the music gets loud and the dancing kicks in.

Popular discos include **Cuenca Tropicana** (*☎ 880 693; 10 de Agosto s/n*); the laid-back **Kaos** (*Honorato Vásquez 6-11*), with couches, pool tables and snacks; and **Ego** (*12 de Abril & Unidad Nacional*), which mixes salsa, merengue and Latin rock. None of these places get moving till after midnight. Taxi drivers know them all.

Cinemas Movies cost about $2 per person. Check Cuenca's newspaper *El Mercurio* for cinema listings. **Teatro Casa de Cultura** (*Luís Cordero at Mariscal Sucre*) has movies as does the **Casa de Cultura** (*cnr Mariscal Sucre & Malo*). For Hollywood flicks in English (with Spanish subtitles) the most convenient cinema in Cuenca is **Cine Cuenca** (*Padre Aguirre near Mariscal Lamar*).

Shopping

Hats Cuenca, the center of the panama hat industry, is one of the best places to buy straw hats. The hat tradition here can be roughly divided into two types: hats made for export (panama hats), and hats made for and used by local indigenous people. The main differences are quality, style and name – Ecuadorians don't wear 'panama' hats, they wear *paja toquilla* hats. See the boxed text 'It's Not a Panama, It's a Montecristi!' in the North Coast & Lowlands chapter.

Throughout Azuay and Cañar Provinces you'll see indigenous people, especially the women, wearing white porkpie-style straw hats. Worn every day in the equatorial sun, these hats last up to six or seven years, mainly because they are refurbished by a hatter every couple of years with a white, natural, sulfuric paint that hardens and protects the hat. There are numerous hatters in Cuenca who refurbish these hats. Most of them despise the idea of 'panama hats,' claiming they are an inferior hat (which, unless you purchase a *superfino,* they are), sold to rich gringos who never wear them. Visit one of these hatters (usually gravel-voiced old-timers) and you'll see hundreds of white, sulfur-painted, porkpie straw hats, tagged for their owners and hanging in rows from the ceiling and all over the walls. They usually have a few top-quality hats for sale, too. Most of them can be found around the intersection of Tarqui and Calle Larga.

Alberto Pulla (*Tarqui*), between Presidente Córdova and Calle Larga, Cuenca's most famous hatter, is 70 years old and has been refurbishing hats since he was six. After he shows you the many hats he has for sale, he'll show you all the magazine articles written about him around the world.

Taller de Sombreros Angel Zhunio (*La Condamine at Tarqui*) is a very traditional shop. It takes eight days to refurbish a hat and these guys (all two of them) are sometimes working on hundreds at a time. Ask Señor Zhunio his opinion on panama hats. You can visit his son's shop, Sombreros Don Migui around the corner on Tarqui, which has some excellent *superfinos* for sale.

For big selections of classic panama hats there are several places to visit. The best known (you'll see the flyers everywhere) is **Homero Ortega P & Hijos** (☎ 809 000; w www.homeroortega.com; *Gil Ramirez Davalos*), whose large shop is behind the bus terminal. The company exports around the world and has a huge selection of superior quality men's and women's straw hats.

Barranco (☎ 831 569; *Calle Larga 10-41; open 9am-12:30pm & 1:30pm-6pm Mon-Fri*) has been finishing (bleaching, trimming, blocking and banding) panama hats since the 1950s, and it recently opened its factory to visitors. There's a small museum of the history of panama hats, and someone will walk you through the factory explaining the entire process of finishing hats. There's plenty of pretty hats for sale, although no pressure to buy (but you should tip your guide if you don't).

Artesanías del Austro (☎ 820 058; *cnr Hermano Miguel & Jaramillo*) sells some stylish straw hats in both men's and women's styles.

Remember that panamas are not just for men – not only are 'men's' styles great on women (take a look around at the indigenous women), but there are plenty of women's styles around as well.

Crafts Other crafts of the Cuenca area include *ikat* textiles, which are made with threads that are tie-dyed before weaving; a method dating to pre-Columbian times. Traditional colors are indigo (a deep reddish blue), but red and black have appeared recently. Handmade ceramic tiles, plates, cups and bowls are also popular, as are baskets. Typical *cuencano* baskets are huge and come with lids – few people can manage to take one of them home. Gold and silver-filigreed jewelry from the nearby village of Chordeleg is for sale, as are the usual weavings, carvings and leatherwork of Ecuador.

Wandering down Gran Colombia and the blocks just north of the Parque Calderón will bring you to several good craft stores. The Thursday **market** (*Mariscal Lamar & Hermano Miguel*), is mainly for locals (which means pigs and polyester, fruit and furniture), but there are a few craft stalls. There's a small daily **crafts market** (*cnr Sangurima & Machuca*) where you can pick up wooden spoons, basketry, pottery and gaudy plastic animals.

Casa de la Mujer (☎ 845 854; *Torres 7-33; open 9:30am-1pm & 3pm-6:30pm Mon-Fri, 9pm-3pm Sat*) represents over 100 artisans and vendors whose stalls make for hours of shopping fun.

Outdoor Equipment Good outdoor supplies are hard to find. Above an appliance store, **Artículos Deportivos** (*cnr Presidente Córdova & Malo*), sells butane for stoves and a few other supplies. **Explorador Andino** (☎ 847 320; *cnr Calle Larga & Malo*) sells knives, sleeping pads and bags and is worth a peak.

Getting There & Away

Air The passenger terminal of **Aeropuerto Mariscal Lamar** (*Avenida España*) is conveniently only 2km from the center of town. **TAME** (☎ 862 400) has an airport desk for inbound/outbound flights and another downtown **office** (☎ 843 222; *Malo 5-08*).

TAME has one morning flight a day to and from Guayaquil, Monday to Saturday. On weekdays, it flies twice a day to and from Quito and once a day on weekends.

For flights to Loja, Machala and some coastal cities, fly into Guayaquil and change; for most other cities, change in Quito. **Austro Aéreo** (☎ 832 677, 848 659; *Hermano Miguel 5-42*) has three or four flights a week to Macas and Guayaquil.

Bus About 1.5km from the town center on the way to the airport is the **bus terminal** (*Avenida España*).

There are dozens of different bus companies with offices in the terminal. Some run two or three buses every hour, while others run two or three every week. Buses vary widely in size, speed and comfort.

Buses leave for Guayaquil ($7, 3½ hours via Parque Nacional Cajas; 4½ to five hours via Cañar) many times daily. Buses leave for Machala ($3.60, four hours) about every hour; a few continue to Huaquillas, or you can go to Machala and change.

Buses for Azogues ($0.50, 45 minutes) leave every 15 minutes, many continuing to Cañar (1½ hours) and Alausí ($3, four hours). Buses for El Tambo (7km beyond Cañar) leave every half-hour and get you within 8km of Ingapirca. **Transportes Cañar** (☎ 844 033) has direct buses going to Ingapirca ($2, 2¼ hours) at 9am and 1pm on Monday to Friday and at 9am on Saturday and Sunday.

For Quito ($10, eight to 11 hours), there are buses about every hour; driving time depends on the route and road conditions. There's several departures each day to Riobamba ($5, six hours), Ambato ($7, seven hours) and Latacunga ($8, eight hours).

There are buses every hour from 6am to 10pm via Saraguro continuing to Loja ($6, four hours). For destinations south of Loja, it is best to change bus in Loja.

If you want to go into the southern Oriente, 11 buses a day go to Macas ($7, 10 to 12 hours) and several others to Gualaquiza (eight hours).

Buses to the Gualaceo Sunday market depart from the corner of Avenidas España and Sebastian de Benalcázar, about 100m southwest of the bus terminal. They leave every few minutes on market day and less frequently on weekdays, and take almost an hour. Some buses go from the terminal through Gualaceo to Sígsig.

There is an **information desk** (☎ 843 888) at the terminal where you can ask about other destinations.

Car A good agency for car rental is **Localiza**, which has two branches – one at the **airport** (☎ 803 198/3) and another **office** (☎ 863 902, ☎/fax 860 174; *España 1485*) near Granada (400m northeast of the airport).

Getting Around

Taxis cost about $2 between downtown and the airport.

Downtown, local buses depart from the stop by the flower market on Padre Aguirre. Not all stops are marked, so ask the drivers.

City buses ($0.12) pass the bus terminal frequently and leave from the front of the bus terminal for the center; buses for the terminal leave from the bus stop on Padre Aguirre. Most (but not all) buses are marked 'Terminal;' ask the driver to be sure.

Local buses ($0.12) for Baños leave from Avenida Torres by the San Francisco market. Local buses for Turi, 4km south of the center, go along Avenida Fray Vicente Solano.

AROUND CUENCA
☎ 07

Several local attractions draw both *cuencanos* and foreign visitors to the area surrounding Cuenca. The region offers plenty of outdoor activities – you can store up your energy by lounging in the hot springs or expend it by taking a strenuous backpacking trip into the mountains.

Baños

This is a much smaller version of the Baños described in the Central Highlands chapter. Here you'll find sulfurous hot springs with public pools and restaurants – a popular getaway for *cuencanos*.

The village is about 5km southwest of Cuenca. Take a local bus there, or take a taxi for $2. Use of the thermal pools costs about $0.40; double that for a private bath.

There are a couple of basic *residenciales* (cheap hotels) by the baths, charging about $4 per person for rooms with hot water. **Hostería Durán** (☎ 892 485/6, fax 892 488; w www.hosteriaduran.com; *singles/doubles $37/49*) is a short distance away and is comfortable, with a private thermal swimming pool and hot pools, pleasant gardens, spacious rooms and the best restaurant in the area. Nonguests can use the facilities for $4. Apart from the Durán, there are several simple restaurants in the area serving inexpensive Ecuadorian food.

Parque Nacional Cajas

This 288-sq-km park (*admission $10*) lies about 30km west of Cuenca and is famous for its many beautiful lakes – well over 200

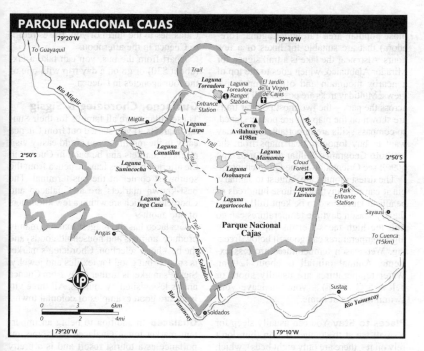

PARQUE NACIONAL CAJAS

have been named, and there are countless smaller ponds, pools and puddles. There are trout in the lakes and fishing is permitted. The terrain is bleak and rough, and the lakes shine like jewels against the harsh countryside. It's rugged hiking and camping country, much of it *páramo* (high Andean grasslands) at around 4000m above sea level. None of the area is above 4500m, so it doesn't normally snow, although the winds and rains can make it very cold. Hikers and campers should be well prepared with warm, windproof gear and plenty of energy. Several readers have written to say that they underestimated the cold weather and had a very cold trip – bring protective clothing!

In sheltered hollows and natural depressions of the terrain, small forests of the *Polylepis* (quenua) tree are seen. This tree grows at the highest altitudes of any tree in the world, and the quenua thickets provide welcome protection from the elements for all kinds of unusual plants and animals. Everything is on a small, tightly packed scale, and forcing your way into one of these dense dwarf forests is like entering a scene from a Grimm fairytale.

Bird-watchers will have a great time looking for the many different species found on the lakes, in the quenua forests and in the surrounding páramo. These are the habitats of such evocatively named birds as the giant conebill, titlike dacnis and gray-breasted mountain toucan. A variety of exotically named hummingbirds can also be seen: the rainbow-bearded thornbill, sapphire-vented puffleg and purple-throated sunangel, just to name a few. Bring binoculars if you have them.

Information The Laguna Toreadora ranger station is on the northern side of Cajas, a few hundred meters from the park entrance. Just a few kilometers before the entrance, on the left, is a park information booth where you pay your entry fee. Many guides will just drive past this booth. You can obtain better information at the ranger station, and they usually have glossy topographical trail maps. You are better off purchasing these maps at the **tourist information office** *(Mariscal Sucre near Malo; Parque Calderón)* in Cuenca before you set out. The maps cost $0.50 each.

There are a number of signed trails in the most popular area (around Laguna Toreadora) that are suitable for hikes of a few hours. Also near the lake is a trail signed for Mirador Ajahuaico, which goes to the top of a nearby mountain and offers impressive views. Multiday treks are possible all the way across the park – the two most popular trails are shown on the map but are poorly signed, so compass skills are important. Hikers may want to buy topographical maps from the **Instituto Geográfico Militar** *(IGM; ☎ 02-254 5090)*; see Orientation in the Quito chapter.

The driest months are August to January, but it can rain anytime – those hundreds of beautiful lakes need to be kept full! During the dry season daytime temperatures can go into the high teens Celsius (up to 70°F); night temperatures can go well below freezing. Wet-season temperatures are less extreme. Annual rainfall is about 1200m. Water temperatures are usually about or below 5°C (40°F) – you can leave your swimming suit at home.

Places to Stay You can usually sleep for a small fee at the ranger station (but don't rely on it – there are only eight beds), which also has a kitchen. Beds have mattresses only, so bring a sleeping bag. Camping is allowed anywhere in the recreation area for $2 per night. The bus passes within a few hundred meters of the ranger station. At Km 25, shortly before the ranger station, there are some cabins that are sometimes closed.

Getting There & Away From Cuenca's bus terminal, **Ejecutivo San Luis** *(☎ 823 230)* buses leave every hour starting at 4am ($2, two hours). There are regular passing buses bound for Cuenca that you should have little trouble flagging down. About 10km before the park, on the right, is El Jardín de la Virgen de Cajas, where the Virgin Mary appeared to a young girl in 1989. There is now a shrine there, and it is a popular picnicking spot with *cuencanos* on weekends.

A southern road passes the park at the villages of Soldados and Angas. This road is in very poor shape, but there are buses on Monday, Wednesday, Friday and Saturday leaving from Del Vado and Loja in Cuenca at 6am.

It is 34km to Soldados and 56km to Angas; the trip takes about four hours. There are small ranger stations but almost no facilities at either of these tiny and remote villages; Cajas lies to the north of you. Buses return to Cuenca in the afternoon.

Apart from the bus, you can take a taxi (about $30) or go on a day trip with one of the tour agencies in Cuenca.

Gualaceo, Chordeleg & Sígsig

These villages are all famous for their Sunday markets. If you started out from Cuenca early in the morning, you could easily visit all three markets and be back in Cuenca in the afternoon. Buses leave Cuenca from the southwest corner of the bus terminal. The best-known markets are at Gualaceo and Chordeleg, which are within a few kilometers of one another.

Gualaceo has the biggest market (mainly produce, animals and household goods) and the best hotel selection. Chordeleg's market is smaller but good for textiles and jewelry. Sígsig's market is further away from Cuenca and is less visited by tourists. All three villages are good examples of colonial towns.

Gualaceo In addition to being an important market town, Gualaceo has some importance as a tourist resort and is a pretty location by Río Gualaceo. It is 25km due east of Cuenca, at about 2370m above sea level. There are several restaurants by the river, and a stroll along the banks is a nice way to spend an afternoon.

The Sunday market is several blocks from the bus terminal. There is also an animal market across the covered bridge, on the east bank of the river. The market is not geared toward tourists (there are very few crafts for sale) but is colorful and fun to visit. Heavy knitted sweaters are a good buy.

There are several places to stay in the town center. **Residencial Gualaceo** *(☎ 255 006; Gran Colombia 3-02; rooms per person with shared/private bath $4/5)* is friendly and sometimes has hot water – it's a basic, reasonably clean, family-run place.

Parador Turístico Gualaceo *(☎ 255 110/126; Gran Colombia; singles/doubles $16/22)*, the best place in the area, is pleasant and about 1km south of town. It's set in attractive gardens with flowers and birds and has a swimming pool and Turkish bath.

Chordeleg This town is 4km or 5km south of Gualaceo and has many stores selling crafts – it is known as a jewelry center throughout Ecuador. Some people complain that it is too 'touristy' and that the quality of the jewelry is lower than in the past. If you're shopping for souvenirs or gifts, you can choose from gold and silver filigree jewelry (by far the most interesting items), as well as a small selection (look hard) of wood carvings, pottery, textiles, panama hats and embroidered clothing.

On the central plaza is a small **museum** (admission free; open 8am-5pm Tues-Sun) that manages to pack more into it than some bigger city museums. There are displays about the history and techniques of many of the local handicrafts. Some of the locally made work is for sale, and guides are available.

There is one basic residencial and several simple restaurants in town.

The tiny village of **San Bartolomé** is between Chordeleg and Sígsig and is famed for its guitar makers and other artisans.

Sígsig A pleasant colonial village, little happens in Sígsig apart from the Sunday market. It is about 25km south of Gualaceo and is the center of a hat-making region. On the outskirts of the village, **Asociación de María Auxiliadora**, in the old hospital, is a hat-making cooperative that sells hats more cheaply than in Cuenca and provides more income for the hat makers. A women's weaving cooperative is also in town. There are a couple of restaurants on the main market plaza, and there is a basic pensión (inexpensive boarding house or place of lodging, often family run), Toral T.

Getting There & Away There are buses from Cuenca leaving regularly with Cooperativa de Transportes Gualaceo and take less than an hour to reach Gualaceo. You can continue the 4km or 5km to Chordeleg on foot or take a local bus. Buses pass the Chordeleg plaza for Sígsig at least once an hour and charge $0.50 for the 40-minute ride. Buses return from Sígsig to Cuenca about every hour for $1.

FROM CUENCA TO MACHALA
☎ 07

About 20km south of Cuenca, the road forks. The Ecuadorian Panamericana heads south to Loja via the towns of Oña and Saraguro. The right fork heads southwest to Machala. This paved road goes through impressive mountain scenery and is well worth doing in daylight. Some 23km from the fork in the Panamericana, you'll pass the small town of **Girón**. As you look down on it from the road, you'll see a neat-looking town of red-tiled roofs interspersed with brightly colored red, blue and green tin roofs. There is a cheap hostal here.

At **Santa Isabel**, 37km beyond Girón, buses may stop for a meal break. There are several restaurants and a basic pensión in this bustling little community. The town is an agricultural center for tropical fruits grown in the area, which is about 1600m above sea level. Banana and papaya plantations are seen interspersed among the cornfields.

Just below Santa Isabel, the scenery changes suddenly and dramatically as the road winds through completely barren mountains with no signs of life. Just as suddenly, a forest of columnar cacti appears, which soon gives way to cloud forest mixed with tropical agriculture.

About 45km beyond Santa Isabel is the town of Pasaje, and 25km further is Machala.

SARAGURO

About 110km south of Cuenca, the road crosses the provincial line into Loja and continues rising and falling through the eerie páramo scenery until it reaches Saraguro, 165km south of Cuenca. This small town is named after the indigenous Saraguro (see the boxed text 'The Saraguro Indians'). Their interesting market day is Sunday, when local Saraguros show up in their traditional black clothing.

There are a few very basic places to stay, none with private bathrooms. Residencial Armigos and Pensión Saraguro are both near the church and are the best places. Local stores or businesses may rent a room – ask around.

There are two or three basic restaurants; the best are Mama Cuchara, on the plaza, and Salón Cristal, behind the church, which serves only lunch.

Loja is 62km to the south, and buses leave Saraguro hourly during the day for the 1½-hour ride. The bus office is a block from the main plaza. Buses also leave for various small villages in the area. For Cuenca, it is best to wait in the plaza for a northbound bus from Loja to pass by.

The Saraguro Indians

The Saraguro originally lived in the Lake Titicaca region of Peru, but they were forced by the Incas to colonize the area around the present-day town of Saraguro. The Saraguro are readily identifiable by their traditional dress. Both men and women (but especially the women) wear flat white felt hats with wide brims. The men sport a single ponytail and wear a black poncho, but perhaps the most unusual part of their attire is their knee-length black or navy-blue shorts that are sometimes covered with a small white apron. They often carry double shoulder bags, with one pouch in front and one behind. The women wear heavy, pleated black skirts and shawls fastened with ornate silver pins called *tupus*, which are highly prized and often passed down from mother to daughter as family heirlooms.

The Saraguro were well known for their jewelry, but this craft is dying out. Today, cattle-raising is their main occupation, and the people can be seen on foot driving their herds to tropical pastures in the 28 de Mayo area. They are the most successful Indian group of the southern Ecuadorian highlands.

LOJA
☎ 07 • pop 160,300 • elevation 2100m

From Saraguro, the road drops steadily to Loja, whose elevation and proximity to the Oriente gives the town a pleasant, temperate climate. Although the town itself is not particularly exciting, it's definitely attractive, and travelers on their way to Peru via the border town of Macará find this a convenient place to stop. Loja is also the departure point for visiting Vilcabamba to the south, Zamora to the east and the beautiful Parque Nacional Podocarpus nearby.

The highland route to Peru through Loja and Macará is slower and rougher, but more scenic than the more traveled route through the towns of Machala and Huaquillas.

Loja was founded by the Spanish captain Alonso de Mercadillo on December 8, 1548, meaning it's one of the oldest towns in Ecuador. Although few of its original buildings survive, the city has some lovely 18th century architecture.

Loja is both an important provincial capital and a college town, with two universities, a music conservatory and a law school.

Information

The **municipal tourist office** (*☎ 570 407; cnr Bolívar & Eguiguren*) is below the town hall across from the Parque Central. There is another, quite helpful tourist information office in the **Almacen Turístico Artesanal** (*☎ 584 219; Bolívar near 10 de Agosto*). The **Ministero del Medio Ambiente** (*☎ 585 421, 571 534; e podocam@impsat.net.ec; Sucre 4-35*) is responsible for administering Parque Nacional Podocarpus and provides information and simple maps.

There is a **Peruvian consulate** (*☎ 571 668, 579 068; Sucre 10-56; open 8:30am-5pm Mon-Fri*) in town.

Banks change money until 1pm or 2pm. **Banco de Guayaquil** (*Eguiguren*) changes traveler's checks and has an ATM. If you are arriving from Peru, get rid of Peruvian currency at the border, as rates are poor in Loja.

There is a **post office** (*cnr Colón & Sucre; open 8am-noon & 2pm-6pm Mon-Fri*). The **Pacifictel** (*Eguiguren*) is a block east of Parque Central; there's also a **branch** (*18 de Noviembre*) across from Hotel Metropolitan.

Internet connections are available at **Jungle Net** (*☎ 575 212; Riofrío 13-64*) for $1 per hour; **Cyber Cenaltec** (*18 de Noviembre 10-44*) at $1.20 per hour; and **World Net** (*Colón 14-69*) also $1.20 per hour.

Hidaltur (*☎ 571 031; e fhidalgo@loja.telco net.net; 10 de Agosto 11-67*) is recommended for international travel services (especially for flights to and within Peru).

Biotours (*☎/fax 578 398, 579 387; e bio tours@loja.telconet.net; 10 de Agosto 10-52*) does day trips to Parque Nacional Podocarpus starting at $35 per person (minimum of two), including lunch. It also arranges overnight camping trips and bird-watching excursions with experienced guides (Rodrigo Tapia is knowledgeable).

Aratinga Aventuras (*☎ 582 434; Lourdes 14-80*) is another place for bird-watching tours and guides; it's more down-to-earth than the others.

There's a **hospital** (*☎ 570 540; Samaniego & San Juan de Diós*) and also a **Red Cross ambulance** (*☎ 570 200*). **Clínica San Agustín** (*☎ 570 314; 18 de Noviembre & Azuay*) also has a good reputation.

The **police** (☎ 573 600) and *migraciones* are on Argentina near Bolivia, southwest of the center.

Things to See & Do

For most of the year, Loja is a quiet but pleasing provincial town with little to do except walk around and enjoy the atmosphere and traditional architecture. There's a weekly **market** on Sunday, but Saturday and Monday also seem to be busy market days. The Plaza de la Independencia is one of several places where market activities go on.

Downtown In the center, both the **cathedral** *(Parque Central)* and the **Church of Santo Domingo** *(Bolívar and Rocafuerte)* have interesting painted interiors and elaborate

statues. Santo Domingo is on a pretty, traditional little plaza. Also found on Parque Central are government buildings and the **Museo del Banco Central** *(10 de Agosto; admission $0.25; open 9am-4pm Mon-Fri)*, which has a small archaeological collection. **Plaza San Francisco** *(Bolívar & Colón)* has a statue of the city's founder on his horse that is attractively framed by the trees. Nearby, the **Casa de la Cultura** *(Colón)* has occasional art shows and cultural events.

Be sure to walk over to the **Plaza de la Independencia** *(Alonso de Mercadillo & Valdivieso)*, where the citizens of Loja gathered on November 18, 1820 to declare their independence from Spain. It's a lovely plaza, that's flanked by old, wooden, colonial-era buildings with pillared overhangs and little

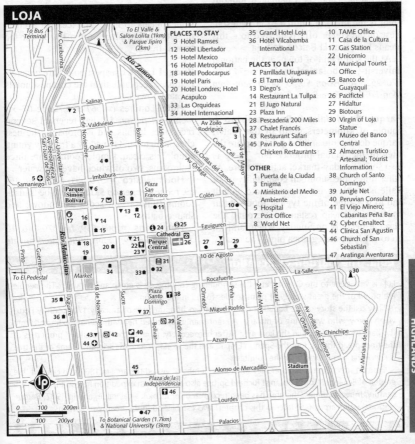

LOJA

PLACES TO STAY
9 Hotel Ramses
12 Hotel Libertador
15 Hotel Mexico
16 Hotel Metropolitan
18 Hotel Podocarpus
19 Hotel Paris
20 Hotel Londres; Hotel Acapulco
33 Las Orquideas
34 Hotel Internacional
35 Grand Hotel Loja
36 Hotel Vilcabamba International

PLACES TO EAT
2 Parrillada Uruguayas
6 El Tamal Lojano
13 Diego's
14 Restaurant La Tullpa
21 El Jugo Natural
23 Plaza Inn
28 Pescadería 200 Miles
37 Chalet Francés
43 Restaurant Safari
45 Pavi Pollo & Other Chicken Restaurants

OTHER
1 Puerta de la Ciudad
3 Enigma
4 Ministerio del Medio Ambiente
5 Hospital
7 Post Office
8 World Net
10 TAME Office
11 Casa de la Cultura
17 Gas Station
22 Unicornio
24 Municipal Tourist Office
25 Banco de Guayaquil
26 Pacifictel
27 Hidaltur
29 Biotours
30 Virgin of Loja Statue
31 Museo del Banco Central
32 Almacen Turístico Artesanal; Tourist Information
38 Church of Santo Domingo
39 Jungle Net
40 Peruvian Consulate
41 El Viejo Minero; Cabanitas Peña Bar
42 Cyber Cenaltect
44 Clínica San Agustín
46 Church of San Sebastián
47 Aratinga Aventuras

shuttered balconies. On the plaza's southern side stands the wooden, baby-blue and white **Church of San Sebastián**, resembling something off a movie set. There's also an incongruous 32m-high clock tower. Walk south of the plaza and hang a right on narrow **Lourdes**, the best preserved and oldest colonial street in Loja. The block was restored about five years ago and its single-story adobe buildings have walls nearly a meter thick. Artisans and art galleries are slowly moving in.

Outside of Town For a short but pleasant walk, head east from the center on Rocafuerte and cross Río Zamora. From there, climb the small hill to see the statue of the **Virgin of Loja**, which is protected by a caged (stone) lion. There is a damaged **lookout** with good city views. Another good lookout point is the hill and **Church of El Pedestal**, west of the center off 10 de Agosto – this area is known as **El Balcón de Loja**.

At the south end of town, at the national university, is a **botanical garden** (*☎ 571 841, 570 252; admission $0.50; open 9am-4pm Mon-Fri, 1pm-5pm Sat & Sun*).

Parque de El Valle & Parque Jiripo A couple of kilometers north of the center, Parque de El Valle and Parque Jipiro are the sites of the annual produce fair. There is also some Sunday-market activity there. At other times, the suburban community of El Valle is worth a visit to see the old church and to try some of the typical food sold in *comedores* (cheap restaurants) around the plaza, especially on Sunday, when families go to eat *cuy* (roast guinea pig). The nearby

Parque de Jipiro has a small lake with a miniature island adorned by a white statue of a larger-than-life Venus. This island is sometimes the scene of symphony performances. Boats can be rented.

Special Events

El Día de La Virgen del Cisne (see the boxed text 'La Virgen del Cisne', later in this chapter) is celebrated in Loja on September 8 with huge processions.

An important fiesta celebrating the independence of Loja takes place on November 18. Festivities may go on for a week, featuring parades and cultural events. The feast of San Sebastián, which coincides with the foundation of Loja, is celebrated annually on December 8.

Places to Stay

Loja appears to have an excess of accommodations, but places often fill up for the annual fiesta.

Budget Loja's cheapest hotels are generally more acceptable than the cheapest hotels in many towns.

Hotel Londres (*☎ 561 936; Sucre 07-51; rooms per person $4*) has received several recommendations and is probably the best cheapie in town. Owned by a friendly young couple, its clean, simple rooms share three bathrooms, two of which have hot water.

Hotel Mexico (*☎ 570 581; Eguiguren 15-89; rooms per person $3*) has hard beds, dark rooms (unless you score a window) and shared baths.

Hotel Paris (*☎ 561 639, fax 570 146; 10 de Agosto 16-49; rooms with shared/private*

Loja: The Garden of Ecuador

Loja is very close to the Oriente, and the surrounding countryside is green and pleasant. The people are proud of the great variety of plant species found in the region.

They tell the story of the beautiful Countess of Cinchón, the wife of an early 17th-century Peruvian viceroy, who was dying of malaria. A Franciscan monk cured her with quinine extracted from the bark of a tree found in the Loja area. After her recovery, fame of the 'miraculous' properties of the tree spread throughout the Spanish Empire and the world. Today, the scientific name of the tree is *Cinchona succirubra*, after the countess.

German scientist and explorer Alexander von Humboldt visited the area in 1802 and called it 'the garden of Ecuador.' British botanist Richard Spruce also mounted an expedition here in the mid-19th century. In recent times, the area has been recognized for its biological value, and in 1982, Parque Nacional Podocarpus (see later in this chapter) was established in the nearby mountains.

bath per person $4/7) is friendly and has OK carpeted rooms with private hot bath and cable TV.

Hotel Internacional (☎ *578 486, 583 609; 10 de Agosto 15-28; rooms per person with shared/private bath $5/6)* is friendly and has a restaurant. Rooms have private bath, TV and plenty of hot water.

Hotel Metropolitan (☎ *570 007/244; 18 de Noviembre 6-41; rooms per person $8)* has friendly and chatty management and comfortable wood-floored rooms with private hot shower and cable TV.

Las Orquideas (☎ *587 008; Bolívar 08-59; rooms per person $8)* offers clean, windowless rooms that aren't as cheerful as the flowery lobby might suggest, but it's friendly and just fine.

Mid-Range Close to the river, the **Hotel Vilcabamba International** (☎ *573 393/645, fax 561 483; Aguirre & Riofrío; singles/doubles $20/27)* is a comfortable but aging place. Rooms have TV and telephone and are clean and comfortable but rather worn. Rates include breakfast.

Hotel Acapulco (☎ *570 651; Sucre 07-61; singles/doubles $12/20)* is clean and popular. Smallish but attractive rooms with TV, private bath and hot water include breakfast in the onsite restaurant.

The following hotels all have restaurants.

Hotel Podocarpus (☎/*fax 581 428, 579 776;* [e] *hotelpod@hotmail.com; Eguiguren 16-50; singles/doubles $20/29)* has comfortable, light, spacious (armchairs surrounding a coffee table) but rather stark-looking rooms with cable TV and telephone. The staff are friendly and breakfast is included in the charge – a good deal.

Grand Hotel Loja (☎ *586 600/1;* [e] *ghloja@ impsat.net.ec; Aguirre & Rocafuerte; singles/ doubles $24/32)* is helpful and friendly and has comfortable rooms with a 1970s golden-bedspread feel. Its only drawback is the street noise (although it's worth getting a window). Breakfast is included.

Hotel Ramses (☎ *571 402, 579 868, fax 581 832; Colón 14-31; singles/doubles $20/ 29)* has nice, big carpeted rooms with huge writing desks and lamps, as well as the usual cable TV and telephone. Rates, which include breakfast, are good value.

Hotel Libertador (☎ *560 779, 578 278;* [e] *hli bloja@impsat.net.ec; Colón 14-30; singles/*

doubles $43/55) is Loja's most upscale hotel. Rooms come with the usual amenities, but some beds are a bit saggy (for this price), so choose carefully. Rates include a buffet breakfast. The highlight is the 4th-floor swimming pool with views. The sauna and Jacuzzi may or may not be functioning.

Places to Eat
A local speciality is *cecina* (salty fried pork – like thick lean bacon – served with yucca).

El Tamal Lojano (☎ *582 977; 18 de Noviembre 05-12; mains $0.60-2; open 9am-8pm Mon-Sat)* serves good almuerzos for $2, but the delicious house specialties are: *quimbolitos* (a sweet cake-like corn dumpling wrapped in *achira* leaves); *humitas* (a lightly sweetened corn dumpling with cheese, wrapped in a corn husk); *empanadas de verde* (a plantain pastry stuffed with seasoned chicken); and, of course, *tamales lojanos* (a sort of savory corn dumpling). Try them all!

Chalet Francés (*Miguel Riofrío near Bolívar; mains $5-9; open lunch & dinner Mon-Fri)* is an eccentric little hideaway with delicious, imaginative food served at candlelit tables. The walls are bedecked with antique musical instruments, animal heads and other oddities from the past. It is one of Loja's best.

El Jugo Natural (☎ *575 256; Eguiguren 14-20; $1-2; open 7am-7pm daily)* serves all-natural juices (no water), yogurt shakes, fruit salads and personalized pizzas ($1.25 each). It's a great choice for a fruity breakfast.

Pescadería 200 Miles (☎ *573 563; Peña 07-41; mains $3-4; open 9am-3:30pm daily)* is the place to go for a good, cheap, seafood lunch (with everyone else).

Parrillada Uruguayas (☎ *570 260; Salinas 16-56; mains $4-8; open 5pm-2am daily)* serves whopping portions of delicious grilled meats.

Diego's (☎ *560 245; Colón 14-88; mains $3-6)* is an attractive restaurant with casual outside tables above an interior courtyard (and nicer tables inside). Choose from plates such as garlic chicken, pastas, lasagne and filet mignon. The almuerzos are the restaurant's best deal.

Salon Lolita (☎ *575 603; Salvador Bustamante Celi at Guayaquil, El Valle; mains $3-8; open 11am-11pm daily)* is *the* place for traditional Lojano food. Try the roast *cuy;* they come whole in $8, $10 or $12 sizes. The bigger ones serve two. They also serve a traditional chicken dish called *gallina cuyada* and *cecina*. It's in the neighborhood of El Valle, just below the church, and it's busiest on weekends. Buses signed 'El Valle' leave Parque Bolívar heading north up Avenida Universitaria; ask to get off at the church.

Plaza Inn *(Parque Central)* is a popular fast-food joint for local students, good for beer and *salchipapas* (sausage with fries).

Restaurant Safari *(☎ 577 456; 18 de Noviembre near Miguel Riofrío; mains $2-3)* is cheap and popular with locals. **Restaurant La Tullpa** *(☎ 570 210; 18 de Noviembre 06-36; open 7:45am-9:30pm daily)* is too.

There are numerous grilled-chicken joints along Mercadillo, west of Bolívar where you can pick up a quarter-chicken with fries for about $2. **Pavi Pollo** *(Alonso de Mercadillo 14-99)* is a good one.

The best hotels are also good for meals.

Entertainment

Although Lojanos are known as good singers and guitar players, nightlife in the town is fairly low key.

El Viejo Minero *(Sucre 10-76)* serves drinks and snacks in a rustic, quiet and friendly environment (making leaving extremely difficult). **Cabanitas Peña Bar** *(Sucre 10-92)*, next door, is somewhat raunchier (and livelier) and has dancing on weekends.

Unicornio *(Bolívar; open 3pm-11pm Mon-Sat)*, on the Parque Central, is a dimly lit lounge with big booths and black-vested waiters. Spot it by the black velvet unicorn on the red wall.

Most of the discos are in the neighborhood east of Orillas del Zamora, walking distance from the center. One of the biggest, loudest and busiest is **Enigma** *(Avenida Zoilo Rodríguez near 24 de Mayo; open Wed-Sat)*.

Shopping

Ceramics and other crafts are sold at the **Almacen Turístico Artesanal** *(☎ 584 219; Bolívar near Rocafuerte)*, in an interesting, old balconied building.

Getting There & Away

Loja is served by La Toma airport, in Catamayo (this village is described later in the chapter), some 30km to the west. TAME has a 5:45am flight from Quito ($49) Monday to Saturday, returning from Loja at 7am. Tuesday through Thursday, a flight leaves from Guayaquil ($36) at 8am and returns at 9am. Check with **TAME** *(☎ 570 248; Avenida Ortega near 24 de Mayo; open 8:30am-1pm & 2:30pm-6:30pm Mon-Fri)* at its office on the east side of town. Note that flights in late August and early September are often booked well ahead of time for the fiestas.

Taxi drivers hang out in front of the TAME office and will arrange to pick you up from your hotel to take you to the airport. They charge about $3 per person in a shared cab (four passengers).

Almost all buses leave from the bus terminal. Transportes Loja has the most buses, but there are many other companies.

There are several buses a day to Quito ($12, 14 to 16 hours) and points in between, such as Riobamba and Ambato. There are also several buses a day to Macará, on the Peruvian border (six hours); Guayaquil ($6, nine hours); Machala (seven hours); Zamora ($2, two hours), for access to the southern Oriente; Cuenca ($5, six hours); and other towns en route to these final destinations. Huaquillas, on the main route to Peru, can also be reached by a night bus in about seven or eight hours, thus avoiding having to backtrack to Machala.

Transportes Sur-Oriente has buses to Vilcabamba ($1.30, 1½ hours) once an hour, and Vilcabambaturis runs faster ($1.30, one hour) minibuses every half-hour from 6:15am to 9:15pm. *Taxis colectivos* (shared taxis; $1, 40 minutes) to Vilcabamba are faster and leave from Aguirre, 10 blocks south of Mercadillo. Buses for Catamayo, which is near the airport (45 minutes), leave the bus terminal frequently from 6am to 9pm.

PARQUE NACIONAL PODOCARPUS

Created in 1982, this is Ecuador's southernmost national park *(admission $10)*. Its 1,463 sq km cover a wide range of habitats, with altitudes ranging from over 3600m, in the páramo and lake-covered mountains southeast of Loja, to about 900m, in the rainforests of Zamora in the southern Oriente. In between, the countryside is wild and rugged, and home to many rare animal and plant species.

The biological diversity of the area has been remarked upon by a succession of travelers and explorers through the centuries. Scientists have found a high degree of endemism (species found nowhere else), apparently because the complex topography combines with the junction of Andean and Amazonian weather patterns to cause unique microclimates throughout the park. These areas give rise to many habitats within the park. Up to 90 different tree species have been recorded in just a single hectare – apparently a world record.

Some of the most important plants here include three species of the park's namesake genus, *Podocarpus,* Ecuador's only native conifer. Also of interest is *Cinchona succirubra*, locally called *cascarilla*, from which quinine, the drug that cures malaria, is extracted (see the boxed text 'Loja: The Garden of Ecuador', earlier). Demand for this product has left few cascarillas outside the park.

Animals include the Andean spectacled bear, mountain tapirs, puma, two species of deer and the Andean fox. All of these animals are hard to see but are prized by local poachers. Birds are abundant and include such exotic-sounding species as the lachrymose mountain-tanager, streaked tufted-cheek, superciliaried hemispingus and pearled treerunner.

Despite being a national park, Podocarpus faces huge problems in protecting the varied habitats within its boundaries. Legal boundaries are not respected by local colonists, and logging often occurs within park limits. Cattle and horses are permitted within the park, and poaching and gold mining are ever-present problems.

Podocarpus receives a lot of rainfall, so be prepared for it. October through December are the driest months.

There are two main entrances (which are at the same locations as those of the ranger stations) for the park, and they're both easy to reach. Access to the highland sector of the park is at the Cajanuma park entrance, near Loja. The main entrance to the lowland sector of the park is at the Bombuscaro entrance, near Zamora (see later in this chapter). Another entrance to the lowland sector, at Romerillos, is rarely used. The park entry fee is valid for five days, so you can use the ticket to visit both areas of the park, which is highly recommended, as Zamora is only a beautiful two-hour bus ride away. You can also visit the park on a guided tour (usually by horseback) from the village of Vilcabamba (see later in this chapter).

Highlands Sector

The main entrance to the highland sector is the **Cajanuma** park entrance, about 10km south of Loja. From the entrance, a trail (which you can take by car or on foot) leads 8.5km uphill to the ranger station. Foot trails from the ranger station head into the páramo region to high-altitude lakes where you can camp. There are also shorter trails around the ranger station, which make for pleasant hikes and decent bird-watching. There are few facilities, so you should be entirely self-sufficient, especially if you're heading out for a longer hike. The **ranger station** (overnight fee $3) has bunk beds and a camping area.

To get to Cajanuma, take a Vilcabamba-bound bus from Loja and get off when you see the large sign on the left-hand side of the road. There is no public transportation from the entrance up to the ranger station, although you could hire a taxi from Loja to the station (about $14) and arrange to be picked up at a later time.

For more information on the western and central parts of the park, visit the Ministerio del Medio Ambiente in Loja. Verbal information, and usually a basic map, are available at the park.

Lowlands Sector

The lush tropical forests of Podocarpus' lowlands are fairly easily accessible from Zamora, and it's well worth tripping down here from Loja to see this side of the park. The climate is hot and humid but beautiful, and the rainiest months are March and April.

The main access to this area of the park is the **Bombuscaro** entrance, 8km south of Zamora by a rough road. The easiest way to get there is by taxi from Zamora, which shouldn't cost more than $3, and you can arrange to be picked up at a later time. From the parking area at the end of the road it's a half-hour walk on an uphill trail to the ranger station where you pay the entry fee. The park rangers are friendly and helpful and can suggest places to **camp** (per person $2); there's a basic **refugio** (beds per person $3), but you'll need a sleeping bag. Alternatively, you can stay in hotels and easily visit the park on day trips.

From the Bombuscaro ranger station, there are several short, maintained (but usually very muddy) trails through the forest. One goes to a waterfall. The longest is the 3km Sendero Los Huigerones. Another trail leads to a deep swimming hole (called the *área fotográfico*) on the Río Bombuscaro, but be careful because the current is swift. Longer trails are not maintained, although the rangers might show you where to take lengthier hikes if you can convince them you won't get lost. The bird-watching is excellent.

There's another infrequently used entrance to the park at the tiny village of **Romerillos**, about 25km south of Zamora (not the same road as the one going to Bombuscaro). Because of illegal mining in the area, park rangers only recommend visiting this area with a local guide, as it can be very dangerous accidentally stumbling across a miner's gold claim. A rugged three-day loop trek leaves Romerillos, but is only recommended for the hardy, experienced and properly equipped hiker. Be prepared for lots of mud.

ZAMORA
☎ 07 • pop 16,074 • elevation 970m

Although the pretty town of Zamora is geographically part of the Oriente, it's most easily reached from Loja, and therefore described here. The road from Loja climbs over a 2500m pass and then drops tortuously along the Río Zamora valley to Zamora, which is 970m above sea level. As you descend, the scenery becomes tropical and the vegetation thicker, and you begin seeing strange plants, such as the giant tree fern. There are good views from both sides of the bus. The spectacular 64km journey takes about two hours.

Zamora was first founded by the Spanish in 1549, but the colony soon died out because of Indian attacks. It was refounded in 1800 but remained very small. In 1953, it became the provincial capital when the province of Zamora-Chinchipe was created, although it was still extremely small and isolated. The first vehicle did not arrive in town until 1962.

Saraguro Indians, wearing their trademark black shorts, are sometimes seen in the Zamora area. They arrive there on foot, driving their cattle on the trail from Saraguro, through 28 de Mayo, to the Zamora–Yantzaza road. North of Zamora, Shuar Indians may also be seen, as well as colonists and miners.

Since the rediscovery of gold in Nambija (a few kilometers to the north) a few years ago, Zamora has been experiencing a boom. The sudden influx of miners has strained the resources of the area somewhat, and food costs are relatively high. Although the town is growing, it still retains somewhat of a frontier feel.

Information
Central streets are signed, but few buildings use numbers. There's a **Banco de Loja** *(Diego de Vaca)* bit it won't cash traveler's checks and has no ATM. There is a **Pacifictel** outlet to the northeast *(cnr Amazonas & José Luis Tamayo)* and southeast *(Francisco de Orellana)* of the main plaza and a **post office** *(cnr 24 de Mayo & Sevilla de Oro)* on the southeast corner of the plaza. The covered indoor market is near the bus terminal. The town's police station is on the northwest corner of the main plaza; there is a **hospital** *(Sevilla de Oro)*.

The weather is not too hot – daytime temperatures average about 20°C, and evenings are pleasant (with few insects).

Things to See & Do
Zamora's main attraction is nearby **Parque Nacional Podocarpus** (see earlier). The Bombuscaro entrance is about 8km south of town. A taxi to the entrance costs about $3, and it can return to pick you up at the end of the day. At the park you can swim in the Río Bombuscaro, hike, bird-watch and dazzle yourself with orchids, bromeliads and other lush tropical plant life. Bring rain gear and expect mud. Hotel Maguna (see Places to Stay following) can arrange guides, some of whom speak a bit of English, for about $4 per person (three-person minimum).

Places to Stay
Hotel Zamora *(☎ 605 253; cnr Pio Jaramillo Alvarado & Sevilla de Oro; rooms per person $3)* is basic but clean, and a few rooms are cheerful and breezy, thanks to their little balconies.

Hostal Seyma *(☎ 605 583; 24 de Mayo; rooms per person $3)*, a block northeast of the plaza, is clean and friendly but can be noisy. Baths are shared, and rooms facing the road are quieter than those facing the

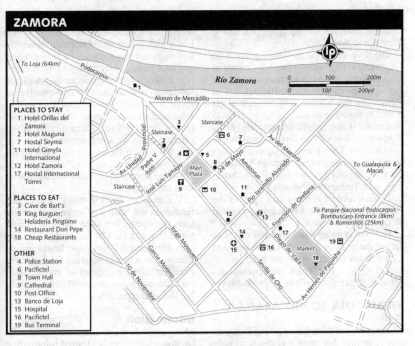

ZAMORA

To Loja (64km)
Podocarpus
Río Zamora
Alonzo de Mercadillo

0   100   200m
0   100   200yd

PLACES TO STAY
1 Hotel Orillas del Zamora
2 Hotel Maguna
7 Hostal Seyma
11 Hotel Gimyfa Internacional
12 Hotel Zamora
17 Hostal Internacional Torres

PLACES TO EAT
3 Cave de Bart's
King Burguer; Heladería Pingüino
14 Restaurant Don Pepe
18 Cheap Restaurants

OTHER
4 Police Station
6 Pacifictel
8 Town Hall
9 Cathedral
10 Post Office
13 Banco de Loja
15 Hospital
16 Pacifictel
19 Bus Terminal

Staircase
Staircase
Staircase
Main Plaza

Provincial
Padre V Isasi
Av Unidad
José Luis Tamayo
Jorge Mosquero
García Moreno
10 de Noviembre
24 de Mayo
Amazonas
Av del Maestro
Pío Jaramillo Alvarado
Francisco de Orellana
Diego de Vaca
Sevilla de Oro
Av Heroes de Paquisha

To Gualaquiza & Macas

To Parque Nacional Podocarpus - Bombuscaro Entrance (8km) & Romerillos (25km)

Market

---

inner courtyard. Neither Zamora or Seyma have hot water.

Hostal Internacional Torres (☎ 605 195; *Francisco de Orellana; rooms per person $5*) offers small rooms with private electric shower, TV, telephone and fan. There is a restaurant, too.

Hotel Maguna (☎ 605 113; *Sevilla de Oro; rooms per person $6*) is friendly and helpful and has 14 basic rooms with private hot baths, TV and fan. Some of the rooms have excellent balcony views of Río Zamora, but the others are not especially appealing. Staff will arrange guides and taxis to the national park. There is a parking area and a garden bar.

Hotel Orillas del Zamora (☎ 605 704, 605 565; *Podocarpus; singles/doubles $12/18*), next to the river, is a spiffy place with four floors of comfortable, modern rooms with private hot-water bath and cable TV. Breakfast is included in the rate, and there's a restaurant and disco.

Hotel Gimyfa Internacional (☎ 606 103; *Diego de Vaca; singles/doubles $8/12*) has modern, comfortable, red-carpeted rooms with private hot showers and TV. Some have city views. There's a small restaurant.

Places to Eat

Most restaurants in Zamora are closed by 8pm, so eat early. The better hotels have decent restaurants.

Restaurant Don Pepe (*Sevilla de Oro; mains $3-6; open daily*) is Zamora's finest (but it's still casual) and serves local specialties such as *ancas de rana* (frog's legs).

Cave de Bart's (*Diego de Vaca; mains $1.50-3; open 10am–midnight daily*) is an ad hoc garden bar-cum-restaurant serving cheap set meals at picnic tables. A few booths are thrown in for good measure. At night it's a mellow place to knock back a few cold ones.

Next to one another on the plaza are King Burguer and Heladería Pingüino. There are several cheap restaurants in and by the bus terminal and market.

Getting There & Away

The bus terminal is at the southeast end of downtown.

Buses leave almost hourly to Loja ($2, two hours) from 3am to 8pm. Pullman Viajeros continues through Loja to Cuenca ($6, 10 hours), departing at 9:45am, 6:15pm and

10:30pm. Transportes Loja has a bus to Quito at 3pm, to Guayaquil at 5pm, and to Machala at 8pm.

The five daily buses heading north to Gualaquiza (five hours) usually originate in Loja and stop at the bus terminal in Zamora. Enough passengers normally get off at Zamora so that it's not very difficult to get a seat to continue north.

Zamora–Chinchipe buses are often *chivas* (open-sided trucks with tiny, uncomfortable bench seats). They provide frequent services to nearby villages as far north as Yantzaza. To visit the wild gold-mining town of Nambija, take Transportes Nambija.

Buses leave at 6:30am and 2pm to the Romerillos entrance of Parque Nacional Podocarpus (two hours).

Buses also go up Río Yacuambi valley as far as the mission town of Guadalupe and (if the rains haven't made the road impassable) on to La Paz. Trucks sometimes continue to the remote village of 28 de Mayo.

FROM LOJA TO VILCABAMBA
☎ 07

The minor road from Loja passing Podocarpus continues due south and drops steadily through green, mountainous scenery to Vilcabamba, some 45km from Loja. En route, you pass through the village of **Malacatos** (elevation 1200m), distinguished by a large church with three blue domes that are visible from a great distance. Malacatos has a Sunday market, and there is a basic hotel and restaurant behind the main plaza.

La Vieja Molina (☎ 673 239; *cabins around $20*) is 2km from the village, on the main road. It has comfortable cabañas with private hot shower (rates listed are for one or two people). The place has attractive gardens, a pool, lawn, sauna, whirlpool and restaurant in an old farmhouse – a popular place for locals to relax on weekend day trips. Reservations can be made at Loja's Hotel Libertador.

VILCABAMBA
☎ 07 • elevation 1500m

People come to Vilcabamba to take a break – an easy task once you're here, considering the tranquility of the village and its stunning mountainous surroundings. The soft and slightly surreal peaks which practically engulf Vilcabamba make for excellent day hikes from town. Furthermore, nearly every other building (and there ain't many of 'em) has a sign out front advertising massages and facials, a trend started by a few hotels and later picked up by the rest of the resident population, a large percentage of which are foreigners who couldn't bring themselves to leave. Most of those who stayed, as well as a handful of locals, now own cafés, offer horse-riding tours or own rustic little hotels offering travelers some serious relaxation. The town also offers access to some of the most biodiverse sections of Podocarpus and is a good stopping point en route to or from Peru via Zumba.

Vilcabamba has for many years been famous as the 'valley of longevity.' Inhabitants supposedly live to be 100 or more, and some claim to be 120 years old. This has been attributed to their simple, hard-working lifestyle, their diet of nonfatty foods and the excellent climate. Scientific investigation has been unable to substantiate these beliefs, but the legend persists.

Information

Most of the town surrounds the main square, where there is a **tourist information office** (*cnr Bolívar & Diego Vaca de la Vega*), a pretty church, **Pacifictel** (*Bolívar; open 7am-10pm daily*), a few simple stores and some basic accommodations. There is a **post office** (*Agua de Hierro*) by the **police station** (☎ 580 896). A block away, **Aventur Net** (*Sucre*) has Internet connections for $3 per hour. There is also a **hospital** (☎ 673 188; *Avenida Eterna Juventud*) in town.

Things to See & Do

Orlando Falco, a trained, English-speaking naturalist guide, can be contacted in his craft shop, Primavera Arts, on the plaza, or at the Rumi-Wilco Ecolodge or Pole House (see Places to Stay later). He is passionate, interesting and experienced, and he leads walking tours to Podocarpus and other areas for about $20 to $35 per person (plus the $10 park fee). Costs depend on the number of people in the group and area visited.

The people at **Cabañas Río Yambala** (**w** www.vilcabamba.cwc.net) have a private reserve, camping gear, horse rental and plenty of hiking and riding opportunities with or without guides. This is an excellent option – see Places to Stay later.

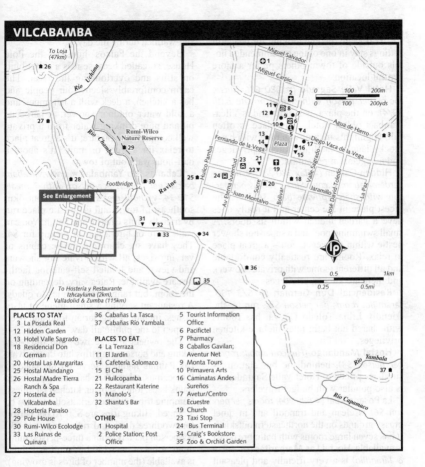

VILCABAMBA

PLACES TO STAY		36	Cabañas La Tasca	5	Tourist Information
3	La Posada Real	37	Cabañas Río Yambala		Office
12	Hidden Garden			6	Pacifictel
13	Hotel Valle Sagrado	**PLACES TO EAT**		7	Pharmacy
18	Residencial Don	4	La Terraza	8	Caballos Gavilan;
	German	11	El Jardin		Aventur Net
20	Hostal Las Margaritas	14	Cafeteria Solomaco	9	Monta Tours
25	Hostal Mandango	15	El Che	10	Primavera Arts
26	Hostal Madre Tierra	21	Huilcopamba	16	Caminatas Andes
	Ranch & Spa	22	Restaurant Katerine		Sureños
27	Hostería de	31	Manolo's	17	Avetur/Centro
	Vilcabamba	32	Shanta's Bar		Ecuestre
28	Hostería Paraíso			19	Church
29	Pole House	**OTHER**		23	Taxi Stop
30	Rumi-Wilco Ecolodge	1	Hospital	24	Bus Terminal
33	Las Ruinas de	2	Police Station; Post	34	Craig's Bookstore
	Quinara		Office	35	Zoo & Orchid Garden

Two- or three-day horse-riding trips are a very popular way of getting into the hills. Tours lasting less than a day go around the village, so the longer ones are recommended. **Caballos Gavilan** (☎ 571 025; e gavilan horse@yahoo.com; Sucre), run by Gavin, a New Zealander who has lived here for years, offers guided three-day treks with overnights in his refuge near the park. **Monta Tours** (☎ 673 186; e solomaco@hotmail.com; Sucre) is run by a Frenchman who also speaks English and Spanish – he has been recommended for horse-riding treks into the mountains with overnights in a simple lodge and big barbeque dinners.

Across from the tourist office, **Avetur/ Centro Ecuestre** (☎ 673 151; Diego Vaca de la Vega) is a cooperative of several local

horse and mule owners offering tours lasting from two hours to three days. The members work together to allow all horse and mule owners to get a fair chance at making money. Most speak only Spanish. This is a good way of helping the local economy.

Several readers and numerous locals have recommended local guide Jorge Mendieta of **Caminatas Andes Sureños** (☎ 673 147; e jorgeluis222@latinmail.com; Parque Central) for his guided hikes. He knows the area well and is especially versed in medicinal plants. A hike with him costs $6 to $15 per person, depending on the length of the walk.

About 1.5km east of town is a small **zoo** (admission $0.50) with local animals, and an excellent collection of orchids.

Places to Stay

Central Many people looking for peaceful settings stay in one of the recommended hotels outside of town; others prefer a more central location.

Hotel Valle Sagrado (☎ 580 686; Sucre; rooms per person with shared/private bath $3/4), on the plaza, is simple and is Vilcabamba's oldest hotel. This place is often full. Highlights include a garden with hammocks, laundry facilities, kitchen privileges and a vegetarian restaurant.

Hidden Garden (☎/fax 580 281; e hidden garden@latinmail.com; Sucre; rooms per person with shared/private bath $6/7) is the nicest place in the center and it really does have a garden hidden within its doors. A small swimming pool and a super-hot shower nestle within the vegetation – a great place to relax. Rooms are rustically comfortable and all different (some with private shower), and there are kitchen privileges.

Residencial Don German (☎ 673 130; Jaramillo; rooms per person $3), run by the friendly Libia Toledo Cueva, has rooms with shared hot bath; rates include kitchen privileges.

Hostal Mandango (Huilco Pamba; rooms per person $3), behind the bus station, is similarly priced to Hotel Valle Sagrado and is also popular with budget travelers.

La Posada Real (☎ 580 904; rooms per person $6) is clean and tranquil and in quiet grassy grounds on the northeastern outskirts. It has seven large rooms with bath; breakfast is available. **Hostal Las Margaritas** (cnr Sucre & Jaramillo) is a very friendly and pleasant guesthouse charging similar prices.

Outside of Town Budget travelers will love the **Rumi-Wilco Ecolodge** (e ofalco ecolodge@yahoo.com; rooms per person $4-4.50) and **Pole House** (doubles/triples $16/18). Both are within the private Rumi-Wilco Nature Reserve, which is owned by naturalist guides Orlando and Alicia Falco, who have many years of local experience and have also guided professionally in the Galápagos and the Amazon. They can also be contacted at Primavera Arts. The ecolodge, near the reserve entrance and a few hundred meters from the Falcos' house, has natural adobe and tile rooms. Three rooms share one bath and a kitchen, another has a private kitchen, and four more up on a hill with nice views also

share a bathroom and kitchen. The water is sun-warmed during the day.

Beyond the Falcos' house is the Pole House, so called because it is a cabin built on stilts and overlooking the river. The cabin comfortably sleeps four people and has a kitchen, a deck with a hammock and a cold-water outdoor shower. A barbecue pit and pure drinking water from a private well complete the picture; it's a great place to relax for a week or more. It's about a half-hour walk out of town.

Cabañas Río Yambala (w www.vilcabam ba.cwc.net; cabins per person with 2 meals $10-14, without meals $5-9) is about 4km southeast of town, and is a rustic place run by friendly Brits Charlie and Sarah. You can walk there or hire a taxi or pickup for $4. They have six charming, rustic cabins of varying sizes, all with private hot showers and views, and limited self-catering facilities are available. Rates vary, depending on the room, but range from singles to quads. A restaurant serving a small menu of tasty dishes, including vegetarian food and beer, is open to the public all day.

The owners arrange two- and three-day hiking and horse-riding trips into their private **Las Palmas** nature reserve on the edge of Podocarpus, where they have a simple lodge (bunk beds, toilet, shower, kitchen facilities). Camping trips into the park itself can also be arranged. Hiking trips are $50/70 per person for two/three days, and riding trips are $30 per person per day, with a three-person minimum. A list of over 150 birds in Las Palmas is available (the number of birds is growing).

Cabañas La Tasca (cabins per person $7), about halfway to Yambala, has five rustic, white-washed, cement cabins with large balconies and hammocks. Three have private baths and two share a bath (all with hot water). The views are good, but be prepared to climb 100m or so to the cabins. Kitchen facilities are available, and it has a recommended restaurant, open to the public until about 7:30pm, with a small but well-prepared menu ranging from $2 sandwiches to $5 French dishes (its specialty). Horse-riding excursions are routinely arranged.

Las Ruinas de Quinara (☎/fax 580 314; e ruinasqui@hotmail.com; dorm beds $7-9, private rooms $10-11) is closer to town, and has a pool, a sauna, a game area, cable TV, tour information, a restaurant and massage services. If anyone steers you here with claims that other hotels are full or dangerous, take the advice with a grain of salt.

Hostería Paraíso (☎ 580 266; *rooms per person $6*) is on the road to Loja, about 1km north of town, and has a charming outdoor pool area, a pyramid-shaped bioenergetic room (remember that this is the 'valley of longevity'), friendly owners, a restaurant/bar and six rooms with warm showers. Rates include breakfast. A sauna and steam room are available for another $2 (open to the public).

Hostería de Vilcabamba (☎ 580 271/72; e *info@vilcabamba.org; singles/doubles $24/34, bungalows around $40*), further out on the Loja road, has a good restaurant, bar, massage services, sauna, Jacuzzi and steam room. The 4.5-hectare grounds feature shaded hammocks, flower gardens and a playground for small children. The 21 rooms and three bungalows are great value.

Hostal Madre Tierra (☎/fax 580 269; e *hmtierra@ecua.net.ec; rooms per person $12-25, cabin doubles $36, cottages per person $20, minimum $80*), a famous and popular place 2km north of town, is a rustic and laid-back hostal that's run by an Ecuadorian/Canadian couple since 1982. Rooms are in a main lodge or in cabins spread over a steep hillside, some reached by long paths (bring a flashlight). Prices include breakfast and dinner (less without dinner), and meals are organic and/or vegetarian. Paying about $25 per person will include massages as well.

The rooms vary in size and comfort; some have shared bathrooms (they all have hot water), and others have private baths and balconies with views. The private cabins are lovely. Local hiking and riding information, a swimming pool with a café/bar, a book exchange, a video room and table games are available at no additional charge.

The full-service spa features clay baths (the clay is changed after every bath), hydromassage, Jacuzzi, contrast steam baths, facials, skin exfoliates, skin-glow treatments, colonic therapy and various massages. Most treatments are about $5 to $10, except for massages, which are about $20 for 1¼ hours. Bus drivers will drop you at the entrance road, which is about a 10-minute walk from town.

Hostería y Restaurante Izhcayluma (e *izhcayluma@yahoo.de; w www.izhcayluma.com; dorm beds $7, rooms with shared/private bath* per person $8/10) is a new place, 2km south of town on the Zumba road. Numerous readers have recommended Izhcayluma for its good value, the friendliness of its young German owners, its excellent restaurant (with sweeping views over the valley) and its 11 comfortable cabañas. There's a bar with a pool table, a garden, a swimming pool and a garden chessboard. All sorts of massage treatments are available. Rates include an American breakfast and use of a mountain bike to ride into town. A taxi from the plaza is $1.50 (or $1 from the bus terminal).

Places to Eat
The hotel eateries at Izhcayluma, La Tasca and Río Yambala are all good.

La Terraza (*cnr Diego Vaca de la Vega & Bolívar; mains $2.50-4*), in town on the northeast corner of the plaza, has a small international menu (Italian, Mexican, Thai) with plenty of vegetarian options. It's good.

El Jardín (*cnr Sucre & Agua de Hierro; mains $3-5; open Wed-Mon*) serves delicious Mexican food (the owner/chef is from Cuernavaca, Mexico) in a lovely garden setting.

El Che (*Bolívar; mains $3-4; open Tues-Sun*) on the plaza is the place to visit for Argentinean food and steaks, pizzas and pastas.

Near the plaza, **Huilcopamba** (*Sucre*) and **Restaurant Katerine** (*Sucre*) are good, small Ecuadorian places.

Cafetería Solomaco (*cnr Sucre & Fernando de la Vega); open 8am-6:30pm daily*), on the plaza, sells loaves of wholegrain bread ($1 each) and does good, healthy breakfasts.

Shanta's Bar (*open noon-3am*), on the road to Río Yambala, serves great trout, pizza and frogs' legs in a laid-back, rustic setting. Be sure to try the house 'snake liquor.' This is also the towns best bar.

On the way out, you'll pass **Manolo's** (*open daily*), a thatched-roof place serving pizzas and sandwiches.

Shopping
The Primavera store, on the north side of the plaza, has lovely T-shirts that are hand-painted by a local artist, as well as a good selection of crafts and souvenirs.

One and a half kilometers east of town is Craig's Bookstore, run by a colorful, friendly, somewhat eccentric American expat; he has a big book exchange, as well as chocolate-chip cookies, local gemstones, homemade jewelry, curios and interesting stories about them.

Getting There & Around

Buses all leave from the tiny **bus terminal** (*cnr Avenida Eterna Juventud & Jaramillo*). Shared taxis depart frequently to Loja ($1, 40 minutes) with five people. There are also buses and minibuses ($1.30, 1½ hours). Several buses a day from Loja continue south to Zumba.

Transportes Mixtos is a cooperative of 15 trucks, which charge $1.50 to $4 for getting to nearby places (most within the $2 range).

Transportes Loja goes three times daily to Piura, Peru ($8, eight hours) via Macará and the driver waits while you get your passport stamped. Transportes Nambija goes to Zumba, on the Peruvian border, at 12:50pm and at midnight.

ZUMBA
☎ 07

The all-weather road continues south of Vilcabamba through the village of Valladolid, which has one basic *pensión*, to the small town of Zumba, about 115km south of Vilcabamba. The drive is through attractive countryside. Zumba, where there is a basic pensión, is about 10km north of the border with Peru. *Ranchera* (truck taxis) can take you to the border at **La Balsa** where you get your exit stamp (or entry stamp if you're coming from Peru), before crossing the river to Peru. Once in Peru, there are *colectivos* to San Ignacio where there are basic places to stay.

CATAMAYO
☎ 07

Loja was founded twice. The first time was in 1546, on what is now Catamayo; the second time was on its present site, two years later. Despite its long history, Catamayo is a totally unremarkable town except for its airport, La Toma, which serves Loja 30km away.

Hotel San Marcos (*rooms per person $4*) on the plaza is basic and quite popular with reasonably clean, large rooms.

Hotel Turista (☎ 677 126), nearby, is similarly priced to Hotel San Marcos and also has some cheaper rooms without a shower. A few other basic places can be found.

Hostería Bellavista (☎ 962 450; *singles/ doubles with bath $12/18*) is 2km or 3km outside of Catamayo to the west. It has a pool, restaurant and bar and can arrange airport transfers or local tours. On Sunday there is a popular buffet lunch featuring local dishes. A taxi from town costs about $1.

There are several simple restaurants on or near the plaza. Dinner on the plaza while watching the center's leisurely activities is usually the best entertainment in town.

The local La Toma airport is about 2km south of town – a taxi will cost about $1. Services are described in Getting There & Away under Loja earlier in this chapter.

Transportes Catamayo, just northeast of the plaza, has frequent buses to and from Loja. Transportes Loja, half-a-block west of the plaza, has numerous buses a day to Machala (six hours), a night bus to Huaquillas, many buses to Guayaquil (nine hours), five a day to Macará and six a day to Quito. Transportes Santa, on the plaza, has a few buses to Quito.

The Panamericana continues west of Loja through Catamayo, Catacocha and on to the Peruvian border at Macará. About 25km west of Catamayo, the road forks. The northwest fork goes to Machala, and the southwest fork goes through Catacocha to the border town of Macará.

EL CISNE & GONZANAMÁ
☎ 07

About 15km west of Catamayo, the Panamericana passes through the village of San Pedro de la Bendita. From here, a road runs north for another 22km to the village of El Cisne, home to the famous Virgin del Cisne (see the boxed text).

About 40km south of Catamayo, Gonzanamá is noted for its weavers and for the production of *alforjas* (saddlebags). You can stay in Residencial Jiménez, which has no hot water. From Gonzanamá, the road continues to the villages of Cariamanga and Sozoranga, which have basic pensiones, before ending in Macará at the border. This road goes through a remote area that is seldom visited by gringos.

CATACOCHA
☎ 07 • elevation 1800m

It's a scenic but bumpy seven-hour ride from Loja to Macará. Catacocha is the halfway

La Virgen del Cisne

This statue, famous throughout Ecuador, is housed in an enormous, Gothic-style church (called El Santuario) surrounded by the unpretentious houses of traditional *campesinos* (peasants).

According to local lore, it was the ancestors of these *campesinos* who made the long and difficult journey to Quito in the late 16th century in search of a fitting religious statue. They returned in 1594 with the carving of La Virgen del Cisne and installed it in a small shrine. Since that time, this icon has been the 'Queen' of the *campesinos*.

The major religious festivals in El Cisne are on May 30 and August 15. After the August festival, thousands of pilgrims from Ecuador and northern Peru carry the statue on their shoulders to Loja (70km away), with many of the pilgrims walking the entire way. The Virgin finally arrives in Loja on August 20, where she is ceremoniously installed in the cathedral. On November 1, the process is repeated in reverse, and the Virgin rests in El Cisne until the following August.

For most of the year, tours and buses make day trips to the village from Loja and Catamayo to see the sanctuary and statue. But on procession days, forget it! You walk like everybody else – the road is so full of pilgrims that vehicles can't get through. This is a very moving religious festival for those who are so inclined.

point on the more frequently used route and is the only place after Catamayo where you can break the journey.

It's a rural village, and on market day (Sunday), it seems as if there are almost as many horses as vehicles in town. From here, the Panamericana drops toward Macará and the Peruvian coast.

There are a few basic hotels and restaurants, all a couple of blocks from the main plaza but in different directions.

MACARÁ
☎ 07 • elevation 450m

From Catacocha, the road continues to drop steadily to Macará at a hot and dusty 450m above sea level. Macará is a small, unimportant town on the Peruvian border. The faster and more convenient coastal route via Huaquillas carries almost 100% of the international traffic. The main advantage to the Macará route is the scenic descent from Loja. There may be police checkpoints on this road, which should be no problem if your passport is in order.

Information
The bank in Macará does not have foreign-exchange facilities. Because of the low volume of border traffic, few people actually change money here. If you ask around, however, you will invariably find someone. There are usually moneychangers hanging out around the market. The town has a Pacifictel office here.

Places to Stay & Eat
Cheap and basic hotels in the town center may have only cold water, but the weather is warm enough that it isn't a great hardship. Afternoon water shortages are common, so plan on a morning wash.

Hotel Guayaquil (*Bolívar*) is over a store between Rengel and Calderón – ask the store owners for rooms.

Hotel Amazonas (*Rengel 418; rooms per person $3*) is poor but it's the cheapest hotel. Rooms are basic but clean and friendly.

Hotel Paraíso (*Veintimilla 553*) and **Hotel Espiga de Oro** (☎ 694 405), by the market, are both better. They both charge about $5 per person.

Hotel Turístico (☎ 694 099; *doubles $12*), on the outskirts of Macará on the way to the border, has simple, clean rooms with private bath and hot water.

There are a few simple restaurants around the intersection of Bolívar and Rengel, most are open only at meal times and have limited menus.

Getting There & Away
Transportes Loja is the main bus company. Buses to Loja ($5, seven hours) leave six times a day, with the last leaving at 3pm. There are morning buses to Guayaquil and to Quito (20 hours). Transportes Cariamanga also has two morning buses to Loja.

For more details about getting to/from Peru, see Land in the Getting There & Away chapter.

The Oriente

El Oriente – the term used by Ecuadorians for all of the Amazon Basin lowlands east of the Andes – is one of Ecuador's most thrilling travel destinations, offering visitors the chance to experience one of the most biodiverse regions on the planet. Once you leave the cloud forests of the eastern Andean foothills, it's all rainforest, home to 50% of Ecuador's mammals, 5% of the earth's plant species and staggeringly prolific bird life. It's a land of forested hills, wetland marshes, big rivers and black-water lagoons, and of exotic animals such as tapirs, manatees, freshwater dolphins, anacondas, caimans, monkeys, sloths, peccaries and jaguars (most of which require luck to spot).

The Oriente is also home to numerous indigenous groups, some of which have had little contact with the outside world until oil exploration in the 1960s brought roads, towns and colonization into areas that were previously accessible only by river travel or light aircraft. Oil exploitation has had an extremely adverse effect on most of these groups, and they continue to struggle for land rights and self-determination. Some have turned to ecotourism as an economic alternative, offering tourists a fascinating blend of intercultural exchange and natural history.

The region is an intriguing mixture of rugged oil towns, pasture lands, conservation struggles, jungle lodges, roving environmentalists, encroaching colonists, tour operators, oil workers, tourists and offbeat characters who, for some reason or another, find themselves making a living in the Ecuadorian jungle. All these things combine and offer the open-eyed visitor a sometimes mind-boggling, but always fascinating, look at the state of one of the earth's greatest rainforests.

North Versus South

The Oriente can be conveniently divided into north and south by the Río Pastaza. The northern Oriente is well connected with the capital and is the most visited part of Ecuador's jungle. It's a combination of sweltering flatlands (from the Coca area north toward Colombia and east to Peru), and slightly cooler upland hills (around Tena, Misahuallí and Puyo). With a long day's travel from the

Highlights

- Experiencing ecotourism at its finest at one of several ecolodges on the Río Napo
- Spotting exotic Amazonian wildlife at the Cuyabeno reserve
- Unwinding in the hot springs of Papallacta, perched on the edge of the Andes and the jungle
- Immersing yourself in Indian cultures through one of several community-based ecotourism projects
- Riding the rapids of Río Misahuallí or upper Río Napo and getting tanked in Tena when you're done
- Visiting a Shuar Indian community in the jungles around Macas
- Staying in the heart of Achuar country at the upscale Kapawi Ecolodge

capital, you can reach Lago Agrio (the access point for Cuyabeno reserve); Coca (the access point for Parque Nacional Yasuní and jungle lodges on the lower Río Napo); the white-water rafting mecca of Tena; or the village of Misahuallí, departure point for jungle lodges on the upper Río Napo. If you're short on time, the northern Oriente is your best bet for a quick look at the Oriente.

The southern Oriente is the least visited part of Ecuador and gives visitors a real sense of remoteness. There's almost no oil drilling

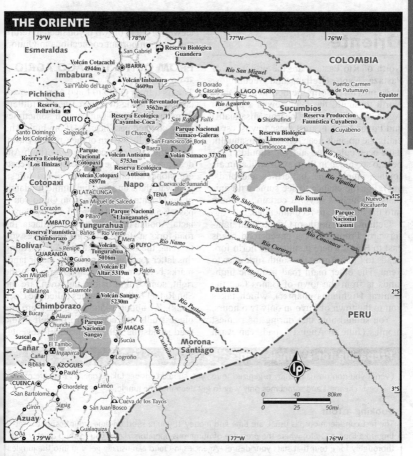

THE ORIENTE

in the region, so there's lots of pristine forest, although mining and cattle are taking their toll. The region's remoteness means its forests are difficult but exciting to explore. To do so, your best bet is to start from the pleasant town of Macas or to visit Kapawi jungle lodge, Ecuador's most isolated lodge.

Visiting the Oriente

Crazy jungle-town bars aside, the main reason to visit the Oriente is to get into the rainforest. Independent travel into the forest, however, is locally discouraged and often impossible. The best way to see the rainforest is by taking an organized tour (see the boxed text 'Preparing for a Jungle Trip') or by staying at a jungle lodge. Jungle tours can be rugged and adventurous,

and can get you deep into the forest where you have a better – although never guaranteed – chance of seeing bigger mammals.

Jungle lodges, on the other hand, are often exquisitely set and generally offer relaxation, comfort, excellent food and daily excursions into the forest. Many lodges have canopy towers, which are by far the best way to see birds and canopy life, and they're usually staffed by multilingual naturalist guides. For details on some of the best lodges, see the Lower Río Napo and Upper Río Napo sections later.

Lodges and tours are both superb ways of experiencing the rainforest, and choosing between the two depends on your interests, needs and pocketbook. Some agencies offer a combination of the two.

The Northern Oriente

North of Río Pastaza are the provinces of Pastaza, Napo, Orellana and Sucumbíos; these provinces form the northern Oriente. North to south, the main towns are Lago Agrio, Coca, Tena (and nearby Misahuallí) and Puyo. Areas nearest these towns, especially the uplands near Tena and Misahuallí, have been colonized and you shouldn't expect to see much in the way of wild animals (plants, amphibians, butterflies and birds, yes). For the chance to see some wild animals – which is never a certainty – tours into the interior are recommended.

Getting to the northern Oriente is straightforward. From Quito, a paved road heads east to Baeza where it splits; the north fork heads to Lago Agrio, the south fork goes to Tena. The other main road from the highlands is from the town of Baños (see the Central Highlands chapter), which takes you to the town of Puyo in only two hours.

You should note that during the rainiest months (June to August), roads can wash out and airports can close. Always allow leeway of a day or two if you need to return and make important connections in Quito.

FROM QUITO TO LAGO AGRIO
☎ 06

The road from Quito to Lago Agrio is spectacular, climbing over the eastern Cordillera from the Valley of Quito via a sometimes snow-covered pass nearly 4100m high. The pass is literally the rim of the Amazon Basin. From the shivering-cold *páramo* (high Andean grasslands), the road descends the eastern slopes through remnant cloud forest, past waterfalls and into the humid lowlands of the Oriente. Two hours from Quito you'll pass Ecuador's best thermal baths, Papallacta. About a half-hour after Papallacta, the road forks at Baeza; the right fork takes you to Tena, the left fork to Lago Agrio. Along this latter road, you'll pass two major landmarks before reaching Lago Agrio. On the right, some 95km before the town, are the San Rafael Falls (sometimes called the Coca Falls). At about 145m high, they are the biggest falls in Ecuador. To the left of the road stands the 3485m Volcán El Reventa-

Preparing for a Jungle Trip

Even if you don't usually enjoy organized tours, you should consider taking one, as they are often the best, cheapest and sometimes only way to get deep into the jungle.

Booking a Tour

The first considerations, as usual, are time and money. If you're short on time, your best bet is setting up a tour in Quito, where the presence of numerous operators allows you to shop quickly and thoroughly for a tour that suits your desires. Agencies in Quito can usually get you into the jungle with only a few days' notice. Once you've booked a tour in Quito, you usually have to make your own way to the town where the tour begins (usually Lago Agrio, Coca, Tena or Misahuallí).

If you have more time, you can sometimes save money (although not a lot) by going directly to Oriente towns such as Coca, Tena or Misahuallí, where you can either hook a last minute deal by joining a departing group that isn't full, or hire a guide directly. One advantage to this approach is that you are often able to meet your guide in person before you slap down your cash. Assembling a group of four or more before hiring a guide will keep the price down.

Types of Tours

Once you've decided where to set up your tour, consider whether you want a trip that emphasizes natural history, intercultural exchange, adventure, wildlife viewing, botany or whatever it is that draws you to the jungle. Different operators emphasize different aspects of the jungle.

Where and how you'll sleep during your tour is another consideration. Sleeping arrangements range from jungle camping to rustic cabins to comfortable lodges. Work the details out carefully beforehand to avoid confusion or disappointment, and thoroughly discuss costs, food, equipment, itinerary and group size before the tour.

dor, which erupted in November 2002 after 26 years of dormancy (see the boxed text 'El Reventador Lives Up to Its Name' later in this chapter). Unfortunately, it's obscured by cloud cover more often than not.

Papallacta
elevation 3300m

The hot springs of Termas de Papallacta are by far the most luxurious, best-kept and probably most scenic thermal baths in Ecuador. The complex, which has over three-dozen pools, is about 3km outside the village of Papallacta itself. It's an excellent place to relax and soak away the aches and pains of a jungle expedition. It's also a good day trip from Quito, only 67km (two hours) away. Sleeping the entire ride back to Quito is hardly a problem.

In the village of Papallacta, there is a slightly cheaper set of baths called Coturpa, although if you're here for the hot springs, you're better off going to Termas de Papallacta, which isn't prohibitively expensive and has far superior services.

Don't forget that at 3300m, Papallacta can get bone-chillingly cold.

Termas de Papallacta About 1.5km before the village, on the left as you approach from Quito, a signed dirt road leads 2km uphill to Termas de Papallacta. The setting is grand: On a clear day, you can see the snow-capped Antisana (5753m) about 15km to the south, and all day every day you can see the green, steep hillsides surrounding the springs. The complex is a comfortable hotel and spa that is popular with upper-class *quiteños* (people from Quito) on weekends. There are two sets of pools: the **Balneario** *(admission $5, free for hotel guests; open 6am-9pm daily)* and the **Spa** *(admission $15; open 6am-9pm daily)*. The *balneario* is simply stunning, with over 25 clean, landscaped pools of varying temperatures, all near the banks of the Río Loreto-Papallacta, which makes for an exhilarating cold plunge. Towels and lockers (both $0.50) are available. There's little reason to spend the extra money on the spa, although it is less crowded (neither are crowded midweek), smaller, has nicer changing facilities and extra sauna facilities. The water in all the pools is changed daily.

If you can afford it, the onsite **Hotel Termas de Papallacta** *(Quito ☎ 02-255 7850,*

Preparing for a Jungle Trip

Guides

One of the most important matters to settle is the guide. A good guide will be able to show you a lot of things you would have missed on your own, whereas an inadequate guide will spoil the trip. Guides should be able to produce a license on request. Find out the guide's specialities and if game will be hunted for the pot. The rainforest is overhunted, and a no-hunting policy is encouraged. Although it's difficult in Quito, try to meet with your guide before you pay.

What to Bring

Most jungle towns only have basic equipment. Bottled water, tarps (for rain) and rubber boots (up to about size 45) are all readily available in the Oriente. Mosquito nets are usually provided in most places that need them. Besides your general travel supplies, essential items for a jungle tour are:

- **insect repellent** Preferably with around 30% DEET
- **sunblock**
- **malaria pills** For more information about malaria see Health in the Facts for the Visitor chapter
- **rain jacket**
- **water-purification tablets** Especially for low-budget tours
- **film** Bring ASA 400 film or faster for the jungle's low lighting
- **flashlight and batteries**
- **binoculars**
- **swimsuit**
- **clothing** A shade hat and thin, long-sleeve shirts and pants to keep the mosquitoes off
- **sense of humor** Essential east of the Andes

256 8989; e term@interactive.net.ec; Foch 635 & Reina Victoria; singles/doubles $55/75, 6-person cabins $125) is a real treat, especially midweek when you're likely to have the place practically to yourself. The cabins and rooms are all rustic and comfortable and – best of all – surrounded by steaming-hot outdoor pools open only to hotel guests, 24-hours a day. Soak yourself silly! All accommodations have private baths, heating and thermal hot showers (and tubs). The six-person cabins have a fireplace, toaster-oven, sink and fridge.

There are two **restaurants** (mains $5-8; both open 8am-8pm daily) – one in the hotel and another at the balneario. Both serve good food (especially the trout which is either farmed locally or caught wild in the lakes around Papallacta), but they're a bit overpriced. You can save money by packing your own food from Quito.

Coturpa Thermal Baths These simple thermal baths (☎ 320 640; admission $2; open 7am-5pm Mon-Fri, 6am-6pm Sat & Sun) are in the village of Papallacta. They are clean and often empty midweek, but they're a far cry from Termas de Papallacta. There are four pools. Bring your own towel.

Places to Stay & Eat If you can't afford the hotel at Termas de Papallacta, you can stay (and eat) just outside the complex at **Hostal Antisana** (☎ 320 626; rooms per person $6), which has private cold-water baths (ouch!), plain rooms and saggy beds. It's friendly and has a cheap restaurant, but bring warm clothes if you spend the night.

Hostería La Pampa de Papallacta (☎ 320 624; rooms $20-40) is a little further from the complex and has rooms and rustic, adobe-style cabins. It's slightly disheveled but fine. It also has a good restaurant (with trout on the menu).

La Choza de Don Wilson (☎ 320 627; rooms per person $5), just below the turnoff to Termas de Papallacta, is a good deal for simple rooms with private hot-water baths. The restaurant here is cozy and friendly.

Residencial Viajero (rooms per person $3), in the village of Papallacta, has simple rooms and shared, thermal hot showers.

Getting There & Away Any of the buses from Quito heading toward Baeza, Tena or Lago Agrio can drop you off in Papallacta, as can the occasional Papallacta bus. If you want to go to the Termas de Papallacta complex, make sure that the driver lets you off on the road to the baths, 1.5km before the village. To leave Papallacta, flag down a bus on the main road.

Baeza & Around

Baeza, about a half-hour beyond Papallacta, is on the junction with the road to Tena and is the most important village between Quito and Lago Agrio. It was an old Spanish missionary and trading outpost, first founded in 1548 and refounded three times since. The pass from Baeza to the Quito valley via Papallacta was known well before the conquest, but the road from Baeza to Lago Agrio was only opened up by the oil boom, so Baeza is both a historical and geographical junction. It is also a quiet, inexpensive spot to stay for walks in the surrounding hills. The plants of the Andean foothills and the bird life are outstanding.

Places to Stay & Eat Facilities are very limited. There is a gas station, a basic hotel and a restaurant in the **Oro Negro complex** (☎ 320 016; rooms per person without bath $5) at the junction of the road going to Tena. Most bus drivers stop here to eat.

About 2km from the junction, heading toward Tena, you reach the village of Baeza proper. **Hotel Samay** (☎ 320 170; rooms per person with shared/private bath $3/5), in the center, is basic but clean, and **Hostal San Rafael** (☎ 320 114; rooms per person with shared/private bath $5/6), at the east end (the end toward Tena), is better. The best place in town is the indecisively named **Casa Posada Hostal Bambu's** (☎ 320 219; Nueva Andalucía; rooms per person $10). It's very friendly and its 12 spotless rooms have TV, hot water and private baths. There's table tennis, a pool table and off-street parking to boot.

El Viejo (☎ 320 146; Nueva Andalucía; mains $1.50-4; open 6am-9pm daily) is a good, clean, friendly restaurant – probably the town's best.

About 10km away on the road to Lago Agrio, at the village of **San Francisco de Borja**, is Cabañas Tres Ríos, which is situated across Río Quijos about 750m east of the village. There are eight cabins, each with private hot showers and patios. It caters mainly to kayakers and is often full with kayaking groups from November to February. Contact **Small World Adventures** (☎ 1-800-585-2925; e info@smallworldadventures.com; PO Box 262, Howard, CO 81233, USA) if you want more information.

About 17km south of Baeza on the road to Tena is the village of **Cosanga**, on the outskirts of which is **Cabañas San Isidro** (Quito ☎ 02-246 5578, 254 7403, fax 02-222 8902; Carrión 555, Quito; singles/doubles $91/158). This is an Ecuadorian-owned cattle ranch on the eastern slopes of the Andes at about 2000m. Some of the land has been left undisturbed, there are good hiking trails, and the bird-watching is first class. You can stay here by advance reservation. Rates include meals served by the friendly family who owns the place. Rooms have private baths and hot water.

Getting There & Away There are no bus stations in these villages. You must flag down passing buses and hope that they have room. Buses to and from Lago Agrio, Tena and Quito pass through regularly.

San Rafael Falls

Beyond Baeza, the road continues dropping, following the trans-Ecuadorian oil pipeline and Río Quijos. There are enchanting views of beautiful cloud forest full of strange species of birds and plants. You pass several small communities, and after six hours, you reach Lago Agrio, 170km from Baeza.

On the way, you can glimpse the San Rafael Falls briefly from the road, but to see them properly, you should stop. The falls are quite impressive, and there is great bird-watching in the area. The Andean cock-of-the-rock is one of the more spectacular species regularly seen here.

To reach the falls, get off the bus just before the bridge crossing Río Reventador. You'll see a concrete-block hut on the right side of the road. Make sure you get off at Río Reventador and not at the bigger community of **El Reventador**, which is about 15km away in the direction of Lago Agrio. Most bus drivers know the entrance; ask for *la entrada para la cascada de San Rafael* (the entrance to San Rafael Falls).

From the hut, it's about 2.5km down a steep trail to the falls. Near the top of the trail is the San Rafael Lodge, and beyond the lodge is the trail to the falls. Reportedly you can camp within sight of the falls for $1.50 per person. The rooms at the lodge (which is not always open) have shared bathrooms, and hot water is available when it's turned on.

Back on the main road, flag a bus down when you want to move on, but be prepared to wait, as buses are sometimes full.

Volcán El Reventador

Until this volcano erupted in 2002 (see the boxed text 'El Reventador Lives Up to Its Name'), it was possible to hike to its summit. At the close of this edition, it was reportedly possible to hike partway up, but ascending to the summit was not advised (if not impossible) because of volcanic activity. Parts of the trail have been destroyed. If El Reventador continues to keep its cool (as was the case at the time of research), this trek may again be possible within a year or two. Check with the South American Explorers (SAE) in Quito for current information (see Information in the Quito chapter).

Just north of the bridge crossing Río Reventador, there are a couple of houses, and just north of those, on the northwest side of the road, there is a trail that climbs up Volcán El Reventador. It is hard to find the beginning of the trail, and there are various confusing little paths, so you should ask anyone you see (note that there are very few people around here). After a few minutes, the trail crosses the river, and about half-an-hour later the trail goes through a grove of palm trees. Beyond that, there is only one trail to the summit, but it is steep and slippery in places. There is almost no water, and the climb takes two days – it's only for experienced hikers who have plenty of extra water bottles and camping gear. Technical climbing is not involved, but it's easy to get lost in the lower slopes, so hiring a guide is a good idea. Try Guillermo Vásquez in the community of Pampas, about 3km west of the San Rafael Falls; Edgar Ortiz at Hotel Amazonas in El Reventador; or Lucho Viteri in Baeza.

This area is within the eastern boundaries of **Reserva Ecológica Cayambe-Coca**, which includes **Volcán Cayambe** (for more information see the Northern Highlands chapter). There are no signs or entrance stations. There is reportedly a guard station located in

El Reventador Lives Up to Its Name

On the morning of November 3, 2002, after lying dormant for 26 years, Volcán El Reventador exploded violently back to life. It was a massive explosion, sending a cloud of gas and some one million tons of ash 16km into the sky. The eruption sent pyroclastic flows (flows of hot volcanic ash and rock) down the southwest side of the volcano, which obliterated several bridges, closed the Quito–Lago Agrio road and destroyed part of the incomplete (and therefore empty) OCP heavy-crude pipeline. Although there was almost no warning, human casualties were few.

El Reventador – which appropriately means 'The Exploder' – lies about 60km northeast of Quito, and within hours of the eruption, the capital was covered in a cloud of ash. Visibility was reduced – the airport was closed, schools were shut, and traffic ground nearly to a halt. It was an post-apocalyptic scene as people tried to get home through the thick, gray haze with handkerchiefs and dust masks covering their faces. In some places, the layer of ash on the ground grew to nearly 5cm thick.

President Gustavo Noboa declared a state of emergency in the provinces of Napo, Sucumbíos, Pichincha and Cotopaxi. The hardest hit areas were farm and pasture lands, especially the agricultural region southeast of the volcano.

Four days after the initial eruption, a second major eruption sent a cloud of ash and gasses over 6km into the sky. Another eruption burped a cloud of sulfuric gas which made Quito stink like a combination of sewage and rotten eggs. After November 20, seismic activity subsided drastically.

In the weeks following the eruption, municipal workers in Quito shoveled ash from the airport runway (which soon reopened) and city streets. Residents swept ash from their roof tops and sidewalks, tourists wrote exciting postcards, and things slowly returned to normal. And what happened to all that ash? People shoveled it into bags (burlap sacks lined city streets for months) and the city shipped it to El Oro Province, home of Ecuador's banana plantations – ash makes excellent fertilizer! El Oro paid Quito back with bananas.

At the close of this edition, volcanic activity was very low, and the road from Quito to Lago Agrio had been reopened. There was no immediate threat of another major eruption, but, as anyone in Ecuador will tell you, you can't predict Mother Nature. To stay abreast of El Reventador's activity, check the website of the Instituto Geofísico's **Escuela Politécnica Nacional** (**W** www.igepn.edu.ec), which posts daily updates of Ecuador's most active volcanoes. The South American Explorers (SAE) in Quito can provide information on how to be prepared for an ashfall (see Information in the Quito chapter).

---

the village of **El Chaco**, about 20km beyond the Río Reventador bridge on the way to Baeza. In El Chaco, there are a couple of very basic *residenciales* (cheap hotels).

Bus drivers on the Quito–Lago Agrio run usually know the San Rafael Falls, but few of them know about the Río Reventador bridge or climbing the volcano. So ask about the falls, even if you plan on climbing Reventador.

LAGO AGRIO
☎ 06 • pop 23,874

Lago Agrio is the main departure point for tours into Cuyabeno reserve and Parque Nacional Yasuní. The town's official name is 'Nueva Loja,' because many of the early Ecuadorians who colonized the area came from Loja. But US oil workers working for Texaco nicknamed the town 'Lago Agrio'

after a small oil town in Texas called Sour Lake, and the nickname has stuck. Locals simply call the town 'Lago.' It became the capital of the province of Sucumbíos in 1989.

Although it's the oldest and biggest of Ecuador's oil towns, Lago Agrio is still just an oil town, and an oil town is an oil town is an oil town. It's got its full quota of seedy bars, prostitutes, drunks and questionable characters, but it's also a bustling provincial capital, and the well-lit hotel area is safe. However, do not stray from this area at night. For most travelers, Lago is simply an overnight stop.

Information
There are few street signs and almost no building numbers.

The **Colombian consulate** (☎ 830 084; *Avenida Quito*) is upstairs at this address.

Look for its sign on the 2nd floor. The **post office** (*Rocafuerte*), **Migraciones** (*immigration office; 18 de Noviembre*), **Andinatel** (*cnr Orellana & 18 de Noviembre*) and the **police station** (*Avenida Quito*) are all within walking distance of the hotel area.

Internet service is available at **Interactive** (☎ 830 529; *Río Amazonas*), inside the entrance to Hotel La Cascada, for $3 per hour.

Banco de Guayaquil (*cnr Quito & 12 de Febrero; open 8am-4pm Mon-Fri*) and **Banco del Pichincha** (*12 de Febrero*) both have ATMs. Banco de Guayaquil changes traveler's checks. The many **casas de cambio** (currency-exchange bureaus) on Avenida Quito near Avenida Colombia will change Colombian pesos.

The best medical attention is at **Clínica González** (☎ 830 728, 831 691; *cnr Avenida Quito & 12 de Febrero*).

With an increased pitch in the conflict in neighboring Colombia, border towns such as Lago Agrio have become safe havens for Colombian guerrillas, antirebel paramilitaries and drug smugglers. Bars can be risky and side streets unsafe, so stick to the main drag, especially at night. Tourists rarely have problems.

Things to See & Do

The Sunday morning **market** can be quite interesting when the local Cofan Indians (see Dureno under Along Río Aguarico later this chapter) come into town to buy staples and sell their handicrafts.

Organized Tours

All the Quito-based companies visiting Cuyabeno go through Lago, and most travelers in town have already booked a tour in Quito or elsewhere by the time they arrive. Finding a guide *in* Lago is harder than in most other jungle towns.

Sionatour (☎ 830 232; *12 de Febrero 267*) was founded to promote direct community-based ecotourism in three local Siona indigenous communities: Orahuëayá, Biaña and Puerto Bolívar. These communities are several hours from Lago by road and canoe, and they provide basic lodging with shared cold showers and toilets. Tours are guided by Spanish-speaking Siona natives, and there are opportunities to interact with, learn about and photograph villagers, as well as explore the rainforest. Tours costs

from $45 to $65 per person per day, depending on the number of people and the services desired.

The **Frente de Defensa de la Amazonía** (FDA; ☎ 831 930; **e** admin@fda.ecuanex.net.ec; *Eloy Alfaro 352*) is a good place to contact guides in local villages, including the Cofan village of Dureno (see Along Río Aguarico later in this chapter). FDA maintains daily radio contact.

Another good and knowledgeable contact for local indigenous and environmental affairs, as well as for arranging tours, is Manuel Silva. You can find him at the **Casa de Cultura library** (☎ 830 624; *2nd floor, cnr Manabí & Avenida Quito*).

Places to Stay

Most hotels are on Avenida Quito. Mosquitoes can be a problem, especially in the rainy months (June to August), so look for fans or mosquito nets in the rooms. Most lack hot water.

Hotel Willigram (☎ 830 163; *Avenida Quito; singles/doubles without bath $4/5, with bath $5/6*) has rooms that are basic but not too bad, but bring a padlock.

Residencial Ecuador (☎ 830 124; *Avenida Quito; rooms per person $6*) has decent-value rooms with private bath, fan and TV. Cheaper rooms with shared bath are also available.

Hotel La Cabaña (☎ 830 608; *Avenida Quito; rooms per person with shared/private bath $4/6*) is clean, friendly and has a laundry basin and rooftop line. Rooms have fans.

Hotel Gran Colombia (☎ 830 601, 831 032; *Avenida Quito; rooms per person with fan $5, singles/doubles with air-con $10/15*) has decent air-conditioned rooms with TV and telephone and a few rooms with fans.

Hotel D'Mario (☎ 830 172; *Avenida Quito 1-171; singles $14-27, doubles $17-32*), in the middle of the hotel strip, is clean and popular and a favorite with tour groups. All rooms have private bath and fan or air-conditioning. Others come with TV, telephone, minifridge and hot water, too. It's the hub of Lago's tourist scene.

Hotel La Cascada (☎ 830 124, 832 229; **e** aliarco@yahoo.com; *Avenida Quito; singles with fan $12, singles/doubles with air-con $17/29, with air-con & fridge $24/34*) is a sparkling new hotel with some of the best rooms in Lago. It's central, there's a clean swimming pool, and all rooms have TVs.

THE ORIENTE

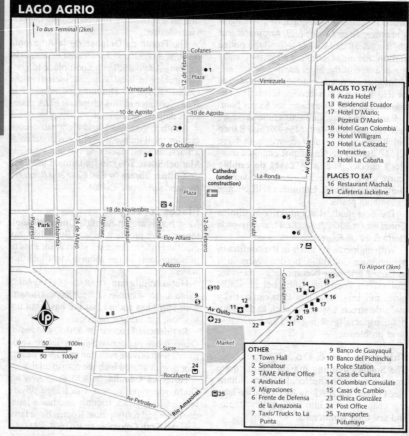

LAGO AGRIO

To Bus Terminal (2km)

Cofanes

Plaza ●1

Venezuela

Venezuela

10 de Agosto

10 de Agosto

●2

9 de Octubre

●3

Cathedral (under construction)

La Ronda

Plaza

⊞4

18 de Noviembre

Progreso

Park

●5

●6

7 ⊞

Eloy Alfaro

Añasco

To Airport (3km)

15 ⊛

14

13 ⊛ ⊡

▼16

9 ⊛

⊛10

12

11 ⊡

19 18 17

Av Quito

⊕23

▼20

●8

22 ● 21

Sucre

Market

Rocafuerte

24 ⊡

Av Petrolera

⊞25

Río Amazonas

0   50   100m
0   50   100yd

24 de Mayo
Vilcabamba
Narváez
Guayaquil
Orellana
12 de Febrero
Manabí
Av Colombia
12 de Febrero
Gonzanama

PLACES TO STAY
8 Araza Hotel
13 Residencial Ecuador
17 Hotel D'Mario;
   Pizzeria D'Mario
18 Hotel Gran Colombia
19 Hotel Williagram
20 Hotel La Cascada;
   Interactive
22 Hotel La Cabaña

PLACES TO EAT
16 Restaurant Machala
21 Cafetería Jackeline

OTHER
1 Town Hall
2 Sionatour
3 TAME Airline Office
4 Andinatel
5 Migraciones
6 Frente de Defensa
   de la Amazonía
7 Taxis/Trucks to La
   Punta
9 Banco de Guayaquil
10 Banco del Pichincha
11 Police Station
12 Casa de Cultura
14 Colombian Consulate
15 Casas de Cambio
23 Clínica González
24 Post Office
25 Transportes
   Putumayo

Araza Hotel (☎ 830 223, 831 247; Avenida Quito; singles/doubles $27/42) is another of Lago's best, with 38 clean, modern rooms that have air-conditioning, private bath, hot water, TV and minifridge. Rates include an American breakfast in the good restaurant.

Places to Eat
Restaurant Machala (☎ 830 161; Avenida Quito) is just one of several outdoor restaurants strung along the south side of the street.

Pizzeria D'Mario (Avenida Quito), below Hotel D'Mario, serves good pizza and other dishes, and is the social hub for travelers and tour groups passing through Lago.

Cafetería Jackeline (Avenida Quito) whips out decent breakfasts, snacks and good fruit salads and hamburgers.

There are many other eateries, chicken rotisserie stalls and fast-food vendors along Avenida Quito.

Getting There & Away
Air At the time of research Lago Agrio's airport handled all passenger service to Coca as well, because Coca's airport was closed. With this increased demand there were about seven daily flights to/from Quito (except on Sundays, when there are no flights). This number is likely to decrease when Coca's airport reopens sometime in 2003. At the close of this edition, **TAME** (☎ 830 113; Orellana near 9 de Octubre) had four daily flights (except Sunday) to/from Quito ($51) and **Icaro** (☎ 832 370/71, 880 546; airport) had five daily flights (except

Sunday), four of which were de facto Coca flights.

Flights fill up fast, so make a reservation. If you can't, it is always worth getting on the waiting list and going to the airport in the hope of cancellations. Tour companies sometimes book up more seats than they can use.

The airport is about 3km east of town, and taxis (which are usually yellow or white pickup trucks) cost about $2.

Bus The drive from the jungle up into the Andes (and vice versa) is beautiful, and it's worth doing in daylight. In late 2002 the Quito–Lago Agrio road via El Chaco was closed temporarily due to mud slides, ash and lava from the erupting Volcán El Reventador. It's an important road and was reopened quickly. Check locally, however, about conditions.

The bus terminal is about 2km northwest of the center. Several companies have buses to Quito ($6 to $8, eight hours). There are one or two daily departures, mainly overnight, to Tena, Cuenca, Guayaquil and Machala.

Buses to Coca aren't usually found in the bus terminal; you have to catch one at Avenida Quito in the center – ask locally for the best spot to wait.

Transportes Putumayo buses go through the jungle towns of Dureno and Tarapoa and have access to Reserva Producción Faunística Cuyabeno. Ask at the office about getting to the jungle east of Lago.

ALONG RÍO AGUARICO
☎ 06

This is one of the few regions within the Cuyabeno reserve that travelers can visit on their own. But it's definitely off the beaten track, so travel prepared.

Dureno

There are two Durenos. The Cofan village of Dureno (described here) lies on the southern banks of Río Aguarico, about an hour east of Lago Agrio by bus or dugout canoe. The Cofan village is 23km east of Lago Agrio; if you miss the turnoff, you will end up at the colonists' village of Dureno, 4km further east. There are basic *comedores* (cheap restaurants) in the colonists' village, and you could find floor space to sleep on if you ask around.

River transportation is infrequent, but Transportes Putumayo has several buses a day to Tarapoa or Tipishca, which pass the Dureno (Cofan village) turnoff, 23km from Lago Agrio. It is marked with a small sign that is not very obvious; it's best to ask the driver for Comuna Cofan Dureno. From the turnoff, follow the path until you reach Río Aguarico, about 100m away. It's best to call ahead by radio to arrange for transportation across the river (see Organized Tours under Lago Agrio earlier in this chapter). Otherwise, you can yell and whistle to attract the attention of the villagers on the other side, although this might not always work.

In the village, you'll be given a roof over your head in an indigenous-style hut – bring a hammock or sleeping mat, as there are no beds. Also, bring your own food and stove, as supplies are not available in Dureno. There is a modest fee for the river crossing and a place to sleep.

The Cofans are excellent wilderness guides and know much about the medicinal and practical uses of jungle plants. You can hire a guide with a dugout canoe for about $35 per day. Up to six people can be accommodated in a dugout, so it's cheaper in a group. The guides Delfin Criollo and Lauriano Quenama have been recommended by readers and have a cabin that sleeps eight people. They speak Cofan, with Spanish as their second language, but they do not understand English. Hector Quenama and Lino Mandua also work as guides. This is off-the-beaten-path tourism and is not for those expecting any comfort. Although you won't see much wildlife, jungle plants will be shown and explained to you; these trips are more for the cultural experience.

Cofan people head to Lago Agrio on weekends for the Sunday morning market. They often wear their distinctive traditional clothing and are easy to spot. The Cofan men wear a one-piece, knee-length smock called a *kushma,* along with a headband (sometimes made of porcupine quills) around their short hair. The women wear very brightly patterned flounced skirts, short blouses and bright-red lipstick and have beautiful, long dark hair. Ask to join them on their return to Dureno after the Sunday morning market – they will then be able to show you where to get off the bus, and you can cross the river with them.

The Cofan are related to the Secoya people, and there used to be tens of thousands of them before early contact with whites decimated them (mainly by disease). This, unfortunately, is the history of most Amazonian Indian groups. Before the discovery of oil, most Cofans' exposure to non-Indian people was limited to the occasional missionary, and they still remain shy, as opposed to the Otavaleño Indians, for example.

Zábalo

This is a small Cofan community on Río Aguarico near the confluence with the smaller Río Zábalo. You can visit an area across the river from the village, where the indigenous Cofan have an interpretive center with a Cofan guide. Souvenirs are sold, and a rainforest walk to see medicinal and other plants, accompanied by the Cofan guide, are part of the programme. Entering and visiting the village itself without advance notice, however, is discouraged, and taking photographs is not allowed.

For an in-depth visit with the Cofan people, you can stay in one of four cabins, each with two double rooms, mosquito nets and a shared outhouse with showers and toilets. It is also possible to arrange trekking/canoeing expeditions into the jungle, with stays in rustic shelters for about $25 to $45 per person per day, depending on group size and trip requirements. Anyone who visits Dureno is expected to pay for and participate in a tour of some sort.

For information and to make reservations contact **Randy Borman** (☎ 02-247 0946; e cofan@uio.satnet.net; w www.cofan.org) in Quito. Randy is the son of American missionaries who came to the Oriente in the 1950s. He was born in Shell, raised as a Cofan, and formally educated in Quito. He later founded the settlement of Zábalo, where he still lives with his Cofan wife and family, along with a handful of other Cofan families. He is highly respected and is the chief of the most traditional remaining group of Cofan. Randy guides occasional groups on excursions into the jungle. He now spends much of his time in Quito working to preserve the Cofan culture and the rainforest. Also check out the informative Cofan website (yes, a traditional culture with a website!).

Getting There & Away

At the time of writing, the community planned to start a canoe-taxi service between Zábalo and Dureno, which should be operating by the time this book goes to print. At about $15 per person, it will be far cheaper than hiring your own canoe (which costs about $200). Ask about the service at the Taller de Eco-canoas in Dureno (the Cofan village). Travelers are discouraged from simply showing up in Zábalo without advance notice, although this is possible if you bring all your own food (there's little extra

---

Faux Dugout Canoes

Transportation for Amazonian indigenous people has always been the traditional dugout canoe, painstakingly crafted from a single tree trunk. Building a large canoe requires a 200-year-old tree – in contrast, the useful life of a dugout canoe rarely exceeds 10 years. Dugouts were formerly used for communal and family purposes, with minimal impact on the rainforest, but as colonists, eco-tourists and others demanded an ever-increasing number of these sturdy craft, the building of dugout canoes has contributed to the depletion of the oldest trees in the rainforest.

Ecuador's Cofan Indians developed a less-damaging way to build dugout canoes. In a project aptly named Ecocanoa and funded by an unusual combination of the European Union, an oil company and a Cofan support group, the Cofans began experimenting in using their wooden dugouts for molds to make similarly shaped canoes out of fiberglass. Three expert fiberglass boatbuilders from Ecuador's Manabí coast were hired to teach the Cofans how to use the material. The Indians learning this new form of dugout-canoe construction were handpicked by Cofan chief Randy Borman (for more details see Zábalo in this chapter), who is savvy to both international concerns and the needs of his people.

The Cofans hope not only to save ancient rainforest trees by using fiberglass canoes, but also to start a tribal cottage industry supplying these boats to tourism companies and other villages and tribes. The Zábalo community has already received several international awards for conservation initiatives – it may be heading toward another one.

out here) and are willing to hang around while a cabin is prepared.

RESERVA PRODUCCIÓN FAUNÍSTICA CUYABENO

This reserve (admission Oct-June/July-Sept $15/20) covers 6034 sq km of rainforest around Río Cuyabeno in northeastern Ecuador. The boundaries of Cuyabeno have been changed several times, and it is now substantially larger than it was originally.

The reserve was created in 1979 with the goals of protecting this area of rainforest, conserving its wildlife and providing a sanctuary in which the traditional inhabitants of the area – the Siona, Secoya and Cofan Indians – could lead their customary way of life. There are several lakes and swamps in Cuyabeno, and some of the most interesting animals found here are aquatic species, such as freshwater dolphins, manatees, caiman and anaconda. Monkeys abound, and tapirs, peccaries, agoutis and several cat species have been recorded. The bird life is prolific.

Its protected status notwithstanding, Cuyabeno was opened to oil exploitation almost immediately after its creation. The new oil towns of Tarapoa and Cuyabeno were built on tributaries of the Río Cuyabeno, and both of these towns and parts of the trans-Ecuadorian oil pipeline were within the reserve's boundaries. Roads were built, colonists followed, and tens of thousands of hectares of the reserve were logged or degraded by spills of oil and toxic waste.

At least six oil spills were recorded between 1984 and 1989, and others occurred unnoticed. Many of the spills found their way into Río Cuyabeno itself, which is precisely the river basin that the reserve was supposed to protect.

Various international and local agencies set to work to try to protect the area, which although legally protected was, in reality, open to development. Conservation International funded projects to establish more guard stations in Cuyabeno, train local Siona and Secoya Indians to work in wildlife management, and support Cordavi, an Ecuadorian environmental-law group that challenged the legality of allowing oil exploitation in protected areas.

Finally, in late 1991, the government shifted the borders of the reserve further east and south and enlarged the area it covered.

The new reserve is both remoter and better protected. Vocal local indigenous groups – which are supported by Ecuadorian and international nongovernmental organizations (NGOs), tourists, travel agencies and conservation groups – are doing a better job of protecting the area than the government did in the original reserve. Although the threat of oil development and subsequent colonization is always present, there is now a solid infrastructure in place to prevent uncontrolled development from ruining the reserve. This is due in part to the hard work of the local people, but also to the positive economic impact of tourism.

The Cuyabeno reserve is now an important tourist destination. It is quite easy to visit the reserve without being aware of the problems it has faced, and many large areas of the reserve remain quite pristine.

Organized Tours

Numerous agencies in Quito offer tours of Cuyabeno. These tours go far beyond the colonized areas, and there is a good chance of seeing some of the wildlife. Travel is mainly by canoes and on foot – except from December to February, when low water levels may limit the areas accessible by canoe.

One such company is **Nuevo Mundo Expeditions** (Quito ☎ 256 4448, 255 3818, w www.nuevomundotravel.com). Its tours are among the best; they're marked by a conservationist attitude and they are led by well-informed, bilingual guides (for further details see Travel Agencies & Tour Operators in the Quito chapter). Nuevo Mundo's tours use the **Cuyabeno River Lodge** (packages per person for 5 days/4 nights about $700) as a base for further exploration. The lodge has comfortable cabins built in native style but featuring private (cold-water) bathrooms. You can arrange trips further into the jungle where you'll stay at a camp near Laguna Grande. 'Ecofishing' trips with a biologist guide are also available. The rate is for five days/four nights including flights from Quito and all food and guiding services.

Neotropic Turis (☎ 252 1212, 09-980 3395, fax 255 4902, e info@neotropicturis.com, w www.cuyabenolodge.com) runs the comfortable and recommended **Cuyabeno Lodge** (packages per person for 4 days/3 nights $220-250, 5 days/4 nights $250-450). Prices vary according to the number of people traveling and the accommodations requested. The lodge (different from the Cuyabeno River Lodge mentioned previously) is staffed by Siona natives and has seven cabins with two double rooms each. Two cabins have private bathrooms, and the rest have shared bathrooms with hot water. Lighting is by gas and kerosene lamps, and a solar panel provides power for warming water and running a radio. Tours are four days/three nights and five days/four nights (or longer if desired), and include transfers from Lago Agrio, native and bilingual naturalist guides, trips by canoe and foot, accommodations, meals, drinking water, coffee and tea. Canoes and kayaks are available to use on the lake. Rates vary depending on the season and availability, but are usually at the lower end; they also include transportation to and from Quito.

Several other companies in Quito and Baños offer cheaper tours to the Cuyabeno reserve, but check carefully that they offer you the type of experience that you are after. Some companies include a day of travel to and from Quito in their itineraries – others don't. Note that while these companies can make arrangements for you in advance, the best rates can usually be obtained by going to their offices to see when their next trip is leaving and asking if there's room. This is particularly true of single travelers or couples who want to join a larger group to save money.

You can visit Cuyabeno independently, but ever since the increase in local indigenous control over tourism in the area, this is no longer a recommended or inexpensive option. Most visitors visit on part of an organized group, which is the best way to go to get the most out of your trip.

Entry to this 655-hectare reserve is usually added to the cost of any tour; ask in advance if you are on a tight budget. In Tarapoa, there is a guard post where you can pay the fee and ask for information. There are a few other guard posts within the reserve.

Most visitors come during the wetter months of March to September. In the less rainy months, river levels may be too low to allow easy navigation. Annual rainfall is between 2000mm and 4000mm, depending on the location, and humidity is often between 90% and 100%. Bring sun protection, rain gear, insect repellent, water-purification tablets and food.

SOUTH FROM LAGO AGRIO
☎ 06

The bus ride from Lago Agrio to Coca shows how the discovery of oil has changed the Oriente. In the early 1970s, this was all virgin jungle, and communications were limited to mission airstrips and river travel. Today, there are roads and buses, and there are always signs of the oil industry – the pipelines, oil wells and trucks.

The bus crosses the Río Aguarico a few kilometers outside Lago and passes occasional small communities. Shortly before reaching Coca, the bus goes through the small oil town of **La Joya de las Sachas**, where Hotel America is the best of a few poor hotels, and then passes the belching wells of the Sacha oil works. The road is narrow but in good condition and almost entirely paved. It follows the oil pipeline for most of the way, and there are several stretches with vistas of the jungle in the distance.

COCA
☎ 06 • pop 17,000

Coca is the capital of the new (in 1999) Orellana Province, which used to be the eastern part of Napo Province. Ecuadorian maps show the town's official name, Puerto Francisco de Orellana, but everyone calls it Coca. Located at the junction of Ríos Napo and Coca (hence its popular name), its official name derives from the fact that Francisco de Orellana came through here on his way to 'discover' the Amazon in 1542.

The Coca of today is a sprawling oil town with little to recommend about it, although it has a strange appeal for some travelers. There are few street signs, and every street except the main street, Napo, is unpaved and hence covered with dust, puddles or mud, depending on the season. Many of the buildings are just shacks, and the place has a real shantytown appearance – there isn't even a town plaza. However, with its new provincial capital status, the town may improve. A local tourist industry has developed because Coca is closer to primary rainforest than Misahuallí. Coca itself may not be especially attractive, but it is the haunt of oil workers and tourists looking for jungle expeditions.

Information

The **tourist information office** (e diturorel lana@andinanet.net; García Moreno; open

Toxic Texaco Legacy

The damage oil companies have wreaked on the Ecuadorian Amazon – both naturally and culturally – is extreme. According to environmentalists, one of the greatest disasters of all lies at the feet of Texaco oil corporation (now ChevronTexaco Corp.), which, in partnership with state-owned Petroecuador, extracted some 1.4 billion gallons of oil from the northern Oriente between 1971 and 1991. The US-based company now faces accusations that it knowingly dumped nearly two times the amount of oil that was spilled by the *Exxon Valdez* in 1989 in Alaska.

In early 2003, ChevronTexaco was trying to ward off a class-action lawsuit, first filed against the company in the US on behalf of some 30,000 Ecuadorians, who say Texaco dumped 20 billion gallons of toxic waste water and 16 million gallons of raw crude into the rainforest; was racist in its disregard for the industry-wide standards practiced in developed nations; decimated the indigenous populations (especially that of the Cofan and Secoya) and the fragile rainforest ecosystems in the region where it drilled; and created a toxic environment resulting in cancer rates up to 1000 times greater than normal. Sound major? It is.

The lawsuit, first filed in 1993, is the first ever class-action environmental suit brought against a multinational oil company on its home turf for actions abroad. US federal courts dismissed the case twice, arguing the victims' claims deserved a full court hearing but that the trial should take place in Ecuador. At the time of writing, the case was weaving its way through Ecuadorian courts, but its outcome was uncertain.

ChevronTexaco says that Texaco complied with Ecuadorian law while operating in Ecuador, and that the company adhered to industry-wide standards. It also says it spent about $40 million in 1995 to clean up its mess. **Amazon Watch** (**W** www.amazonwatch.org) and the plaintiffs in the case estimate damages to be around $1 billion. Amazon Watch reports Texaco made approximately $6 billion during its 20-odd years of drilling. When the *Exxon Valdez* spilled its oil off the US coast, Exxon had to pay about $2.1 billion to clean it up – over 50 times what Texaco says it spent.

Although Texaco closed shop in the northern Oriente in 1991, there are reportedly over 300 open oil pits still leeching toxins into local ecosystems. According to Amazon Watch, some 800 hectares of rainforest were polluted.

To learn more about the case and how to get involved check out Amazon Watch's website, **ChevronToxico** (**W** www.chevrontoxico.com) or its **Texaco Rainforest** (**W** www.texacorainforest.org). You can read ChevronTexaco's side of the story on the **Texaco website** (**W** www.texaco.com).

8:30am-1pm & 2pm-5:30pm Mon-Fri) can provide you with information about Coca and the province of Orellana.

There is an **Andinatel office** *(cnr Eloy Alfaro & 6 de Diciembre)* and a **post office** *(9 de Octubre)*. Internet service is available at **Imperial Net** *(García Moreno; open 9am-10pm daily)* for $1.80 per hour.

Casa de Cambio 3R *(☎ 881 229; cnr Napo & García Moreno; open 8am-8pm Mon-Sat)* charges 4% commission to cash traveler's checks. Medical services are limited; **Clínica Sinai** *(cnr Napo & García Moreno)* is better than the hospital.

Organized Tours

Coca is a good place to set up a jungle tour. Guides charge around $40 to $45 per person per day for three- to five-day tours and about $60 per person per day for longer tours deeper into the jungle. Group sizes are usually four to six people. Smaller groups have to pay more per person. It is easier to find people to make up a group in Quito, but prices may be higher if the trip is booked in Quito. Trips usually last three to 10 days. You may have to bargain to get the best rate, but make sure everything you expect is included. Note that some outfits may charge as little as $20 or as much as $70 a day. The cheapest outfitters have unreliable boats, poor food, and guides that don't speak English. If you go with a cheap one, don't be surprised if you have to spend the night on the side of the river because your boat's engine breaks down, or you find yourself drinking boiled river water.

Hotel El Auca doesn't arrange tours but is probably one of the best places in town to

THE ORIENTE

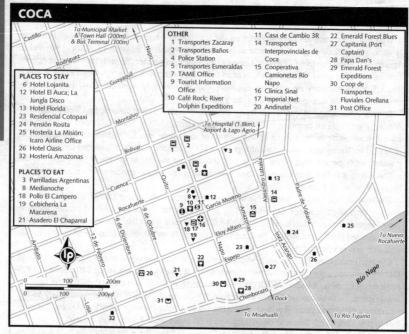

COCA

To Municipal Market
& Town Hall (200m)
& Bus Terminal (300m)

Castillo

Rodriguez

Napo

PLACES TO STAY
6 Hotel Lojanita
12 Hotel El Auca; La
   Jungla Disco
13 Hotel Florida
23 Residencial Cotopaxi
24 Pensión Rosita
25 Hostería La Misión;
   Icaro Airline Office
26 Hotel Oasis
32 Hostería Amazonas

PLACES TO EAT
3 Parrilladas Argentinas
8 Medianoche
16 Pollo El Campero
19 Cebichería La
   Macarena
21 Asadero El Chaparral

OTHER
1 Transportes Zacaray
2 Transportes Baños
4 Police Station
5 Transportes Esmeraldas
7 TAME Office
9 Tourist Information
   Office
10 Café Rock; River
   Dolphin Expeditions

11 Casa de Cambio 3R
14 Transportes
   Interprovinciales de
   Coca
15 Cooperativa
   Camionetas Río
   Napo
16 Clínica Sinai
17 Imperial Net
20 Andinatel

22 Emerald Forest Blues
27 Capitanía (Port
   Captain)
28 Papa Dan's
29 Emerald Forest
   Expeditions
30 Coop de
   Transportes
   Fluviales Orellana
31 Post Office

Guayaquil

Montalvo

To Hospital (1.8km);
Airport & Lago Agrio

Bolívar

Cuenca

Quito

Rocafuerte

9 de Octubre

6 de Diciembre

12 de Febrero

Ambato

Loja

Alejandro Labaka

Padre de Vidania

García Moreno

Amazonas

Eloy Alfaro

Napo

Espejo

Inez Arango

Chimborazo

Dock

Río Napo

To Nuevo
Rocafuerte

0   100   200m
0   100   200yd

To Misahuallí

To Río Tiguino

meet guides looking for work, as well as to meet other travelers who can tell you of their experiences or help form a group. Ask here about guides to the rarely visited **Parque Nacional Sumaco-Galeras**.

One of Ecuador's foremost jungle guides is the friendly, English-speaking Luís García, who runs **Emerald Forest Expeditions** (☎ 882 285; ⓦ www.emeraldexpeditions.com; Napo). Most tours last four to five days and are based at a lodge in Pañacocha (great for boa spotting). Trips to places deeper into the jungle (such as along the Río Shiripuno-Cononaco or to the Río Tiputini in Parque Nacional Yasuní) can be arranged but require at least 10 days. Accommodations consist of camping or, in the case of Pañacocha, rustic cabins. All trips are best arranged through the Emerald Forest Expedition **Quito office** (☎ 254 1278, ☎/fax 254 1543, ⓦ www.emeraldexpeditions.com); see Travel Agencies & Tour Operators in the Quito chapter for more details. However, you might get in with another group by stopping by the Coca office. Also look for Luís at his bar Emerald Forest Blues (see Entertainment later).

An excellent source of information about the Huaorani is Randy Smith at **River Dolphin Expeditions** (☎ 880 600, 880 127, 09-917 7529; ⓔ rde4amazon@yahoo.com; ⓦ www.aamazon-green-magician.com; García Moreno). Randy is a Canadian who has more than a decade of experience living and working with and for the Huaorani. He's also one of the Oriente's best-known (and somewhat controversial) environmentalists. Randy lives in Coca, but he's sometimes in the jungle for weeks, so allow time to arrange a tour with him. Randy is knowledgeable and opinionated and he leads a somewhat alternative lifestyle, partly as a result of living like a Huaorani for years – if you can deal with it, you can have a very rewarding experience. Randy has two books available at Abya Yala Bookstore in Quito and is working on a third. If he's not around, his knowledgeable and friendly Quechua partner, **Ramiro Viteri** (the former director of tourism), can give you information and help you set up a tour. River Dolphin Expeditions offers a unique 10-day tour in which you and your companions row traditional four-person canoes down the Río

Napo to Iquitos Peru, fishing for piranhas and visiting tributaries and indigenous communities en route. The trip costs $600 per person with a group of four.

Tropic Ecological Adventures (☎ 222 5907, w www.tropiceco.com) also does tours to Huaorani territory. See Travel Agencies & Tour Operators in the Quito chapter and Vía Auca later in this chapter.

Kem Pery Tours (☎ 222 6583, 222 6715, w www.kempery.com) does tours to Bataboro Lodge, on the edge of Huaorani territory. See Travel Agencies & Tour Operators in the Quito chapter and Vía Auca in this chapter.

Witoto Tours is a Quechua-run operator run by friendly folks, but its tours have received mixed reports. People who like rugged sleeping conditions and don't mind spontaneous itinerary changes or the possibility of surviving on treated river water will probably do fine. Some rave about the tours, which incorporate purification rituals, medicinal plant identification and visits to local communities. It's supposedly opening a new office on Espejo between 6 de Diciembre and 12 de Febrero. If you can't find it, ask around.

Whimper Torres (☎ 880 336, 880 017, 881 196, Quito ☎ 02-265 9311; e ronoboa@latin mail.com) is a well-known local guide with over 18 years experience. He's been highly recommended and offers trips to Pañacocha, Río Tiputini, Parque Nacional Yasuní and the Shiripuno-Cononaco area.

Fausto Tapuy has been recommended as an excellent bird-watching guide. He lives in Coca, but you have to ask around to find him.

Places to Stay

The best of Coca's cheapies – and one of the few that gets more travelers than oil workers – is **Hotel Oasis** (☎ 880 206; e yuturilodge@yahoo.com; rooms per person with cold/hot private bath $5/7), down on the river. The no-frills rooms are a good deal for Coca, and the staff can arrange trips to the Yuturi and Yarina Lodges further down Río Napo (see Lower Río Napo later in this chapter).

Hotel El Auca (☎ 880 127, 880 600; e hel auca@ecuanex.net.ec; Napo; singles $12-35, doubles $20-50) is Coca's most popular hotel for tour groups and oil workers alike. The restaurant here is the best place to meet other travelers and guides and dial into the

local scene. The cheapest rooms have fans and electric hot showers and are just fine. The mid-range rooms are in lovely new cabañas and the suites are luxurious and have air-conditioning. It also has the nicest garden in Coca. The hotel is often full by mid-afternoon.

Hostería Amazonas (☎ 880 444, 881 215; Espejo; singles/doubles with fan $14/22, with air-con $20/34) has sparse but clean rooms with electric hot shower, TV and fan or air-conditioning. Some rooms have river views or refrigerators.

Hostería La Misión (☎ 880 260/544, fax 880 263; singles/doubles with fan $17/25, with air-con $20/29), on the riverfront, vies with Hotel El Auca for title of 'best hotel.' Its strongest punches are its river-side restaurant and bar (a great place to relax) and the swimming pool. All rooms have hot water and cable TV. The air-conditioned rooms are in high demand and are often booked ahead.

Hotel Lojanita (☎ 880 032; cnr Napo & Cuenca; rooms per person with/without bath $5/4) is just bearable if you're in a pinch, and **Hotel Florida** (☎ 880 177; Alejandro Labaka; singles/doubles with $6/12, with private bath $10/18) is way overpriced but secure. **Pensión Rosita** (☎ 880 167; rooms per person $4) and **Residencial Cotopaxi** (cnr Amazonas & Espejo; rooms per person $3) are cheap, basic and probably unpleasant for lone women travelers.

Places to Eat
The restaurants at Hostería La Misión and Hotel El Auca are considered among the best in town – hanging out at the Auca's outdoor tables is part of hanging out in Coca.

Medianoche (☎ 880 026; Napo; mains $2-2.50; open 6pm-1am daily) has four plates of chicken on the menu, and it's extremely popular. There's no sign (it's called *medianoche* because it's open after midnight).

Pollo El Campero (García Moreno; mains $2-3) is good for rotisserie chicken, while **Asadero El Chaparral** (Espejo; mains $2-3) is good for grilled meats. **Parrilladas Argentinas** (2nd floor, cnr Amazonas & Cuenca) is locally popular and is the best place for a steak, but there's not much else on the menu. **Cebichería La Macarena** (Eloy Alfaro) is good for fish.

Entertainment
La Jungla Disco (admission $10, hotel guests free; open Wed-Sat), above the restaurant of Hotel El Auca, is the place to dance on weekends. The $10 admission includes six beers or four *cuba libres* (rum and Coke drinks) – and you can probably talk yourself in for cheaper if you don't plan to slurp that much.

Emerald Forest Blues (☎ 882 280; Quito; open 9am-late daily) is a welcoming little bar owned by Luís García of Emerald Forest Expeditions. The music is good, and the atmosphere is conducive to meeting other folks.

Café Rock (García Moreno; open 10am-late daily) is a popular hangout, good for absorbing the Coca-ness of Coca.

Papa Dan's (Napo; open 4pm-2am daily) is a longtime favorite, has rickety walls, a thatched roof and a down-home tropical feel.

Getting There & Away
Air Coca's airport was due to be closed until mid-2003 (and it may still be closed). Until it reopened, all flights went through Lago Agrio, about two hours north by bus. Tickets could be purchased in Coca. At the close of this edition, if you bought your ticket with Icaro, the airline shuttled you for free to Lago Agrio's airport to meet your flight. With TAME, you had to get to Lago Agrio on your own – allow *at least* three hours for the whole journey if this is still the case. The following schedule may change when the airport reopens.

Icaro (☎ 880 997, 880 546) flies three times daily Monday through Saturday to Quito ($56; last flight at 12:45pm). Its office is in Hostería La Misión (see Places to Stay earlier). **TAME** (☎ 881 078, 880 768; cnr Napo & Rocafuerte) has four flights to Quito ($51) Monday through Saturday. **AeroGal** (☎ 881 450/1/2/3), at the Coca airport, may also fly to Quito.

The airport terminal is almost 2km north of town on the left-hand side of the road to Lago Agrio. A taxi ride there (when it's open) costs about $1.

Bus There is a bus terminal is at the north end of town, but several buses still leave from offices in the town center. The situation is likely to change, so make careful inquiries about the departure point of your bus.

Transportes Baños (☎ 880 182; cnr Napo & Bolívar) has several daily buses to Quito ($8, nine to 13 hours, depending on the route). Transportes Jumandy, in the bus terminal, has several buses a day to Tena ($6, six hours). **Transportes Esmeraldas** (☎ 881 077; cnr Napo & Cuenca) has two night buses to Quito. All three companies have buses to Lago Agrio ($2, three hours). **Transportes Zacaray** (☎ 880 286; cnr Napo & Bolívar) heads daily to Santo Domingo de Los Colorados ($8, 10 hours), Manta ($13, 15 hours), Guayaquil ($12, 17 hours) and Quito ($8, nine hours). Transportes Loja, at the terminal, has evening departures to Santo Domingo, Quevedo, Babahoyo, Machala and Loja. Transportes Interprovinciales de Coca, at the bus terminal, has buses that go south to Río Tiguino.

Open-sided trucks called *rancheras* or *chivas* leave from the terminal for various destinations between Coca and Lago Agrio, and to Río Tiputini to the south. Pickup trucks and taxis at **Cooperativa Camionetas Río Napo** (Eloy Alfaro) provide service to just about anywhere you want to pay to go.

Boat Travelers arriving and departing by river must register their passport at the *capitanía* (port captain), by the landing dock. If you're on a tour, your guide usually takes care of this.

Since the completion of the new Tena–Coca road, there is no passenger canoe service to Misahuallí. You could hire a private canoe (they hold at least 10 people) to take you there for about $250. The upriver trip takes about 14 hours (it's only six coming the other direction).

Coop de Transportes Fluviales Orellana *(Napo)* offers passenger service to Nuevo Rocafuerte ($15, nine to 15 hours) on the Peruvian border at 7am Monday and Thursday. It returns to Coca, departing Nuevo Rocafuerte at 7am on Sunday and Thursday. Although there's usually a stop for lunch, be sure to bring food and water for the long trip. For information on crossing to Peru by river and continuing to Iquitos in Peru (see Nuevo Rocafuerte later in this chapter).

VÍA AUCA
☎ 06

This road from Coca crosses Río Napo and continues south across Río Tiputini and Río Shiripuno, ending near the small community of **Tiguino**, on Río Tiguino. There are daily *rancheras* that go as far as Tiguino. This used to be Huaorani territory and virgin jungle. Vía Auca is an oil-exploitation road that was built in the 1980s. The Huaorani have been pushed eastward (some groups went westward) into their new reserve. The area is being colonized, and cattle ranches and oil rigs are replacing the jungle. Conservationists are trying to prevent the same thing from happening along the road built by Maxus in Parque Nacional Yasuní (for more details see later in this chapter).

The rivers crossed by the road provide access to remote parts of both the Huaorani Reserve and Yasuní, but you should seek the local advice of authorized guides about the advisability of taking trips down these rivers. Some tours may be possible, but others enter the territories of Huaoranis, who either are strongly opposed to tourism or want to manage it on their own terms. Taking the road to Tiguino in the morning and returning to Coca the same day is no problem if you are interested in seeing what it looks like. The trip takes about three or four hours and costs about $3.

Three to four hours downriver on Río Tiguino is the remote and simple **Bataboro Lodge** *(rooms per person with/without bath $75/55)*, which is sometimes inaccessible during very high or low water levels. There is only river transportation on Monday and Friday. The lodge has rooms with shared bath, and there are two rooms with private bath; rates include meals and transportation from Coca. It's in a remote area, and upkeep of the trails is erratic. Safari Tours and Kem Pery Tours (see Organized Tours in Coca earlier) have information about this lodge.

LOWER RÍO NAPO
☎ 06

East of Coca, the wide Río Napo flows steadily toward Peru and the Amazon River. Some of Ecuador's best jungle lodges are reached by boat from Coca. East of the settlements of Pompeya and Limoncocha, the river flows just outside the northern border of Parque Nacional Yasuní and finally enters Peru at Nuevo Rocafuerte, now an official border crossing.

Yarina Lodge

Just an hour downstream from Coca, this lodge *(rooms per person $45)* has 20 rustic cabins with private baths, and is a good choice for budget travelers seeking a comfortable introduction to the jungle. The surroundings offer river views, short trails and the opportunity to watch birds and paddle canoes. Rates are reasonable and include meals and tours with Spanish- and English-speaking local guides. Information and reservations can be obtained at Hotel Oasis (see Places to Stay under Coca earlier) or in Quito at **Yuturi Jungle Adventure** *(☎ 250 4037, 250 3225;* w *www.yuturilodge.com; Amazonas N24-236 & Colón)*. Discounts are available for SAE members.

Pompeya and Limoncocha Area

Pompeya is a Catholic mission about two hours downriver from Coca on Río Napo. It has a school and a small archaeology museum, and basic food and lodging can be arranged. The museum has a fine collection of indigenous artefacts from the Río Napo area and pre-Columbian ceramics. A small admission fee is charged. Some archaeologists believe that before the arrival of Europeans, the indigenous population of Río Napo (and other parts of the Amazon Basin) was many times greater than it is today.

From Pompeya, you can walk 8km north on a new road to the ex–North American mission of Limoncocha *(per person $2)*, which is a basic place to stay and eat. Nearby, the locally run **Limoncocha Biological Reserve** has a lake that is recommended for bird-watching.

Limoncocha is best reached by bus (several a day) from the oil town of **Shushufindi**, a two- or three-hour trip from either Coca or Lago Agrio. In Shushufindi, there are several basic places to stay – Hotel Shushufindi is better than most. A local guide charmingly describes the town as having 40 prostitutes and no doctors. Be sure to stay alert; in particular, watch your valuables at passport checkpoints. Two daily buses from Shushufindi to Limoncocha continue on to Pompeya.

Sacha Lodge

Opened in 1992, this Swiss-run lodge *(packages per person for 3/4 nights doubles $580/720, singles $695/870)* provides comfortable accommodations in the deep jungle. Sacha Lodge is built on the banks of Laguna El Pilche, a lake about 1km north of Río Napo. Getting there is half the fun – a three-hour ride in a fast motor-canoe from Coca is followed by a walk through the forest on an elevated boardwalk and then a 15-minute paddle in a dugout canoe to the lodge.

The main building – which has a restaurant, bar and small library – is three stories high and has a little observation deck at the top. It is linked by boardwalks to 10 cabins, each with two rooms. Each room has a private bath and hot water, as well as a deck and hammock with fine forest views. All rooms are screened (although mosquitoes don't seem to be a problem) and have electric lights and ceiling fans. Buffet-style meals are plentiful and delicious, and both vegetarians and meat-eaters are well catered for.

Hikes and canoe trips are made in small groups, typically consisting of about five tourists and two guides. One guide is a local, and the other is usually a bilingual naturalist guide. Trails in the area vary in length, and destinations include flat rainforest, hilly rainforest, and various lakes, rivers and swamps. A 43m-high observation deck atop a huge ceiba tree is a few minutes' walk away from the main lodge. Special interests, such as bird-watching, photography, plants or fishing, can be catered to with advance request, and a bird-watching list is available.

Most guests come either on a four-day/three-night or a five-day/four-night package – the first option is Friday to Monday, and the second is Monday to Friday. Once you arrive, you won't be disturbed by a new influx of guests until it's time to leave. Airfare is an additional $120 round trip from Quito to Coca, or you can travel by bus.

Reservations should be made at Sacha Lodge's **Quito office** *(☎ 02-256 6090, 250 9504, 250 9115; ⓦ www.sachalodge.com; Zaldumbide 375 & Toledo)*.

Napo Wildlife Center

Opened in early 2003, this jungle lodge *(ⓦ www.tropicalnaturetravel.com; doubles per person for 3/4 nights $655/785, singles $785/945)* lies within the boundaries of Parque Nacional Yasuní, on the south side of Río Napo. It's set on the shore of the drainage lake Añangucocha, an hour by paddle-canoe up a small tributary from the Napo. The lodge is a joint ecotourism project between the Quechua community of Añangu (which owns the 88 hectares of land where the lodge is set) and the US-based nonprofit organization Tropical Nature. It was not opened at the time of research, but Tropical Nature has a reputation for doing things right, and the lodge sounds very promising.

On the property itself are two parrot clay licks, where between late October and early April Tropical Nature guarantees you'll see between eight and 10 species of parrot – they visit the licks by the thousands. The rare zigzag heron is also reportedly seen on the property. Jiovanny Rivandeneyra, a renowned bird-watching guide, works here as a guide. So bird-watchers might like it here.

The lodge has 10 spacious three-person cabañas, each with electricity, private hot baths and balconies with views of the lake. Departures to the lodge are on Monday (for the four-night stay) and Friday (for the three-night stay). Rates include lodging, meals, guided excursions and canoe transport from Coca. You can make reservations and get more information from the website listed earlier. If you're already in Quito, email Norby López at **EcoTours** *(ⓔ ecotours@uio.satnet.net)*.

Sani Lodge

Less than four hours downstream from Coca, Sani Lodge *(packages per person for*

3/4/7 nights $285/380/665) is a lovely new 20-person lodge built on the shore of a beautiful oxbow lake, just off the Río Napo. Its small size makes it especially attractive for those who want a more intimate experience, and its location is excellent for wildlife viewing. Monkeys, sloths and black caiman are regularly spotted, and the lodge's bird list records over 550 species of birds in the area (the 30m-high tree tower will help you find them). Nocturnal mammals such as tapirs and capybara live in the area, but are rarely seen. Even jaguar tracks have been spotted on the property.

The eight handsome, thatched-roof cabins each sleep two to three people and have private cold-water baths, comfortable beds, mosquito screens and a small porch. Oil lamps provide the light at night, except in the lodge which has solar electricity.

The lodge was founded and is owned by the Sani community, the Quechua inhabitants who together own the 160 sq km of land around the lodge. The tourism side of the business is run – with conservation, community and comfort all in mind – by the North American/Ecuadorian owners of El Monte Sustainable Lodge (see Mindo in the Northern Highlands chapter). Employees are all members of the community. Profits earned by the lodge go directly to the community, which intends to build a school in Coca and devote itself to the sustainable use of the forest and preservation of its culture.

Tours are for three, four or seven nights, and the very reasonable rates include three meals a day, canoe transport to/from Coca, and daily excursions with both a native guide and an English-speaking naturalist guide.

Reservations can be made online, by phone or at Sani Lodge's **Quito office** (☎ 02-255 8881; w www.sanilodge.com; Roca 736 & Amazonas, Pasaje Chantilly).

La Selva Jungle Lodge

This North American–run lodge (packages per person for 3/4 nights $576/700) provides a high-quality, responsible tourism experience. Many local people are employed, and the staff offers excursions into the rainforest with informed and interested guides. In 1992 the lodge won the 'World Congress on Tourism and the Environment' award.

Accommodations are in 16 double cabins and one family cabin (three rooms), each with private hot bath and mosquito screens. Kerosene lanterns light the rooms. Meals are excellent by any standards and absolutely outstanding for Oriente standards.

There is also a small research facility, where scientists and students can work on their projects by advance arrangement. One project that has been successful is the breeding of butterflies near the lodge. Visitors are able to see this operation, which affords excellent opportunities to photograph rainforest butterflies, and learn about their life cycles.

Excursions are accomplished both by dugout canoe and hiking. There is a 35m-high canopy platform located about 20 minutes away from the lodge on foot. Bird-watching is a highlight – over 500 species have been recorded in the La Selva area, including the rare zigzag heron, which bird-watchers from all over the world come to see. About half of Ecuador's 44 species of parrots have been recorded near here, as well as a host of other exotic tropical birds. Monkeys and other mammals are frequently seen. Of course, there are tens of thousands of plant and insect species.

The lodge is five to six hours downriver from Coca by regular passenger canoe, but La Selva's private launches make the trip in about half that time. It is set on Laguna Garzacocha, which, with its several tributaries and varying vegetation, must surely be one of the prettiest small jungle lakes anywhere.

The lodge has a four-day/three-night minimum, and prices include river travel from Coca, accommodations, all meals and all guide services. The bar tab, laundry service and airfare ($120 round trip) are extra.

There is a three-night package and a four-night package, which can be combined for longer stays. The lodge can also arrange a one-week 'Light Brigade' tour, which involves camping in the jungle – but in style! Rates for this are about $1325 per person.

Information and reservations are available from the La Selva's **Quito office** (☎ 02-255 4686, 255 0995, fax 02-256 7297; w www.la selvajunglelodge.com; 6 de Diciembre 2816).

Pañacocha

Pañacocha, which in Quechua means 'Lake of Piranhas,' is a stunning black-water lake reached by turning north up the Río Pañayacu from the Río Napo. It's most easily visited by tour from Coca, although you can get here by passenger canoe from Coca as well (see Getting There & Away under Coca earlier in this chapter). There is a small community near the shore where you can stay. A popular activity here, of course, is piranha fishing – the fish are fairly easy to catch and make for good eating (but watch out for those teeth!).

Cheap accommodations are available at a variety of small local places and private houses, where rates start as low as $5 for a double.

Cabañas Pañacocha (*tour packages per person per day about $50*) is nestled into a cove at the north end of the lake and offers exquisitely situated (although basic) accommodations in rustic cabañas with private, cold-water bathrooms and mosquito nets. You can tool around the lake on paddleboats, and there is a network of trails through primary forest. The site was recently purchased by Fundación Pañacocha, a nonprofit organization working to create the Bosque Protector Pañacocha, a reserve which would link the two bigger parks of Cuyabeno and Yasuní to create one of the largest, officially protected areas in South America. You can arrange a visit (which includes boat transportation, guides, food and lodging) by contacting the Quito office of **Fundación Pañacocha** (☎ *02-223 1768;* e *cibt@ecuanex.net.ec*).

Pañacocha is approximately five hours downstream from Coca, or about halfway to Nuevo Rocafuerte.

Yuturi Lodge

This lodge (*packages per person for 3/4 nights $240/300*) is built on Río Yuturi, a southern tributary of Río Napo about 20 minutes beyond Pañacocha. There are 15 rustic cabins with private cold showers, mosquito nets and good views. Guided trips through the forest with both an indigenous and an English-speaking guide are included in the price, as are meals and transport from Coca to the lodge. The last night of the trip is spent at Yarina Lodge (see earlier) so guests don't have to get up two hours before dawn to meet their flights out of Coca. We've received several recommendations for the place. Reservations can be made at Hotel Oasis (see Places to Stay under Coca earlier in this chapter) or in Quito at **Yuturi**

Jungle Adventure (☎ *02-250 4037, 250 3225;* w *www.yuturilodge.com; Amazonas N24-236 & Colón*). The four-day/three-night trips depart Monday; the five-day/four-night trips depart Friday.

Nuevo Rocafuerte

This small river town is on the Peruvian border about 12 hours from Coca along Río Napo. This is a legal border crossing with Peru, although basic infrastructure such as regular boats and simple hotels are still lacking. It is possible to travel by boat from Coca to Iquitos, Peru, but it takes time (anywhere from one to three weeks, depending on your planning and luck), patience and the willingness to rough it. Bring adequate supplies if you make the trip on your own, that is, water-purification tablets, bug repellent and food. River Dolphin Expeditions in Coca offers a 10-day tour in which you paddle canoes from Coca to Iquitos, Peru along the Río Napo. Guides are available in Nuevo Rocafuerte for trips into Parque Nacional Yasuní.

A basic **pensión** (*rooms per person with shared bath $3-5*) in Nuevo Rocafuerte provides beds, and a small store has basic supplies, but you should bring most of what you will need with you. A few simple *comedores* sell food.

Getting There & Away Passenger canoes from Coca depart at 7am on Monday and Thursday mornings and take about 12 hours to reach Nuevo Rocafuerte; the trip is usually broken at Pañacocha for a meal, but you should bring your own food and water as well.

The return canoe leaves Nuevo Rocafuerte early Sunday and Thursday mornings. Because travel is against the flow of the river, the round trip may require an overnight stop. The fare is $15 each way.

To/From Peru Exit and entry formalities on the Ecuador side are taken care of in Nuevo Rocafuerte; in Peru they're settled in Iquitos. The official border crossing is at Pantoja, a short ride downstream from Nuevo Rocafuerte. Timing is the key: a cargo boat called the *Torres Causana* leaves Iquitos, Peru around the 18th of every month, arriving in Pantoja around the 24th. You need to catch this boat in Pantoja for its six-day round trip to Iquitos. To get to Pantoja, ask for a ride with the Peruvian *militares* (soldiers) who go daily by boat to Nuevo Rocafuerte to shop;. You'll find their boats at the Rocafuerte marina, and they charge about $5 for the lift.

The *Torres Causana* charges about $70 for the six-day trip to Iquitos. It's a cargo boat, so you sleep in hammocks and conditions are extremely basic. Food is available, but you're better off bringing your own from Coca or Nuevo Rocafuerte. Definitely bring water-purification tablets.

PARQUE NACIONAL YASUNÍ

Yasuní *(admission $20)* lies south of Río Napo and includes most of the watersheds of Ríos Yasuní and Nashiño, as well as substantial parts of Río Tiputini. This 9620-sq-km national park is by far the largest in mainland Ecuador and was established in 1979 (and expanded in 1990 and 1992) to conserve a wide variety of different rainforest habitats.

These habitats can be divided into three major groups: 'terra firme' or forested hills, which are never inundated even by the highest floods; 'varzea' or lowlands, which are periodically inundated by flooding rivers; and 'igapó,' which are lowlands that are semi-permanently inundated. Thus, Parque Nacional Yasuní has wetlands, marshes, swamps, lakes, rivers and rainforest.

The biodiversity of this varied and remote tropical landscape is staggeringly high. Not many scientists have had the opportunity to visit the park, but those that have report much higher species counts than they had expected – including many new species. The animals there include some of the rarer and more difficult to see jungle wildlife, such as jaguars, harpy eagles, pumas and tapirs.

Because of the importance of the park's incredible biodiversity, Unesco has declared Yasuní an international biosphere reserve.

Except for about 20 Huaorani families, the national park is almost uninhabited. Most of the Huaorani live outside the park's boundaries – especially in the Reserva Huaorani, which acts as an ecological buffer zone for the national park. This was created in 1991, encompassing much of what used to be the western part of Yasuní and providing the Huaorani with a suitable area of rainforest in which to live in a traditional way.

Meanwhile, the eastern and southern borders of Parque Nacional Yasuní were extended to Río Cururay, so that the size of the park remains about the same.

On the face of it, this huge, remote national park surrounded by a buffer zone seems a modern conservation success story. Unfortunately, this is not entirely the case. Oil has been discovered within the boundaries of the park. In 1991, despite Yasuní's protected status, the Ecuadorian government gave the US-based oil company Conoco the right to begin oil exploitation. Conoco was soon replaced by the Maxus Oil Consortium, a subsidiary of Du Pont. It is understandable that the Ecuadorian government wants to make money from its oil reserves, but much of the profit will benefit foreign interests rather than Ecuador's. There has also been a great deal of logging recently within the Huaorani territory (the park buffer zone) by Colombian lumber companies which purchase trees (primarily cedar) from the Huaorani.

Where drilling begins, a road soon follows, thus opening up pristine rainforest to colonization, deforestation and degradation. It is the roads and the subsequent colonization that cause greater long-term damage than the oil drilling itself. A 110km road has been built into the park, but in an attempt to avoid the problems associated with colonization, the road is open only to oil-company workers, local indigenous people and a few scientists with permits.

Degradation caused by the oil-drilling process itself does occur. This includes contamination of soil and drainage systems by oil and the waste products associated with oil exploitation, as well as the noise pollution and destruction of vegetation causing the exodus of wildlife from the region. Nevertheless, this degradation has so far been reasonably well contained, and wildlife is reportedly very abundant – but you can't go there to see it unless you're a researcher or an oil worker.

Various international organizations – such as the Nature Conservancy, Conservation International and the Natural Resources Defense Council – in coalition with Ecuadorian groups such as Fundación Natura and local grassroots conservation groups, have worked hard to minimize the oil company's impact in Yasuní. Although Parque Nacional Yasuní remains threatened by oil exploitation, hope remains that the threat will not develop into as destructive a pattern as has occurred in other parts of the Amazon.

In common with the majority of Ecuador's preserved areas, Yasuní is woefully understaffed. At present, the only permanently staffed ranger station is at Nuevo Rocafuerte, with some other seasonal stations on the southern boundaries of the park. Some of the guides in Coca can take you on trips into the park (see Nuevo Mundo Expeditions under Travel Agencies & Tour Operators in the Quito chapter).

The annual rainfall is about 3500mm, depending on which part of the park you are in. May to July are the wettest months; January to March are the driest. This is one of the few remaining true wildernesses in Ecuador. The beauty of this area is its remoteness and inaccessibility, which allows the wildlife to remain in the region relatively undisturbed.

VOLCÁN SUMACO

The 3732m cone of Sumaco is surrounded by rainforest and plagued by wet weather, and it is the remotest and least studied of Ecuador's volcanoes. It is within Parque Nacional Sumaco-Galeras, one of Ecuador's remotest national parks. The volcano is dormant at this time, although volcanologists believe it is potentially active. It lies about 27km north of the Coca–Tena road, from which it can be climbed in about a five or six day round trip. About 20km east of the Tena–Baeza road, a short dirt road leads north from the Coca–Tena road to the village of **Huamaní**.

In Huamaní, guides can be hired for the climb to the summit, which involves poorly marked trails and chopping through the jungle with a machete. It is easy to get lost, and therefore guides are strongly recommended if you plan to do this. Francisco Chimbo and Benjamin Shiguango (ask for them in the village) are experienced. The going rate is about $15 per day for a guide – plus you have to provide food and shelter for the guide, as well as for yourself. In addition, a $12 fee per climber is charged; it goes to the community of Huamaní.

Facilities in Huamaní are quite minimal, so bring food and equipment from Tena (see later in this chapter). The rainiest months

(May to August) turn the trail into a mud bath, and the mountain views are clouded over. The driest months are reportedly October to December and this is also the best time to go.

ARCHIDONA
☎ 06

Archidona is a small mission village that was founded in 1560 – the same year as Tena, 10km to the south. The town has grown little in the intervening centuries.

The main plaza is a small, attractive and well-laid-out forest of tropical palms, vines, ferns, flowers and trees. Such a pretty plaza is a surprise in so small a village. The carefully but strangely painted concrete-block church is also very colorful. A good day to visit Archidona is Sunday, when the local Quijo Indians come to their weekly market and to hear mass.

There are a couple of cheap and basic hotels near the plaza. **Residencial Regina** (☎ 889 144; rooms per person with shared/private bath $5/6) has rooms with private bath and a friendly staff. The cheaper Residencial Carolina is also OK. There are a few simple and inexpensive places to eat.

From the plaza, you can take a bus to Cotundo and ask to be dropped at the entrance to the **Cuevas de Jumandí** (admission $0.50), about 4km north of Archidona. There are three main branches in the cave system, which apparently have not yet been fully explored. There is a snack bar and small amusement park (not always open), as well as a place to stay by the caves. The entrance to the cave is lighted, but you must bring your own lights and equipment to see the stalagmites and other formations further in. The cave is muddy, and rubber boots and old clothes are recommended. If you plan on going deep into the cave, you should have a local guide and equipment. Guides in Tena arrange expeditions into the caves with an overnight stay by the cave entrance. These are by far the best known of the many caves in the area.

TENA
☎ 06 ● pop 20,215 ● elevation 518m

Tena has become the de facto white-water rafting and kayaking capital of Ecuador. It's a cool little town where kayaks lay around hotel-room entrances and boaters hang out

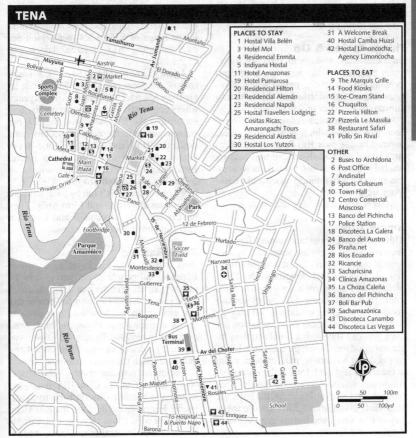

TENA

PLACES TO STAY
1 Hostal Villa Belén
3 Hotel Mol
4 Residencial Enmita
5 Indiyana Hostal
11 Hotel Amazonas
19 Hotel Pumarosa
20 Residencial Hilton
21 Residencial Alemán
23 Residencial Napoli
25 Hostal Travellers Lodging;
   Cositas Ricas;
   Amarongachi Tours
29 Residencial Austria
30 Hostal Los Yutzos
31 A Welcome Break
40 Hostal Camba Huasi
42 Hostal Limoncocha;
   Agency Limoncocha

PLACES TO EAT
9 The Marquis Grille
14 Food Kiosks
15 Ice-Cream Stand
16 Chuquitos
22 Pizzería Hilton
27 Pizzería Le Massilia
38 Restaurant Safari
41 Pollo Sin Rival

OTHER
2 Buses to Archidona
6 Post Office
7 Andinatel
8 Sports Coliseum
10 Town Hall
12 Centro Comercial
   Moscoso
13 Banco del Pichincha
17 Police Station
18 Discoteca La Galera
24 Banco del Austro
26 Piraña.net
28 Ríos Ecuador
32 Ricancie
33 Sacharicsina
34 Clínica Amazonas
35 La Choza Caleña
36 Banco del Pichincha
37 Boli Bar Pub
39 Sachamazónica
43 Discoteca Canambo
44 Discoteca Las Vegas

in pizza joints rapping about their day on the rapids. You can set up a rafting trip easily, and there are several tour operators offering trips into the jungle. Situated at the junction of the lovely Río Tena and Río Pano, Tena has a comfortable climate, thanks to the moderating effect of the rivers on the temperature.

Now the capital of Napo Province, Tena was founded in 1560. There were several Indian uprisings in the early days, notably in 1578, when Jumandy, chief of the Quijos, led a fierce but unsuccessful revolt against the Spaniards. Today, the area is largely agricultural – cattle ranches and coffee and banana plantations abound.

The anniversary of Tena's foundation is celebrated on November 15.

Information

The **Andinatel** (Olmedo) and **post office** (cnr Olmedo & García Moreno) are both northwest of the footbridge. Internet facilities are available at the friendly **Piraña.net** (Orellana) for $3.50 per hour.

Banco del Austro (15 de Noviembre) changes traveler's checks from 9am to 1pm Monday to Friday. **Centro Comercial Moscoso** (☎ 886 029; Amazonas; 8am-8pm Mon-Sat, 8am-2pm Sun) will also change traveler's checks, but only when there's enough cash in the till. Both branches of Banco del Pichincha have ATMs, as does Banco del Austro.

Clínica Amazonas (☎ 886 495; Santa Rosa) is open 24 hours. The **hospital** (☎ 886 302/304) is south of town on the road to

Puerto Napo. The **police station** (☎ 886 101) is on the main plaza.

Things to See & Do

On a clear day, visitors to Tena are sometimes puzzled by the sight of a volcano looming up out of the jungle some 50km away to the north–northeast – this is Volcán Sumaco (see earlier in this chapter).

Parque Amazónico (admission $2; open 8am-5pm daily), which is across a gated, covered bridge over Río Pano, is a 27 hectares island with a self-guided trail passing labeled local plants and animal enclosures. Picnic areas, a swimming beach and a bathroom are available.

Market days are Friday and Saturday.

Jungle Trips

Although much of the land around Tena has been colonized, there are some nearby sections of uncut primary forest that can still be visited. The popular **Amarongachi Tours** (☎/fax 886 372; w www.amarongachi-tours .com; 15 de Noviembre 438) offers various good-time jungle excursions. During its tours (which cost about $40 per person per day), you can stay with a family in the jungle, eat good local food, go for nature hikes, rappel down waterfalls, pan for gold, swim in the rivers and get a look at the rainforest. Amarongachi also operates the lovely Amarongachi and Shangrila cabins; the latter are on a bluff 100m above Río Anzu (a tributary of Río Napo) and feature great views of the river and forest.

Also recommended are the local guides listed with **Ricancie** (Indigenous Network of Upper Napo Communities for Cultural Coexistence and Ecotourism; ☎ 887 953; w http://ric ancie nativeweb.org; 15 de Noviembre 774). Almost all of the guides speak Quechua and/or Spanish, but few speak English. The staff can arrange stays in local villages, as well as the usual jungle trips; they also know the locations of the numerous caves and petroglyphs found in the Tena region. About nine villages are represented, and stays cost $35 to $70 per person per day, depending on the distance traveled, the size of the group and the services required.

Sacharicsina (☎ 886 839; e sacharicsina tour@yahoo.com; Montesdeoca 110) is also recommended. It's run by Olmedo, Oswaldo and Fausto Cerda – a knowledgeable and

friendly local Quechua family. They have eight different tours, and rates are generally in the range of $35 to $50 per person per day, depending on group size and the length of the trip.

Agency Limoncocha (☎ 887 583; e limon cocha@andinanet.net; Sangay 533) is run by German Michael Welschinger. His agency offers one- to five-day tours to nearby forest around the Río Jatanyacu for $28 per person per day. He also offers day runs down the Río Napo (Class III) for $40 per person. Michael owns the cheap Hostal Limoncocha (see Places to Stay, later).

You'll find **Sachamazónica** (☎ 887 979) in the bus terminal. It's run by local indigenous guides Domingo and Lirio Andy. They have worked in Misahuallí and Coca for years and have a lot of experience.

River-Rafting

Tena is the rafting and kayaking capital of Ecuador, and people come here to ride the rapids from all over the world. If you didn't bring your own gear (which many people do), you can join the white-water fun by signing up for a guided trip. If you *did* bring your own gear (which usually means a kayak), you can hire guides or arrange for transport and put-ins through the places mentioned here.

The most popular river is the Upper Napo, which features Class III rapids – big waves and big fun – and can be run year-round. For more excitement, the Río Misahuallí has wild Class IV+ rapids (seasonal November or December to March) and includes a portage around a waterfall. This is some of Ecuador's most challenging rafting, and you should have an expert and certified guide for this. Because of a landslide at the put-in, this river had only just become accessible to kayakers at the time of research for this edition.

Ríos Ecuador/Yacu Amu (☎ 886 727, Quito ☎/fax 02-223 6844, 290 4054; w www .riosecuador.com; 15 de Noviembre) is owned by Australian Steve Nomchong, a professional kayaker who has competed internationally. Ecuadorian Gynner Coronel, the head guide, is certified by the Ecuadorian White-Water Guides Association (AGAR; Asociación de Guías de Aguas Rapidas del Ecuador) and has competed internationally and speaks excellent English. Several European languages are also spoken.

Various rivers are run, both with rafts (no experience necessary) and kayaks. A run down the Upper Napo costs $50 per person, normally with a three-person minimum, although there are guaranteed departures every Saturday. Trips down the Misahuallí cost about $65 per person (when there's access). Transportation and lunch are included in both costs.

A four-day white-water kayaking school (suitable for beginners) is offered for $260 (a bargain compared to rates in the US or Europe). Rental kayaks ($15 per day, or $30 with helmet, skirt, jacket and paddles) are available for experienced kayakers. Ask about other rivers and multiday trips.

Also inquire at Amarongachi Tours who is working with professional guides to start another company. Agency Limoncocha also runs the Río Napo and usually guarantees single rafters can get on a boat on Fridays during high season (a good place to check if you're alone). See Jungle Trips earlier for more details.

Caving
A recommended caving guide is Fernando Noriega Reyes; ask for him at Ricancie (see Jungle Trips earlier). Another good guide is **Manuel Moreta** (☎ 889 185; e manuel.moreta@eudoramail.com), who does waterfall and caving tours and can also arrange tours of Cuevas de Jumandí (see Archidona earlier), along with accommodations by the caves. Note that you should carry your own flashlights (torches) – including backups and extra batteries.

Places to Stay
Budget Most of the cheapest places lack hot water.

A Welcome Break (☎ 886 301; e cofanes@hotmail.com; Agusto Rueda 331; rooms per person $4) is owned by a friendly family and has 10 simple, clean rooms, which share six showers. There's a guest kitchen, laundry facilities and a garden. It's basic but budget travelers love it.

Hostal Limoncocha (☎ 887 583; e limoncocha@andinanet.net; Sangay 533; rooms per person with shared/private bath $3.50/5) is a white house up on a hill to your right as you arrive from the south; it has cheerful, clean rooms (with or without bath) and firm beds. The shared baths are spotless

and hammocks grace the outside deck with lovely views over town. Breakfast and beer are available on request, and there's a guest kitchen.

Residencial Napoli (☎ 886 194; rooms per person $3) is, if nothing else, cheap.

Hostal Travellers Lodging (rooms per person $6, with views $12) is clean and popular, and has comfortable rooms with private hot showers. There is a variety of rooms; the $12 rooms have windows and great views, while the cheaper ones are small, thin-walled, and dark (but still comfortable). All have private baths and hot water. The lodge is run by **Amarongachi Tours** (☎ 886 372; 15 de Noviembre 438). It's a good place to get information and assemble a tour group.

Residencial Alemán (☎ 886 409; 15 de Noviembre 210; singles/doubles with cold bath $5/6, doubles with hot showers $11.50) is clean and friendly, and has rooms with cold bath and fans, or doubles with cable TV and hot showers. There is a parking area.

Residencial Hilton (☎ 886 329; 15 de Noviembre; rooms per person with shared/private bath $4/6) is a tidy little place with small, simple rooms that are actually quite cheerful if you have a window. Those with private baths have good beds.

Residencial Austria (☎ 887 205; Tarqui; singles/doubles $7/11) is small and friendly, and has clean, airy rooms with fan, bath and hot water. It's a great deal.

Indiyana Hostal (☎ 886 334; Bolívar 349; rooms per person $8) is a small, family-run hotel, and with the orange carpet and satiny couches in the living room, it feels sort of like grandma's house. It has eight clean bedrooms with fan, cable TV and private hot showers.

Hostal Villa Belén (☎ 886 228; Avenida Jumandy; rooms per person with hot bath $8), north of town, has very clean rooms which open on to a pleasant garden area.

Hotel Amazonas (☎ 886 439; cnr Juan Montalvo & Mera; rooms per person $3), **Residencial Enmita** (☎ 886 253; Bolívar; rooms per person $4) and **Hostal Camba Huasi** (☎ 887 429; rooms per person under $3) are fine if you just want a place to crash, sans the hot water and other mod cons.

Mid-Range The clean and modern **Hotel Mol** (☎ 886 808; Sucre 432; singles/doubles $16/24) has spacious, pleasant rooms with cable TV, air-conditioning, private bath and hot water; many have balconies. There is a small pool and a restaurant.

Hostal Los Yutzos (☎ 886 717/769/458; *Agusto Rueda 190; rooms per person with fan/air-con $12/15*), in a quiet river-side location, has comfortable, clean, modern rooms with fans or air-conditioning. Rooms have cable TV, hot shower and telephone; some have river views.

Hotel Pumarosa (☎/fax 886 320; Orellana; rooms per person $12.50) is down by the river and has large, attractive rooms with firm beds, reliably hot water, cable TV and telephone. There's a disco and a roller rink right next door which means noise on the weekends.

Places to Eat

Tena has plenty of small and inexpensive restaurants.

Cositas Ricas (15 de Noviembre; mains $3-4.50; open 7:30am-9:30pm daily), next to Amarongachi Tours, is a favorite of travelers and serves vegetarian and Ecuadorian plates and good juices made with boiled water.

Chuquitos (☎ 887 630; mains $3-5; open 7:30am-9pm Mon-Sat), just off the main plaza, has a balcony with river views, a large menu of local food (especially fish) and the best lemonade in town.

Pizzería Le Massilia (cnr Orellana & Pano; pizzas $4-6; open 5pm-11pm daily) serves some of the best thick- and thin-crust pizzas in the Oriente. **Pizzería Hilton** (pizzas $2-7; open 5pm-11pm daily) is also good, with slightly cheaper options.

The Marquis Grille (☎ 886 513; Amazonas 251; full dinners $9; open noon-3pm & 6pm-11pm Mon-Sat), with its starched white tablecloths and slick waiters, is Tena's finest restaurant. The *quiteño* chef cooks up delicious, thick steaks, lamb, chicken, grilled trout and other delectable dishes. Most cost $9 and include salad, wine and dessert.

Restaurant Safari (☎ 888 257; mains $1.50-3; open 7am-11pm daily), near the bus terminal, is plain, bright and very cheap.

Pollo Sin Rival (open Mon-Sat; mains $1.50-3), two blocks south of the bus terminal, is where travelers and locals alike go for roast chicken.

There's an ice-cream stand on the main plaza by the river (on the northeast side of the footbridge) with outdoor tables. Nearby

are several cheap food kiosks serving burgers, *papi-pollo* (chicken with fries) and other greasy snacks in the evening.

Entertainment

Kids take to the discos on weekends, but bobbing straight-faced on the dance floor is about as crazy as things get. It's still worth going out. Discos open 8pm to 2am or 3am Thursday through Saturday. **La Choza Caleña** (15 de Noviembre; admission $2) gets packed; people like it for its bamboo-wall, thatched-roof, down-home atmosphere. **Discoteca La Galera** (admission $2), next to Hotel Pumarosa, is a poppy little disco with a roller rink attached. Women get in free on Friday. Those in the know (ie, most of the town's youth) head south of the bus terminal to **Discoteca Canambo** (admission $1) and **Discoteca Las Vegas** (admission $1), where they do the communal light-shake to pop tunes.

Boli Bar Pub (15 de Noviembre) is good for a mellow night of pool, beer and rock and roll. There are also several little riverside bars on either side of the river where folks suck down Pilseners and smoke the night away at outdoor tables.

Getting There & Away

The **bus terminal** (15 de Noviembre) is in the southern end of town. There are numerous departures a day for Quito ($5, five hours) via Baeza, and 11 a day to Coca ($6, six hours). There are regular departures to Puyo ($2.50, three hours) and Ambato ($4, five hours). Jumandy has a night bus to Lago Agrio ($7, eight to nine hours). Most of these main routes are paved, but unpaved sections, old buses and inclement weather still make trip lengths in the Oriente notoriously unpredictable.

Getting Around

The local buses for Archidona ($0.20, 15 minutes) leave about every half hour during daylight hours from the west side of the market. Buses for Misahuallí ($0.75, one hour) leave about every hour from 15 de Noviembre, outside the bus terminal. There are about nine buses a day from the terminal to La Punta ($0.60, 1½ hours), from where boats cross the river to Ahuano. About five buses a day go to Santa Rosa ($0.70, two hours). Other local destinations are also served.

MISAHUALLÍ

☎ 06

East of Tena, this small village (also called Puerto Misahuallí) is at the end of the road running from Puerto Napo along the north bank of Río Napo. Along with Tena, it is a popular place from which to see some of the Oriente, because you can easily get here by bus from Quito in a day.

However, before you grab your hammock and pith helmet and jump on the next bus, you should realize that this isn't virgin jungle. The area has been colonized for decades, and most mammals have been either hunted out or had their habitats encroached upon to the point where they cannot survive.

What you will see, if you keep your eyes open – or better still, if you hire a local guide – is a variety of jungle birds, tropical flowers, army ants, dazzling butterflies and other insects.

In addition, you will see the people who live in the jungle – colonists, gold-panners, oil workers, farmers, ranchers, military personnel, people in the tourism industry and entrepreneurs. The remaining Indian tribes live deeper in the jungle and, for the most part, prefer to be left alone. Most of the Indians in the area are either transplanted highlanders or acculturated locals.

The physical geography of this area remains rolling and rather rugged. The elevation is about 400m (with hills twice that high within a few kilometers), and there are many more ridges and valleys around here than in the flatlands around Coca, which is barely 100m above sea level. The more complex geography means that there are still some small areas that haven't been disturbed by colonists because they are hard to get to.

Buses can usually reach Misahuallí in any weather, but roads can be in poor shape during the wettest period (June to August).

If you want an excursion deep into the jungle, it can be arranged in Misahuallí, although this will require time, patience, flexibility and money.

Information

There is no bank, nor any post office or Internet facilities (go to Tena for all that). You need to carry your passport on buses, boats and tours in the region.

Things to See & Do

It's fun to pack a lunch and walk the pleasant graveled roads out of Misahuallí and visit the nearby villages.

There's a nearby **waterfall** that makes a nice place for a swim and a picnic. It often figures into one-day tours offered by some guides, although you can reach it easily enough on your own. Take a Misahuallí–Puerto Napo bus and ask the driver to drop you off at Río Latas, about 15 or 20 minutes away from Misahuallí. All the drivers know *el camino a las cascadas* ('the trail to the falls'). Follow the river upstream to the falls, passing several swimming holes en route. Be prepared to wade. It takes about an hour to reach the falls, depending on how fast you walk.

Be sure to visit the **butterfly farm** *(Centro de Reproducción de Mariposas; admission $2; open 9am-4pm daily)*, located a block off the plaza. It's run by Pepe and Margarita of Ecoselva (see Organized Tours following), and it offers a close look at rainforest butterflies and their equally dazzling stages as cocoons and caterpillars. The mature butterflies are released into the forest. Volunteers are needed.

Organized Tours

Misahuallí was once one of the best towns in the Oriente to spend a few days hanging out, meeting other travelers, putting a group together, hiring a guide and heading off into the jungle. These days, however, more people are arranging tours in Quito and passing quickly through jungle-entry points such as Misahuallí. This makes it harder for independent travelers to organize their own group, but it can still be done, and you'll get a slightly cheaper rate than going from Quito – and get to enjoy this relaxing, riverside jungle town in the process. You'll find an accommodating guide (and price) far more quickly if you already have a small group together (four or more) when you arrive in Misahuallí. The larger your group, the more economical the price.

Guides will approach you in the main plaza offering tours – most of these are inexperienced and unlicensed, and you're best off hiring a guide recommended here or by other travelers.

There are several good guides and tour operators available in Misahuallí. The tours range from one to 10 days in duration and prices should include the guide, food, water, accommodations (from jungle camping to comfortable lodges) and rubber boots. Tours cost $25 to $50 per person depending on the destination, season, number of persons and length of the tour. Four people can get a good tour for $25 to $35 per person per day.

Aventuras Amazónicas (☎ 890 031, 890 113) Based in Residencial La Posada, on the plaza, this is run by Carlos and María del Carmen Santander. The staff do a good job.

Douglas Clarke's Expeditions (☎ 887 584; **e** douglasclarkeexpediciones@yahoo.com) Contact the Hostal Marena Internacional. This operator has been around for years, and one- to 10-day tours are available. Several of the guides speak some English. Most overnights involve camping. We've received many good reports.

Ecoselva (☎ 890 019; **e** ecoselva@yahoo.es) This outfit is run by Pepe Tapia González, who has a biology background and speaks English. He's extremely knowledgeable about plants and insects, is often used by researchers and is great fun. His office is on the plaza. One- to 10-day tours are offered with overnights at his rustic lodge or jungle camps. With four people he charges $25 per person per day.

Expediciones El Albergue Español (☎ 890 127; **w** www.albergueespanol.com) This outfit is based at the hotel of the same name (see Places to Stay & Eat following), and several of its guides have been recommended. Trips are usually based out of the comfortable Jaguar Lodge on the Río Napo.

Fluvial River Tours (☎ 228 2859, Quito ☎ 02-228 2859) Héctor Fiallos runs this company, which is also called Sacha Tours. It has been around for years. Fiallos himself is a good guide, but he's rarely in Misahuallí. Inquire at Hostal Sacha (see the Places to Stay & Eat following).

Jaime Recalde (☎ 890 077/087; **e** jaimerecalde@yahoo.com) Jaime is a friendly licensed guide who has lots of experience guiding for the bigger operators. He charges $35 per person for tours near Misahuallí and $50 per person to areas further abroad, such as Cuyabeno. Ask for him at Restaurant Doña Gloria (see Places to Stay & Eat following).

Misahuallí Tours On the corner of the plaza, this agency is run by the cheerful and knowledgeable Carlos Lastra Lasso, who speaks some English.

Places to Stay & Eat

None of the accommodations in Misahuallí are expensive or particularly luxurious. Water and electricity failures are frequent. Although the cheapest places may look pretty run down, don't let their appearances make you think they are dangerous. They aren't – they are just cheap, beat-up jungle hotels.

Residencial El Balcón del Napo (☎ 890 117, 890 045; rooms per person $2), on the plaza, has small, concrete-block rooms – some of which look like jail cells. The rooms with windows are OK.

Hotel Shaw (rooms per person $3) is situated above, and run by, Ecoselva (see Organized Tours, previous). It's basic and has shared baths.

Residencial La Posada (☎ 890 113; rooms per person $5), nearby, is a rambling old place with clean, recently renovated rooms; some have private baths.

El Paisano (☎ 890 027; rooms per person $5) is popular with travelers and has clean doubles with private baths, fans and mosquito nets. There is a pleasant garden with hammocks, and the open-air restaurant will provide vegetarian dishes if requested in advance. It's just off the plaza.

Hostal Sacha (☎ 886 679; rooms per person with shared/private bath $3/4), owned by Fluvial River Tours (see Organized Tours previous), is a very rustic little place down by the river. There are hammocks out front and a nice open-air bar, good for afternoon beers by the river. Bring a mosquito net if you stay the night.

Hostal Marena Internacional (☎ 890 002; rooms per person $6) is half a block from the plaza and has a 4th-floor rooftop restaurant with a view and large rooms with private bath and hot water. It's owned by Douglas Clarke's Expeditions.

Hotel Albergue Español (☎ 890 127; **w** www.albergueespanol.com; rooms per person $8) is Spanish run and offers rooms with private bath and solar-heated hot water. Rooms are clean and have fans; some have river views. There is a restaurant, and the management is helpful. It is about 200m off the plaza, past Hostal Marena Internacional. It's owned by the owners of Jaguar Lodge, about 90 minutes away by boat (see Jaguar Lodge later in this chapter).

France Amazonia (☎/fax 887 570; rooms per person $10), also a few minutes from the plaza, has six stone cabins with thatched roof and private hot bath. Four are doubles and two are triples. Local tours can be arranged. The French owner provides decent meals.

Hostería Misahuallí (w *www.misahualli jungle.com; singles/doubles $30/41*) is just across Río Misahuallí, on the north side of Río Napo. Reservations can be arranged through its **Quito office** (☎ *02-252 0043, 252 4322;* e *miltour@accessinter.net; Ramírez Dávalos 251*). It's a comfortable but sprawling place, with a restaurant, swimming pool, tennis court, pool table, electricity, private baths, hot water and a number of trails.

There are several little eateries on the plaza. One of the best is **Restaurant Doña Gloria** (*mains $2-3.50; open daily*), where the juice is always made with boiled water.

Getting There & Away

Buses leave from the plaza about every hour during daylight hours; the last bus is at 6pm. The main destination is Tena ($0.75, one hour), where you can make connections to other places. Transportes Jumandy has a direct bus from Quito at 11am, returning from Misahuallí at 8:30am ($5, seven hours).

Since the opening of the Tena–Coca road and the construction of roads east along Río Napo, river traffic has dwindled to the point that passenger canoes are no longer available. Hiring a canoe to take you to Coca costs $250 to $300. If you're staying at a lodge on the Río Napo, transport will be arranged by the lodge.

UPPER RÍO NAPO
☎ 06

The Río Napo flows northeast from Misahuallí toward Coca and has nature reserves, communities and excellent jungle lodges along its verdant shores. Public canoe transportation down the Napo to Coca has been completely replaced by transportation on the Tena–Coca road. There is also a road along the south bank of the Río Napo from Puerto Napo to La Punta, which passes some of the places described below.

Reserva Biológica Jatun Sacha

Jatun Sacha (*admission $6*) means 'Big Forest' in the Quechua language. This is a biological station and rainforest reserve of 20 sq km on the south side of Río Napo, 23km east of Puerto Napo. It is run by **Fundación Jatun Sacha** (*Quito* ☎ *02-243 2240, 243 2173;* w *www.jatunsacha.org; Pasaje Eugenio de Santillán N34-248 & Maurián, Urbanización Rumipamba*), an Ecuadorian nonprofit organization founded in 1985 with the goal of promoting rainforest research, conservation and education.

At Jatun Sacha, scientists are currently carrying out surveys listing which species are present, a complicated task considering the area is one of the most species-rich regions on earth. Some of the plants and animals found here are unknown to science – exciting stuff! Herpetologists (scientists who study reptiles) claim that there are more species of 'herps' here than almost anywhere on the globe. Botanists echo this with regards to flowering plants. Much of it is primary forest, although it is broken up by cleared sections. There are a few kilometers of trails and a small botanical garden. A local guide can be hired for a few dollars.

Unfortunately, neighboring areas are being rapidly cleared for logging and agriculture, and it is not known how long the incredible biodiversity of Jatun Sacha will remain. One of the goals of the foundation, however, is the furthering of rural development projects, which will help residents engage in economically viable and sustainable activities as an alternative to deforestation. Volunteers (who pay $300 for a minimum one-month stay) are welcome to apply for a variety of projects.

At the research station itself, there are four unscreened buildings that sleep about 30 people. Accommodations are primitive – bunk beds, mosquito nets and outdoor showers and latrines. A dining room and meals are available. Researchers, students and tourists can stay here for $25 a day, including meals and access to the reserve trail system.

Jatun Sacha can help arrange transportation from Quito if your group takes one of its multiday tours. To get here independently see Cabañas Aliñahui following.

Cabañas Aliñahui

Also known as **Butterfly Lodge** (w *www .ecuadorexplorer.com/alinahui; room & board per person per day $25-35*), this is where most tourists stay when visiting the Jatun Sacha area. Aliñahui's eight comfortable, screened cabins are spaced throughout a 2-hectare tropical garden and have solar electricity, shady patios with hammocks and upstairs verandas with river views. Most cabins have two double rooms and a private bathroom with a flush-toilet and a solar-heated shower.

There's also an open-air buffet restaurant serving good, healthy Ecuadorian and international meals, a small bar and a gift shop.

The site is on a bluff above the river, and there are several thatched shelters with excellent views of the river and (on clear days) four of the Andean volcanoes – hence the name Aliñahui, which means 'good view' in Quechua. These shelters are great places to relax.

Aliñahui offers naturalist-led walking tours (day and night), guided canoe excursions, visits to local communities, and opportunities for swimming, photographing, gold panning and relaxing. Of course, the bird-watching is outstanding – 537 species have been recorded in the area! There are often educational programmes lead by local and international specialists in botany, biology, mammalogy, entomology, ecology, herbalogy or shamanism.

Several readers have recommended Aliñahui as one of Ecuador's best environmentally conscious lodges. It's owned primarily by the US-based nonprofit organization **Health & Habitat** (w www.butterflylodge.org) in partnership with its immediate jungle neighbor, Jatun Sacha. Rates include three meals and vary slightly, depending on the size of your group and length of stay. Guided tours cost about $15 extra per person per day. Multiday packages can also be arranged.

Reservations can be made at Cabañas Aliñahui's **Quito office** (☎ 02-256 4012, 222 7094, fax 222 7095; e alinahui@interactive.net.ec; Pinto 240; open 10am-5pm Mon-Fri), between Reina Victoria and Diego de Almagro, by email, or by mail at Cabañas Aliñahui, PO Box 17-11-6353, Quito, Ecuador.

To get to either Jatun Sacha or Cabañas Aliñahui from Tena, take an Ahuano or Santa Rosa bus and ask the driver to drop you at either entrance (they all know them). Aliñahui is about 3km east of the Jatun Sacha research station, or 27km east of Tena on the road to Santa Rosa.

Ahuano

This small mission village is about one hour downriver from Misahuallí and can also be reached by bus from Tena to La Punta, followed by a river crossing. This is the end of the road, and travel by boat from here to Coca is expensive and difficult to arrange, so you're best off returning to Tena and

going by bus. There is not much to do in Ahuano itself, although there are some nearby jungle lodges. There are a couple of basic stores but little other infrastructure in this village.

Places to Stay Ask in the village about basic *pensiones* (boarding houses). **Hostal Samantha** (beds about $2) is the cheapest. **Casa de Stefan** (rooms per person $10) has four rooms with private bath and four with shared bath.

Casa del Suizo (Quito ☎ 02-256 6090, 250 9504/115; w www.casadelsuizo.com; Zaldumbide 375 & Toledo; rooms per person per night $70, packages per person for 4 days/3 nights doubles $210, singles $273) is a comfortable jungle lodge that can accommodate up to 170 guests, offering travelers a taste of the rainforest without the discomfort. The spacious cabins and rooms are very pleasant, with balconies or terraces, views, private showers, hot water, electricity and ceiling fans. There is a large, free-form pool and a good restaurant and bar – all in a scenic location by the river, which can be appreciated from a tower above the restaurant. There is a variety of tours available, including river trips, jungle hikes, visits to missions and local communities, and wildlife walks. Both package and daily rates include meals and tours with bilingual guides.

Cabañas Anaconda (Quito ☎/fax 02-222 4913; e anacondaec@andinanet.net; rooms per person $35-45, packages per person for 3 days/2 nights $80), on Anaconda Island, a few minutes from Ahuano, is a jungle-style lodge with bamboo walls and thatched roofs. Rooms have mosquito screens and private bath but no electricity or hot water. Rates include good meals and a daily canoe trip or jungle excursion from the island. English-speaking guides are available with advance request. You'll see pet animals such as monkeys and peccaries; some of the caged exhibits have been criticized as being too small.

Getting There & Away Buses from Tena run eight times a day to La Punta, about 28km east of Puerto Napo on the south side of Río Misahuallí. Although the bus doesn't actually go to Ahuano, it's still called the Ahuano bus locally, because there isn't much happening at La Punta. There is no problem crossing Río Napo from La Punta to Ahuano.

Dugout canoes wait at La Punta to take you across to Ahuano. The fare is about $1 per person, and there are frequent boats, particularly after a bus arrives. Chartering your own boat costs more. These boats can drop you off at Casa del Suizo or Cabañas Anaconda (the latter costs several dollars).

Selva Viva & Liana Lodge

This is a preserve of about 10 sq km of primary forest surrounding the well-known animal-rehabilitation center AmaZOOnico (W www.amazoonico.org; admission $2). It's on a tributary of Río Napo about 3km east of Ahuano. The center was founded in 1994 by Angelika Raimann and Remigio Canelos (a Swiss/Quechua couple) to care for rainforest animals that have been confiscated from illegal traffickers or are otherwise injured. Healthy animals are released back into the rainforest. There are dozens of animals on the premises at any time, ranging from toucans to tapirs.

Since the center opened, the owners have bought the surrounding rainforest and opened Liana Lodge (fax 887 304; e amazoon@na .pro.ec; rooms per person about $39) to help fund both the rehab center and the new preserve. The lodge has six cabins, each with two double rooms with private hot shower and a view of the river. Rates include meals, taxes and local tours.

To get to Selva Viva, take one of several daily buses from Tena to Santa Rosa. Ask the driver to stop at the Selva Viva entrance, and hike almost 2km downstream to the lodge. Quechua, English, Spanish, German and French and are spoken here.

Jaguar Lodge

This comfortable, modern lodge (☎ 890 127, 890 004; w www.alberguespanol.com; packages per person for 3 days/2 nights $105, 4 days/3 nights $135, 5 days/4 nights $155, group of 4 or more per person per day $35) sits within 10 sq km of privately owned primary forest (and is surrounded by more) on the bank of the Río Napo, about 1½ hours from Misahuallí. It has about a dozen rooms with solar-heated hot-water baths, a swimming pool, an attractive main lodge with good views, a decent restaurant and bar, and a cable-TV lounge. It's a good deal, considering the price includes meals, kayaks for tooling around the river, and activities such

as visits to nearby indigenous communities and gold panning. There's a small farm and three lookouts on the property, and guides are available for a variety of tours.

Yachana Lodge

This ecotourism lodge (packages for 3/4 nights July, Aug & Dec $325/400, other months $224/314) is part of an impressive project called Funedesin (Foundation for Integrated Education and Development), a NGO whose mission statement is finding workable solutions in the struggle between the ideals of rainforest preservation and the realities of life in the Ecuadorian Amazon. The lodge not only uses local labor to provide visitors with a rainforest experience, it also is the center of other projects, including organic agriculture, beekeeping, agricultural training, food processing, a clinic and health education, and radio broadcasting. Visitors are encouraged to tour the various facilities. The community is strongly involved in the projects – locals don't just accept them as handouts.

The Yachana Lodge complex is in the tiny community of Mondaña, almost halfway between Misahuallí and Coca on Río Napo. The lodge itself has 11 rooms (each room sleeping two or three people) and three family cabins with a double and a triple room. Each room has a private hot shower and a balcony, and lighting is by solar power. There is a small conference center and library, a deck with a view and a restaurant serving tasty meals.

Visitors typically stay for three or four nights, with set departures from Quito on Tuesdays and Fridays. Both four-day/three-night and five-day/four-night options are available. Children aged 12 and under are charged half price. Costs include everything except alcohol, soft drinks, personal expenses and (optional) air transportation from Quito to Coca. From Coca, it is a two-hour motorized canoe ride to the lodge.

During the stay at the lodge, you can take part in a traditional healing ceremony, go on guided hikes along 20km of trails, take day or night rides in a canoe, take a class in basket weaving from a local expert, visit the projects in the area or just relax in a hammock. Local guides and Yachana's naturalists are treasure troves of information and speak excellent English.

Reservations should be made in Quito at **Funedesin/Yachana Lodge** (☎ 02-256 6035, 252 3777, 250 3275; **w** www.yachana.com; Baquedano 385 & JL Mera).

PUYO

☎ 03 • pop 25,362

With a growing population, Puyo is the provincial capital of Pastaza. Until the early 1970s, it had a real frontier atmosphere and was the most important town in the Oriente. Since the discovery of oil, however, the frontier has been pushed deep into the jungle, although Puyo remains an important Oriente town.

Fiestas de Fundación de Puyo, the week-long celebrations of Puyo's founding day, takes place in early May.

Information

For basic tourist information you can visit the **Cámara de Turismo** (☎ 886 737; 2nd floor, Marín Centro Commercial Zuñiga; open 8:30am-12:30pm & 3pm-6pm Mon-Fri).

Amazonía Touring (☎ 883 064; Atahualpa; open 9am-8pm Mon-Sat, 9am-noon Sun) is the only place to change traveler's checks. It charges a 3% commission. **Banco del Austro** (Atahualpa) has an ATM. The **post office** (27 de Febrero) is northwest of the market. Telephone services are available at **Andinatel** (Orellana; open 8am-10pm daily).

Cyber Té (Marín 5-69; open daily) has the fastest Internet connection at $2 per hour, but **Guanábanet** (Atahualpa; open daily) is livelier and also slightly cheaper ($1.80 per hour).

The **Voz Andes mission hospital** (☎ 795 172) in Shell (see later in this chapter) is the best bet for medical emergencies. The **Red Cross** (☎ 885 214) in Puyo is on the north side of the main plaza.

Things to See & Do

Early risers may see a spectacular view of jagged snowy peaks rising up over a jungle covered with rolling morning mist. Later in the morning, the mountains usually disappear into the clouds. The jagged peaks belong to **El Altar** (5319m), the fifth-highest mountain in Ecuador, which is about 50km southeast of Puyo. Occasionally, you can also catch a glimpse of **Sangay** (5230m), southwest of Puyo. A good view can be had from the main plaza on a clear day.

Less than 1km north of the center, by Río Puyo, is **Parque Omaere** (☎ 886 764; admission $3; open 8am-4pm daily), which calls itself a pedagogical ethnobotanical park. The park offers tours (free with admission) guided by local natives who explain the importance of the many plants of the rainforest. Life-sized replicas of the houses of several Oriente tribes are in the park. Get there by following Loja north of town for about half a kilometer, until you reach the bridge over the river, and follow the sign. A pleasant **trail** (locally called the paseo turístico) continues past Omaere for 2.5km along the river to the Puyo–Tena road, where you can flag the very occasional bus back into town, hitch, or walk back along the trail.

Centro Fatima (☎ 884 105; admission $2; open 8am-5pm daily) is 9km from Puyo on

Community Tourism

Papangu-Atacapi Tours (☎ 883 875; **e** papangu@andinanet.net; 27 de Febrero, near Sucre) is a unique Quechua-run tour operator specializing in cultural tourism, offering travelers the opportunity to visit Quechua villages, stay with local families and learn about Quechua lifestyles. It was founded by **Organización de Pueblos Indígenas de Pastaza** (OPIP; ☎ 883 019), a community organization representing about 130 small Quechua communities in Pastaza Province, totaling about 20,000 people. The philosophy of Papangu-Atacapi Tours is to provide communities with the opportunity to develop and benefit from their own forms of ecotourism. The money tourists spend on these tours goes directly to the communities they visit.

Guided tours with small groups (two-person minimum) cost $35 to $40 per person per day. Popular options include day tours in the Puyo area and three-day/two-night excursions to local villages. There are also more expensive options ($70 to $80 per person per day) that last for several days and include light-aircraft flights to remote villages. You can also ask here about possibilities for work in volunteer projects in the area.

Catedral de la Inmaculada Concepción, Cuenca

ALICE GRULICH-JONES

Making panama hats, Cuenca

AARON MCCOY

Inca wall, Ingapirca

ROB RACHOWIECKI

Colorful panama hats, Cuenca

DAVID PEEVERS

Traditional healer, Río Napo, Oriente

ROB RACHOWIECKI

Urania butterflies, Oriente

BRENT WINEBRENNER

Canoeing, Oriente

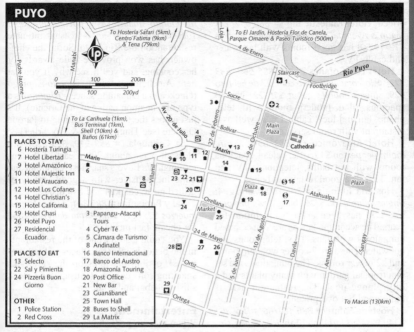

PUYO

To Hostería Sáfari (5km),
Centro Fátima (9km)
& Tena (79km)

To El Jardín, Hostería Flor de Canela,
Parque Omaere & Paseo Turístico (500m)

Loja

Río Puyo

Staircase
Footbridge

4 de Enero

Sucre

Río Puyo

To La Carihuela (1km),
Bus Terminal (1km),
Shell (10km) &
Baños (61km)

Av. 20 de Julio

27 de Febrero

Bolívar

9 de Octubre

Main Plaza

Cathedral

Marín

Plaza

Marín

Orellana
Market

Atahualpa

Plaza

24 de Mayo

10 de Agosto

5 de Junio

Dávila

Amazonas

Sangay

Ortiz

To Macas (130km)

Ortega

PLACES TO STAY
6 Hostería Turingia
7 Hotel Libertad
9 Hotel Amazónico
10 Hotel Majestic Inn
11 Hotel Araucano
12 Hotel Los Cofanes
14 Hotel Christian's
15 Hotel California
19 Hotel Chasi
26 Hotel Puyo
27 Residencial
    Ecuador

PLACES TO EAT
13 Selecto
22 Sal y Pimienta
24 Pizzería Buon
    Giorno

OTHER
1 Police Station
2 Red Cross

3 Papangu-Atacapi
   Tours
4 Cyber Té
5 Cámara de Turismo
8 Andinatel
16 Banco Internacional
17 Banco del Austro
18 Amazonía Touring
20 Post Office
21 New Bar
23 Guanábanet
25 Town Hall
28 Buses to Shell
29 La Matrix

the Tena road. This wildlife-rescue and research center covers 28 hectares and is involved in such projects as reproducing endangered species and domesticating and raising rainforest animals as livestock for local communities. The center is staffed by a friendly biologist and volunteers (who pay a small weekly fee for a bed and use of the kitchen facilities). Call for information. Visitors can take a guided tour of the facilities and see the animals that are being bred, which include tapirs, capybaras and other rodents, various monkeys (which are very friendly), parrots and reptiles. You can get there from Puyo by taking a taxi ($4) or any bus to Tena.

Places to Stay

Budget One of the cheapest places in town is **Residencial Ecuador** (☎ 883 089; 24 de Mayo; rooms per person $3), which has dark but clean rooms with shared bath.

Hotel Libertad (☎ 883 282; Orellana; rooms per person $5) is new, sparkling clean and one of the best-value hotels in town. The rooms have good beds and TVs, but all have shared baths (although these are clean and have hot water).

Hotel Chasi (☎ 883 059; 9 de Octubre; rooms per person $5) and **Hotel California** (☎ 885 189; 9 de Octubre; rooms per person $5) are both worn-down but clean places with private cold-water baths.

Hotel Araucano (☎ 883 834, 885 686, fax 885 227; Marín 575; rooms per person $6.50-11.50) is clean, very friendly and helpful. All rooms have a private hot bath and a fan, and some have TV and fridge (depending on the price you pay). Top-floor rooms have views of Sangay, and rates include a tiny breakfast.

Hotel Puyo (☎ 884 497, 886 525; 9 de Octubre; rooms per person $8) is another new hotel. Its spotless rooms have firm beds, TV, telephone and private hot-water baths – quite a deal for Puyo.

Hotel Christian's (☎/fax 883 081; Atahualpa; rooms per person $9) is a bit like sleeping in a small, empty shopping mall. It's clean but odd for a hotel. Street-side rooms have huge windows, and all have private baths and hot water.

Hostal Lo Copales (☎ 795 290; Km 51 vía Baños-Puyo) is a lovely little place to stay outside of town, but it's about 1km west of Shell (see Shell later in this chapter).

THE ORIENTE

Mid-Range Although it seems a bit over-priced, **Hotel Majestic Inn** (☎ 885 417; cnr Marín & Avenida 20 de Julio; singles/doubles $12/19.50) has good rooms with hot water and cable TV.

Hotel Los Cofanes (☎/fax 885 560, 883 772; e loscofanes@yahoo.com; 27 de Febrero 629; singles/doubles about $15/22) has 30 spacious, tiled, modern rooms with telephone, fan and local cable TV, as well as a restaurant with room service.

Hotel Amazónico (☎ 883 094; Marín; rooms per person $12) offers clean, spacious rooms with hot baths, telephone, TV and fan. There's a good restaurant below.

Hostería Turingia (☎ 885 180; Marín 294; singles/doubles $15/25, bungalows per person $18) has been a Puyo institution for years. The accommodations are a bit cramped bungalows with fans, TVs, telephones and hot water. There are 24 older wooden rooms and 22 newer rooms. The bungalows are set in a tropical garden with many plants and a tiny plunge pool. The restaurant here is quite good but overpriced.

Hostería Safari (☎ 885 464/66, ☎/fax 851 424; e safarifloreshotel@andinanet.net; singles/doubles $25/43) is a modern, comfortable hotel, about 5km away on the road to Tena. It has a nice garden with a pool, a Jacuzzi and sauna which operate on weekends, a games area, a gift shop and a restaurant and bar. Rooms have private bath and hot water and rates include breakfast and dinner.

Hostería Flor de Canela (☎ 885 265; e hosteriaflordecanela@hotmail.com; Paseo Turístico, Barrio Obrero; rooms per person $14-18) offers relaxing cabañas surrounded by lush foliage near the Río Puyo. The exorbitant cabañas seem wasteful of tropical hardwoods, but they sure are pretty. It's right next door to Parque Omaere (see Things to See & Do previous). There's a swimming pool too.

Places to Eat

A few restaurants in the center are adequate, if not memorable. **Selecto** (Marín; mains $1.50-2.50; open 7:30am-9pm daily) serves simple, filling almuerzos (set-lunch menu) and set-dinner menus for $1.50, as well as plates from the menu.

Pizzería Buon Giorno (☎ 883 841; Orellana; pizzas $4.50-6; open 1pm-10pm Mon-Sat) serves good, heavily cheesed pizzas in a chipper dining room.

El Jardín (☎ 886 101; Paseo Turístico, Barrio Obrero; mains $4-5; open noon-10pm Tues-Sat, noon-5pm Sun) is a casual, intimate restaurant on the Río Puyo. Sofia, the chef-owner, has won province-wide awards for her cooking, and you'll see why if you eat here. A delicious specialty is pollo ishpingo (chicken in a cinnamon sauce – ishpingo is a type of cinnamon native to the Oriente). It's just across the footbridge leading to Parque Omaere (see Things to See & Do earlier).

La Carihuela (☎ 883 919, 823 920) is a pleasant place about 200m east of the bus terminal. It's Puyo's snazziest restaurant and quite inexpensive, with a good variety of grilled meat, chicken and fish dishes.

Sal y Pimienta (☎ 885 821; Atahualpa; almuerzos $2; open 7am-11pm daily) is good for cheap, fast meals.

You could also try one of the restaurants in the better hotels (see Places to Stay previous), or join the folks on the sidewalks snacking on chuzos (sausage-and-steak shish kebabs) and hotdogs.

Entertainment

When the sun goes down, everyone seems to take to the streets downtown, and then at around 9pm or 10pm, they disappear just as quickly. When that happens, try **New Bar** (27 de Febrero; open 6pm-2am Mon-Sat). It's convenient and has plenty of tables (and sometimes dancing and karaoke). Where 27 de Febrero turns to dirt, you'll find the popular little back-alley disco **La Matrix** (open Thur-Sat). There are several open-air bars down by the river, before the footbridge leading to Parque Omaere (see Things to See & Do, previous), although they're most appealing for afternoon drinks.

Getting There & Away

The provincial airstrip is in Shell (see Shell later).

The bus terminal is about 1km southwest of town. There are buses via Baños ($1.50, two hours) to Ambato ($2.50, three hours). Buses to Quito leave about every hour and go either via Baños or Baeza. Buses to Tena ($2.50, three hours) also leave hourly.

Buses to Macas ($3.75, five hours) leave five or six times a day and go as far as Río Pastaza, where you have to transfer (see Macas later in this chapter). Flota Pelileo has a 6:30am departure to Coca ($8, 8½ hours).

Centinela del Oriente runs ancient buses to various small villages in the surrounding jungle.

Getting Around
Small local buses go to Shell ($0.20) about every 30 minutes or so from south of the market along 27 de Febrero. A taxi ride from downtown to the bus terminal costs about $0.80 and to Shell about $3.

SHELL
Shell is a US missionary center about 10km southwest of Puyo on the road to Baños. Its airstrip is the most important airstrip in the province of Pastaza, but is used only by missions, the Ecuadorian Air Force and folks with enough money to charter their own plane. You won't get lost in this place – it's a one-street town, and the airport is at the west end, on the way to Baños.

There are a couple of basic but adequate hotels along the main drag. About 1km out of town, on the road to Baños, **Hostal Lo Copales** *(☎ 795 290; Km 51 vía Baños-Puyo; cabins per person $8, with 3 meals $20)* is the best place around. It has four spotless wooden cabins with private baths and, behind them, 20 hectares of forest and a creek to explore.

The best restaurant here is **El Capitán/La Bromeliad** *(☎ 759 386; mains $2-4; open daily)*, midway down the main drag. It's popular with the pilots.

The Ecuadorian Air Force (FAE; Fuerza Aerea Ecuatoriana) flies weekdays to Quito and larger jungle towns, but civilians only get on in medical emergencies. You can charter a five-seater plane at many of the companies along the strip for a measly $900 to Quito or $320 to destinations in the Oriente.

Buses charge $0.20 to Puyo (about 20 minutes) and $1.50 to Baños. There is no bus terminal; wait on the main road and flag a bus that's heading your way.

The Southern Oriente

There are two main surface routes into the southern Oriente. The most frequently used route is from Cuenca through Limón (officially named General Leonidas Plaza Gutiérrez) to Macas, the main town in the southern

Oriente. The other route runs from Loja through Zamora (both described in the Cuenca & the Southern Highlands chapter) and continues north to Limón, where it joins the first road heading north to Macas. You can also get to Macas in about five hours from Puyo in the northern Oriente. Almost all the roads in this region are unpaved and subject to landslides and delays during the rainy season, so don't plan a tight schedule in this area. June to August are the rainiest months.

MACAS
☎ 07 • pop 30,177
Macas, the capital of Morona-Santiago Province, could very well be the most dignified town in the Oriente. It has four centuries of history as a Spanish trading and missionary outpost, and an old mule trail still joins Macas with the highlands near Riobamba. A road that would follow this trail is planned, and large segments of it have now been completed. The road north to Puyo requires crossing Río Pastaza on two bridges (there's an island between them); the bridges can take cars but not large vehicles. Buses meet travelers at either end.

Despite its history, Macas is essentially a modern and developing town. The bus terminal and airport are both relatively new, and the main plaza was completed only in 1983.

Information
Tourist Offices For general information, stop by the helpful **Cámara de Turismo** *(☎ 701 606, 700 300; Bolívar; open 8:30am-12:30pm & 2:30pm-6pm Mon-Fri)*. The **Centro de Interpretación** *(cnr Juan de la Cruz & 29 de Mayo)* has a small exhibit and information about Parque Nacional Sangay.

Money You may be able to change traveler's checks at **Banco del Austro** *(cnr 24 de Mayo & 10 de Agosto)*, which offers cash advances on Visa and has an ATM.

Post & Communications There is a **Pacifictel** *(24 de Mayo; open 8am-10pm daily)* and a **post office** *(9 de Octubre; open 7:30am-noon & 1:30pm-6pm Mon-Fri)*.

Internet service is available for about $1.50 per hour at **Cyber Vision** *(☎ 701 212; Soasti; open 9am-1pm & 1:30pm-10pm Mon-Fri, 10am-3pm Sat & Sun)* and **Cyber Ventura** *(Soasti; open 7am-10pm daily)*.

THE ORIENTE

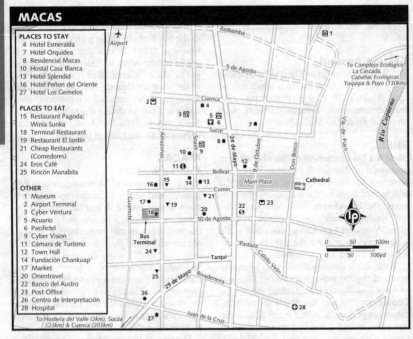

MACAS

PLACES TO STAY
4 Hotel Esmeralda
7 Hotel Orquidea
8 Residencial Macas
10 Hostal Casa Blanca
13 Hotel Splendid
16 Hotel Peñon del Oriente
27 Hotel Los Gemelos

PLACES TO EAT
15 Restaurant Pagoda;
   Winia Sunka
18 Terminal Restaurant
19 Restaurant El Jardín
21 Cheap Restaurants
   (Comedores)
24 Eros Café
25 Rincón Manabita

OTHER
1 Museum
2 Airport Terminal
3 Cyber Ventura
5 Acuario
6 Pacifictel
9 Cyber Vision
11 Cámara de Turismo
12 Town Hall
14 Fundación Chankuap'
17 Market
20 Orientravel
22 Banco del Austro
23 Post Office
26 Centro de Interpretación
28 Hospital

Airport

Riobamba

5 de Agosto

To Complejo Ecológico
La Cascada,
Cabañas Ecológicas
Yuquipa & Puyo (130km)

Cuenca

Sucre

Amazonas

Soasti

24 de Mayo

9 de Octubre

Don Bosco

Via de Puyo

Río Cuyaco

Bolívar

Main Plaza

Cathedral

Comin

Guamote

10 de Agosto

Bus
Terminal

Pastaza

Calisto Velin

Tarqui

29 de Mayo

Rivadeneira

Juan de la Cruz

To Hostería del Valle (2km), Sucúa
(23km) & Cuenca (203km)

0   50   100m
0   50   100yd

Travel Agencies & Tour Operators To
book national and international airline tickets,
visit **Orientravel** (☎ 700 371; **e** ortravel@cue
.satnet.net; cnr 10 de Agosto & Soasti).

Ikiaam Shuar Travel (☎ 701 690, 700 120;
e ikiaamjungle_tour@yahoo.com; Barrio Las
Palmeras, Sevilla) is a Shuar-run operator offering tours into the southern Oriente. These
require a flight by light aircraft to the jungle
village of Yaupi, from where the tour begins;
subsequent travel is by foot, canoe and horse.
Shuar communities are visited, and there's
plenty of time for wildlife searching. The tour
has a five-day minimum and costs $50 to $70
per person per day, depending on the number
of people in your group. They also offer less
expensive tours lasting one to three days in
Parque Nacional Sangay. Owners Andrés
Vizuma and Bolívar Caita have excellent reputations. Ikiaam does not have an office.
Arrangements should be made in advance by
email or phone, or you could stop by Andrés'
house in nearby Sevilla, the village on the
other side of the river from Macas.

Winia Sunka (☎ 700 088; **e** pablovhuias@
hotmail.com; cnr Comin & Amazonas) offers
two-day excursions into the jungle near

Macas ($35 per person per day) and six-day
trips near the Río Morona ($55 per person
per day). The biggie, however, is the eight-
day trip to Iquitos, Peru ($75 to $80 per person per day); the tour starts with a flight
from Macas to Puerto Morona, from where
you continue by boat down Río Morona to
Río Marañón and on to the Amazon River
and Iquitos. There's a 10-person minimum
and arrangements should be made up to two
months in advance.

Yacu Amu Rafting (☎ 223 6844, 290 4054,
w www.yacuamu.com) offers eight-day trips
on the nearby Río Upano, which has Grade
III and IV rapids, lots of waterfalls and
magnificent scenery; it is also suitable for
kayaking expeditions if you are an experienced kayaker. See Travel Agencies & Tour
Operators in the Quito chapter.

Things to See & Do
The **cathedral**, built fairly recently on a small
hill above the main plaza, is dedicated to the
400th anniversary of the miraculous changes
that happened to a painting of the Virgin of
Macas in 1592. The story is told in a series
of stained-glass windows, and the painting

itself can be viewed on the altar. On the night of August 4, a procession in honor of the Virgin goes the 23km from Sucúa.

The **views** from behind the cathedral of the wide Río Upano valley are impressive. On a clear day from the cathedral's hill, you can glimpse Volcán Sangay, some 40km to the northwest. At 5230m, it is the seventh-highest mountain in Ecuador and is one of the most active volcanoes in the world.

A few blocks northeast of the center, is a small **children's park** (Don Bosco & Zabala) with a library and tiny **museum**. Ask the librarian to open it for you. It has a few archaeological artefacts dating to 2700 BC, a handful of ethnographic exhibits and some old photos of Macas.

Complejo Ecológico La Cascada is a locally popular picnic area and pool on the road to Puyo, about a 90-minute walk from the center. Don't swim in the river here, as there are strong currents. Carry your own drinking water.

Places to Stay

Residencial Macas (☎ 700 254; 24 de Mayo; rooms per person with shared/private bath $3/4) has tiny but spotless rooms. Those with shared bath (which are kept immaculate) have freshly painted wooden walls. If you don't mind miniscule rooms, it's a great deal.

Hotel Splendid (☎ 700 120; Soasti; rooms per person shared/private bath $4/8) has basic old rooms with electric showers and some better rooms with TV and hot showers.

Hotel Orquidea (☎ 700 970; 9 de Octubre; rooms per person with cold/hot water $7/8) has clean, spacious rooms, although all doubles have twin beds only (sorry, no snuggling).

Hotel Los Gemelos (☎ 701 770; Amazonas; rooms per person $8) is a modest new hotel with five immaculate rooms with firm beds and cable TV. Downside? Bathrooms are shared (but they're clean and have hot water).

Hotel Esmeralda (☎ 700 130; Cuenca; rooms per person $9.50) has clean, nondescript rooms with private hot showers, TV and telephone. Breakfast is included.

Hostal Casa Blanca (☎ 700 195; Soasti; rooms per person $8) is a fairly new place with eight clean rooms with hot showers and TV.

Hotel Peñon del Oriente (☎ 700 124; rooms per person $8) is one of the best places

in the center, although its rooms are pretty worn. All rooms have private bath, hot water, TV, fan and decent views.

Hostería del Valle (☎ 700 226, 701 143; singles/doubles/triples $8/14/18) is a friendly place about 2km south of town on the road to Sucúa. It has clean, bungalow-style accommodations with private hot bath, TV and breakfast. Other meals can be prepared on request.

Finally, to experience some of the jungle near Macas, try the **Cabañas Ecológicas Yuquipa** (rooms per person $40) near Río Yuquipa, a small tributary of Río Upano. The simple cabins are reached from Km 12 on the road to Puyo, followed by a 4km walk. Facilities are minimal, with latrines and simple sleeping huts, and you have to wash in the river. Rates include meals and Spanish-speaking guides.

Places to Eat

Restaurant Pagoda (☎ 700 280; cnr Amazonas & Comín; mains $4-6; open 9:30am-10:30pm daily), a chifa (Chinese restaurant) opposite Hotel Peñon del Oriente, is the town's best restaurant.

Restaurant El Jardín (☎ 701 311; Amazonas; mains $2.50-3.50; open 7am-10pm daily) is locally popular and sells Ecuadorian standards and cheap sandwiches.

Eros Café (Amazonas; mains $2-3; open 7am-11pm daily) is good for hamburgers, ice cream, snacks and beer.

Rincón Manabita (Amazonas; mains $1.50-3; open 7am-10pm Mon-Fri, 7am-3pm Sat & Sun) serves filling set meals for $1.50 and some simple variants of coastal specialities.

There are several comedores on Comín near Soasti, where women sell ayampacos, a local speciality of either chicken, beef or fish, wrapped in bijao leaves and cooked on a grill. The cheapest food is available at the bus terminal.

Entertainment

Weekends are pretty mellow in Macas, but if you're just itching to dance, try **Acuario** (Sucre), a small, popular disco in the center.

Shopping

Fundación Chankuap' (☎ 701 176, 701 375; cnr Bolívar & Soasti; open 9am-noon & 2pm-6pm Mon-Fri, 8am-1pm Sun) is a Shuar/Achuar-run shop selling local crafts, snack foods and essential oils, including *sangre de drago* (literally 'dragon's blood,' which is drawn from the eponymous tree and has all sorts of curative uses, from cuts and scrapes to ulcers and diarrhea).

Getting There & Away

Air On Monday and Thursday TAME (☎/fax 701 162, 701 978; airport) flies from Quito to Macas ($56) at 1:30pm and returns at 2:30pm. If flying from Macas to Quito, the left-hand side of the plane offers the best mountain views, including Sangay and Cotopaxi if the weather is clear. **Austro Aéreo** (☎ 700 939; airport) flies to/from Cuenca (about $40) on Monday and Friday.

Small aircraft can sometimes be chartered to various jungle villages, but are expensive; ask a local tour agency or guide.

Bus All departures are from the bus terminal. Various companies offer several departures a day for Cuenca ($7, nine hours) and Gualaquiza ($4, eight to 10 hours). Buses to Sucúa ($0.75, one hour) run every 30 minutes from 6am to 7pm.

Buses north to Puyo ($4, five hours) leave several times a day. About halfway to Puyo, Río Pastaza must be crossed at the settlement of Chuitayo. Cars can cross a small bridge, but buses are too heavy, so passengers have to cross on foot and continue by a second bus waiting on the other side, a distance of almost a kilometer. A small restaurant at the bridge provides drinks and snacks. Some buses continue on to Tena ($5.50, eight hours from Macas).

Transportes Macas runs small buses and pickup trucks to various remote parts of the province, including 9 de Octubre (for Parque Nacional Sangay) and Morona.

PARQUE NACIONAL SANGAY

This national park (admission $10) is more fully described in the Central Highlands chapter. Most access to the park is from the north and west; access from the south and east is very difficult.

You can get buses from Macas to 9 de Octubre, where you can stay in the schoolhouse or camp. The people are friendly and can tell you where the dirt road continues to San Vicente and then on to Purshi by footpath. Allow about eight hours to hike from 9 de Octubre to Purshi (although this section

should be passable to vehicles). This small settlement is the official entrance to Parque Nacional Sangay. There is usually a ranger here, but the local people are also helpful. Trails lead a short distance into the park, but peter out quickly, and continuing requires a machete and a lot of perseverance. It's recommended for very experienced explorers only. The rainfall is high, the vegetation thick, and the terrain steep and broken.

It is possible to continue on foot beyond Purshi to Atillo in the highlands, from where a dirt road eventually connects with the Panamericana. A road is under construction and will eventually link Macas with Cebadas and Guamote in the highlands. At the time of research, this road was complete except for the stretch through the national park.

There is a park information center in Macas (see Information under Macas earlier in this chapter).

THE JUNGLE FROM MACAS

There are various ways to see more of the Oriente from Macas. It should be said, however, that the best-known centers for tourism in the jungle are in the northern Oriente.

Many Ecuadorian maps show tracks or trails leading from Macas into the interior. These often lead to Shuar Indian villages and missions further into the Oriente. The trails are usually overgrown, however, because transportation is mainly by light aircraft these days. It is difficult, but not impossible, to visit some of these villages.

You can charter an *expreso* light aircraft to take you to some of the better-known centers, such as **Taisha**, 70km due east of Macas by air. There is a basic place to stay there. With luck or the right contacts, flights can be arranged with the Salesian mission aircraft, but flights are often full, and inclement weather may cause days of delay. Hiring your own aircraft is subject to the availability of planes, and it costs about $60 per person per hour for a five-seater, usually with at least a $200 minimum fee.

Visiting nearby Shuar centers on foot or by bus is fairly straightforward. There are frequent buses to the mission of **Sevilla** (Don Bosco), about an hour's walk away on the other side of Río Upano.

From Sevilla, you can head south on foot along a broad track to the village of San Luís, about a four-hour walk. This makes a

Kapawi Ecolodge & Reserve

Built in a pristine area of Achuar Indian land in the remotest part of the Ecuadorian Amazon, Kapawi (*packages per person for 3/5/7 nights $600/720/1100, students for 3/4 nights $480/600*) is a culturally sensitive and unique ecotourism project. It's owned by the Achuar themselves, in partnership with Canodros, the lodge developers. At every step, Canodros consulted the community and freely provided important advice – both cultural and technical.

The lodge buildings were constructed following traditional ideas of Achuar architecture and used no nails of any kind. Achuar workers helped build the place and are now lodge employees. The land for the buildings remains Achuar, and Canodros pays a monthly rent. In 2011, Canodros will turn the entire project over to Achuar hands.

Kapawi uses low-impact technology – such as solar power, trash management and recycling, and biodegradable soaps. The lodge has 20 individual double cabins built around a lake, and each has a private bath and a balcony with lake views. The food served is a mixture of locally provided produce, with some international food flown in. Local fruits are a highlight. A bar provides a relaxing area with a library and games section. Locally made handicrafts are for sale.

Guests visit the rainforest in small groups accompanied by an Achuar guide and a bilingual naturalist, who work in tandem to explain the intricacies of the rainforest, both from an ecological and a cultural point of view. Visits to an Achuar family can be arranged, but photography is not allowed. Instead, the Achuar provide bowls of the traditional welcoming *nijiamanch* (manioc beer) and ask guests questions about their lives in addition to explaining some aspects of their own lifestyle – it's a great cultural interchange. Kapawi received Conservation International's 'Ecotourism Excellence Award' and the British Airways 'Tourism for Tomorrow' award.

The lodge is just off Río Pastaza, on an oxbow lake on Río Capahuari. The only way to practically reach Kapawi is by light aircraft, followed by a boat ride. Flights cost $150 for the round trip. Package rates are based on double occupancy and include all meals and guided tours. To get the student rate, you must proffer a valid ISIC student ID card. All visitors pay a tax of $10 per person levied by the Achuar community.

Reservations can be made at the main **Canodros office** (*Guayaquil ☎ 04-228 0880, 251 4750;* **e** *kapawi@canodros.com;* **w** *www.canodros.com*) or at the **branch office** (*Quito ☎ 02-222 203, 220 947; Portugal 448 at 6 de Diciembre*). Major travel agencies can also make reservations. More information is available in an article called 'Kapawi,' by Arnaldo Rodríguez, published in *Cultural Survival Magazine, Summer 1999*.

---

good day trip, and en route you'll pass cultivated areas and Indian huts, where you may be invited to try some *chicha de yuca*. This traditional Shuar drink is made by the women, who grind up the yucca by chewing it and then spit it into a bowl, where it is left to ferment. If this doesn't appeal to you, bring a bottle of water. There are no facilities of any kind beyond Sevilla.

SUCÚA
☎ 07 • pop 6000

Sucúa is a Shuar Indian center about 23km south of Macas. The Shuar were formerly called the Jivaro and were infamous for shrinking the heads of their defeated enemies. This practice still occurred as recently as two generations ago, and the *tsantsas*

(shrunken heads) can occasionally be seen in museums. Most of today's Shuar have become missionized and look very Ecuadorian in their jeans and T-shirts, but you still might see older Indians, especially women, with elaborate facial and body tattoos.

There is a small plaza with shady trees, flowers, cicadas and birds. From the plaza, walk down the main street and you'll come to the **Shuar Cultural Center** on your left, about a kilometer away. It's of little interest to casual visitors, but useful to people working with the Shuar. Market day is Sunday.

There are a few basic hotels, but most travelers stay in nearby Macas. Frequent buses or pickups leave for Macas ($0.75, one hour) from dawn until dusk at the corner of the main plaza.

FROM MÉNDEZ TO MORONA
☎ 07

South of Sucúa, the road passes through the quiet little village of Méndez (population 2000), near the junction of a road heading east to the Peruvian border. Méndez' official name is Santiago de Méndez, and the town's houses have red-tiled roofs and flowery gardens. Half a block from the corner of its shady plaza are three simple *pensiones* – Anita, Miranda and Amazonas – all charging about $2 per person. Nearby, Hotel Los Ceibos looks a little better. There are only a couple of restaurants.

The road heading east from Méndez goes to the remote settlement of Morona, on Río Morona, near where it crosses the border with Peru. The trip takes about 10 hours – ask around in Méndez for trucks going to Morona, or take a bus from Macas. There is only one place to stay, and it's extremely basic. This is a remote and poorly explored area, and readers trying this route are encouraged to write in with their experiences for the next edition of this book.

About halfway on the road between Méndez and Morona lies the small settlement of **Santiago**, on Río Santiago. There, you can hire dugout canoes to go upriver to Río Coangos for about $30. From the Coangos, there is a trail to **La Cueva de los Tayos** (The Cave of the Oilbirds – see the 'Oilbirds' boxed text). The trail is in poor condition, and you should hire a guide for the two- to three-hour hike. You'll need to be self-sufficient for this expedition, so bring sleeping gear and food.

LIMÓN
☎ 07 • approximate pop 3000 • elevation 1400m

Heading south from Méndez toward Gualaquiza, the road passes through Limón, a small, unprepossessing jungle town. It is also known as General Leonidas Plaza Gutiérrez, its primary importance is that it lies near the junction of the roads to Cuenca, Macas and Zamora. There's a Pacifictel office and one main street with a few hotels, several simple restaurants and some bus offices.

An hour south of Limón the road passes through the missions of San Juan Bosco and Indanza (also known as Plan de Milagro), and then continues through pretty but sparsely populated countryside until it reaches Gualaquiza, four hours from Limón.

Residencial Domínguez and Santo Domingo are basic but clean, and each charges about $2 per person. **Residencial Limón** (☎ 770 114; rooms per person with shared/private bath $4/5), next to Pacifictel, has large, clean rooms, but only one bathroom for the rooms with shared bath. **Hotel Dream House** (☎ 770 166; rooms per person $2) has rooms with shared bathrooms and a restaurant.

Several times a day, various bus companies along the main street have bus services to destinations north, south and west. The road

Oilbirds

There is only one species of oilbird, and it is so unusual that it is placed in its own family, the Steatornithidae, related to the nightjars. The world's only nocturnal fruit-eating birds, oilbirds spend most of the day roosting in caves in colonies that may number thousands of birds. La Cueva de los Tayos is one such cave. At dusk, they leave the cave in search of fruit, particularly that of palm trees.

Palm fruits are known for having a high fat content, which gives the oilbirds an incredibly fatty or oily flesh. For centuries, the birds have been captured in their roosting colonies and boiled down into a valuable oil used for cooking and lighting. The most highly prized birds of all are nestlings, which, fed only regurgitated fruit for up to four months, can reach a weight of 1½ times that of an adult. Once the chicks leave the nest, they lose all that juicy baby fat. Hunting oilbirds is now discouraged, although it still occurs occasionally.

Because of their dark environment, oilbirds have well-developed eyes and exceptional night vision. They also have a sensitive sense of smell, which may help them detect the palm fruits' distinctive fragrance. The caves they roost in are often pitch black. To avoid crashing into the cave walls (and into other birds), oilbirds emit audible clicks used for echolocation, much as bats do. In addition, they have a loud screaming call, which they use for communication. The combination of screams and clicks made by thousands of birds within the confines of a cave can be deafening.

up to Cuenca climbs steeply from Limón to a pass over 4000m in elevation – the ride is spectacular and should be done in daylight.

If you are going north to Macas, sit on the right-hand side of the bus, as there are good views of Río Upano.

GUALAQUIZA

☎ 07 • approximate pop 4000 • elevation 950m

Gualaquiza is a pretty little village surrounded by forested hills. The church on the main plaza looks like a toy building, and the cobbled streets and balconied houses give the town a Spanish colonial air. Pleasant walks lead into the surrounding countryside. Gualaquiza closes down early and is definitely *tranquilo*. The Pacifictel office closes for lunch, and weekend hours are limited.

A rough road heads west out of town for about 15km to the village of Nueva Tarquí, where caves can be explored (it is essential to carry spare flashlights and batteries). There are reportedly some poorly explored Inca sites in the Gualaquiza area – ask the locals for guidance.

Accommodations are limited, as this town is rarely visited. On the main plaza, the simple **Residencial Amazonas** (☎ 780 715; *rooms per person $2*) has rooms with shared baths. **Hotel Turismo** (☎ 780 113; *Calle Gonzalo Pezantes Lefebre; rooms per person with shared/private bath $3/4*) is a clean place and charges an extra $1 for TV. One reader reports that it's favored by short-stay couples and suggests that the new **Hotel Wakiz** (*Orellana 08-52; rooms per person $4.50*) is the best in town; the manager is friendly and helps with arranging cave tours.

There are several bus companies on the main street with two or three departures a day for various destinations. The next significant town to the north is Limón (four hours), and after that Sucúa and Macas ($4.50, eight to 10 hours). Buses go south to Zamora and Loja and west to Cuenca ($5 to $7); those that go via Indanza (Plan de Milagro) take about eight hours, but a new, more direct road via Sígsig cuts the trip to six hours.

FROM GUALAQUIZA TO ZAMORA

☎ 07

Several kilometers south of Gualaquiza, a turnoff to the right leads to Bomboiza, where a **Salesian mission** can be visited.

Soon thereafter, the road crosses the provincial line into Zamora-Chinchipe Province and then rises before passing through the village of **El Panguí**, where there is one basic hotel on the main street. The road continues through the village of **Los Encuentros** and, about 3½ hours from Gualaquiza, reaches the village of **Yantzaza**, the only sizable village before Zamora, 1½ hours further south. In Yantzaza there are restaurants and some basic places to stay (which are likely to be full of gold miners) near the main plaza.

From Yantzaza, the road follows the east bank of Río Zamora. There are beautiful vistas of the river and heavily forested hills on either side, often with tropical trees flowering in bright reds, yellows and purples. The bus goes through many little Indian hamlets and *fincas* (farms) growing tropical produce such as coffee, sugarcane and citrus fruit. The road also goes near a gold-mining area, so the journey is enlivened by the various interesting characters getting on and off the bus.

Just before Zamora you pass through the gold-mining town of **Nambija**. Around 1980, gold was discovered in the area. This led to a gold rush, and Nambija became a wild mining town, with lots of heavy drinking, prostitution, gunfights, open sewers, muddy streets and constant frenzied mining action. A landslide in the late 1980s killed many people, and the town has calmed down somewhat in recent years. There is a noisy and basic hotel.

About five hours from Gualaquiza, you finally reach the pretty town of Zamora, the best base from which to explore the lower regions of Parque Nacional Podocarpus. Although Zamora is geographically part of the Oriente, it is most easily reached from the highland city of Loja (only two hours west by bus – for more information see the Cuenca & the Southern Highlands chapter).

North Coast & Lowlands

For foreign visitors the coast usually takes a backseat to the rest of the country, which is unfortunate because it has some truly astounding attractions. The northern coast (comprised of Esmeraldas and Manabí Provinces) boasts some of the country's most popular beach destinations, where you can char yourself in the tropical sun and swim in the warm water that bathes the Ecuadorian coast year-round.

Culturally, the northern coast is an entirely different trip than the rest of the country. Esmeraldas has the highest percentage of Afro-Ecuadorians of any province in the country, lending the region a markedly different feel. And when it comes to food – step aside highlands and Oriente – the coastal cuisine of Esmeraldas and Manabí is simply rockin'.

In northern Esmeraldas, the infrequently visited Reserva Ecológica de Manglares Cayapas Mataje and the Reserva Ecológica Cotacachi-Cayapas protect important areas of what scientists call the Chocó bioregion. This severely threatened region of staggering biodiversity stretches north along Colombia's Pacific coast, south to the equator and east into the Andes' western slopes. It is an extremely poor area, as tourism is undeveloped and travel (often by boat) is challenging, but the rewards (both natural and cultural) can be incomparable.

South of Esmeraldas city, the beaches are the main attractions. The towns of Atacames, Same, Súa, Muisne and especially Canoa are all good for soaking up the sun.

Parque Nacional Machalilla, Ecuador's only coastal national park, is a definitely a highlight, especially to see the humpback whales which mate just offshore between mid-June and early October. The park's access point is the relaxing fishing village of Puerto López, which is a day's bus ride from the capital.

South of Puerto López, verdant forested hills bump up against the coastline, and the highway winds through the low-key little villages of Salango, Puerto Rico and Ayampe, which have long empty beaches and some of the most unique and appealing places to stay on the coast. At Ayampe the road crosses into Guayas Province, the beginning of the south

Highlights

- Exploring the rarely visited mangroves, fishing villages and reserves in northern Esmeraldas Province
- Sampling the coast, culture, archaeology and ornithology of Parque Nacional Machalilla
- Watching humpback whales do it like they do off the small island of Isla de la Plata from mid-June to early October
- Visiting the 'ecocity' of Bahía de Caráquez and taking advantage of various alternative tour opportunities
- Eating seafood, seafood, seafood

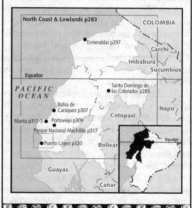

coast (see the Guayaquil & the South Coast chapter for more information).

When to Go

There are two definite seasons on the coast. On the northern coast, the rainy season lasts from December to May, and the dry season the rest of the year. However, the sunniest, hottest days are during the rainy season, which has daily downpours but also daily sun. The dry season is often overcast, gray and cool. Ecuadorians flock to the beaches during the rainy season, especially during the July and August school vacations and from January to Easter when the water is warmest. The quietest months are from September to November.

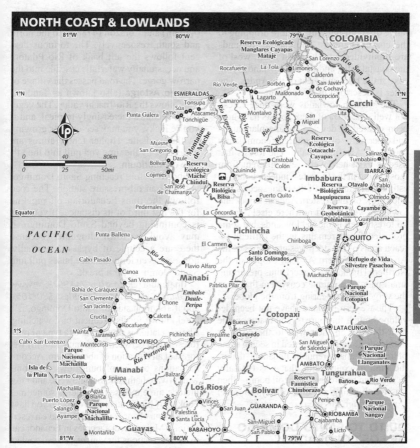

NORTH COAST & LOWLANDS

Malaria is prevalent in the northern region mostly during the rainy season. It's less of a problem south of Esmeraldas Province.

Getting There & Around

Most places along the northern coast can be reached by direct bus ride from Quito in just a day. Santo Domingo de los Colorados, in the western lowlands, is the main transportation hub between the Andes and the coast. From Quito, two roads reach Santo Domingo: the new road, which does the trip in about three hours, and the old road via Mindo, which takes about five hours and has some fabulous attractions on the way (for more information on this route, see Western Andean Slopes in the Northern Highlands chapter).

San Lorenzo can be reached by paved road from Ibarra (in the northern highlands) in only four hours. From Latacunga in the central highlands, a spectacular five-hour bus ride will take you to Quevedo in the western lowlands, from where it's about four hours to Portoviejo.

Nearly the entire coastal highway is now paved south from Esmeraldas city.

Western Lowlands

The descent down the western slopes of the Andes to the lowlands (at about 300m) is dramatic and steep. It does not stay low all the way to the coast, however. After dropping to almost sea level, the land rises again in a barren, scrubby and almost uninhabited range of 700m-high hills before dropping to the coast. Therefore, the coastal lowlands are subdivided into the coast itself, west of the coastal hills, and the flat lowlands lying east of the hills and west of the Andes. The latter is described in this section.

The western lowlands were once forest, but well over 90% of these forests have now been cleared to develop banana plantations and other forms of agriculture, predominantly cacao and African oil palm. The forests that used to exist here were very different from those found in the Oriente – indeed, botanists estimate that about half the plant species that once grew on the western Andean slopes and lowlands were found nowhere else! Almost no forest is left in the flat lowlands, but some protected forest remains in the difficult-to-reach areas of the steep western slopes of the Andes (see Western Andean Slopes in the Northern Highlands chapter), thus preserving small parts of a unique ecosystem that is on the verge of disappearing from the globe.

The western lowlands have not been developed much for tourists, and many people rush through on their way to the coast or highlands. If you're interested in seeing some of tropical, banana-republic Ecuador – that is, the kind of countryside that was typically Ecuadorian before the recent oil boom – then it is worth taking a couple of days to travel slowly through this area.

QUITO TO SANTO DOMINGO DE LOS COLORADOS
☎ 02

The most common route from the highlands to the coast is the road from Quito through Santo Domingo de los Colorados. From Santo Domingo, you can head south through Quevedo and Babahoyo, in the lowland province of Los Ríos, and on to Guayaquil, on the south coast; or you can go northwest toward Esmeraldas, on the north coast.

The descent into the lowlands is a spectacular and sometimes terrifying one. It is best to make the journey in the morning, because in the afternoon the views are often obscured by fog. Despite almost nonexistent visibility, the drivers hurtle down the western slopes of the Andes at breakneck speeds. Amazingly, accidents are very rare.

The road to Santo Domingo begins in high *páramo* (Andean grasslands), with nice

views of the extinct **Volcanes Atacazo** (4463m) and **Corazón** (4788m) to the north and south, respectively. The tortuous descent follows the left bank of Río Pilatón, and occasionally waterfalls cascade into the narrow gorge. The road passes the village of **Cornejo Astorga** (also known as Tandapi) and follows the Río Toachi valley. The vegetation becomes increasingly tropical, and if you're lucky, you may see orchids growing on the roadside. Higher temperatures are noticeable by the time you pull into the village of **Alluriquín**.

Shortly before reaching Santo Domingo, you pass an oil-pressure station. The road follows the trans-Ecuadorian oil pipeline for the last third of its distance. If your bus is continuing beyond Santo Domingo, it may avoid the town altogether, because there are a couple of bypasses; normally, however, even long-distance buses pull into Santo Domingo for a break.

Tinalandia (Quito ☎/fax 244 9028; w www.tinalandia.net; singles/doubles $80/105), about 16km outside of Santo Domingo, is a hotel known for its excellent bird-watching. The vegetation is premontane (a type of rainforest found between 500m and 1500m) wet forest at an elevation of about 600m. Accommodations consist of bungalows or cabins with private baths and hot showers, and rates include three meals. The hotel is sometimes booked by bird-watching groups, so you have to take your chances if you don't have a reservation. (Major travel agencies in Ecuador can make reservations for you, or you can contact the place yourself.) The driest months (May and June) are particularly popular with bird-watchers. You can make day visits to the grounds for $10. Tinalandia is about 86km after the turn-off from the Panamericana in Alóag. There is a small stone sign on the right side of the road as you drive from Quito, and the hotel itself is about 500m up a track on the left side of the road. If you are on a bus to Santo Domingo, ask the driver to let you off at Tinalandia – all the drivers know it.

SANTO DOMINGO DE LOS COLORADOS
☎ 02 • pop 184,000

Better known as Santo Domingo, this fast-growing city is an important transportation hub, with major roads heading north, south, east and west. Just 500m above sea level and

SANTO DOMINGO DE LOS COLORADOS

PLACES TO STAY	PLACES TO EAT	OTHER
2 Hotel El Colorado	6 Cebichería Calet	1 Banco del Pichincha
4 Hotel Diana Real	8 Chifa Happy	3 Local Bus Plaza
5 Hostal Jennefer	11 Restaurante	7 Town Hall
9 Residencial San	Timoneiro	10 Banco del Pichincha
Martín	13 Pollo Colorado	12 Net Express
		14 Andinatel

only 130km from Quito, Santo Domingo is the nearest lowland tropical town that is easily accessible from the capital, so it is a popular weekend destination for *quiteños* (people from Quito) – but it's of limited interest to travelers. Santo Domingo is a convenient city in which to make bus connections or break a long journey.

Santo Domingo is the capital of its canton and celebrates its cantonization day on July 3, when there are fairs and agricultural festivals; the town and its hotels get quite crowded during this period.

Information

Sunday is Santo Domingo's main market day, and therefore the town closes down on Monday. For phone calls head to **Andinatel** *(Avenida Quito near Río Toachi)*. The **post office** *(Avenida Tsachilas near Río Baba)* is just north of downtown. **Banco de Guayaquil** *(Avenida Quito)*, east of downtown, has a MasterCard/Cirrus ATM. Both branches of **Bancos del Pichincha** *(Iturralde, Main Plaza • Avenida Quinindé)* also have ATMs.

For Internet service, try **Net Express** *(29 de Mayo near Los Tsachilas; open 9am-8pm daily)*. Access costs $1 per hour.

Things to See & Do

There are lively **street markets** and a busy Sunday market, when activities spill out onto surrounding streets, but watch your belongings carefully in these areas. These markets are for locals, and mainly mundane things – such as clothing, produce and kitchen utensils – are sold.

The **Río Toachi** is nearby, and city buses will take you there. Just across the river is a modest resort with a few restaurants, a swimming pool (you may prefer to swim in the river) and some games courts.

Places to Stay

The town is crowded during the July 3 celebrations and on weekends, when prices may be higher.

If you're just passing through and want a hotel near the bus terminal, **Hostal Patricia** *(☎ 276 1906; rooms per person $4)* has cheap rooms with private cold showers. The best near the terminal is **Hotel Sheraton** *(☎ 275 1988; singles/doubles $7/10)*, which offers private hot showers, cable TV and fans.

Most of the cheapest hotels are in the center, near the market area, which is not very safe at night. A fair choice is the clean, helpful and very basic **Residencial San Martín** *(☎ 750 813; cnr 29 de Mayo & Tulcán; rooms per person $3)*.

Hotel El Colorado *(☎ 275 0226, 275 4299; cnr 29 de Mayo & Esmeraldas; rooms per person $6)* is friendly and has clean, plain rooms with private bathrooms.

Tsachila (Colorado) Indians

Santo Domingo de los Colorados used to be famous for its resident Tsachila (better known as the Colorado Indians, after whom the town is named), who painted their faces with black stripes and dyed their bowl-shaped haircuts with a brilliant red using a natural dye from the *achiote* plant. You can buy postcards of them all over Ecuador, but the Indians are now fairly Westernized, and you are unlikely to see them in their traditional finery unless you go to one of their nearby villages and pay them to dress up. Photographers are expected to give 'tips,' but the Tsachila are becoming increasingly unhappy with their roles as models for foreign photographers. Please be sensitive to this.

The best-known Colorado village is Chihuilpe, about 7km south of Santo Domingo on the road to Quevedo and then about 3km east on a dirt road. Some of the older Indians, notably the *gobernador* (headman) Abraham Calazacon (who died in the 1980s) and his brother Gabriel, earned reputations as *curanderos* (medicine men), and people still come from all over Ecuador to be cured. Nearby, the house of Agosto Calazacon is a tourist center, and there's now a small museum here that describes Tsachila history and culture.

There are other Colorado villages in the area south of Santo Domingo, but for the most part the villagers prefer to be left alone. Apart from going to the tourist center in Chihuilpe, you can also visit one of the *curanderos* who advertize their trade in the first 15km of the route to Quevedo. They mainly sell curative herbs, but some may offer other healing treatments. A taxi from Santo Domingo to Chihuilpe should cost around $15 for a two- to three-hour trip.

Hostal Jennefer (☎ 275 0577; 29 de Mayo near Ibarra; singles/doubles $6/10) is the best of downtown's budget hotels, offering large clean rooms with hot showers and cable TV. Some bathrooms have big bathtubs, too.

Hotel Diana Real (☎ 275 1380, 275 1384; cnr 29 de Mayo & Loja; singles/doubles $14/18), a bit more upscale, has clean rooms with fan, cable TV, hot shower and telephone. There is also a restaurant.

The better hotels are east of the center on Avenida Quito, and the best of these is **Hotel Zaracay** (☎ 275 0316, 275 0429, 275 1023, 275 4873; Avenida Quito; singles/doubles with air-con $23/28). It's a well-known place about 1.5km east of town, and has spacious rooms with bath, air-conditioning, TV, telephone and balcony. You'll pay less for rooms with fans. The food is pricey but good, and the rooms are in jungle-style cabins with thatched roofs. The gardens have a swimming pool, and there is a tennis court and casino. This hotel is popular, and reservations are a good idea (but not always necessary).

Places to Eat

For good meals (breakfast, lunch and dinner) try the friendly **Restaurante Timoneiro** (Avenida Quito 115; mains $2-4). **Chifa Happy** (mains $2-4), on the western corner of the main plaza, serves decent Chinese food.

Cebichería Calet (Ibarra 137; mains $3-6) serves good *ceviche* (marinated, uncooked seafood) and traditional seafood.

Parrilladas Argentinas (Avenida Quito; mains $3-5), on the traffic circle, has good grills but not much else. There's another branch on Km 5 on Vía a Quevedo – this one has more choices but closes by 8:30pm; take a taxi.

Fried and grilled chicken are a staple of local dining – chicken rotisseries are everywhere. A good one to try is **Pollo Colorado** (Avenida Quito; mains $2-3). It's one of several around the *'cinco esquinas'* (five corners) intersection at Avenida Quito and Iturralde.

Entertainment

Head out along Avenida Quito. For salsa dancing, **Salsoteca The Jungle** is probably your best bet. **Colorados Pool Bar**, a few blocks further east, has good recorded music and a pool table, and is suitable for women and men alike. A few other bars and cafés can also be found along this street.

Getting There & Away

The bus terminal is almost 2km north of town and has frequent buses to many major towns. Quito ($2, three hours) and Guayaquil ($4, five hours) are the most frequent destinations, and buses of several companies leave to those cities at least once an hour. It's easy to catch buses to intermediate points such as Quevedo or Daule, but you'll find fewer buses to Babahoyo, as most southbound buses take the Daule road after passing through Quevedo.

Transportes Occidentales has several departures a day to Machala ($5 to $6, six to eight hours). There are buses about every hour to the north-coast town of Esmeraldas ($3, 3½ hours), stopping at La Concordia and Quinindé. After going through Esmeraldas, some may continue to Atacames or Muisne. Buses also go to Bahía de Caráquez ($3.50, six hours) and Manta ($4.30, seven hours).

There are also departures to Cuenca ($5, 10 hours), Riobamba ($3.50, five hours), Ambato ($3, four hours) and Latacunga.

There is a local bus plaza at the west end of 3 de Julio, where you can find beat-up old bone-shakers to take you to nearby villages. It can be interesting to take one of these buses just to see the countryside, but make sure that there is a return bus, as these villages often don't have restaurants (let alone a place to stay). You can also find buses here returning to Quito via La Concordia and Mindo – an uncomfortable but beautiful five-hour ride.

Getting Around

The most useful city bus is signed 'Centro.' It runs past the bus terminal, through the center and out along Avenida Quito past Hotel Zaracay on the way to the Río Toachi swimming area. The fare is $0.12. The return bus, signed 'Terminal Terrestre,' heads west along 29 de Mayo, picking up passengers for the terminal.

NORTH OF SANTO DOMINGO DE LOS COLORADOS
☎ 02

The main road north of Santo Domingo heads to the port of Esmeraldas (see that section later in this chapter), almost 200km away. About 42km from Santo Domingo along this road, the **Bosque Protectora La Perla** (☎ 272 5344, 275 9115; admission $5) is a 250-hectare reserve, that is good for bird-watching and nature walks; guided hikes and camping are also possible. Visits include a guide, and advance reservations are requested. Exact directions can be obtained at the time of reservation.

A few kilometers beyond is the village of **La Concordia**, which has a basic *hostal* (small, cheap hotel). About 50km northwest of Santo Domingo (just past La Concordia), a paved road leads eastward toward Mindo via Puerto Quito and Pedro Vicente Maldonado (see the Northern Highlands chapter) and eventually reaches Mitad del Mundo.

About 87km northwest of Santo Domingo, is the small town of **Quinindé** (also known as Rosa Zárate; the area code is 06). There are a couple of basic hotels in this town.

Approximately 40km west of Quinindé is the **Reserva Biológica Bilsa**, a 30-sq-km reserve in the Montañas de Mache (a small range of coastal mountains) at an elevation of between 300m and 750m. Administered by **Fundación Jatun Sacha** (☎ 243 2240/46, 243 2173; w www.jatunsacha.org; Pasaje Eugenio de Santillán N34-248 & Maurián, Urbanización Rumipamba, PO Box 17-12-867), one of Ecuador's primary research and conservation organizations, the reserve preserves some of the last remaining stands of premontane tropical wet forests. The biodiversity here is exceptionally high: howler monkeys are common, jaguars and pumas have been recently recorded, isolated populations of endangered birds have been found, and new species of plants have been discovered. The reserve is open to researchers, volunteers and tour groups. During the wet months from January to June, access is only on foot or mule via a 25km muddy trail, but vehicular access may be possible in the dry months. Contact Jatun Sacha for reservations and volunteer or research information.

SOUTH OF SANTO DOMINGO DE LOS COLORADOS

It's 100km from Santo Domingo to Quevedo on a gently descending paved road through banana plantations and, as you get closer to Quevedo, African palm and papaya groves. During the first 15km you see frequent signs on the side of the road advertizing the homes of Colorado Indian *curanderos* (medicine men). You can visit them, but expect to pay both for cures and for taking their photo. There are villages about every 20km along this road.

About 46km south of Santo Domingo, you'll see a sign for the **Río Palenque Science Center** (*Centro Científico Río Palenque;*

day-use $5), a small, private reserve owned by renowned orchid expert Dr Calaway Dodson. Although it is only 180 hectares, it is one of the largest tracts of western lowlands forest left in the area, forming a habitat island surrounded by agricultural land. There are facilities for researchers, about 3km of trails, and excellent bird-watching. The elevation is about 200m.

A flora checklist published in 1978 lists 1100 plants at the center, and of these, about 100 species were new to science. This gives an indication of how important it is to preserve what little there is left of this unique habitat. Bird lists include over 360 species. However, because of the small size of the preserve, there are no large and few small mammals present.

Visitors can sleep in the **field station** *(Guayaquil* ☎ *04-220 8670/80;* e *fundacion@grupowong.com; rooms per person with/without food $30/15)*, which is adequate but not luxurious, and cheaper if you bring your own food. Reservations should be made, but if the place is not full of researchers (it usually isn't), you can just show up. The nearest store is in the village of Patricia Pilar, about 2km north of the entrance to the science center. Any bus between Santo Domingo and Quevedo can drop you off or pick you up at the entrance road to the center.

About 15km before Quevedo you roll through the village of **Buena Fe**, which has a couple of basic hotels on the main street.

QUEVEDO
☎ 05 • pop 100,000

Quevedo is an important road hub and market town, but few travelers spend more time here than they absolutely have to. At only 145m above sea level, Quevedo is oppressively hot. For most people, the main attraction is the drive to Quevedo from Latacunga in the highlands – a spectacular trip – on the way to the coast.

Quevedo has quite a significant Chinese-Ecuadorian community, so you'll see lots of Chinese-run businesses. Many people claim the town has the best Chinese food in the country.

Orientation & Information
The main plaza is two blocks west of the Río Quevedo and just a few blocks south of the various independent bus terminals.

Banco del Pichincha, on the corner of the main plaza, changes traveler's checks. There are plenty of ATMs around. The **post office** *(cnr Decimasegunda & Bolívar)* is poorly marked and entered through an alley in a business block near Bolívar. **Pacifictel** *(7 de Octubre near Decimatercera)* is almost two blocks south of there.

Places to Stay
There are plenty of hotels in Quevedo, but they're a rather sorry lot. Many of the cheaper hotels suffer from water shortages, so check if you want a shower immediately.

Hotel Imperial *(☎ 751 654; Séptima 104; rooms per person $4)*, by the river, is shabby but secure and has basic rooms with fans and cold-water private bathrooms. The market nearby may preclude sleep early in the morning, but the views of the goings-on are interesting. Other places for about $3 to $5 can be found within a few blocks, but they are definitely worse.

Hotel Ejecutivo Internacional *(☎ 751 781; Quarta near 7 de Octubre; singles/doubles $8/12)* has reasonably sized air-conditioned rooms that vary somewhat in quality – the interior rooms are nicer and quieter.

Hotel Quevedo Internacional *(☎ 751 875/6; Decimasegunda 207; singles/doubles about $20/21)* has fair rooms with TV, air-conditioning, telephone, minifridge and private hot showers. The restaurant here is quite good.

Hotel Olímpico *(☎ 750 455, 750 210, fax 751 314; Decimanovena at Bolívar; singles/doubles about $30/45)*, on the eastern edge of town, is the best place to stay. This is a tourist complex, complete with an Olympic-sized swimming pool, water slides, tennis courts, a casino, a good restaurant and a bar. It's popular and often full, so call ahead.

Places to Eat
With its large Chinese community, Quevedo has plenty of *chifas* (Chinese restaurants). There are several along 7 de Octubre, of which **Chifa Peking** is one of the most popular. **La Casa del Rey** *(cnr Bolívar & Novena)* is another inexpensive, locally popular place. **Restaurant Tungurahua** *(7 de Octubre)*, near Séptima, is always packed for its cheap set lunches. **Las Redes** *(June Guzman 801)* is good for seafood. The restaurant in Hotel Olímpico has been recommended as the best

in town. The hotel restaurants of Quevedo Internacional and Ejecutivo Internacional are also acceptable (see Places to Stay earlier).

Getting There & Away
There is no central bus terminal, so you have to roam the streets looking for the various terminals; they are nearly all north of the main plaza and west of the river. **Transportes Macuchi** (cnr Guayaquil & Bolívar) has regular direct buses to Quito ($3.25, four hours). **Transportes Sucre** (7 de Octubre), between Quinta and Quarta, has buses to Santo Domingo, from where there are frequent buses to Quito. Transportes Sucre also has buses to Portoviejo.

Transportes Sucre and **TIA** (7 de Octubre), between Quarta and Tercera, go frequently to Guayaquil ($2.25, 2½ to four hours) both via Daule or Babahoyo. The route via Daule is faster. **Transportes Valencia** (cnr Bolívar & Segunda) goes via Babahoyo ($1.30, 1½ to two hours) every 20 minutes from 3:15am to 7:45pm.

Transportes Cotopaxi (Avenida Progreso near Séptima), on the west side of the market, has hourly departures from 3am to 5pm to Latacunga ($3, 5½ hours), as well as an 8am and a 1pm bus to Portoviejo ($3.50, four hours). This route, from Latacunga via Quevedo to Portoviejo, is one of the least frequently traveled and also one of the prettiest highland-to-coast routes.

QUEVEDO TO GUAYAQUIL
If your southbound bus crosses Río Quevedo, then you are going to Babahoyo; if it doesn't, then you are heading to Daule, which is the most frequent route to Guayaquil (see the Guayaquil & the South Coast chapter).

About 20km away from Quevedo on the road toward Daule is **Empalme**, or Velasco Ibarra, as it's officially called. Here the road forks; the westbound route is an unpaved road to Portoviejo, and the southbound route is a paved road to Guayaquil. Empalme is a busy little junction town with several basic restaurants and *pensiones*. You're in the heart of banana country here, and it continues that way to **Balzar**, another small market town with a basic hotel.

Near **Palestina**, the banana plantations give way to rice paddies, and *piladoras* are frequently seen along the road. *Piladoras* are husking-and-drying factories, and you'll see tonnes of rice spread out on huge concrete slabs to dry in the sun (assuming you're traveling in the dry season).

About three quarters of the way to Guayaquil, you'll reach **Daule**. This is another small commercial and agricultural center that has basic hotels. Three hours after leaving Quevedo, the bus reaches Guayaquil.

BABAHOYO
☎ 05 • pop 79,393
Babahoyo is the capital of the flat agricultural province of Los Ríos. North of the town lie banana and palm plantations, while south of it are rice paddies and some cattle. Huge flocks of white cattle egrets can make the ride from Babahoyo to Guayaquil very pretty.

Babahoyo was once an important town on the route between Guayaquil and Quito. In the 19th century, passenger and cargo boats regularly steamed up Río Babahoyo as far as this town and then transferred to mules for the ride up to Quito. Perhaps because of its low elevation and propensity for flooding, the area was called Babahoyo, which translates as 'slimepit.'

Although it's not exactly exciting, Babahoyo is a bustling and energetic town with much commercial activity. The central streets are very busy and gringos are an uncommon sight.

Information
Banco de Guayaquil (cnr Malecón 9 de Octubre & Bolívar) has a MasterCard/Cirrus ATM. The **post office** (Barona), between Bolívar and Sucre, is in the government buildings facing the central plaza. There's a **Pacifictel office** (10 de Agosto) between Bolívar and Calderón.

Places to Stay & Eat
There are several accommodations options – none of which are very fancy or expensive.

Hotel Riberas de Babahoyo (Malecón at Carbo; rooms per person with/without bath $3/ 2.25) is run down and has rooms with fans.

Hotel Cachari (☎ 730 749; Bolívar 111; singles/doubles with bath $6/7, with air-con $8/10), half a block off the river, is fair value for rooms with private bath and fans or air-conditioning. Some rooms have river views, and there is a sauna and Jacuzzi.

Hotel Emperador (☎ 730 535, 731 373; Barona near 27 de Mayo; singles/doubles with fan $8/13, with air-con $11/19) has 32 modern rooms with TV, telephone and private hot shower. It has a popular Chinese restaurant, too.

There are many *chifas* in the town center, especially on Barona east of the central plaza.

Getting There & Away

Babahoyo has no proper bus terminal, but most companies have buses departing from a couple of blocks southwest of the plaza. There are frequent services to Guayaquil ($0.80, 1½ hours). There are also services into the highlands to Ambato ($3.25, five hours) and Riobamba ($3.25, 4½ hours). It's a beautiful trip, climbing from the humid lowlands to the scenic flanks of Chimborazo.

The North Coast

SAN LORENZO
☎ 06

Until the mid-1990s, San Lorenzo was accessible only by boat or train and had an isolated feel. Now, roads from highland Ibarra and coastal Esmeraldas have made San Lorenzo easily accessible, and the town is growing. Until recently, most travelers arrived by an exciting train ride down from Ibarra; now, the train doesn't run, because the bus is quicker and cheaper, and San Lorenzo – although it's prospering with its newfound road connections – is no longer on a popular tourist route.

San Lorenzo is not very well laid out, but it is small and it's easy to find your way around. The main reason to come here is to travel along the coast. You can head north into Colombia or south toward Reserva Ecológica Cotacachi-Cayapas. Boat travel is still possible.

Orientation & Information

As you roll into town, you'll pass the old train station and follow San Lorenzo's main street, Calle Imbabura, for several blocks to the Parque Central (the town's main park/ plaza) near the water. On the way, you'll pass most of the better hotels on your left. The boat dock is a couple of blocks beyond the park.

The police station faces the park, and the *capitanía* (port captain) is at the boat dock; if you're traveling into or out of Colombia,

take care of passport formalities at one of these. **Andinatel** (open 8am-10pm Mon-Sat, 8am-noon & 7pm-9pm Sun) is opposite Gran Hotel San Carlos on the other side of Calle Imbabura; there's no sign.

San Lorenzo's Catholic hospital is reputedly the best in the area north of Esmeraldas.

The **Ministerio del Ambiente** (☎ 780 184; usually open 9am-12:30pm & 2pm-7pm Mon-Fri), on the far side of the park, has pamphlets on Reserva Ecológica de Manglares Cayapas Mataje and will let you look at maps. Information is minimal, however.

Places to Stay

Try to get a room with a mosquito net and a fan – the mosquitoes can be bad, especially in the wet months. The town suffers from occasional water shortages, so take showers when you can. The following places all have mosquito nets.

Gran Hotel San Carlos (☎/fax 780 284/ 306/240; cnr Imbabura & José Garcés; rooms per person with shared/private bath $4/6) is the first obvious place to stay as you arrive in town. You'll see it a few blocks after the train station on the left. It is clean and safe and has 35 rooms with fans, nets, firm beds, TV and shared or private bath. **Residencial Vilma**, across the street, is cheaper and basic.

Hotel Pampa de Oro (☎ 780 214, 780 263; Calle Tácito Ortíz; rooms per person $5) is a friendly place, two blocks further toward the boat dock, on a side street to the left. Rooms have fan, bath and TV, and are small but cheerful. A few rooms have air-conditioning.

Hotel Continental (☎ 780 125, 780 304; Imbabura; rooms per person with fan/air-con $6/10) is another long block toward the park. Its plain, clean rooms with TV and warm shower are about as swanky as San Lorenzo gets.

Hotel Imperial (☎ 780 242; Imbabura; singles/doubles without bath $2.50/3, with bath $3.50/6) is beyond Hotel Continental, across the street on the right, but a nearby dance hall is sometimes noisy at night.

Hotel Carondolet (☎ 780 202; Parque Central; rooms per person with shared/private bath $3.50/4) is on the inland side of the plaza. It's a simple, friendly place with small, clean rooms that have private baths and a communal balcony overlooking the park.

Places to Eat

La Red (☎ 780 710; Isidro Ayora near Imbabura; mains $3-10; open 7am-10pm daily) serves good seafood, as well as the usual chicken dishes. Put in your order in the morning if you want something special for dinner. It's to the right just before Hotel Imperial.

Ballet Azul (Imbabura; mains $2-6; open 8:30am-10pm Mon-Sat) is a little, open-air restaurant perfect for watching the evening unfold as you sit on the street outside while sucking down a plate of shrimp ($4.50) and a cold beer. It's known for its *ceviche de camarón* (shrimp ceviche) and *camarones al ajillo* (garlic shrimp).

El Condorito (Eloy Alfaro; mains about $2; open daily) is popular for its $2 *almuerzo* (set-lunch menu).

Hotel Carondolet (Parque Central) also has a restaurant (see Places to Stay earlier).

Getting There & Away

Bus La Costeñita and Transportes del Pacífico alternate departures for Borbón ($1.20, 1½ hours) and Esmeraldas ($4, five hours). They leave the Parque Central hourly from 5am to 4pm. The road is mostly paved but has some badly potholed or unpaved sections.

Aerotaxi buses leave at 1pm and 3pm to Ibarra ($4, four hours) from the corner of Imbabura and Tácito Ortiz. Both buses continue on to Quito ($5, five to six hours).

Train The spectacular train ride between Ibarra and San Lorenzo has been replaced by buses, although there is always talk of reopening the line.

Boat Since the opening of the road to Borbón and Esmeraldas, boat traffic has declined. La Costeñita and Transportes del Pacífico, alternate departures between 7am and 3pm to Limones ($3.50, 1½ hours). From Limones boats leave hourly for La Tola ($2, 40 minutes). If you get to La Tola early, you can connect with a bus to Esmeraldas. The bus takes about four or five hours from La Tola to Esmeraldas, so the whole trip from San Lorenzo to Esmeraldas can be done in one day and costs about $8. This is slower and more expensive than taking the bus directly from San Lorenzo, but buzzing through the mangroves past little settlements, with black scissor-tailed frigatebirds circling overhead, is an unforgettable experience.

From La Tola, there are also boats to Borbón at 7am and 4pm.

North to Colombia There are boats at 7am and 2pm to Palmareal ($2.50, two hours) on the Colombian border. From Palmareal you get another boat to Monte Alto, then a bus to the Río Mira, which you must cross to get a truck to Tumaco, Colombia. The journey can be done in one day. If you need a Colombian visa, get it in Quito. Passport formalities for exiting and arriving in Ecuador can be handled either at the *capitanía*, on the dock, or at the police station, two blocks away. Few foreigners take this route, and boats are subject to regular drug and weapon searches. Due to the conflict in Colombia and the movement of contraband, crossing the border here is not recommended. Check with the Colombian embassy or the South American Explorers in Quito for the latest information.

RESERVA ECOLÓGICA DE MANGLARES CAYAPAS MATAJE

This 51,300-hectare reserve supports six species of mangroves, including the tallest mangrove forest in the world, Manglares de Majagual, near the villages of La Tola and Olmedo (see later). The town of San Lorenzo lies in the middle of the reserve and makes a good base. Most of the reserve is at sea level and none of it is above 35m. In June and July millions of migratory birds pass through here. A highlight of the reserve is the 11km island beach of **San Pedro** near the Colombian border. There are basic, community-run **cabañas** (rooms per person $2), nearby at the settlement of **Palmareal**. If you stay, bring a mosquito net and water (or purification tablets). Food is available. Be sure to check locally on the safety of traveling in the remote border region near Colombia. The reserve is accessible almost solely by boat.

Tours can be arranged in San Lorenzo. **Coopseturi** (☎ 06-780 161) is run by Andres Carvache, who will take you just about anywhere you want to go in the nearby mangroves by boat (day trips per person $30 to $35). Ask him to show you his map and explain the routes. He speaks Spanish only. His office is in the Transportes del Pacífico office down near the pier.

If you're really interested in the area, contact **Jaime Burgos** (☎ 06-731 410, 09-982 3666, 09-726 0499) in Atacames; he owns La Estancia, the best restaurant in Atacames (see Places to Eat under Atacames later in this chapter). Señor Burgos is very knowledgeable about the area (and loves it profoundly) and was a principal force behind the formation of local reserves.

LIMONES
☎ 06 • pop 7000

Limones is a small town at the mouth of the deltas of Río Santiago and Río Cayapas. It's basically an island, reached only by boat, which is why the San Lorenzo–Limones–La Tola boat service keeps running despite the new road. It's an interesting place, with weather-beaten buildings stilted over the water and a little plaza at the foot of the pier. You can sometimes see Chachi Indians (formerly known as the Cayapas). Most of the timber logged in this area is floated down the river to Limones, where there's a sawmill. There are few amenities in town, but you can get some sleep at **Hotel Mauricio Real** (rooms per person with shared/private bath $3/6), a tolerable place at the end of the pier.

See Getting There & Away under San Lorenzo earlier for details about boat travel.

LA TOLA
☎ 06

People traveling by boat from San Lorenzo and Limones arrive at La Tola and continue by bus to Esmeraldas, or by foot to nearby Olmedo. Arrive early if you're trying to make it to Esmeraldas. There is little reason to stay in La Tola. If you do need to stay the night, you're better off in Olmedo.

There is a Tolita archaeological site on the nearby island of **Manta de Oro**, but the gold ornaments that were found here are now in museums, and there is not much to see unless you are an archaeologist.

La Costeñita and Transportes del Pacífico run buses to and from Esmeraldas ($3, four hours) and boats to and from Limones ($1.50, about 40 minutes); see Getting There & Away under San Lorenzo, earlier. If you take a morning bus from Esmeraldas, you can connect here with a boat to San Lorenzo, and vice versa.

OLMEDO
☎ 06 • approximate pop 150

A 20-minute walk from the pier at La Tola, Olmedo is a predominantly Afro-Ecuadorian

fishing village on a spit of land surrounded by estuary, mangroves, shrimp farms and the sea. Here you'll find the small **Cabañas de los Manglares de Olmedo** (San Lorenzo ☎ 780 357, La Tola ☎ 786 133, Olmedo ☎ 786 126; rooms per person $5), a community-run hostal right on the estuary – when the tide is up, the water's beneath the deck. The bathrooms and cold showers are shared, and meals are available for $3 to $4 each. The hostal began as an ecotourism project by Action for Mangrove Reforestation (Actmang), a Japanese nongovernment organization. The women who run the place will take you clamming when the tide is out (and the silty beach is over 1km wide) for $6 per person. You can also organize boat and fishing tours.

Nearby are the **Manglares de Majagual**, reportedly the tallest mangrove forest in the world. You can visit the forest on your own or hire a guide in Olmedo. You can also ask for Señora Orin Flores in La Tola, who works as a guide.

BORBÓN
☎ 06

This small river port on Río Cayapas has about 5000 inhabitants, most of whom are the descendants of African slaves brought here by the Spanish. The town is the best place to get boats up Río Cayapas before continuing up Río San Miguel to the Reserva Ecológica Cotacachi-Cayapas – an interesting trip to a remote area. It is also the entry point for trips up the equally interesting Río Santiago. Market day is Sunday.

Information

Angel Ceron runs the hotel La Tolita Pampa de Oro and is a good source of information about the area; he can tell you how to get to some of the local archaeological sites that pertain to the Tolita culture, which existed here around 2000 years ago. There is not much to see – these sites are mainly of interest to professional archaeologists.

The US-run mission in Borbón can be of assistance to travelers. Ask for directions in town – most people know where it is.

Places to Stay & Eat

The two hotels in Borbón are very basic. **La Tolita Pampa de Oro** (rooms per person $3) is friendly and the best place to stay. The other, **Residencial Capri** (rooms per person

Riches from the Rainforest

In the rainforests around Borbón, a small tagua-nut industry has developed. Known as 'vegetable ivory,' tagua nuts come from a palm tree that grows in the local forest. The 'nuts,' which are actually seeds, are the size of chicken eggs and soon become extremely hard. They can be carved into a variety of novelties, such as animal statuettes, miniature cups, chess pieces, rings and buttons. By providing economically viable alternatives to cutting the forest down, harvesting only the nuts is a sustainable alternative to harvesting the whole rainforest.

Apart from in the Borbón market, you will find tagua-nut products for sale in other areas along the coast, in Riobamba and in Quito gift shops. The ornaments are reminiscent of ivory and make good and inexpensive souvenirs of the rainforest – buying them actually helps to preserve that forest. Local carvers are becoming increasingly proficient, but quality varies, so look carefully for the best pieces.

$3) has basic rooms with mosquito nets and primitive toilet facilities.

There is a comfortable jungle lodge called Steve's Lodge some distance away by the river – see Along Río Cayapas later.

Most places to eat are basic *comedores* (cheap restaurants) that don't bother with a menu – ask them what they have. Some can get raucous with checker or domino playing and beer drinking in the evening.

Getting There & Away

La Costeñita and Transportes del Pacífico run buses to Esmeraldas ($3, four hours) or San Lorenzo ($2, two hours) about every hour from 7am to 6pm. Most of the roads are paved, although some sections are badly potholed.

A daily passenger boat leaves at 11am for San Miguel ($8, five hours). This boat can drop you at any location on Río Cayapas or at San Miguel. Various boats run irregularly to other destinations – ask around at the docks. *Fletes*, or private boats, can usually be hired if you have the money, but these are not cheap – expect to pay at least $100 per day per group.

ALONG RÍO CAYAPAS
Borbón to San Miguel

The most reliable boat service from Borbón is the daily passenger boat to San Miguel (see following), which is often used by travelers rather than locals – although you certainly won't find hordes of tourists. There are several stopping places along the way.

Steve's Lodge (*Stephan Tarjanyi, Casilla 187, Esmeraldas, Ecuador; rooms per person per night $45, 3-day packages $280*) at the mouth of Río Onzole, about an hour from Borbón, is the first you'll come to. Run by a friendly Hungarian named Steve Tarjanyi, the lodge has six comfortable double rooms with great river views. The lodge doesn't have a phone so you'll have to write to the above address. Both overnight and three-night stays include meals, and the three-night stay also includes a guided boat tour up Río Cayapas to the Reserva Ecológica Cotacachi-Cayapas (camping in the reserve is also an option). There are discounts for groups of four or more. Guides speak English.

Beyond Steve's Lodge, the boat to San Miguel stops at a number of communities and missions. River travel is made interesting by passengers ranging from Catholic nuns to Chachi Indians embarking or disembarking in the various tiny ports, which are usually no more than a few planks at the water's edge.

The first mission is the Catholic **Santa María**. Here, there is a clean dormitory that sleeps six people. There is also a basic residencial, or you can camp. The next mission is the Protestant **Zapallo Grande**; you can find a basic place to sleep here, too. Chachi crafts are often for sale. Both missions have medical clinics and local people will offer to take you on tours. There are also a number of other communities, such as Pichiyacu, Playa Grande, Atahualpa and Telembi, that are the homes of mainly Chachi Indians or Afro-Ecuadorians.

Finally, you'll reach San Miguel.

San Miguel

This small, friendly village is the main base from which to visit the lowland sections of the Reserva Ecológica Cotacachi-Cayapas.

There is a ranger station on a small hill overlooking the village – the view of the rainforest and river from here is quite spectacular. There are about 30 houses in the village, one of which is a small store selling soft drinks, crackers, sardines, candy, oatmeal and little else. The inhabitants of the village are Afro-Ecuadorians. Chachi Indians' houses are scattered along the shores of the river nearby.

The *guardaparque* (park ranger) will let you stay in the **ranger station** *(per person $5)*, which has four beds, but no running water or mosquito nets. Larger groups can sleep on the floor or camp outside. The grass in front of the station is a haven for chiggers though, so load up on repellent. The station has a cold shower, a toilet and kitchen facilities. A shop sells a few very simple food supplies, or you can buy basic meals (rice and fried bananas with a little soup) for about $5. The people are friendly.

The driver of the daily passenger canoe from Borbón spends the night about 15 minutes downriver from San Miguel. He will not come back to San Miguel unless he knows for sure that he has a passenger, so be sure to make arrangements. The canoe leaves San Miguel around 4am.

PLAYA DE ORO

The other river leading inland from the Borbón is Río Santiago. The furthest community up the river is the remote settlement of **Playa de Oro**, near the border of Reserva Ecológica Cotacachi-Cayapas. Playa de Oro means 'Beach of Gold' and was so coined because gold has been panned in the region for centuries. There are some community-run **cabañas** *(beds per person $25)* in the village, which are totally hit-or-miss, depending on whose turn it is to run the place. Food is included in the price, but purified/boiled water often is not.

Half an hour upstream from Playa de Oro is the **Playa de Oro Reserva de Tigrillos**, a 10,000-hectare reserve owned and operated by the community of Playa de Oro. The reserve, which borders Cotacachi-Cayapas, protects some of each species of jungle cat found in the area – jaguars, pumas, ocelots, margays, oncillas and jaguarundis. The only way to really experience the reserve is by staying at the river-side **jungle lodge** *(private rooms per person $30, dorm beds $25)*.

Prices include three meals, laundry service and local guides.

The village of Playa de Oro is about five hours upstream from Borbón, but there are no boats. You have to take the 7:30am bus from Borbón to Selva Alegre ($2, two hours). From Selva Alegre, if you made a reservation, a boat from Playa de Oro will motor you up to the village or the reserve. The two-hour river trip (2½ hours if you're going to the reserve) from Selva Alegre costs $50, split among the number in your group. Reservations must be made at least a month in advance with **Rosa Jordan** *(e rosaj@look.ca)* who speaks English.

RESERVA ECOLÓGICA COTACACHI-CAYAPAS

This 204,420-hectare reserve *(admission $5)* is by far the largest protected area of western Andean habitats in Ecuador. It covers an altitude range of about 200m above sea level in the San Miguel area to 4939m above sea level at the summit of Cotacachi. Thus, the type of habitat changes rapidly from lowland, tropical, wet forest to premontane and montane cloud forest to páramo, with many intermediate habitat types. This rapid change of habitat produces the so-called 'edge effect' that gives rise to an incredible diversity of flora and fauna.

These are the haunts of such rarely seen mammals as giant anteaters, Baird's tapirs, jaguars and, in the upper reaches of the reserve, spectacled bears. The chances of seeing these animals are remote, however. You may see monkeys, squirrels, sloths, nine-banded armadillos, bats and a huge variety of bird species. It is certainly a great area for bird-watching.

There are two principal ways to visit the reserve. You can go in from the highlands (as described in the Northern Highlands chapter), or you can go in from San Miguel, as described later in this chapter. It is extremely difficult (if not impossible) to hike between the two regions; the steep and thickly vegetated western slopes of the Andes in between are largely trackless and almost impenetrable. This is bad news if you want to visit the interior of the reserve but good news for the species existing there – they will probably be left alone for a little while longer.

Both the lower reaches of the reserve and the rivers leading into this area are the home of the indigenous Chachi, of which about 5000 remain. The Chachi are famous for their basketwork, and there are stores in Borbón, Limones, Esmeraldas and Quito selling their crafts. You can buy them far more cheaply directly from people on the river. Many of the Chachi live in open-sided, thatched-roof houses built on stilts near the river. Fishing and subsistence agriculture are their main sources of food, and many speak only the Chachi tongue. Some groups now live on or close to missions; others are largely beyond missionary influence. In these groups, both men and women go bare breasted.

Over the last few decades, the Chachi have been swept by a form of river blindness that is supposedly carried by blackfly, which is particularly prevalent in April and May. Some 80% of the Indians have the disease to a greater or lesser extent. Insect repellent works to keep the insects off you, and taking chloroquine as a malarial prophylactic also helps to prevent the disease.

When to Go
The area is very wet. Up to 5000mm of rain has been reported in some of the more inland areas, although it is somewhat less wet around San Miguel. The rainy season is from December to May. River levels are high then, and the local people consider this to be the best time to travel. It is also the season with the highest concentrations of mosquitoes, blackflies and other insects, but they tend to be really bad only at dawn and dusk, so cover up then. Even during the rainy months, mornings are often clear. The drier months of September to December are usually less buggy, and there is a better chance of seeing wildlife, although river navigation may be limited.

Getting There & Around
Entrance into the reserve is payable at the ranger station in San Miguel. The rangers will act as guides, and charge about $10 per day, plus food. Two guides are needed for many trips – one for each end of the dugout canoe. These canoes are paddled and poled – not many people have engines out here. Alternatively, you can visit on a guided tour with one of the lodges. Note that the lodge in Playa de Oro is also an access point for the reserve.

It is about two or three hours by canoe from San Miguel to the park boundaries.

Another one or two hours brings the visitor to a small but pretty waterfall in the jungle. There are a few poorly marked trails, for which a guide is almost essential. There are places to camp if you have tents and all the necessary gear.

THE ROAD TO ESMERALDAS
☎ 06
The bus journey to Esmeraldas from San Lorenzo via Borbón is dusty in the dry season, muddy in the wet season and bumpy all year long. The section between San Lorenzo and Borbón starts along the Ibarra road and then turns inland through the forest. A short side road stops at the village of **Maldonado**.

Beyond Borbón, there are a number of villages, most with a basic residencial if you get stuck. One of these villages is **Lagarto**, where Río Lagarto is crossed. Soon after crossing Río Lagarto, the routes from Borbón and La Tola unite. Then the road passes through the village of **Montalvo**, which has no hotel, and on to the coastal village of **Rocafuerte**, which has very basic residenciales and simple restaurants selling tasty fresh seafood. People from Esmeraldas drive out here on weekends for a good meal in a rural setting.

A few kilometers further on the road passes through the two coastal villages of Río Verde: **Palestina de Río Verde**, just beyond the river, and then **Río Verde**, a few kilometers further. Río Verde was the setting of Moritz Thomsen's book *Living Poor* – see Books in the Facts for the Visitor chapter. At the river crossing, look for a large frigatebird colony visible in the trees along the banks. Palestina de Río Verde has a few simple hotels.

Between the two coastal villages **Hostería y Restaurante Pura Vida** (☎ 744 203, 744 204; e pura_vida_verde@yahoo.com; rooms per person $10-15) is the best place to stay between San Lorenzo and Esmeraldas. This quiet and remote hostal arranges rental bikes, fishing, excursions and volunteering in local schools. Some rooms have private baths, and there's a **restaurant** (meals $3-5) is on the premises. It's a lovely place. The phone lines are sometimes out, so try emailing or just show up.

Almost 20km beyond Río Verde is the village of **Camarones**, which, as its name implies, sells delicious shrimp lunches in its simple beachfront restaurants during the weekends and vacations. Ask around about cabins for rent if you want to stay by the beach; Cabañas Fragatas is one such place.

A few kilometers beyond Camarones, the road passes the Esmeraldas airport on the east side of Río Esmeraldas. The city is on the west side, but there is no bridge until San Mateo, about 10km upriver. It is a half-hour drive from the airport to Esmeraldas.

ESMERALDAS
☎ 06 • pop 126,000

This important city is the capital of the province of Esmeraldas. It was near here that the Spanish conquistadors made their first landfall in Ecuador. Esmeraldas has been an influential port town throughout Ecuador's history, and it is now the largest port in northern Ecuador. Although fishing and shipping are important, the oil refinery near the terminal of the trans-Ecuadorian oil pipeline has given Esmeraldas another source of income and employment, as well as its share of noise and pollution. This, combined with the fact that Esmeraldas is considered Ecuador's most dangerous major city, makes it an unattractive destination.

Most tourists just spend the night (if they have to) and continue southwest to the towns of Atacames, Súa and Muisne, where the best beaches are found. Esmeraldas also has beaches in the northern suburb of Las Palmas, but they're nothing special.

Information

There is no tourist office. The **immigration office** (☎ 710 156, 724 624) is at the Policía Civil Nacional, 3km out of town (take a taxi). You should have your passport stamped here if you are leaving or entering Ecuador via the rarely used coastal route to Colombia.

Banco del Pichincha (cnr Bolívar & 9 de Octubre) and **Banco Popular** (cnr Piedrahita & Bolívar) change traveler's checks and have ATMs.

The **post office** (Colón near 10 de Agosto) is two blocks east of the main plaza. Make phone calls at **Andinatel** (cnr Malecón Maldonado & Montalvo).

The **hospital** (☎ 710 012; Avenida Libertad) is between Esmeraldas and Las Palmas, at the north end of town. The **police station** (cnr Bolívar & Cañizares) is two blocks south of the plaza.

Esmeraldas has a reputation for being the most dangerous city in Ecuador. True or not, there are definitely drug problems and thieves. Avoid arriving in Esmeraldas after dark, and stick to well-lit streets if you do. Be careful in the market areas (especially the south end of the Malecón Maldonado) and anywhere away from the main streets. Single women have reported that they get hassled more often in Esmeraldas than elsewhere in Ecuador. Incidences of malaria are high during the wet months.

Places to Stay

Hotels are plentiful here, but the cheapest ones are depressing. Mosquitoes are a problem, particularly during the wet months, when you should have a fan or a mosquito net in your room to keep the insects off.

Hotel Diana (☎ 710 333; Cañizares 224; rooms per person $3-5) has decent, small rooms with private bath and fan. It's the best of the cheapies and its management is friendly and helpful.

Hotel Asia (☎ 714 594, 710 648, 711 852; 9 de Octubre 116; rooms per person $4), a couple of blocks north of Hotel Diana, is fine. Rooms are clean and have private baths.

Sandry Hotel (☎ 713 547; Libertad near Montalvo; rooms with/without air-con $5/4), across from the market, is clean and has rooms with private bath, fan and TV. Some have air-conditioning. The hotel is secure, but the market area isn't, so be careful.

Hotel El Galeón (☎ 713 116, 723 820, fax 714 839; rooms per person $4), near the corner of Olmedo and Piedrahita, is a bit run down, but has rooms with fan and private bath.

Apart Hotel Esmeraldas (☎ 728 700/1/2/3; Libertad 407; singles/doubles $19/25) is the best hotel close to the town center. Air-conditioned rooms have minifridges, phone, TV and room service. There is a casino, a guarded parking lot and a restaurant/bar.

You could also stay in the nicer and pricier resort-suburb of Las Palmas, 3km north of the center. Almost all of the hotels are on Avenida Kennedy, which is the main street parallel to the beach. Reach it by heading north on Libertad.

Hotel Cayapas (☎ 721 318, 721 319; Avenida Kennedy 401; singles/doubles $15/20) has a nice garden and simple but clean, air-conditioned rooms with telephone, TV and hot water. It also offers room service.

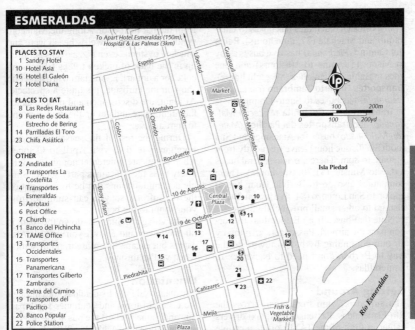

ESMERALDAS

PLACES TO STAY
1 Sandry Hotel
10 Hotel Asia
16 Hotel El Galeón
21 Hotel Diana

PLACES TO EAT
8 Las Redes Restaurant
9 Fuente de Soda
Estrecho de Bering
14 Parrilladas El Toro
23 Chifa Asiática

OTHER
2 Andinatel
3 Transportes La
Costeñita
4 Transportes
Esmeraldas
5 Aerotaxi
6 Post Office
7 Church
11 Banco del Pichincha
12 TAME Office
13 Transportes
Occidentales
15 Transportes
Panamericana
17 Transportes Gilberto
Zambrano
18 Reina del Camino
19 Transportes del
Pacífico
20 Banco Popular
22 Police Station

NORTH COAST & LOWLANDS

Places to Eat

The better hotels in Esmeraldas and Las Palmas have decent restaurants; the one in Hotel Cayapas (see earlier) is above average. The food in the many small and cheap pavement cafés and *comedores* is often good – try along Olmedo between Mejía and Piedrahita.

Las Redes Restaurant *(Bolívar)*, on the east side of the central plaza, is good for seafood. **Fuente de Soda Estrecho de Bering** *(Bolívar)*, also facing the plaza a few doors down, is a good place for snacks, ice cream and people-watching. The best place if you feel like Chinese food is **Chifa Asiática** *(Cañizares near Sucre)*. **Parrilladas El Toro** *(9 de Octubre near Olmedo)* does decent grilled meats.

Entertainment

The northern coast is known for its lively African-influenced marimba music, of which Esmeraldas is the center. There are no particular places where you go to listen to shows; impromptu gatherings are the norm. The best way to find out what's happening is to ask the locals. There are several discos – most are in Las Palmas. Note: Women should not go to any of these places unescorted by a man.

Getting There & Away

Air TAME flies from Quito to Esmeraldas and back on Monday, Wednesday, Thursday, Friday and Sunday afternoons. The one-way fare is $37. TAME may have flights to Cali, Colombia, twice a week, but only during the beach high season (December to April).

The **TAME office** *(☎ 726 863; Bolívar near 9 de Octubre)* is just off the central plaza. You can also purchase a plane ticket at the **airport office** *(☎ 727 058)* if the flight isn't full; arrive early and make sure you get a seat assignment.

Bus There is no central bus terminal. The fastest service to Quito ($6, five hours) is with **Aerotaxi** *(Sucre)*, which is between Rocafuerte and 10 de Agosto. Transportes Occidentales and Transportes Esmeraldas, both near the central plaza, are slower and a little cheaper. **Transportes Panamericana** *(Piedrahita)*, between Colón and Olmedo, has the most luxurious buses to Quito, but the fare is a couple of dollars more expensive, and the trip takes seven to eight hours.

Transportes Occidentales and Transportes Esmeraldas also have frequent buses to

Guayaquil ($5 to $7, seven to eight hours). Transportes Occidentales has buses to Guayaquil and Machala ($7, nine hours). **Reina del Camino** *(Piedrahita)* has five buses a day to Manta ($8, nine to 10 hours) and one goes to Bahía de Caráquez ($7, eight hours). **Transportes Gilberto Zambrano** *(cnr Sucre & Piedrahita)* has buses to Santo Domingo.

Transportes La Costeñita *(Malecón Maldonado)* and **Transportes del Pacífico** *(Malecón Maldonado)* buses for Atacames and Súa (both $0.70, one hour) leave frequently from 6:30am to 8pm. There are also several buses a day to Muisne ($1.70, two hours). These companies also go to Borbón (four hours) and on to San Lorenzo ($4, five hours). Buses also go to other small provincial villages.

Note that buses from Esmeraldas to Borbón pass the airport. Passengers arriving by air and continuing by bus to towns on the way to Borbón don't need to backtrack to Esmeraldas.

Getting Around

The airport is 25km from town, across the Río Esmeraldas. Passengers and taxi drivers gather in front of the TAME office a couple of hours before the flight, and four or five passengers are crammed into each taxi at a cost of about $3 per person. Incoming passengers get together to do the same thing at the airport. At the airport, you can hire a taxi for about $25 to take you directly to Atacames, thus avoiding Esmeraldas completely.

To get to the airport cheaply, take a La Costeñita or Transportes del Pacífico bus to Borbón (it stops at the airport). Pay on board ($0.50).

Take a Selectivo bus signed 'Las Palmas No 1' northbound along Bolívar to get to the port of Esmeraldas and to the beaches of Las Palmas. The fare is $0.15. A taxi charges about $1.

ATACAMES

☎ 06

Atacames is at its rip-roaring riotous best (or worst, depending on your fancy) when *serranos* (people from the highlands) pour into town to party. They arrive in droves during the high season (July to mid-September, Christmas through New Year, Carnaval and Easter) and the beach turns into a chaotic family fiesta. The open-air bars along the Malecón (waterfront) serve milkshakes and

tropical drinks and try to out-blast the music from the bar next door. Along the Malecón, vendors sell candy, jewelry, beach ware and shucked oysters – even pizza ovens get fired up in the back of pickup trucks ('Slice and coke for a dollar!') – and tattoo artists set up shop on the curbside. It's quite a spectacle. At night, the discos open and people dance the night away and get up the next morning to start all over.

During the rest of the season, it's dead. Foreigners tend to visit April to October, when things are quieter, although you definitely miss the Atacames party scene. Simple accommodations can be found right on the oceanfront, so you can stumble from your room to the beach.

The village of **Súa**, just down the road, is far mellower and allows you to visit Atacames but escape to a more tranquil setting when you're through.

Orientation

The main road from Esmeraldas goes through the center of town and continues south past Súa and Same. Get off the bus at the beaten-up bus-stop sign. A block off the highway toward the ocean, a footbridge crosses the Río Atacames to the beach and hotel area. Hotels and restaurants line the east-west Malecón. The street behind the Malecón is the Calle Principal. Buses do not go down to the beach, but, if you're feeling lazy, you can hail an 'ecotaxi' (tricycle) to take you (via the other bridge) to your hotel for under $1. The actual center of town is on the inland side of the highway. There is little reason to go into the town center except to catch a bus, go to the bank or use the phone or Internet.

Information

On the highway, just northeast of the bus stop, **Banco del Pichincha** *(Roberto Luis Cervantes s/n; open 8am-2pm Mon-Fri)* changes traveler's checks and has an ATM. **Andinatel** *(cnr Luis Tello & Juan Montalvo; open 8am-9:45pm daily)* is on the main plaza in the town center. Get online at **Comisariato del Cuaderno** *(☎ 731 521; Luis Tello, Parque Central; open 7am-9pm Mon-Sat, 9am-2pm Sun)*, also on the main plaza; it charges $2.40 per hour.

The beach has a powerful undertow and no lifeguards. People drown here every year, so stay within your limits.

Thieves work the beach, especially at night. Assaults and rapes have also been reported by people walking along the beach at night. Do not stray from the well-lit areas in front of the hotels. During the day, exercise caution if walking the isolated stretch to Súa, as knifepoint robberies have been reported. The main beach is fine during the day, but keep an eye on your stuff. Camping is definitely not recommended.

Places to Stay

There are over 50 hotels to choose from within a few blocks of the beach. They can get packed on weekends, especially holiday weekends, when prices rise to what the market will bear and single rooms are unavailable. During high-season weekends you must pay for the number of beds in the room (upward of four or six) regardless of the number in your party. Rates are best from Sunday to Wednesday, when you can try bargaining, especially if you plan on staying a few days. Single travelers usually pay the double rate.

Addresses are not used, so you need to ask or walk around to find a hotel. The following are described in west-to-east order. If you're facing the ocean, west is to your left.

Cabañas Rincon del Mar (☎ 731 064; 2- to 10-person cabañas $25-100), at the west end of town on the beach, rents a variety of simple, relaxing cabañas tucked in among the palm trees. They all have fans and private baths, and the pricier ones have kitchens. Most cabañas sleep from six to eight people. During the low season two people could probably rent one for $25.

At the west end of the Malecón, Calle Las Acacias runs away from the beach toward the highway. Along this street you'll find Atacames' oldest and cheapest hotels. Most of them are simple, but just fine. **Hotel El Reina Isabel** (☎ 731 665; Calle Las Acacias; low/high season rooms per person $4/7) is a good choice, and doubles are always available.

La Casa del Manglar (☎ 731 464; rooms per person with shared/private bath $6/7) is clean, friendly and simple. The cheaper rooms lack fans, but its bamboo walls and mangrove trimming give it a tropical feel. It's to your left immediately after crossing the footbridge.

Cabañas Los Bohios (☎/fax 731 089; Calle Principal; low/high season rooms per person $7/9) has nice, little, double cabins with baths and fans. The parking area outside the cabins detracts from the scenery, but it's fine.

Rincón Sage (☎ 731 246; doubles $12) has decent rooms with bath and a nice rooftop patio.

Hostal Jennifer (☎ 731 055; low/high season rooms per person $5/8), on a side street two blocks east of the footbridge, usually has single rates midweek and in the low season. It's clean, well managed, secure, modern and popular, and it fills up fast. There's a four-person minimum charge during the high season.

Cabañas Sol y Mar (☎ 731 524, 726 649; low/high season rooms per person $7/10), next door to Hotel Jennifer, is one of the few places that actually *has* double rooms and *charges* for double rooms. It's a great deal. Rooms are clean and airy and have private baths and fans. There's a small terrace with hammocks and off-street parking.

Hotel El Tiburon (☎ 731 145, 731 622; e antonia_tiburon@hotmail.com; Malecón; low/high season rooms per person $5/10) is a large, clean hotel smack in the center of the Malecón (2½ blocks east of the footbridge). Rooms have TV, bath and fan. It has a popular restaurant and off-street parking.

Hotel Vista Hermosa (☎ 731 547, 731 306; rooms per person $4-6) is clean, comfortable and has 18 rooms for two to eight people that vary in price depending on the season and the room.

Villas Arco Iris (☎ 731 069, 09-924 3417; e arcoiris@andinanet.net; low season singles/ doubles/triples $20/22/39, high season $54/ 54/64), toward the east end of the beach, offers lovely cabañas with TV, air-conditioning, and individual decks with hammocks and lounge chairs. The larger cabañas have kitchens. There's a swimming pool, the restaurant is excellent, the service is friendly, and the atmosphere is very relaxing. Prices are about 20% lower if you pay cash.

Hotel Casa Blanca (☎/fax 731 031/96, Quito ☎ 02-569 029; rooms with fan during week/weekend $30/50, with air-con $40/60) has clean rooms with TV and telephone and either air-conditioning or a fan. A pool and restaurant are on the premises.

Places to Eat

To the west of the footbridge you'll see a big *choza* (thatch-roof building). It is filled with **ceviche stalls** serving all types of ceviche (surprise) and oysters. A bowl of *ceviche de* *concha* (shellfish ceviche) or *ceviche de pescado* (fish ceviche) starts at around $3. (Careful with all that raw fish.)

Cocada (a chewy coconut sweet) is a local specialty that is sold everywhere. It's almost as prolific as the ubiquitous *batido* (fruit shake).

There are many simple *comedores* on the beach near the footbridge. They all tend to serve the same thing – *batidos* and the catch of the day. A whole fish dinner will start at around $4 or $5. Most of these double as bars in the evenings.

The best restaurant in town is **La Estancia** (☎ 09-968 8777; *Malecón; mains $6-13; open 5:30pm-10pm Mon-Thur, 12:30pm-11pm Fri-Sun*). Its eclectic decor and papier-mâché walls give the place a cozy ambience, and the food is excellent. Seafood, of course, is the specialty.

La Cena (*Malecón; mains $2-4*), a few doors east, serves good, cheap almuerzos ($1.50) and inexpensive seafood dishes. **Pizzería No Name** (*Malecón; pizzas $4-12; open 6:30pm-1am daily*) is the place for pizza.

Walfredo (*Calle Principal; mains about $2-4; open 8am-10pm daily*) has one of the biggest seafood menus in town. The prices are good, the food's good, it's casual, and it's always busy. Walfredo is next to the police station, west of the footbridge, one street back from the Malecón.

Entertainment

On high-season weekends the Malecón stays jammed with people well into the night. Revelers pour into the competing beach-side bars (walk along and take your pick) and swill fruity rum cocktails to blaring music. The only discos in town are on the Malecón so they're easy to stumble into after you've barhopped. During the low season and mid-week, things are mellow, if not dead.

Getting There & Away

All buses stop at the rusty, old bus-stop sign on the main road to/from Esmeraldas; there is no bus terminal. Buses for Esmeraldas ($0.70, one hour) normally begin from Súa, and there are plenty of seats. Most buses from Esmeraldas to Atacames continue on to Súa, Same and Tonchigüe for about $0.50. There are regular buses to Muisne ($1, 1½ hours).

Transportes Occidentales (☎ 09-981 9743) and **Aerotaxi** (☎ 731 112), whose offices are near the highway, both go daily to Quito ($8, six to seven hours). If you're returning to Quito on a Sunday in the high season be sure to buy your ticket in advance.

SÚA
☎ 06

This small fishing village is more bustling than Atacames from a fishing point of view, but it's a much quieter place to stay if you'd rather watch the boats at work than just hang out on the beach. The fishing industry attracts its attendant frigatebirds, pelicans and other seabirds, and the general setting is attractive, although the beach is less clean because of fishing activities. Súa is quieter and less popular than Atacames and it is easier to find weekend prices that aren't inflated. There is an Andinatel office.

Súa is about a 6km walk by road from Atacames. You can walk along the beach at the lowest tides, but if you try this, be careful not to get cut off by the tide, and go with several friends to avoid getting robbed.

There's much less to choose from than in Atacames, but prices are lower. **Hotel Chagra Ramos** (☎ 731 006, 731 070; *rooms per person $6-8*) is good value and has a little beach, nice views and pleasant rooms with bath. It also has a good, inexpensive restaurant.

Hotel El Peñón de Súa (☎ 731 013; *rooms per person $5*) is 300m away from the beach but has nice rooms with a private shower and a little patio.

Hotel Buganvillas (☎ 731 008; *rooms per person about $5*) is also an enjoyable little place.

There are a handful of other places to stay.

Buses to and from Esmeraldas run about every 45 minutes. It takes 10 minutes to get to Atacames ($0.30) and about an hour to get to Esmeraldas ($0.70).

If you want to go further along the coast to Muisne, you have to wait out of town along the main road for a bus passing from Esmeraldas.

SAME & TONCHIGÜE
☎ 06

The small village of Same (pronounced 'sah-may') is a quiet beach resort about 6km southwest of Súa. Same lacks the crowds of Atacames and is slightly more expensive. The attractive gray-sand beach is palm fringed and clean.

Tonchigüe is a tiny fishing village about 3km west of Same. Its beach is a continuation of the Same beach.

Cabañas Seaflower (*☎ 733 369; 2- to 5-person cabañas $25*) has four rustic, wooden cabañas, which are all connected to each other behind the Seaflower's restaurant just a shell's throw from the beach.

La Terraza (*☎ 733 320; rooms for 2-4 persons $45, cabañas $35*) offers spacious, stark rooms with terraces, two of which face the beach. The cabañas are cement with wooden decks and floors. La Terraza's restaurant and bar is popular, but is open irregularly.

The tiny **Rincón del Sabor** (*mains $3-5*) does delicious seafood, especially *encocado* (fish in coconut sauce).

Azuca (*☎ 733 343; Entrada Las Canoas, Carretera*), on the highway, is the cheapest place in town. It's a Colombian-owned, eclectic, artsy place with just a few rooms over an excellent restaurant. The two women who run the place play great music and take good care of their guests. Ask about their cabaña on the beach.

Hotel Club Casablanca (*Quito ☎ 02-225 2077; e casablan@uio.satnet.net; doubles $50-70*) is a 1st-class resort with swimming pool, tennis courts and games facilities.

On a cliff overlooking a small but private beach between Same and Tonchigüe, **El Acantilado** (*☎ 733 466, Quito ☎ 02-245 3606; high season cabañas $48, low season for 2/3/4 persons $29/40/48*) offers comfortable cabañas that sleep two to four people and have hot water. It has a good restaurant, too.

In Tonchigüe, **Hotel Luz del Mar** (*rooms per person $6*) is one of the cheapest options in the area.

Playa Escondida (*☎ 09-973 3368; camp sites per person $5, rooms per person $8-12*) is 3km west of Tonchigüe and 10km down the road to Punta Galeras. It's an isolated, quiet, beautiful spot, run by a Canadian named Judy. It has a restaurant and lots of empty, hidden beach.

Buses heading east to Esmeraldas and south to Muisne pick up and drop passengers at both Same and Tonchigüe.

MUISNE & AROUND
☎ 05

This small port is on an island at the end of the road from Esmeraldas and it has a minor banana-shipping industry. It is relatively remote and far fewer people come here compared to the more popular beaches, such as Atacames.

There are some mangroves remaining in the area, and this is one of the few places where mangroves are, to some extent at least, protected (see the boxed text 'Maltreated Mangroves').

Orientation & Information
At the end of the road from Esmeraldas, motorized dugouts frequently cross Río Muisne to the island ($0.15). When you disembark at Muisne, you'll see the main road heading directly away from the pier through the town 'center' to the beach. It's about 1.5km along the main road from the center to the beach, a walk that's made far easier by hiring an 'ecotaxi' (as the tricycle taxis have proudly deemed themselves).

There is an **Andinatel office** (*open 8am-10pm daily*) just off the main plaza. The post office, nearby, is open sporadically.

Dangers & Annoyances
There have been reports of theft from beach cabins, some of which are not very secure. Bring your own padlock, and be sure to check the windows. Single travelers, women especially, are strongly advised not to wander along the beach away from the hotels and restaurants.

Organized Tours
Hotel Playa Paraíso and Hotel Calade (see Places to Stay & Eat following) offer boat trips up Río Muisne to see the **mangrove forests** (see the boxed text 'Maltreated Mangroves'). They can also take you by boat to the nearby beach at **Mompiche** where there's a world-class wave – it's a left point-break that breaks only during big swells.

Passenger canoes go once or twice a day to the settlement of **San Gregorio**, 1½ hours up Río Muisne. You can get information about the area from Antojitos Bar & Café, about three blocks from the boat landing in Muisne – ask for the Cotera brothers, who know a lot about the area.

Places to Stay & Eat
There are only budget hotels in Muisne. Although there are a handful of hotels near the river and the bus stop, most travelers cross the river to the island and stay in beachfront

cabañas. During the rainy months, mosquitoes can be bad, so look for mosquito nets over your bed.

Hotel Galápagos (☎ 480 158; rooms per person $6) is about 400m before you arrive at the beach and one block to the right of the 'main road.' It's the only proper hotel in Muisne, with plain, concrete rooms and private baths. The owner is friendly.

Hotel Playa Paraíso (☎ 480 192; rooms per person $4) is pleasant and friendly, rustic and wooden, and its little rooms have shared baths and mosquito nets. The restaurant serves good food (including vegie options), and its tables are perfect for comfortable, beach-side reading and beer drinking all day long. There's table tennis, a pool table and a big bar in the grassy backyard. You can pitch a tent on the grass for $2.

Hotel Calade (☎ 480 279; rooms per person with shared/private bath $4/5), just down the beach, is friendly and has clean but basic rooms with mosquito nets. The rooms without private baths are better because they face the ocean. It's a nice place and has a restaurant, too.

A couple of other cheap places to stay and several inexpensive restaurants and bars are found along the beach. Everything is within a five-minute walk; look around for what looks best for you.

Getting There & Away

Several companies have buses departing about every 30 minutes to Esmeraldas ($1.50, 2½ hours) passing Same, Súa and Atacames en route. There are five buses a day to Santo Domingo de los Colorados ($4, five hours) where connections to Quito or Guayaquil are made. Transportes Occidentales has a nightly bus at 10:30pm to Quito ($8, 8½ hours); it runs a night bus from Quito at 10:45pm

Maltreated Mangroves

Ecuador's coastal mangroves are an important habitat. In addition to helping to control the erosion of the coast, they provide homes, protection and nutrients for numerous species of fish, birds, mollusks and crustaceans (see Flora & Fauna in the Facts about Ecuador chapter). Unfortunately, mangroves have been in no-man's land, and it has been difficult to say who owns these coastal tropical forests that are semipermanently inundated. Squatters took over areas of mangroves as their own, but this was not a problem in itself, because they were able to use the mangroves sustainably. The mangroves also supported cottage industries, such as fishing, shrimping and crabbing, as well as some sport fishing. Thousands of families along the coast were gainfully employed in these industries without impacting the mangroves.

This all changed in the 1980s with the arrival of shrimp farms, which produced shrimp in artificial conditions in numbers many times greater than could be caught by traditional shrimping methods. To build the farms, it was necessary to cut down the mangroves. The prospective owner of a shrimp farm simply took over an area of mangrove forest, paid off anyone who was living there, cut down the mangroves, and began the shrimp-farming process. The net profits of the shrimp farms were very high, and the idea soon caught on and spread rapidly along the coast, resulting in the complete destruction of 80% to 90% of Ecuador's mangroves during the 1980s and early 1990s.

Although there are now laws controlling this destruction, it has continued because the laws are difficult to enforce in the remote coastal areas. There have been many negative short- and long-term effects of the shrimp farms. Previously many families could find a sustainable livelihood in the mangroves, whereas shrimp farms employ only a handful of seasonal workers. Where before there were mangroves protecting a large diversity of species, now there's just commercial shrimp. Coastal erosion and pollution from the wastes of the shrimp farms have become serious problems. It is yet another case of a handful of entrepreneurs getting very rich at the expense of thousands of families' livelihoods and the environment.

In 1999, the shrimp industry suffered dramatically when diseases such as *mancha blanca* (whitespot) wiped out entire shrimp farms in a matter of days. Many farms now lie abandoned. Meanwhile, desperate efforts are being made in Muisne, Bahía de Caráquez and a few other coastal towns to start replanting mangroves.

which arrives in Muisne at 7am. Buses or pickups (depending on road conditions) go south to Daule about every hour, from where boats go on to Cojimíes. It's easier, however, to take an Esmeraldas bus to El Salto (a road junction with a basic *comedor*) and wait there for southbound traffic heading to Daule. To get further south, get a bus to El Salto and then a bus to Pedernales, from where there are buses heading in all directions. Between El Salto and Pedernales, you often have to change buses in San José de Chamanga (you'll know you're in Chamanga by the floating piles of garbage and stilted houses). Ask your driver.

COJIMÍES
☎ 05

Cojimíes, a dirt-road village port, is set precariously on a headland that's constantly being washed away into the ocean. The village has to keep moving inland, and the locals say that the cemetery, now near the shoreline, was once way at the back of the town. There is a Pacifictel office here.

There are a few very basic wash-in-a-bucket-type places to stay on or just off the one main drag in Cojimíes. A few basic restaurants serve pricey meals. Ask around for small *comedores* in people's houses – the meals are cheaper and often better.

Hotel Coco Solo (☎ 09-586 952, Quito ☎ 02-240 404, 461 677; e cocosolo25@hot mail.com; cabins per person $8) is 14km south of Cojimíes – it's a hotel lost in the coconut groves that's great for lovers of deserted beaches and the noise of the wind whistling through the palm leaves. Rooms are in cabins and there is a restaurant with a limited menu and a pool table. Horse riding can be arranged. Apart from making reservations using the contact information provided here, you can also reserve through **Guacamayo Bahíatours** – see Travel Agencies under Bahía de Caráquez later in this chapter.

The Costa del Norte bus office is on the main street and can give you transportation information. Trucks run along the beach, racing the tide at breakneck speeds, to Pedernales ($2, 40 minutes). Departures depend on the tide, so they usually occur in the morning. Buses take the 'road' (1½ hours); the last one leaves at around 3pm.

To head north, you have to take a boat across to Daule, from where there are buses to the junction, El Salto. At El Salto you can get a bus to Muisne or Esmeraldas (those to Esmeraldas pass Atacames and other coastal towns).

PEDERNALES
☎ 05 • approximate pop 12,000

Pedernales is about 40km south of Cojimíes and is the most important market town between Muisne and Bahía de Caráquez. It's also an important transportation hub. In the 1990s, the shrimp industry expanded from the south, giving Pedernales a freewheeling boomtown atmosphere – for a while. Farms have lately been abandoned because of *mancha blanca* (whitespot), a shrimp disease that has pummeled the local industry and further illustrated the catastrophic unsustainability of shrimp farming as it's currently practised.

The town gets lively on weekends when *serranos* flood into town and drag their pounding sound systems on to the Malecón. The beach is unsightly but interesting, although there are better beaches to the north.

Hotel Playas (☎ 681 092; rooms per person $4) is the best budget hotel in town, but you have to bargain hard. **Hostal Villa Martín** (rooms per person $4), down on the beach, is also good and has an excellent restaurant.

Among the best hotels in town are **Hotel América** (☎ 681 174; García Moreno), on the road down to the beach, and **La Catedral del Mar** (☎ 681 136; rooms per person $12).

Buses leave the main street for destinations south along the coast including the uninteresting village of Jama ($1.50, 1½ hours), Canoa ($3, three to 3½ hours) and San Vicente ($3.50, four hours). Full-speed trucks take the beach north to Cojimíes during low tide. The road via Chamango to El Salto and Daule avoids Cojimíes; if you take a bus in the morning you can easily connect at El Salto for buses to Muisne and further north.

A paved road heads inland to El Carmen and on to Santo Domingo. There are regular buses to Santo Domingo ($3.40, three hours), Quito ($5, six hours) and Guayaquil ($6, seven hours).

CANOA
☎ 05

This growing little beach village, about 18km north of San Vicente, has a long, wide and usually empty beach. The swimming is good when the waves are down – when they're up, people drag out their surfboards. At the north end of the beach are some caves with hundreds of roosting bats inside. You can reach them at low tide.

There are no banks, but there is a public phone, and Internet access is available at La Posada de Daniel (see below). Hotel Bambu and La Posada de Daniel both rent surfboards for about $6 per hour. Buses between Pedernales and San Vicente come through Canoa about every hour.

Hotel Bambu (*☎ 616 370; w www.ecuador explorer.com/html/coast_hotels; camp sites $2, singles/doubles with shared bath $7/10, with private bath $12/14, with private bath & balcony $15/18*) is a beachfront beauty and a great place to stay. The rooms (with firm beds and mosquito nets) are immaculate. There's a breezy communal lounge, hammocks all over the place, a volleyball area, a bar and an excellent restaurant. The bathrooms have hot water to boot. The hotel rents surfboards, boogie boards and a beach sailer. English and Dutch are spoken.

La Posada de Daniel (*☎ 616 373; e pos adadedaniel@hotmail.com; cabañas per person low/high season $6/9*) is a few blocks inland and is a friendly place with a restaurant, travel agency and 20 clean, rustic-looking wooden cabañas spread around a large swimming pool.

Hostal Shelmar (*rooms per person with shared/private bath $2/4*), one block inland from Bambu, is just fine for the cheapest place in town.

Restaurant Torbellino (*mains $1.50-3*) is probably the best bang for your buck, serving excellent local specialties from a charcoal-fired kitchen, presided over by Doña Sofía Hernandez. Her *biche* (a local soup of several tropical vegetables flavored with peanuts) can't be beat; you can get it vegetarian, or with fish or shrimp. Her excellent ceviches and other seafood lure locals all the way from Bahía de Caráquez. It's three blocks back from the beach.

Arenabar (*☎ 692 542; Malecón; pizzas $2-3*) serves good pizza and has dancing on Saturday nights.

The wide beaches of the area are slowly being developed. South of town you'll find several unimpressive (but clean) hotels along the beach.

Río Muchacho Organic Farm

The Río Muchacho Organic Farm is a working farm that offers much more than just organic tropical produce. It also practises sustainable permaculture and has built a primary school, where, apart from learning their ABC, children are taught sustainable farming practices, reforestation and waste management. The family who lives on the farm welcomes visitors, who are encouraged to participate in the daily activities of Río Muchacho.

The farm lies along the river of the same name and is reached by a rough 8km track branching inland from the road north of Canoa. Transportation to the farm is normally on horseback, which is how the local *montubios* (coastal farmers) get around. After touring the farm, inspecting the crops and learning about permaculture and organic farming, visitors are free to choose from a variety of activities. They can help milk the cows and make cheese; harvest and prepare crops; roast and grind coffee; fish for river shrimp; make ornaments from tagua nuts; relax with a mud-facial mask; or go hiking, riding or bird-watching.

Accommodations (*packages per person 1 night/2 days $64, 2 nights/3 days $90*) are in very rustic cabins (including a great tree house). Showers and clean composting toilets are shared. Guest groups are kept small, and reservations are a good idea.

Volunteers are welcome to stay longer and work in the school or on the farm, and are charged $260 a month for food and lodging. This is an excellent ecocultural experience for travelers who want to learn about real *montubio* life.

The farm is owned and managed by Guacamayo Bahíatours (*☎ 691 107, 691 412; e ecopapel@ ecuadorexplorer.com; w www.riomuchacho.com*); see Bahía de Caráquez, later. Rates include transportation from Bahía de Caráquez, activities, meals and accommodations. Day visits cost $20 per person. Guacamayo earmarks 10% of tour fees to support the school and other conservation work.

Hauling the catch, Esmeraldas

Río San Miguel, Esmeraldas

Local fishermen, Mompiche

Public art at Malecón 2000, Guayaquil

Las Peñas, Guayaquil

Las Peñas, Guayaquil

SAN VICENTE
☎ 05

Most people visit San Vicente simply to catch the ferry across the Río Chone to the more important town of Bahía de Caráquez (or vice versa). San Vicente itself has a busy river-side market and a beach-side church with interesting murals and stained-glass work. It has a few hotels and bus transportation heading north.

Hostal San Vicente (☎ 674 182, 674 160; rooms per person with shared/private bath $5/4), near the center, is the best of the basic places.

Hotel Vacaciones (☎ 674 116; rooms per person $9) is good and has air-conditioned rooms, a pool and a decent restaurant.

On the northern outskirts of town, on the way to Canoa, there are several hotels, such as **Hotel Monte Mar** (☎ 674 197; rooms $20-30), which has the best views of Bahía de Caráquez across the bay, as well as a pool, a restaurant, and the option of air-conditioning.

Buses leave hourly from near the market (by the passenger-ferry dock) to Pedernales (three hours), and some continue to Cojimíes. Reina del Camino has several buses a day to Chone (see Inland from Portoviejo later in this chapter), Santo Domingo and Guayaquil ($5 to $6, five to six hours), as well as morning and evening buses to Quito ($7, eight hours). Buses head regularly to Canoa ($0.25, 30 minutes).

Passenger ferries take 10 minutes to reach Bahía de Caráquez and leave several times an hour between 6am and 10pm ($0.25). A car ferry leaves about every half-hour – foot passengers can cross at no charge.

BAHÍA DE CARÁQUEZ
☎ 05 ● pop 20,000

This small coastal town looks bigger than it is, thanks to the high-rise condos and holiday homes that remain empty for much of the year. In the first half of the 20th century, this was Ecuador's most important port, but problems with sandbanks led to the development of the ports in Guayaquil and Manta, and Bahía (as the locals call it) became a backwater. It regained fame during the early 1990s, when President Sixto Durán (1992–96) had a holiday home here, and many upper-class Ecuadorians followed suit.

The 1998 El Niño hit Bahía particularly badly; the city was cut off by landslides,

and streets turned into rivers of mud. This was followed, in August 1998, by a 7.2 earthquake, which toppled or severely damaged some buildings. Only one person was killed in the quake, but at least 20 died in the horrendous mudslides that followed, literally wiping out the poorer neighborhoods on the edge of town.

By late 1999, numerous buildings still had earthquake damage, but the town's economic and touristic infrastructure was back in swing. Several interesting local tours are worth taking, but beach lovers will have to go elsewhere, as Bahía's beaches have been eroded and can only be used at low tide.

In 1999, Bahía declared itself an 'eco-city.' The town market may very well be the only one in Ecuador that recycles rather than throws away its waste. There are two organic farms nearby, as well as what is said to be the world's first organic shrimp farm. Reforestation projects are aimed both at the hillsides that were damaged after the 1998 El Niño and at mangroves that were damaged by shrimp farms. Various other agro-ecological and recycling ventures are being promoted by a handful of visionary locals.

Information
Tourist Offices Only somewhat helpful is the **tourist office** (☎ 691 124; e mturlitoral@ ec-gov.net; Bolívar near Mateus; open 8:30am-5pm Mon-Fri). Both Guacamayo Bahíatours and Bahía Dolphin Tours, listed under Travel Agencies later, are good about providing information even if you don't take a tour with them.

Money Cash your traveler's checks at the **Banco de Guayaquil** (☎ 692 205; cnr Bolívar & Riofrío; open 8:30am-6pm Mon-Fri); it has a MasterCard/Cirrus ATM.

Post & Communications You'll find the **post office** (Aguilera 108; open 8am-5pm Mon-Fri, 8am-noon Sat) between Bolívar and the Malecón. Make phone calls at **Pacifictel** (cnr Intriago & Arenas; open 8am-10pm daily).

Genesis Net (☎ 692 400; Malecón Santos 1302; open daily) offers Internet access for $2 per hour.

Travel Agencies The following agencies are both friendly and helpful and offer local information and tours. Both can provide information on volunteering in local schools and other types of local community work (there are some excellent opportunities here).

Guacamayo Bahíatours (☎ 691 107, 691 412; e ecopapel@ecuadorexplorer.com; w www.riomuchacho.com; Bolívar at Arenas; open 7:30am-7pm Mon-Fri, 9am-5pm Sat, 10am-2pm Sun) is owned by an Ecuadorian/New Zealand couple and is a good source of local information. The company arranges tours to Río Muchacho Organic Farm (see the boxed text earlier for more information on this farm). The staff can also arrange day trips to visit other agroecological projects, such as an organic shrimp farm.

You can take a tour through mangrove forests in a canoe paddled by a local fisherman to see coastal wildlife, especially birds. Trips to local islands with seabird colonies (including one of the biggest frigatebird colonies on this coast) are combined with an explanation of the problems facing the mangrove habitat and a visit to a private zoo that has Ecuador's largest collection of domesticated fowl from all over the world. Other trips include hikes through coastal tropical dry forest and whale watching (from late September to early October). Prices are $12 to $30 per person, depending on the tour and the number of people.

Bahía Dolphin Tours (☎ 692 097/86/88; w www.bahiadolphin.com; Bolívar 1004) owns the Chirije archaeological site (see Things to See & Do), and day visits or overnight tours to the site can be arranged. The company has English-, French- and German-speaking guides. The staff can arrange packages with overnight stays at Chirije and in Bahía, combined with visits to panama-hat workshops, an organic shrimp farm, frigatebird islands and other local places. Interesting city tours focus on Bahía as an 'eco-city' and cost $8 to $15. Tours to local islands cost $11 to $25.

Medical Services Both the Clínica Bahía (Hidalgo near Intriago) and Clínica Viteri (Riofrío near Montúfar) are recommended by locals.

Things to See & Do

The **Casa de Cultura** is worth a quick peek simply because it's in a century-old building. The **Museo Bahía de Caráquez** (☎ 692 285/86; cnr Malecón Santos & Peña; open 10am-5pm Mon-Fri, 11am-3pm Sat & Sun), right across the street, has a small collection of pre-Columbian pottery. The **mirador** (lookout) at the south end of town gives good views of the area and can be reached on foot or by a short taxi ride.

Chirije archaeological site, 15km south of Bahía and 3km north of San Clemente, is an earthen hill riddled with artefacts – such as ceramics, burials, cooking areas, garbage dumps and jewelry – dating mainly from the Bahía culture (500 BC–AD 500). The site is owned by Bahía Dolphin Tours (see Travel Agencies), and to visit you must arrange a guided trip through the agency. The sheer number of remains leads archaeologists to think this was once an important ancient port. Only small sections of the site have been professionally excavated, and some pieces are exhibited in the tiny on-site museum, but visitors will find shards of pottery all over the place.

Chirije is cut off by high tides, so visits have to be planned with this in mind. You can spend the night and take advantage of trails into the coastal, tropical, dry forest. Five large cabins sleep up to eight (a squeeze) and have a porch, private bath and kitchen if you want to spend a few days and cook for yourself. Rates are $50 to $75 per cabin and meals cost extra and are available on request. Because you are cut off by high tides, this really is 'getting away from it all.' You can take a day tour and then add a night if you like the place.

Places to Stay

Some cheap places have water-supply problems. **Bahía B&B** (☎ 690 146; Ascázubi 322; rooms per person with shared/private bath $4/7) is a decent choice for the price, and has a friendly, helpful staff and an English- and French-speaking owner. Rooms are small and rather musty but have fans and clean beds. Rates include a full breakfast.

Hostal Los Andes (☎ 690 587; Ascázubi; doubles $3), next door to Bahía B&B, is a thin-walled dump, but it's cheap. **Hotel Palma** (☎ 690 467; Bolívar 910; rooms per person $2) is slightly better and still dirt cheap.

Bahía Hotel (☎ 690 509, ☎/fax 693 833; Malecón Santos at Vinueza; rooms per person without/with TV $7/9) has 40 clean, straightforward rooms with firm beds, private bath, fan and, if you want, TV.

BAHÍA DE CARÁQUEZ

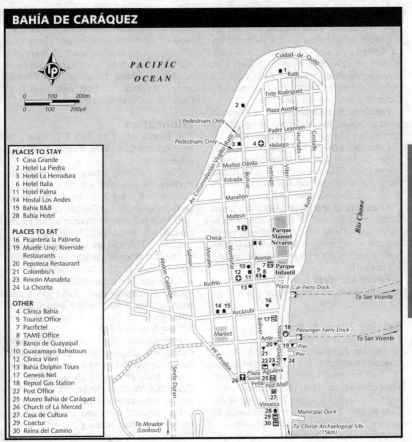

PACIFIC
OCEAN

Cuidad de Quito

Río Chone

PLACES TO STAY
1 Casa Grande
2 Hotel La Piedra
3 Hotel La Herradura
6 Hotel Italia
11 Hotel Palma
14 Hostal Los Andes
15 Bahía B&B
28 Bahía Hotel

PLACES TO EAT
16 Picantería la Patineta
19 Muelle Uno; Riverside Restaurants
20 Pepoteca Restaurant
21 Colombiu's
23 Rincón Manabita
24 La Chozita

OTHER
4 Clínica Bahía
5 Tourist Office
7 Pacifictel
8 TAME Office
9 Banco de Guayaquil
10 Guacamayo Bahíatours
12 Clínica Viteri
13 Bahía Dolphin Tours
17 Genesis Net
18 Repsol Gas Station
22 Post Office
25 Museo Bahía de Caráquez
26 Church of La Merced
27 Casa de Cultura
29 Coactur
30 Reina del Camino

To San Vicente

To San Vicente

To Mirador (Lookout)

To Chirije Archaeological Site (15km)

Hotel Italia (☎ 691 137; cnr Bolívar & Checa; singles/doubles $15/25) is a four-story hotel with small but spotless, comfy rooms with private hot showers, cable TV, telephones and fans. Downstairs is a decent restaurant.

Hotel La Herradura (☎ 690 446; Bolívar at Hidalgo; singles/doubles with fan & cold water $15/20, with air-con & hot water $25/35) has friendly staff and one of the town's better restaurants. It's an old, white, brick building with lots of character and country antiques. Air-conditioned rooms have telephone, TV and private hot showers, and two rooms have balconies with ocean views.

Hotel La Piedra (☎ 690 780, 691 463; e apartec@uio.satnet.net; Avenida Circunvalación Virgilio Ratti near Bolívar; singles/

doubles $67/79) has spacious, wallpapered rooms with flowery bedspreads, private bath, air-conditioning, telephone and cable TV. The seaside swimming pool, restaurant and bar help kick up the price.

Casa Grande (Avenida Circunvalación Virgilio Ratti at Viteri; doubles $50) is a stylish, private, 1960s-era house, with faded mod decor to match and walls adorned with original Kingman paintings. The seven rooms are comfortable and spacious, and the backyard overlooks the sea. Make reservations through Bahía Dolphin Tours (see Travel Agencies earlier). Rates include breakfast.

Places to Eat

Of the several restaurants overlooking the river, **Muelle Uno** (☎ 692 334; Malecón

Santos; mains $3-6; open 9am-midnight daily) is the fanciest and priciest; it's good but not necessarily the best. A few doors down, **La Chozita** (☎ 692 729; Malecón Santos; mains $3-6; open 8am-11pm daily) feels a bit more organic with its black faded floors. It's right on the water and the food – especially the grilled seafood – is delicious.

Pepoteca Restaurant (Ante & Malecón Santos), across the Malecón, serves cheap set lunches and good à la carte meals.

Colombiu's (☎ 690 537; Bolívar near Ante; mains $1.50-4; open 8:30am-10pm daily) serves good, filling almuerzos for $1.30 and tasty plates of seafood for under $4. It's cheap, comfortable and popular.

Picantería la Patineta (Ascázubi; soups $0.80; open 8:30am-12:30pm) serves delicious encebollado, which is a seafood, yucca and onion soup garnished with chifles (crispy banana slices). It's a breakfast tradition (and it's cheap!).

Rincón Manabita (cnr Malecón Santos & Aguilera; mains about $2) is the place to go for grilled chicken.

Getting There & Away

Two bus companies have offices next to one another on the south end of the Malecón. **Coactur** (☎ 690 014) has buses to Portoviejo ($1.50, two hours) hourly from 4am to 8pm; some continue to Manta ($2.20, three hours) and Guayaquil ($4.50, six hours). **Reina del Camino** (☎ 690 636) offers two classes of service – regular and ejecutivo (1st class) – to Quito ($6/8, eight hours) and Guayaquil ($4.50/6, six hours). The company also serves Ambato ($9, nine hours) and Santo Domingo ($4, four hours). Buses to local towns such as Chone are often rancheras (open-sided buses or trucks) and they leave from various places in town.

To Canoa and points north, cross the river to San Vicente – see San Vicente, earlier in this chapter, for boat information. The passenger and car-ferry docks are on the eastern side of town, off Malecón Santos.

PORTOVIEJO

☎ 05 • pop 180,641

This large city is the capital of Manabí Province and is important for coffee, cattle and fishing. Founded on March 12, 1535, it is one of the oldest cities in Ecuador and is the sixth largest. Portoviejo has a thriving agricultural-processing industry and is an important commercial center, with good road connections to Quito and Guayaquil. Although it's a bustling town, Portoviejo is not visited much by tourists, who prefer to head to the coast. However, it is friendly and is a reasonable overnight stop from Quito en route to the coast.

Information

The **tourist office** (☎ 630 877; Gual 234; open 8:30am-5pm Mon-Fri) can provide basic information.

There are many banks. Both **Banco del Pacífico** (☎ 639 300; cnr 10 de Agosto & Chile; open 8:30am-3pm Mon-Fri) and **Banco de Guayaquil** (Parque Central; open 8:30am-4pm Mon-Fri) change traveler's checks and have ATMs. Branches of Banco del Pichincha have ATMs and are found around town.

The **post office** (Ricuarte; open 8am-6:30pm Mon-Fri, 8am-12:30pm Sat) is between Sucre and Bolívar. The main **Pacifictel** (cnr 10 de Agosto & Pacheco; open daily) has longer hours than the more centrally located **branch office** (cnr 9 de Octubre & Rocafuerte; open 8:30am-4pm Mon-Fri).

Internet access is available at **Miky Cyber Café** (Chile 621; open daily) and **Webeando** (cnr 9 de Octubre & Morales; open daily), which both charge $1.20 per hour, and **Cybercafé Mr Chat** (Sucre 715; open Mon-Sat), which charges $1 per hour.

For standard tours and airline ticketing, try **Metropolitan Touring** (☎ 651 070, 631 761; Olmedo 706; open 8:30am-1pm & 3pm-7pm Mon-Fri).

The **public hospital** (☎ 630 766, 630 555, 630 087) is at the southeast end of Rocafuerte, 1km from the center; take a taxi or call the **Red Cross ambulance** (☎ 652 555). **Clínica Metropolitana** (☎ 634 207; cnr 9 de Octubre & Rocafuerte) is another choice.

Things to See

Despite the town's colonial history, there's little to see. Wander down to the pleasant **Parque Eloy Alfaro**, which has what may well be the starkest, barest modern **cathedral** in Ecuador. Next to the cathedral is a **statue of Francisco Pacheco**, who is the founder of Portoviejo.

The **street market** (Chile), between Duarte and Gual, makes for an interesting stroll; it's impassable to cars during the day.

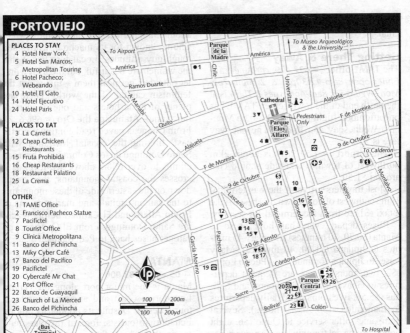

PORTOVIEJO

PLACES TO STAY
4 Hotel New York
5 Hotel San Marcos;
   Metropolitan Touring
6 Hotel Pacheco;
   Webeando
10 Hotel El Gato
14 Hotel Ejecutivo
24 Hotel Paris

PLACES TO EAT
3 La Carreta
12 Cheap Chicken
   Restaurants
15 Fruta Prohibida
16 Cheap Restaurants
18 Restaurant Palatino
25 La Crema

OTHER
1 TAME Office
2 Francisco Pacheco Statue
7 Pacifictel
8 Tourist Office
9 Clínica Metropolitana
11 Banco del Pichincha
13 Miky Cyber Café
17 Banco del Pacífico
19 Pacifictel
20 Cybercafé Mr Chat
21 Post Office
22 Banco de Guayaquil
23 Church of La Merced
26 Banco del Pichincha

NORTH COAST & LOWLANDS

Places to Stay

Hotel Paris (☎ 657 272; Sucre 513; rooms per person $4) is one of Portoviejo's oldest hotels (check out the early-20th-century pressed-tin ceiling in the entry). It's simple, friendly, safe and clean, but it looks rather dilapidated. There is, however, a spacious public lobby with a balcony and views of Parque Central. Rooms have private bath.

Hotel Pacheco (☎ 651 788; 9 de Octubre 512; rooms per person $3-5) is yet another cheapie – it's tolerable.

Hotel San Marcos (☎/fax 630 650/651; e porturis@gye.satnet.net; Olmedo 706; singles/doubles with fan $10/16, with air-con 15/22) is an older hotel. The rooms have phone, TV, fan and private bath.

Hotel El Gato (☎ 636 908, 632 856; Gual at Olmedo; singles/doubles with fan $7/11, with air-con $11/15) has large clean rooms with electric showers, TV, telephone and fan/air-conditioning.

Hotel New York (☎ 632 037, 631 998; cnr Olmedo & F de Moreira; singles/doubles $18/25, with window $20/28) offers fair rooms with fan, air-conditioning, private bath, hot water and TV. It has a restaurant.

Hotel Ejecutivo (☎ 632 105, 630 840, fax 630 876; 18 de Octubre; singles/doubles $40/46), between Gual and 10 de Agosto, is the town's best hotel. It provides car rental, has a good but pricey restaurant, and fully equipped, carpeted rooms.

Places to Eat

La Carreta (☎ 652 108; Olmedo; mains $1.50-4; open 7am-10pm Mon-Fri, 7am-3pm Sat), by the cathedral, is a slick little eatery with tie-clad waiters, starched tablecloths and good, inexpensive food.

Restaurant Palatino (10 de Agosto near Chile; mains $2-4; open 8am-6pm daily) is the place to head for cheap, filling Ecuadorian standards.

La Crema (Sucre 513), below Hotel Paris, is also cheap and good.

Fruta Prohibida (☎ 637 167; Chile 607; open 9:45am-11pm daily) has indoor and outdoor tables and serves a good variety of snacks, including fruit salads, excellent juices, hamburgers, ice cream and desserts.

Rows of **cheap restaurants** serving roasted chicken, as well as other meals are found on Gual between 18 de Octubre and Pacheco, as well as on the block of Morales south of Gual.

Getting There & Away

The **TAME office** (☎ 632 429; cnr América & Chile; open 8am-12:30pm & 2:30pm-7pm Mon, Wed & Fri, 8am-4pm Tues & Thur) is at the north end of the town center. TAME has one afternoon flight to/from Quito on Monday, Wednesday and Friday. The one-way fare is $48.

The **airport** (☎ 650 361) is about 2km northwest of town; a taxi ride should cost around $1.50.

Most travelers arrive at the bus terminal 1km southwest of downtown. It's best to take a taxi ($1) to/from the terminal for security.

Buses depart every half-hour or so to Manta ($0.70, 40 minutes) and every 45 minutes to Jipijapa ($1.20, 40 minutes). Many buses to Jipijapa continue on to Puerto López ($2, two hours). There are frequent departures to Guayaquil ($3, 3½ hours) and Salinas ($5.50, five hours), and daily departures to Esmeraldas ($6.50, 10 hours). Several companies offer service to Quito ($6, eight hours); Reina del Camino has *ejecutivo* buses to Quito if you want a little more comfort.

Other small nearby villages are frequently served by small bus companies.

INLAND FROM PORTOVIEJO
☎ 05

Manabí is an important agricultural province, and a good road system links Portoviejo with a number of canton capitals. The towns, often quite large, act as market centers for coffee, cattle, citrus, corn, cotton, yucca and bananas. They are colorful and bustling, and the people are hardworking, tough, old-fashioned and friendly. Tourists rarely visit these towns, even though the region is easy to travel in using local buses, and you can find cheap and basic hotels in the bigger towns. This area provides a glimpse of rural and provincial Ecuadorian life for those travelers who want to get off the beaten track.

Approximately 20km north of Portoviejo, **Rocafuerte** is known for its confectionery made of coconuts and caramel. **Calceta**, 43km northeast of Portoviejo, is known for sisal production. Sisal is the fiber gathered from the spiny-leaved agave plant that grows in the region. The sisal fibers are used for ropes and sandals, among other things.

From Calceta, a good road continues about 25km northeast to the sizable town of **Chone**, known for its macho cowboys and tough-guy attitudes. Local lore has it that the women are beautiful, but the men won't let outsiders get near them – this is not the feminism capital of the world. There are plenty of basic hotels and one good mid-range one – **Atahualpa the Oro** (☎ 696 627). From Chone, a paved road continues northeast, linking the coastal lowlands with Santo Domingo de los Colorados. This road climbs to over 600m above sea level as it crosses the coastal mountains, then drops down on the eastern side of these mountains to the canton capitals and market towns of **Flavio Alfaro** and **El Carmen** before reaching Santo Domingo. From El Carmen, you can get buses back to Pedernales.

MANTA
☎ 05 • pop 183,000

Manta is the major port along the central Ecuadorian coast and an important local tourist resort. Despite its popularity among Ecuadorian tourists, foreign travelers tend to zip through on their search for quieter and cleaner beaches. Surely Manta's not the place for empty, paradisiacal beaches, but it's an interesting place to soak up the atmosphere of a relatively safe and always busy Ecuadorian port town. The city has a strong seafaring tradition, and giant wooden fishing boats are still built by hand on Tarqui beach. Nearby, fishing crews drag their daily catches onto the sand each morning, turning the beach into a bustling, impromptu fish market with lots of chatter, barter and standing around in the sun. The town has a good local archaeology museum, some great seafood restaurants and a handful of fun bars and clubs to keep you rolling through the night. If you're dying for sun and sand, you'll find some attractive beaches just northwest of town.

Manta now hosts a de facto US military base, which the US Airforce – in return for a $30 million expansion of Manta's airstrip – uses as an operations point for its crackpot Plan Colombia (a coca-eradication plan based on some $3 billion in military and weapons assistance for the Colombian armed forces). *Manteños* (people from Manta) feel mixed about the US presence. Some believe it will help the local economy; others feel it

1500 Years of Seafaring

Manta has a long history. Even before its Spanish foundation in 1535, Manta (named 'Jocay' by the local Indians) was an important port. The Manta culture thrived throughout the whole western peninsula from about AD 500 until the arrival of the conquistadors, and many artefacts made by these early inhabitants have been found.

The pottery of the Manta culture was well made and was decorated with pictures of daily life. Through these pictorial decorations, archaeologists have learned that the Manta people enhanced their appearance by skull deformation and tooth removal, thus increasing the backward slope of their foreheads and chins and emphasizing their large, rounded, hooked noses.

Also evident in their pottery was the Mantas' astonishing skill in navigation (this was also recorded in detail by the early conquistadors). They were able to navigate as far as Panama and Peru, and claims have been made that they reached the Galápagos. There are records claiming that the Manta seafarers sailed as far north as Mexico and as far south as Chile.

Not only were their navigational and ceramic skills well developed but the Mantas were also skilled stonemasons, weavers and metalworkers. People wishing to learn more about the Manta culture should visit the museum in town.

After the conquest, the town of Manta had a history of attack and destruction by pirates from various European countries. Attacks in 1543, 1607 and 1628 left the city ruined, and many survivors fled inland (to Montecristi in particular).

Today, the descendants of the seafaring Manta people continue to demonstrate their superb marine skills as fishermen, navigating their small open boats many kilometers out in the open ocean for days at a stretch.

drags Ecuador into the conflict in neighboring Colombia while increasing US dominance over Ecuador.

Orientation

The town is divided into two by Río Manta. Manta, on the west side, and Tarqui, on the east side, are joined by road bridges. Manta has the main offices, shopping areas, 1st-class hotels and the bus terminal. Tarqui has more hotels, but they are older and more run down, and Tarqui beaches are more prone to theft and similar problems. Streets with numbers over 110 are in a particularly insalubrious neighborhood. The main residential areas are to the southwest of Manta business district, while the cleanest beaches are to the northwest of Manta. Addresses are rarely used.

Information

The staff are friendly and helpful at the municipal tourist office (☎ 611 471, 611 479; Calle 9, Municipio; open 8am-5pm Mon-Fri); ask for Maribel. The Cámara de Turismo (☎ 620 192; Malecón de Manta & Circunvalación, Tramo 1; open 9am-6pm daily) also provides tourist information.

Change traveler's checks at Banco del Pacífico (☎ 623 212; cnr Avenida 2 & Calle 13; open 8:30am-5pm Mon-Fri) or Banco del Pichincha (☎ 626 844; Avenida 2 at Calle 11; open 8am-2pm Mon-Fri); both have ATMs. There's a Banco del Pacífico ATM (cnr Avenida 107 & Calle 103) in Tarqui.

The post office (Calle 8; open 8am-5:30pm Mon-Fri, 8am-1pm Sat) is at the town hall, and Pacifictel (Malecón de Manta; open 8am-10pm daily) is on the Manta waterfront. You can get online at Publicomp (☎ 610 306; Avenida 3 245; open 8:30am-11pm Mon-Sat, 10:30am-8:30pm Sun) or at Cyber Café (Avenida 1 near Calle 14); both charge $0.70 per hour.

The reliable Metropolitan Touring (☎ 623 090, 613 366; Avenida 4 at Calle 12) is a full-service travel agency.

There is a public hospital (☎ 611 849, 611 515; Avenida 24 & Calle 13), and Clínica Manta (☎ 921 566) has doctors of various specialties.

You can extend your embarkation (tourist) card in the immigration office at the police station (☎ 920 900 4 de Noviembre) – this street is a continuation of Malecón de Manta.

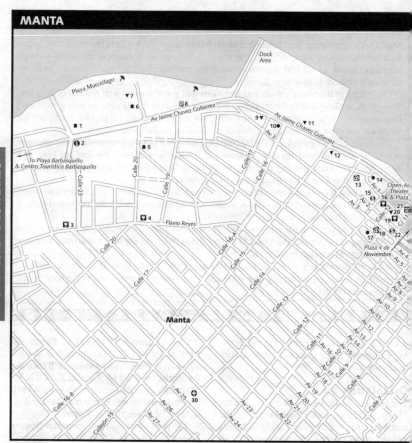

MANTA

Playa Murciélago

To Playa Barbasquillo
& Centro Turístico Barbasquillo

Av Jaime Chavez Gutierrez

Av Jaime Chavez Gutierrez

Dock
Area

Flavio Reyes

Open-Air
Theater
& Plaza

Plaza 4 de
Noviembre

Manta

Things to See & Do

The **Museo del Banco Central** *(Malecón de Manta; admission $1 Mon-Sat, free Sun; open 9am-5pm Mon-Sat, 11am-3pm Sun)* is worth a visit to understand more of the Manta culture. The exhibit is small, but it is well laid out and labeled in Spanish.

In Tarqui, there is a huge **statue of a Manabí fisherman**, and beyond it is the protected sandy **Tarqui beach**. Early in the morning, the east end of this beach is a hive of activity as scores of fishermen drag their catch ashore. There's lots of haggling to be heard as buyers negotiate the rows upon rows of shark, tuna, swordfish, dorado and other fish (all of which have slowly decreased in size over the years). Vendors push their carts around to take advantage of

the morning crowd. Also on the beach is Manta's **boatyard**, where giant wooden fishing boats are built by hand on the edge of the sand. The whole scene is worth getting up early to see. The **fishing-boat harbor**, between Manta and Tarqui, is busy and picturesque at high tide and dead in the mud at low tide.

In Manta, **Playa Murciélago** is a less protected beach and has bigger waves (although they're still not very big, there's a powerful undertow). It is a couple of kilometers northwest of the town center and is the town's most popular beach, backed by snack bars and restaurants and places to rent umbrellas. Further northwest there is **Playa Barbasquillo**, which is quieter still and has a tourist-resort complex.

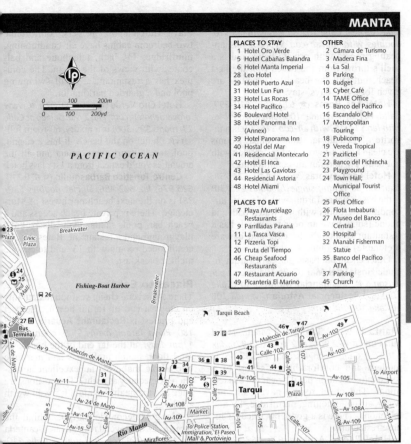

MANTA

PLACES TO STAY
1 Hotel Oro Verde
5 Hotel Cabañas Balandra
6 Hotel Manta Imperial
28 Leo Hotel
29 Hotel Puerto Azul
31 Hotel Lun Fun
33 Hotel Las Rocas
34 Hotel Pacífico
36 Boulevard Hotel
38 Hotel Panorma Inn (Annex)
39 Hotel Panorama Inn
40 Hostal del Mar
41 Residencial Montecarlo
42 Hotel El Inca
43 Hotel Las Gaviotas
44 Residencial Astoria
48 Hotel Miami

PLACES TO EAT
7 Playa Murciélago Restaurants
9 Parrilladas Paraná
11 La Tasca Vasca
12 Pizzería Topi
20 Fruta del Tiempo
46 Cheap Seafood Restaurants
47 Restaurant Acuario
49 Picantería El Marino

OTHER
2 Cámara de Turismo
3 Madera Fina
4 La Sal
8 Parking
10 Budget
13 Cyber Café
14 TAME Office
15 Banco del Pacífico
16 Escandalo Oh!
17 Metropolitan Touring
18 Publicomp
19 Vereda Tropical
21 Pacifictel
22 Banco del Pichincha
23 Playground
24 Town Hall; Municipal Tourist Office
25 Post Office
26 Flota Imbabura
27 Museo del Banco Central
30 Hospital
32 Manabí Fisherman Statue
35 Banco del Pacífico ATM
37 Parking
45 Church

NORTH COAST & LOWLANDS

Places to Stay

Prices rise during holiday weekends and during the high seasons (December to March and June to August), when single rooms can be hard to find. At other times of the year you can bargain for cheaper rates. The cheaper hotels are in Tarqui.

Tarqui Although it's not dirt cheap, one of the best budget choices is **Hotel Panorama Inn** (☎ 611 552; Calle 103 near Avenida 105; rooms per person $6-12), which has rather worn but spacious rooms with private baths, TV and large windows. You pay more for air-conditioning. There are pool privileges at the **annexe** across the street, which is more expensive and has a restaurant, but smaller rooms.

Boulevard Hotel (☎ 625 333, 620 627, 621 836; Calle 103; rooms per person $6), across the street, is a student-oriented place with decent, tiled rooms with TV and bath. Choose carefully as some rooms are pretty dismal.

Hotel Miami (☎ 611 743; cnr Malecón de Tarqui & Calle 108; rooms per person $4), on the east end of the Malecón, is a quirky, old wooden place near the beach that has tolerable rooms with TV and bath. It's pretty basic, but has an alluring nostalgia.

Hotel El Inca (☎ 620 440, 610 986; Calle 105; singles with fan $13, doubles with fan/air-con $25, $30 or $34), near the beach, has decent doubles with fan and cold-water bath, or with air-conditioning, cable TV and phone. Some rooms have ocean views and there is an attached restaurant.

Hotel Pacífico (☎ 623 584, 622 475; Avenida 106 near Calle 102; singles with fan $10, doubles with fan/air-con $15/20) has appealing rooms with private baths and is a shell's throw from the beach (not the best beach, but still the beach). Discounts are given for a few days' stay.

Hotel Las Rocas (☎ 612 856, 610 299; Calle 101 at Avenida 105; singles/doubles with fan $12/16, with air-con $16/22) is a favorite of Ecuadorian tour groups. Rooms are clean but a bit worn and overpriced with hot bath, TV and fan/air-conditioning.

Hotel Las Gaviotas (☎ 620 140, 624 738; Malecón de Tarqui; singles/doubles $25/30) is the best hotel in Tarqui, with adequate air-conditioned rooms with hot water, bath and phone (some have an ocean view). It has a restaurant (although the café and bar are preferable) and a tennis court.

Other cheap but basic places in Tarqui include **Hostal del Mar** (Calle 104; rooms per person $4), **Residencial Montecarlo** (Calle 105) and **Residencial Astoria** (Avenida 105 at Calle 106).

Manta Between Tarqui and Manta, **Hotel Lun Fun** (☎ 622 966, 612 400, 622 976, fax 610 601; Calle 2; singles/doubles $35/45) is modern and comfortable. It's sort of a fence-sitter location but it's near the bus terminal. The clean rooms have bath, hot water, air-conditioning, minifridge, TV and telephone. There is a good, but pricey, Chinese restaurant.

Hotel Puerto Azul (☎ 623 167; 24 de Mayo; singles with shared bath $6, doubles with private bath & fan/air-con $20/30) has clean, carpeted, no-frills rooms. It's right next to the bus terminal so it is very convenient if you're just passing through.

Leo Hotel (☎ 610 617; cnr Avenida 9 & 24 de Mayo; rooms per person with fan/air-con $15/20), next door to Hotel Puerto Azul, has spacious new rooms with private baths.

Hotel Manta Imperial (☎ 621 955, 622 016; rooms $18-30) is next to Manta's Playa Murciélago. Rooms are rather worn and have private bath, cable TV and either fan or air-conditioning, and some have a beach view. A swimming pool, a disco on weekends and a mediocre restaurant complete the scene.

Hotel Cabañas Balandra (☎ 620 316, 620 915; w www.hotelbalandramanta.com; Calle 20; singles/doubles/triples $80/88/95) is north of downtown Manta, two blocks away from Playa Murciélago. The very comfortable two-bedroom cabins have air-conditioning, minifridge, TV, bath, telephone and balconies with views of the ocean. The complex has a restaurant, a small swimming pool and a guarded parking lot.

Hotel Oro Verde (☎ 629 200/209; w www.oroverdehotels.com; Playa Murciélago at Calle 23; rooms $95-300) is a luxury, 60-room full-service hotel on the beach. It has a casino, pool, tennis court, gym, sauna and all the amenities you'd expect from a 1st-class hotel.

Centro Turístico Barbasquillo (☎ 620 718, 625 976, fax 622 456; singles/doubles $30/38) is on the next beach northwest of Murciélago. There is private beach access and a beach bar, pool, sauna, gym, disco, kid's playground and a restaurant. Rates for air-conditioned rooms with TV and telephone include breakfast.

Places to Eat

There are several **cheap seafood restaurants** on the east end of Tarqui beach. The best and priciest is **Restaurant Acuario** (☎ 623 180; Playa Tarqui; mains $5-9; open 10am-11pm daily), at the far end of the beach. Its sand floor, thatch umbrellas and maritime bric-a-brac make for an excellent atmosphere (especially at night). The portions are huge and the quality is high. It's well worth a splurge.

Along Malecón de Tarqui, behind the comedores, are several restaurants. **Picantería El Marino** (Malecón de Tarqui & Calle 110; open 8am-5pm) is one of the best and has a salty-dog, seafaring feel.

Fruta del Tiempo (☎ 625 920; cnr Avenida 1 & Calle 12; mains $1-3; open 7:30am-2am Mon-Sat, 4pm-10pm Sun) is good for filling, cheap almuerzos, fruit juices, shakes, and ice cream.

Pizzería Topi (☎ 621 180; Malecón de Manta; mains $3-6; open noon-1am daily) is open late and has a variety of pizzas and other Italian dishes.

La Tasca Vasca (☎ 627 804; Avenida Jaime Chavez Gutierrez; mains $6-10; open noon-4pm & 7pm-midnight Mon-Sat) is an outstanding Spanish restaurant with dark brick walls, starched white tablecloths, dim lighting and sublime food. Chalkboard menus hang from the walls and the waiters dress in traditional Spanish garb. Note that Malecón de Manta is called Avenida Jaime Chavez Gutierrez near the dock area.

Parrilladas Paraná (☎ 610 885; Malecón de Manta at Calle 17; mains $3-6; noon-3pm & 6pm-11:30pm daily) is one of Manta's favorite grills. The portions are big and the steaks are good.

Numerous beach-side restaurants back Playa Murciélago, all of which serve reasonably priced seafood. The location is relaxing.

Entertainment

The epicenter of Manta's lively nightlife is the area around the intersection of Flavio Reyes and Calle 20, uphill from Playa Murciélago. Here you will find Manta's most popular *discotecas*, bars and karaoke joints, which are hoppin' Thursday through Saturday nights. Everyone swears by *discoteca* **La Sal** (Flavio Reyes & Calle 20; admission $3-8), which has all types of dance music but leans heavily on house and techno. **Madera Fina** (☎ 626 573; Flavio Reyes) rivals La Sal but has a more tropical feel (both inside and out), favoring salsa, reggae and tropical rhythms.

Closer to the town center, *discoteca* **Escándalo Oh!** (☎ 623 653; Calle 12) is a longtime favorite. Nearby, *discoteca* **Vereda Tropical** (☎ 625 920) is smaller and decent.

Getting There & Away

Air On the Manta waterfront, past the open-air theater, is the **TAME office** (☎ 622 006, 613 210; Malecón de Manta). TAME has daily flights to/from Quito ($50 one way). You can buy tickets at the airport on the morning of the flight, but the planes tend to be full on weekends and vacations.

The **airport** (☎ 621 580) is some 3km east of Tarqui, and a taxi costs about $1.

Bus There is a large, central bus terminal in front of the fishing-boat harbor in Manta, and almost all buses leave from there. Buses to nearby Manabí towns and villages such as Montecristi ($0.20, 15 minutes) also leave from the terminal.

Trans Crucita goes hourly to Crucita ($1.10, 1½ hours). Reales Tamarindo has frequent departures to Portoviejo ($0.70, 40 minutes), Jipijapa ($1, one hour), Puerto López ($2.40, 2½ hours), Montañita ($4.70, 3½ hours), La Libertad ($6, five hours) and Quevedo ($5, four hours). Coactur goes

regularly to Pedernales ($4.60, seven hours) and Canoa ($4, 3½ to four hours).

Flota Imbabura goes daily to Guayaquil ($4.50, five hours), Quito ($8.50, eight hours), Esmeraldas ($9, 10 hours) and Ambato ($7, 10 hours).

Car You can rent cars through **Localiza** (☎ 622 434; cnr Flavio Reyes & Avenida 21) and **Budget** (☎ 629 919; Malecón de Manta & Calle 16).

CRUCITA AREA
☎ 05

The fishing village of **Crucita** is reached by going north from Portoviejo. There, you'll find several good seafood restaurants, a very long, narrow beach (best at low tide) and hang gliders (there are competitions every few months). The beach in front of town is not very clean, but heading north or south brings you to much better ones. There are several places to stay, including: **Hostal Hipocampo** (☎ 676 167/65; rooms per person $6), which has been there for years and offers adequate rooms with private bath; and the newer motel-like **Hostería Zucasa** (☎ 676 133/37; rooms per person with cold/hot water $14/17), which has a shady pool area with hammocks and comfortable rooms.

Northward, the next villages are **San Jacinto**, about 13km beyond Crucita and slightly inland, and **San Clemente**, about 3km beyond San Jacinto and on the coast. There are good, sandy beaches between these villages, both of which have restaurants and cheap or mid-range places to stay. Beyond San Clemente, a road continues northeast along the coast to Bahía de Caráquez, about 20km away.

Crucita, San Jacinto and San Clemente can be easily reached from Portoviejo and Manta. All have been developing a tourist industry since the 1990s. Most visitors are Ecuadorians.

MONTECRISTI
☎ 05

Montecristi is known throughout the world for producing the finest straw hat on the planet, the 'Montecristi,' better known as – and mistakenly labeled – the panama hat; see the 'It's Not a Panama, It's a Montecristi!' boxed text. In Ecuador they're called *sombreros de paja toquilla* (hats made of

NORTH COAST & LOWLANDS

It's Not a Panama, It's a Montecristi!

Made from a palm fiber, shade hats have been woven in (and exported from) Ecuador since the 17th century. Workers on the Panama Canal in the 19th century used these light but strong hats to protect themselves from the tropical sun and travelers in the area came to call them panama hats.

The toquilla palm (*Carludovica palmata*) which is harvested for panama hats grows at its best in the humid, hilly inland regions of the central Ecuadorian coast. Three-year-old palms can be harvested year-round and only the shoots (before the palm leaf opens up) are used; an average hat requires seven shoots. Tied into bundles of 112 shoots, they are transported by donkey and truck to coastal villages where the fibers are prepared – a long process.

First, the shoots are beaten on the ground and then split by hand to remove the long, thin, flat, cream-colored leaves; green leaves are discarded. The leaves are tied into bundles of eight and boiled in huge vats of water for about 20 minutes before being hung to dry for three days. Some are soaked in sulfur for bleaching. As they dry, the leaves shrink and roll up into the round strands that are used for weaving. Some of the straw stays on the coast, but most is purchased by buyers from Cuenca where the straw is woven into hats.

Weaving begins by simply crossing eight straws and making a central 'button' – it's much harder than it looks. Weaves vary from a loose crochet to a tighter 'Brisa' weave, used for most panama hats, to the tightest weave of all, using the highest-quality straw. This weave is called a 'Montecristi' and the proud owner of such a hat will tell you that 'It's not a panama, it's a Montecristi!'

---

paja toquilla, a fine, fibrous straw endemic to this region). There are many stores along the road leading into town and around the plaza selling hats, but most of the hats you'll see are loosely woven and inexpensive. For a proper *super-fino* (the finest, tightest weave of all) visit the shop and home of **José Chávez Franco** (☎ 606 343; e ste lios@manta.telconet.net; Rocafuerte 386), between Eloy Alfaro and 10 de Agosto, behind the church. Here you can pick up high-quality hats for under $100, but check them closely. None are blocked or banded but they're cheaper than just about anywhere else in the world. You'll find other good shops if you investigate.

Montecristi is also an important center for wickerwork, and basketry shops line the highway as you approach town.

The town is an old colonial one, founded around 1628, when many of the inhabitants of Manta fled inland to avoid the frequent plundering by pirates. The many unrestored colonial houses give the village a rather tumbledown and ghostly atmosphere.

The main plaza has a beautiful church dating back to the early part of the last century. It contains a statue of the Virgin (to which miracles have been attributed) and is worth a visit. In the plaza is a statue of Eloy Alfaro, who was born in Montecristi and

was president of Ecuador at the beginning of the 20th century. His tomb is in the town hall by the plaza.

Montecristi can be reached during the day by frequent buses ($0.20, 15 minutes) from the bus terminal in Manta.

JIPIJAPA
☎ 05

Pronounced 'Hipihapa,' this town is an important agricultural center. Sunday is market day and it is busy – signs outside many merchants' stores in the center read 'Compro Café' (Coffee Bought Here). *Paja toquilla* hats are sold. The bus terminal on the outskirts facilitates fast onward travel. A few very basic hotels are available.

From the terminal, buses to Portoviejo, Manta and Puerto López leave frequently; fares are about $1. Buses to Guayaquil and Quito leave several times a day.

PUERTO CAYO
☎ 05

About 30km west of Jipijapa, the road meets the Pacific Ocean at the fishing village of Puerto Cayo. **Hostería Luz de Luna** (*Quito* ☎ 02-407 279, 405 602, 400 563; doubles $15) is near the beach, a few kilometers north of town, and has over 20 clean cabins with baths, a pool, a restaurant (the best in the area) and tours to Isla de la Plata and Parque Nacional Machalilla. Hotel Puerto Cayo, at the south end along the beach, is more expensive but no better. **Hostería Los Frailes** (*Jipijapa* ☎ *601 365; doubles $12*) is more central and offers reasonable rooms with private baths; there's a restaurant. Residencial Zavala's and Cabañas Alejandra, also nearer the center, are cheaper.

PARQUE NACIONAL MACHALILLA
☎ 05

This is Ecuador's only coastal national park, preserving a small part of the country's rapidly disappearing coastal habitats. The park was created in 1979 to protect about 50km of beach (less than 2% of Ecuador's coastline), some 40,000 hectares of tropical dry forest and cloud forest, and about 20,000 hectares of ocean (including offshore islands, of which **Isla de la Plata** is the most important).

From December to May, it is sunny and uncomfortably hot, with frequent short rainstorms. From June to November, it is cooler and often overcast.

Most **archaeological sites** within and near the park date from the Manta period, which began around AD 500 and lasted until the conquest. There are also remains of the much older Machalilla and Chorrera cultures, dating from about 1500 BC to 500 BC, and the Salango culture, which dates from 3000 BC. None of the sites are striking.

The tropical dry forest found in much of the inland sectors of the park forms a strange and wonderful landscape of characteristically bottle-shaped trees with small crowns and heavy spines – a protection against herbivores. In the upper reaches of the park, humid cloud forest is encountered. Some of the most common species include the *leguminous algarrobo*, which has green bark and is able to photosynthesize even when it loses its leaves.

The kapok (or ceiba) tree, with its huge planklike buttresses surrounding the base of the gray trunk, has fruits that yield a fiber that floats and doesn't get waterlogged. The kapok fiber was used in life jackets before the advent of modern synthetics. Fig, laurel and palo santo trees are also commonly seen. The tall spindly candelabra cactus

NORTH COAST & LOWLANDS

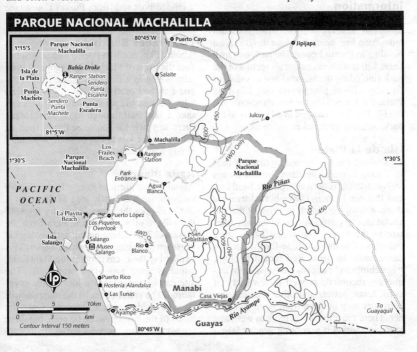

PARQUE NACIONAL MACHALILLA

grows profusely on some hillsides. Also common is the prickly pear.

Within this strange-looking forest, a variety of bird and animal life is found. Well over 200 species of birds have been recorded, including a variety of coastal parrots, parrotlets and parakeets, as well seabirds, such as frigatebirds, pelicans and boobies – some of which nest in the offshore islands. Other animals include deer, squirrels, howler monkeys, anteaters and a variety of lizards, snakes and iguanas.

This unique tropical dry forest once grew along much of the Pacific coast of Central and South America, but it has suffered from human interference more than most other tropical forests. It has now almost entirely disappeared and is one of the most threatened tropical forests in the world.

Fortunately, Machalilla's uniqueness has led to it being better managed than some parks. It has a park superintendent and several rangers who work with the local people to establish better protection of the park. Locals are trained to work as guides and to maintain a museum and archaeological area.

Information

The **park headquarters** (☎ 604 170; open 8am-5pm Mon-Fri) and the small **museum** (admission free; open 8am-5pm daily) share a building in Puerto López. The park-entrance fee is $20 and covers any or all sectors of the park (including the islands) and is valid for five days. If you plan to visit only Isla de la Plata, the fee is $15; the mainland-only fee is $12. The fee is charged in all sectors of the park, so carry your ticket.

Isla de la Plata

This island can be reached by hiring a boat in Puerto López. The name, which means 'Silver Island,' is derived from the local legend that Sir Francis Drake buried treasure there, although other stories suggest that the abundance of guano shining in the sun gives rise to the name. The island has nesting colonies of seabirds – blue-footed boobies can usually be seen. Red-footed boobies, frigatebirds and pelicans have also been frequently recorded, as well as a variety of gulls, terns, petrels and other seabirds. Albatrosses may be seen from April to October. There are a few coral reefs as well, and you can snorkel if you bring gear or take a tour that features snorkeling. Dolphins are often seen on the trip over to the island. The attraction of the island itself has been dwarfed by the spectacle of mating **humpback whales** which abound in the waters around the island between mid-June and early October (especially July and August). During this time, sightings are almost guaranteed, and the boats stop for photography and observation. Some biologists now claim that the number of boats cruising around the whales (the boats get frighteningly close) is negatively affecting their mating patterns.

Isla de la Plata has been locally and aptly dubbed 'the poor person's Galápagos,' although the animal life on the island is nowhere near the abundance of that on the Galápagos. From the boat landing, a steep climb up almost 200 steps takes you to the middle of the island, from where two loop trails, the 3.5km Sendero Machete and the 5km Sendero Punta Escaleras, can be hiked. Most guides choose the shorter one, saying there are better animal sightings. Either way, the trail is rough, and good footwear is advised. There's no shade so come prepared. The only way to visit the island is by taking a guided boat tour from Puerto López (see Organized Tours under Puerto López later).

Los Frailes Beach

About 10km north of Puerto López, just before the town of Machalilla, a ranger station admits you to a dirt road going 3km to the coast at the beautiful beach of Los Frailes, which is suitable for swimming. Hikers can take a 4km trail through the coastal forest; there are two lookouts. Seabirds such as blue-footed boobies can be seen, especially if you have binoculars.

Agua Blanca

About 5.5km north of Puerto López, a park entrance is on the right side of the road. A dirt road goes through tropical dry forest to the village of Agua Blanca, 6km from the entrance. The village has an **archaeological museum** (admission $2; open 8am-6pm daily) explaining the excavation of the Manta site, which is about a half-hour away. The site can be visited, but a local guide is required. The entrance fee to the museum will cover a guided visit to the site. Only the bases of the buildings can be seen, but there are plans to restore some of the approximately

400 buildings excavated at the site, which is thought to have been an important political capital of the Manta people.

San Sebastián & Julcuy

From Agua Blanca, a four-hour hike to the southeast goes up through a transition zone to an area of remnant cloud forest at San Sebastián, about 600m above sea level and 10km away. Guides ($20) are required and are available in Agua Blanca to take you to either the archaeological site or San Sebastián. Horses ($5 per person) can be hired if you don't want to hike. The hike up to San Sebastián gives you a good look at the transitional forests as you climb close to 800m in elevation; overnight trips are recommended. Camping or staying with local people are the only accommodations.

Instead of taking this hike, you can continue through Agua Blanca up the Río Julcuy valley to the northeast. From Agua Blanca, it is a six- to seven-hour hike up this road through the park, coming out at the village of Julcuy, just beyond the park boundary. From Julcuy, it's about another three hours to the main Jipijapa–Guayaquil road. Four-wheel drives may be able to pass this road in good weather, but it is mainly a horse trail.

Places to Stay

You can camp in several places within the park, but check with park authorities about the availability of water – particularly during the May-to-December dry season.

At the village of **Machalilla**, a little over 10km north of Puerto López, you can stay at the budget- to mid-priced Hotel Internacional Machalilla, which has a decent beach nearby.

People in Agua Blanca will put you up in their houses. Basic food is available on request, but it's best to bring some of your own if you have special requirements. Spending two nights with a family in Agua Blanca, including meals and a guide, should cost around $30 for two people (plus the park-entrance fee). You can also camp near Agua Blanca. In San Sebastián, you can stay with locals, and camping is allowed, but there is no camping ground per se. Most people stay in hotels in Puerto López.

Getting There & Away

At least every hour, buses run up and down the coast between Puerto López and Jipijapa.

You should have no difficulty, therefore, in getting a bus to drop you off at the park entrance or in finding one to pick you up when you are ready to leave.

Trucks occasionally go from the main road to Agua Blanca and back; most likely, you'll have to walk or hire a taxi in Puerto López to get to Agua Blanca. This costs about $12 (you can share the price among other riders).

You can arrange boat trips to Isla de la Plata through the tour agencies in Puerto López (see following).

PUERTO LÓPEZ

☎ 05 • pop 15,000

This is the nearest town of any size to Parque Nacional Machalilla, and it houses the park headquarters. It's a busy fishing village, and you can watch the fishermen come in and unload their catch most mornings – the fish are gutted on the spot, and the air is full of wheeling frigatebirds and vultures trying to grab the scraps. If you make friends with the local fishers, they may take you out on a fishing trip.

Buses running from La Libertad (on the south coast) to Jipijapa often stop here for about 10 minutes while passengers buy snacks. Sometimes, children get on the bus, yelling *'Corviche caliente!'*. This coastal specialty consists of a dough made of flour and mashed plantains, and stuffed with salty fish. They're quite tasty, especially with a dash of salsa.

Information

There's no ATM in town, but **Banco del Pichincha** (*cnr Machalilla & General Córdova*) changes traveler's checks and gives cash advances on Visa.

Pacifictel (*cnr Machalilla & Eloy Alfaro; open 8am-12:15pm, 2pm-5pm & 7pm-9pm Mon-Sat, 8am-noon Sun*) is near the market. The post office and police station are on the same block. Internet access for $2 per hour is available at **Sunset Cybercafé** (*General Córdova; open 8am-10pm daily*).

There's a small clinic north of town.

Organized Tours

Numerous agencies offer tours to Isla de la Plata and/or the mainland part of the park. Some are licensed, some aren't.

From June through September, whale-watching tours combined with visits to Isla

NORTH COAST & LOWLANDS

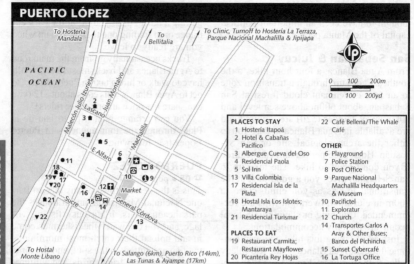

PUERTO LÓPEZ

To Hostería Mandala

To Bellitalia

To Clinic, Turnoff to Hostería La Terraza, Parque Nacional Machalilla & Jipijapa

PACIFIC OCEAN

0   100   200m
0   100   200yd

To Hostal Monte Libano

To Salango (6km), Puerto Rico (14km), Las Tunas & Ayampe (17km)

PLACES TO STAY
1 Hostería Itapoá
2 Hotel & Cabañas Pacífico
3 Albergue Cueva del Oso
4 Residencial Paola
5 Sol Inn
13 Villa Colombia
17 Residencial Isla de la Plata
18 Hostal Isla Los Islotes; Mantaraya
21 Residencial Turismar

PLACES TO EAT
19 Restaurant Carmita; Restaurant Mayflower
20 Picantería Rey Hojas

22 Café Bellena/The Whale Café

OTHER
6 Playground
7 Police Station
8 Post Office
9 Parque Nacional Machalilla Headquarters & Museum
10 Pacifictel
11 Exploratur
12 Church
14 Transportes Carlos A Aray & Other Buses; Banco del Pichincha
15 Sunset Cybercafé
16 La Tortuga Office

---

de la Plata are popular. During July and August, good whale sightings are pretty much guaranteed, and in June and September, sightings may be brief, distant or just of single animals. Once you reach the island, lunch is provided, a guided hike is taken and there is a short time for snorkeling. Whatever the agencies tell you, however, snorkeling is not a major part of the tour. The trip to the island takes well over an hour going flat out, and can be rough, so take motion-sickness medication if necessary, and bring a rain jacket for the wind and spray.

Licensed companies charge a standard price (recently, $30) plus the park-entry fee. They all have boats with two outboard engines (both are used for speed, but the boat can return on one if the other breaks down), and are equipped with life jackets, radios and basic toilet facilities. These agencies are found along General Córdova down to and along Malecón Julio Izurieta. They offer similar services and take turns, so just ask in any agency.

On the Malecón, you'll be approached by folks offering a much cheaper whale-watching expedition on fishing boats. Prices go as low as $15 and there is no park fee (because the island is not visited). Be wary of these trips. The boats are slow, they roll a lot, and people prone to seasickness are almost guaranteed to throw up. There are

limited life jackets, no radio and only one engine, and rarely are there any toilet facilities. Outside of the whale-watching season, similar tours to the island are offered to see birds and sea lions, and dolphins may well be spotted.

Most of the operators will also arrange a variety of other local trips, such as camping and/or horse riding in the Agua Blanca/San Sebastián areas and visits to local beaches. It is usually cheaper to make your own way to Agua Blanca and hire locals there whose tours aren't any worse, but may take longer to arrange.

Two companies, **Exploratur** (☎ 604 123; *Malecón Julio Izurieta*) and **Mantaraya** (☎ 604 233; *Malecón Julio Izurieta*), both offer scuba-diving trips to people with certification; both have received good reports, and all equipment is provided. Exploratur also offers PADI dive courses. Note that these companies are not necessarily better than others for nondiving trips.

Places to Stay

Hotels can fill up quickly during the busy whale-watching season, and during the coastal high season from January to April.

In Town If you want nothing more than a cheap place to crash the night, try the very basic **Residencial Isla de la Plata** (☎ 604 114;

General Córdova; rooms per person $2) or **Residencial Paola** *(☎ 604 162; rooms per person with shared/private bath $2/3).*

Sol Inn *(Juan Montalvo near Eloy Alfaro; rooms per person with shared/private bath $3/ 4)* definitely has a *buena onda* (good vibe), thanks to its young and friendly owners. It's an attractive two-story bamboo-and-wood structure with colorfully painted rooms and a communal outdoor kitchen, dining area and several hammocks. The shared baths are kept spotless.

Hostería Itapoá *(☎ 09-984 3042, Quito ☎ 02-255 1569; Calle Abdón Calderón; cabañas per person $5)* is a wonderfully friendly Brazilian/Ecuadorian-owned place that has three little bamboo cabañas with private baths. Two more are planned. María, the owner, will prepare mouth-watering Brazilian dinners by arrangement for $3 to $4 per person. Breakfast is included in the room rate.

Albergue Cueva del Oso *(☎ 604 124; Lascano 116; rooms per person $4)* is a small hostel catering to backpackers. The three dorm rooms and one double are simple, but clean, and have shared baths. Hot showers, a TV lounge and an equipped kitchen are provided.

Residencial Turismar *(Malecón Julio Izrieta; rooms with private bath per person low/high season $4/6, with shared bath $3)* has friendly owners and worn-out rooms with private bath. The small communal balcony has ocean views, and there's a laundry basin. Guests can usually use the owners' kitchen.

Hostal Monte Libano *(☎ 601 850; Malecón Julio Izrieta; rooms per person $3-5)* is a friendly little place on the south end of the Malecón (past the creek). It's quiet and close to the beach.

Villa Colombia *(☎ 604 189, 604 105; dorm beds $3, singles/doubles $4/6)* is several blocks from the beach and is friendly and popular with budget travelers. It offers kitchen and laundry facilities and most rooms have baths. There is hot water.

Hostal Isla Los Islotes *(☎/fax 604 108; Malecón Julio Izrieta at General Córdova; rooms low/high season $14/20, with ocean views $25/30)* has seven clean but spartan (and slightly overpriced) rooms with private hot bath. Some have ocean views.

Hotel & Cabañas Pacífico *(☎ 604 147; e hpacific@manta.ecua.net.ec; Lascano at Malecón Julio Izrieta; rooms per person with shared/private bath $6/12, with ocean view per person $20)* offers immaculate, comfortable rooms with firm beds and private hot baths – if you spring for the better ones. The rooms with shared bath are rather dismal. There's a restaurant, a garden area, a swimming pool and off-street parking. Whale-watching tours are also on offer.

North of Town A 10-minute walk up the beach, **Hostería Mandala** *(☎/fax 604 181; cabins singles/doubles/triples $7/15/21)* is unique and relaxing. You can't miss it – a huge sculpture of three whale flukes waving in the air marks the spot and can be seen from the main road if you arrive by bus. It's run by an Italian/Swiss couple and is very clean and attractively decorated by the owners' art. Several languages, including English, are spoken, and a restaurant in the attractive main lodge serves excellent Italian and local seafood. There is also a bar, a games room and a library. The thatched-roof cabins all have private hot showers and a porch, and all are by the ocean. Private parking is offered.

Hostería La Terraza *(☎ 604 235; singles/ doubles $14/24)* is about 1km northeast of town on a hill behind the clinic. The steep climb up is rewarded by sweeping views of the whole coastal area. Peter, the German owner (who speaks English too), will drive down to pick you up if you call. The *hostería* offers six cabins; all have one double bed plus a bunk bed, a hot private shower, and a porch with a hammock and those great ocean views. There's guarded parking. Breakfasts (with views of course) are available, and dinners can be arranged.

Places to Eat

Restaurant Carmita *(☎ 604 149; Malecón Julio Izrieta; mains $2-3; open 8am-11pm daily)*, on the shorefront, is a good, reasonably priced restaurant that serves seafood and other dishes. It's been around for years and is a favorite standby.

Restaurant Mayflower *(☎ 604 161; Malecón Julio Izrieta; mains $2-5; open 8am-9pm daily)*, next door to Carmita, is a locally popular restaurant with a few Chinese dishes and plenty of seafood.

Picantería Rey Hojas *(mains $2-4; open 6am-midnight daily)*, a few doors down from the Mayflower, has outdoor tables, longer hours (good for pre-whale-watching breakfasts) and lots of seafood.

Café Bellena/The Whale Café (*Malecón Julio Izurieta; mains $2-5; open 8am-10pm Tues-Sun*), further down the Malecón, is a friendly café with a great balcony overlooking the beach. American owners Diane and Kevin personally prepare excellent breakfasts (the apple cinnamon pancakes are divine), fresh-brewed coffee, lattes, and imaginative lunches and dinners. Pizza and vegetarian options also grace the menu, but the real specialty here is dessert: yummy apple pie, chocolate cake, milkshakes and yogurt smoothies – you get the point.

Bellitalia (*open from 6pm*), in a private house a few blocks north of the center, serves delicious dinners in an enchanting candlelit garden environment. The Italian owners have a short menu of Italian and local specialties, all of which are cooked to order. This place has received rave reviews from local cognoscenti. Prices are not much more than anywhere else, and it's definitely worth it.

Hostería Mandala (*☎/fax 604 181*) is also a relaxing place for delicious Italian dinners and pizzas and local seafood specialties in a dreamy location by the beach (see Places to Stay earlier).

Getting There & Away

Transportes Carlos A Aray (*General Córdova & Machalilla*) has direct buses (one in the morning, one in the evening) to Quito ($5, 11 hours). It also has the only direct bus from Quito, which is a night bus. According to locals, a recent spate of armed robberies have occurred on this night bus. Alternatively you can catch the bus to Puerto Viejo or Manta and come from there.

Several other companies between Jipijapa and La Libertad stop at the corner of General Córdova and Machalilla at least every hour during daylight hours. These buses will drop you off at any point you want along the coast. There are also buses to and from Santa Elena (on the south coast) about every hour.

SALANGO
☎ 04

About 6km south of Puerto López, Salango is a mellow little fishing town, whose main attraction is **Isla Salango**, a small island less than 2km out to sea. People scuba dive

around the island or hire fishing boats to buzz out and see the seabirds. It's a rather nondescript place, but worth a visit for the small **Museo Salango** (*☎/fax 901 195, 901 208; admission $1.50; open 9am-5pm Wed-Sun*), which has exhibits about local archaeological sites. Many signs are in English, and the accompanying gift shop sells work by local artisans.

Salango also has one of the best seafood restaurants around, **El Delfín Mágico** (*☎ 278 0291; Parque Central; mains $3-8; open 10am-7pm daily*). Service is notoriously slow, so you can place your order and visit the museum while it's prepared. Try the *camarones con salsa de maní* (shrimp in peanut sauce) or *al ajillo* (in garlic sauce). *Spondylus* (a spiny, red oyster) is a local delicacy that is sometimes available. **El Pelicano** (*☎ 278 3752; open 8am-8pm daily*), near the church, also serves excellent seafood.

There's a good hotel 2km south of Salango called the **Hostería Piqueros Patas Azules** (*☎ 604 135; singles/doubles from $15/25*). It has a small archaeological museum and some tastelessly amusing features, such as statues in the showers where it appears that the water is falling from the legs. If you can live with that, the rooms and restaurant/bar are quite good, and there is a nice beach nearby, as well as a mud bath, all of which makes it popular with *guayaquileños* (people from Guayaquil) looking for a getaway. Readers have recommended this place.

PUERTO RICO
☎ 04

About 8km south of Salango, the road passes through the village of Puerto Rico, whose claim to fame is the **Hostería Alandaluz** (*☎ 278 0690; Quito ☎/fax 02-254 3042; e info@alandaluz.com; camp sites with/ without own tent $3/4, singles/doubles with shared bath $16/26, with private bath $36/26, beach cabins $46/30*), one of Ecuador's very first self-sustaining, low-impact resorts. Located about 1km south of the village, it's an alternative, Ecuadorian-run hotel, built mainly of local, fast-growing, easily replenishable materials, such as bamboo and palm thatch. The organic gardens on the grounds produce some of the spices, herbs, fruits and vegetables that are served at meal times. The lavatories are self-composting, and everything that can be recycled is.

Much has been invested in local community projects as well.

There is a bar and a dining room that serves good meals (with a predominantly seafood and vegetarian menu). The beach is close by, and you can bathe undisturbed, although the waves are rather wild. Most of the cabins have private baths and sitting rooms, while some are smaller and some are on the beach. The ambience is relaxed, and some people end up staying and unwinding for days.

Often, there are spaces available if you just show up at the hotel, and prices for walk-ins can be somewhat cheaper, although the place may be booked full for Friday and Saturday nights.

Any bus going up or down the coast can drop you off in front of the hotel (see Getting There & Away under Puerto López earlier for more details).

LAS TUNAS
☎ 04

The next village south (blink and you'll miss it) is Las Tunas. The beach here is long, wide and empty. You'll know you're in Las Tunas when you spot the grounded bow of a giant wooden boat, which is actually the restaurant-half of a hotel built by an inspired (or wacky) Swiss expat. It's appropriately called **La Barquita** (☎ 278 0051, 278 0683; e barquita2000@yahoo.com; dorm beds $6, doubles/triples $24/30), and has clean, comfortable doubles with hammocks out front, a few nice cabañas, or dorm beds for budget travelers. It's a big place.

AYAMPE
☎ 04

Sandwiched between verdant tropical hills and another long, wide beach, the sandy little village of Ayampe is 17km south of Puerto López, right on the Guayas-Manabí provincial line. People are friendly and it's a good place to kick off your shoes and spend a few days relaxing on the beach or exploring the wooded banks of the Río Ayampe. The two small islands just offshore are known locally as 'La Tortuga' (tortuga means 'turtle') and 'La Iguana,' because, without too much stretch of the imagination…hey! They look like a turtle and an iguana.

The following are all down-to-earth, friendly, unique places to stay.

Cabañas de la Iguana (☎ 278 0605; w www.designalltag.com/ayampe; rooms per person with shared/private bath $6/8) is a delightfully modest Ecuadorian/Swiss-owned place with four small, spotless cabañas, two with private bath and two with shared bath. They're built together, behind a flowery garden and an outdoor common area. Home-cooked meals are available on request.

Cabañas La Tortuga (☎ 278 0613, 09-995 6015; singles/doubles/triples $15/24/30) has nine lovely cabañas just off the beach, each with room for five. They all have firm beds, mosquito nets and private hot showers. The owners rent kayaks f or paddling up the Río Ayampe and can arrange bird-watching guides. There's a restaurant, bar and a lounge with satellite TV. It's a tough place to leave. You can also make reservations at its office in Puerto López.

Finca Punta Ayampe (☎ 278 0616; w www.fincapuntaayampe.com; doubles/triples $16/21, cabañas singles/doubles/triples $30/32/39) is set on a hillside just south of town, and has outstanding views. The four, comfortable, two-bedroom cabañas are built of caña de guadúa (a local, fast-growing bamboo species), and have private baths, balconies and, of course, excellent views over the sea. There's a sundeck, an organic garden, a restaurant in the main lodge and plenty of hammocks around. Surfing, scuba diving, bird-watching and other tours can be arranged. Prices rise during the high season.

If you're traveling south toward Montañita and Guayaquil, see the Guayaquil & the South Coast chapter.

Guayaquil & the South Coast

Most foreign travelers are drawn to Ecuador's south coast by the long empty beaches and laid-back villages that dot the coast north of Guayaquil. If you are cruising south from Puerto López and Parque Nacional Machalilla (see the North Coast & Lowlands chapter), the next logical stop is Montañita, home of Ecuador's most famous wave (and an international blend of hippies, freaks, surfers and sunbathers all diggin' the mellow vibe and cheap accommodations of the place). Some of Ecuador's oldest archaeological sites are found in this area, especially near the villages of Manglaralto and Valdivia.

The heart of the south coast is Guayaquil, Ecuador's biggest city, last stop before the Galápagos Islands. Although the country's most important port fails to make the must-see lists of most travelers, its urban revival and edgy spirit definitely make it worth a couple days if you're passing through. *Guayacos* (people from Guayaquil; also known as *guayaquileños*) are surely the country's most boisterous folks.

West of Guayaquil, Bosque Protector Cerro Blanco protects some of the coast's last remaining tropical dry forest and has some excellent bird-watching. Further west, the barren Santa Elena Peninsula is the home of the country's most famous (and chichi) beach resort, Salinas. Southeast of Guayaquil, the infrequently visited Reserva Ecológica Manglares Churute protects some of the southern coast's last stands of mangroves and is starting to get more and more attention.

The next province south is El Oro, Ecuador's banana-growing heartland. Its capital, Machala, is an important (and rather unattractive) port city and the common gateway to Peru.

When to Go

The south coast is generally drier than the north coast, and the rainy season lasts only from January to April. During this time the coast is oppressively hot and humid, but it's also sunny, unlike the dry season which is often overcast and pleasantly cool. During the dry season, visitors are often disappointed to find its just a little too nippy out

for laying on the beach. Ecuadorians visit the coast during the rainy season and in July and August.

Getting There & Away

From Quito, most travelers head first to Manta (about nine hours from the capital) or Puerto López (nearly 11 hours from the capital) and work slowly down the coast from there (although there are direct buses to Guayaquil, too). Guayaquil is about five spectacular hours from Guaranda (in the central highlands) and less than four hours from Cuenca via the new road through Parque Nacional Cajas.

Highlights

- Strolling the new *malecón* (waterfront), dining in fabulous restaurants and meeting the lively people of Guayaquil – Ecuador's largest city
- Learning what it means to *farrear* (to party) in Guayaquil
- Riding the waves at Montañita, then yapping the night away with the rest of the sandy foreigners in the village
- Wandering the petrified forests of Puyango
- Sighing at 'the lovers' – two 8000-year-old embracing skeletons in Santa Elena
- Eating *more* seafood

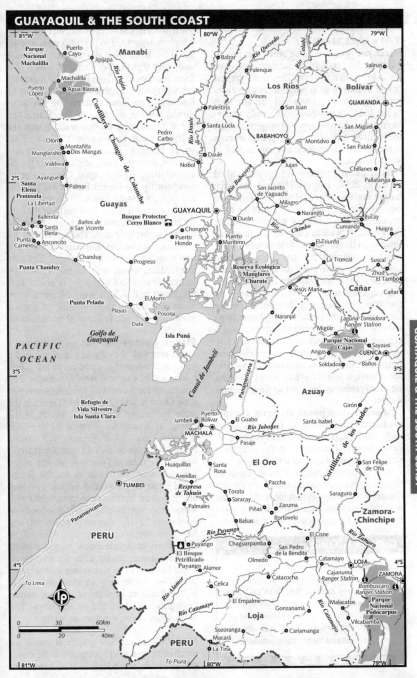

GUAYAQUIL & THE SOUTH COAST

Guayaquil

☎ 04 • pop 2,117,553

Guayaquil is one of those cities that travelers either love or hate. These days, however, it's a lot easier to love: Ecuador's largest city is wrestling its reputation as a sweltering, dangerous port town and standing it on its hot head. Guayaquil has recently undertaken massive urban renewal projects (which are focused primarily on attracting tourists to the city) on a scale nearly unmatched in South America.

Its flagship development project, called Malecón 2000, has transformed the once dangerous waterfront along the wide Río Guayas into a 2.5km outdoor architectural showpiece. The historical neighborhood of Las Peñas, as well as Guayaquil's principal downtown thoroughfare, 9 de Octubre, have also been restored. All these areas, as well as the city's downtown parks, plazas and museums, merit a day or two of exploration.

Sure, Guayaquil is still an oppressively hot, noisy, chaotic city, but *guayacos* are damn proud of the place (and of themselves) and it's well worth hanging out for a while to figure out why, especially if you're a city person. And when it comes to nightlife and dining out, this city is hard to beat in Ecuador, although you'll have to journey around the city (probably by taxi) to find the best places.

Although most people fly to the Galápagos Islands from Quito, all flights to the islands either stop or originate in Guayaquil. Subsequently, Guayaquil is the next best place after Quito to set up a Galápagos trip.

Besides being Ecuador's most populous city, the provincial capital is also, by far, the country's most important port. More exports and imports pass through Guayaquil than all other Ecuadorian ports combined.

Guayas & Quill

Guayaquil takes its name from two names: from Guayas, the great Puna Indian chief who fought bravely against the Incas and then later against the Spanish, and Quill, the wife of Guayas, whom he is said to have killed before drowning himself, rather than allowing her to be captured by the conquistadors.

ORIENTATION

Most travelers stay in the center of town, which is organized in a gridlike fashion on the west bank of Río Guayas. The main east–west street is 9 de Octubre, which runs from the Estero Salado (a brackish estuary bordering the east side of the center) to La Rotonda (the famous statue of liberators Simón Bolívar and José de San Martín) on the Río Guayas. La Rotonda marks the halfway point of the new Malecón 2000 which stretches along the bank of the Río Guayas, from the Mercado Sur (near the diagonal Blvd José Joaquín Olmedo) at its southern tip, to Barrio Las Peñas and the hill of Cerro Santa Ana to the north.

The airport is about 5km north of the center and the bus terminal is about 2km north of the airport entrance. The suburbs of La Garzota, Los Sauces and Alborada are just north and west of the bus terminal. The suburb Urdesa, which is frequently visited for its restaurants and nightlife, is about 4km northwest and 1.5km west of the airport. There are many other suburbs, of course, most of which are residential or industrial.

Street Names As part of Guayaquil's urban renewal, the city has implemented a new street-naming system based upon north, south, east and west quadrants. The quadrants are formed by the intersection of 9 de Octubre and Quito, which meet at the large Parque del Centenario, smack in the center of downtown. Numbered *avenidas* (avenues) and *calles* (streets) will replace (or at least coincide with) traditional street names. *Avenidas* run north–south and *calles* run east–west. To further orient the disoriented stranger, street and avenue numbers are followed by the coordinates NO (for *noroeste* or northwest), NE (for *noreste* or northeast), SE (for *sureste* or southeast) and SO (for *suroeste* or southwest). Many signs downtown (and some new maps) include the new names along with the traditional ones, but everyone (including cab drivers) still know streets only by their old names; we've therefore kept the traditional names throughout the text and on the maps. The maps show the new names as well.

Maps Excellent topographical maps for much of the country (but especially the coast) are available for $2 each at the **Instituto**

GUAYAQUIL AREA

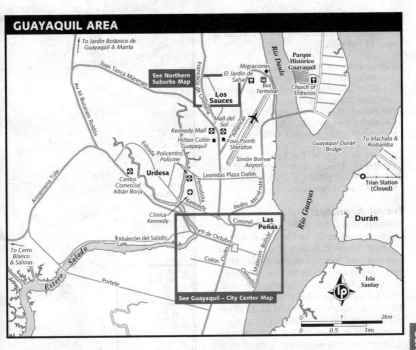

To Jardín Botánico de Guayaquil & Manta

Juan Tanca Marengo

Av. M. Bucaram Roldós

Francisco de Orellana

See Northern Suburbs Map

Los Sauces

Migraciones
El Jardín de Salsa
Bus Terminal

Río Daule

Parque Histórico Guayaquil

Church of Entrerios

Mall del Sol

Kennedy Mall

Hilton Colón Guayaquil

Four Points Sheraton

Estrada Policentro; Policine

Guayaquil-Durán Bridge

To Machala & Riobamba

Arosemena Tola

Centro Comercial Albán Borja

Urdesa

Simón Bolívar Airport

Leonidas Plaza Dañín

Pedro Menéndez

Periodista

Kennedy

Clínica Kennedy

Malecón del Salado

9 de Octubre

Coronel

Las Peñas

Río Guayas

Durán

Trian Station (Closed)

Colón

Quito

Malecón Bolívar

Olmedo

To Cerro Blanco & Salinas

Estero Salado

Portete

See Guayaquil – City Center Map

Isla Santay

0   1   2km
0   0.5   1mi

GUAYAQUIL & THE SOUTH COAST

Geográfico Militar (IGM; ☎ 239 3351; Quito & Padre Solano, Edificio MAG, ground floor).

INFORMATION
Tourist Offices

There are several tourist information kiosks along the Malecón that provide information and brochures about Guayaquil. If you can't get what you need at one of the kiosks, pop your head into the **Dirección Municipal de Turismo** (☎ 252 4100, ext ☎ 3477/9; e dtur gye@telconet.net; w www.guayaquil.gov.ec; Malecón & 10 de Agosto) in the Municipio; the staff are very friendly and some speak English.

The **Subsecretario de Turismo Litoral** (☎ 256 8764; e infotour@telconet.net; Paula de Icaza 203, 6th floor; open 9am-5pm Mon-Fri) provides general tourist information about the coastal attractions of Guayas and Manabí Provinces.

Money

The banks listed here all change traveler's checks. There are many more (most with ATMs) in the financial area, near the intersection of Paula de Icaza and Pichincha.

Banco de Guayaquil Cnr Rendón & Panamá. Visa/Plus ATMs.

Banco del Pacífico (☎ 232 8333) Paula de Icaza 200. Open 8:30am to 3:30pm Monday through Friday. MasterCard/Cirrus ATMs.

Banco del Pacífico (☎ 232 9831) Cnr 9 de Octubre & Ejército. Open 8:30am to 5pm Monday through Friday. MasterCard/Cirrus ATMs.

Banco del Pacífico Plaza Mayor Shopping Center, Rodolfo Baquerizo Nazur near Avenida José Maria Egas, Los Sauces. Open 8:30am to 4pm Monday through Friday. MasterCard/Cirrus ATMs.

Post & Communications

Pacifictel (open 8am-9:15pm daily) and the main **post office** (open 8am-7pm Mon-Fri, 8am-noon Sat) share the same huge building bounded by Ballén and Carbo. There is also a **Pacifictel** (Avenida José Maria Egas near Rodolfo Baquerizo Nazur; open 8am-9pm daily) in Los Sauces.

An additional '2' has been added to the beginning of all telephone numbers (except cellular numbers) within Guayas Province; see the boxed text 'New '2' for Telephone Numbers' in the Facts for the Visitor chapter for more detailed information.

For Internet access, try any of the following reliable Internet cafés. They all charge about $1 per hour.

American Cyber (☎ 264 7112) Oxandaberro near Isidro Ayora, La Alborada

Cyber@City Unicentro Shopping Center, Ballén near Chile. Open daily.

Cyberin@Net (☎ 224 1196) Located just off Guillermo Pareja Rolando, a few blocks south of the Garzocentro Shopping Center, La Garzota. Open 8am to 1:30am daily.

Cyber Tek (☎ 232 4738) Cnr 9 de Octubre & Chimborazo. Open 8:30am to midnight daily.

SCI Cyber (☎ 232 6993) Cnr Chile & Ballén. Open 8:30am to 8pm daily.

Travel Agencies

Although Guayaquil is the last stop for the Galápagos, prices are no lower than they are in Quito. Quito definitely has more travel agencies (and therefore more choices). However, you do save about $45 on the flight to the islands (and over an hour's time on the plane). Tours from either city to the Galápagos are generally expensive. More details are given in The Galápagos Islands chapter.

Ecuadorian Tours (☎ 228 7111; **w** www .ecuadoriantoursgye.com.ec; 9 de Octubre 1900; open 9am-1pm & 2pm-6pm Mon-Fri) is the American Express agent and a good all-purpose travel agency.

Centro Viajero (☎ 230 1283, 256 4064, 09-975 2433; **e** centrovi@telconet.net; Baquerizo Moreno 1119 at 9 de Octubre, Office 805, 8th floor; open 9am-7:30pm daily) is a travel agency that readers recommend for its excellent service in assembling Galápagos packages; the agency only handles larger boats. Spanish, English and French are spoken.

Bookstores

For English-language (and other) books, the best store is **Librería Científica** (☎ 232 8569; Luque 225).

Laundry

Most laundries in Guayaquil specialize in dry cleaning rather than washing, drying and folding. One that does both is **Lava Express** (☎ 256 7284; Carbo 302), between Paula de Icaza and Rendón.

Medical Services

The best hospital in Guayaquil (and the whole coastal region) is **Clínica Kennedy**

GUAYAQUIL – CITY CENTER

OTHER
1 Lighthouse
2 Capilla Santa Ana church
3 Church of Santo Domingo
4 La Taberna
7 Asociación Cultural Las Peñas
8 Museo Antropológico y de Arte Contemporáneo
9 Parking
10 Holiday
11 Instituto Geográfico Militar
13 Chasquitur
15 Ecuadorian Tours
16 Olympic Pool
17 Banco del Pacifico
20 Budget
21 US Consulate
22 Museo de Arqueología del Banco Central (Art Gallery & Cinema)
23 Casa de Cultura
28 Dr Ángel Sáenz Serrano
30 Galápagos Sub-Aqua
33 Church of La Merced
41 Supercines 9 de Octubre
43 Dr Alfonso Guim León
45 Cyber Tek
46 Centro Viajero
48 TAME Office; Galasam Tours
49 Peruvian Consulate
51 Church of San Francisco
52 Subsecretario de Turismo Litoral
53 Lava Express
54 Banco del Pacifico
55 Banco de Guayaquil
56 Museo Arqueológico del Banco del Pacifico
57 La Rotonda
58 Librería Científica
66 Post Office; Pacifictel
66 Palacio de Gobierno & Police Station
67 Sucre Monument
68 Palacio Municipal; Dirección Municipal de Turismo
71 Cathedral
73 Bus Stop for Chongón & Bosque Protector Cerro Blanco
74 Museo Municipal & Library
75 Clock Tower
79 Olmedo Monument

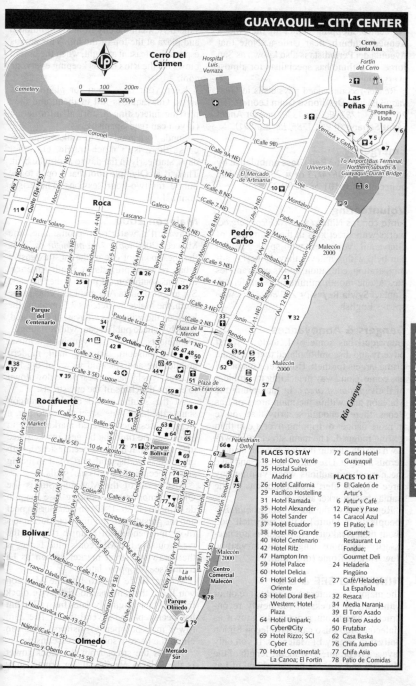

GUAYAQUIL – CITY CENTER

PLACES TO STAY
18 Hotel Oro Verde
25 Hostal Suites Madrid
26 Hotel California
29 Pacifico Hostelling
31 Hotel Ramada
35 Hotel Alexander
36 Hotel Sander
37 Hotel Ecuador
38 Hotel Río Grande
40 Hotel Centenario
42 Hotel Ritz
47 Hampton Inn
59 Hotel Palace
60 Hotel Delicia
61 Hotel Sol del Oriente
63 Hotel Doral Best Western; Hotel Plaza
64 Hotel Unipark; Cyber@City
69 Hotel Rizzo; SCI Cyber
70 Hotel Continental; La Canoa; El Fortín
72 Grand Hotel Guayaquil

PLACES TO EAT
5 El Galeón de Artur's
6 Artur's Café
12 Pique y Pase
14 Caracol Azul
19 El Patio; Le Gourmet; Restaurant Le Fondue; Gourmet Deli
24 Heladería Pingüino
27 Café/Heladería La Española
32 Resaca
34 Media Naranja
39 El Toro Asado
44 El Toro Asado
50 Frutabar
62 Casa Baska
76 Chifa Jumbo
77 Chifa Asia
78 Patio de Comidas

(☎ 228 6963, 228 9666; *Periodista*), by the Policentro shopping center in the Nueva Kennedy suburb, near Urdesa. Note that Avenida del Periodista is also known as San Jorge. The clinic has specialists for almost everything.

Reader-recommended physicians in Guayaquil include **Dr Alfonso Guim León** (☎ 253 2179, 253 1783; *Boyacá 1320*) and **Dr Ángel Sáenz Serrano** (☎ 256 1785; *Boyacá 821*).

Emergency
You can reach the **Red Cross ambulance** by calling ☎ 256 0674/75 or ☎ 256 1077. The **police** are at ☎ 101 or ☎ 239 2221/30.

Volunteering
Junto con los Niños (**W** www.juconi.org.ec) works with street kids in the slum areas of Guayaquil. Volunteers who speak Spanish can help with whatever they do best – administration, education, sports programmes etc. A one-month minimum is preferred. Contact **Sylvia Reyes** (☎ 220 8093/95) who speaks English.

Dangers & Annoyances
Guayaquil has some of Ecuador's worst poverty and discombobulated tourists make prime targets for theft. However, Guayaquil has come a long way in tackling its problem of theft *in tourist areas*. In fact, along the Malecón and within the main areas of Las Peñas, there's enough security that you're in more danger of tripping over a cop than getting mugged. The main streets of downtown are OK during the day, but can be dangerous at night. Use common sense and take the normal precautions when visiting any large city. Be alert for pickpockets in the Bahía street market area.

Regardless of the horror stories *quiteños* (people from Quito) will gladly tell you about their rival city, Guayaquil is not necessarily any more dangerous than visiting New York or Rome (or Quito).

THINGS TO SEE & DO
The majority of interesting sights are on or within a few blocks of the newly reconstructed waterfront promenade known as Malecón 2000 (also called Malecón Simón Bolívar or simply El Malecón). If you only have a day, be sure to walk the length of the Malecón and visit the neighborhood of Las Peñas and Cerro Santa Ana. The latter has superb views of the city from the lighthouse and plaza at the top of the hill. This area is especially pleasant at night, when the breeze blows off the Río Guayas keeping everyone cool.

Keep your eyes open for plaques and signs. Guayaquil is full of them, and they provide interesting historical information (if you can read Spanish).

Sunday is a good day to walk around, because there isn't much traffic. On other days, start early in the day to avoid the heat. There is an **Olympic pool** that is open to the public for two-hour sessions. There is a nominal fee.

Malecón 2000
Guayaquil's waterfront promenade, the Malecón 2000 (*open 7am-midnight daily*), is the focal point of one of the most extensive urban renewal projects in South America. From its southernmost point at the Mercado Sur to Cerro Santa Ana and Las Peñas in the north, the Malecón stretches 2.5km along the bank of the wide Río Guayas. It's a gated, heavily policed public space with restaurants, monuments, gardens, playgrounds, a music hall and museum, shopping mall, modern architecture and splendid views of the Río Guayas. It is by far the best place downtown to escape the chaos of the city streets.

At the southern end of the Malecón stands the handsome, steel **Mercado Sur**, a Belgium-designed covered market built in 1907 – at the time the biggest marketplace in Guayaquil. It has now been restored, with giant glass walls, and part of it is being slowly occupied by artisans' stalls.

Just north of the Mercado Sur is the **Olmedo monument** honoring José Joaquín de Olmedo (1780–1847) an Ecuadorian poet and the president of the first Ecuadorian territory independent of Spanish rule. To the west, outside the Malecón's blue fence, is the sprawling street market known as **La Bahía** (see Shopping later).

Where 10 de Agosto hits the Malecón you'll see the famous **Moorish-style clock tower**, which originally dates from 1770 but has been replaced several times. The 23m tower may be open to visitors, who can climb the narrow spiral staircase inside.

Across the street from the clock tower is the **Palacio Municipal**, an ornate, gray building that is separated from the simple and solid **Palacio de Gobierno** by a small but pleasant pedestrian mall. Both buildings date from the 1920s. The Palacio de Gobierno replaced the original wooden structure, which was destroyed in the great fire of 1917.

Continuing north along the Malecón, you will soon come to the famous statue of **La Rotonda**, one of Guayaquil's more impressive monuments, particularly when it is illuminated at night. Flanked by small fountains, it depicts the historic but enigmatic meeting between Bolívar and San Martín that took place in 1822. Bolívar was the Venezuelan who liberated Venezuela, Colombia and Ecuador from Spanish colonial rule. San Martín was the Argentinean liberator who defeated the Spanish in Chile and Peru. After their secret meeting in Guayaquil, San Martín returned to Argentina before moving to France, while Bolívar continued his triumphs in Bolivia. Few people realize that the curved wall behind the statue acts as an acoustic reflector. If two people stand at either end of it, the whisper of one into the wall will be carried around to the other person. Give it a try.

From La Rotonda, there are good views north, along the riverfront, of the colonial district of Las Peñas and Cerro Santa Ana and, far beyond, the impressive Guayaquil-Durán bridge – the biggest in the country. To the east of La Rotonda, **9 de Octubre**, downtown Guayaquil's main commercial street (which is absolutely jammed with pedestrians on weekdays), stretches off toward Parque del Centenario.

Heading north from La Rotonda you'll pass a long stretch of gardens and then, on your right, the new **Museo Antropológico y de Arte Contemporáneo** (MAAC; Malecón at Loja), a museum of anthropology, archaeology and contemporary art (planned to open in stages through 2003). Much of the museum's archaeology collection (due to open in July 2003) came from the former **Museo de Arqueología del Banco Central**, which had an excellent collection of Valdivia figurines and other ceramics, textiles, metallurgy and ceremonial masks. MAAC also has a 400-seat, noncommercial art cinema. Behind the museum is an open-air stage, where musical and theatrical performances are occasionally given. Right beside the museum are several clean, brightly lit fast-food restaurants.

Las Peñas & Cerro Santa Ana

The historic street of **Calle Numa Pompillo Llona**, named after the *guayaquileño* (1832–1907) who wrote the national anthem, begins at the northern end of the Malecón, to the right of the stairs that head up the hill called Cerro Santa Ana. The narrow, winding street has several unobtrusive plaques set into the walls of some its houses, indicating the simple residences of past presidents. The colonial architecture has not been restored per se, but it has been well looked after, and the elegantly decaying wooden houses are interesting to see. Several artists now live in the area, and there are a few art galleries, including the **Asociación Cultural Las Peñas** (☎ 235 1891; Numa Pompillo Llona 173; admission free; open 10am-4pm daily) in a lovely old house over the river. Paintings by numerous local artists are sold inside; peek in if only to get a glimpse of one of these old houses and the view over the river.

Numa Pompillo Llona is a dead-end street, so retrace your footsteps and, instead of continuing back along the Malecón, hang a sharp right and head up the steps of **Cerro Santa Ana**. The stairs lead past dozens of refurbished, brightly painted homes, cafés, bars and souvenir shops (all very touristy) and up to the hilltop fort **Fortín del Cerro** ('Fort of the Hill'). Cannons, which were once used to protect Guayaquil from pirates, aim over the parapet toward the river and are still fired today during celebrations. You can climb the **lighthouse** (admission free; open 10am-10pm daily) for spectacular 360-degree views of the city and its rivers. The views are especially enchanting at night (the area is totally safe).

Back at the bottom of the hill, if you walk inland from the stairway, you'll see the open-air theater **Teatro Bogotá**. Behind the theater is the oldest church in Guayaquil, the **Church of Santo Domingo**. The church was founded in 1548 and restored in 1938; it's worth a look.

Downtown Area

Along the streets south of Las Peñas the colonial buildings blend into the modern ones. The **Church of La Merced** (Rendón at Rocafuerte) is comparatively modern (constructed in 1938), but the original wooden church dated back to 1787 and, like most of

Guayaquil's colonial buildings, was destroyed by fire. The modern version is worth seeing for its richly decorated golden altar.

Nearby, the **Museo Arqueológico del Banco del Pacífico** (☎ 256 6010; Paula de Icaza 113; admission free; open 9am-6pm Tues-Fri, 11am-1pm Sat & Sun) is quiet and air-conditioned, which in itself is a welcome break from the hot hustle of downtown. The well-displayed collections have labels in Spanish and English. The main exhibit has ceramics and other artefacts documenting the development of Ecuadorian coastal cultures from 3000 BC to AD 1500. There is also a contemporary art gallery with shows that change every few weeks.

The **Church of San Francisco** (9 de Octubre near Chile) was originally built in the early 18th century, destroyed by fire in 1896, reconstructed in 1902 and beautifully restored recently. The plaza in front contains Guayaquil's first public monument, unveiled on New Year's Day in 1880. It is a **statue of Vicente Rocafuerte**, Ecuador's first native president who held office from 1835–39. (Ecuador's first president, Juan Flores, was a Venezuelan.)

Parque Bolívar Area

Parque Bolívar (also known as Parque Seminario) is one of Guayaquil's most famous plazas. In its small, but well-laid-out, ornamental gardens live prehistoric-looking land iguanas of up to a meter in length – they are a different species from those found on the Galápagos. They're a surprising sight here, right in the center of the city. Around Parque Bolívar are many of Guayaquil's 1st-class hotels.

On the west side of Parque Bolívar is the **cathedral**. The original building on this site dates from 1547, but – as is common with most of Guayaquil's original wooden buildings – it burnt down. The present structure was completed in 1948 and renovated in 1978. The front entrance is extremely ornate, but inside it is simple, high-vaulted and modern.

A block south of Parque Bolívar, you find **Museo Municipal** (☎ 252 4100; Sucre; admission free; open 8:30am-4:30pm Tues-Fri, 10am-2pm Sat & Sun) and the municipal **library**. The museum is small but has varied exhibits. On the ground floor, there is an archaeology room, a colonial room and a

changing display of modern art. The archaeology room has mainly Inca and pre-Inca ceramics, with some particularly fine pieces from the Huancavilca period (c. AD 500) and several figurines from the oldest culture in Ecuador, the Valdivia (c. 3200 BC). The colonial room has mainly religious paintings and a few household items from colonial times.

Upstairs, there are modern art and ethnography rooms, inexplicably joined. Besides jungle artefacts, you'll see regional costumes and handicrafts. All in all, it's a varied collection with which to pass the time.

Parque del Centenario

This is Guayaquil's largest plaza, covering four city blocks and featuring several monuments. The most important monument is the great central column topped by Liberty and surrounded by the founding fathers of the country – a monument to patriotism. The best way to get there is along 9 de Octubre.

Casa de Cultura

On the west side of Parque del Centenario is the Casa de Cultura **archaeology museum** (☎ 230 0500; cnr 9 de Octubre & Moncayo; admission $0.50; open 10am-6pm Tues-Fri, 9am-3pm Sat). The main attraction is the small gold collection. Only about two-dozen pieces remain of the original 500-piece collection, most of which was stolen in 1987. There is also a **cinema** (admission $1) on the premises that shows good movies. Foreign films are very popular and the cinema is small, so get there early. Other cultural events, such as art shows and lectures, occur regularly. Stop by for a programme.

Parque Histórico Guayaquil

This new 8.5-hectare park (☎ 283 3807, 287 2033/34/35; Spanish only ₩ www.parque historico.com; adult/child under 13 Mon-Sat $3/1.50, Sun $0.50; open 9am-4:30pm Tues-Sun) is across the Guayaquil-Durán bridge, on the east side of Río Daule. Don't confuse this with Parque Guayaquil. The park is divided into three 'zones,' and exploring them makes for a relaxing and interesting walk. The Endangered Wildlife Zone has 45 species of birds (including the odd-looking harpy eagle), animals and reptiles in a seminatural habitat taking up over half the park's space. An interpretive trail/boardwalk

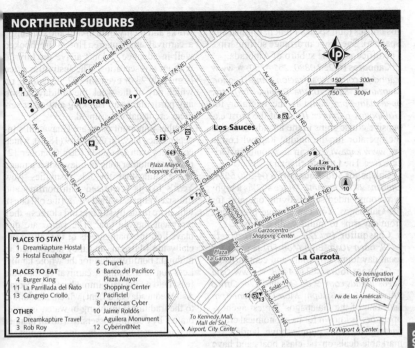

NORTHERN SUBURBS

PLACES TO STAY
1 Dreamkapture Hostal
9 Hostal Ecuahogar

PLACES TO EAT
4 Burger King
11 La Parrillada del Ñato
13 Cangrejo Criollo

OTHER
2 Dreamkapture Travel
3 Rob Roy

5 Church
6 Banco del Pacífico;
  Plaza Mayor
  Shopping Center
7 Pacifictel
8 American Cyber
10 Jaime Roldós
  Aguilera Monument
12 Cyberin@Net

introduces the visitor to coastal habitats and wildlife. The Urban Architecture Zone, which has a restaurant, showcases the development of early 20th-century architecture in Guayaquil, with reproductions of turn-of-the-century buildings and audiovisual displays. The Traditions Zone focuses on local traditions, with an emphasis on rural customs, crafts and agriculture.

Wheelchair access, children's areas and a general information area are all part of the infrastructure. The city plans to operate a ferry service beginning in 2004, from the Malecón (near MAAC), across the river to this park.

City Cemetery

This dazzling white cemetery (*Coronel & Moncayo*) contains hundreds of tombs, monuments and huge mausoleums. A walk, lined with palm trees, leads to the impressive grave of President Vicente Rocafuerte. It's best reached by a short cab ride.

Jardín Botánico de Guayaquil

About a half-hour drive north of town, this botanical garden (☎ 241 7004; admission about $5; open 8:30am-4pm daily, closed Dec 24, 25, 31 & Jan 1) has an excellent orchid collection and hundreds of other plants. Paths and trails lead you past plant exhibits and there is a gift shop, café, butterfly garden and an auditorium.

Insect repellent is recommended in the rainy months. With three days' advance notice, a guided tour can be arranged.

Call the gardens for information about getting there (recently, the No 63 bus went there and the No 22 bus dropped you off a 10-minute walk away), or take a taxi and ask for Urbanización de Los Orquídeas. **Chasquitur** (see Organized Tours following) offers tours and has information.

ORGANIZED TOURS

Local day tours (to nearby beaches, city tours etc) are often available. To nearby beaches, however, taking a bus or hiring a taxi (if you have a small group) is more economical.

Dreamkapture Travel (☎ 224 2909; w www .dreamkapture.com; Alborada 12a etapa, Avenida Benjamín Carrión at Avenida Francisco de Orellana) is run by a French-Canadian

GUAYAQUIL & THE SOUTH COAST

woman who offers good deals on Galápagos cruises (and speaks French, English and Spanish). She also can arrange surfing trips. The office is in the suburb of Alborada.

Canodros (☎ 228 0880, 251 4750; **w** www .canodros.com; Urbanización Santa Leonor, Manzana 5, Solar 10, Vía Terminal Terrestre; open 9am-6pm daily) is the operator for Galápagos Explorer II one of the most expensive cruise ships in the islands. It is also the operator for the unique **Kapawi Lodge** (**w** www.kapawi.com) in the southern Oriente (see The Oriente chapter).

Galápagos Sub-Aqua (☎/fax 04-230 5514; Orellana 211 & Panamá, Office 402) is a highly recommended scuba-diving operator for the Galápagos. You can arrange everything from day trips to multiday dive cruises.

Chasquitur (☎ 228 1084/85; Urdaneta 1418; open 10am-6pm Mon-Fri) is good for local day tours, city tours and ecotourism.

Galasam Tours (☎ 230 4488; **w** www.Gala pagos-islands.com; 9 de Octubre 424, Office 9A; open 9am-6:30pm Mon-Fri, 10am-1pm Sat), one of the Galápagos' largest agency-operators, is known for its economical cruise packages. Some people have landed remarkable deals on 1st-class boats and have had superb experiences. Go in with your eyes open.

Nancy Hilgert (☎ 228 4712, 09-723 0864) is a bird-watching guide who can help you search for the more elusive local species. She works with professional and academic tour groups and may be available for individual bird-watchers.

Ecuandino (☎ 232 6375, 232 5339; **e** ecua ndin@telconet.net) is both a panama-hat exporter and an organizer of local tours, especially to see how toquilla (fine, fibrous straw) is split, boiled, bleached and dried in preparation for weaving, followed by the weaving process itself. Ask for Alejandro Lecaro who speaks English. See the boxed text 'It's Not a Panama, It's a Montecristi!' in the North Coast & Lowlands chapter.

SPECIAL EVENTS

All the national holidays are celebrated vigorously in Guayaquil, but one stands out as the major annual festival – it is, in fact, a combination of two holidays: Simón Bolívar's birthday, on July 24 (1783), and the Founding of Guayaquil, on July 25 (1538). The already lively city goes wild with many parades, art shows, beauty pageants, fireworks and plenty of drinking and dancing – a carnival atmosphere. Hotels are booked well in advance – don't arrive on July 24 without a reservation. The festivities often begin July 23 or even July 22, depending on which day of the week the holiday falls in any particular year. Banking and other services are usually disrupted.

Other important dates are Guayaquil's Independence Day, on October 9 (1820), which combines with Día de la Raza (October 12) to create another long holiday, but it's much less exciting than the July festivities. New Year's Eve is celebrated with bonfires and life-sized puppets called viejos (the old ones), which are made by stuffing old clothes – they represent the old year. The viejos are displayed on the main streets of the city, especially the Malecón, and they are burned in midnight bonfires – fun for the whole family. Less fun is the annual carnival (a movable feast held on the days immediately preceding Ash Wednesday and Lent) which, in addition to the traditional throwing of water, is 'celebrated' by dousing passersby with all manner of unpleasant liquids – no one is exempt.

PLACES TO STAY

The Guayaquil Tourist Board controls hotel prices and each hotel is required to post its approved prices near the entrance. You may be charged up to 22% tax on their listed price, but most of the cheaper hotels don't bother. Better hotels often have a two-tiered pricing system in which foreigners are charged about twice as much as residents.

Hotels downtown are convenient for sightseeing, but they're a good $4 taxi ride from the airport or bus terminal. Hotels in the middle-class northern suburbs are quieter and, because they're closer to the airport and bus terminal, are convenient if you're only spending one night. The suburbs also have a slower pace.

During holiday periods, finding a room can be problematic, especially in the better hotels, and prices are usually higher than the listed price. Outside the holiday season, single travelers can often weasel a double or triple room at the price of a single.

The heat and humidity in Guayaquil are especially oppressive from January to April, when air-conditioning in your hotel room is highly desirable.

Downtown

Budget Cheap hotels in Guayaquil are generally of a higher price and lower standard than in other cities. Budget hotels have cold water only unless noted otherwise.

Hotel Ecuador (☎ 232 1460; *Moncayo 1117; singles/doubles $8.50/10*) is a decent place for a basic room with cramped bath, a fan and TV. Dark interior rooms are slightly quieter and cheaper than the lighter outside rooms and all are a bit musty. A few rooms are air-conditioned and a small restaurant is attached.

Hotel Delicia (☎ 232 4925; *Ballén 1105; singles with shared bath $5, rooms with fan/ air-con $10/15*) is secure, clean and good value, but it fills up fast. Unfortunately, the neighborhood the hotel is in is not too good, but the friendly manager will suggest the safest streets for walking around the area.

Hostal Suites Madrid (☎ 230 7804, 231 4992; *Quisquis 305; singles with fan/air-con $10/12, doubles $12/15*) offers decent rooms with hot bath and TV. Some rooms are dark and cramped but, overall, it's fair value.

Hotel Sander (☎ 232 0030, 232 0944; *Luque 1101; rooms per person with fan/air-con $9/11*) is one of the best budget options downtown. It's a big place with plain but pleasant rooms, tiled floors, private baths and TV.

Pacífico Hostelling (☎ 256 8093, 230 2077; *Escobedo 811; rooms per person $9*) doesn't belong to a hostel chain but does provide good clean rooms with firm beds, bath, TV and fan – another good-value place. Some have air-conditioning for the same price.

Hotel Centenario (☎ 252 4467, 251 3744; *Garaycoa 931; rooms $12*) has the same rates for one or two people. Rooms vary – some have fans and others have air-conditioning; most have TVs and telephones and some are definitely better than others.

Hotel Río Grande (☎ 251 8972; *Luque 1035; singles/doubles $12/14, doubles with window $15*) is a bit gloomy, but the rooms are clean and have air-conditioning, cable TV and bath.

Hotel California (☎ 230 2538; *Urdaneta 529; doubles with cold/hot water $18/24*) is a friendly place with adequate rooms that have private baths, air-conditioning, and TV. The cheaper rooms (without hot water) are actually more appealing; take a look at both before deciding.

Mid-Range All mid-range hotels have private baths, hot water, air-conditioning, telephone, TV and restaurants on the premises.

Hotel Ritz (☎ 253 0120, 251 6610; *9 de Octubre 709; singles/doubles $19/22*) offers clean rooms with air-conditioning, private hot baths, TV and telephone. They're bare but big enough to play soccer in.

Hotel Alexander (☎ 253 2000, 253 2651; **e** *hotelalexander@hotmail.com; Luque 1107; singles/doubles $21/25, doubles with window $32*) is fair value considering the carpeted rooms are all immaculate and have cable TV, sparkling bathrooms (hot water included) and air-conditioning. It has a good restaurant and is favored by Ecuadorian businesspeople.

Several decent mid-range (and top-end) places are found near Parque Bolívar. Prices given can vary substantially. And booking by email can be almost twice as expensive as simply walking in and seeing what is available.

Hotel Plaza (☎ 232 7140, 232 7545; **e** *igafe@telconet.net; Chile 414; singles/doubles $25/30*) is modern and clean and has rooms with minifridges. There are a few pricier suites.

Hotel Rizzo (☎ 232 5210; *Ballén 319; standard rooms $40, suites $62*) is another decent choice. Rooms are a bit worn, but they're comfortable and continental breakfast is included.

Hotel Doral Best Western (☎ 232 8490, 232 4456; *Chile 402; doubles $44*) is clean and secure, but try to choose from a few rooms as some are bigger and better than others. It has a good restaurant and the price includes breakfast.

Hotel Palace (☎ 232 1080; **e** *hotpalsa@impsat.net.ec; Chile 216; singles/doubles $49/61*) is clean and comfy and, with almost 200 rooms, it usually has space available. The hotel has business and fax services, as well as a travel agency. The street-side rooms are noisy but more cheerful. The rates listed above are for foreigners, but walk-ins speaking Spanish get quoted $36/43.

Hotel Sol del Oriente (☎ 232 5500; *Aguirre 603; singles/doubles $47/51*) is an excellent choice for its price range. The rooms are comfortable and huge and, if you get a window on one of the upper floors, the views are fabulous. It has a decent Chinese restaurant as well.

Top End There is a big jump in prices from mid-range to top-end hotels. This is artificially created by the top-end hotels themselves, who consider themselves luxury class and charge nonresident tourists twice the rate as for residents.

If you have any kind of residency status, use it. The prices given below are for nonresidents and include the obligatory 22% tax. All these hotels have good restaurants. If you don't have a reservation, discounts may be negotiated at reception.

Grand Hotel Guayaquil (☎ 232 9690; e grandhot@gye.satnet.net; Boyacá & 10 de Agosto; doubles $85-125), located behind the cathedral, has a pool, two squash courts, a gym and two saunas. They have outdoor barbecues by the pool, as well as good indoor restaurants.

Hotel Continental (☎ 232 9270; w www .hotelcontinental.com.ec; Chile 510; singles $74-122, doubles $116-140) is right on Parque Bolívar. It is the oldest of the city's luxury hotels and is known for its restaurants: one restaurant has won international gastronomy awards, another specializes in Ecuadorian cuisine and a third is open 24 hours. A few rooms have Internet connections complete with computer!

Hotel Ramada (☎ 256 5555; Malecón 606; singles/doubles $142/154) has great views over the Malecón and Río Guayas. There's an indoor pool, a sauna, restaurants, a bar and a casino. The rooms have niceties such as hairdryers and radio-alarm clocks, and a business center offers (outrageously priced) Internet access. You can often get a promotional deal at a $79 rate. The best part about the place is that you can stroll across the street to the Malecón for a nighttime wander. Some rooms have direct river views, others angled and some have no view at all – ask.

Hotel Unipark (☎ 232 7100; w www.oro verdehotels.com; Ballén 406; singles $116-147, doubles $147-183, suites $183-269) is one of Guayaquil's most luxurious centrally located hotels – it's all about elegance. Facilities include a sauna and gym, restaurants, a children's recreation area, many stores and a casino. One of the restaurants has delightful views of Parque Bolívar. Weekend rates can be half the price quoted here and you can often score package deals online.

Hampton Inn (☎ 256 6700; w www.hamp ton.com.ec; 9 de Octubre 432 & Baquerizo

Moreno; rooms $85-350) is the newest of the downtown five-star hotels. With just 95 rooms and suites on 12 floors, it boasts good sized rooms and personalized staff. The hotel has a deli, sushi bar and restaurant and includes a spa, gym, business center and free buffet breakfast for its guests.

Hotel Oro Verde (☎ 232 7999; w www .oroverdehotels.com; 9 de Octubre & García Moreno; standard rate singles $152-293, doubles $165-317) is slightly away from the center, about four blocks east of Parque de Centenario. It has over 250 rooms and suites and is considered the best place to stay downtown – although the rooms aren't really much better than other luxury hotels for the price. Here, you're paying for the service and the facilities, which include a pool, gym, sauna, casino, shops and several excellent restaurants. You can sometimes get walk-in rates for as low as $104 for a double.

Northern Suburbs

The northern suburbs of La Garzota, Los Sauces and Alborada are closer to the airport and bus terminal than downtown and many travelers opt to stay out here. It's much quieter and safer and closer to attractions such as the modern Mall del Sol, the bars of Kennedy Mall and the restaurants of Urdesa (another suburb to the east). If you plan to spend more than a day running around downtown, however, you may prefer a hotel there. Buses connect all suburbs with downtown and a cab ride to the Malecón costs about $4.

Dreamkapture Hostal (☎ 224 2909; w www .dreamkapture.com; Alborada 12a etapa, Manzana 2, Villa 21; singles/doubles with shared bath $12/20, with private bath $15/23) is a small, friendly Canadian/ Ecuadorian-owned hostal with spotless rooms, a breakfast room (with tables you can sit around all day), TV room and a small garden with a tiny pool for cooling off. There's lots of travel information lying around and a wholesome breakfast is included in the price. The communal baths are clean and the amiable owner speaks French, English and Spanish. The hostal is on Juan Sixto Bernal near the intersection of Avenida Benjamín Carrión and Avenida Francisco de Orellana. There's no sign, so look for the dreamy fantasy paintings. To help your cab driver find it, show them the block number given in the address information above. Airport pickup is available for $5.

Hostal Ecuahogar (☎ 224 8357; e youth host@telconet.net; Avenida Isidro Ayora, Los Sauces 1, Manzana F-31, Villa 20; dorm beds for 1/2 people $15/22, singles/doubles $20/25) is in Los Sauces neighborhood, close to the airport. It's part of the Hostelling International chain, so members get a small discount and prices include breakfast. Perks include hot baths, kitchen privileges, an on-site travel agency and pick-up service from the airport or bus station. The No 22 city bus goes by from the bus terminal.

Tangara Guest House (☎ 228 4445, fax 228 5872; Ciudadela Bolivariana, Manuela Sáenz & O'Leary, Block F, Casa 1; singles/doubles $37/49) is a quiet, friendly, family-run guesthouse out in the suburbs and fairly close to the airport. The rooms have private bath and hot water and are simple, but clean, bright and air-conditioned. There are kitchen privileges and a TV room. Discounts are available for longer stays. Breakfast is included. Take a taxi the first time, then the owners can help you figure out the bus system.

Hilton Colón Guayaquil (☎ 268 9000; w www.hiltoncolon.com; Avenida Francisco de Orellana; rooms $175-325) is another top-notch luxury hotel, with almost 300 rooms and suites. Its location – near the airport, the Mall del Sol shopping center and the bars of Kennedy Mall – is very convenient. Two restaurants, a 24-hour café, two bars and a deli all serve good meals and a pool provides a place to relax. It has a shop, casino and gym and sauna facilities.

Four Points Sheraton (☎ 269 1888; w www.fourpoints.com; frente a Mall del Sol; singles $100-170, doubles $112-183) is also close to the airport and Mall del Sol. A large outdoor pool, small gym and sauna, restaurant, café and 144 rooms offer comfort for airport travelers. Rates are lower than the Hilton, the bathrooms are smaller and there are fewer restaurants, but this is good value for the location.

PLACES TO EAT

Downtown Guayaquil has loads of little, cheap restaurants catering to working folk on lunch breaks, but they're all pretty run-of-the-mill. The best dining experiences – the ones that end with, 'hey, this is what eating in Guayaquil's all about!' – are in the northwestern suburb of Urdesa. That's where you go to treat yourself.

Guayacos love their *encebollado*, a tasty soup made with seafood, yucca and onion and garnished with popcorn and *chifles* (crispy fried bananas). The best *encebollados* are sold in cheap mom-and-pop restaurants – keep your eyes peeled for a busy one. They usually sell out by 11am. *Cangrejo* (crab) is another local favorite.

There's a slough of bright, clean fast-food restaurants in the **Patio de Comidas** (*Malecón near Olmedo*) where you can feed on all sorts of high-cholesterol grub; several in front of MAAC (see Malecón 2000 earlier); and dozens more in the Mall del Sol, north of downtown. Calle 9 de Octubre has a lots of modern cafeterias, restaurants and fast-food joints, although none are very cheap. There are several cafés on the steps of Cerro Santa Ana catering to tourists.

Downtown

Casa Baska (☎ 253 4599; Ballén 422; mains $6-10; open noon-11pm Mon-Sat), on Parque Bolívar, is one of Guayaquil's most memorable eateries. It's a genuine Spanish restaurant with a smoky European atmosphere and award-winning food (literally). From chalkboard menus on the brick walls you'll choose from plates such as grilled octopus, *zarzuela de mariscos* (seafood stew) and baby eels. Prices are higher than average but well worth it. Ring the bell to get in and be prepared to wait for a table.

El Toro Asado (*cnr Chimborazo & Vélez • cnr Garaycoa & Luque; mains $1.50-4; open noon-1:30am daily*) serves good, reasonably priced grilled meats. Both its locations are casual and busy and *almuerzos* (set-lunch menus) only cost $1.50. *Asado y menestra* (grilled beef with lentils or beans) is the specialty.

Media Naranja (*9 de Octubre & Avilés*) is another good place for cheap *asado* – if you don't mind the noise from 9 de Octubre (it's an open-air joint with picnic tables). There's beer on tap, too.

Chifa Asia (☎ 232 8088; Sucre 321 at Chile; mains $2-5; open 11am-9:30pm daily) is the better of several cheap *chifas* (Chinese restaurants) around this area. You can get a huge lunch combo for $5 or go with cheaper items from the menu. **Chifa Jumbo** (☎ 232 9599; Sucre 309), a few doors down, is also good. There's another *chifa* in **Hotel Sol del Oriente** *(Aguirre 603)*, which is a bit more upscale (see Places to Stay earlier).

Pique y Pase *(☎ 229 3309; Lascano 1617 near Carchi; mains $2.50-7; open noon-midnight Tues-Thur & Sun, 11am-1am Fri & Sat)* serves excellent *menestra* (lentils or beans) with chicken or beef for only $2.50. Vegetarians can go straight for *menestra* with rice. It's one of the best deals around.

Caracol Azul *(☎ 228 0461; 9 de Octubre 1918; mains $10-20; open noon-3:30pm & 7pm-midnight Mon-Sat)* is a gourmet French-Peruvian restaurant. The prices are high, the atmosphere is elegant and the food is outstanding. Try the *corvina a lo macho* (sea bass smothered in a rich shellfish sauce; $13). The *ceviches* (raw seafood marinated in lemon, onion and seasonings) are delicious as well.

Artur's Café *(☎ 231 2230; Numa Pompillo Llona 127, Las Peñas; mains $3-7)* is a long-time local favorite for its unbeatable hideaway atmosphere and superb location over the Río Guayas in Las Peñas. Ecuadorian cuisine is the specialty, and there's often live music on weekends.

El Galeón de Artur's *(☎ 230 3574; Cerro Santa Ana; mains $4-6; open 6pm-1:30am daily)* is under the same management as Artur's Cafe (see previous) and it's good for *comida típica* (traditional Ecuadorian food). The atmosphere is cozy, but avoid the upstairs tables unless you like eating *seco de chivo* (a sort of goat stew) to the cacophony of karaoke singers.

Resaca *(☎ 09-942 3390; Malecón at Roca; mains $4-6; open 11am-midnight Sun-Thur, 11am-3am Fri & Sat)* is a hip new restaurant/bar on the Malecón that serves tasty, fairly priced food, most of it delicious seafood and salads. Make a reservation if you hope to dine after 8pm. It's also a popular bar, so it's packed (and fun) on weekend nights, too.

La Canoa *(Chile 510; mains $3-5; open 24 hrs)*, in the Hotel Continental, has an extensive menu of excellent traditional Ecuadorian dishes from all over the country. The prices are reasonable, too. There's a branch in the Mall del Sol (see Shopping later). Also in the hotel is the expensive **El Fortín**, which has won international gastronomic awards.

Frutabar *(☎ 282 0609; 9 de Octubre 410, 1st floor; drinks about $1.50; open 9am-9:30pm Mon-Sat)* serves over 20 types of *batidos* (fruit shakes) and dozens of juice creations. It has a cool beach-scene feel and a small balcony over 9 de Octubre.

Café/Heladería La Española *(☎ 230 2710; Junín 705; ice creams about $0.50, sandwiches about $1.50; open 8:15am-7:30pm Mon-Fri, 8:15am-2:30pm Sat)* is a good little café serving cheap pastries and sandwiches. It's worth a stop if you're in the area.

Heladería Pingüino *(cnr 1 de Mayo & Moncayo)* is the spot for ice cream.

Many of the city's best restaurants are in the better hotels (all of which are open to the public). Most of the better hotels offer good breakfasts – even if you are on a budget, it's a good chance for a lovely breakfast in comfortable surroundings.

Grand Hotel Guayaquil *(Boyacá & 10 de Agosto)* has breakfast specials from $4. Up in **Pepa de Oro** *(open 24 hrs)* the coffee is excellent and refills are free. The hotel's **1822 Restaurant** serves excellent international food in a delightfully old-fashioned, wood-paneled setting.

Hotel Oro Verde *(9 de Octubre & García Moreno)* has several excellent restaurants: **El Patio** serves delicious Ecuadorian dishes at upscale prices; it's open for breakfast, lunch and dinner. If you really feel like emptying your wallet, try the French restaurant, **Le Gourmet** *(open 7pm-1am daily)*. A bit easier on the pocket book is the hotel's **Restaurant Le Fondue** *(open 7pm-1am daily)*, which serves Swiss food; the specialty, of course, is fondue. Finally, there's the **Gourmet Deli** *(open 8:30am-8pm daily)*, down at street level, which serves mouth-watering cakes and pastries for about $1.50 a pop.

Northern Suburbs

If you are adventurous enough to explore beyond the hotels and restaurants of the downtown area, you'll be well rewarded. The suburb of Urdesa, 4km northwest of the city center, is one of the best areas for eating well. The main drag, Estrada, is lined with slick restaurants and trendy bars. Walk along and take your pick. Other good eateries are scattered throughout the suburbs of Alborada, La Garzota and Los Sauces.

La Parrillada del Ñato *(☎ 238 7098; Estrada 1219 at Laureles; mains $6-10)* is Guayaquil's most famous grill. Everything the chefs pull off the barbecue is excellent. The steaks are massive (some are big enough for three), the chicken is juicy and the seafood is excellent. It's a giant place and mealtime is always busy. It's an institution. Splurge. There's also a **branch** (cnr Demetrio Aguilera Malta & Avenida Rodolfo Baqurizo Nazur) in Alborada.

Trattoria da Enrico (☎ 238 7079, 238 8924; Bálsamos 504; mains $9-20; open 7pm- midnight daily) is another hallmark eatery (and it has nothing to do with the aquarium in the ceiling or the size of the owner's moustache). It's eclectic yet romantic and well worth the price. The food, mostly Italian, is sublime. The sea bass sent us over the edge.

Trattoría La Carbonara (☎ 238 2714, 238 7079; Bálsamos 108; mains $7-15) is another good Italian restaurant which is a bit more sedate and slightly less expensive than Trattoria da Enrico's.

El Cangrejo Criollo (☎ 223 2018; Avenida Principal, Villa 9, La Garzota; mains $7-12; open 10:30am-1am Mon-Sat, 10:30am-10pm Sun) is the restaurant with the giant crab over the door. Why? Because crab is the house specialty – and it's good. If you like crab, eat here. There's plenty of other delicious seafood plates on the menu as well. Avenida Principal is also known as Guillermo Pareja Rolando.

La Balandra (☎ 288 3147; Calle Quinta 504) is one of Urdesa's most highly recommended seafood restaurants.

Tsuji (☎ 288 1183; Estrada 816, Urdesa) is an upscale Japanese restaurant. It's pricey, but the food is excellent.

Lo Nuestro (☎ 238 6398, 288 2168; Estrada 903; mains $6-12) is like a step back in time. Housed in a century-old mansion complete with wooden shutters and period furniture, Lo Nuestro is one of the most atmospheric places in Guayaquil to eat seafood dishes typical of the region. Musicians play on Friday and Saturday evenings when reservations are recommended and the place fills at lunch time with local bigwigs.

Cantonés Internacional (☎ 223 6333; Avenida Guillermo Pareja Rolando at Calle 43, La Garzota; mains $7-11) is considered Guayaquil's best Chinese restaurant. The large dining room is comfortable but unexciting – the food makes up for it.

ENTERTAINMENT

The farra (nightlife or party) in Guayaquil is spread around town, but the best clubs are in the neighborhoods of Alborada, Kennedy Norte and Urdesa. The local newspapers El Telégrafo and El Universo are your best bet for entertainment listings. The city's luxury hotels all have casinos.

Bars & Nightclubs

Resaca (Malecón at Roca) is the only bar on the Malecón. It's new, it's trendy and it's packed on weekends. The food is great, too. Resaca, incidentally, means 'hangover.'

Holiday (Rocafuerte 410; admission $7; open 8pm-4am Thur-Sat, from 6pm Fri) is the best discoteca downtown, where international DJs tickle three floors of happy dancers with house, electronica, beat, jungle and so on. Fire breathers, go-go dancers and smart drinks keep the energy high.

La Taberna (Cerro Santa Ana) is a nice bar with a dance floor; it's open late.

Rob Roy (Avenida Demetrio Aguilera Malta 739) is a British-style pub that draws a hospitable blend of expats, travelers and locals. It's a few blocks off Avenida Baquerizo Nazur, Alborada.

GUAYAQUIL & THE SOUTH COAST

A Different Tale of a Long, Black Veil

A legend in Guayaquil tells of a mysterious, beautiful woman who walks the streets of old Guayaquil at night. Known as la dama tapada (the veiled woman), she wears a long, black veil over her face and has a body that drives men wild. According to the legend, a man stumbled from a cantina (bar) long ago, spotted this enchanting woman and could not help but follow her down the dark side streets. When he could hold back no longer, he ran to stop her and, beneath the moon and her veil, saw the most resplendent face he'd ever seen. When he tried to kiss her, the shadows shifted and her skin melted away revealing a horrifying skeletal face that sent the drunk scurrying back to his wife and home. La dama tapada is supposedly the spirit of a woman who had many lovers and, after dying a violent death, was condemned to wander the streets at night. Whether you take or leave the moral of this story is entirely up to you!

Barhopping is easy at **Kennedy Mall** in Kennedy Norte. Rather than a shopping mall, however, it's a bar and disco mall. You have a cabbie drop you off and the plan is to visit several bars during the night. They're all right next to each other. Most of them charge a cover but have an open bar, meaning you drink for free after paying admission. **Bamboo** is one of the few bars without a cover charge (but there's a $5 per person minimum consumption). It's a friendly place where people sit around and sing karaoke until the wee hours. **Café Olé** (admission $7.50) has four dance floors, an open bar and lots of Latin music. **Jarro ckafé** (admission $10) pumps out techno, salsa, merengue and cumbia. **Café Bolero** often has live music.

The main drag in Urdesa, Estrada, was once the epicenter of middle- and upper-class farra in Guayaquil – it got so good that local authorities shut down many of the bars and nightclubs to appease the neighborhood's whining upper-class residents. Unfortunately, much of Guayaquil's nightlife may be headed this direction as authorities have promised to close down all bars and discos that aren't in areas zoned for nightlife (which means most of the best bars in town, including Kennedy Mall). **El Manantial** (Estrada & Monjosa) survived the cut and is popular and crowded, and it has outdoor tables. **Infinity** (Estrada 505) is another one.

La Creme (Centro Comercial Albán Borja, Avenida Carlos Julio Arosemena, Km 2.7; admission $10-15) is one of the hottest discotecas in town. It gets international DJs, has several dance floors, couches and a good mix of techno, house, trance and other beats. **Suruba** (Francisco de Orellana 796) is another multiroom discoteca that draws the crowds. It's a good one.

El Jardín de Salsa (☎ 239 6083; Américas), on the road between the airport and the bus terminal (every cab driver knows it) is extremely popular. The dance floor here is one of the biggest in Ecuador and it's salsa, salsa, salsa. You don't have to dance as there's plenty of seating for drinking and people watching.

Cinemas

El Telégrafo and *El Universo* publish show times. English-language movies with Spanish subtitles are usually shown, although downtown there are plenty of B-rate movie houses screening porno flicks and schlock such as *Cannibals of the Amazon*. For subject matter slightly less riveting, try the newly revamped, six-screen **Supercines 9 de Octubre** (☎ 252 2054; 9 de Octubre 823 at Avilés), one of the few downtown cinemas showing Hollywood blockbusters. For state-of-the-art, surround-sound, big-screen thrills, go to the multiscreen **Cinemark** in the Mall del Sol (see Shopping following). **Casa de Cultura** (cnr 9 de Octubre & Moncayo) has a small cinema and shows good foreign films and art flicks.

SHOPPING

Guayacos like to shop at the sprawling street market called **La Bahía** (Carbo & Villamil; open daily), between Olmedo and Colón. It's crowded, busy and colorful and you'll find everything from knock-off name-brand watches to barbwire, brassieres and bootleg CDs. It's a great place to explore, but watch for pickpockets.

If you prefer a more sedate shopping atmosphere, try one of the several flashy indoor shopping malls. **Unicentro**, downtown by Parque Bolívar, is the smallest. **Policentro**, in the Kennedy suburb at the end of Avenida del Periodista (San Jorge), is bigger and has many modern stores, as well as restaurants and a movie theater. Also in Urdesa is **Centro Comercial Albán Borja**. The biggest and newest mall in Guayaquil – actually the whole country – is **Mall del Sol**, near the airport. Plenty of shops, restaurants and cinema screens are found there. Just north of Olmedo is the **Centro Comercial Malecón**, a flashy indoor shopping mall.

El Mercado de Artesanía (Loja & Moreno; open daily) is large artisans' market in a building taking up a whole block. It has a huge variety of crafts from all over Ecuador.

GETTING THERE & AWAY
Air

Guayaquil's Simón Bolívar Airport is one of Ecuador's two major international airports and is about as busy as Quito's. It's located on the east side of Avenida de las Américas, about 5km north of the city center; the international and national terminals are side by side. Anyone flying to the Galápagos Islands either leaves from here or stops here on their way from Quito; those flying from Quito rarely have to change planes.

There's a *casa de cambio* (currency-exchange bureau) at the airport, which pays about as much as the downtown rate and is open for most incoming international flights. There are also the usual cafeterias, car-rental agencies, gift shops and international telephone facilities.

About 1km south of the main airport is the Terminal de Avionetas (small-aircraft terminal).

Domestic There are many internal flights to all parts of the country, but times, days and fares change constantly, so check the following information. The most frequent flights are to Quito with TAME, which charges about $58 one way. There are up to 12 flights a day. For the best views, sit on the right side when flying to Quito.

TAME also flies to Cuenca ($58) daily, Loja ($37) on Tuesday and Thursday, Machala ($32) on weekday mornings and Lago Agrio ($80, via Quito). There are usually flights to Tulcán and Esmeraldas as well.

TAME operates the only scheduled flights to Baltra Airport in the Galápagos. There are two morning flights every day, costing $344 per round trip ($300 in the low season – from mid-January to mid-June and September through November). It also flies to San Cristóbal in the Galápagos (same price) twice daily on Monday, Wednesday and Friday. Ecuadorian residents pay $85 all year.

Icaro flies to Quito ($57) three times a day Monday through Friday and once daily on weekends. It flies once daily (except Saturday and Monday) to Cuenca ($45) and to Loja ($45).

AeroGal flies Wednesday and Saturday to San Cristóbal, Galápagos ($344 round trip).

Austro Aéreo, at the airport, has flights to Cuenca ($40) three times a week.

All the aforementioned flights leave from the main national terminal. Several small airlines have flights leaving from the Terminal de Avionetas. These airlines use small aircraft to service various coastal towns, such as Portoviejo and Esmeraldas. Flights are subject to passenger demand, and charters are possible. Because some of these flights are in five-passenger aircraft, baggage is limited to a small 10kg bag and passenger weight is limited to 100kg.

The following is a list of domestic airline offices in Guayaquil.

AECA (☎ 228 8110) Terminal de Avionetas
AeroGal (☎ 228 4218, 228 7710, 228 4799) Main airport
Aerolitoral (☎ 228 0864) Terminal de Avionetas
Austro Aéreo (☎ 229 6685/87, 228 4084) Main airport
Icaro (☎ 229 4265, 239 3408) Main airport
TAME (☎ 256 0778, 256 0920) P de Icaza 424, Gran Pasaje, enter from 9 de Octubre. Also at the main airport (☎ 228 2062, 228 7155).

International If you are leaving on an international flight, you'll be charged a $10 departure tax.

Many airlines have offices in Guayaquil. Their addresses and phone numbers change frequently; check with a travel agency. Some of the most important are listed below.

Aerolíneas Argentinas (☎ 269 0012/13) Quisquis 1502, Office 202, Tulcán
Air France (☎ 268 7149/98/99) MH Alcívar, Edificio Torres del Norte B, Mz 506, Office 701
Alianza Summa/Avianca (☎ 253 2093) Francisco de Orellana, Mz 111; (☎ 228 7850) Hilton Colón Guayaquil hotel, Avenida Francisco de Orellana
American Airlines (☎ 256 4111) Córdova 1021 at 9 de Octubre, 20th floor
Avensa/Servivensa (☎ 232 7082/85) Aguirre 116 at Pichincha, Office 14
Continental Airlines (☎ 256 7241) 9 de Octubre 100, at the Malecón, 29th floor; (☎ 228 8987) Hilton Colón Guayaquil hotel, Avenida Francisco de Orellana
Copa (☎ 230 3227/39/11; 9 de Octubre 100 & Malecón, 25th floor)
Iberia (☎ 232 9558) 9 de Octubre 101 & Malecón
KLM (☎ 269 2876/77) Hilton Colón Guayaquil hotel, Avenida Francisco de Orellana
Lacsa/Grupo Taca (☎ 562 950, 293 880) 9 de Octubre 100 & Malecón, 25th floor
Lufthansa (☎ 232 4360, 252 2502) Malecón 1400, Illingworth

Bus
The bus terminal is just north of the airport. It boasts many simple restaurants, a bank, hairdresser etc. There are scores of bus company offices and you can get just about anywhere. The following selection gives an idea of what's available – there are many more options. Fares will almost certainly change, but not drastically.

Local For the Santa Elena Peninsula (see later), you can take Transportes Villamil or Transportes Posorja, which have buses every

10 minutes to Playas ($1.90, 1¾ hours) and Posorja ($2.10, two hours). Co-op Libertad Peninsular (which has air-conditioned buses) and CICA both have buses to Salinas ($2.25, 2½ hours) every 15 minutes.

To get to Bosque Protector Cerro Blanco (see later in this chapter), you can take a bus marked 'Chongón' from the stop at Moncayo and Sucre. All the drivers know where to stop for the entrance to the reserve.

National The best services to Quito are with the companies **Transportes Ecuador** (☎ 229 7592; $7), **Flota Imbabura** (☎ 229 7649; $8) and **Panamericana** (☎ 229 7638; $9). They all do the trip in eight hours.

Several companies run buses to Cuenca, but if you want to get there fast, try the vans run by **Supertaxis Cuenca** (☎ 229 7026); they charge $7. The fastest route (3½ hours) is via Parque Nacional Cajas.

Most bus companies sell tickets in advance, which will guarantee you a seat. Otherwise, just show up at the terminal and you'll often find a bus to your destination leaving soon. Friday nights and holidays can get booked up, so plan in advance if traveling then. The following table should give you an idea of fares and travel times.

destination	cost (US$)	duration (hrs)
Ambato	4.80	6
Atacames	8	8
Babahoyo	1	1
Bahía de Caráquez	4.50	5½
Cuenca	4 to 6	3½ to 4½
Esmeraldas	5	7
Guaranda	3.20	4½
Huaquillas	4.50	4
Ibarra	10	11
Lago Agrio	10	16
Las Piñas	4.50	5
Loja	6	9
Macará	9	11
Machala	3	3
Manta	3	3½
Muisne	9	9
Portoviejo	3	4
Puyo	7	7
Quito	7	7 to 10
Riobamba	3.50	4½
San Lorenzo	10	10
Santo Domingo	4	5
San Vicente	5	6
Tulcán	12	13
Zaruma	5	5

International Ecuadorian bus companies such as CIFA, Transportes Rutas Orenses and Ecuatoriana Pullman go to Machala and Huaquillas on the Peruvian border. Transportes Loja has one bus at 6:30pm to the border at Macará.

The easiest way to Peru, however, is with one of the international lines. **Rutas de America** (☎ 245 2844, 245 0342; Los Rios 3012 at Letamendi), whose office and terminal is southeast of downtown, has direct buses to Lima ($50, 24 hours) every day at 6am. **Expresso Internacional Ormeno** (☎ 229 7362, Centro de Negocios El Terminal, Bahia Norte, Office 34, Bloque C) goes daily to Lima ($55) at 2pm, stopping in Tumbes ($20, five hours). Their office and terminal is on Americas just north of the main bus terminal. These services are very convenient because you do not have to get off the bus (let alone change buses) at the border – formalities are taken care of on the bus. Both companies also go to several other South American countries.

Boat

Cruise lines occasionally call at Guayaquil, and passengers may make brief forays ashore. A few cargo boats will take passengers to and from North America or Europe (for more information see the Getting There & Away chapter). Generally though, sailing between Guayaquil and a foreign port is more expensive and less convenient than flying.

Cargo boats steam for the Galápagos about once or twice a month. The round trip from Guayaquil takes about 12 to 20 days, of which about three to four days are spent crossing the ocean from Guayaquil to the islands and the rest is spent in the archipelago. The trips are designed to deliver and pick up cargo from various Galápagos ports and are not very comfortable. Passengers are accepted, however, and although this is not a recommended way of getting to the islands, it is possible. See Getting There & Away in The Galápagos Islands chapter for more details.

GETTING AROUND
To/From the Airport

The **airport** (Américas) is about 5km north of the town center. A taxi from the airport to the center will cost about $4. Taxi drivers may try to charge higher fares from the airport – be sure to bargain. Taxis are always cheaper if you hail one from the street outside the airport.

If you cross the street in front of the airport, you can take a bus downtown. From the center, the best bus to take to the airport is the No 2 Especial, which only costs $0.20 and takes under an hour. It runs along the Malecón but is sometimes full, so you should leave yourself plenty of time or take a taxi. Taxis at airports tend to overcharge gullible new arrivals.

To/From the Bus Terminal

From the airport, the bus terminal is about 2km away. You can walk the distance if you want – turn right out of the airport and head for the obvious huge terminal. Or you can take a bus or taxi (about $1.50).

Buses from the center to the bus terminal leave from Parque Victoria, near 10 de Agosto and Moncayo.

Several buses leave from the terminal for the center. The No 71 bus charges a few cents more and is a little less crowded than the others. A taxi to the center is about $4.

Bus

City buses are cheap (about $0.20) but are always crowded and the system is complicated. They are mainly designed to get workers and commuters from the housing districts to downtown and back again and they are not much use for riding around the city center. They never seem to go exactly where you want to go and what with waiting for them and battling the traffic, you'd better off walking. The downtown area is less than 2 sq km, so it's easy to walk anywhere.

Car

If you're feeling affluent, you can rent a car; if you're not then forget it, because it's not cheap. There are several car-rental agencies at the airport. Make sure that insurance, tax and mileage are included in your rate. If you find a cheap deal, make sure the car isn't about to break down. See the Getting Around chapter for more details.

Taxi

Always agree on the fare before you get into the cab as Guayaquil taxi drivers have quite a bad reputation for overcharging. You

should be able to get between any two points downtown for about $1.50 and to the airport, the bus terminal or Urdesa for about $3 to $4.

West of Guayaquil

☎ 04

This region is a fairly dry, relatively barren and sparsely populated area, but contains *guayaquileños'* favorite beach resorts. Foreign travelers tend to make a bee line for the beaches north of Guayaquil along the coast.

BOSQUE PROTECTOR CERRO BLANCO

About 15km west of Guayaquil is the Cemento Nacional factory, which owns nearly 6000 hectares of protected tropical dry forest on the Cerro Blanco, north of the main coastal highway. This is a private reserve (*admission $3; open 8am-4:30pm daily*) administered by Fundación Pro-Bosque, in co-operation with the cement works, and there are several trails that take you into this area of rolling coastal hills. The reserve may expand to 16,000 hectares in the future.

The reserve contains over 210 species of bird (including the endangered great green macaw, seven other endangered species and many endemic species), as well as 33 species of mammal, such as howler monkeys, peccaries, kinkajous, tamanduas, ocelots and jaguars. There are stands of dry forest with huge *ceiba* (kapok) trees and over 100 other tree species, as well as views of coastal mangrove forests in the distance. This is one of the most interesting places to visit close to Guayaquil if you are interested in natural history.

Other features include a wildlife **rescue center** (*admission $2*), where endangered species are cared for and reared. Many of the center's animals have been recovered from illegal poaching. There is also a plant nursery.

During the wet season, there are lots of mosquitoes, so bring repellent. There are few insects in the dry season and it is easier to see wildlife, as the animals concentrate in the remaining wet areas and the vegetation is less thick. Early morning and late afternoon are, as always, the best times to see wildlife.

Information

Cerro Blanco has a visitors center and a **camping ground** *(camping included in admission, 3-person tent rental $8)* with barbecue grills, bathrooms and running water (even showers). Cabins are planned for mid-2003. The visitors center sells a bird list and booklets, and dispenses information and trail maps. Back-country camping may be permitted and early entry to the reserve can be arranged in advance for avid birdwatchers. Reservations are requested for weekday visits (two days' advance warning is required); however on weekends you can just show up.

Spanish-speaking guides are available for $6 to $10 per group; for weekday visits it is best to arrange one in advance in Guayaquil through **Fundación Pro-Bosque** *(☎ 241 6975; Eloy Alfaro & Cuenca, Edificio Promocentro, Office 16)*. The guides' training is general – they don't specialize in any one subject – and they can take groups of up to eight people. The reserve can be contacted directly through the director, **Eric Horstman**, who speaks English *(☎ 287 1900, ext ☎ 32280; e| vonhorst@ecua.net.ec)*.

Getting There & Away

Cooperativa de Transportes Chongón buses leave Guayaquil's bus terminal heading west and will drop you at the park entrance at Km 16; the drivers know it. Get off before the cement factory; you'll see a sign. Chongón buses also leave from Moncayo at Sucre in downtown Guayaquil, allowing you to avoid the trip out to the terminal if you're already downtown. A taxi will cost about $13, depending on your bargaining ability.

From the reserve entrance, it is about a 10-minute walk to the information center and camping area.

PUERTO HONDO

A little west of Cerro Blanco is the small community of Puerto Hondo, at Km 17 on the south side of the Guayaquil–Salinas highway. It can be reached the same way as Cerro Blanco. There are basic stores and supplies. Club Ecológico Puerto Hondo will take visitors on canoe rides ($9) into the mangroves in the area, which can be arranged through Fundación Pro-Bosque (see Bosque Protector Cerro Blanco previous).

This has to be arranged in advance, as tours can only happen at high tide.

PLAYAS
☎ 04

Called General Villamil on some maps, Playas is the closest beach resort to Guayaquil, which makes it crowded and littered during the high season, but the municipal authorities are trying to combat the Latin American habit of littering.

Playas is also an important fishing village. A generation ago, many of the fishing craft were small balsa rafts with one sail, similar to the boats that were used before the Spanish conquest. Now, more modern crafts are mainly used, but a few of the old balsa rafts can be seen in action. These interesting vessels usually come in at the west end of the beach, depending on winds and tides. Large flocks of frigatebirds and pelicans hoping for scraps wheel dramatically around the fishing fleet as it comes in to unload the catch.

As a result of its proximity to Guayaquil, there are many holiday homes in Playas. It is busy from December to April but quiet at other times. It can be depressing on an overcast midweek day in the low season. Weekends are much busier than midweek.

In the high season, all the hotels are open and prices rise a little – especially on weekends. Holiday weekends see prices as high as the market will bear. In other months, some of the cheaper hotels may close down. Those that are open have few guests and will sometimes lower their prices to have you stay there – try bargaining.

Information

Banco de Guayaquil *(Central Plaza; open 9am-4:30pm Mon-Fri)* changes traveler's checks and has a MasterCard/Cirrus ATM. **Pacifictel** *(Avenida Jaime Roldos Aguilera)* is 1km west of town. There is no post office.

Locals warn that the beach is dangerous at night – muggings have been reported even around dusk. During the day it's fine, but don't leave your belongings unattended.

Activities

There's some good surfing around Playas and the best place for information is the local surf club, **Playas Club Surf** *(☎ 09-725 9056; cnr Avenidas Paquisha & 7)*, based at

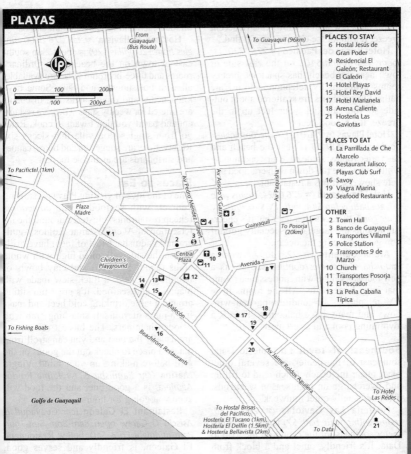

PLAYAS

From Guayaquil (Bus Route)

To Guayaquil (96km)

0   100   200m
0   100   200yd

To Pacifictel (1km)

Av Pedro Mendez Gilbert

Av Asisclo G Garay

Av Paquisha

Plaza Madre

Children's Playground

Central Plaza

Guayaquil

To Posorja (20km)

Avenida 7

Malecón

To Fishing Boats

Beachfront Restaurants

Golfo de Guayaquil

To Hostal Brisas del Pacífico, Hostería El Tucano (1km), Hostería El Delfín (1.5km) & Hostería Bellavista (2km)

To Data

To Hotel Las Redes

Av Jaime Roldos Aguilera

PLACES TO STAY
6   Hostal Jesús de Gran Poder
9   Residencial El Galeón; Restaurant El Galeón
14 Hotel Playas
15 Hotel Rey David
17 Hotel Marianela
18 Arena Caliente
21 Hostería Las Gaviotas

PLACES TO EAT
1   La Parrillada de Che Marcelo
8   Restaurant Jalisco; Playas Club Surf
16 Savoy
19 Viagra Marina
20 Seafood Restaurants

OTHER
2   Town Hall
3   Banco de Guayaquil
4   Transportes Villamil
5   Police Station
7   Transportes 9 de Marzo
10 Church
11 Transportes Posorja
12 El Pescador
13 La Peña Cabaña Típica

Restaurant Jalisco (see Places to Eat later). Juan Gutierrez, the club president, is very friendly and can turn you on to the local breaks. He can also take you water skiing, dolphin spotting or hiking up to the top of nearby Cerro del Muerto.

Places to Stay

The cheapest places may have water shortages and normally lack furniture beyond a bed. During high season, room rates may rise by 10% to 30%.

Central Playas The cheapest hotels are scattered around the central plaza but can be noisy on weekends due to the proximity of loud dance music thumping into the wee hours.

Residencial El Galeón (☎ 276 0270; cnr Guayaquil & Asisclo G Garay; rooms per person with shared/private bath $4/5) is clean and very friendly and has a good, cheap restaurant downstairs. Rooms are worn-out but have mosquito nets and fans.

Hostal Jesús de Gran Poder (☎ 276 0589; cnr Guayaquil & Avenida Asisclo G Garay; rooms per person with shared/private bath $10/12) has clean, matchbox-size rooms. The place is adorned with pictures of Christ, plastic flowers and little signs on the doors saying 'For the love of God, close the door quietly.' They'll sell you a cold beer, though, so they aren't overly evangelical. Rooms with shared baths are far more cheerful.

Hotel Marianela (☎ 276 0058; Avenida Jaime Roldos Aguilera; rooms per person with shared/private baths $3/4) has very basic rooms but a few with windows catch a decent breeze. It's about the cheapest you'll find.

Hotel Brisas del Pacífico (☎ 276 1730/31; rooms year-round $10), on the east side of town near the beach, has spacious, breezy rooms with fan, TV, telephone and private baths. Plastic chairs are scattered about outside so you can kick your feet up in the breeze. It's a good deal.

Hotel Playas (☎ 276 0121; Malecón; singles/doubles from $8/12) is near the beach and has varied rooms; some have air-conditioning while others are run down with cramped private showers. It has a restaurant.

Hotel Rey David (☎ 276 0024; rooms with private bath & fan $14, with TV $20, with TV & air-con $28) lacks character but it's cheerful. Rooms are large and especially good if you get one facing the ocean.

Arena Caliente (☎ 228 4097; Avenida Paquisha s/n; singles/doubles $28-35) is a new four-story hotel with spotless tiled rooms that have large baths. All the rooms have TV, telephone, air-conditioning and windows and many have balconies. There's a swimming pool and a restaurant, too.

Southeast of Town En route to Data, southeast of the center, are several quiet places near the beach which tend to fill up and overcharge on high-season weekends. They're usually quiet midweek.

Hostería Las Gaviotas (☎ 276 0133; rooms with private bath $7) is nearly a kilometer southeast of the center on the road to Data. It's friendly, quiet and a block from the beach, but the rooms are pretty basic. It has a decent restaurant.

Hotel Las Redes (☎ 276 0222; Km1 via a Data; rooms with fan/air-con $10/18), near Hostería Las Gaviotas, is a popular place and its best rooms have air-conditioning and TV; prices rise dramatically on holiday weekends. It has a restaurant.

Hostería El Tucano (☎ 276 0127; singles/doubles $37/46, 5-person rooms about $50) is 1km southeast of the center and has a big swimming pool, sauna, spa and good restaurant. The large, clean, air-conditioned rooms have TV and hot showers. It's about 100m off the beach and the management will give you hammocks to sling over the sand.

Hostería El Delfín (☎ 276 0125; doubles $18), 1.5km southeast of the center, has large

rooms with bath, some with a sea view. It's on the beach and has a restaurant and bar.

Hostería Bellavista (☎/fax 276 0600; singles from $20, villas $70) is about 2km southeast of town on the beachfront. Ordinary rooms and three-bedroom villas are available, all with hot showers and fans. Some have kitchenettes and dining areas and discounts are offered for weekly stays. There's a restaurant and bar if you don't want to cook. Rates go from singles to a villa that sleeps six. Reservations are suggested and bikes, canoes and surfboards are available for rent.

Places to Eat

One of the joys of visiting Playas is stuffing yourself with seafood at the *comedores* (cheap restaurants) clustered around the intersection of Avenida Jaime Roldos Aguilera and Paquisha. Most of them have grills out on the sidewalk piled high with whole crabs (about $1 each) and clay bowls of bubbling *cazuela,* a thick stew made with plantains and seafood. It's great fun sitting around a table drinking cold beer and making a mess of yourself smashing crab with wooden hammers. The busiest restaurants are usually the best and you can stroll from place to place to check out the goods on the grill before making up your mind. **Viagra Marina** (cnr Paquisha & Av Jaime Roldos Aguilera) is a good one, and the food will keep you going for hours.

Restaurant El Galeón (cnr Guayaquil & Asisclo G Garay; open 8am-8pm Sun-Thur, 8am-midnight Fri & Sat), below Residencial El Galeón, is friendly and serves good, cheap, standard Ecuadorian fare.

Savoy, down on the beach, does excellent *ceviche de camarón* (raw but well-marinated shrimp) and good French fries. It's one of several *comedores* along the beach.

Restaurant Jalisco (cnr Avenidas Paquisha & 7) does good, cheap almuerzos and seafood plates. It's a simple place but the food's good enough that it's been in business for some 40 years. It's also the home of Playas Club Surf, the local surf club (see Activities earlier).

If you need a change from seafood, try the town's best grill-house, **La Parrillada de Che Marcelo** (Avenida Jaime Roldos Aguilera). The specialty is steak, although there's pork and chicken on the menu as well.

The better hotels all have restaurants.

Entertainment

During high season, *discotecas* are open every night. During low season, they only function on weekends. Most of them (and they come and go like tourists from Guayaquil) are near the central plaza or downhill toward the beach. The dancing doesn't really kick in till after 10pm.

La Peña Cabaña Típica *(Avenida Jaime Roldos Aguilera)* has been around for ages and still draws the crowds.

El Pescador *(Avenida Jaime Roldos Aguilera; open 9am-2am daily)* is a small bar-cum-café good for a drink and meeting people.

Getting There & Away

Transportes Villamil *(☎ 276 0190; Avenida Pedro Mendez Gilbert)* and Transportes Posorja have buses to Guayaquil ($1.90, 1¾ hours). Buses leave every 20 minutes with either company from before dawn until about 7pm. **Transportes 9 de Marzo** *(Guayaquil at Avenida Paquisha)* have frequent buses to Posorja (S0.50, 30 minutes) during the day.

The best way to get to Santa Elena is to go to Progreso and change buses there. Buses from Guayaquil to Santa Elena are often full during the holidays.

On Sunday afternoons in the December-to-April high season, everybody is returning to Guayaquil. The road becomes a one-way busfest and few (if any) vehicles can travel south into Playas.

AROUND PLAYAS

There are two roads south of Playas – one follows the coast and the other heads inland. The coastal road goes through the villages of Data de Villamil and Data de Posorja, which are often collectively called **Data**. These places are known for boat building. The inland road passes through the old village of **El Morro**, which has a huge old wooden church with dilapidated bamboo walls and three white wooden towers.

Both the inland and coastal roads lead to **Posorja**, a fishing village with many working boats and hundreds of seabirds wheeling overhead the a dirty beach. Posorja is best visited on a day trip – it is about 20km southeast of Playas. Buses frequently go there from Playas with 9 de Marzo.

Stretching northwest from Playas, **Punta Pelada** is a long and fairly deserted beach backed by salt flats, cliffs and cacti. There is reportedly good surfing here. The dirt road along the beach is a popular drive for those with their own vehicles – there is no public transportation here.

SANTA ELENA PENINSULA
☎ 04

The land west of Progreso becomes increasingly dry and scrubby and the *ceiba* trees give way to 5m-high candelabra cacti. Few people and animals are seen, although herds of tough, half-wild goats seem to thrive. Some of the few inhabitants scratch a living from burning the scrub to make charcoal and, once in a while, you see someone on the side of the road with bags of charcoal to sell.

Just over halfway between Progreso and Santa Elena, a signed road to the left indicates the archaeology museum in the coastal village of **Chanduy**, 12km from the main road. Archaeological excavations nearby led to the opening of the small **Museo Real Alto** *(☎ 230 6683; admission $1; open 9am-4pm Mon, 9am-5pm Tues-Sun)*, on the outskirts of the village, which has displays on the 6000-year-old archaeology of the area. Chanduy is reached by bus or taxi from La Libertad (see later).

Baños de San Vicente

About 20km east of Santa Elena (see following) and 8km north of the main Guayaquil–Santa Elena road, these **thermal hot springs** *(admission $1)* are about the cheapest soak you'll find in Ecuador. The temperatures of the baths are between 89.6°F and 109.4°F (32°C and 43°C) and you can get a massage with aloe or mud for an extra $2.50. There's also a volcanic mud bath. It's a rather drab, government-operated tourist complex, but it's relaxing.

Hotel Florida *(☎ 228 2195, 228 1464; rooms per person $15)* offers the only accommodation; the price includes three meals. On weekends, go early or late in the day to avoid the crowds. Any bus heading to Santa Elena from Guayaquil can drop you at the entrance road, from where you'll have to hitch about 8km north from the main road to the complex. All bus drivers know where to drop you off. The road is also signed.

Santa Elena

The area around Santa Elena toward the end of the peninsula is almost one complete dusty urban zone with few open spaces. The road forks at Santa Elena, where you can head west to La Libertad and Salinas, east to Guayaquil or north along the coast. If you're en route to/from the beach towns north along the coast, it's easier to change buses at the fork than going into La Libertad (see following). The bus driver will drop you at the fork.

Besides an oil refinery and the peninsula's radio station, Santa Elena is home to the archaeological museum **Los Amantes de Sumpa** (☎ 278 6149, 278 5216; admission $1; open 9am-1:30pm & 2:30pm-5pm Mon-Tues & Thur-Fri). It has a fascinating display of 8000-year-old skeletons shown in the positions that they were found, including two embracing as *amantes* (lovers). This is currently the oldest archaeological exhibit in the country and it is well laid out and labeled in Spanish. The museum is a couple of blocks from the main road on the west side of town – ask any bus driver.

Hotels are limited. **Residencial El Cisne** (☎ 294 0038; per person with private bath $6) is a clean, basic hotel on the main square. Most people stay in other towns on the peninsula.

La Libertad

La Libertad, the largest town on the peninsula, has about 50,000 inhabitants. It is an important fishing port, has a nearby oil refinery and is the transportation hub for the area. It is a busy, noisy, dirty town with a reputation for theft. Few travelers like it, but it has an undeniably lively air. The beach here is mainly rubble and the main reason to be here is to change buses (although this is often easier in Santa Elena).

The Banco del Pacífico, near the plaza at the town's east end, has a MasterCard/Cirrus ATM. Pacifictel is also on this plaza.

Two decent lodging choices are **Hotel Viña del Mar** (☎ 278 5979; Avenida 3 & Guayaquil; singles/doubles $6/10) and the cheaper **Residencial Turis Palm** (☎ 278 5159, 278 4546; 9 de Octubre 626; singles/doubles $4/8). The best places are away from the town center. **Hotel Samarina** (☎ 278 5167, ☎/fax 278 4100; 9 de Octubre at 10 de Agosto; rooms $30), by the waterfront, about 1.5km northwest of the town, has an adequate restaurant, a swimming pool and air-conditioned rooms and bungalows.

La Libertad is the center of bus service on the peninsula. To get to Guayaquil ($2 2½ hours) you can take buses with eithe **Cooperativa Libertad Peninsular** (CLP; cnr 9 de Octubre & Guerro Barreiro) or **Cooperativ Intercantonal Costa Azul** (CICA; 9 de Oc tubre & Diagonal 2) opposite the Residencia Turis Palm. Buses from Guayaquil continue to Salinas and then return to Guayaquil vi La Libertad.

To get to Santa Elena, flag down one o the minibuses that run frequently along 9 d Octubre. Frequent buses to Salinas run al day from Calle 8 and Avenida 2.

Transportes San Agustín is in a bus ter minal near the market and has buses to Chanduy (see Santa Elena Peninsula ear lier). Various small local coastal village (including Ballenita, Valdivia, Ayangue an Palmar) are served by transportation from the market area. Cooperativa Manglaralto and CITM have several daily buses to Manglaralto and Montañita (both just unde an hour from La Libertad), Puerto Lópe ($2.80, three hours) and on to Jipijap ($3.50, five hours). Note that buses may b booked up in advance during weekends i the high season.

Punta Carnero

This is a point of land in the middle of wild and largely deserted beach some 15km in length. The ocean in front of the hotel may be too wild for swimming, but th beach is good for walks. Sportfishing is popular activity and boats and equipmen can be chartered from Salinas. The area ha also been recommended for bird watching Whales may be observed in July, Augus and September.

Out on the point, the resort-hotel **Punt Carnero Inn** (☎ 277 5450, 294 8477; e pca nero@gye.satnet.net; high season double $70) overlooks the ocean from a cliff top Comfortable, balconied rooms have bat and air-conditioning. There is a restauran and a swimming pool. Nearby, **Hosterí Vista del Mar** (☎ 277 5370, 294 8370; dou bles $20-50) has cheaper rooms and cabin with or without air-conditioning (but al have hot showers). It has a restauran swimming pool and tennis court.

Buses from La Libertad will get you t Punta Carnero, but most visitors come wit their own vehicle.

Salinas

On the tip of the Santa Elena Peninsula, Salinas is the biggest resort town on the south coast. About 150km west of Guayaquil, it is also the most westerly town on the Ecuadorian mainland. The westernmost point is a hill called La Chocolatera, which lies within a military base. Reportedly, you can visit it by taxi if you leave identification with the guards until you leave.

Salinas is considered to be the best resort in Ecuador and its modern hotels and high-rise condos make it the seasonal haunt of affluent Ecuadorians. It's relatively overpriced yet quite crowded during the high season (mid-December through April) and still fairly expensive and dead in the off season. The water is warmest for swimming from January to March. During Carnaval, the place is completely full with beachgoers playing volleyball, sailing and enjoying themselves. The beaches are not spectacular and are backed by high-rise hotels and condos. In July and August, the place is overcast and dreary. Although the sunbathing is lousy during this time, whale- and bird-watching is fairly good.

There is a Yacht Club, and the *capitanía* (port captain), on the west end of the waterfront, is where you are supposed to register if arriving or leaving by yacht. During the January-to-April high season, international yachts come through and occasionally need a crew member.

The streets are haphazardly arranged and poorly signed. Most locals go by landmarks rather than street names. Salinas is a long town and its streets parallel the beach for just a few blocks inland. Most businesses are found within two or three blocks of the coast.

Information A block from the beach, **Banco del Pacífico** (*Calle 18 & Gallo*) has a MasterCard/Cirrus ATM. Make phone calls at **Pacifictel** (*Calle 20 at Gallo*).

Organized Tours Bird-watchers need to seek out the **Oystercatcher Bar** (☎ 277 8329, 277 7335; **e** bhaase@ecua.net.ec; Av 2), between Calle 47 and Calle 50. The owner, Ben Haase (who speaks Spanish, Dutch, and English), knows more about coastal birds than anyone in the area. Ben is permitted to lead tours to the private Ecuasal lakes by the Salinas salt factory, where 109 species

of birds have been recorded. The bar is an equally good place to set up whale-watching trips (June through October only).

Pesca Tours (☎ 277 2391, Guayaquil ☎ 244 3365; **w** www.pescatours.com.ec) charters fishing boats (8.5m to 13.5m long) for about $350 a day (6am to 4:30pm). Boats take up to six anglers and include a captain, two crew members and all fishing gear. You have to provide your own lunch and drinks, but they'll provide a cooler. The best season (for marlin, dorado and wahoo) is September to December.

Macchiavello Tours (*Malecón*), in the Hotel Casino Calypsso (see Places to Stay following), arranges various local sightseeing tours, including fishing, bird-watching, area museums and, from July to October, whale-watching ($25 per person). Of several companies, this agency appears to have the safest boats, English- and German-speaking guides and provides a slide show the night before the tour to help you understand what you will see.

Places to Stay The locals stay at holiday homes rather than at hotels. There are no very cheap accommodations and hotels may close down in the off season. Prices quoted here are for the high season – they often drop 20% to 30% May through mid-December.

Sportfishing from Salinas

Beginning about 13km offshore from Salinas, the continental shelf drops from 400m to over 3000m (about 40km offshore), so a short, one-hour sail can take you into really deep water. Swordfish, sailfish, tuna, dorado and marlin are some of the fish to chase. Black marlin, occasionally weighing over 600kg, are the world's third-biggest sport fish, topped only by a couple of shark species. The world record for black marlin is 707kg, set in 1953 in Peru. But that's child's play compared to the lone 800kg black marlin that locals claim is swimming around the Ecuadorian coast. Bet you can't catch it!

Salinas occasionally hosts world fishing competitions. The best fishing is from September to December, when boats may be booked up several days in advance.

Prices will be higher than those quoted here during Easter week, Christmas, New Year and Carnaval.

Hotel Albita (☎ 277 3211, 277 3662; Avenida 7; rooms per person $10), between Calle 22 and 23, is a good budget choice with slightly musty but habitable rooms with fans, private baths and hot water.

Residencial Rachel (☎ 277 2501, 277 2526; Calle 17 & Avenida 5; singles/doubles $10/16) has decent rooms with private bath, fan and TV.

Hotel Yulee (☎ 277 2028; rooms with fan $23-34, with air-con $45), in an old, rambling building near the main plaza, is a friendly place with air-conditioned rooms that have private bath, hot water and TV. There is a good restaurant and a garden.

Hotel Francisco 1 (☎ 277 4106; Enríquez near Rumiñahui; singles/doubles $25/35) has 11 air-conditioned rooms with hot showers, telephone and cable TV. There is also a pool and restaurant.

Hotel Salinas Costa Azul (☎ 277 4268/69, fax 277 4267; Enríquez & Calle 27; singles/doubles $25/30), at the eastern end of Salinas, is modern and has decent air-conditioned doubles that have bathrooms and TV. There is also a small restaurant and swimming pool.

Hotel El Carruaje (☎ 277 4282; Malecón 517; singles with/without ocean view $30/34, doubles $60/51) is small and has pleasant, modern rooms – most with an ocean view. The restaurant is very good, and the hotel is usually full in the high season.

Hotel Casino Calypsso (☎ 772 425/35, fax 773 583; w www.hotelcalypsso.com.ec; Malecón; singles $73, doubles $88-175) has spacious, tiled, comfortable and air-conditioned but characterless rooms with TV, telephone, fridge and (if you drop the cash) good ocean views. The hotel has a pool, Jacuzzi, sauna, restaurant, travel agency and (if you have any money left) a casino. Low-season prices are considerably less.

Barceló Colón Miramar (☎ 277 1610, 277 1620; w www.barcelo.com; Malecón; doubles $177, with full board $268), between Calle 38 and Calle 40, is Salinas' most opulent hotel. It boasts three restaurants, several bars and lounges, a swimming pool, Jacuzzi, complete gym and spa facilities and a tennis court. Deep-sea fishing trips, jet-skiing, water-skiing, windsurfing and all manner of organized tours can be arranged

through the hotel. During the low season you can often get all-inclusive deals for around $60 per person, which includes three good meals, snacks, all the Ecuadorian and Colombian booze you want and use of the sauna and gym facilities.

Places to Eat The food is quite good at **Cevichelandia**, the local nickname for a series of cheap seafood stalls at Calle 17 and Enríquez, but they are mainly for lunch.

There are various restaurants, bars and *discotecas* along the waterfront east of the center, but they're mostly closed in the low season. The names, prices and quality of other places changes from year to year, but a walk along the waterfront will yield a number of choices.

Entertainment During weekends in the high season, the place comes alive with discos and clubs, mainly near the Malecón. Also check the **Oystercatcher Bar** (see Organized Tours earlier). Salinas is pretty dead during the low season.

Getting There & Away Buses enter town along the Malecón and continue to the naval base, where they turn around and head back along Enríquez to La Libertad and Guayaquil. There's a **CLP bus office** (Calle 7 near Avenida 5). During the high season, there are direct buses to Guayaquil; during low season they usually stop for about an hour in La Libertad (and you may have to change buses).

NORTH ALONG THE COAST
☎ 04

The coast stretching north of Guayaquil as far as Parque Nacional Machalilla (see the North Coast and Lowlands chapter) has been deemed the 'Ruta del Sol' ('Route of the Sun'). It's a beautiful stretch of coast, especially north of Valdivia, where lush, tropical-humid forest often reaches nearly to the shoreline. But don't let the name fool you. A more honest name (as the Ayampe band Johnny y la Familia titled their album) would be *La Ruta del Sol y la Garúa* ('The Route of Sun and Mist'). The coast is often overcast and cool during the dry months of May to December and can be soggy with mist in July and August. It's still beautiful, but it's something to consider if you're chasing the sun.

Ballenita to Valdivia

From La Libertad, many buses run north along the coast. Some go only a short way, but many make it as far as Puerto López and Jipijapa, in the province of Manabí (see the North Coast & Lowlands chapter). The beaches en route are often very good and there are several fishing villages where *guayaquileños* have holiday homes – these places are becoming increasingly well known among foreign travelers.

The first place of interest is the village of Ballenita, just north of Santa Elena. On the outskirts of Ballenita is **Farallón Dillon** (☎ 278 6643, 278 5611; e ddillon@gu.pro.ec; singles/doubles about $24/38), where there is a nautical museum, unique shop of marine antiques and artefacts, and a lookout point from which migrating whales can be seen from June to September. English is spoken and food and tourist information is available. There are also five varied rooms sleeping two to six people, some with private bath and air-conditioning.

Valdivia, a village 50km north of La Libertad, has a small **museum** displaying artefacts from the Valdivia period (around 3000 BC), but the best pieces of antiquity are in Guayaquil museums. About 5km before reaching Valdivia, you pass the fishing village of **Ayangue** and, 5km before that (40km north of La Libertad), the village of **Palmar**. Both are close to pleasant beaches. The area is fairly crowded with visitors during high-season weekends, but only Ayangue has a couple of small hotels, including the budget **Un Millón de Amigos** (☎ 291 6014; singles/ doubles $5/10) and the mid-range **Cumbres de Ayangue** (☎ 291 6040).

North of Valdivia, the dry landscape begins to get a little wetter. The cactus and scrub give way to stunted trees and the occasional banana plantation.

Manglaralto

Manglaralto is the main village on the coast of Guayas Province north of La Libertad. It's a quiet place with a long beach, but it tends to lose visitors to its popular neighbor Montañita just 5km north. The surfing out front is decent. You can walk here from Montañita (or vice versa) along the beach at low tide.

The community has developed some interesting ecotourism and community projects, and there are some unique homestay and volunteer opportunities. **Fundación Pro Pueblo** (see the boxed text) arranges stays with local families; it's office is opposite the church.

There are a few simple pensiones, particularly near the north end of the beach. **Hostería Marakayá** (☎ 290 1294; singles/doubles with fan $6/8), 100m from the beach, is a good choice and has clean rooms with private hot bath. Rooms with air-conditioning are about twice as much as those with fan.

Kamala Hostería (e kamalahosteria@hot mail.com), on the beach just north of town, is a friendly, easy-going hostería owned by four backpackers (two Ecuadorian, one Australian and one Israeli) who just 'didn't really want to go home in the end.' They offer PADI dive courses and guided dives, horse riding and a monthly full-moon party.

GUAYAQUIL & THE SOUTH COAST

Fundación Pro-Pueblo

With some interesting community-tourism programmes under its belt, this nongovernment organization, or **NGO** (☎ 04-290 1208/1195/1114/1343; e propueblo1@propueblo.org.ec), offers travelers the opportunity to visit remote coastal villages off the beaten track, where local families provide simple accommodations, meals, guides and mules for a nominal fee.

The villages involved are usually an easy day's walk or horse ride from Manglaralto and from each other. Visiting them gives travelers a chance to experience some rural hospitality and lifestyle while putting tourist dollars into local pockets. Overnight tours into the coastal hills can be arranged for bird-watching, visiting remote waterfalls or seeing orchids and other natural delights.

Pro-Pueblo also supports the sustainable economic development of the region by encouraging the production of arts and crafts – including tagua-nut jewelry, panama hats, sandstone and wood carvings, reproductions of ancient ceramics and products made from recycled paper. Beekeeping and organic farming are also important projects.

Accommodations are in bungalows and there's a restaurant to boot.

Restaurant Las Pangas, on the beach, is a good place to eat.

Dos Mangas

A few kilometers inland from Manglaralto is the village of Dos Mangas. Here, the land begins to rise into the Cordillera de Colonche – coastal hills reaching an elevation of 834m and covered by tropical, humid forest. Tagua carvings and *paja toquilla* (*toquilla* straw) crafts can be purchased in the village.

Guides and horses can be hired at the Centro de Información Sendero Las Cascadas, a small kiosk in the village. The friendly guides speak Spanish only and will take you on a four- to five-hour hike through the forest to an elevation of 60m and to the 80m waterfalls (these dry up in the dry season). They charge $10 for up to three people and an extra $3 per person for horses. The park entrance is $1. Lunch can be arranged in local homes for about $1 per person.

By purchasing crafts and hiring guides here, visitors directly supply income to villagers who are seeking alternatives to logging the forests around Dos Mangas. Trucks to Dos Mangas ($0.25, 15 minutes) leave the highway from Manglaralto every hour or so.

Montañita

Approximately 5km north of Manglaralto, Montañita is a perfect example of what epic surfing can do to a tiny fishing village. What was once a rickety little fishing village is now a rickety little surfing village with more budget hotels than you can shake your surfboard at. The pancakes are good, the feet are always bare, the bodies are tanned and the surf – well – it's best from December to May (when hotel prices rise with the waves).

The beach break is rideable most of the year, but the real wave is at the north end of the beach, at *la punta* (the point). It's a rippin' right that can reach 2m to 3m on good swells. An international surf competition is usually held around Carnaval.

There is a Pacifictel office in town and you can usually find someone to rent you a board or give you lessons.

Montañita's waves can get big and riptides are common – swimmers drown each year. Be careful!

Places to Stay First you need to decide whether you want to stay near the point, where hotels are more expensive, quieter and perfect for stumbling out into the waves, or in town, where hotels are cheaper, closer to restaurants and perfect for stumbling home from the bar. There are also several places along the highway just north of town. Regardless of where you stay, you're always within a 15-minute walk of Montañita.

Unless specified, the prices quoted here are for high season (mid-December through April). Almost all hotels cut their rates in half for the rest of the year.

The Calle Principal is the main drag down to the beach. Most hotels in town are on the streets leading away from the Calle Principal.

La Casa Blanca (☎ 290 1340; e *lacasa blanca@hotmail.com; rooms per person low/ high season $5/10*), in town, is a good, reliable place. The three floors of rooms have private, hot baths, mosquito nets and hammocks outside the doors. Six of the rooms have sea views.

Cabañas Tsunami (☎ 09-714 7344; *rooms per person with shared/private baths $8/10, low-season $3/4*), next door to Casa Blanca, has three floors of small, clean, cane-wall rooms. It's similar to Casa Blanca, but a little more cramped.

Pre-Columbian Coastal Ceramics

Some of Ecuador's oldest archaeological sites (dating back to about 3000 BC) are found in the Valdivia–Manglaralto area. Although there is little to see for the traveler, you might see villagers in the Valdivia area selling pre-Columbian artefacts. Many of these are replicas and those that *are* genuine are illegal to export out of Ecuador (or to import into most other countries).

If you're after ceramics, buy those that are advertised as replicas. Many are very attractive and quite authentic looking and not only do they make good souvenirs, but purchasing them supports the work of local artisans and discourages the exploitation of genuine archaeological artefacts.

Cabañas Pakaloro *(☎ 290 1366; rooms per person low/high season $5/6)*, behind Casa Blanca, is a beautifully crafted, two-story, wooden place, hand-built by its French owner. The rooms are immaculate, with excellent baths, firm beds, mosquito nets and individual small terraces with a hammock.

El Centro del Mundo *(dorm beds low/ high season $2/5, rooms per person with shared/private bath $6/8, low season $3/4)*, also in town, is a three-story structure close to the beach. Its highlights are the small communal balconies facing the ocean and the pool table. The dorm area is a loft with about 20 flattened mattresses on the floor.

Hotel Montañita *(☎ 290 1296; rooms per person low/high season $6/13)* is slightly out of the Montañita vein: It's big, cement and has a swimming pool and 2nd-floor restaurant. The rooftop terrace has lots of hammocks and good views.

Hostal D' Lucho *(Calle Principal; rooms per person $5, low season $2-3)* is a tin-roof dump, but it's the cheapest in town.

Hotel Brisas Marina *(rooms low/high season $7/15)*, just south of the Calle Principal, has paper-thin walls but a great little balcony right over the seawall.

North of town toward the point, you'll find several more comfortable but down-to-earth hotels. These are accessed by walking along the beach (except at high tide) or by one of several access roads from the highway north of town.

Paradise South *(☎ 290 1185; rooms per person with shared/private bath $15/20)*, just north of the river on the way to the point, offers handsome attached cabañas built of stone and wood. There's a large grassy area with a volleyball court and pool table.

Cabañas Arena Guadua *(☎ 290 1285; e mtlive@lycos.com; 5-person cabañas low/ high season $35/50)* has four large cabañas right on the sand, each with private bath, hot water and mosquito nets.

La Casa del Sol *(☎ 290 1302, 09-975 5711; w www.casasol.com; rooms per person $4-10)*, toward the point, is luxuriously rustic, very popular and has comfortable, fan-cooled rooms all with private baths. The restaurant is good, the bar is relaxing and massages and Reiki are available.

Hotel Las Tres Palmeras *(☎ 09-975 5711; rooms per person $10)* is across the street from La Casa del Sol and has six modern

rooms with mosquito nets and hot showers. Tres Palmeras Restaurant is run by a Texan/ Mexican couple who likely make the best Tex-Mex food in Ecuador. There is also a full beach-side bar.

Hotel Baja Montañita *(☎/fax 290 1218/9; singles/doubles/triples $30/35/50, 4-6 person cabañas $130)* is the closest to the point. It's a characterless upscale hotel with about 35 air-conditioned rooms and cabins (some sleeping up to six) with hot showers, TV and air-conditioning. It has a swimming pool, Jacuzzi and a restaurant (which is only open in the high season).

Places to Eat The following restaurants – and many others – are on or around the Calle Principal.

Funky Monkey *(mains $1.50-4; open 7am-9:30pm daily)* serves tasty vegetarian specials such as soy burgers and stir-fry, good breakfasts and bottomless cups of coffee. The bar is open until 11pm and the cocktails are potent. There's a pool table, too.

Restaurant Aura's *(almuerzos $2)* serves good, home-style cooking and the set meals are one of the best deals in town. It has a TV and videos that you can watch while you eat.

Restaurant Lojanita *(mains $3-7)* is a chain from Guayaquil that does excellent seafood.

Pizzería de Wilson *(pizzas from $5; open 8am-midnight daily)* serves decent pizzas.

Olón

A few kilometers further north from Montañita is the coastal village of Olón, which has a long beach and a couple of inexpensive hotels. **Agrolón** *(☎ 09-738 6750; open 8am-6:30pm daily)*, on the highway above a hardware store, sells products made of *caña de guadua*, a fast growing bamboo grown along the coast.

Seven kilometers north of Olón, the provincial line between Guayas and Manabí is crossed – see the North Coast & Lowlands chapter for travel to places north of Olón.

South of Guayaquil

Places in Guayas Province south of Guayaquil are of little interest to *guayaquileño* vacationers compared to the area west of the city. For the most part, this area is visited by travelers on their way to Peru.

RESERVA ECOLÓGICA MANGLARES CHURUTE
☎ 04

This 50,000-hectare national reserve (admission $10) protects an area of mangroves southeast of Guayaquil. Much of the coast used to be mangrove forest – an important and unique habitat (see Flora & Fauna in the Facts about Ecuador chapter). This is one of the few remaining mangrove coastlands left – the rest have been destroyed by the shrimp industry. Inland is some tropical dry forest on hills reaching 700m above sea level.

This is a poorly researched region, but preliminary studies of the area within the reserve indicate that the changing habitat from coastal mangroves to hilly forest supports a wide biodiversity with a high degree of endemism. Dolphins have frequently been reported on the coast and many other animal and bird species are seen by wildlife-watchers, who are the main visitors.

Contact Dreamkapture Hostal in Guayaquil (see Places to Stay under Guayaquil earlier) about the new cabañas the owners are building in the reserve.

The reserve entrance is on the left side of the main Guayaquil–Machala highway, about 46km south of Guayaquil. At the entrance is an **information center** (☎ 09-763 653) where you pay the entrance fee. The park rangers can arrange boats for you to visit the mangroves (about $60 for the whole day for four or five people). There are also several kilometers of hiking trails. The best season for boats is January to May, when water levels are high (but there are more insects then). There is room at the information center for a few people to sleep.

Bordering the reserve is another area protected by Fundación Andrade. Nancy Hilgert is the contact and she can guide you. Chasquitur does tours to Manglares Churute (for both, see Organized Tours under Guayaquil).

Any bus between Guayaquil and Naranjal or Machala can drop you off at the information center. When you are ready to leave, you can flag buses down. There is a sign on the road and drivers know it.

MACHALA
☎ 07 • pop 216,901

South of Guayaquil (after driving through 200km of banana plantations) is the city of Machala. It's the capital of El Oro Province and the commercial heart of Ecuador's main banana-producing region. Despite (or because of) its economic importance, Machala is not of great tourist interest. Most travelers on their way to and from Peru pass through here, but few people stay more than a night.

Machala isn't totally devoid of interest, however, as the local international port of Puerto Bolívar, only 7km away, is worth visiting (see Puerto Bolívar & Jambelí later in this chapter). Machala has a highly touted **International Banana & Agricultural Festival** during the third week in September, when an international contest is held to elect La Reina del Banano ('The Banana Queen').

On the main road to Machala, southeast of the city, stands the statue of El Bananero – a man carrying a large branch of bananas. This is Machala's most telling monument. Watch for it as you arrive in town.

Information
The **tourist information office** (☎ 932 106; 9 de Octubre 1017, Edificio Galarza, 1st floor; open 8:30am-5pm Mon-Fri) offers basic information about El Oro Province. **Orotour** (☎ 931 557; Bolívar 922) and **Glendatur** (☎ 921 855, Bolívar 912) are both reliable travel agencies.

The **Peruvian consulate** (☎ 930 680; cnr Bolívar & Colón) is open on weekday mornings and you can organize visas to Peru here.

Most banks near the central plaza change money. **Banco de Guayaquil** (cnr Rocafuerte & Guayas) changes traveler's checks and has a MasterCard/Cirrus ATM. Banco del Pichincha, across the street, also changes traveler's checks. **Banco del Pacífico** (cnr Junín & Rocafuerte) has a Visa/Plus ATM.

The most convenient **Pacifictel branch** (Montalvo near 9 de Octubre; open 8am-10pm daily) is a block southeast of the plaza. The **post office** (cnr Montalvo & Bolívar) is one block south of the plaza. For Internet access try **Copy@Comp** (Sucre near Montalvo), **Ciber Yogur** (9 de Mayo near Pichincha) or **Planeta Net** (Junín near Sucre). They all charge $0.80 per hour and are open daily.

There is a **hospital** (☎ 930 420, 937 581; cnr Colón & Boyacá), as well as numerous clinics and pharmacies nearby.

Places to Stay
Machala has far better hotels than the border town of Huaquillas (see later). Prices may

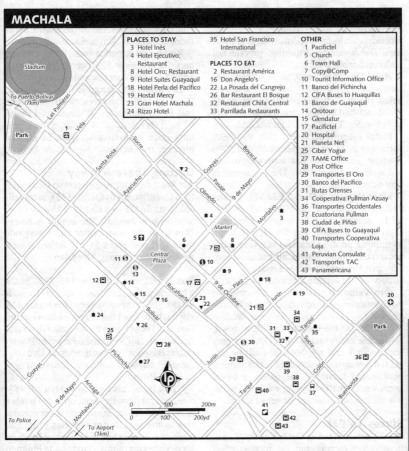

MACHALA

PLACES TO STAY
3 Hotel Inés
4 Hotel Ejecutivo;
   Restaurant
8 Hotel Oro; Restaurant
9 Hotel Suites Guayaquil
18 Hotel Perla del Pacifico
19 Hostal Mercy
23 Gran Hotel Machala
24 Rizzo Hotel

35 Hotel San Francisco
   International

PLACES TO EAT
2 Restaurant América
16 Don Angelo's
22 La Posada del Cangrejo
26 Bar Restaurant El Bosque
32 Restaurant Chifa Central
33 Parrillada Restaurants

OTHER
1 Pacifictel
5 Church
6 Town Hall
7 Copy@Comp
10 Tourist Information Office
11 Banco del Pichincha
12 CIFA Buses to Huaquillas
13 Banco de Guayaquil
14 Orotour
15 Glendatur
17 Pacifictel
20 Hospital
21 Planeta Net
25 Ciber Yogur
27 TAME Office
28 Post Office
29 Transportes El Oro
30 Banco del Pacifico
31 Rutas Orenses
34 Cooperativa Pullman Azuay
36 Transportes Occidentales
37 Ecuatoriana Pullman
38 Ciudad de Piñas
39 CIFA Buses to Guayaquil
40 Transportes Cooperativa
   Loja
41 Peruvian Consulate
42 Transportes TAC
43 Panamericana

rise for September's Banana Festival and national holidays.

Most cheap hotels have only cold water, but the weather is hot enough that it's not a great hardship. In fact, air-conditioning and fans are much more appealing than a hot shower!

Hostal Mercy (☎ 920 116; Junín 609; rooms per person with fan/air-con $4/5) is one of the best budget hotels and is often full by lunch. It's friendly and the rooms all have private baths (some rooms also have air-conditioning). Parking is available.

Hotel Suites Guayaquil (☎ 922 570; Montalvo near 9 de Octubre; rooms per person $5) has large wood-floor rooms with private bath. Choose carefully as they vary greatly – some are pretty ugly.

Gran Hotel Machala (☎ 930 530; Montalvo near Rocafuerte; rooms per person with shared/private bath $4/5) has bare-bone but clean rooms. Some have fans and most have seatless toilets.

Hotel Inés (☎ 932 301, fax 931 473; Montalvo 1509; singles/doubles $4/7, with air-con $7/11) is a decent place and has rooms with private bath and fan or air-conditioning. Rooms with cable TV cost a little more; there is parking.

Hotel San Francisco International (☎ 930 445, 930 457; Tarqui near Sucre; singles/doubles with fan $12/18, with air-con $17/23) has five floors of large, clean rooms. They all have TV and phone and most have big windows; it's a good choice. The restaurant is comfortable and popular.

Hotel Perla del Pacífico (☎ 930 915, 931 472; Sucre 613; singles/doubles $15/26) offers tidy, comfortable rooms with firm beds, tiled floors, air-conditioning, private hot baths and cable TV.

Hotel Oro (☎ 937 569; Sucre & Montalvo; singles/doubles $18/24) has pleasant, carpeted rooms with air-conditioning, cable TV, direct-dial phones, minifridges and lots of hot water. There's a restaurant, too.

Hotel Ejecutivo (☎ 923 162, 933 992; Sucre & 9 de Mayo; singles/doubles $18/25) is clean, secure and has air-conditioning, hot water and cable TV. The restaurant is tiny but decent.

Rizzo Hotel (☎ 933 651, 921 511; Guayas 2123; singles/doubles $28/42) is a great hotel by Machala standards and it's surprisingly quiet for its central location. It has a swimming pool, sauna and relaxing patio area. The rooms – with air-conditioning, TV, private baths and hot water – vary widely in size but are all comfy.

Oro Verde (☎ 933 140; e ov_mch@oro verdehotels.com; Circunvalación Norte & Calle Vehicular V7, Urbanización Uniorno; doubles from $120), in the suburbs outside of town, is Machala's only luxury hotel. Double rooms are spacious and the hotel has all the expected amenities, including a swimming pool, sauna facilities, car rental, a travel agency and small shopping mall. It's a 10-minute cab ride from the center of town.

Places To Eat

All the hotels listed earlier have slightly expensive restaurants, but the food is good and most are air-conditioned. If you have time, consider heading over to Puerto Bolívar (see later) for a fresh seafood lunch.

Restaurant Chifa Central (Tarqui near Sucre; mains $2-5; open 11am-10pm daily) is a clean, well-lit place for Chinese food. The portions are huge and the rice and noodle dishes are good.

Around the corner on Sucre are several cheap **parrillada restaurants** serving inexpensive grilled chicken and steaks. They're best for dinner.

Bar Restaurant El Bosque (9 de Mayo near Bolívar; mains $2-3; open 8am-3pm daily) has outdoor tables and serves simple but decent meals.

Don Angelo's (9 de Mayo; open 7am-4am daily), just south of the Central Plaza, is an unembroidered little restaurant with a reputation for serving some of the town's better food, namely chicken and seafood.

Restaurant América (☎ 931 752; Olmedo near Guayas; mains $2-3) gets packed for the good $1.50 set lunches and dinners.

La Posada del Cangrejo (Rocafuerte near Páez; mains $2-3) serves mostly fast food and $2.50 almuerzos. It's best on Fridays when it serves caldo de bolas, a thick peanuty soup with floating balls of cooked plantain and cheese.

Getting There & Away

Air Weekday morning flights to Guayaquil ($31), continuing to Quito ($65), are available with **TAME** (☎ 930 139, 932 710; Montalvo near Pichincha). The airport is barely 1km from the town center and a taxi ride there will cost about $1. If you're on foot, walk southwest along Montalvo.

Bus There are **CIFA** (☎ 933 735) buses which go to the Peruvian border at Huaquillas ($1.30, 1½ hours) every 20 minutes during daylight from the corner of Bolívar and Guayas. These buses go via Santa Rosa and Arenillas (see To/From the Peruvian Border later). Buses with **Transportes El Oro** (Rocafuerte), between Junín and Tarqui, go only to Santa Rosa.

CIFA buses also go to Guayaquil ($3, three hours) from its depot on 9 de Octubre near Tarqui. There are several other companies in the area. **Rutas Orenses** (9 de Octubre near Tarqui) has efficient and frequent services to Guayaquil. **Ecuatoriana Pullman** (9 de Octubre near Colón) also goes there in larger air-conditioned coaches.

Panamericana (Colón & Bolívar) has regular daily buses to Quito ($7, 11 hours). It also has buses to Santo Domingo ($6, eight hours) and an evening bus to Tulcán. **Transportes Occidentales** (Buenavista & Olmedo) has regular buses to Quito and a night bus to Esmeraldas ($7, nine hours).

Ciudad de Piñas (Colón & Rocafuerte) has hourly buses from 4:30am to 7:30pm to Piñas ($1.80, two hours).

Cooperative Pullman Azuay (☎ 930 539; Sucre at Tarqui) has many buses daily to Cuenca ($3.60, four hours). A few direct buses take three hours.

Transportes Cooperativa Loja (☎ 932 303; Tarqui near Rocafuerte) goes to Loja ($4.50) several times a day; the ride takes six to seven hours on the old (but very scenic) dirt road via Piñas and four to five hours on the newer paved road. Nearby, Transportes TAC goes hourly to Zaruma ($2, three hours) from 4am to 7pm.

Getting Around

The No 1 bus, which is usually crowded, goes northwest from the central plaza along 9 de Octubre to Puerto Bolívar ($0.20, 15 minutes). It returns along Pichincha and goes southeast as far as the statue of El Bananero, almost 2km from the center.

At the airport, **Localiza** (☎ 935 455) rents cars. Oro Verde also arranges car rental (see Places to Stay earlier).

PUERTO BOLÍVAR & JAMBELÍ
☎ 07

The international port, Puerto Bolívar, is 7km from Machala and an important outlet for the southern coast's banana and shrimp exports. There are some simple but decent seafood restaurants by the waterfront, where you can enjoy a freshly prepared lunch while watching seabirds wheeling overhead and ships sailing by. However, this place is best avoided at night.

The port is protected from the ocean by islands and mangroves (most of which have been cleared for shrimp farms). Motorized dugouts can be hired for cruising the mangroves for **bird-watching** or to go to the nearby island beach at Jambelí.

The silty beach at Jambelí (mosquito-ridden during the wet months) is the favorite resort of holidaymakers from Machala; it can be busy on weekends and completely overcrowded during Carnaval and Semana Santa. If you are a bird-watcher, a good reason to visit is to see the wide variety of coastal and pelagic birds and to search for the rufous-necked wood-rail, a rarely seen bird of the mangroves. Boats can be hired for rides through the mangroves.

Numerous beach-side shacks serve seafood on weekends, but many are closed midweek. You can stay at one of several cheap hosterías.

To get to Puerto Bolívar take the No 1 bus from Machala's central plaza; it runs frequently. A taxi should cost about $2. To Jambelí you can either charter a boat from Puerto Bolívar or take one of the passenger shuttle boats. The shuttle boats head to Jambelí ($1, 20 minutes) about four times a day (more frequently on weekends and holidays). The boats drop you off on a canal on the mainland side of the island and you have to walk the few hundred meters to the beach.

ZARUMA
☎ 07 • elevation 1150m

In the mountains southeast of Machala, Zaruma is an old gold-mining town with some exquisite, century-old, wooden architecture. In fact, the quaint timber buildings with elaborate balconies are the only real reason to come here (aside from the lovely mountain views and the joy of having nothing to do).

As far as mining is concerned, the gold is almost all worked out, although visits to a mine can be arranged by asking for permission at the *municipalidad* (town hall). Some archaeological ruins have been discovered in the area; people have probably been mining gold here since pre-Columbian times.

Roland Hotel (☎ 972 800; *singles/doubles* $7/10), on the outskirts as you arrive from the coast, is the best place in Zaruma. Rooms have TV and hot shower.

There is an inexpensive country hotel, Pedregal, about 3km outside Zaruma. **Los Rosales de Machay** (*doubles* $20) is roughly 12km north of Zaruma and is a good country resort which boasts a pool, pretty gardens, a decent restaurant and comfortable doubles. Take a taxi or drive there.

Transportes TAC has frequent buses to to/from Machala ($2, three hours).

PIÑAS
☎ 07 • elevation 1014

Set in a hilly coffee-producing area, Piñas is another lovely little mountain town with colonial wooden architecture. In 1980, a new bird species – the El Oro parakeet – was discovered near here. The best place to see the bird is Fundación Jocotoco's **Reserva Buenaventura**, a 1500-hectare cloud-forest reserve about 9km from Piñas.

A local Peace Corps volunteer wrote in to recommend the **Orquideario** (*Sucre & Olmedo*), a 2.5-hectare orchid garden with bromeliads, heleconias and a talapia-fish breeding pond. There are also a couple of orchid collectors in town who will show you their plants. You can walk or take a taxi to a cross on a nearby hilltop for good views of the surrounding hills.

Residencial Dumari (☎ 976 118; *rooms per person without/with TV & private bath $4/7*), in the town center, is the best place in Piñas. The rooms are clean and some have TV and private warm shower.

Hotel Las Orquídeas (☎ 976 355; *Abdón Calderón & J Montalvo; rooms $5-10*) is also fine and has a decent restaurant next door.

Ciudad de Piñas bus company runs frequent buses to/from Machala ($1.80, two hours).

EL BOSQUE PETRIFICADO PUYANGO
☎ 07

This petrified forest became a reserve in 1988 to protect the fossil remains and wildlife of the area. Fossilized Araucaria tree trunks – many of them millions of years old and up to 11m long and 1.6m in diameter – have been found. This is the largest petrified forest (2659 hectares) in Ecuador and probably the whole continent. Puyango is also known for its birds and over 130 species have been listed – there are undoubtedly more. A bird list should be available at the reserve.

Puyango is in a valley at about 360m above sea level, some 55km inland from the coast. The valley is separated from the ocean by the Cordillera Larga, which reaches over 900m above sea level. Despite the separation, the area experiences a coastal weather pattern, with warm temperatures and most of the annual 1000mm of rainfall occurring from January to May.

Camping is allowed for a small fee; ask at the information center. A lookout point and trails have been constructed.

The nearby village of **Puyango** is composed of some 20 families. There is no hotel as such, although the villagers will find you a bed or floor space if asked. Locals know the reserve and some will act as guides for you. The nearest village with basic hostales is **Alamor**, just south of Puyango.

For more information, call the **Machala office** (☎ 930 012).

Transportes Cooperativa Loja buses from Machala and Loja will drop you in Puyango. Alternatively, take a CIFA bus to the town of Arenillas, where you can catch an infrequent local bus to Puyango. Puyango is close to the border, so there may be passport checks.

TO/FROM THE PERUVIAN BORDER

It's about 80km from Machala to the border town of Huaquillas, the route taken by most overland travelers to Peru. There are two or three passport checks en route (not including the stop at immigrations near the border), but these take only a minute, assuming your passport is in order. At these checks, foreign travelers usually have to get off the bus and register their passports – the drivers know the routine and will wait for you.

Santa Rosa & Arenillas
☎ 07

The bus to Huaquillas passes through banana and palm plantations, as well as through the dusty market towns of Santa Rosa and Arenillas, of which Santa Rosa is the most important. Buses between Machala and Huaquillas pass by frequently.

In Santa Rosa you can sleep at **Hotel Santa Rosa** (☎ 943 677; *Vega Dávila & Colón; rooms with fan/air-con $8/10*) or **Hotel América** (☎ 943 130; *Colón & El Oro*), which is slightly cheaper.

Huaquillas
☎ 07 • pop 30,000

This dusty town's only claim to fame is its location at Ecuador's principal border-crossing with Peru. There is a busy street market by the border and the place is full of Peruvians shopping on day passes (Ecuador is still cheaper than Peru). It's a bustling but not particularly attractive introduction to Ecuador if you're arriving from Peru. Huaquillas continues across the border into Peru, where it becomes known as **Aguas Verdes**. The two sides are divided by Río Zarumilla.

Money Banks in Huaquillas or Aguas Verdes do not normally do exchange transactions, so you have to rely on street moneychangers, identified by their black briefcases.

If leaving Peru, it's best to get rid of as much Peruvian currency as possible before arriving in Ecuador. If leaving Ecuador, your US currency is easily exchanged in Peru. Traveler's checks can also be exchanged, but with some difficulty and at lower rates than cash.

Places to Stay & Eat Most travelers leaving Ecuador sleep in Machala and go straight through to Tumbes (or vice versa); both places have plenty of hotels. If you do need to spend the night, try **Hotel Lima** *(☎ 907 900, 907 794; Machala & Portovelo; singles/ doubles with fan $4/6, with air-con $6/8)*, three blocks from the border. **Hotel Vanessa** *(☎ 907 263; 1 de Mayo 323; doubles $10)*, about seven blocks from the border, is reasonably quiet and has clean, air-conditioned doubles. There are several little hole-in-the-wall restaurants around town.

Getting There & Away Huaquillas does not have a main bus terminal, but you will see buses on the main street a few blocks from the border. CIFA buses run frequently to Machala ($1.30, 1½ hours). Panameri-

cana, behind the *migraciones* (immigration office), has several buses a day to Quito ($10, 12 hours), some via Santo Domingo and others via Ambato. Ecuatoriana Pullman has frequent buses to Guayaquil ($4.50, 4½ hours). A few buses go to Cuenca and Loja ($4, six to seven hours).

Note that from Guayaquil, the international bus companies Rutas de America and Expresso Internacional Ormeno (see Getting There & Away under Guayaquil earlier) offer direct services to Tumbes and Lima in Peru, allowing you to avoid changing buses at Huaquillas or the border.

See Land in the Getting There & Away chapter earlier in this book for information about crossing the border into Peru.

The Galápagos Islands

☎ 05 • pop 18,640

A visit to the Galápagos Islands is the wildlife experience of a lifetime, a mind-blowing lesson in natural history set in a barren, volcanic land with a haunting beauty all its own. Here, you can swim with sea lions, float eye-to-eye with a penguin, scuba dive with hammerhead sharks, stand next to a blue-footed booby feeding its young, watch a giant 200kg tortoise lumbering through a cactus forest, and try to avoid stepping on iguanas scurrying over the lava.

That this little string of islands, 1000km from mainland Ecuador, has so profoundly influenced human thought, that the handful of animals which somehow made it out here and, isolated for so long lost all fear of predators and developed into species entirely their own, and that today you can see these unique animals living practically as they have for aeons, is simply astounding.

But a trip to the Galápagos isn't cheap. Flying from Quito and spending a week cruising the islands during the high season will cost at least $900, even for the most thrifty of budget travelers. You can pay over three times that for the most expensive of the top-end tours. It's possible to visit the islands on your own and see some beautiful sights, but without taking a cruise you won't come close to experiencing what the archipelago has to offer.

People who get the most out of a trip to the Galápagos (and few walk away unmoved) are those who have an interest in natural history, a love of wildlife and the ability to bury the bothers of hopping around on a fixed itinerary with a group of fellow tourists (although even the most hardened, antigroup skeptics soften into gooey-eyed gazers at their first glimpse of a seal pup). For most, visiting the Galápagos turns out to be the highlight of their trip to Ecuador.

The Islands

Five of the islands are inhabited. The total population is certainly higher than the official figure and growing – it has at least tripled since the early 1980s. The inhabitants make a living mainly from tourism, fishing and farming. About half the residents live in Puerto Ayora, on Isla Santa Cruz.

Highlights

- Hiking the cliff-top trail on South Plaza – a superb vantage point for watching seabirds
- Walking on uneroded, century-old lava flows on Isla San Salvador
- Climbing to the summit of Isla Bartolomé for a picture-perfect view of the islands
- Snorkeling among playful sea lions
- Scuba diving with hammerhead sharks at Gordon Rocks

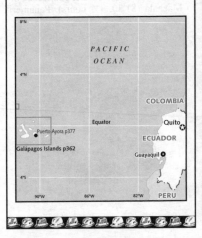

Santa Cruz, in the middle of the archipelago, is the most important island from the travelers' point of view. On the south side of this island is Puerto Ayora, the largest town in the Galápagos and the place from which most tours are based. North of Santa Cruz, separated by a narrow strait, is Isla Baltra, which is home to the islands' major airport. A public bus and a ferry connect the Isla Baltra airport with Puerto Ayora (see Getting Around the Islands later in this chapter).

Isla San Cristóbal, the easternmost island, has the provincial capital (Puerto Baquerizo Moreno), a few hotels and an airport. Despite its political status, more tours start from Isla Baltra and Puerto Ayora.

The other inhabited islands are Isla Isabela, with the small port of Puerto Villamil;

The Galápagos – Evolution in Action

When the Galápagos were formed, they were barren volcanic islands, devoid of all life. Because the islands were never connected to the mainland, all the species now present must have somehow crossed 1000km of open ocean. Those that could fly or swim long distances had the best chance of reaching the islands, but other methods of colonization were also possible (but more difficult).

Plant seeds or insect eggs and larvae may have been brought over in an animals' stomach contents or attached to the feathers or feet of birds. Small mammals, land birds and reptiles, as well as plants and insects, may have been ferried across on floating vegetation.

Galápagos wildlife is dominated by birds (especially seabirds), sea mammals and reptiles. There are no amphibians, because their moist skin is unable to withstand the dehydrating effect of salt water (although humans have recently introduced a couple of frog species). And, of course, there are plenty of tropical fish and marine invertebrates.

Compared to the mainland, there are few small land mammals and insects. The well-known fearlessness of the islands' animals probably comes from having no large predators to fear – there simply weren't any until pigs, goats, cats and other domesticated animals were introduced by human colonists. Domestic animals that escaped found little competition – now, their offspring is feral and has become a major problem for the islands' native species.

When the first migrating species arrived millions of years ago, they found the islands different from the mainland in two important ways: First, the islands were physically different, and second, there were few other species to compete with. Some colonizers were able to survive, breed and produce offspring. Obviously, the young were the same species as their parents, but some had subtle differences.

A classic Galápagos example of this situation is a bird that produces a chick with a bill that is slightly different from those of its parents or siblings. In the different environment of the islands, some chicks with slightly different bills are more able to take advantage of the environment. These birds are said to be better adapted and are more likely to survive and raise a brood of their own.

These better-adapted survivors may pass on favorable genetic traits (in this case, a slightly better adapted bill) to their offspring, and thus, over many generations, certain favorable traits are selected for and other less favorable traits are selected against. Eventually, the difference between the original colonizers and their distant descendants is so great that the descendants can be considered a different species altogether. This is the essence of Darwin's theory of evolution by natural selection.

The earliest colonizers had little competition and a variety of different habitats to choose from, and so adaptive changes could occur in different ways to take advantage of different habitats or islands. Thus it wasn't only that a longer or broader or smaller bill would be better adapted – it could be that various types of bills could confer adaptive advantages to birds in different ecological niches. One ancestral species could therefore give rise to several modern species in this evolutionary process, which is called adaptive radiation. This explains the presence in the Galápagos of 13 similar, endemic species of finches – called 'Darwin's finches' in honor of the founder of evolutionary theory.

Charles Darwin, during his visit in 1835, noted the differences in bills in these 13 species of finches; he also noted similar differences in other groups of animals. These observations, combined with many others, led to the 1859 publication of Darwin's *The Origin of Species*, which is one of the most influential books ever published and remains the mainstay of modern biological thought.

These evolutionary processes take thousands or millions of generations – new species don't normally appear over a single generation. For many years, evolutionary biologists were puzzled over how so many unique species could have evolved in the Galápagos over the relatively short period of about four million years (the age of the oldest islands). The answer has recently been provided by the geologists and oceanographers who found nine-million-year-old remnants of islands under the ocean to the east of the existing islands. Presumably, the ancestors of the present wildlife once lived on these lost islands, and therefore had at least nine million years to evolve – a figure that evolutionary biologists find acceptable.

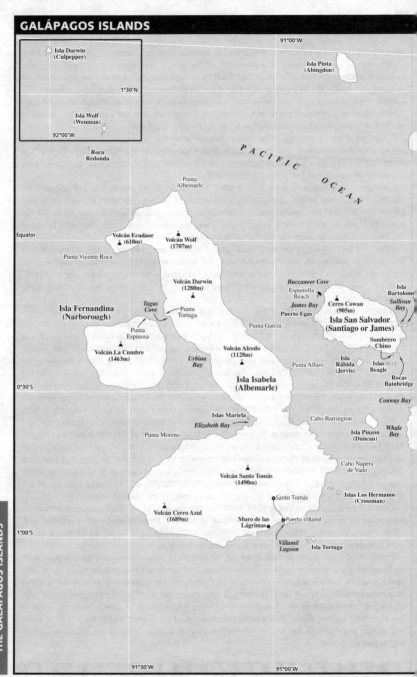

GALÁPAGOS ISLANDS

91°00'W

Isla Darwin
(Culpepper)

1°30'N

Isla Pinta
(Abingdon)

Isla Wolf
(Wenman)

92°00'W

Roca
Redonda

PACIFIC OCEAN

Punta
Albemarle

Equator

Volcán Ecudaor
(610m)

Volcán Wolf
(1707m)

Punta Vicente Roca

Volcán Darwin
(1280m)

Buccaneer Cove
Espumilla
Beach

Isla Fernandina
(Narborough)

Tagus
Cove

Punta
Tortuga

James Bay

Puerto Egas

Cerro Cowan
(905m)

Isla
Bartolomé

Sullivan
Bay

Punta García

Isla San Salvador
(Santiago or James)

Punta
Espinosa

Volcán La Cumbre
(1463m)

Urbina
Bay

Volcán Alcedo
(1128m)

Sombrero
Chino

Isla
Rábida
(Jervis)

Islas
Beagle

Punta Alfaro

Rocas
Bainbridge

0°30'S

Isla Isabela
(Albemarle)

Conway Bay

Islas Mariela

Elizabeth Bay

Cabo Barrington

Whale
Bay

Punta Moreno

Isla Pinzón
(Duncan)

Cabo Nápera
de Vado

Volcán Santo Tomás
(1490m)

Islas Los Hermanos
(Crossman)

Santo Tomás

Volcán Cerro Azul
(1689m)

Muro de las
Lágrimas

Puerto Villamil

1°00'S

Villamil
Lagoon

Isla Tortuga

91°30'W

91°00'W

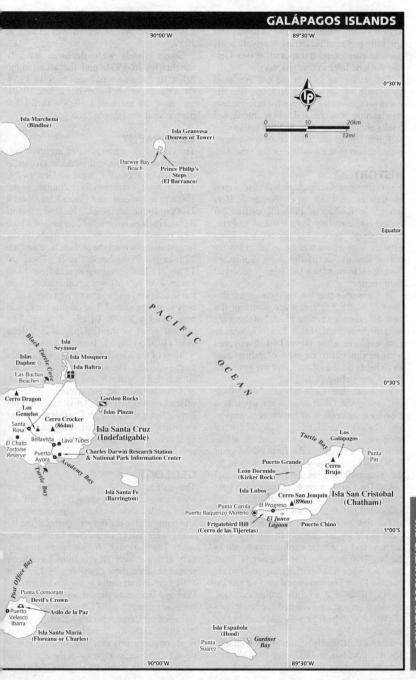

GALÁPAGOS ISLANDS

90°00'W 89°30'W

0°30'N

0 10 20km
0 6 12mi

Isla Marchena
(Bindloe)

Isla Genovesa
(Douwes or Tower)

Darwin Bay
Beach

Prince Philip's
Steps
(El Barranco)

Equator

P A C I F I C   O C E A N

Isla
Seymour

Islas
Daphne

Isla Mosquera

Isla Baltra

Las Bachas
Beaches

Cerro Dragon

Los
Gemelos

Gordon Rocks

Islas Plazas

Black Turtle Cove

Santa
Rosa

Cerro Crocker
(864m)

El Chato
Tortoise
Reserve

Bellavista

Lava Tubes

Isla Santa Cruz
(Indefatigable)

Puerto
Ayora

Academy Bay

Charles Darwin Research Station
& National Park Information Center

Turtle Bay

Isla Santa Fe
(Barrington)

Turtle Bay

Los
Galápagos

Punta
Pitt

Cerro
Brujo

Puerto Grande

León Dormido
(Kicker Rock)

Isla Lobos

Cerro San Joaquín
(896m)

Isla San Cristóbal
(Chatham)

Punta Carola
Puerto Baquerizo Moreno

El Progreso

El Junco
Lagoon

Frigatebird Hill
(Cerro de las Tijeretas)

Puerto Chino

0°30'S

1°00'S

Post Office Bay

Punta Cormorant

Devil's Crown

Puerto
Velasco
Ibarra

Asilo de la Paz

Isla Santa María
(Floreana or Charles)

Isla Española
(Hood)

Gardner
Bay

Punta
Suárez

90°00'W 89°30'W

and Isla Santa María (Floreana), with Puerto Velasco Ibarra – both have places to stay and eat. Infrequent public ferries or private boats provide inter-island transportation (see Getting Around later in this chapter).

The remaining islands are not inhabited by people but are visited on tours. See the Facts for the Visitor chapter for information on planning your trip and for recommended books about the islands. See the Galápagos Wildlife Guide special section for a brief introduction to the wildlife of the islands.

HISTORY

The Galápagos Archipelago was discovered by accident in 1535, when Tomás de Berlanga, the Bishop of Panama, drifted off course while sailing from Panama to Peru. The bishop reported his discovery to King Charles V of Spain and included in his report a description of the giant *Galápago* (tortoise), from which the islands received their name.

It is possible that the indigenous inhabitants of South America were aware of the islands' existence before 1535, but there are no definite records of this. In 1953, Norwegian explorer Thor Heyerdahl discovered what he thought to be pre-Columbian pottery shards on the islands, but the evidence seems inconclusive.

For more than three centuries after their discovery, the Galápagos were used as a base by a succession of buccaneers, sealers and whalers. The islands provided sheltered anchorage, firewood, water and an abundance of fresh food in the form of the giant Galápagos tortoises, which were caught by the thousands and stacked, alive, in ships' holds. The tortoises could survive for a year or more and thus provided fresh meat for the sailors long after they had left the islands.

The first rough charts of the archipelago were made by buccaneers in the late 17th century, and scientific exploration began in the late 18th century. The Galápagos' most famous visitor was Charles Darwin, who arrived in 1835. Darwin stayed for five weeks, making notes and wildlife collections that provided important evidence for his theory of evolution, which he was just then beginning to develop.

Ecuador officially claimed the Galápagos Archipelago in 1832. For roughly one century thereafter, the islands were inhabited by only a few settlers and were used as penal colonies, the last of which was closed in 1959.

Some islands were declared wildlife sanctuaries in 1934, and the archipelago officially became a national park in 1959. Organized tourism began in the late 1960s, and now, an estimated 50,000 to 60,000 people visit the islands each year.

GEOGRAPHY

The Galápagos are an isolated group of volcanic islands that lie in the Pacific Ocean on the equator about 90° west of Greenwich. The nearest mainland is Ecuador, some 1000km to the east, and Costa Rica, almost 1100km to the northeast. The land mass of the archipelago covers 7882 sq km, of which well over half consists of Isla Isabela, the largest island within the archipelago and the 12th-largest in the South Pacific. There are 13 major islands (ranging in area from 14 sq km to 4588 sq km), six small islands (1 sq km to 5 sq km) and scores of islets, of which only some are named. The islands are spread over roughly 50,000 sq km of ocean. The highest point in the Galápagos is Volcán Wolf (1707m), on Isla Isabela.

Most of the islands have two – sometimes three – names. The earliest charts gave the islands both Spanish and English names, and the Ecuadorian government assigned official names in 1892. An island can thus have a Spanish name, an English name and an official name. The official names are used here in most cases; the few exceptions will be indicated.

GEOLOGY

The earliest of the islands visible today were formed roughly four to five million years ago by underwater volcanoes erupting and rising above the ocean's surface (the islands were never connected to the mainland). The Galápagos region is volcanically very active – over 50 eruptions have been recorded since their discovery in 1535. In 1991, the infrequently visited northern island of Marchena erupted, as did the westernmost large island of Fernandina in 1995, followed by Cerro Azul on Isabela in October 1998. Thus, the formation of the islands is an ongoing process; the archipelago is relatively young compared to the age of the earth (which is about 1000 times older).

Geologists generally agree that two relatively new geological theories explain the islands' formation. The theory of plate tectonics holds that the earth's crust consists of several rigid plates that, over geological time, move relative to one another over the surface of the earth. The Galápagos lie on the northern edge of the Nazca Plate, close to its junction with the Cocos Plate. These two plates are spreading apart at a rate of about 1km every 14,000 years, and the Galápagos Islands are slowly moving southeast. How fast is 1km every 14,000 years? It's about the same rate at which your fingernails grow – pretty fast by plate-tectonic standards.

The hotspot theory states that deep within the earth (below the moving tectonic plates) are certain superheated areas that remain stationary. At frequent intervals (measured in geological time), the heat from these hotspots increases enough to melt the earth's crust and produce a volcanic eruption of sufficient magnitude to cause molten lava to rise above the ocean floor and, eventually, above the ocean's surface.

The Galápagos are moving slowly to the southeast over a stationary hotspot, so one would expect the southeastern islands to have been formed first and the northwestern islands to have been formed most recently. This has proven to be the case. The most ancient rocks yet discovered on the islands are about 3.25 million years old and come from Isla Española in the southeast. In comparison, the oldest rocks on the western islands of Isla Fernandina and Isla Isabela are less than 750,000 years old. The northwestern islands are still in the process of formation and contain active volcanoes, particularly Isabela and Fernandina. In addition to the gradual southeastern drift of the Nazca Plate, the northern drift of the Cocos Plate complicates the matter, so that the islands do not get uniformly older from northwest to southeast.

Most of the Galápagos are surrounded by very deep ocean. Less than 20km off the coasts of the western islands, the ocean is over 3000m deep. When visitors cruise around the islands, they can see only about the top third of the volcanoes – the rest is underwater. Some of the oldest volcanoes in the area are, in fact, completely underwater. The Carnegie Ridge, a submerged mountain range stretching to the east of the Galápagos, has the remnants of previous volcanic islands, some were as much as nine million years old. These have been completely eroded away; they now lie 2000m beneath the ocean surface and stretch about half the distance between the Galápagos and the mainland.

Most of the volcanic rock forming the Galápagos Islands is basalt. Molten basalt has the property of being more fluid than other types of volcanic rock, so when an eruption occurs, basalt tends to erupt in the form of lava flows rather than in the form of explosions. Hence the Galápagos Islands have gently rounded shield volcanoes rather than the cone-shaped variety most people associate with the formations.

While not every visitor has the time or energy to climb a volcano, a visit to one of the lava flows is within everyone's reach. Several can be visited, but the one at Sullivan Bay, on the east end of San Salvador (also known as Santiago or James Island), is especially rewarding. This lava flow is about a century old and remains uneroded.

Here you can see *pahoehoe*, or 'ropy,' lava, which is formed by the cooling of the molten surface and the wrinkling of the skin into ropy shapes by the flow of the molten lava beneath. Impressions of trees can be found in the solidified lava, and some of the first colonizing plants – the *Brachycereus* cactus and the *Mollugo* carpetweed – can be seen beginning the slow conversion of a lava field to soil.

ECOLOGY & ENVIRONMENT

As early as 1934, the Ecuadorian government set aside some of the islands as wildlife sanctuaries, but it was not until 1959 that the Galápagos were officially declared a national park. The construction of the Charles Darwin Research Station, on Isla Santa Cruz, began soon after, and the station began operating in 1964 as an international non-government organization (NGO). (The Galápagos National Park Service began operating in 1968 and is the key institution of the Ecuadorian government responsible for the park. The National Park Service and the Charles Darwin Research Station work together to manage the islands.) In 1986, the Ecuadorian government granted more protection to the islands by creating the Galápagos Marine Resources Reserve.

THE GALÁPAGOS ISLANDS

The national park covers approximately 97% of the total land mass – the rest is taken up by urban areas and farms that existed prior to the creation of the park. The Galápagos Marine Resources Reserve covers the 133,000 sq km of ocean and seabed within which the islands are located, plus a 20,000-sq-km buffer zone. A law that passed in 1998 enables the park and reserve to protect and conserve the islands and surrounding ocean; the law also encourages educational and scientific research while allowing sustainable development of the islands as an Ecuadorian province.

Tourism

Few tourists had visited the islands before the station opened, but by the mid-1960s, organized tourism began, with a little over 1000 visitors a year. This figure soon increased dramatically. In 1970, an estimated 4500 tourists arrived, and by 1971, there were six small boats and one large cruise ship operating in the islands. In less than two decades, the number of visitors had increased tenfold; in the early 1990s, an estimated 60,000 visited annually. The most current figures indicate that 47,356 foreign tourists and 24,211 mainland Ecuadorians visited the islands in 2001.

To cope with the increased demands of tourism, a second airport with regular flights to the mainland opened in the mid-1980s, and a third is currently being discussed. The number of hotels in Puerto Ayora and Puerto Baquerizo Moreno doubled from 15 in 1981 to about 30 a decade later. New hotel growth is now restricted. There are over 80 boats (with sleeping accommodations) carrying four to 96 passengers; the majority carry fewer than 20 passengers. The resident population of the islands is growing at about 10% annually to provide labor for the booming tourism industry.

While this is good for the economy of Ecuador, inevitable problems have resulted. Among the more serious are entrepreneurial proposals of building luxurious high-rise hotels and introducing as many more cruise ships into the islands as possible. Fortunately, the Ecuadorian government has seen the sense of preventing these projects.

The wildlife of the Galápagos is unique. The islands have been called 'a laboratory of evolution' and are of immense importance to our understanding of the natural world. The incredible assemblage of wildlife is threatened not only by tourism, but also by the increased colonization that accompanies the booming tourist industry.

Overfishing

Overfishing has been a major problem in recent years. One of the most notorious examples was the taking of a reported seven million sea cucumbers in two months during 1994, after the Ecuadorian government authorized a quota of 550,000. Although sea-cucumber fishing became illegal in December 1994, the Charles Darwin Foundation reports that close to one million sea-cucumbers per month continued to be exported in 1995,

Charles Darwin Foundation

Most tourists have the opportunity to visit the Charles Darwin Research Station. Visitors are encouraged to make donations to the organization, which carries out research and advises government and tourist agencies on minimizing the impact of tourism on the islands. (None of the $100 park fee goes toward the research station.)

Outside of the islands, the research station is supported by contributions to the Charles Darwin Foundation. Donors contributing $25 or more each year receive the English-language bulletin *Galápagos News* and the English-language scientific journal *Noticias de Galápagos*. These journals are great for keeping up with the latest happenings on the islands, including information about conservation issues, as well as interesting recent research and unusual wildlife observations.

Donations are tax deductible for citizens of the USA and several European countries. Addresses for donations are easily obtained in the research station and at most boats or hotels in the Galápagos. US citizens may contact the **Charles Darwin Foundation** (*407 N Washington St, Suite 105, Falls Church, VA 22046, USA*). The best source of information about the Charles Darwin foundation and related organizations is at [W] www.galapagos.org.

chiefly for their purported aphrodisiac properties. Other illegal fishing activities include taking shark fins for shark-fin soup, killing sea lions for bait, and overfishing lobster (the population of which has dropped far below normal numbers) to feed tourists and locals.

Fishermen hoping to make money fast reacted in a hostile manner to the government ban on fishing for sea cucumbers and other animals. In January and September of 1995, armed fishermen urged on by two unscrupulous local government officials occupied the Charles Darwin Research Station and threatened to kill tortoises, beat up station personnel and burn portions of the park. Fortunately, the tense situation was defused with help from the Ecuadorian military and pressure from the US embassy.

Since then, there have been isolated protests by fishermen unhappy with restrictions on various fisheries in the islands. In November, 2000, fishermen protesting quotas on lobsters disrupted work at the Charles Darwin Research Station on Santa Cruz and ransacked the park headquarters on Isla Isabela. Another major protest took place in April, 2002, when over 800 fishermen in Santa Cruz blocked the road linking Puerto Ayora and Baltra airport. They were protesting quotas on sea cucumbers, which are again legal to harvest during certain months of the year.

Other Problems

The introduction of domestic animals into the islands is only one of various difficulties the archipelago faces. Feral goats and pigs and introduced rats decimate (or cause the extinction of) native species in a few years.

Some islanders who recently arrived see the national park as a barrier to making a living; arson fires set by some newly arrived colonists burned about 10,000 hectares on Isla Isabela in 1994.

One of the most serious recent abuses within the reserve occurred in January 2001, when the Ecuadorian oil tanker *Jessica* ran aground near Puerto Baquerizo Moreno, San Cristóbal, spilling between 150,000 to 180,000 gallons of fuel. Fortunately, much of it was carried away from the islands by favorable winds and ocean currents. Dozens of sea lions, blue-footed boobies and brown pelicans had to be rescued, but in late 2002

the Charles Darwin Research Station reported the effects were widespread but minimal. The empty *Jessica* was left where it grounded, and tourism is back to normal.

Conservation Efforts

There are various solutions to the problems facing the Galápagos Islands. One extreme view is to prohibit all colonization and tourism – an option that appeals to few. Many colonists act responsibly and actively oppose the disruptive and dangerous tactics of the protesting fishermen. The tourist industry is important for Ecuador's economy, and the best solution is a combination of environmental education for both residents and visitors and a programme of responsible tourism.

Management of tourism is an important part of the function of the park service. Various successful programmes have been implemented to minimize the impact of tourism on the national park while increasing tourists' enjoyment and learning. Most visitors understand that these regulations protect the islands as a unique living laboratory.

In 1998, a Special Law for the Galápagos was enacted. It enabled 95% of the Visitor Entry Fee ($100) to be retained by the Galápagos, with 40% going to the park, 40% to local authorities and the rest to other local interests. The 40% for the park is a significant amount and is much more than is collected for mainland parks. Also, the Galápagos Marine Resources Reserve has more than doubled in size.

By law, all tour boats must be accompanied by certified naturalist guides that have been trained by the National Park Service. On the better boats, these are 'Naturalist III Guides' – bilingual, university-educated biologists with a very real interest in preserving and explaining the wildlife. On the cheapest boats, 'Naturalist II Guides' are provided – they speak little English and may know less about the wildlife but will (at least in principle) keep visitors from littering or molesting the wildlife, and they may be able to identify species. Visits to the islands are restricted to the official visitor sites.

Important park rules protect wildlife and the environment; these are mostly a matter of courtesy and common sense: Don't feed or handle the animals; don't litter; don't remove any natural object (living or not); do not bring pets; and do not buy objects made of sea lion teeth, black coral, tortoise or turtle shells, or other artefacts made from plants or animals. You are not allowed to enter the visitor sites after dark or without a qualified guide, and a guide will accompany every boat. On all shore trips, the guide will be there to answer your questions and show you the best sites – and also to ensure that you stay on the trails and follow park rules.

With approximately 65,000 annual visitors, it is essential to have a system of protection for the islands. The rules are sensible and necessary and do not infringe upon your enjoyment of the Galápagos. The wildlife is so prolific that you'll see just as much on the trail as you would anywhere else, and staying on the trails helps ensure that other areas are properly protected.

ORGANIZED TOURS

There are basically three kinds of tours in the Galápagos: day trips returning to the same hotel each night, hotel-based trips staying on different islands, and – to see the most of the islands – boat-based trips with nights spent aboard. Once you decide on what kind of tour you want, you can either fly to the islands and find a tour there, or make reservations in advance on the mainland or through a travel agency in your home country. Public transportation between the islands is very limited, so visiting the islands without taking a tour is a waste of time and money.

You can go to almost any island, but it takes time to reach the more outlying ones. It is best to visit a few central islands and inspect them closely rather than trying to cram as many ports of call as possible into your cruise. Inter-island cruising takes up valuable time, and you don't see very much while at sea. Boats now have fixed itineraries, so you need to think ahead if you want a tour that visits a specific island. Most fixed itineraries go to several of the most interesting visitor sites. Make sure you aren't stuck in Puerto Ayora for more than one night at the most.

Day Tours

Day trips are usually based in Puerto Ayora. A few operators work out of Puerto Baquerizo Moreno, but their trips are more expensive and choices are limited.

A typical day trip begins at dawn, with either a walk down to the dock or a bus ride across the island to meet a boat at the north side of Santa Cruz. Several hours are spent sailing to the day's visitor site(s), which you will visit during the middle of the day with a large group. Only a few central islands are close enough to be visited on day trips.

Because a lot of time is spent going back and forth, the downside of this kind of tour is that there is no chance of visiting the islands early or late in the day. The cheapest boats may be slow and overcrowded; their island visits may be too brief; the guides may be poorly informed; and the crew may be lacking an adequate conservationist attitude. Therefore, the cheapest day trips are not recommended. Nevertheless, day trips are useful for people who cannot stand the idea of sleeping in a small rocking boat at night.

There are plenty of day-trip operators in Puerto Ayora who charge from $40 to $115 per person per day. The one you choose will depend on which destinations they offer. Ask other travelers about the quality of the guides and boats of the local agencies.

Better and more expensive day trips – using fast boats with knowledgeable guides and staying in good hotels – can be arranged on the mainland. These trips are normally booked as a series of day trips lasting a week; they give a greater choice of islands to visit and are OK if you must take day trips. Prices range from $800 to over $1000 per week, including guided trips, hotel and meals, but not airfare or park fee. Book through **Metropolitan Touring** (**W** www .metropolitan-touring.com) – see Travel Agencies & Tour Operators in the Quito chapter – which uses Hotel Delfín in Puerto Ayora, or through Hotel Galápagos and Red Mangrove Inn (both in Puerto Ayora, covered later in this chapter).

Hotel-Based Tours

These tours go from island to island, and you sleep in hotels on three or four different islands (Santa Cruz, San Cristóbal, Floreana, Isabela). Tours typically last a week and cost $800 to over $1000 per person, plus airfare and park fee. However, few companies offer this kind of tour. Ask the agencies in Quito until you find one that does. This kind of tour may be possible to arrange more cheaply in Puerto Ayora, but again, only a few boats do this. Red Mangrove Inn arranges trips, mixing both hotel nights on different islands with some nights aboard a boat (see Places to Stay under Puerto Ayora later in this chapter).

Boat Tours

Most visitors (non-Ecuadorians in particular) tour the Galápagos on boat tours, sleeping aboard the boat. Tours can last from three days to three weeks, although tours lasting from four to eight days are the most common. It's difficult to do the Galápagos justice on a tour lasting less than a week, but five days is just acceptable. If you want to visit the outlying islands of Isabela and Fernandina, a 10-day or two-week cruise is recommended. On the first day of a tour, you arrive from the mainland by air at about lunchtime, so this is only half a day in the Galápagos, and on the last day, you have to be at the airport in the morning. Thus, a five-day tour gives only three full days in the islands. Shorter tours are advertised, but with the travel time at either end, they are not recommended.

Boats used for tours range from small yachts to large cruise ships. By far the most common type of boat is the motor sailer (a medium-sized motor boat), which carries eight to 20 passengers.

It is customary to tip the crew at the end of a trip. A tip may be anywhere between $20 and $50 per passenger per week, depending on the quality and cost of the tour. On an exceptionally good boat, you might tip more than $50; on some of the cheapest boats, passengers tip less than $20. The total tip is divided among the crew; the guide (if they're an experienced bilingual naturalist) may get as much as half (less, though for non-English-speaking guides who know little natural history). The cook and captain both get larger portions than the other crew members. Passengers should do the dividing – giving the money to one crew member and having that person deal with it is asking for complaints from other crew members.

Arranged Locally Most people arrive at the islands with a prearranged tour, although shoestringers come hoping to hook up with a tour when they get there. It's a bit cheaper to arrange a tour for yourself in Puerto Ayora than to pay for a prearranged tour from the mainland. Generally, only the cheaper boats are available in the Galápagos; the better

> ## Land Ho!
>
> Almost all Galápagos visitor sites are reached by boat, and normally landings are made in a *panga* (small boats), which every boat carries for shore trips (the larger boats carry several). Most landing sites are on sandy or rocky beaches – there are few docks. Landings are called 'wet' or 'dry.' During a wet landing, you will have to wade ashore in shallow water – sometimes up to your knees (occasionally deeper if you don't pay attention to your guide and what the waves are doing). Dry landings are made on to rocky outcrops or jetties – you probably won't get wet unless a rogue wave comes up and splashes you, or unless you slip on some seaweed and fall into the ocean (it happens).

boats are almost always booked. Therefore, don't fly to the Galápagos hoping to get on a really good boat for less money – it rarely works that way.

Flying to the Galápagos and arranging a tour is not uncommon, but neither is it as straightforward as it sounds. It can take several days – sometimes a week or more – and is therefore not an option for people with a limited amount of time. It is, however, a reasonable option for those with extra time and limited funds.

The best place to organize a tour for yourself is from Puerto Ayora. It is sometimes possible to do this in Puerto Baquerizo Moreno, but there are fewer boats available.

After arrival in Puerto Ayora, first find somewhere to sleep (especially during the high season, when the choice of rooms may be limited), and then start looking for a boat. If you are alone or with a friend, you'll need to find more people, as even the smallest boats take no fewer than four passengers. There are usually people in Puerto Ayora looking for boats, and agencies (see Puerto Ayora, later) can help in putting travelers and boats together.

Finding boats in August and around Christmas and Easter is especially difficult. The less busy months have fewer travelers on the islands, but boats are often being repaired or overhauled at this time, particularly in October. Despite the caveats, travelers who arrive in Puerto Ayora looking for a boat can almost always find one within a week (often in just a few days) if they work at it. Some travelers have said that this method sucks – by the time they pay for hotels and meals in Puerto Ayora, they don't save anything. Others have said they enjoyed the adventure of hanging out in Puerto Ayora and waiting to see what happened. Bargaining over the price is acceptable and sometimes necessary.

The cheapest and most basic boats are available for about $60 per person per day, which should include everything except park fees, alcohol and tips. The cheaper the boat, the more rice and fish you can expect to eat, and the more crowded the accommodations. A few boats even charge for bottled water. Check this before you leave.

Conditions on the cheapest boats can be cramped and primitive. Ask about washing facilities – they can vary from deck hoses on the cheapest boats to communal showers on the better boats and private showers in more expensive boats. Also inquire about water – on the cheaper boats, you may need to bring your own large containers of water. Bottled drinks are carried but cost extra – agree on the price before you leave, and make sure that enough beer and soda is loaded aboard. There's nothing to stop you from bringing your own supply.

The most important thing to find is a crew with a good and enthusiastic naturalist guide who can point out and discuss the wildlife and other items of interest. It is worth paying more for a good guide. All guides must carry a license, which qualifies them as Naturalist I, II or III. Naturalist I guides have limited foreign-language and biology training, while Naturalist III guides are usually fluent in a foreign language and have a good academic background in natural sciences. Naturalist II lies in between.

Owners, captains, guides and cooks all change frequently; in addition, many boats make changes and improvements from year to year. Generally speaking, a boat is only as good as its crew. You should be able to meet the naturalist guide and captain and to inspect the boat. You can deal with a crew member or boat representative during your search, but don't hand over any money until you have an agreed itinerary.

You should get the itinerary in writing to avoid disagreements with other passengers and the crew during the cruise. Boats must register their itineraries with the National Park Service and with the port captain. Most itineraries are fixed in advance and cannot be changed. Generally, itineraries are good and include visits to some of the best visitor sites.

Prearranged Most visitors arrange tours before arriving at the islands. You can do this in your home country (expensive but efficient), or you can arrange something in Quito or Guayaquil (cheaper, but you sometimes have to wait several days or weeks during the high season). See the Quito and the Guayaquil & the South Coast chapters for more information on agencies that book Galápagos tours.

If you are trying to economize, you may find that you can get a substantial discount by checking various agencies and seeing if they have any spaces to fill on departures leaving in the next day or two. This applies both to the cheaper tours and to some of the pricier ones. Particularly out of the high season, agencies may well let you travel cheaply at the last minute rather than leave berths unfilled. This depends on luck and your skill at bargaining. We've heard stories of travelers paying $500 in Guayaquil for an eight-day tour aboard a first-class yacht, and then chatting on the deck with someone who paid over $1500 back home. But this won't happen in high season.

Safari Tours (e admin@safari.com.ec) has a database of tours and can often get you on a boat quickly at a reasonable price. **Sangay Touring** (w www.sangay.com) also has a good range of choices at fair prices. For both companies, see Travel Agencies & Tour Operators in the Quito chapter. **Galasam** (w www.Galapagos-islands.com) has offices in Quito and Guayaquil (see those chapters) and is well known for its economic cruises.

Seven-day economy tours use small boats with six to 12 bunks in double, triple and quad cabins. All bedding is provided, and accommodations are clean but spartan, with little privacy. Plenty of simple, fresh food and juice is served at all meals. Guides may speak English or may be educated in biology. There are toilets aboard, and fresh water is available for washing your face and drinking. Bathing facilities might consist of hosed sea water, but showers are available on some. Itineraries are preset and include visits to most of the central islands, allowing enough time to see the wildlife.

A one-week (eight-day) economy tour costs about $500 to $600 per person.

Shorter, cheaper tours are available – four days or five days for under $400. The $100 park fee, airfare and bottled drinks are not included. Typically, for a one-week tour, you will leave Quito on a specific morning (say Monday) and begin the boat tour Monday afternoon or evening. The tour may finish Sunday night or, possibly, Monday morning at the airport for your flight back.

Sometimes, a one-week tour is a combination of two shorter tours; for example, a Monday-to-Thursday tour combined with a Thursday-to-Monday tour. People that paid for a full week on this kind of tour spend most of Thursday dropping off and picking up passengers, so try to avoid this.

If you add up the cost of the cheapest one-week tour plus airfare and park fees, you get almost no change out of $1000. If you're going to spend this much, then seeing the Galápagos is probably important to you, and you will want to get as much out of it as possible. If economy class is all you can afford, and you really want to see the Galápagos, go! It'll probably be the adventure of a lifetime. But you might consider spending an extra few hundred dollars to go on a more comfortable, reliable boat and getting a decent guide (although the more expensive boats have their problems, too).

For about $700 to $800 for eight days, you can take a more comfortable tourist-class tour – the usual extra costs (airfare, fees and tips) apply. Many companies in Quito offer tours at about this price.

More luxurious boats are also available through agencies in Quito and Guayaquil. These typically are over (sometimes way over) $1000 per person per week, plus the usual extras. The most expensive boats are reasonably comfortable and have superb food and excellent crews. Many of these boats run prearranged tours with foreign groups; you are not likely to find them available for budget or independent travel. If you want this kind of luxury, a good travel agency in Ecuador or at home will be able to help you with information.

There are a few large cruise ships carrying up to 80 passengers. These ships have the advantage of having comfortable double cabins with private showers, and they are spacious and more stable than the smaller boats. Each ship carries at least four experienced, multilingual naturalist guides, and passengers divide into four groups and land on the islands at half-hour intervals, thus avoiding the horrendous scene of 79 other people trooping around a visitor site all at once. Tours can be for three, four or seven nights. Rates can range from $100 to over $200 per person per night, depending on your cabin and whether or not you share it. Information and reservations are available from any major travel agency in Quito or Guayaquil.

Dangers & Annoyances Lonely Planet has received some letters criticizing the economy-class tours, and even people traveling on more expensive boats have reported problems – anything from sinking boats to sexual harassment. The more common complaints include last-minute changes of boat (which the contractual small print allows), a poor crew, a lack of bottled drinks, changes in the itinerary, mechanical breakdowns and overbooking. Passengers share cabins and are not guaranteed that their cabin mates will be of the same gender; if you are uncomfortable sharing a cabin with a stranger of the opposite sex, make sure you are guaranteed in writing that you won't have to do this.

Because a boat is only as good as the crew running it, and because crews change relatively often, it is difficult to make blanket recommendations. Lonely Planet has not received consistently poor reports about any one boat, which suggests that problems are usually solved in the long run. Things go wrong from time to time, and when they do, a refund is difficult to obtain. If you have a problem, report it to the port captain at the *capitanía* (port captain) in Puerto Ayora. If you are unable to do so while in the islands, reports can be mailed to **El Capitán del Puerto** (*La Capitanía, Puerto Ayora, Galápagos, Ecuador*). Reports are taken seriously, and repeat offenders do get their comeuppance – voice your complaints. You should also report problems (in person or by email) to the **Cámara de Turismo** (*tourist information office;* **e** *infocptg@capturgal.org .ec*) in Puerto Ayora, which keeps a database of complaints to share with agencies and tourists.

GETTING THERE & AWAY
Air
TAME operates two daily morning flights from Quito via Guayaquil to the Isla Baltra airport, just over an hour away from Puerto Ayora by public transportation (see Getting Around the Islands later). It also flies on Monday, Wednesday and Saturday mornings from Quito via Guayaquil to San Cristóbal. AeroGal flies from Quito to San Cristóbal via Guayaquil on Wednesday and Saturday. All round-trip flights are in the afternoons of the same days.

Flights from Guayaquil cost $344 round trip and last 1½ hours. From Quito, flights cost $389 round trip and last 3¼ hours, due to the stop in Guayaquil (you do not have to get off the plane). Flights are slightly discounted in the low season.

Ecuadorian nationals can fly from Guayaquil for half the price foreigners pay, and Galápagos residents pay half that again. Some foreign residents of Ecuador or workers in the islands are also eligible, so if you have a residence visa you should make inquiries. Cheap flights to the islands are very difficult to get unless you are a resident.

There is a military logistic flight on every other Wednesday that occasionally has room for passengers. Ecuadorians are given priority, but they get cheap flights with TAME anyway, and so there are sometimes seats available for foreigners. Make inquiries at Avenida de la Prensa 3570, a few hundred meters from the Quito airport (ask for Departamento de Operaciones, Fuerza Aerea del Ecuador). Flights go from Quito via Guayaquil and stop at both San Cristóbal and Baltra. Foreigners pay about $300 roundtrip for either destination.

Flights to the Galápagos are sometimes booked solid well in advance, but you'll often find that there are many no-shows. Travel agencies book blocks of seats for their all-inclusive Galápagos tours. They will release the seats on the day of the flight when there is no longer any hope of selling their tour.

If you are tied to a definite itinerary, you should make a reservation; if you're flexible, you can buy your ticket at the airport when you want to fly. You have a better-than-even chance of getting a ticket, and it's unlikely that you'll be turned away two days in a row.

Boat
It's very hard to find boats to the Galápagos.

Cargo ships leave the Guayaquil's Muelle Sur Naval every few weeks and charge about $150, one way. Conditions are tolerable. The journey to the islands takes about 3½ days, and you should be prepared to bring a sleeping bag or hammock, although a bunk in a cabin may well be available. These ships are mainly for cargo purposes, not for wildlife viewing. If you stay aboard while the boat spends about a week making deliveries around the islands, you are charged about $50 a day, or you can get off and return later.

In 2003, the old, rusty *Marina 91* (*Guayaquil* ☎ 04-239 7370) was the only boat authorized to carry passengers. The *Virgen de Monserrat* (*Guayaquil* ☎ 04-229 6785) used to take passengers, but had no authorization at this time; this may change so it's worth a try. Be sure you see these boats before you drop any cash.

GETTING AROUND THE ISLANDS
Most people get around the islands by organized boat tours, but it's entirely possible to visit some of the islands independently. Santa Cruz, San Cristóbal, Santa María (Floreana) and Isabela all have accommodations and are reachable by inter-island boat rides or flights (which are pricey). Keep in mind, however, that although these islands have some splendid attractions, you'll only scratch the surface of the archipelago's natural wonders traveling independently.

To/From Baltra Airport
Most visitors (whether on a tour or traveling independently) fly to Isla Baltra, a small island practically touching Isla Santa Cruz. Outside the airport, you will be met by a boat representative (if you are on a pre-arranged tour) and taken by bus on a five-minute drive to the boat dock.

If you are traveling independently, don't take these buses. Instead, take the public bus that's signed 'Muelle' to the dock (a 10-minute ride) for the ferry to Isla Santa Cruz. A 10-minute ferry ride will take you across to Santa Cruz, where you will be met by a bus to take you to Puerto Ayora, about 45 minutes away. This drive (on a paved road) provides a good look at the interior and highlands of Santa Cruz – dry in the north and greener and wetter in the highlands and on the southern slopes. The ferry and second bus are scheduled to coincide with the departure of the first bus from the airport, so there isn't much waiting involved. You should be in Puerto Ayora about an hour after leaving the airport.

The combined bus/ferry/bus trip costs about $2.50. You can buy your ticket on the bus or one of the ticket booths near the airport exit. The ride is always crowded.

Buses from Puerto Ayora to Baltra (via the ferry) leave early every morning to meet the first flight from Baltra, and again later if there is a second flight. Tickets are sold at the CITTEG office. These same buses return from the airport after the plane from the mainland has landed. A second and third bus will run if there is enough demand.

Air

The small airline, **EMETEBE** (Puerto Ayora ☎ 526 177, San Cristóbal ☎ 520 036, Puerto Villamil ☎ 529 155), flies a five-passenger aircraft between the islands. It offers two to three flights a week between Baltra and Puerto Villamil (Isla Isabela), between Baltra and San Cristóbal, and between San Cristóbal and Puerto Villamil. Fares are about $120 one way, and there is a 13kg baggage-weight limit per person (although this is flexible if the plane isn't full). EMETEBE also has an **office** (☎ 04-229 2492) in Guayaquil.

Boat

Ingala (Puerto Ayora ☎ 526 151, 526 199) operates passenger ferry services aboard the *Ingala II*. It goes from Santa Cruz to San Cristóbal about three times per week, from Santa Cruz to Isabela about twice monthly (usually on a Friday) and once a month from Isabela to Floreana. The office in Puerto Ayora can give you up-to-date details, as can the Camará de Turismo (tourist information office) in Puerto Ayora. Departure times change often.

Fares are $50 for foreigners (sometimes cheaper in low season if you bargain) on any passage and are purchased the day of departure. For more information, see the respective town sections, later. If you can't get on an Ingala boat, ask around for private trips, which are more expensive. The port captain knows which boats are scheduled to depart soon, as well as their destinations.

The cheapest rides are usually on the smaller (but often faster) private boats that zip between the islands with supplies and occasional passengers. Ask around the harbors. These are easiest to find in the busier ports of Puerto Ayora and Puerto Baquerizo Moreno (San Cristóbal).

FEES & TAXES

The $100 Galápagos national-park fee – payable only in cash – must be paid at one of the airports after you arrive. You will not be allowed to leave the airport until you pay. Make sure you have your passport available when you pay your fees and hang on to your ticket until you leave.

ISLA BALTRA

Most visitors' first experience of the Galápagos is from the archipelago's main airport at Isla Baltra. Baltra is a small island (27 sq km) off the north coast of Santa Cruz. Nearly all tours begin here or in the town of Puerto Ayora, about one hour away (by a bus-boat-bus combination) on Isla Santa Cruz. There are no visitor sites or accommodations, but both public and private transportation from the airport to Puerto Ayora is available. Those on a prearranged tour are often met at the airport and taken to their boats – a host of pelicans and noddies will greet you as you arrive at the harbor, and you can begin your wildlife watching within minutes of leaving the airport. Public transportation is described under Puerto Ayora (see Isla Santa Cruz following).

ISLA SANTA CRUZ

With an area of 986 sq km, this is the second-largest island in the archipelago. A road crosses Santa Cruz from north to south and gives the visitor the easiest opportunity of seeing some of the highland interior of the island. The highest point is Cerro Crocker (864m).

This island has the highest population and the greatest number of tourist facilities. The main town is Puerto Ayora, where most visitors either stay while arranging a boat or anchor sometime during their cruise in the famous harbor of Academy Bay. In addition to the tourist facilities, there are about 10 national-park visitor sites and one privately owned visitor site on Santa Cruz.

Visitor Sites

About a 20-minute walk by road northeast of Puerto Ayora, the **Charles Darwin Research Station** *(open 7:30am-5pm daily)* can also be reached by dry landing from Academy Bay. It contains a national-park information center; an informative museum in the Van Straelen Exhibition Center (where a video in English or Spanish is presented several times a day); a baby-tortoise house with incubators, where you can see hatchlings and young tortoises; and a walk-in adult tortoise enclosure, where you can meet the Galápagos giants face to face. The tiny tortoises in the baby tortoise house are repatriated to their home islands when they weigh about 1.5kg (or are about four years old) – some 2000 have been repatriated so far. In the adult enclosures you can get close enough to touch the tortoises, but touching is not allowed. An elevated wooden boardwalk goes through the most interesting areas.

Several of the 11 remaining subspecies of tortoise can be seen here. **Lonesome George**, the only surviving member of the Isla Pinta subspecies, is also here and can be viewed from the boardwalk. Although the chances of finding a Pinta female to breed with George are remote, attempts are being made to allow him to mate with a female from a closely related subspecies from Volcán Wolf. So far, he hasn't shown much interest, but things move slowly in the tortoise world.

Other attractions include paths through arid-zone vegetation, such as salt bush, mangroves and prickly pear and other cacti. A variety of land birds, including Darwin's finches, can be seen. T-shirts and other souvenirs are sold to support the research station.

Southwest of Puerto Ayora, a 3km trail takes you to **Turtle Bay**, where you'll find a very fine white-sand beach and a spit of land providing protected swimming (there are strong currents on the exposed side of the spit). There are sharks, marine iguanas and a variety of waterbirds – including pelicans and the occasional flamingo. There are also mangroves. This is one of the few visitor sites where you can go without a guide, although there is no drinking water or other facilities. To get there, find the trail and hike out for about half an hour.

Several sites of interest in the highlands of Santa Cruz can be reached from the trans-island road. Access to some sites is through colonized areas, so respect private property. From the village of Bellavista, 7km north of Puerto Ayora by road, one can turn either west on the main road continuing to Isla Baltra or east on a road leading in about 2km to the **lava tubes** *(admission $2)*. These underground tunnels are more than a kilometer in length and were formed by the solidifying of the outside skin of a molten lava flow. When the lava flow ceased, the molten lava inside the flow kept going, emptying out of the solidified skin and thus leaving tunnels. Because they are on private property, they can be visited without an official guide. The owners of the land provide information, guides and flashlights (bring your own flashlight to be sure) included in the entrance fee. Tours to the lava tubes are offered in Puerto Ayora.

North of Bellavista is the national-park land known as the **highlands**. A footpath from Bellavista leads toward Cerro Crocker and other hills and extinct volcanoes. This is a good chance to see the vegetation of the Scalesia, Miconia and fern-sedge zones (see Habitats, under Flora & Fauna, in the Facts about Ecuador chapter) and to look for birds such as the vermilion flycatcher or the elusive Galápagos rail and paint-billed crake. It is around 5km from Bellavista to the crescent-shaped hill of Media Luna and 3km further to the base of Cerro Crocker. This is national-park, so a guide is required.

A part of the highlands that can be visited from the road are the twin craters called **Los Gemelos**. These are actually sinkholes, not volcanic craters, and they are surrounded by Scalesia forest. Vermilion flycatchers are often seen here, as well as short-eared owls on occasion. Los Gemelos are reached by taking the road to the village of Santa Rosa, about 12km west of Bellavista, and continuing about 2km beyond Santa Rosa on the trans-island road. Although the craters lie only 25m and 125m on either side of the road, they are hidden by vegetation, so ask your driver to stop at the short trailhead.

Near Santa Rosa, is **El Chato Tortoise Reserve**, where you can observe giant tortoises in the wild. The reserve is also a good place to look for short-eared owls, Darwin's finches, yellow warblers, Galápagos rails and paint-billed crakes (these last two are difficult to see in the long grass).

A trail from Santa Rosa leads through private property to park land about 3km away. The trail is downhill and often muddy. Horses can be hired in Santa Rosa – ask at the store/bar on the main road for directions to the outfitter's house. The trail forks at the park boundary, with the right fork going up to the small hill of Cerro Chato (3km further) and the left fork going to La Caseta (2km). The trails can be hard to follow, and you should carry water. The reserve is part of the national park, and a guide is required. In 1991, a tourist entered the reserve without a guide, got hopelessly lost and died of thirst.

Next to the reserve is a **private ranch** *(admission $2)* owned by the Devine family. This place often has dozens of giant tortoises on it, and you can wander around at will and take photos for a fee. The entrance is beyond Santa Rosa, off the main road – ask locals for directions. Stay on the main tracks to avoid getting lost. Remember to close any gates that you go through. There is a café selling cold drinks and hot tea, which is welcome if the highland mist has soaked you.

The remaining Santa Cruz visitor sites are reached by boat and with guides. On the west coast are **Whale Bay** and **Conway Bay**, and on the north coast are **Black Turtle Cove** (Caleta Tortuga Negra) and **Las Bachas**. Between these two areas is the relatively new visitor site of **Cerro Dragón**. Conway Bay has a 1.5km trail passing a lagoon with flamingos; Whale Bay isn't visited very often. North of Conway Bay, Cerro Dragón has two small lagoons that may have flamingos and a 1.75km trail that leads through a forest of *palo santo* trees and opuntia cacti to a small hill with good views. There are some large repatriated land iguanas here.

There is no landing site in Black Turtle Cove, which is normally visited by *panga* (small boats) ride. The cove has many little inlets and is surrounded by mangroves, where you can see lava herons and pelicans. The main attraction is in the water: marine turtles are sometimes seen mating, schools of golden mustard rays are often present, and white-tipped sharks may be seen basking in the shallows. It makes a very pleasant change to visit a marine site in a *panga* instead of walking. This site is occasionally visited by day boats from Puerto Ayora. The nearby Las Bachas beach, although popular for sunbathing and swimming, is often deserted.

Puerto Ayora
pop 12,000
This town is on the central island of Santa Cruz, and it is where most visitors stay and visit. The population is growing (too) fast and has doubled in less than a decade. This is because of immigration from mainland Ecuador, and new laws are attempting to control the growth. There are the usual amenities: hotels, bars and restaurants, stores, a Pacifictel office, a post office, a TAME office, tourist agencies and information, a basic hospital, churches and a radio station. The airport is at Isla Baltra, about an hour away.

Tourist Offices You can get hotel information, maps and schedules for local boat transportation at the friendly **Cámara de Turismo** *(tourist information office; Capturgal;* ☎ *526 206;* e *infocptg@capturgal.org.ec;* w *www.galapagoschamberoftourism.com; Avenida Charles Darwin; open 7:30am-noon & 2pm-5:30pm Mon-Fri).* Perhaps more importantly, you should report any complaints here about boats, tours, guides or crew – it's kept on file to provide ratings to other tourists and agencies. The **municipal tourist office** *(Av Charles Darwin)* is moderately helpful at best.

Money The only bank is **Banco del Pacífico** *(Avenida Charles Darwin)*, which gives cash advances on MasterCards, changes traveler's checks and has an ATM. The better hotels accept major credit cards.

Post & Communications There's a **post office** near the harbor and a **Pacifictel office** *(Avenida Padre Julieo Herrera)*. The Internet service is cheapest and fastest at **Compumatic** *(Bolívar Naveda)* where connections cost $2 per hour; otherwise try **Pelikan.net** *(Avenida Charles Darwin)* at $3 per hour. The bar **Limón y Café** *(Av Charles Darwin)*, also charges $3 per hour and you can drink a beer while you type.

Travel Agencies & Tour Operators There are several self-styled 'information centers' near the waterfront that will give you information about day trips and boat charters. It cannot be overemphasized that a cheap tour based at Puerto Ayora, visiting other islands on day trips, gives you only a superficial look at the Galápagos. Stay in Puerto Ayora by all means, but make every effort to visit the islands by taking a cruise of at least several days' duration – preferably a full week or more.

Most travel agencies are found along Avenida Charles Darwin. **Moonrise Travel** (☎ 526 402/03, 526 348, 526 589; e *sde vine@pa.ga.pro.ec*) is run by the Devine family, who are well established as Galápagos experts and guides. They can help with finding a tour boat or with confirming a flight, in addition to other things.

Other travel agencies that may be able to help with cheap, last-minute tours are **Galapatour** (☎ 526 088; *Avenida Rodriguez Lara & Genovesa*), behind the municipal market, and **Galaven** (☎ 526 359; e *galaven@ pa.ga.pro.ec*), at the harbor.

Hotel Lobo del Mar (see Places to Stay) operates the 'tourist-superior' class motor yacht *Lobo del Mar*, so it's a good place to check for last minute cruise deals. The hotel also organizes various day trips to other islands.

Hotel Delfín (☎ 526 297/8), along with Metropolitan Touring, operate the fastest day-tour yacht at Santa Cruz, the *Delfín II*. It visits some of the closer islands, and, because it's fast, you spend less time on the boat. The price is $115, and includes snorkeling (and gear), a buffet lunch and guides. Visit Hotel Delfín for more information – also see Places to Stay later.

Galápagos Tour Center (*cnr Pelícano & Avenida Padre Julio Herrera*) offers half-day snorkeling trips and half-day trips to the highlands (each $25 per person). It also rents mountain bikes (half day/full day $8/15), surfboards ($8/18), snorkel equipment and boogie boards.

Red Mangrove Inn (☎/fax 526 277) offers day tours to Islas Plazas, Seymour and Santa Fe. It also rents sea kayaks, surfboards, mountain bikes and snorkel equipment (see Places To Stay).

Laundry You can have your clothes washed and dried in about three hours at **Lavandería Central** (*Charles Binford; open 7am-10pm daily*) for $1 per kg.

Medical Services The town's hospital is not very sophisticated and is poorly supplied. **Protesub** (☎ 526 911, 09-985 5911, 09-928 3994; *18 de Febrero*) has a state-of-

the-art recompression chamber for divers with the bends and offers 24-hour emergency service and medical consultations, including gynecology. It has a good reputation, and several languages are spoken. Hotel calls cost $30 and drop-in consultations cost $25.

Diving Companies all over the world can arrange diving tours on boats in the Galápagos. In Puerto Ayora, two professional dive centers have been frequently recommended. Rates vary from about $100 to $120 for two dives per day, depending on the destination. A popular nearby dive site is **Gordon Rocks** where there's a good chance of seeing hammerhead sharks and other large fish; you should have at least 20 dives under your belt, however, before you dive here.

Galápagos Sub-Aqua (☎/fax 526 350, 526 633; w *www.galapagos-sub-aqua.com*; *Avenida Charles Darwin*) also has an **information office** (☎/fax 04-230 5514; *Orellana 211 & Panamá, Office 402*) in Guayaquil. Galápagos Sub-Aqua is a full-service dive center. If you have never dived before, they can supply you with all the equipment and teach you what you need to know. Certified divers (who must have their PADI or NAUI cards) can take anything from a couple of dives to tours of various numbers of days. You can also get any PADI certification, from open-water to dive master. Most of the instructors are licensed Galápagos guides, very friendly and speak English.

Scuba Iguana (☎/fax 526 497, ☎ 526 296; w *www.scubaiguana.com*), in the Hotel Galápagos, is run by experienced dive master Mathias Espinosa, who has guided Galápagos dives since the 1980s and is an underwater photographer, and by Hotel Galápagos owner, Jack Nelson, who has guided in the Galápagos for over 30 years. Full certification courses are offered, and you can arrange for guides to pick you up on your cruise to take you diving. Trips can also be booked online or at the Quito office (see Travel Agencies & Tour Operators in the Quito chapter).

Places to Stay Hotels in Puerto Ayora range from cheap and basic to 1st class – by Galápagos standards, at least. Prices tend to rise during the heaviest tourism seasons (December to January and June to August).

Street numbers aren't used in Puerto Ayora.

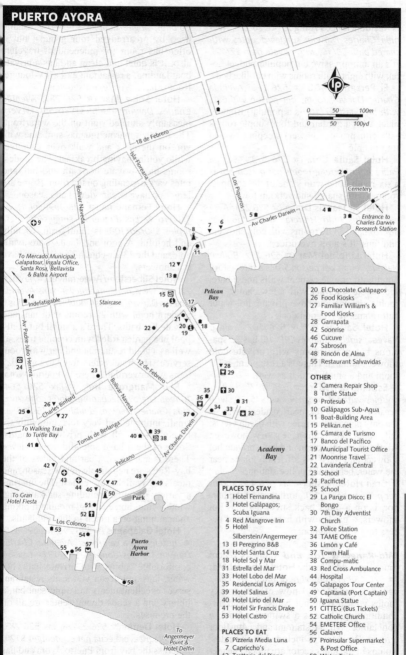

PUERTO AYORA

Cemetery

Entrance to Charles Darwin Research Station

To Mercado Municipal, Galapatour, Ingala Office, Santa Rosa, Bellavista & Baltra Airport

Pelican Bay

Staircase

Indefatigable

Academy Bay

Puerto Ayora Harbor

To Walking Trail to Turtle Bay

To Gran Hotel Fiesta

Park

Los Colonos

To Angermeyer Point & Hotel Delfin

20 El Chocolate Galápagos
26 Food Kiosks
27 Familiar William's & Food Kiosks
28 Garrapata
42 Soonrise
46 Cucuve
47 Sabrosón
48 Rincón de Alma
55 Restaurant Salvavidas

OTHER

2 Camera Repair Shop
8 Turtle Statue
9 Protesub
10 Galápagos Sub-Aqua
11 Boat-Building Area
15 Pelikan.net
16 Cámara de Turismo
17 Banco del Pacífico
19 Municipal Tourist Office
21 Moonrise Travel
22 Lavandería Central
23 School
24 Pacifictel
25 School
29 La Panga Disco; El Bongo
30 7th Day Adventist Church
32 Police Station
34 TAME Office
36 Limón y Café
37 Town Hall
38 Compu-matic
43 Red Cross Ambulance
44 Hospital
45 Galapagos Tour Center
49 Capitanía (Port Captain)
50 Iguana Statue
51 CITTEG (Bus Tickets)
52 Catholic Church
54 EMETEBE Office
56 Galaven
57 Proinsular Supermarket & Post Office
58 Water Taxis

PLACES TO STAY

1 Hotel Fernandina
3 Hotel Galápagos; Scuba Iguana
4 Red Mangrove Inn
5 Hotel Silberstein/Angermeyer
13 El Peregrino B&B
14 Hotel Santa Cruz
18 Hotel Sol y Mar
31 Estrella del Mar
33 Hotel Lobo del Mar
35 Residencial Los Amigos
39 Hotel Salinas
40 Hotel Lirio del Mar
41 Hotel Sir Francis Drake
53 Hotel Castro

PLACES TO EAT

6 Pizzería Media Luna
7 Capriccho's
12 Trattoria del Pippo

0   50   100m
0   50   100yd

18 de Febrero
Isla Floreana
Los Piqueros
Av Charles Darwin
Bolivar Naveda
12 de Febrero
Bolivar Naveda
Charles Binford
Tomás de Berlanga
Pelicano
Av Padre Julio Herrera
Av Charles Darwin

THE GALÁPAGOS ISLANDS

Budget One of the cheapest places to stay is **Residencial Los Amigos** (☎ 526 265; Avenida Charles Darwin; singles/doubles with shared bath $6/10, with private bath $7/12). It's an unimpressive but popular budget hotel, with eight plain rooms with cot-like beds.

El Peregrino B&B (☎ 526 323; Avenida Charles Darwin; rooms per person without/with breakfast $7/10) is a popular, friendly place with a garden and four simple rooms (all with private shower) sleeping two to four people.

Hotel Santa Cruz (☎ 526 573; Avenida Padre Julio Herrera; rooms per person $5) is a six-room hotel with some of the cheapest rooms (with shared showers) in town.

Hotel Sir Francis Drake (☎ 526 221; Avenida Padre Julio Herrera; singles/doubles $8/15) has 13 OK rooms with cold showers and fans. It's a bit overpriced.

Hotel Lirio del Mar (☎ 526 212; Bolívar Naveda; rooms per person $8) is a three-story hotel with orange cement walls and a bare, second-story terrace with a few chairs. The rooms are fine and have private, hot-water bathrooms. It's a good deal.

Hotel Salinas (☎/fax 526 107; Bolívar Naveda; singles/doubles $10/16) has 22 spacious but plain rooms with private cold shower and fans. There is a restaurant, a TV room and a small garden as well.

Estrella del Mar (☎ 526 427; singles/doubles without ocean views $15/20, with ocean views $18/30), near Academy Bay, is the only place at this price with ocean views; only about four rooms have a view, however. All the rooms are clean and have private hot showers and fans. It's a friendly place near the water, behind the police station.

Gran Hotel Fiesta (☎/fax 526 440; rooms per person about $12), northwest of the harbor, is on a quiet back street and has hot showers, a garden with hammocks and access to a small lagoon.

Mid-Range & Top End With its recent four-story addition, the **Hotel Lobo del Mar** (☎ 526 188; 12 de Febrero; rooms in older/newer sector $17/50) now offers swanky rooms with private hot baths, TV and air-conditioning. There's a swimming pool, a pool table, a bar, a restaurant and a 4th-floor terrace. Breakfast is included in the rates. Rooms in the older sector are much cheaper and have fans and private hot baths.

Hotel Castro (☎ 526 508/9, 526 113; Los Colonos; singles/doubles $34/44) is usually used by prearranged tour groups, but it often has room for independent travelers also. It is quiet and clean and has a private boat landing, a restaurant and a TV lounge. Rooms have private hot showers.

Hotel Sol y Mar (☎ 526 281; Avenida Charles Darwin; doubles $30-55) is very pleasantly situated right on the waterfront. The resident marine iguanas sunbathe with you on the deck and walk over your feet while you're having breakfast. The modest rooms have private hot bath and fan, and rates vary depending on the room (some are larger or have ocean views) and season.

Hotel Fernandina (☎ 526 499; cnr 18 de Febrero & Los Piqueros; singles/doubles/triples $50/80/108) is family-run, friendly and helpful. A pool and Jacuzzi are available, and the 13 air-conditioned rooms have hot showers.

Hotel Silberstein/Angermeyer (☎/fax 526 277; w www.hotelangermeyer.com; Avenida Charles Darwin; singles/doubles $79/120) is a modern hotel with 22 rooms with fans and private hot baths. There's a small but pretty pool in a garden filled with coconut trees, as well as a good restaurant and bar with room service. The hotel offers four- to eight-day tours with overnights here in Puerto Ayora.

Red Mangrove Inn (☎/fax 526 564; e redmangrove@ecuadorexplorer.com; Avenida Charles Darwin; doubles $116-213) is small, intimate and very relaxing, with six lovely rooms, all with private hot baths. Some of them have splendid ocean views. There is a Jacuzzi, a bar and views of the bay. Rates are negotiable in low season, and meals are available on request. The inn runs a variety of tours, including sea-kayaking, windsurfing, horse riding, mountain biking and camping on a ranch in the highlands.

Hotel Galápagos (☎ 526 296, fax 526 330; e hotelgps@pa.ga.pro.ec; Avenida Charles Darwin; singles/doubles $79/137) has 14 comfortable cabins with private bath, hot water, fans and ocean views. Its restaurant serves excellent meals and a pleasant bar, a library and a scuba-diving center are all on the premises.

Hotel Delfín (☎ 526 297/8, fax 526 283; e indefagi@ayora.ecua.net.ec; doubles $125) is across the bay from Puerto Ayora and has a small semiprivate beach, which is visible from many of its 21 rooms. All rooms have private bathrooms, and rates are slightly lower than those of the other good hotels and include breakfast. It's a fairly large place, with a restaurant/bar and a pool. The hotel is a quick zip across the harbor by boat (walk down to the harbor and hail a water taxi). The hotel is used as a base for day tours organized by **Metropolitan Touring** (W www.metropolitan-touring.com); see Travel Agencies & Tour Operators in the Quito chapter.

Places to Eat Puerto Ayora's restaurants and bars are good places to meet people. You can buy food and drinks in stores, but the choice is limited and expensive compared to the mainland. The cheapest is **Proinsular Market** (Avenida Charles Darwin) by the harbor. Lobster is sold in some restaurants but has been dramatically overfished, so consider foregoing lobster meals on the islands.

The cheapest places to eat are found out along Avenida Padre Julio Herrera. **Cucuve** (Avenida Padre Julio Herrera), at the southeast end, sells a variety of hot snacks, and **Sabrosón** (Avenida Padre Julio Herrera), across the street, does open-air parrilladas (grilled meats).

Soonrise (Avenida Padre Julio Herrera) is good for breakfasts of yogurt and fruit salad, as well as cheap set lunches.

East from this street, along Charles Binford, are a number of very popular kiosks selling cheap and well-prepared meals – mainly fish and meat dishes. The most popular of all is **Familiar William's** (encocados $4-7; open 6pm-10pm Tues-Sun) which is famous for its mouthwatering encocados (fish, shrimp or lobster smothered in a savory coconut sauce).

El Chocolate Galápagos (Avenida Charles Darwin; mains $3-6; open 7:30am-10pm Mon-Sat) is great for breakfast, and there's always a chocolate cake on hand.

Trattoria del Pippo (Avenida Charles Darwin; pizzas $3-5; open 5pm-10pm daily) has a wide selection of pizzas and other Italian and international dishes. It's a relaxing place with good food.

Capriccho's has organic food and vegetable salads. **Pizzería Media Luna** (mains $4-8; open 3pm-10pm Wed-Mon), near Capriccho's, has decent pizzas, as well as sandwiches and brownies.

Angermeyer Point (☎ 527 007; Punta Estrada; mains $8-10.50; open 7am-11pm Tues-Sat, 11am-4pm Sun) has an unbeatable location out on the point, just across the harbor mouth. It's in the former home of painter Carl Angermeyer, and there are patio tables over the water and a full bar. Service is tops and the food is geared toward tourists – Cajun fish and Jack Daniels Steak, to give you an idea. The all-you-can-eat Sunday brunch ($18.50) is reportedly outstanding. Saturday's happy hour means two-for-one drinks. To get there, hail a water taxi ($0.50) from the harbor.

Restaurant Salvavidas (☎ 526 416; mains $6-11; open 9am-8pm Mon-Sat), down by the dock, has, under various names, been the standard daytime dockside meeting place for years. You can grab a beer, snack or meal here while waiting for your panga.

Rincón de Alma (☎ 526 196; Avenida Charles Darwin; mains $6-8; open 7am-9pm daily) is popular for breakfasts, fast food and cheap set lunches.

Garrapata (☎ 526 264; Avenida Charles Darwin; mains $7-9; open 7pm-10pm Mon-Sat), next to the La Panga disco, is considered to be the best restaurant in town – it serves seafood, imaginative chicken dishes and nine different pastas. The service is friendly and it has a bar.

Most of the hotels have restaurants as well (see Places to Stay earlier).

Entertainment The following places are on Avenida Charles Darwin. The most popular disco in town is **La Panga** (Avenida Charles Darwin), next to Garrapata. Most people start out with drinks at the equally popular bar **El Bongo** (Avenida Charles Darwin), downstairs. Always busy on weekends, **Limón y Café** (Avenida Charles Darwin) is a laid-back little hang-out with a pool.

La Taberna del Duende, in Barrio Miraflores, has live music Thursday through Saturday nights. A taxi ride there should cost $0.80 – cab drivers know the place.

Shopping You can purchase the famous Galápagos T-shirts in most souvenir shops, but the profits from those sold at the Charles Darwin Research Station go to support this worthwhile institution. Avoid buying objects made from black coral, turtle and tortoise shell. These threatened species are protected, and it is illegal to use these animal products for the manufacture of novelties.

Many postcards are photographs or drawings by Tui de Roy, a resident famous for her beautifully illustrated books on Galápagos wildlife. Her mother, Jacqueline, and brother, Gil, make silver jewelry of the Galápagos animals. Their work is not cheap but it's well worth it – keep your eyes peeled.

You are advised to stock up on sunblock, insect repellent, toiletries, film and medications on the mainland. These are available in Puerto Ayora, but selection is slimmer and more expensive than on the mainland.

Getting There & Away Reconfirming your flight departures at the **TAME office** (☎ 526 165, 526 527; *Avenida Charles Darwin; open 7am-noon Mon-Sat & 1pm-4pm Mon-Fri*) is essential. Flights are often full, and there is sometimes difficulty in changing your reservation or buying a ticket. **EMETEBE** (☎ 526 177; *Avenida Charles Darwin*) flies at least twice weekly to Puerto Baquerizo Moreno (San Cristóbal) and Puerto Villamil (Isabela). Both flights cost $120 one way and are in five-seat light aircraft; there's a 13kg (30 lb) baggage-weight maximum per passenger (although this is flexible if the plane isn't full). You must reserve your ticket at least a few days in advance and then purchase it the day before the flight. Departure times vary flight to flight.

The *capitanía* has information about (infrequent) boats to the mainland (see Getting Around the Islands earlier in this chapter) and has details of every boat sailing from Puerto Ayora.

The passenger ferry *Ingala II* sails two to three times a week to San Cristóbal and two Fridays each month to Isabela. Both trips are about four hours and cost $50. Tickets are sold the day of departure below the EMETEBE office near the harbor. You can pick up schedules for the *Ingala II* at the Cámara de Turismo (tourist information office), at the *capitanía* and at the main **Ingala office** (☎ 526 151, 527 001, 526 199), north of the harbor off Avenida Padre Julio Herrera.

Ask at Restaurant Salvavidas about open skiffs that usually head daily to Isabela and San Cristóbal. They reach the islands in less than three hours and charge about $30. There are no toilets on these little boats and the ride can be rough.

Getting Around The CITTEG buses that leave from Puerto Ayora for the Baltra airport (see To/From Baltra Airport under Getting Around the Islands earlier) will drop you off at the villages of Bellavista or Santa Rosa to explore some of the interior. Also, CITTEG buses from Puerto Ayora to Santa Rosa (about $1) leave from the corner of Padre Julio Herrera and Charles Binford four or five times a day Monday to Saturday and less often on Sunday. Charters can be arranged for groups.

Note that neither of these villages had hotels at this time. The most convenient way of seeing the interior and ensuring that you don't get stuck is to hire a bus or truck for the day with a group of other travelers.

ISLAS PLAZAS

These two small islands are just off the east coast of Santa Cruz and can be visited on a day trip from Puerto Ayora. The heavy volume of visitors has led to some trail erosion.

The two islands were formed by uplift due to faulting. Boats anchor between them, and visitors can land on **South Plaza** (the larger of the islands), which is only about 13 hectares in area. A dry landing on a jetty brings you to an opuntia cactus forest, where there are many land iguanas. A 1km trail circuit leads visitors through sea lion colonies and along a cliff-top walk where swallow-tailed gulls and other species nest. The 25m-high **cliffs** are a superb vantage point to watch various seabirds, such as red-billed tropicbirds, frigatebirds, pelicans and Audubon's shearwaters. Snorkeling with the sea lions is a possibility, and out to sea, you may glimpse a manta ray 'flying.' Cactus forest, land iguanas, sea lions, seabirds galore – no wonder this is a favorite wildlife-watching site.

ISLAS SEYMOUR & MOSQUERA

Separated from Isla Baltra by a channel, Isla Seymour is a 1.9-sq-km uplifted island with a dry landing. There is a circular trail (about 2.5km) leading through some of the largest and most active seabird-breeding colonies in the islands. Magnificent frigatebirds and blue-footed boobies are the main attractions. Whatever time of year you come, there is always some kind of courtship, mating, nesting or chick rearing to observe. You can get close to the nests, as there is always at least one pair of boobies that chooses the middle of the trail as the best place to build their nest. Swallow-tailed gulls also nest here, and other birds are often seen as well. Sea lions and marine iguanas are common, and occasional fur seals, lava lizards and Galápagos snakes are seen too. This is a small island, but it is well worth visiting for the wildlife.

Isla Mosquera is a tiny sandy island (about 120m by 600m) that lies in the channel between Islas Baltra and Seymour. There's no trail, but visitors land on the sandy beach to see the sea lion colony. Swimming and snorkeling with the sea lions is a popular activity.

ISLAS DAPHNE

These two islands of obviously volcanic origin are roughly 10km west of Seymour. **Daphne Minor** is the one that is very eroded, while **Daphne Major** retains most of its typically volcanic shape (called a tuff cone). A short but steep trail leads to the 120m-high summit of this tiny island.

There are two small craters at the top of the cone, and they contain hundreds of blue-footed booby nests. Masked boobies nest on the crater rims, and a few red-billed tropicbirds nest in rocky crevices in the steep sides of the islands.

The island is difficult to visit because of the acrobatic landing – visitors have to jump from a moving *panga* on to a vertical cliff and scramble their way up the rocks. The steep slopes are fragile and susceptible to erosion, which has led the national park authorities to limit visits to the island. Either you have to be lucky or you'll have arrange your visit well in advance.

ISLA SANTA FÉ

This 24-sq-km island, about 20km southeast of Santa Cruz, is a popular destination for day trips. There is a good anchorage in an attractive bay on the northeast coast, and a wet landing gives the visitor a choice of two trails. A 300m trail takes you to one of the tallest stands of opuntia cactus in the islands. Some of the cacti here are over 10m high. A somewhat more strenuous 1.5km rough trail goes into the highlands, where the Santa Fé land iguana may be seen if you are lucky. This species of iguana is found nowhere else in the world. The endemic rice rat is sometimes seen under bushes by the coast. Other attractions include a sea lion colony, excellent snorkeling, marine iguanas and, of course, birds.

ISLA SAN CRISTÓBAL

This 558-sq-km island is the fifth-largest in the archipelago and has the second-largest population. The provincial capital, Puerto Baquerizo Moreno, is on the southwest point. Despite being the capital, there is less tourist traffic here than in the larger town of Puerto Ayora, on Isla Santa Cruz.

There are several visitor sites on or near San Cristóbal, but they are not frequently visited by boats from Santa Cruz. The Chatham mockingbird, is common throughout the island and found nowhere else.

Visitor Sites

About 1.5km southeast of Puerto Baquerizo Moreno is **Cerro de las Tijeretas** (Frigatebird Hill). It can be reached without a guide via a foot trail. From the hill, there is a view of a bay below and the town behind. Both species of frigatebirds have nested here, but pressure from the nearby town appears to be driving them away.

A road leads from the capital to the village of El Progreso, about 8km to the east and at the base of the 896m-high Cerro San Joaquín, the highest point on San Cristóbal (buses go here several times a day from Puerto Baquerizo Moreno). Rent a jeep or walk east along a dirt road about 10km further to **El Junco Lagoon** – a freshwater lake at about 700m above sea level. It's one of the few permanent freshwater bodies in the Galápagos. Here you can see white-cheeked pintails and common gallinules and observe the typical highland Miconia vegetation and endemic tree ferns. The weather is often misty or rainy.

Smaller than its name suggests, **Puerto Grande** is a well-protected little cove on San Cristóbal's northwestern coast. There is a good, sandy beach suitable for swimming. Various seabirds can be seen, but the site is not known for any special colonies.

About an hour northeast of Puerto Baquerizo Moreno by boat is the tiny, rocky **Isla Lobos**, the main sea lion and blue-footed booby colony for visitors to San Cristóbal. There is a 300m-long trail where lava lizards are often seen. Both the boat crossing and the trail tend to be rough, and there are better wildlife colonies elsewhere.

About a two-hour boat ride northeast of Puerto Baquerizo Moreno, is another little rocky island that, because of a resemblance to a sleeping lion, is named **León Dormido**. The English name is Kicker Rock. The island is a sheer-walled tuff cone that has been eroded in half; smaller boats can sail between the two rocks. Because the sheer walls provide no place to land, this site can only be seen from a passing boat.

At the northern end of the island is **Los Galápagos**, where you can often see the giant Galápagos tortoises in the wild, although it takes some effort to get to the highland area where they live. One way to get there is to land in a bay at the north end of the island and hike up – it takes about two hours to reach the tortoise area by the trail. Some visitors report seeing many tortoises, others see none. Good luck! The road from Puerto Baquerizo Moreno through El Progreso and on to El Junco Lagoon is slowly being pushed northeast. It may be possible to get to Los Galápagos by taking this road to the end and hiking in – ask in town.

The northeasternmost point of the island is **Punta Pitt**, where volcanic tuff formations are of interest to geologists (and attractive in their own right), but the unique feature of this site is that it is the only one on which you can see all three Galápagos booby species nesting. The walk is a little strenuous, but it is rewarding.

Other visitor sites on this island include **Cerro Brujo**, near the coast, and **Turtle Bay**. Both are at the northeast end and can be visited in association with Punta Pitt and Los Galápagos. Flamingos and turtles are among the attractions.

Puerto Baquerizo Moreno
pop 5400
This is the capital of the Galápagos and everyone here just calls it 'Cristóbal' (even though that's the name of the island). It's a laid-back little fishing port village with a vacuum-like ability to suck you in and not let you leave. The surfing is world-class, and you can explore many places on the island from here on your own. It's much smaller than Puerto Ayora.

Orientation From the airport it's a short walk to town along Avenida Alsacio Northia.

The waterfront Avenida Charles Darwin (usually called the Malecón) is the main drag. If you stand on the Malecón facing the sea, to your right (east), you'll see the small hill called Cerro de las Tijeretas (Frigatebird Hill). To your left is the naval base. The two streets behind you, running parallel to the Malecón, are Cobos and then Avenida Alsacio Northia, which leads west back to the airport.

Information You'll usually find that the **tourist information office** (☎ 521 124, 520 592; **e** aguerrero@galapagoschamberoftourism.org; Avenida Charles Darwin) has tourist maps of town and the island.

Banco del Pacífico (Avenida Charles Darwin; open 8am-3:30pm daily) changes traveler's checks and has a MasterCard-only ATM. Phone service is poor, but this is being improved.

Slow, expensive Internet service is available at **Cyber Jean Carlos** (Calle Española) for $4.50 per hour.

Chalo's Tours (☎ 520 953; Avenida Charles Darwin) offers local day trips on San Cristóbal and more expensive day trips to nearby islands; it also rents snorkel equipment. The owner of **La Casona** (Avenida Charles Darwin) is a guide, speaks English and can take people on day trips when he isn't flippin' burgers (see Places to Eat).

You can rent bikes from **Nahin Zavala** (☎ 520 696; Padre Luís Morales) who lives on a side street between Hotel Chatham and the naval base. He's also a good one to ask about day trips to nearby islands.

Things to See & Do You can visit the following places without a guide. There's an interesting **interpretation center** (☎ 520 358, ext ☎ 102) on the north side of the bay that has exhibits about the biology, geology and human history of the islands. From the center there are various well-marked trails that wind around the cactus- and scrub-covered **Cerro de las Tijeretas** (Frigatebird Hill). One trail leads over the hill to the small Las Tijeretas bay, which has excellent **snorkeling**. Another trail leads west toward the narrow beach of **Playa Cabo de Horno**, nicknamed 'Playa del Amor' ('Beach of Love') because the sheltering little mangrove trees are favorite make-out spots. From this beach you can often see surfers ripping up the waves peeling off **Punta Carola**, the nearby point. The surf here is excellent (and extremely fast) and there are three other breaks nearby.

From beside the airport a road leads several kilometers (about half-an-hour's walk) to **La Lobería**, a rocky beach with a lazy sea lion colony. There are lots of land iguanas along the trail leading past the beach. Bring water and protection from the sun. Taxis charge about $3 to take you out here and you can walk back (or pay an extra $4 for the driver to wait).

It's fun to take the bus to the village of **El Progreso** and then hitch, walk or hire a car up to **El Junco Lagoon** (see Visitors Sites earlier). You can hire a taxi to take you out there from Cristóbal, wait and return for about $20. Ask to stop to pick oranges (or whatever's in season) on the way – your driver should know the best spots. The road to El Junco continues across the island to the isolated beach of **Puerto Chino**. Other local visitor sites are described under Visitor Sites earlier.

Places to Stay Spending more money at the pricier hotels doesn't buy much more luxury than you'll find at the mid-range places. Most places offer discounts if you stay four or more days.

Hotel San Francisco (☎ 520 304; Avenida Charles Darwin near Villamil; rooms per person $6) is clean and basic with private coldwater baths and a tendency for water shortages – but it's cheap.

Hotel Flamingo (☎ 520 240; rooms per person $7) is another no-frills cheapie, but it's clean and friendly and rooms have private cold-water baths.

Mar Azul (☎ 520 139, fax 520 107; Avenida Alsacio Northia at Avenida Quito; singles/doubles $12/20) is friendly and has pleasant patios and rooms with private hot shower, TV and fan.

Hotel Chatham (☎/fax 520 137; Avenida Alsacio Northia at Avenida de la Armada; doubles $15) has plain, clean rooms with corrugated tin roofs, comfortable beds, TV and private hot shower. Rooms open on to a hammock-filled patio.

Los Cactus (☎ 520 078; J Jose Flores near Avenida Quito; singles/doubles/triples $9/14/20) is clean, friendly and has private hot showers.

Cabañas Don Jorge (☎ 520 208; e waves05@hotmail.com; Avenida Alsacio Northia; rooms per person $8-10) is a rustic, laid-back place with small, simple cabins built on the lava rocks, directly across from Playa Man, northeast of the Malecón (on the way to Cerro de las Tijeretas). It's quiet and there's a guest kitchen.

Hotel Orca (☎/fax 520 233; singles/doubles about $45/55), on Playa de Oro, is the largest hotel, but tends to rent rooms only to tour groups or people who make reservations through the Quito office (Quito ☎ 02-256 4565). It's near the beach, and its 20 rooms have hot water and fans.

Hostal Galápagos (☎/fax 520 157; singles/doubles $43/55) is air-conditioned and clean but unimpressive considering the price. Its location near the Playa de Oro is its finest feature.

In the highlands at El Progreso, you'll find lodging at **Casa del Ceibo** (☎ 520 248; rooms per person $4), which has two rooms. Simple kitchen privileges are available, and a restaurant is open on weekends.

Places to Eat In the evening, women sell *chuzos* (thinly sliced steak grilled on a stick) along Alsacio Northia, near the school – good, cheap protein. On the same street, between 7am and 10am, you'll find a cart selling the town's best *encebollado* (a seafood, yucca and onion soup). More cheap and tasty protein.

Rosita's (☎ 520 106; cnr Villamil & Cobos; mains $5-10; open daily) is considered to be the best restaurant, serving tasty *bacalao* (a local cod), good $3 *almuerzos* (set-lunch menus), chicken dishes and *ceviche* (marinated, uncooked seafood).

Restaurant Albacora (☎ 520 712; Alsacio Northia & Española; mains $3-7; open Mon-Sat) is a good place to stuff yourself for about $5. Seafood plates go for about $4, and the French fries are excellent. It has a rock floor, bamboo walls and a TV for cheer.

La Casona (☎ 520 292; Avenida Charles Darwin), a popular evening hang-out on the Malecón, is the place to go for burgers.

Barracuda (Cobos; almuerzos $1.50; open lunch Mon-Sat) has some of the cheapest almuerzos in town.

El Grande (Villamil; drinks $0.90-1.50), named after its *big* owner, is famous for its array of *batidos* (fruit shakes). Surfers swear the '4x4' – made with *borojó* (a gooey, bitter Colombian fruit), alfalfa, malt, raw egg and your choice of one other fruit – keeps them energized all day.

Miconia (☎ *520 035; Avenida Charles Darwin; mains $6-12)* has an excellent 2nd-story patio dining room and serves good pizza, pasta and seafood.

Cebichería Langostino *(Hernán Melville)* is a local favorite for lunchtime ceviche; it is in a small house 1½ blocks inland from the Malecón toward the east end of town.

Entertainment   The laid-back local surf bar is **Escuba Bar** *(Avenida Charles Darwin; open 8pm-1am)*, complete with foosball and a pool table. **Barquero** *(Cobos)* is a good hang-out with outdoor tables for watching the world go by. Side by side, **Neptuna** and **Yolita** are the local discos; both are on the Malecón near the *capitanía*.

Getting There & Away   The airport is about half a kilometer from town – about a five-minute walk. **TAME** (☎ *521 089; open 8:30am-noon & 2pm-4pm Tues, Thur & Fri, 10am-noon Mon, Wed & Sat)* is at the airport. For information on flights to Guayaquil and Quito see Air under Getting There & Away earlier. There are twice-weekly flights on five-seat light aircraft to Baltra (for Puerto Ayora, Santa Cruz) with **EMETEBE** (☎ *520 036);* the office is at the airport. (See Getting There & Away under Puerto Ayora for rates and restrictions.)

The passenger ferry *Ingala II* sails two to three times per week to Puerto Ayora, Santa Cruz ($50, about four hours). Small boats head regularly to Santa Cruz and occasionally to Floreana and Isabella; ask at the *capitanía*. Rates are $20 to $30.

Getting Around   A few buses leave each day to the farming center of El Progreso, 8km into the highlands. From here, you can hire a vehicle (or walk or hitch hike) for the final 10km ride to the visitor site of El Junco Lagoon. Some buses go further than El Progreso.

In Puerto Baquerizo, taxis hang out along the Malecón and have fixed rates to island destinations, but don't always stick to them. They'll take you to La Lobería, El Progreso, El Junco Lagoon, La Galapaguera, Puerto Chino – anywhere there's a road.

ISLA ESPAÑOLA
This 61-sq-km island (also known as Hood) is the most southerly in the archipelago and has two visitor sites. Because Española is somewhat outlying (about 90km southeast of Santa Cruz), reaching it requires a fairly long sea passage; captains of some of the smallest boats may be reluctant to go this far. The island is well worth visiting from late March to December, because it has the only colony of the waved albatross, one of the Galápagos' most spectacular seabirds.

The best visitor site on Española is **Punta Suárez**, at the western end of the island; a wet landing is necessary. A 2km trail takes visitors through masked and blue-footed booby colonies and past a beach full of marine iguanas before reaching the main attraction – the waved albatross colony.

Just beyond the colony is a blow hole through which the waves force water to spout about 20m into the air. If you sit on top of the cliffs between the waved albatrosses and the blow hole, you can watch seabirds performing their aerial ballet (and their less elegant attempts to land and take off).

Other birds to look out for are the Hood mockingbird (found nowhere else), swallow-tailed gulls, red-billed tropicbirds and oyster-catchers. The large cactus finch can also be seen and is found on few other islands.

There is a beautiful white-sand beach at **Gardner Bay**, at the east end of Isla Española. It is reached with a wet landing, and there is good swimming to be had and a sea lion colony. An island a short distance offshore provides good snorkeling – there's one rock that often has white-tipped reef sharks basking under it.

ISLA SANTA MARÍA
Officially known as Santa María but often called Floreana or Charles, this is the sixth-largest of the islands at 173 sq km. There's accommodations in the village of Puerto Velasco Ibarra.

Visitor Sites
From the village of Puerto Velasco Ibarra, a road runs inland for a few kilometers to an area where you can see the endemic medium tree finch (this finch exists only on Floreana). Early settlers once lived in the nearby caves. This area, called **Asilo de la Paz**, is an official visitor site.

The Chronicles of Floreana

This island of Floreana (also known as Santa María or Charles) has had an interesting history. The first resident of the Galápagos was Patrick Watkins, an Irishman who was marooned on Floreana in 1807 and spent two years living there, growing vegetables and trading his produce for rum from passing boats. The story goes that he managed to remain drunk for most of his stay, then stole a ship's boat and set out for Guayaquil accompanied by five slaves. No one knows what happened to the slaves – only Watkins reached the mainland.

After Watkins' departure, the island was turned into an Ecuadorian penal colony for some years. In the 1930s, three groups of German settlers arrived on Floreana, and strange stories have been told about them ever since.

The most colorful of the settlers was a baroness who arrived with three lovers. Another settler, Dr Friedrich Ritter, an eccentric who had all of his teeth removed before arriving so as to avoid having dental problems, was accompanied by his mistress. The third group was a young couple from Cologne, the Wittmers.

Despite their common nationality, there was a great deal of friction among the groups, and mysteriously, one by one, the settlers died. The baroness and one of her lovers simply disappeared, while another lover died in a boating accident. The vegetarian Dr Ritter died of food poisoning after eating chicken. The only ones to survive were the Wittmers.

Margaret Wittmer, one of the original settlers, died in 2000 at the age of 95. Her children and grandchildren run a small hotel and restaurant in Puerto Velasco Ibarra. Although several books and articles have been written about the strange happenings on Floreana (including one by Wittmer herself), no one is really sure of the truth.

It is an all-day hike up there and back – you can hire a guide (local biologist/guide Felipe Cruz rented the town's dumptruck for my trip). There are no taxis.

There are three visitor sites on the north coast of Floreana. **Post Office Bay** used to have a barrel where whalers left mail. Any captain of a boat that was heading to where the mail was addressed would deliver it. The site continues to be used, but obviously, the barrel has been changed many times. About 300m behind the barrel is a lava cave that can be descended with the aid of a short piece of rope. Nearby is a pleasant swimming beach and the remains of a canning factory; a wet landing is necessary.

Also reached with a wet landing is **Punta Cormorant**. There is a greenish beach (green because it contains crystals of the mineral olivine) where sea lions play and the swimming and snorkeling are good.

A 400m trail leads across an isthmus to a white-sand beach where turtles sometimes lay their eggs. The beach is also good for swimming, but beware of stingrays – shuffle your feet when entering the water.

Between the two beaches is a flamingo lagoon, which is probably the main attraction of this visitor site. Several dozen flamingos are normally seen. This is also a good place to see other wading birds, such as the black-necked stilt, oystercatchers, willets and whimbrels. White-cheeked pintail ducks are often seen in the lagoon, and Galápagos hawks wheel overhead.

Another Floreana visitor site is the remains of a half-submerged volcanic cone poking up out of the ocean a few hundred meters from Punta Cormorant. Aptly named the **Devil's Crown**, this ragged semicircle of rocks is one of the most outstanding marine sites in the Galápagos.

A *panga* ride around the cone will give views of red-billed tropicbirds, pelicans, herons and lava gulls nesting on the rocks, but the greater attraction is the snorkeling in and around the crater. There are thousands of bright tropical fish, a small coral formation, sea lions and (if you are lucky) sharks.

Puerto Velasco Ibarra

This port is the only settlement on Isla Santa María (Floreana), which has only about 70 permanent inhabitants. There is not much to do in this tiny town, but a black beach nearby boasts a sea lion colony, and there's a

THE GALÁPAGOS ISLANDS

flamingo lagoon within walking distance. A road goes into the highlands – there is very little traffic (a school bus goes up and back at 6am and 3pm) but it's easy walking.

The family of Margaret Wittmer (see the boxed text 'The Chronicles of Floreana') run a small **hotel and restaurant** (☎ 520 250; singles/doubles/triples $30/50/70), where there is the island's only phone. They also have a small gift shop and post office. Beachfront rooms have hot water and fans, and three meals cost about $20 a day. The hotel is rarely full, and even if they were, you could ask the staff to show you somewhere to crash.

Once a month, the passenger ferry *Ingala II* goes from Isabela to Floreana to Santa Cruz. Other boats can be arranged, especially between Floreana and Santa Cruz.

ISLA SAN SALVADOR

This official name is used less often than the old Spanish name (Santiago), or the English name (James). Santiago is the fourth-largest of the islands and has several excellent visitor sites within its 585 sq km.

The best site is **Puerto Egas**, on James Bay, on the west side of Santiago. Here, there is a long, flat, black lava shoreline where eroded shapes form lava pools, caves and inlets that house a great variety of wildlife. This is a great place to see colonies of marine iguanas basking in the sun. The tide pools contain hundreds of red Sally Lightfoot crabs, which attract hunting herons of all the commonly found species.

The inlets are favorite haunts of the Galápagos fur seal, and this site is one of the best places on the islands to see them. You can snorkel here with fur seals and many species of tropical fish. Moray eels, sharks and octopuses have also been seen during snorkeling trips here.

Behind the black lava shoreline is Sugarloaf Volcano, which can be reached via a 2km footpath. Lava lizards, Darwin's finches and Galápagos doves are often seen on this path. It peters out near the top of the 395m summit, but from here, the views are stupendous. There is an extinct crater in which feral goats are often seen (the wild goats are a major problem on Santiago), and Galápagos hawks often hover a few meters above the top of the volcano. North of the volcano is a crater where a salt mine used to be; its

remains can be visited by walking along a 3km trail from the coast.

Puerto Egas is one of the most popular sites in the islands – so popular that it was temporarily closed in late 1995 by the National Park Service because too many people were visiting it. It has since reopened.

At the north end of James Bay, about 5km from Puerto Egas, is the brown-sand **Espumilla Beach**, which can be reached with a wet landing. The swimming is good here, and by the small lagoon behind the beach you can see various wading birds – including, at times, flamingos. A 2km trail leads inland through transitional vegetation where there are various finches and the Galápagos flycatcher.

At the northwestern end of Santiago, another site that is normally visited by boat is **Buccaneer Cove**, so called because it was a popular place for 17th- and 18th-century buccaneers to careen their vessels. The cliffs and pinnacles, which are used as nesting areas by several species of seabirds, are the main attraction these days. This is best appreciated from the sea, but it is possible to land in the cove, where there are beaches.

Sullivan Bay is on Santiago's east coast. Here, a huge, black, century-old lava flow has solidified into a sheet that reaches to the edge of the sea. A dry landing enables visitors to step on to the flow and follow a trail of white posts in a 2km circuit on the lava. You can see uneroded volcanic formations, such as *pahoehoe* lava, lava bubbles and tree-trunk molds in the surface. A few pioneer colonizing plants, such as *Brachycereus* cactus and *Mollugo* carpetweed, can be seen. This site is of particular interest to those interested in volcanology or geology.

ISLA BARTOLOMÉ

Just off Sullivan Bay (see Isla San Salvador earlier) is Isla Bartolomé, which has an area of 1.2 sq km. Here you can see the most frequently photographed and hence most famous vista on the islands. There are two visitor sites and footpaths. One begins from a jetty (dry landing), from where it is about 600m to the 114m summit of the island. This good but sandy trail leads through a wild and unearthly looking lava landscape; a wooden boardwalk and stairs have been built on the last (steepest) section, both to aid visitors and to protect the trail from erosion. There are a few pioneering plants on either side of the trail, but the main attraction is the view toward Santiago, which is just as dramatic as the photographs suggest.

The other visitor site is a small, sandy beach in a cove (wet landing). Here you have good snorkeling and swimming opportunities, including a chance to swim with the endemic Galápagos penguins that frequent this cove. Marine turtles and a gaudy variety of tropical fish are also frequently seen.

The best way to see and photograph the penguins is by taking a *panga* ride close to the rocks on either side of the cove – particularly around the aptly named Pinnacle Rock, to the right of the cove from the seaward side. You can often get within a few meters of these fascinating birds – the closest point to Puerto Ayora where you can do so. Other penguin colonies are on the western side of Isabela.

From the beach, a 100m trail leads across the narrowest part of Bartolomé to another sandy beach on the opposite side of the island. Marine turtles may nest here between January and March. Both beaches are clearly visible from the viewpoint described earlier.

SOMBRERO CHINO

This tiny island just off the southeastern tip of Santiago is less than a quarter of 1 sq km in size. It is a fairly recent volcanic cone, which accounts for its descriptive name (it translates as 'Chinese Hat'). The hat shape is best appreciated from the north. There is a small sea lion cove on the north shore, where you can anchor and land at the visitor site. Opposite Sombrero Chino, on the rocky shoreline of nearby Santiago, penguins are often seen.

A 400m trail goes around the cove and through a sea lion colony – marine iguanas scurry everywhere. The volcanic landscape is attractive, and there are good views of the cone. There are snorkeling and swimming opportunities in the cove.

ISLA RÁBIDA

This approximately 5-sq-km island, also known as Jervis, lies 5km south of Santiago. There is a wet landing on to a dark red beach where sea lions haul out and pelicans nest. This is one of the best places to see these birds nesting.

Behind the beach, there is a saltwater lagoon where flamingos and white-cheeked pintails are sometimes seen (although the flamingos were not seen much during the 1990s). This lagoon is also the site of a sea lion bachelor colony where the *solteros* (lone males), deposed by the dominant bull, while away their days.

There is a 750m trail with good views of the island's 367m volcanic peak, which is covered with *palo santo* trees. At the end of the trail, there is a great snorkeling spot.

ISLA GENOVESA

This island is known more often by its English name of Tower. It covers 14 sq km and is the northeasternmost of the Galápagos Islands. As it is an outlying island, Tower is infrequently included on a one-week itinerary. If you have the time, however, and are interested in seabirds, this island is well worth the long trip. It is the best place to see a red-footed booby colony, and it provides visitors with the opportunity to visit colonies of great frigatebirds, red-billed tropicbirds, swallow-tailed gulls, masked boobies and many thousands of storm petrels. Other bird attractions include Galápagos doves and short-eared owls. Both sea lions and fur seals are present, and there are exciting snorkeling opportunities – hammerhead sharks are here.

The island is fairly flat and round, with a large, almost landlocked, cove named Darwin Bay on the south side. There are two visitor sites, both on Darwin Bay. **Prince Philip's Steps** (also called El Barranco) is on the eastern arm of the bay and can be reached with a dry landing. A steep and rocky path leads to the top of 25m-high cliffs, and nesting seabirds are sometimes found right on the narrow path.

At the top of the cliffs, the 1km-long trail leads inland, past dry-forest vegetation and various seabird colonies, to a cracked expanse of lava, where thousands of storm petrels make their nests and wheel overhead. Short-eared owls are often seen here, and it is an excellent hike for the bird enthusiast.

The second visitor site, **Darwin Bay Beach**, is a coral beach reached by a wet landing. There is a 750m trail along the beach that passes through more seabird colonies.

You can take a pleasant *panga* ride along the cliffs. The *panga* is often followed by playful sea lions. This recommended excursion gives a good view from the seaward side of the cliffs and of the birds nesting on them.

Finally, this is the only regularly visited island that lies entirely north of the equator (the northernmost part of Isabela also pokes above the line). Cruises to Tower well involve various ceremonies for passengers who have never crossed the equator at sea before.

ISLAS MARCHENA & PINTA

Isla Marchena is also known as Bindloe. At 130 sq km, this is the seventh-largest island in the archipelago and the largest one to have no official visitor sites. There are some good scuba-diving sites, however, so you may get to see the island up close if you are on a dive trip.

The 343m-high volcano in the middle of the island was very active during 1991 – ask your guide about its current degree of activity. In the past, it was possible to see the eruptions from boats cruising in the northern part of the islands.

Isla Pinta is the original home of Lonesome George, the tortoise described earlier under Isla Santa Cruz. Pinta is the ninth-largest of the Galápagos Islands and is further north than any of the bigger islands. Its English name is Abingdon. There are landing sites, but the island has no visitor sites, and researchers require a permit to visit.

ISLA ISABELA

The largest island in the archipelago is the 4588-sq-km Isabela (occasionally called Albemarle), which occupies over 58% of the entire land mass of the Galápagos. It's a relatively recent island and consists of a chain of five fairly young and intermittently active volcanoes, one of which, Volcán Wolf, is the highest point in the Galápagos at 1707m (some sources claim 1646m). There is also one small older volcano, Volcán Ecuador.

Although Isabela's volcanoes dominate the westward view during passages to the western part of Santa Cruz, the island itself is not frequently visited by smaller boats because most of the best visitor sites are on the west side of the island. The reverse 'C' shape of the island means that the visitor sites on the west side are reached only after a very long passage (over 200km) from Santa Cruz, and so either you have to make a two-week cruise or you visit Isabela without seeing many of the other islands.

This island is a marvelous one, however. There are a large number of Galápagos

tortoises, and it looks like Isabela is going to become more important in Galápagos tourism in the years to come.

Visitor Sites

There are many visitor sites on Isabela. One of these is the summit of **Volcán Alcedo** (1128m), which is famous for its 7km-wide caldera and steaming fumaroles, where hundreds of giant tortoises can be seen, especially from June to December. The view is fantastic. Until 1998, it was possible to hike to and camp near the summit (two days were required). This long, steep, waterless and very strenuous trail was closed for several years, but it now may be reopened – you'll need to check. If it is, advance permits will likely be required.

A few kilometers north of the landing for Alcedo is **Punta García**, which consists mainly of very rough *aa* lava, a sharp, jagged lava; there are no proper trails, but you can land. Until recently, this was the only place where you could see the endemic flightless cormorant without having to take the long passage around to the west side. Recently, however, these birds have been present only intermittently, and visits to this site have declined.

At the northern tip of Isabela is **Punta Albemarle**, which used to be a US radar base during WWII. There are no trails, and the site is known for the flightless cormorants, which normally are not found further to the east. Further west are several points where flightless cormorants, Galápagos penguins and other seabirds can be seen, but there are no visitor sites. You must view the birds from your boat.

At the west end of the northern arm of Isabela is the small, old Volcán Ecuador (610m), which comes down almost to the sea. **Punta Vicente Roca**, at the volcano's base, is a rocky point with a good snorkeling area, but there is no official landing site.

The first official visitor-landing site on the western side of Isabela is **Punta Tortuga**, a beach at the base of Volcán Darwin (1280m). Part of the land here was formed through a recent uplift. Locals report that one day in 1975, the uplift just appeared. One day there was nothing, and the next day there was an uplifted ledge – no one saw it happen.

Although there is no trail, you can land on the beach and explore the mangroves for the mangrove finch, which is present here but not always easy to see. This finch is found only on Islas Isabela and Fernandina.

Just south of the point is **Tagus Cove**, where early sailors frequently anchored. You can still see some of the names of the vessels scratched into the cliffs around the cove. A dry landing will bring you to a trail, which you follow for 2km past a saltwater lagoon and on to the lower lava slopes of Volcán Darwin, where various volcanic formations can be observed. There are some steep sections on this trail. A *panga* ride along the cliffs will enable you to see the historical graffiti and various seabirds, usually including Galápagos penguins and flightless cormorants. There are snorkeling opportunities in the cove.

Urbina Bay lies around the middle of the western shore of Isabela and is a flat area formed by an uplift from the sea in 1954. Evidence of the uplift includes a coral reef on the land. Flightless cormorants, pelicans and marine iguanas can be observed on land, and rays and turtles can be seen in the bay. A wet landing on to a beach brings you to a 1km trail that leads to the corals. There is a good view of Volcán Alcedo.

Near where the western shoreline of Isabela bends sharply toward the lower arm of the island, there is a visitor site that's known for its marine life. **Elizabeth Bay** is best visited by a *panga* ride, as there are no landing sites. Islas Mariela are at the entrance of the bay and are frequented by penguins. The end of the bay itself is a long, narrow and convoluted arm of the sea surrounded by three species of mangroves. Marine turtles and rays can usually be seen in the water, and various seabirds and shorebirds are usually present.

West of Elizabeth Bay is **Punta Moreno**. You can make a dry landing on to a lava flow, where there are some brackish pools. Flamingos, white-cheeked pintails and common gallinules are sometimes seen, and various pioneer plants and insects are found in the area. There is a rough trail.

On the southeastern corner of Isabela, there is the small village of Puerto Villamil. Behind and to the west of the village is the **Villamil Lagoon**. This visitor site is known for its migrant birds – especially waders, over 20 species have been reported here. The surrounding vegetation is dense and

without trails, but the road to the highlands and the open beach do give reasonable access to the lagoons. Also west of Puerto Villamil is a visitor site, **Muro de las Lágrimas** (Wall of Tears), which was built by convicts.

To the northwest lies the massive **Volcán Santo Tomás** (1490m), which is also known as Volcán Sierra Negra. The tiny settlement of Santo Tomás is on the lower flanks of the volcano. Trucks or jeeps can be hired for the 18km ride from Puerto Villamil. From Santo Tomás, it is 9km further up a steep trail to the rim of the volcano – horses can be rented in the village.

The caldera is roughly 10km in diameter and is a spectacular site with magnificent views. An 8km trail leads around the east side of the volcano to some active fumaroles. It is possible to walk all the way around the caldera, but the trail peters out. You should carry all your food and water or rent horses. Galápagos hawks, short-eared owls, finches and flycatchers are among the birds commonly seen on this trip. The summit is often foggy (especially during the June-to-December garúa season) and it is easy to get lost – stay in a group. Nearby is Volcán Chico, a subcrater where you can see more fumaroles. These volcanoes are very infrequently visited.

Puerto Villamil
pop 1200

The small port of Puerto Villamil on Isabela is where most of the island's inhabitants live (the island's total population is around 1500). It is not much visited by travelers, although some tours do stop here.

For those wanting to visit Volcán Santo Tomás (see earlier), there are several men in Puerto Villamil who work as guides – ask around.

There's nowhere to change traveler's checks; bring US cash. There is a Pacifictel office.

Places to Stay & Eat Clean, recommended and also often full is **San Vicente** (☎ 529 140; singles/doubles $3/4). It has six rooms with cold showers. Meals are provided upon request. Other cheapies are pretty run-down and basic; try **Hostal Loja** (☎ 529 174; rooms per person $2), or **Los Delfines** (☎ 529 129; singles/doubles $3/4), both have hot water.

Tero Real (☎ 529 195; singles/doubles $5/8) has clean rooms with private cold showers and a fridge. Meals are provided on request.

Hotel Ballena Azul (☎/fax 529 125; e isa bela@ga.pro.ec or e isabela@hosteriaisabela .com.ec; rooms per person $8) is the best budget place in town. The singles have shared bathrooms, the doubles and triples have private bathrooms and solar hot water, and some rooms have beach views. Meals are available upon request.

La Casa Marita (☎ 529 238, fax 529 201; e hcmarita@ga.pro.ec; singles/doubles/triples/ quads $35/50/65/80) is attractive and has pleasant beachfront rooms sleeping up to four. All have hot showers and kitchenettes, and some have air-conditioning. Rates include breakfast, and other meals are available upon request.

Restaurants tend to provide menus without prices, so always check on price (and taxes) before ordering. El Encanto de la Pepa, is the best (and priciest) place to eat and serves a good variety of dishes in a tropical setting.

Costa Azul is clean and cheaper, but has a more limited menu and lacks atmosphere. Ballena Azul has good food with many choices but very slow service – it's cooked to order, so order ahead of time. La Iguana has limited hours (weekends and vacations) and serves good pizzas and drinks under the palm trees. There are a few basic *comedores* (cheap restaurants).

Getting There & Away Two times a week, **EMETEBE** (☎ 529 155) flies from Baltra to San Cristóbal to Isabela to Baltra. Its office is at the airport. See Getting Around the Islands near the beginning of this chapter for more information. The Isabela stop may be canceled if there are no passengers who want to go there.

Getting Around Buses to/from Villamil to Santo Tomás and further into the highlands

leave at 7am and noon, returning two hours later. Trucks can be rented at other times.

ISLA FERNANDINA

At 642 sq km, Fernandina (infrequently called Narborough) is the third-largest island and the westernmost and youngest of the main islands. The recently formed volcanic landscapes are most impressive. Many eruptions have been recorded since 1813, the most recent being in 1995. This is the island on which you are most likely to see a volcanic eruption.

There is one visitor site at **Punta Espinosa**, just across from Tagus Cove on Isabela. The point is known for one of the greatest concentrations of the endemic marine iguanas, which are found by the thousands. Also, flightless cormorants, Galápagos penguins and sea lions are common here.

A dry landing brings you to two trails: a 250m trail to the point and a 750m trail to recently formed lava fields. Here you can see various pioneering plants, such as the *Brachycereus* cactus, as well as *pahoehoe* and *aa* lava formations.

OTHER ISLANDS

The one sizable island in the central part of the archipelago that has no visitor sites is **Isla Pinzón**, also called Duncan. It is a cliffbound island, which makes landing difficult, and a permit is required to visit it (permits are usually reserved for scientists and researchers).

The northernmost islands are the two tins islands of **Isla Wolf** (Wenman) and **Isla Darwin** (Culpepper). They are about 100km northwest of the rest of the archipelago and are very seldom visited, except occasionally on scuba-diving trips. Both have nearly vertical cliffs that make landing difficult; Isla Darwin was first visited in 1964, when a helicopter expedition landed on the summit. Various other rocks and islets are present in the archipelago, but all are extremely small.

Language

Spanish is the official language of Ecuador, however, travelers to the region will encounter a mix of other European tongues, indigenous languages and colorful dialects.

Most Indians are bilingual, with Quechua (also known as Quichua) being their mother tongue and Spanish their second language. There are also several small lowland groups that speak their own languages. Note that Quechua spoken in Ecuador is quite different from that spoken in Peru and Bolivia, so it can be difficult for highland Indians from these countries to communicate easily. It's rare to encounter Indians who understand no Spanish at all, although they certainly exist in the more remote communities.

PHRASEBOOKS & DICTIONARIES

Lonely Planet's compact *Latin American Spanish phrasebook* is a good addition to your backpack. Another useful resource is the *University of Chicago Spanish-English, English-Spanish Dictionary* – its small size, light weight and thorough entries make it ideal for travel. It also makes a great gift for any newfound friends upon your departure.

Lonely Planet's *Quechua phrasebook* is based on the Cuzco variety of the language (southern Quechua), but can still be useful in getting your basic message across, and any attempts to speak Quechua in Ecuador will be greatly appreciated.

SPANISH

The basic elements of Spanish are easily to pick up, and a month-long language course taken before departure can go a long way toward facilitating communication and comfort on the road. Making the effort to learn a few basic phrases and pleasantries will be met with enthusiasm and appreciation.

The Spanish of Ecuador sounds different from the Spanish of Spain and includes regional vocabulary, much of which is derived from indigenous languages. Throughout Latin America, the Spanish language is referred to as *castellano* more often than *español*. Unlike in Spain, the plural of the familiar *tú* form is *ustedes* rather than *vosotros;* the latter term will sound quaint

and archaic in the Americas. In addition, the letters **c** and **z** are never lisped in Latin America; attempts to do so could well provoke amusement or even contempt.

Pronunciation

Pronunciation of Spanish is not difficult, given that many Spanish sounds are similar to their English counterparts and there is a clear and consistent relationship between pronunciation and spelling. The best way to familiarize yourself with the pronunciation of the area you're traveling in is to chat with locals, keeping an ear out for regional variations.

Traditionally, there were three Spanish letters that didn't exist in English: **ch**, **ll** and **ñ**. These followed **c**, **l** and **n** respectively in the alphabet, and had their own corresponding sections in the dictionary. In the mid-1990s, Spain's Academia Real de la Lengua Española abolished these as separate letters; hence, newer Spanish dictionaries list them in their English alphabetical order. The practice varies from region to region, so look for a **ch** section in the phone book if you can't find 'Chávez' under **c**.

Vowels

a	as in 'father'
e	between the 'e' in 'met' and the 'ey' in 'hey'
i	as the 'ee' in 'feet'
o	as in 'note'
u	as the 'oo' in 'boot;' silent after **q** and in the pairings 'gue' and 'gui,' unless it carries a dieresis (eg, **ü** in *güero*)

Diphthongs

A diphthong is one syllable made up of two distinct vowel sounds that glide from one into the other.

ai	as in 'Thailand'
au	as the 'ow' in 'how'
ei	as the 'ay' in 'hay'
ia	as the 'ya' in 'yard'
ie	as the 'ye' in 'yes'
oi	as the 'oy' in 'boy'
ua	as the 'wa' in 'wash'

LANGUAGE

ue   as the 'we' in 'well' (unless preceded
       by 'q' or 'g')

Consonants

Many consonants are pronounced in much
the same way as in English, but there are
some exceptions:

b   resembles English 'b,' but is a softer
       sound produced by holding the lips
       nearly together. At the beginning a
       word or when preceded by **m** or **n**,
       it's pronounced as the 'b' in 'book'
       (eg, *bomba, embajada*). Spanish **v** is
       pronounced almost identically; for
       clarification, Spanish speakers refer
       to **b** as 'b larga' and to **v** as 'b corta'
c   as the 's' in 'sit' before **e** and **i**; else-
       where, as English 'k'
d   produced with the tongue against the
       front teeth, almost like the 'th' in
       'feather;' as English 'd' after **l** and **n**
g   as a guttural English 'h' before **e** and
       i; elsewhere, as in 'go'
h   always silent
j   as a guttural English 'h'
ll   as the 'y' in 'yes'
ñ   as the 'ny' in 'canyon'
r   similar to the 'dd' in 'udder;' at the
       beginning of a word or following **l**, **n**
       or **s**, it's rolled strongly
rr   a very strongly rolled 'r'
v   as **b** (see above)
x   as in 'taxi' except for a few words in
       which it's as **j** (eg, *México*)
z   as the 's' in 'sit'

Semiconsonant

y   as the 'i' in 'hit' when alone or at the
       end of a word; elsewhere, as the 'y'
       in 'yes'

Word Stress

Stress is extremely important as it can
change the meaning of words. In general,
words ending in vowels or the letters 'n' or
's' have stress on the penultimate (next-to-
last) syllable, while those with other end-
ings have stress on the last syllable. Thus
vaca (cow) and *caballos* (horses) are both
stressed on their penultimate syllables,
while *catedral* (cathedral) is stressed on its
last syllable. Any deviation from these rules
is indicated by an accent, eg, *sótano* (basement), *América* and *Panamá*

Gender

Nouns in Spanish are either masculine or
feminine (indicated in this language guide
by 'm/f' respectively). Nouns ending in **-o**,
-e or **-ma** are usually masculine. Nouns
ending in **-a**, **-ión** or **-dad** are usually feminine. Some nouns can take either a mascu-
line or feminine form; eg, *viajero/viajera*
(male/female traveler). An adjective takes
the same gender as the noun it describes and
usually comes after it.

Greetings & Civilities

In their public behavior, Latin Americans
are cordial yet polite, and expect others to
reciprocate. Never, for example, address a
stranger without first extending a greeting
such as *buenos días* or *buenas tardes*. When
in doubt about whether to use the informal
tú or the more formal *usted*, it's better to err
on the side of caution and use the latter. You
must always use *usted* when addressing the
police or people in authority.

Hello/Hi.	*Hola.*
Good morning/	*Buenos días.*
Good day.	
Good afternoon.	*Buenas tardes.*
Good evening/	*Buenas noches.*
Good night.	

(The above three phrases are often short-
ened to *Buenos/Buenas*.)

Goodbye.	*Adiós.*
See you later.	*Hasta luego.*
Please.	*Por favor.*
Thank you.	*Gracias.*
You're welcome.	*De nada.*
It's a pleasure	*Con mucho gusto.*
Excuse me.	*Discúlpeme/Perdón.*
Excuse me. (when	*Permiso.*
squeezing past)	
I'm sorry.	*Lo siento.*
How are you?	*¿Como está?*
(to one person)	
How are you?	*¿Como están?*
(to more than one person)	
I'm fine.	*Estoy bien.*
What's your name?	*¿Cómo se llama usted?*
My name is ...	*Me llamo ...*
Pleased to meet	*Mucho gusto.*
you.	

Useful Words & Phrases

Yes.	*Sí.*
No.	*No.*

with	*con*
without	*sin*
before	*antes*
after	*después de*
soon	*pronto*
already	*ya*
now	*ahora*
right away	*ahorita, en seguida*
here	*aquí*
there	*allí* or *allá*

I	*yo*
you (informal)	*tú/vos*
you (polite)	*usted*
he/it	*el*
she/it	*ella*
you (pural, polite)	*ustedes*
we	*nosotros/nosotras* (m/f)
they	*ellos/ellas* (m/f)
Sir/Mr	*Señor*
Madam/Mrs	*Señora*
Miss	*Señorita*

Language Difficulties

Do you speak English?	*¿Habla inglés?*
Does anyone here speak English?	*¿Alguien habla inglés aquí?*
I don't speak Spanish.	*No hablo castellano.*
I understand.	*Entiendo.*
I don't understand.	*No entiendo.*
Do you understand?	*¿Entiende usted?*
What did you say?	*¿Mande?* (colloq)
Please speak more slowly.	*Por favor hable más despacio.*
Could you repeat that, please?	*¿Puede repetirlo, por favor?*
What does it mean?	*¿Qué significa?/ ¿Qué quiere decir?*
Please write that down.	*Por favor escríbalo.*

Where?	*¿Dónde?*
When?	*¿Cuándo?*
What?	*¿Qué?*
Which (ones)?	*¿Cuál(es)?*
Who?	*¿Quién?*
Why?	*¿Por qué?*
How much?	*¿Cuánto?*
How many?	*¿Cuántos?*

Getting Around

Where is ...?	*¿Dónde queda/está ...?*
How can I get to ...?	*¿Cómo puedo llegar a ...?*

Road Signs

Traffic signs will invariably be in Spanish and may not be accompanied by internationally recognized symbols. Pay especially close attention to *Peligro* (Danger), *Cede el Paso* (Yield, or Give Way; especially prevalent on one-lane bridges), and *Hundimiento* (Dip; often a euphemistic term for an axle-breaking sinkhole!). Disregarding these warnings could result in disaster.

Adelante	Ahead
Alto	Stop
Cede el Paso	Yield/Give Way
Curva Peligrosa	Dangerous Curve
Despacio	Slow
Derrumbes en la Vía	Falling Rocks
Desvío	Detour
Hundimiento	Dip
Mantenga su Derecha	Keep Right
No Adelantar	No Overtaking
No Rebasar	No Overtaking
No Estacionar	No Parking
No Hay Paso	No Entrance
Peligro	Danger
Trabajos en la Vía	Roadwork
Tránsito Entrando	Entering Traffic

When does the next bus leave for ...?	*¿Cuándo sale el próximo bus para ...?*
I'd like a ticket to ...	*Quiero un boleto/ pasaje a ...*
What's the fare to ...?	*¿Cuánto cuesta el pasaje a ...?*
Are there student discounts?	*¿Hay descuentos estudiantiles?/ ¿Hay rebajas para estudiantes?*

plane	*avión*
train	*tren*
bus	*bus/camioneta/ ómnibus*
small bus	*colectivo/micro*
ship	*barco/buque*
boat	*lancha/bote/panga*
car	*auto/carro*
taxi	*taxi*
truck	*camión*
pick-up truck	*camioneta*

bicycle	bicicleta
motorcycle	motocicleta
hitchhike	hacer dedo/
	pedir un ride
airport	aeropuerto
bus stop	paradero/parada
bus terminal	terminal de buses/
	terminal terrestre
port	puerto
train station	estación de ferrocarril
wharf/pier	muelle
city	ciudad
town	pueblo
village	pueblito, caserío
freeway	autopista
tourist office	oficina de turismo
gas/petrol station	bomba de gasolina
police station	estación de policía
embassy	embajada
consulate	consulado
bank	banco
public toilet	baño público
entrance	entrada
exit	salida
open	abierto/a (m/f)
closed	cerrado/a (m/f)
ticket	boleto, pasaje
ticket office	taquilla
first/last/next	primero/último/
	próximo
1st/2nd class	primera/segunda clase
one way/round trip	ida/ida y vuelta
left luggage	guardería de equipaje

Accommodations

Do you have rooms available?	¿Hay habitaciones?
I'd like (a) ...	Quisiera ...
May I see the room?	¿Puedo ver la habitación?
What does it cost?	¿Cuánto cuesta?
Does it include breakfast?	¿Incluye el desayuno?
Can you give me a deal?	¿Me puede hacer precio/promoción?
	¿Me puede rebajar?
hotel	hotel/residencial/
	hospedaje
room	habitación
single room	habitación sencilla

double room	habitación doble
bed	cama
double bed	cama matrimonial
toilet/bath	baño
shared bath	baño compartido
private bath	baño privado
shower	ducha
per night	por noche
full board	pensión completa
air conditioning	aire acondicionado
blanket	manta, cobija
the bill	la cuenta
fan	ventilador
key	llave
padlock	candado
pillow	almohada
sheets	sábanas
soap	jabón
toilet paper	papel higiénico
towel	toalla
clean	limpio
dirty	sucio
good	bueno
poor	malo
noisy	ruidoso
quiet	tranquilo
hot	caliente
cold	frío
too expensive	demasiado caro
cheaper	más económico/barato

Post & Communications

post office	correo
letter	carta
parcel	paquete
postcard	postal
airmail	correo aéreo
registered mail	correo certificado
stamps	estampillas
email	correo electrónico
public telephone	teléfono público
local call	llamada local
person to person	persona a persona
telephone number	número telefónico
phonecard	tarjeta telefónica
telephone call	llamada (telefónica)
collect call (reverse charges)	llamada a cobro revertido
long-distance call	llamada de larga distancia
international call	llamada internacional
busy	ocupado
Don't hang up.	No cuelgue.

Toilets

The most common word for 'toilet' is *baño*, but *servicios higiénicos* or just *servicios* (services) is a frequent alternative. Men's toilets will usually be signaled by *hombres*, *caballeros* or *varones*. Women's toilets will say *señoras* or *damas*.

Shopping

I'd like ...	*Me gustaría .../*
	Quisiera ...
Do you have ...?/	*¿Hay ...?*
Are there ...?	
How much is it?	*¿Cuánto cuesta/vale?*
I (don't) like it.	*(No) me gusta.*

shop	*almacén/tienda*
shopping center	*centro comercial*
price	*precio*
change	*vueltas*
money	*dinero/plata*
coin	*moneda*
banknote	*billete*
cash	*efectivo*
cheque	*cheque*
credit card	*tarjeta de crédito*
expensive	*caro*
cheap	*barato*
big	*grande*
small	*pequeño*

Geographical Terms

The list below covers the most common terms you'll encounter in Spanish-language maps and guides.

avenida	avenue
bahía	bay
calle	street
camino	road
campo, finca	farm
carretera, ruta	highway
cascada, salto	waterfall
cerro	hill/mount
cordillera	mountain range
estero	marsh, estuary
granja, rancho	ranch
lago	lake
montaña	mountain
parque nacional	national park
paso	pass
puente	bridge
río	river
seno	sound
valle	valley
volcán	volcano

Food

I (don't) eat/drink ...	*(No) como/tomo...*
I'm a vegetarian.	*Soy vegetariano/a.*

water	*agua*
purified water	*agua purificada*
bread	*pan*
meat	*carne*
cheese	*queso*
eggs	*huevos*
milk	*leche*
juice	*jugo*
vegetables	*vegetales/legumbres*
fish	*pescado*
seafood	*mariscos*
coffee	*café*
tea	*té*
beer	*cerveza*
alcohol	*alcohol*

Health

I'm ill.	*Me siento mal.*
I have a fever.	*Tengo fiebre/*
	temperatura.

clinic	*clínica*
dentist	*dentista/odontólogo*
doctor	*doctor/médico*
medicine	*medicina/remedio*
pharmacy	*droguería*

Time & Dates

Times are modified by morning *(de la mañana)* or afternoon *(de la tarde)* instead of am or pm. Use of the 24-hour clock, or military time, is also common, especially with transportation schedules.

What time is it?	*¿Qué horas son?/*
	¿Qué hora es?
It's one o'clock.	*Es la una.*

It's ... o'clock.	*Son las ...*
two	*dos*
eight	*ocho*

At three o'clock ...	*A las tres ...*
It's late.	*Es tarde.*
It's early.	*Es temprano.*

There are a number of ways to express minutes past or to the hour. Half-past eight is expressed as *las ocho y treinta* (eight and thirty) or *las ocho y media* (eight and a half). However, 7:45 is *las ocho menos quince*

Emergencies

Help!	¡Socorro!/¡Auxilio!
Help me!	¡Ayúdenme!
Fire!	¡Fuego!
police	policía
doctor	doctor
hospital	hospital
Leave me alone!	¡Déjeme!
Go away!	¡Váyase!
Thief!	¡Ladrón!
I've been robbed.	Me han robado.
They took my ...	Se me llevaron ...
money	el dinero
passport	el pasaporte
bag	la bolsa

(eight minus fifteen) or *las ocho menos cuarto* (eight minus one quarter).

yesterday	*ayer*
today	*hoy*
tomorrow	*mañana*
day after tomorrow	*pasado mañana*
morning	*mañana*
tomorrow morning	*mañana por la mañana*
afternoon	*tarde*
night	*noche*
now	*ahora*
right now (meaning in a few minutes)	*horita/ahorita*
already	*ya*
Monday	*lunes*
Tuesday	*martes*
Wednesday	*miércoles*
Thursday	*jueves*
Friday	*viernes*
Saturday	*sábado*
Sunday	*domingo*
January	*enero*
February	*febrero*
March	*marzo*
April	*abril*
May	*mayo*
June	*junio*
July	*julio*

August	*agosto*
September	*septiembre*
October	*octubre*
November	*noviembre*
December	*diciembre*

Numbers

1	*uno*
2	*dos*
3	*tres*
4	*cuatro*
5	*cinco*
6	*seis*
7	*siete*
8	*ocho*
9	*nueve*
10	*diez*
11	*once*
12	*doce*
13	*trece*
14	*catorce*
15	*quince*
16	*dieciséis*
17	*diecisiete*
18	*dieciocho*
19	*diecinueve*
20	*veinte*
21	*veintiuno*
22	*veintidós*
30	*treinta*
31	*treinta y uno*
32	*treinta y dos*
40	*cuarenta*
50	*cincuenta*
60	*sesenta*
70	*setenta*
80	*ochenta*
90	*noventa*
100	*cien*
101	*ciento uno*
200	*doscientos*
500	*quinientos*
1000	*mil*
one million	*un millón*
1st	*primero/a*
2nd	*segundo/a*
3rd	*tercero/a*
4th	*cuarto/a*
5th	*quinto/a*

Glossary

abrazo – backslapping hug exchanged between men

AGAR – Asociación de Guías de Aguas Rapidas del Ecuador (Ecuadorian White-Water Guides Association)

aguardiente – sugarcane alcohol

almuerzo – inexpensive set-lunch menu

apartado – post office box (also called 'apdo')

ASEC – Asociación Ecuatoriana de Ecoturismo (Ecuadorian Ecotourism Association)

ASEGUIM – Asociación Ecuatoriana de Guías de Montaña (Ecuadorian Mountain Guides Association)

autobus – large intercity bus; also called *bus grande*

balneario – literally 'spa', but any place where you can swim or soak

baño – bathroom or toilet

batidos – fruit shakes

buseta – small intercity bus which usually has about 22 seats

cabañas – cabins found both on the coast and in the *Oriente*

caldo – clear soup

camioneta – pickup or light truck

campesino – peasant

capitanía – port captain

casas de cambio – currency-exchange bureaus

casilla – post-office box

censo – temporary-residence cards

centros comerciales – often abbreviated to 'CC'; shopping centers

ceviche – local dish of uncooked but well-marinated seafood

chifa – restaurant serving Chinese food

chifles – crispy fried bananas

chiva – open-sided bus, or truck mounted with uncomfortably narrow bench seats; also called *ranchera*

chugchucara – tasty dish consisting of fritada (fried chunks of pork); mote (hominy) with chicharrón (fried bits of pork skin); potatoes; fried banana; tostada (toasted corn); popcorn; and cheese empanadas

churrasco – popular dish of fried beef, rice, a fried egg or two, avocado, cold vegetable salad and fried potatoes

colectivos – shared taxis

comedores – cheap restaurants

Conaie – Confederation of Indigenous Nationalities of Ecuador

cuartel – army barracks

curanderos – medicine men

cuy – roast guinea pig

encebollado – seafood, yucca and onion soup garnished with *chifles*

endemic – species which breed only in one place – in the Galápagos Islands, for instance

entrada – entrance

FARC – Revolutionary Armed Forces of Colombia

guardaparque – park ranger

helados de paila – ice cream handmade in large copper bowls

hostal – small and reasonably priced hotel; not a youth hostel

hostería – small hotel, which tends to be a midpriced country inn; often, but not always, found in rural areas

IGM – Instituto Geográfico Militar, the Ecuadorian government agency which produces and sells topographic and other maps

indígena – indigenous person

Ingapirca – most famous Inca archaelogical site in Ecuador

kushma – one-piece, knee-length smock worn by Cofan men

llapingachos – fried pancakes of mashed potatoes with cheese

malecón – waterfront

merienda – inexpensive set-dinner menu

mestizo – person of mixed indigenous and Spanish descent

migraciones – immigration offices

música folklórica – traditional Andean folk music

nevado – permanently glaciated or snow-capped mountain peak

Oriente – Ecuador's Amazonian lowlands east of the Andes

pachamama – earth mother

Panamericana – Pan-American Highway, which is the main route joining Latin American countries with one another; it is called the Interamericana in some countries

panga – small boat used to ferry passengers, especially in the Galápagos Islands, but also on the rivers and lakes of the *Oriente* and along the coast

páramo – high-altitude Andean grasslands of Ecuador, which continue north into Colombia with relicts in the highest parts of Costa Rica

parque nacional – national park

peña – bar or club featuring live folkloric music

pensión – inexpensive boarding house or family-run lodging

playa – beach

pucarás – pre-Inca hill fortresses

puente – bridge

quinta – fine house or villa found in the countryside

ranchera – see *chiva*

refugios – mountain refuges

residencial – cheap hotel

SAE – South American Explorers

salsoteca – nightclub where dancing to salsa music is the main attraction

serranos – people from the highlands

shigra – small string bag

soroche – altitude sickness

SS.HH. – servicios higiénicos, or public toilets

tagua nut – from a palm tree grown in local forest; the 'nuts' are actually hard seeds that are carved into a variety of ornaments

terminal terrestre – central bus terminal for many different companies

Thanks

Many thanks to the travelers who used the last edition and wrote to us with helpful hints, useful advice and interesting anecdotes:

Tim Abbott, Bob Adams, Pamela Adams, Tamar Adelaar, Peggy Aerts, Dorianne Agius, Jose Carlos Aguilar Malaga, Sarah Akber, Andy Alcock, Ximena Alfaro, Marjorie Allard, Lisbeth Allemann, Suzyn Allens, Colleen Alspaugh, Colleen and Tom Alspaugh, Xavier Amigo, Fredrik Anderson, Laura Anderson, Steve Anderson, Folke Andersson, Nici Andhlam-Gardiner, Vaughan Andrews, B Androphy, Neville Antonio, Alice Archer, Siri Ardal, Carine Attias, Heather Atwood, Nicolas Atwood, Maria Augustijns, Nicole Avallone, Aria Avdal, Levi Avnon, Robert Ayers, Fouad G Azzam, Dirk Bachmann, Myriam Baechler, Janina Baeder, Vivi Baek Jensen, Ken Bail, Brooke Bailey, Helen Balcombe, Erik Munk Ballegaard, Andrew Balmain, Townsend Bancroft, Philip Barclay, Peter Barker, Silke Baron, Malvina Baron Bechor, Richard Barragan, Richard and Kathy Barragan, Nestor Barrero, Felix Bartelke, Stéphane Barthe, Alice Barton, Joshua Baruch, Luc Bas, Alistair Basendale, Patrizia Bathge, Reinhard Baumann, Marc Beaudin, Felicia Beavar, Lars Bech, Martina Becker, Perry Beebe, John Beeken, Eppo Beertema, Sara Beesley, Kim Beeson, Gina Behrens, Jan-Willem Beijen, Aart Beijst, AMA Beijst, Mary Bell, Ben Bellows, Chris Benenilts, Mira Benes, Maria and Tony Benfield, Shomron Ben-Horin, Julian Bentham, Rachel Bentley, Gaia Ben-Zvi, Anna Beran, Leah Berg, Thore Berg, David Bergman, Mauricio Bergstein, Edwin Bernbaum, Rene and Melissa Beukeboom, Paul Biegler, Anne Bierman, Karlheinz Biesinger, Claudio Binotto, Iain Bird, Rob Blackwell, Mireille Blais, Jeff Blanchard, Sally Blaser, Erica Blatchford, Allison Blaue, Pascal Bleuel, Pascal and Sandra Bleuel, Nienke Bobbert, Frank Boellert, Markus Bohnert, Stephan Bollen, Frank Bollert, Robin Bollweg, Jenefer Bonczyk, Gabriela Bonifaz, Yolanda Bons, Jasper Boon, Ashley Booth, Piero Boschi, Andy Boscoe, Christoph Bossard, Pierre Bouchard, Guillaume Bouche, James Bourke, Peter Bowie, Lois Bowman, Hope Boylston, Ben Brabazon, Nicholas Branch, Nicolien Bredenoord, Casey Brennan, Ross Brevitt, Nathalie Bridey, Nathalie Bridley, Gert Brienne, Marleen Brils, Marla Brin, Zach Brittsan, Montserrat Briz, Jane Brodthagen, Caroline Bronkars, Liora Brosbe, Paul Brown, Paul and Stefany Brown, Alison Bruce, Thomas Bruck, Bouke Bruinsma, Martin Brukman, Nicole Buettner, Jorgen Buhr, Jean-Thomas Bujard, Nathalie Bultinck-Brimmel, Nathalie and Peter Bultinck-Brimmel, Nicky Bunting, Miriam Burneo, Roberto Burocco, Agi and Shanf Burra, Matthew Burtch, Sanfous Calsaz, Rohan Calvert, Darby Cameron, Kirsteen Campbell, Louise Campbell, Heather Cantwell, Jason Cardwell, Stephen Carlman, Johanna Carpenholm, Hugh Carroll, Rosmary Carrubba, John Carter, Inti Carvajal, Jacqueline Casteleins, Jerome Catz, Justine Cawley, Jeff Cenaiko, Sarah Cenaiko, Dr. Gonzalo Cevallos, Sonia Chadha, Harcharan Chandhoke, Eric Charmet, Morag Chase, Shakeel Chaudhry, Jonathan Cheek, Julie Ann Cheshire, Michael Chewter, Andrea Christ, Banzon Christoffel, Maria Nordstedt, Ann Christofferson, Marie Chry, Marie Chrysander, Piero Ciccarelli, Herman Claeys, Paul Class, Dan Clayton, Molly Clerk, Bob Coats, Bob and Hydroikos Associates Coats, Karen and Andrew Cockburn, Ying Xiong, Richard Cody, Miguel Coello, Ian Coeur, Marcus Coleman, Rosa Comas, Frank Connor, Ralph Cook, Robon Cook, Jack P Cooley, Vera Cooley, Geoff Copland, Diane V Corbett, Kevin Corcoran, Arnaud Corin, Missy Cormier, Albert Cortüs, Edvina and Frank Costley, David Coultas, Georgina Cox, Mary Cox, Su Coyne, Su and Ranald Coyne, Brooke Crabb, Nina Craig, Helen M Crawford, Philippe Créange, Alessandro Crisanti, Emma Crowe, Helen Cullington, Benoit Cunningham, Carman Cunningham, Michael Cunningham, Alexander Czarncbag, Anna and Jacek Czarnoccy, Wojciech Dabrowski, Ali Dale, Carol Damm, Rachel Daniels, Jennie-Lee Davis, Tierza Davis, Bertha Dawang, Chris Dawson, Joanie Dawson, Rachel de Grey, Maria de los Angeles Berg, Eliane de Nicolini, Lisa De Paoli, Marc De Schepere, Laura de Vries, Marc De Vries, Rini de Weijze, Ian Dean, Erwin Deckers, Liz Deeks, Anke Dehne, Hector Del Olmo, John Denison, CB Denning, Vina Devi, Anne Dias, Tomas Diaz Mathe, Beth Dibben, John Dickinson, Claudia-Verena Diedler, Eric Diepstraten, Frank Dierkes, Thomas Dietsche, Marc DiGiacomo, Kathleen Dirkens, Ruth Ditlmann, Siarl Dixon, Sasch Djumena, Jamie Donald, Annick Donkers, Karin Donner, Maureen Dooley, Sherry Doucette, Robin Doudna, Deborah Dray, Daniel Drazan, Semeli Drymoniti, Lee Dubs, Marlene Dunn, Agnieszka Dziarmaga, Yasmin Ebrahim, Annie and Marcel Edixhoven, Ian Edwards, Josse Eelman, Oivind Egeland, Naomi Eisenstein, Jocelyn Elliot, Misty Ellis, Giver Emmanuel, Jeroen en Esther,

399

Honora Englander, Judy Ridgway Epp, Geoff and Ruth Erickson, Rob Erickson, Niklas Erixon, TJ Ernst, Miguel Espinoza, Miguel Estrada, Pily Estrada, Ian Evans, Pamela Ewasink, Camiel Faber, Kristen Faith, Krista Farey, Michael Fassbender, Csaba Feher, Judy Fennessy, Bjorn Fiedler, John Finnerty, Christa Finsterer, Martina Eva Fischer, Nadine Fischer, Patricia A Fitzpatrick, Janet and Peter Flatley, Barbara Fleck, Julia Fleminger, John Fontaine, Emke Fopma, Richard Forrest, Johanna Forsell Ray, Malin Forsgren, Gianni Fortuna, Dave Foster, Katy Foster, Kent Foster, Shanti Foster, Frederic Francken, Nicole Franken, Peter Fraser, Beat Frauenfelder, Reto and Sandra Frei, Erith French, Erika Fricke, Beth Fridinger, Jorg Friese, Jorg and Tina Friese, Anita Frohli, Ondrej Frye, Dave Fuller, Judy Gabriel, Tim Gagan, Eleasha Gall, Anita Gallagher, Jim Gallagher, Robert Galvan, Juan Galvan D, Michelle Gambino, Cassandra Garcia, Susan Garcia, Patrick Garland, Jacques Gauguin, Anna Genet, Axarlis Georgios, Daniela Gerson, Stecv Gerv, Stacy Gery, Lara Giavi, Julie Gibson, Marlene Gilland, Philippe Gillet, Olivier Girard, Alex Girdwood, Katherine Glen, Jean-Francois Gloux, Pat Glowa, Christian Goettler, Paul Goldberg, Kevin Golde, Laurie Goldsmith, Juan Carlos Gonzalez, Julian Gonzalez, Kim Gonzalez, d Good, David Goode, Diane B Goodpasture, Charles Gordon, Gus Gordon, Julie Gorshe, Jim and Lisa Grace, Dan Grady, Jochen Graff, M Graff, Terry Grant, Pat Gray, Laura Grefa, Gregory Grene, Charlotte Grimbert, Angela Grimm, Nienke Groen, Philip Groth, Monica Guerra, Salvador Guerra, Mary Gulldege, Willie Gunn, Charles Gutnaud, Joel Guzman, Ferdinand Höng, Gary W Hahn, Franz Haiboeck, Sarah Louisa Hails, Frans Hakkemars, Tony Hall, Matthew Halwes, Michael Hancock, Olivia Hanley, Kelly Hann, Christiane Hanstein, Yso Hardy, Julie Harris, Paul Harris, Christopher Hart, Ramsey Hart, Andre Hartlief, Nils Hartmann, Helga Hartsema-Bartelds, Rachel Hartsough, Colin Harvey, Jessica Hastings, Helen Haugh, Peter Hausken, Julienne Heath, Annette Hebestreit, Kai Hecheltjen, John Heidema, Christian Heindel, Raphaela Heinen, Els Helsen, Caroline Hennin, Lothar Herb, Sharon Herkes, Peter Hermens, F Hertzberger, Margaret Hessel, Marie Heylen, M Hiemstra, Dominic Higgins, John J Higgins, Michael Hilburn, Cliff Hilpert, Eva Himmelberg, Jillian Hirasawa, Nicholas and Jayne Hird, Rado Hnath, Ward Hobert, Geraldine Hodgkins, Liesbeth Hoek, Gigi Hoeller, Gösta Hoffmann, Simon Hoffmann, Paul Hofman, Esther Hofstede, Janette Hol, Daniela Holguin, Andrew Holmes, Matthew Holmes, Neil Holmes, Ian Holt, Jeff Holt, Janine Holtman, Wayne Hooper, Wim Hooymans, Amy Horwitz, Tom Hoskin, Adrian Hoskins, Alan Howard, Laura Howell, Susanne Hrinkov, Connie Hughes, Mark Hughes, Amber Hulls, Fer Hurk, Esther Hurwitz, Lele and Wigolf Huss, Jennifer Hutchings, Cameron Hutchison, Mia Huysmans, Patricia Inarrea, Freddy Irusta, Nicolas Isnard, Legarth Iversen, Bastiaan Jaarsma, Wilson Jackson, Yves Jackson, Annette Jacobs, Gavin Jacobs, Emma Jansen, Eve Jansen, Thomas Jansseune, Jitske Jettinghoff, Steve Job, Ann Jochems, Eva Dagrun Johaug, Carina Johnson, Niels Johs, Alison Jones, Brent Jones, Clive Jones, Jake Jones, ES de Jong, Marika De Jong, Werner Joos, Arnold Joost, Tim Joshlin, Hartmut Köhler, Helena Kantola, Maurice Kaplan, Schmid Karlheinz, Christine Karrer, Maierhofer Karoline, Deborah Kashdan, Allan Kelly, Jessica Kennedy, Petra Kessler, Esther Keusch, Hilary Kingston, Diana Kirk, Robert Kirk, Michael Kiwoor, Jutta Kiworr, Oliver Klein, Dirk de Kleuver, Alexandra Klitsch, Bill Klynnk, Tina Knipping, Phil Knoll, Martin Knolle, Bjorn Knuthammar, Jaap Koerce, Steve Kohler, Lynn Kohner, Rob Kok, Edo Kolmer, Heinke Konnerth, Sanjay Konur, Donald Koolisch, HN Koomen, Claus Kori-Linder, Natasa Kovacic, Margaret Kozmin, Uwe Kraft, Andreas Krampe, Peter Kreuzaler, Gary Kris, Emma Kristensen, Olga Kroes, Susie Krott, Ann-Birte Krueger, Stefan Kuhle, Jessica Kuijper, Will Kumar, Matthias Kunz, Jaroslav Lübl, Inga Labuhn, CR Lacy, David Lacy, Sandra Lafforgue, Mike Laing, Luce Lamy, Mark Lander, Lisa Laria, Erik Larsen, Claudette Laundry, Palle Laursen, Angiolo Laviziano, Chung Law, Emma Lawlor, JC Le Berre, Rose Lea, A Leach, Chris Leary, Christine Lee, Davis Lee, Shannon Lee-Rutherford, Dave Lefkowitz, Bernard Lefrancois, Anneliese Lehmann, Isabel Lehmann, Gemma Leighton, Zoe Leighton, Janick Lemieux, Jesper Lemmich, Bernard and Marlene Leroudier, Michel Leseigneur, Chris Leuhery, Mikkel Levelt, Julie Levy, Colin Lewis, Isabel Liao, Steve Lidgey, Sigrid Liede, Louise Limoge, Ulf Lindün, Andreas Lindberg, Claudia Linders, David Linford, Trish Lister, Katie Lo, Isabelle Lochet, Stephanie Lock, Martin Loew, Carola Lotz, Alexander Louis, Jos Louwer, Nadia Louzao, Cosette Loviat, Markus J Low, Denise Loykens, Lene Lubbert Hansen, Fernando and Forsberg Lucena, Simone Ludwig, Brian Alan Luff, A Lukowsky, Karl Lundberg, Michael Lustenberg, Tanja Lutolf, Katie Luxton, Annabelle Lyon, June MacDonald, Ian Mace, Robert MacLellan, Ms G MacTaggart, Jody Madala, Karla Mader, Karla and Paul Mader, Hansjoerg Maier, Igor and Julia Makovetzki, P Maler, Erika Malitsky, Erika Malitzky,

Katrin Mangold, Jorg Manser, Kathleen Mantel, Sandro Marchesi, Regina Marchi, Ann Marie Scanlan, Torsten Markert, Claire Marks, Alyssa Martin, John Martin, Isabelle Martineau, Al Mason, Sebastien Masson, Jacob Massoud, Jay Matsya, Hanni Matt, Kylie Matterson, Michele Mattix, Oliver Maurath, Charles and Christiane May, Ilse Mayer, Simone M, Lina McCain, Kelly McCarthy, Jill and Bernie McClean, Dan McDougall, Twid McGrath, Pat McGregor, Alan McIntosh, Kenneth McIntosh, Weze McIntosh, Sheridan S McKinney, Alexandra Scotti McLaren, James McLaughlin, Stuart McLay, Craig McVicar, Craig P McVicar, Jeffrey Mease, Andreas Meese, Sylvia Meichsner, Sharon Meieran, Liesbeth Meijnckens, Bernarda Mejia, Linda Mendelson, Kerstin Menze, Jane Mercer, Thomas Messerli, Steve Metcalfe, Ellen Mette Finsveen, Frixos Michael, Matthias Michael, Corinne Michel, Alan Michell, Greg Middleton, Judy Midgley, Sabrena San and Demian Miguel, Jakob Elm Mikkelsen, Cherise Miller, James Miller, Jonathan and Jayme Miller, Mike Missle, Henrik Mitsch, Astrid and Hoger Muller, Jörg Mnnzenberg, Tanya Mohammadi, Jock and Janice Moilliet, Julio Molineros, Brigitte Monfils, Arturo Mora, Aksel Morch, Lucille Moreau, David Morenoff, Brian Morgan, Helen Morgan, Pierre Morin, Cyndi Morley, Lisa Morris, Andrea Mosler, Larry Moss, Lisa Moss, Elaine Mowat, Nick Moxham, Annabelle Mueller, B Muldrow, Kerry Mullen, Edmund Muller, Jorg Muller-Tows, Ian Munro, Jamie Murray, Christina and Brigitta Mutke, Mark Myles, Michelle Nahar, Eban Namer, ET Nance, Jr, Alex Nash, Tino Naumann, Auke Nauta, Lou Neal, Kim Nearpass, Justin Nearpass-Pollack, Paige Newman, Lisanne Newport, Helen Newton, Joanna Newton, Colleen Nicholson, Defossez Nicolas, Gitte Nielsen, Judith M. Night, Connie and Ted Ning, Richard Nixon, Paolo Notarantonio, Andrzaj Nowak, Edith Nowak, Pieter Nuiten, Matthias Nussbaum, Lisa Oakes, Bas Oank, Christopher Obetz, Ignacio Ochoa, Chris OConnell, Neil O'Connell, Deirdre O'Donnell, Patrick O'Donnell, Theodor Oest, Maria and Paul Offermans, Martin Ohman, Helge Olav Svela, Chris Olin, David Olson, Katie O'Neill, Karen Oorthuijs, Rebecca Oppenheimer, Kara O'Reilly, Cathal O'Riordain, Zita O'Rouke-Wigger, Melanie Ortlieb, Christian Osvald, Stefan Otti, Winfrid Ottmers, Carol Outwater, Julie Overnell, Hannah Owens-Pike, Ton Paardekooper, Louise Pabe, Patricia Pache, Frantois Panchard, Antje Pannenbecker, Spiras and Julie Pappas, Don Parris, Arnold Parzer, Shuli Passow, Nirav V Patel, Ruth Patricia, Helle Pederson, Nicola Peel, Suzan Peeters, Robert Peeterse, Vicente Martin Peluffo, Victoria Pennell, Sabina Pensek, Jane A Lyons de Perez, Vinicio Perez, Luis Periera, Celine Swanson Perilhou, Darcy Peters, J Pettiward, Rafael Pfaffen, Dominique Pfeifer, Laurens C Philippo, Jason Phillips, Doug and Janet Phillops, Giuseppe Piacentino, Alain Piche, Phill Piddell, Dennis Piedra, Wenceslao Pigretti, Jessica Pilkington, Inger Pinkowsky, Graham Pither, Marco Plaatje, Gary Plamer, Susanne Poeisch, Chris Pollard, Nathalie Pollier, John Polo, Ken Polspoel, Inge Pool, Desmond Poon, Diane De Pooter, Aase Popper, Antonio Postigo, Katja Potzsch, Gaetan Poulin, Martin Powell, Lorena Pozzo, Pablo Prado, Yves Prescott, Nick Prihoda, Mark Probst, Mirjam Pronk, Luharky Puig Placeres, Varsha Puri, Sebastian Querner, Rik Quint, Paddy Radford, Andreas Raeder, Mike Rahill, Andy Sweet, Nancy Rainwater, Emil Rasmussen, Sherry Rauh, Gaby Raynes, Marilyn Ream, Dave Redmond, Monique Reeves, Batia Regev, Harald Reil, Ralf Reinecke, Ernst Reiner, Natalie Rempel, Doris Renggli, Helena Rex, Diego Ribetto, Liza Richards, Mollie Richford, Christoph Richter, Darine Riem, Michel Riemersma, Susanne Ritz, Carlyn Ritzen, BA Rix, Ann Robertson, Eric Robette, Becki Robinson, PC Robinson, Shane Robinson, Denys Robitaille, Noel Rochford, Tim Roden, Margaret Roemer, Toby Roeoesli, Deborah Rohrer, Mary Roos, Simon Rose, Steffen Rossel, Mary and Mike Rossignoli, Andrea Rostek, Deborah Roth, Catherine Rourke, DM Rovers-Bos, Nick Rowlands, Mattias Rudh, Dan Ruff, Fred Runkel, Barbara Rusch, David Ryan, Erica Ryberg, Filippo Saccardo, Terry Salguero, Gil Salomon, Jorge Samaniego, R Samuelson, Ian Samways, Fernando Sanchez-Heredero Gonzalez, Jim Sarro, Bettina Schatzl, Michaela Schau, Stephane Scheyven, Franz Schiemer, Eva Schmidt, Robin Schmidt, Caroline Andrews and Schmutz, Amy Schneider, EV Schofield, Uwe Schröder, Jon Schroeder, Björn Schroth, Liam Schubel, Ralph Schurink, Deborah Schwagerman, Eric Schwartz, Sam Scott, Dick Scroop, Karsten Seeber, Christina Seidler, Ulrike Seiler, Jacob Seligmann, Shelly Selin, Padi Selwyn, Claudia Senecal, Monika Senn, Moran Serr, Bobbi Setter, Gavin Sexton, Yshay Shachar, Nadav Shashar, Warren Shauer, Eleanor Shield, Peter Shinglewood, Julia Shirtliff, Pamela Shriman, Kalpana Shyamapant, Neta Siboni, Jonathan Sibtain, Christian Silkenath, Nathalie Simpson, Alli Sinclair, Milo Sjardin, Hilde Sleurs, Ludwik Sliwa, Monica Small, Mrs E Smeeton, Anna Smet, Gary Smith, Melissa Smith, Shalin Smith, Joyce and Joris Snijders, Catherine and Kennedy Somerton, Tim

Sorby, James Spencer, Stephanie Spivack, Charles W Stansfield, Silke Stappen, Erik Stark, Gerhard Stebich, Ernst Steigenga, Stele Stenersen, Sue Sterling, Jean Stevens, Andrew Stewart, Jonathan Stewart, Jo Stockhill, JM Stockill, Samantha and Adam Stork, Andreas Strein, Ragnhild Strommen, Jo Surtees, Clare Suter, Heather Sutherland, Judy and Ariana Svenson, Kathryn Swan, Nicole Sweeney, Peter Sweeny, Jennifer Swenson, Isaac Sylvander, Ilona Szemzo, Eli Ragna Taerum, Vinay Talwar, Patricio Tamariz, Ruth Tammaro, Lian Tan, Matthias Von Der Tann, Graham Taylor, John Taylor, Kathleen Taylor, Keith Taylor, Lucy Taylor, Michael Taylor, Sarah R Taylor, Jan Tenzer, Vanessa Teplin, Neal Teplitz, Carol Tepper, Laura Terborgh, Lars Terje Holmaas, Barbara Terpin, Dr James Terry, Rosemary Theroux, Marie-Josee Therrien, Philippe Theys, Sabine Thielicke, Jens Thoben, Carol Thomas, Fern Thomas, Ewan and Caroline Thompson, Gordon Thompson, J Thompson, Jan Timmer, Medardo Toctaquiza, Helena Toctaquiza-van Maanen, Amy Tonn, Irene Torres, Nghia Tran, Fabrizzio Trivino, Meinrad Tschann, Nickol Turak, Sue Turner, Monika Tüscher, Susan Twombly, Steven Tyerman, Christian D Ulrich, Andrea Untergutsch, Cheyenne Valenzuela, Xavier Valino, Hugo van Answaarden, Aukje van den Bent, Louis van den Berg, Jaap van den Burg, Sofie Van Den Hende, Ron Van Den Hurk, Theo van der Avoird, Lee Van Dixhorn, Natalie van Eckendonk, Arjan van Egmond, Susanne Van Gorp, Dorine van Haselen, Pieter and Iris van Hoeken-Rusz, Agnes van Hulst, Jan-Eidse van Melle, Christien van Meurs, Wim Van Rompay, Ron van Rooijen, Katrien Vanden Eynde, Pieter Vanhoeken, Alison Van Horn, Peter Vanquaille, Martin Veenendaal, Colette Venderick, Sophie Verhagen, Frank Verheggen, JP Verkade, Jeroen Vermeulen, Susan Vetrone, Catherine Vial, Jennifer and Julie Vick, Aurelie Vieillefosse, Fredy Villamarin, Helen Vint, Leonor Vodoz, Erich Voegtli, Marc-Andre Voll, JJH Vollenberg, Ruud Vollenberg, Sven von der Ohe, Judith Vonwil, Gregory Voss, Jadranka Vrsalovic, Kay Waefler, Carsten Waider, Sandra Waldmann, N C Walker, Peter Walla, Mike Wallace, Regina Walter, Nathan Ward, Lucy Wardle, Peter Wardle, Nick Water, James Watson, Deborah Watt, Nancy Watts, Mark Weaver, Sheila Webb, Eugene Welling, Sandi Wermes, Winnie Wernicke, Thorun Werswick, Petra Wester, Annemieke Wevers, Sharon Whalley, Martin Whearty, Michael Wheelahon, MC Whirter, Christianne White, Linda White, Teresa White, Sam Whitley, Martina Wiede, Ulrike Wiedenfels, Julie Wiedman, Thomas Wilhelm, Krsita Willeboer, Jo Williams, Piers Williams, Lori Willocks, Lawrence Wilmshurst, Lizzie Winborn, Ralph Winkelmolen, Thomas and Judith Winter, Leora Wise, Paul Wittrock, Fritz Woldt, Andreas Wolf, Stefanie Wong, Marjorie Wonham, David Wood, Peter Wouter, Jack Woy, Allison Wright, Slaney Wright, Jennifer Yantz, Brian Yates, Xiang Yi, Simone Yurasek, Galit Zadok, Sandra Zaramella, John Zeeb, Andrea Zeichner, Lital Zelinger, Filippo Zimbile, Susanne Zimmer, Judith Zingg, Nataschja Zoet, Byron Niama Zurita

LONELY PLANET

You already know that Lonely Planet produces more than this one guidebook, but you might not be aware of the other products we have on this region. Here is a selection of titles that you may want to check out as well:

South America on a Shoestring
ISBN 1 86450 283 5
US$29.99 • UK£17.99

**Healthy Travel
Central & South America**
ISBN 1 86450 053 0
US$5.95 • UK£3.99

Chile & Easter Island
ISBN 1 74059 116 X
US$21.99 • UK£14.99

Venezuela
ISBN 1 86450 219 3
US$19.99 • UK£12.99

**Latin American
Spanish Phrasebook**
ISBN 0 86442 558 9
US$6.95 • UK£4.50

Peru
ISBN 0 86442 710 7
US$17.95 • UK£11.99

Trekking in the Central Andes
ISBN 1 74059 431 2
US$19.99 • UK£14.99

Quechua Phrasebook
ISBN 1 86450 381 5
US$7.99 • UK£4.50

Colombia
ISBN 0 86442 674 7
US$19.99 • UK£14.99

**Full Circle:
A South American Journey**
ISBN 0 86442 465 5
US$10.95 • UK£5.99

Bolivia
ISBN 0 86442 668 2
US$21.99 • UK£13.99

**Available wherever books
are sold**

LONELY PLANET

Guides by Region

Lonely Planet is known worldwide for publishing practical, reliable and no-nonsense travel information in our guides and on our Web site. The Lonely Planet list covers just about every accessible part of the world. Currently there are 16 series: Travel guides, Shoestring guides, Condensed guides, Phrasebooks, Read This First, Healthy Travel, Walking guides, Cycling guides, Watching Wildlife guides, Pisces Diving & Snorkeling guides, City Maps, Road Atlases, Out to Eat, World Food, Journeys travel literature and Pictorials.

AFRICA Africa on a shoestring • Botswana • Cairo • Cairo City Map • Cape Town • Cape Town City Map • East Africa • Egypt • Egyptian Arabic phrasebook • Ethiopia, Eritrea & Djibouti • Ethiopian Amharic phrasebook • The Gambia & Senegal • Healthy Travel Africa • Kenya • Malawi • Morocco • Moroccan Arabic phrasebook • Mozambique • Namibia • Read This First: Africa • South Africa, Lesotho & Swaziland • Southern Africa • Southern Africa Road Atlas • Swahili phrasebook • Tanzania, Zanzibar & Pemba • Trekking in East Africa • Tunisia • Watching Wildlife East Africa • Watching Wildlife Southern Africa • West Africa • World Food Morocco • Zambia • Zimbabwe, Botswana & Namibia
Travel Literature: Mali Blues: Traveling to an African Beat • The Rainbird: A Central African Journey • Songs to an African Sunset: A Zimbabwean Story

AUSTRALIA & THE PACIFIC Aboriginal Australia & the Torres Strait Islands •Auckland • Australia • Australian phrasebook • Australia Road Atlas • Cycling Australia • Cycling New Zealand • Fiji • Fijian phrasebook • Healthy Travel Australia, NZ & the Pacific • Islands of Australia's Great Barrier Reef • Melbourne • Melbourne City Map • Micronesia • New Caledonia • New South Wales • New Zealand • Northern Territory • Outback Australia • Out to Eat – Melbourne • Out to Eat – Sydney • Papua New Guinea • Pidgin phrasebook • Queensland • Rarotonga & the Cook Islands • Samoa • Solomon Islands • South Australia • South Pacific • South Pacific phrasebook • Sydney • Sydney City Map • Sydney Condensed • Tahiti & French Polynesia • Tasmania • Tonga • Tramping in New Zealand • Vanuatu • Victoria • Walking in Australia • Watching Wildlife Australia • Western Australia
Travel Literature: Islands in the Clouds: Travels in the Highlands of New Guinea • Kiwi Tracks: A New Zealand Journey • Sean & David's Long Drive

CENTRAL AMERICA & THE CARIBBEAN Bahamas, Turks & Caicos • Baja California • Belize, Guatemala & Yucatán • Bermuda • Central America on a shoestring • Costa Rica • Costa Rica Spanish phrasebook • Cuba • Cycling Cuba • Dominican Republic & Haiti • Eastern Caribbean • Guatemala • Havana • Healthy Travel Central & South America • Jamaica • Mexico • Mexico City • Panama • Puerto Rico • Read This First: Central & South America • Virgin Islands • World Food Caribbean • World Food Mexico • Yucatán
Travel Literature: Green Dreams: Travels in Central America

EUROPE Amsterdam • Amsterdam City Map • Amsterdam Condensed • Andalucía • Athens • Austria • Baltic States phrasebook • Barcelona • Barcelona City Map • Belgium & Luxembourg • Berlin • Berlin City Map • Britain • British phrasebook • Brussels, Bruges & Antwerp • Brussels City Map • Budapest • Budapest City Map • Canary Islands • Catalunya & the Costa Brava • Central Europe • Central Europe phrasebook • Copenhagen • Corfu & the Ionians • Corsica • Crete • Crete Condensed • Croatia • Cycling Britain • Cycling France • Cyprus • Czech & Slovak Republics • Czech phrasebook • Denmark • Dublin • Dublin City Map • Dublin Condensed • Eastern Europe • Eastern Europe phrasebook • Edinburgh • Edinburgh City Map • England • Estonia, Latvia & Lithuania • Europe on a shoestring • Europe phrasebook • Finland • Florence • Florence City Map • France • Frankfurt City Map • Frankfurt Condensed • French phrasebook • Georgia, Armenia & Azerbaijan • Germany • German phrasebook • Greece • Greek Islands • Greek phrasebook • Hungary • Iceland, Greenland & the Faroe Islands • Ireland • Italian phrasebook • Italy • Kraków • Lisbon • The Loire • London • London City Map • London Condensed • Madrid • Madrid City Map • Malta • Mediterranean Europe • Milan, Turin & Genoa • Moscow • Munich • Netherlands • Normandy • Norway • Out to Eat – London • Out to Eat – Paris • Paris • Paris City Map • Paris Condensed • Poland • Polish phrasebook • Portugal • Portuguese phrasebook • Prague • Prague City Map • Provence & the Côte d'Azur • Read This First: Europe • Rhodes & the Dodecanese • Romania & Moldova • Rome • Rome City Map • Rome Condensed • Russia, Ukraine & Belarus • Russian phrasebook • Scandinavian & Baltic Europe • Scandinavian phrasebook • Scotland • Sicily • Slovenia • South-West France • Spain • Spanish phrasebook • Stockholm • St Petersburg • St Petersburg City Map • Sweden • Switzerland • Tuscany • Ukrainian phrasebook • Venice • Vienna • Wales • Walking in Britain • Walking in France • Walking in Ireland • Walking in Italy • Walking in Scotland • Walking in Spain • Walking in Switzerland • Western Europe • World Food France • World Food Greece • World Food Ireland • World Food Italy • World Food Spain **Travel Literature**: After Yugoslavia • Love and War in the Apennines • The Olive Grove: Travels in Greece • On the Shores of the Mediterranean • Round Ireland in Low Gear • A Small Place in Italy

LONELY PLANET

Mail Order

Lonely Planet products are distributed worldwide. They are also available by mail order from Lonely Planet, so if you have difficulty finding a title please write to us. North and South American residents should write to 150 Linden St, Oakland, CA 94607, USA; European and African residents should write to 72-82 Rosebery Ave, London, EC1R 4RW, UK; and residents of other countries to Locked Bag 1, Footscray, Victoria 3011, Australia.

INDIAN SUBCONTINENT & THE INDIAN OCEAN Bangladesh • Bengali phrasebook • Bhutan • Delhi • Goa • Healthy Travel Asia & India • Hindi & Urdu phrasebook • India • India & Bangladesh City Map • Indian Himalaya • Karakoram Highway • Kathmandu City Map • Kerala • Madagascar • Maldives • Mauritius, Réunion & Seychelles • Mumbai (Bombay) • Nepal • Nepali phrasebook • North India • Pakistan • Rajasthan • Read This First: Asia & India • South India • Sri Lanka • Sri Lanka phrasebook • Tibet • Tibetan phrasebook • Trekking in the Indian Himalaya • Trekking in the Karakoram & Hindukush • Trekking in the Nepal Himalaya • World Food India **Travel Literature** The Age of Kali: Indian Travels and Encounters • Hello Goodnight: A Life of Goa • In Rajasthan • Maverick in Madagascar • A Season in Heaven: True Tales from the Road to Kathmandu • Shopping for Buddhas • A Short Walk in the Hindu Kush • Slowly Down the Ganges

MIDDLE EAST & CENTRAL ASIA Bahrain, Kuwait & Qatar • Central Asia • Central Asia phrasebook • Dubai • Farsi (Persian) phrasebook • Hebrew phrasebook • Iran • Israel & the Palestinian Territories • Istanbul • Istanbul City Map • Istanbul to Cairo • Istanbul to Kathmandu • Jerusalem • Jerusalem City Map • Jordan • Lebanon • Middle East • Oman & the United Arab Emirates • Syria • Turkey • Turkish phrasebook • World Food Turkey • Yemen **Travel Literature**: Black on Black: Iran Revisited • Breaking Ranks: Turbulent Travels in the Promised Land • The Gates of Damascus • Kingdom of the Film Stars: Journey into Jordan

NORTH AMERICA Alaska • Boston • Boston City Map • Boston Condensed • British Columbia • California & Nevada • California Condensed • Canada • Chicago • Chicago City Map • Chicago Condensed • Florida • Georgia & the Carolinas • Great Lakes • Hawaii • Hiking in Alaska • Hiking in the USA • Honolulu & Oahu City Map • Las Vegas • Los Angeles • Los Angeles City Map • Louisiana & the Deep South • Miami • Miami City Map • Montreal • New England • New Orleans • New Orleans City Map • New York City • New York City City Map • New York City Condensed • New York, New Jersey & Pennsylvania • Oahu • Out to Eat – San Francisco • Pacific Northwest • Rocky Mountains • San Diego & Tijuana • San Francisco • San Francisco City Map • Seattle • Seattle City Map • Southwest • Texas • Toronto • USA • USA phrasebook • Vancouver • Vancouver City Map • Virginia & the Capital Region • Washington, DC • Washington, DC City Map • World Food New Orleans **Travel Literature**: Caught Inside: A Surfer's Year on the California Coast • Drive Thru America

NORTH-EAST ASIA Beijing • Beijing City Map • Cantonese phrasebook • China • Hiking in Japan • Hong Kong & Macau • Hong Kong City Map • Hong Kong Condensed • Japan • Japanese phrasebook • Korea • Korean phrasebook • Kyoto • Mandarin phrasebook • Mongolia • Mongolian phrasebook • Seoul • Shanghai • South-West China • Taiwan • Tokyo • Tokyo Condensed • World Food Hong Kong • World Food Japan **Travel Literature**: In Xanadu: A Quest • Lost Japan

SOUTH AMERICA Argentina, Uruguay & Paraguay • Bolivia • Brazil • Brazilian phrasebook • Buenos Aires • Buenos Aires City Map • Chile & Easter Island • Colombia • Ecuador & the Galapagos Islands • Healthy Travel Central & South America • Latin American Spanish phrasebook • Peru • Quechua phrasebook • Read This First: Central & South America • Rio de Janeiro • Rio de Janeiro City Map • Santiago de Chile • South America on a shoestring • Trekking in the Patagonian Andes • Venezuela **Travel Literature**: Full Circle: A South American Journey

SOUTH-EAST ASIA Bali & Lombok • Bangkok • Bangkok City Map • Burmese phrasebook • Cambodia • Cycling Vietnam, Laos & Cambodia • East Timor phrasebook • Hanoi • Healthy Travel Asia & India • Hill Tribes phrasebook • Ho Chi Minh City (Saigon) • Indonesia • Indonesian phrasebook • Indonesia's Eastern Islands • Java • Lao phrasebook • Laos • Malay phrasebook • Malaysia, Singapore & Brunei • Myanmar (Burma) • Philippines • Pilipino (Tagalog) phrasebook • Read This First: Asia & India • Singapore • Singapore City Map • South-East Asia on a shoestring • South-East Asia phrasebook • Thailand • Thailand's Islands & Beaches • Thailand, Vietnam, Laos & Cambodia Road Atlas • Thai phrasebook • Vietnam • Vietnamese phrasebook • World Food Indonesia • World Food Thailand • World Food Vietnam

ALSO AVAILABLE: Antarctica • The Arctic • The Blue Man: Tales of Travel, Love and Coffee • Brief Encounters: Stories of Love, Sex & Travel • Buddhist Stupas in Asia: The Shape of Perfection • Chasing Rickshaws • The Last Grain Race • Lonely Planet ... On the Edge: Adventurous Escapades from Around the World • Lonely Planet Unpacked • Lonely Planet Unpacked Again • Not the Only Planet: Science Fiction Travel Stories • Ports of Call: A Journey by Sea • Sacred India • Travel Photography: A Guide to Taking Better Pictures • Travel with Children • Tuvalu: Portrait of an Island Nation

Mail Order

Lonely Planet books are comprehensively updated. They are also available by mail order from Lonely Planet, so if you have difficulty finding a title please write to us. North and South American residents should write to 150 Linden St, Oakland, CA 94607, USA; European and African residents should write to 10a Spring Place, London NW5 3BH, UK; and residents of other countries to Locked Bag 1, Footscray, Victoria 3011, Australia.

Index

Text

Boxed Text

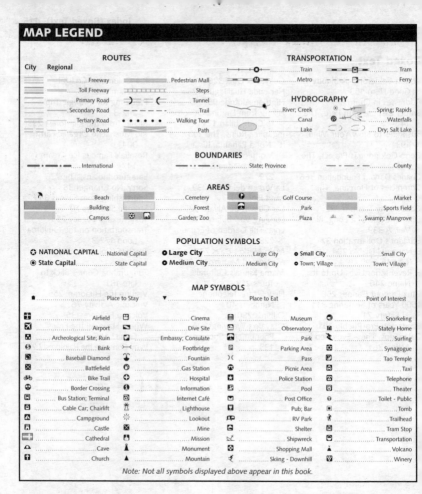

MAP LEGEND

ROUTES

City   Regional

Freeway
Toll Freeway
Primary Road
Secondary Road
Tertiary Road
Dirt Road

Pedestrian Mall
Steps
Tunnel
Trail
Walking Tour
Path

TRANSPORTATION

Train
Metro

Tram
Ferry

HYDROGRAPHY

River; Creek
Canal
Lake

Spring; Rapids
Waterfalls
Dry; Salt Lake

BOUNDARIES

International

State; Province

County

AREAS

Beach
Building
Campus

Cemetery
Forest
Garden; Zoo

Golf Course
Park
Plaza

Market
Sports Field
Swamp; Mangrove

POPULATION SYMBOLS

○ NATIONAL CAPITAL ... National Capital
◉ State Capital ... State Capital

● Large City ... Large City
● Medium City ... Medium City

● Small City ... Small City
○ Town; Village ... Town; Village

MAP SYMBOLS

■ ... Place to Stay

▼ ... Place to Eat

● ... Point of Interest

Airfield
Airport
Archeological Site; Ruin
Bank
Baseball Diamond
Battlefield
Bike Trail
Border Crossing
Bus Station; Terminal
Cable Car; Chairlift
Campground
Castle
Cathedral
Cave
Church

Cinema
Dive Site
Embassy; Consulate
Footbridge
Fountain
Gas Station
Hospital
Information
Internet Café
Lighthouse
Lookout
Mine
Mission
Monument
Mountain

Museum
Observatory
Park
Parking Area
Pass
Picnic Area
Police Station
Pool
Post Office
Pub; Bar
RV Park
Shelter
Shipwreck
Shopping Mall
Skiing - Downhill

Snorkeling
Stately Home
Surfing
Synagogue
Tao Temple
Taxi
Telephone
Theater
Toilet - Public
Tomb
Trailhead
Tram Stop
Transportation
Volcano
Winery

Note: Not all symbols displayed above appear in this book.

LONELY PLANET OFFICES

Australia
Locked Bag 1, Footscray, Victoria 3011
☎ 03 8379 8000 fax 03 8379 8111
email: talk2us@lonelyplanet.com.au

USA
150 Linden St, Oakland, CA 94607
☎ 510 893 8555 TOLL FREE: 800 275 8555
fax 510 893 8572
email: info@lonelyplanet.com

UK
72-82 Rosebery Ave, London, EC1R 4RW
☎ 020 7841 9000 fax 020 7841 9001
email: go@lonelyplanet.co.uk

France
1 rue du Dahomey, 75011 Paris
☎ 01 55 25 33 00 fax 01 55 25 33 01
email: bip@lonelyplanet.fr
www.lonelyplanet.fr

World Wide Web: www.lonelyplanet.com *or* AOL keyword: lp
Lonely Planet Images: www.lonelyplanetimages.com